SCHAUM'S
OUTLINE OF

RUSSIAN GRAMMAR

JAMES S. LEVINE, Ph.D.

*Associate Professor of Russian
and Director of Russian Studies
George Mason University*

Schaum's Outline Series

McGRAW-HILL

New York   San Francisco   Washington, D.C.   Auckland   Bogotá   Caracas
Lisbon   London   Madrid   Mexico City   Milan   Montreal   New Delhi
San Juan   Singapore   Sydney   Tokyo   Toronto

JAMES S. LEVINE received his B.A. in History and Russian from the State University of New York at Buffalo, and his M.A. and Ph.D. in Slavic Linguistics from the University of Illinois at Urbana–Champaign. Dr. Levine also studied Russian language, literature, and culture at Moscow University and St. Petersburg University, Russia. He has taught Russian for the past twenty-five years at several universities, including the University of Illinois, the University of Maryland at College Park, and George Mason University in Fairfax, Virginia. He is currently Associate Professor of Russian at George Mason University, where he is also Director of Russian Studies. He has served as a consultant on foreign language education projects for the American Council on Education, and as a specialist reviewer and panelist for the National Endowment for the Humanities, the National Security Education Program, and the American Council of Teachers of Russian. He is cotranslator of the *Black Book* (Holocaust Library), coeditor of *Case in Slavic* (Slavica Publishers, Inc.), and author of numerous articles on Russian language and linguistics.

Schaum's Outline of Theory and Problems of
RUSSIAN GRAMMAR

9 10 11 12 13 14 15 16 17 18 19 20 CUS CUS 9 0 9 8

ISBN 0-07-038238-7

Sponsoring Editor: Barbara Gilson
Production Supervisor: Tina Cameron
Editing Supervisor: Maureen B. Walker
Project Supervision: Keyword Publishing Services Ltd.

Library of Congress Cataloging-in-Publication Data

Levine, James S.
    Schaum's outline of Russian grammar / James S. Levine.
        p.   cm.— (Schaum's outline series)
    Includes index.
    ISBN 0-07-038238-7
    1. Russian language—Grammar. I. Title. II. Title: Outline of Russian grammar.
III. Title: Russian grammar.
PG2112.L394 1999
491.782′421—dc21
                                                99-30512
                                                CIP

McGraw-Hill

A Division of The McGraw-Hill Companies

To Jody, Sasha, and Erica

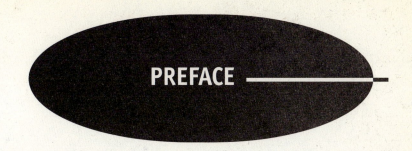

PREFACE

Schaum's Outline of Russian Grammar is intended as a study aid to assist English speakers in their acquisition of contemporary Russian. It is designed for students from the beginning to advanced levels: beginning students can use this book as a companion to any basic Russian language textbook, while intermediate–advanced students will find the book useful as a review text and reference for grammar. For individuals learning the language outside of an academic setting, the numerous practice exercises and answer key make it possible to use the Outline as a text for independent study.

The book consists of eight chapters: The Sounds of Russian; Nouns; Prepositions; Pronouns; Adjectives and Adverbs; Numbers, Dates, and Time; Verbs; and Conjunctions.

The first chapter, "The Sounds of Russian," introduces the Cyrillic alphabet and presents a guide to the pronunciation of Russian consonants and vowels. This chapter also presents aspects of the Russian writing system, e.g., spelling rules, peculiarities of capitalization, transliteration from English to Russian, as well as a brief section on different Russian letter styles.

Chapters 2–8 present all the essentials for a solid foundation in Russian grammar. Grammatical terms, including the basic parts of speech and associated grammatical concepts (e.g., gender, number, and case in the noun; tense, aspect, mood, and voice in the verb), are clearly explained and illustrated with numerous examples. Comparisons between English and Russian—their similarities and differences with respect to particular grammatical features—are made throughout the book. In the author's view, such comparisons will provide native speakers of English with greater insight into the structure of their own language, which in turn will enhance their understanding and ultimate mastery of the grammatical structure of Russian.

One of the most challenging tasks for English speakers is mastering the variable forms of Russian words, for example, the declensional endings of nouns, pronouns, adjectives, and numbers, as well as the changes undergone by verbs in conjugation. In *Schaum's Outline of Russian Grammar* the task of learning grammatical endings is made easier by highlighting them in declension tables throughout the text. The presentation of verb conjugation addresses the dual audience of Russian learners: those who have learned verbs the traditional way, and others who have been exposed to the "single-stem system." Verbs are classified according to their suffixed or nonsuffixed "basic (single) stem," an approach which has become increasingly common in American textbooks at the first- and second-year levels. In addition, a representative example of each verb class is fully conjugated in a special box, and is then followed by a description of its stress and consonant alternation properties. All students will benefit from the thorough coverage of verbal aspect, and of the other major topics in the Russian verb, e.g., the conditional and subjunctive, verbs in **-ся**, verbs of motion, participles, and verbal adverbs.

The development of grammatical accuracy requires a good deal of practice in manipulating the structures of the language. In this book numerous drills and exercises follow the explanations of each grammatical point and provide practice and reinforcement of the covered material. Together with the answer key, the practice exercises enable students to gauge their own understanding and progress. Finally, the comprehensive index provides quick and easy access to information.

JAMES S. LEVINE

ACKNOWLEDGMENTS

I am indebted to the many Russian language specialists whose work I consulted, and benefited from, in writing various portions of this book. In particular, I would like to acknowledge my debt to the following: G. G. Timofeeva's *Новые английские заимствования в русском языке* in the discussion of English-to-Russian transliteration (Chapter 1); Johanna Nichols' *Predicate Nominals: A Partial Surface Syntax of Russian* in the description of predicate nominatives and predicate instrumentals after forms of **быть** (Chapter 2) and in the description of the two types of **это** sentences (Chapter 4); Derek Offord's *Using Russian: A Guide to Contemporary Usage* in the presentation of prepositions (Chapter 3); Genevra Gerhart's *The Russian's World* in the presentation of numbers and fractions (Chapter 6); Alexander Nakhimovsky's *Overview of Russian Conjugation* in the description of the single-stem verb system (Chapter 7); and O. P. Rassudova's *Aspectual Usage in Modern Russian* in the discussion of the meaning and uses of the aspects (Chapter 7). A valuable source of information on topics throughout the book was Terrence Wade's *A Comprehensive Russian Grammar*. Complete references for these works, and for other sources consulted, are given in the Bibliography.

I would like to thank the following friends, colleagues, and students who helped in various ways in the preparation of this book. Particular thanks must go to William S. Hamilton (Wake Forest University), whose teaching first inspired me to learn Russian, and who has been a mentor and friend throughout my career. His advice and comments on an earlier draft of this book resulted in several improvements. I am also grateful to Thomas R. Beyer, Jr. (Middlebury College), who reviewed the manuscript and wrote a detailed report with many helpful recommendations. To Marybeth Spain go my sincere thanks for her help in the preparation of Chapter 8. Certain formulations on the use of conjunctions originated with her, as did many of this chapter's illustrative examples. Ekaterina Mosolevskaya kindly contributed the sample of Russian cursive letters in Chapter 1. The book has fewer errors thanks to careful proofreading by Mikhail Feldman, who read an early draft, and by Tatiana Vasilyeva, who read the page proofs for Chapter 3. I am also deeply grateful to Viktor Zabolotnyi, with whom I frequently consulted on questions of style and usage. He gave most generously of his time, sharing his native intuitions and judgments on my examples, often suggesting adjustments, or replacing my examples with his own.

I would like to express my appreciation to the editorial staff of Schaum Publications of McGraw-Hill: Barbara Gilson (Editorial Director), who initiated the process of having a Russian volume added to the foreign language grammars in the Schaum's Outline Series; Mary Loebig Giles (Associate Editor), who handled correspondence and coordinated the initial review of the manuscript; Maureen Walker (Editing Supervisor); and Meaghan McGovern (Editorial Assistant), who coordinated the final review of the manuscript, and was always helpful in responding to my questions and concerns. I am also grateful to the staff at Keyword Publishing Services Ltd, London: Alan Hunt, who expertly managed the copyediting and typesetting of the manuscript, and Olga Abbott, who read the final proofs and helped eliminate a number of errors that I had missed. This book is certainly a better one for the efforts of all those mentioned, but any inaccuracies and mistakes that remain are mine alone.

On a more personal note, I would like to thank my wife, Jody, and my daughters, Sasha and Erica, for generously tolerating my frequent absences and my near monopoly of the computer over the past year and a half. Their love and enthusiasm make everything possible. This book is dedicated to them.

J.S.L.

CONTENTS

CHAPTER 1   **The Sounds of Russian**   **1**

The Russian (Cyrillic) Alphabet   1

Alphabet. Shapes and sounds. Letters similar to English letters in form and pronunciation. Letters similar to English letters in form, but not in pronunciation. Letters corresponding to letters in Greek. Remaining letters. The two "signs."

The Vowels   4

Stressed vowels. Unstressed vowels. Vowel reduction rules.

The Consonants   7

Paired consonants: hard and soft. Unpaired consonants. Clusters of unpaired consonants. Voiced and voiceless consonants. Voicing rules.

Syllabification   10
Spelling Rules   10
Capitalization   11
Transliteration: English to Russian   11

English consonants and their Cyrillic counterparts. English consonant letters lacking one-to-one phonetic equivalents. English letter combinations transliterated by a single letter in Cyrillic.

Russian Letter Styles   13

Italic letters. Cursive letters.

CHAPTER 2   **Nouns**   **19**

Articles   19
Noun Structure   19
Gender   20

Grammatical gender. Masculine nouns. Feminine nouns. Neuter nouns. Why gender is important.

Gender Identification by Noun Groups   22

Masculine nouns of natural gender in **-а** and **-я**. Masculine nouns with a stem ending in the soft sign. Feminine nouns with a stem ending in the soft sign.

Nouns of Common Gender   23
Gender of Nouns Denoting Professions   24
Gender Differentiation by Suffix   25

Nouns denoting people.

ix

Gender of Indeclinable Nouns of Foreign Origin 26
Number 28
Nominative Plural of Nouns 28

Spelling Rule 1 and nominative plurals. Stress shifts in nominative plurals. Fleeting vowels in the nominative plural. Nominative plurals in **-á (-я́)**.

Irregular Plurals 30

Irregular nominative plurals in **-ья**. Irregular plurals from different words. Plurals of neuter nouns in **-мя**.

Nouns Used Only in the Singular 32
Nouns Used Only in the Plural 33
Declension of Nouns 34

First declension. Second declension. Third declension.

Case 35
Animacy 35
The Cases of Russian 35

Nominative case. Accusative case. Genitive case. Prepositional case. Dative case. Instrumental case.

Personal Names (Part I) 64

First names and patronymics.

Summary Table of Case Endings of Nouns in the Singular 65
Summary Table of Case Endings of Nouns in the Plural 65

CHAPTER 3   **Prepositions**   **67**

Prepositions Governing the Nominative Case 67
Prepositions Governing the Accusative Case 68
Prepositions Governing Either the Accusative or the Prepositional Case 70

Verbs governing the preposition **в** + accusative. Verbs governing the preposition **на** + accusative.

Prepositions Governing Either the Accusative or the Instrumental Case 74
Prepositions Governing the Genitive Case 77

Core prepositions governing the genitive case. Verbs followed by the preposition **от** + genitive case. Verbs followed by the preposition **у** + genitive case. Other prepositions governing the genitive case.

Prepositions Governing the Prepositional or Locative Case 87

Verbs governing the preposition **в** + prepositional case. Nouns requiring the preposition **на** to express location. Verbs followed by the preposition **на** + prepositional case.

Prepositions Governing the Dative Case 94

Verbs followed by the preposition **к** + dative case.

Prepositions Governing the Instrumental Case   97

Verbs followed by the preposition **за** + instrumental case. Verbs followed
by the preposition **с** + instrumental case.

CHAPTER 4   **Pronouns**   **101**

Personal Pronouns   101

Nominative case. Accusative case. Genitive case. Prepositional case. Dative
case. Instrumental case.

The Reflexive Personal Pronoun **Себя**   109

Idiomatic uses of **себя**.

The Reciprocal Pronoun **Дру́г дру́га**   110
Interrogative Pronouns: **Кто́**, **Что́**   112

The pronoun **кто́**. The pronoun **что́**.

Possessive Pronouns   114

The possessive pronouns **че́й?, мо́й, тво́й, на́ш, ва́ш**. The possessive
pronouns **его́, её, их**. The reflexive possessive pronoun **сво́й**.

Demonstrative Pronouns   119

The demonstrative pronouns **э́тот** and **то́т**. The indeclinable pronoun **э́то**.
The "identifying" **э́то**. The "characterizing" **э́то**. The demonstrative
pronoun **тако́й**.

Determinative Pronouns   123

The emphatic pronoun **са́м**. The pronoun **са́мый**. The pronoun **ве́сь**.

Relative Pronouns   127

The relative pronoun **кото́рый**. The relative pronoun **како́й**. The relative
pronouns **кто́** and **что́**.

Indefinite Pronouns   134

The pronouns **кто́-то/кто́-нибудь, что́-то/что́-нибудь,
како́й-то/како́й-нибудь, че́й-то/че́й-нибудь**.

Negative Pronouns   136

Negative pronouns in **ни-: никто́, ничто́, никако́й, ниче́й**. Negative
pronouns in **не-: не́кого, не́чего**.

CHAPTER 5   **Adjectives and Adverbs**   **140**

Adjectives   140

Qualitative and relational adjectives.

The Long Form of Adjectives   141

Attributive and predicative. Adjective structure. Declension of adjectives.
Adjectives whose stem ends in a hard consonant. Adjectives whose stem
ends in a soft **-н**. Adjectives whose stem ends in **-г, -к, -х**. Adjectives whose
stem ends in **-ж, -ч, -ш, -щ**.

The Short Form of Adjectives   146

Use of short-form adjectives. Choosing the short form or the long form in the predicate. Use of **какóй** vs. **какóв** and **такóй** vs. **такóв**. Use of **такóй** vs. **тáк** and **какóй** vs. **кáк**.

Adjectives Used as Nouns   155

Neuter singular adjectives used as nouns.

Possessive Adjectives   157

Possessive adjectives of the type **птúчий**. Possessive adjectives in the suffix **-ин**.

Personal Names (Part II)   159

Family names in **-ин** and **-ов**, **-ев**, **-ёв**. Family names in **-ий** and **-óй**.

Comparison of Adjectives and Adverbs   159

The degrees of comparison. Russian comparatives. Formation of the compound comparative. Use of the compound comparative. Formation of the simple comparative. Use of the simple comparative. The compound superlative: form and use. The simple superlative: form and use.

Adverbs   168

Adverbs of manner. Adverbs of time. Adverbs of place. Adverbs of measure or degree. Indefinite adverbs. Negative adverbs.

CHAPTER 6   **Numbers, Dates, Time**   **177**

Numbers   177

Cardinal numbers. Use of **нóль/нýль** 0. Declension and use of 1. Declension and use of 2, 3, and 4. Declension of 5–20 and 30. Declension of 50, 60, 70, and 80. Declension of 40, 90, and 100. Declension of 200, 300, and 400. Declension of 500, 600, 700, 800, and 900. Use of cardinal numbers 5–999. Declension and use of **тýсяча**. Declension and use of **миллиóн** and **миллиáрд/биллиóн**. Money and prices. Telephone numbers. Numerical nouns formed from cardinal numbers. Collective numbers. Ordinal numbers. Use of Russian ordinals for English cardinals. Fractions. Decimal fractions.

Dates   199

Days of the week. Weeks. Months. Seasons. Years and centuries. Dates with months and years. Order of numbers in dates. Expressing age.

Time   205

Conversational clock time. Official time: 24-hour system. Approximation.

CHAPTER 7   **Verbs**   **209**

Overview of Verbs   209

Transitive and intransitive verbs. Personal endings. Forms of address: informal and formal. Verb tenses. Verb aspects. Verb moods.

Conjugation   211

The infinitive. The past tense. The present tense. First and second conjugation endings. Stress patterns in the non-past. Consonant alternations in conjugation. Verbal stem structure: (prefix) + root + (suffix). The basic stem: suffixed and nonsuffixed. Rules for combining basic stem + endings. Stems with a suffix. Suffixes that build first conjugation verbs. Suffixes that build second conjugation verbs. Irregular verbs of mixed conjugation. Summary table of suffixed stems. Nonsuffixed stems. Irregular verbs with nonsuffixed stem. Summary table of nonsuffixed stems.

Verb Tenses: Formation   238

Present tense. Past tense. Future tense.

Verb Aspects: Formation   240

Prefixation. Suffixation. Suppletion.

Verb Aspects: Meanings and Uses   242

Aspect choice and context. Aspect in the past and future. Contexts for using perfective verbs. Contexts for using imperfective verbs. Aspect in questions. Aspect in the infinitive. Negation and imperfective infinitives. **Не** + imperfective infinitives. Absence of necessity (**не надо**) + imperfective infinitives. **Нельзя́** and aspect in the infinitive.

Imperatives   254

Second-person imperative: formation. Aspect and the second-person imperative. Affirmative imperatives. Negated imperatives. First-person imperative. Third-person imperative.

The Conditional   260

Real and unreal conditionals.

The Subjunctive   262

The subjunctive with **бы** + past tense. The subjunctive with **что́бы** + past tense.

Transitive and Intransitive Verbs   266
Verbs with the Particle -ся (-сь)   266

Principal groups of verbs in **-ся**. Voice and the particle **-ся**. Active voice. Passive voice. Middle voice.

Verbal Government   271
Verbs of Motion   271

Unidirectional and multidirectional verbs. Intransitive verbs of motion. Principal uses of unidirectional verbs. Principal uses of multidirectional verbs. Transitive verbs of motion. Prefixed verbs of motion. Unidirectional verbs in the prefix **по-**. Multidirectional verbs in the prefix **по-**. Directional prefixes. Aspectual usage of prefixed motion verbs.

Verbal Adjectives (Participles)   280

Active participles. Present active participles. Past active participles. Passive participles. Present passive participles. Past passive participles. Short past passive participles.

Verbal Adverbs (Gerunds)   285
Imperfective verbal adverbs. Perfective verbal adverbs.

CHAPTER 8   **Conjunctions**   **289**
Coordinating Conjunctions   289
Copulative (connective) coordinating conjunctions. Disjunctive coordinating
conjunctions. Adversative coordinating conjunctions. The adversative
conjunction **a**: contrastive and contradictory. Choosing **и**, **a**, or **но**.

Subordinating Conjunctions   295
Temporal conjunctions. Causal conjunctions. Purposive conjunctions.
Subordinating conjunctions **что** and **как**. Resultative conjunctions.
Conditional conjunctions. Concessive conjunctions. Comparative
conjunctions.

Answers to Exercises   **306**
Bibliography   **324**
Index   **327**

The Sounds of Russian

THE RUSSIAN (CYRILLIC) ALPHABET

The Russian alphabet is also known as the Cyrillic alphabet, named in honor of St. Cyril, the Greek monk and scholar who is credited with devising an early version of it. The Russian alphabet contains 33 letters, most of which represent sounds similar to those of English.

Alphabet

Cyrillic Letter	Name of Letter	English Equivalent (approximate)	Cyrillic Letter	Name of Letter	English Equivalent (approximate)
А а	a	*a as in father*	Р р	er	*r as in better*
Б б	be	*b as in bet*	С с	es	*s as in sun*
В в	ve	*v as in very*	Т т	te	*t as in Tanya*
Г г	ge	*g as in get*	У у	u	*u as in flu*
Д д	de	*d as in dog*	Ф ф	ef	*f as in fun*
Е е	ye	*ye as in yes*	Х х	kha	*ch as in Bach*
Ё ё	yo	*yo as in York*	Ц ц	tse	*ts as in cats*
Ж ж	zhe	*z as in azure*	Ч ч	che	*ch as in cheese*
З з	ze	*z as in zoo*	Ш ш	sha	*sh as in shoe*
И и	i	*i as in visa*	Щ щ	shcha	*shsh as in fresh sheen*
Й й	i kratkoye (short i)	*y as in boy*	ъ	tvyordiy znak (hard sign)	*no sound value*
К к	ka	*k as in skate*	ы	yeri	*i as in vigor*
Л л	el	*l as in lot*	ь	myagkiy znak (soft sign)	*no sound value*
М м	em	*m as in Mike*			
Н н	en	*n as in net*	Э э	e oborotnoye (reversed e)	*e as in echo*
О о	o	*o as in ought*			
П п	pe	*p as in span*	Ю ю	yu	*yu as in Yukon*
			Я я	ya	*ya as in yacht*

The alphabet chart above lists approximate English equivalents for the sound values of the Cyrillic letters as well as the *Russian names* of the letters in the Cyrillic alphabet. It is important to learn the pronunciation of the letter names, as well as the order in which they occur, for several reasons. First, in order to pronounce the many acronyms that occur in Russian, one must know the names of the Cyrillic letters, since many acronyms are pronounced as a succession of individual letters, e.g., **МБ** is pronounced "em-be" and stands for **Мирово́й ба́нк** *World Bank*, **ЦБР** is pronounced "tse-be-er" for **Центра́льный ба́нк Росси́и** *Central Bank of Russia*, and **РФ** is pronounced "er-ef" for **Росси́йская Федера́ция** *Russian Federation*. Second, knowing the names of the letters is important for those situations when it is necessary to spell words such as names and addresses, for example, when traveling in Russia, or when speaking to Russians on the telephone. Finally, when looking up words in a dictionary, knowing the correct sequence of the letters will make the search for words easier and faster.

Shapes and Sounds

Several Cyrillic letters are immediately recognizable from their similarity to English letters, and some of these are also pronounced close to their English counterparts. However, rarely are there exact sound equivalents between languages, and so the comparisons between Russian and English sounds given in this pronunciation key should be viewed only as a guide to correct pronunciation in Russian. In order to acquire native-like pronunciation it is important not only to study the differences between English and Russian sounds, but also to *practice* the correct Russian pronunciation with audiotapes and videotapes, and, of course, to take every opportunity to listen to, and talk with, native speakers of Russian.

In illustrating the sounds of Russian consonants and vowels, we use a *phonetic transcription* which is shown in square brackets [ ]. The transcription used in this book will employ the Latin letters of English and, when needed, a few diacritical marks, e.g., the sounds associated with the letter combinations *sh* and *ch* in English *shop* and *cheese* will be represented as [š] and [č], respectively, with the "haček" symbol ˇ above the letter. Also, Russian stressed vowels (discussed below) will be represented by an acute accent mark [´]. It should be noted that the English equivalents of the Russian vowels in the alphabet chart are for the pronunciation of these vowels when they are stressed. If they are not stressed, they may shift to less distinct values, as we shall see below.

Letters Similar to English Letters in Form and Pronunciation

Letter	Sound	Russian	Example	Approximate Pronunciation
А а	[á]	а́кт	act	like *a* in English *father*, but with the mouth open a bit wider
О о	[ó]	ко́т	cat	like *o* in English *ought*, but with the lips more rounded and protruded
Е е	[é]	те́ма	theme	like *e* in English *tempo*
М м	[m]	ма́ма	mom	just like English *m*
К к	[k]	ко́мик	comic	like English *k*, but without the puff of air following it; like English *skate*
Т т	[t]	то́м	tome	like English *t*, but a pure dental, with the tip of the tongue touching the lower teeth, not the teeth ridge as in English

Letters Similar to English Letters in Form, but Not in Pronunciation

Other Cyrillic letters correspond in shape to letters in English, but they correspond in pronunciation to *different* English letters. These are examples of *faux amis*, or "false friends," in the alphabet.

Letter	Sound	Russian	Example	Approximate Pronunciation
У у	[ú]	у́тка	duck	like in English *flu*, but shorter and the lips more rounded and protruded

В в	[v]	во́дка	vodka	just like English *v*
Н н	[n]	не́т	no	like *n* in English, but a pure dental, with the tip of the tongue touching the lower teeth (like Russian т)
Р р	[r]	ка́рта	map	like in English *better* or *ladder*, i.e., a flapped [r], produced by the tip of the tongue tapping against the teeth ridge
С с	[s]	но́с	nose	like the *s* and *c* in English *sauce*, but a pure dental, the tongue touching the lower teeth; never like the *c* in English *cat* or *contact*

Letters Corresponding to Letters in Greek

In addition to the letters that are shaped like those in English, a few Cyrillic letters resemble letters in the Greek alphabet, on which they were modeled. The following letters were fashioned after the Greek letters *gamma*, *delta*, *lambda*, *pi*, *phi*, and *chi*, respectively (also, Greek *rho* served as a model for Cyrillic **P**, listed in the previous group due to its misleading similarity to English *p*).

Letter	*Sound*	*Russian*	*Example*	*Approximate Pronunciation*
Г г	[g]	га́з	gas	like *g* in English *get*; never like the first or second *g* in *George*
Д д	[d]	до́м	house	like *d* in English, but a pure dental, with the tip of the tongue touching the lower teeth (like Russian т and н)
Л л	[l]	Ла́ра	Lara	like *l* in English *pill*, but with the tongue farther back in the mouth
П п	[p]	па́спорт	passport	like *p* in English *span*; not like the "aspirated" *p* in English *pan*
Ф ф	[f]	кафе́	cafe	like *f* in English
Х х	[x]	са́хар	sugar	like *ch* in German Bach

Remaining Letters

The remaining Cyrillic letters do not resemble letters in English or Greek. At least one letter, **ш** [š], is modeled after the Hebrew letter *shin*. Three others look like the reverse of English letters: Cyrillic **я** [ya] has the shape of a backwards English **R**. Cyrillic **и** [i] is the reverse of English **N**. And Cyrillic **э** [e] is shaped like a reverse, but more rounded, English **E**.

Letter	*Sound*	*Russian*	*Example*	*Approximate Pronunciation*
Б б	[b]	бана́н	banana	like *b* in English, but not aspirated (like Russian п)
З з	[z]	ва́за	vase	like *z* in English, but with the tip of the tongue touching the lower teeth (like Russian с)
Ё ё	[yo]	ёлка	fir tree	like *yo* in English *York* and *yore*
Ж ж	[ž]	журна́л	magazine	like *z* in English *azure*, but with the tongue farther back and the lips rounded
И и	[i]	ди́ск	disk	like *i* in English *visa*
Й й	[y]	ма́й	May	a "glide," like *y* in English *toy*, *boy*
Ц ц	[c]	ца́рь	tsar	similar to the *ts* in English *nuts*, but pronounced together as one sound
Ч ч	[č']	ча́й	tea	like *ch* in English *cheese* but softer, with the tongue raised higher

Ш ш	[š]	шо́к	shock	like *sh* in English, but with the tongue farther back in the mouth
Щ щ	[šš']	бо́рщ	borsch	similar to *shsh* in English *fresh sheen*, but softer, with the tongue higher and more forward in the mouth
ы	[ɨ]	сы́н	son	no close English equivalent; similar to *i* in English *sin*, *vigor*, but with the tongue drawn further back and the lips spread
Э э	[e]	э́ра	era	similar to *e* in English *echo*, but with the mouth open wider
Ю ю	[yu]	ю́мор	humor	similar to English *yu* in *Yukon*, and *u* in *use*
Я я	[ya]	Я́лта	Yalta	similar to English *ya* in *Yalta* or *yacht*

The Two "Signs"

Finally, Russian has two "signs" which, by themselves, have no sound value, but serve important functions, especially the "soft sign":

ь   soft sign—indicates that a preceding consonant is "soft" or "palatalized," which in transcription will be represented by an apostrophe after the consonant, e.g., **со́ль** *salt* [sól'] (see section below on Palatalized Consonants). Between a soft consonant (C) and a vowel (V) the letter **ь** indicates the sequence C + [y] + V, e.g., **Татья́на** is pronounced **Та** [t' + y + á] **на**.

ъ   hard sign—occurs only after a prefix ending in a consonant before a root beginning with a vowel, e.g., **въе́зд** *entrance* **в** + **ъ** + **езд** where **в** is a prefix meaning "in" and **езд** is a root meaning *drive*; **ъ** also indicates the presence of [y] before a vowel, e.g., **въ** [ye]зд.

To summarize, of the 33 letters in the Cyrillic alphabet, 10 are vowels, 20 are consonants, 1 is a "glide" **й** [y], and 2 are "signs," the "soft sign" (**ь**) and the "hard sign" (**ъ**).

THE VOWELS

There are 5 vowel *sounds* represented by 10 vowel *letters*, two letters for each sound. The vowel letters can be divided into 2 series: the "hard series" and the "soft series."

Hard Series	**a** [a]	**э** [e]	**o** [o]	**y** [u]	**ы** [ɨ]
Soft Series	**я** [ya] ['a]	**e** [ye] ['e]	**ё** [yo] ['o]	**ю** [yu] ['u]	**и** [i] ['i]

The terms "hard" and "soft" do not refer to the vowels themselves, but to the consonants that precede them. A hard consonant is the basic articulation of the consonant, just as it is described above in this pronunciation key. A *soft*, or *palatalized*, consonant is identical except for one important modification—in pronouncing a soft consonant the tongue is simultaneously raised toward the palate, or roof of the mouth. Most Russian consonants have these two forms of pronunciation. When a consonant is capable of occurring either hard or soft, it will be hard before the letters **a э o у ы**, and soft before the letters **я е ё ю и**. The soft series vowels with a preceding soft consonant are indicated in transcription by ['a] ['e] ['o] ['u] ['i], the apostrophe indicating the soft pronunciation of the consonant. In addition, the soft series vowels **я е ё ю** (but not **и**) are pronounced with a preceding [y] (as [ya] [ye] [yo] and [yu]) in the following positions:

1. Word-initially: **Я́лта**   [yá]   **Е́льцин**   [yé]   **ёлка**   [yó]   **ю́мор**   [yú]
2. After a vowel: **моя́**   [yá]   **пое́л**   [yé]   **моё**   [yó]   **мою́**   [yú]
3. After **ь** and **ъ**:   **друзья́**   [yá]   **въе́зд**   [yé]   **бельё**   [yó]   **ма́терью**   [yu]

Stressed Vowels

Russian, like English, is characterized by a heavy *stress* within a word. A stressed vowel is one which is emphasized by pronouncing it with greater force, or louder, than unstressed vowels. The stressed vowels are also tense and a bit longer than unstressed vowels in the word. However, even when stressed, Russian vowels are shorter than the long vowels in English, which may begin as one sound and *glide* into another sound, producing a diphthong. In pronouncing Russian vowels it is important to avoid pronouncing them like English diphthongs. Compare, for example, the vowel sound [uw] in English *boots* with Russian [u] in **бу́тсы** *soccer boots*; the sound [oə] in English *cork* with [o] in Russian **ко́рка** *crust*; and the sound [iy] in English *mere*, *feel*, and *fear* with [i] in Russian **ми́р** *peace*, **филе́** *fillet*, and **фи́рма** *firm*. The Russian vowels in these examples, and in Russian words generally, are monophthongs, that is, they begin and end with the same sound.

Stress in Russian, as in English, is "free," that is, it can fall on any vowel in the word: first (**до́ктор** *doctor*), second (**профе́ссор** *professor*), third (**рестора́н** *restaurant*), fourth (**университе́т** *university*), etc. Russian stress is also "mobile," i.e., the stress may shift from one syllable to another within the grammatical forms of the same word, for example within the singular and plural forms of a noun: **а́дрес** *address* and **адреса́** *addresses*. Also, stress can determine the meaning and/or the part of speech of certain words that are spelled alike, e.g., **мука́** *flour* and **му́ка** *torture*, the adverb **до́ма** *at home* and the plural noun **дома́** *houses*. (The same phenomenon occurs in English: only the stress differentiates the noun *récord* and the verb *recórd*.) For these reasons, it is very important when learning new words to learn the stress of the word as well. Stressed vowels are not normally marked in a Russian text, but they are marked in dictionaries and textbooks of Russian. Note also that the vowel letter **ё** [yo]/['o] always indicates a stressed vowel, so it is the only vowel whose stress is not indicated by the acute accent ´.

Unstressed Vowels

The stressed vowel in a word is emphasized at the expense of the other, unstressed vowels. Thus, in relation to the stressed vowel, unstressed vowels are usually shorter, and lax, i.e., pronounced in a more "relaxed" way. These changes are referred to as *vowel reduction*. Not all vowels in Russian are reduced. For example, the vowels **ю/у** and **и/ы** when unstressed remain essentially the same. Nor can the vowel **ё** ever be reduced, since this vowel is *always* stressed. Therefore, the only vowels that may have a reduced pronunciation are **а о э я** and **e**. The first two vowels, **a** and **o**, are reduced to varying degrees, depending on their location in relation to the stressed syllable. The least amount of reduction occurs in the syllable immediately preceding the stressed syllable—called the "pretonic" syllable—and in word-initial position. In any other syllable before or after the stress, the vowels **a** and **o** undergo a further reduction. It is important to keep in mind that a preposition and its object are pronounced as if they were a *single* phonetic unit, i.e., as one word. As a result, unstressed vowels in prepositions are reduced according to their position in relation to the stressed vowel of the following word. Examples are given below.

Vowel Reduction Rules

1. *Reduction of the Vowels* **a** *and* **o**

    (*a*)   **a** [a] and **o** [o] → [ʌ]

    (*b*)   **a** [a] and **o** [o] → [ə]

(a)   in pretonic (i.e., the syllable immediately preceding the stressed syllable) and/or word-initial
      position both **a** and **o** are pronounced as a slightly shorter and more lax *a* sound. In phonetic
      transcription it is customary to represent this sound with the symbol [ʌ].

        Pretonic: **бана́н** [bʌnán] *banana*   **доска́** [dʌská] *blackboard*
                          Москва́ [mʌskvá] *Moscow*   **вопро́с** [vʌprós] *question*
                          над до́мом [nʌddómǝm] *above the house*
                          до за́втра [dʌzáftrǝ] *until tomorrow*
                          под но́сом [pʌd nósǝm] *under the nose*
        Word-initial: **она́** [ʌná] *she*   **окно́** [ʌknó] *window*
                          отве́т [ʌtv'ét] *answer*   **оборо́т** [ʌbʌrót] *turn*
                        анана́с [ʌnʌnás] *pineapple*   **об э́том** [ʌbétǝm] *about this*

(b)   in any position other than pretonic or word-initial, Russian **a** and **o** are pronounced even shorter
       and more lax, similar to the sound of the first and last vowel, respectively, of English ***about*** and
       sofa. This sound is represented with the symbol [ǝ].

        ма́ма [mámǝ] *mom*   **до́ктор** [dóktǝr] *doctor*
        соба́ка [sʌbákǝ] *dog*   **хорошо́** [xǝrʌšó] *good*
        молоко́ [mǝlʌkó] *milk*   **городо́к** [gǝrʌdók] *town*
        ко́мната [kómnǝtǝ] *room*   **панора́ма** [pǝnʌrámǝ] *panorama*
        под водо́й [pǝdvʌdóy] *under water*   **на мосту́** [nǝmʌstú] *on the bridge*

Note: When preceded by the consonant **ч**, unstressed **a** is pronounced [i], e.g., in **часы́** [č'isí] *watch*,
части́ца [č'ist'ícǝ] *particle*, **частота́** [č'istʌtá] *frequency*.

Note: When preceded by the consonant **ж**, unstressed **a** is pronounced [ɨ], e.g., in the words **жале́ть**
[žɨl'ét'] *to regret*, **к сожале́нию** [ksǝžɨl'én'iyu] *unfortunately*.

2.   *Reduction of the Vowel* **э** [e]

    э [e] → [i]

In many words the vowel **э** [e] when unstressed is pronounced [i]. This vowel occurs primarily in words
of foreign origin, and almost always at the beginning of the word.

        экле́р [ikl'ér] *eclair*   **эпо́ха** [ipóxǝ] *epoch*
        эгои́ст [igʌíst] *egoist*   **эконо́мика** [ikʌnóm'ikǝ] *economics*
        эле́ктрик [il'éktr'ik] *electrician*   **экза́мен** [igzám'in] *examination*
        экспре́сс [ikspr'éss] *express*   **эта́п** [itáp] *stage*

3.   *Reduction of the Vowels* **я** [ya] *and* **e** [ye]
(a)   **я** [ya] and **e** [ye] → [yi]/[i]
(b)   **я** [ya] and **e** [ye] → [yǝ]/[ǝ]

(a)   Except in certain grammatical endings, unstressed **я** [ya] and **e** [ye] are both pronounced [yi] in
       word-initial position, or after a vowel; after a soft consonant, these vowels are pronounced as [i],
       without the initial [y].

   Word-initial:

        язы́к [yizík] *language*   **япо́нка** [yipónkǝ] *Japanese female*
        ягуа́р [yiguár] *jaguar*   **яйцо́** [yiycó] *egg*
        яку́т [yikút] *Yakut*   **еда́** [yidá] *food*
        езда́ [yizdá] *ride*   **ено́т** [yinót] *raccoon*

After a vowel:

по́яс [póyis] *belt*   **краси́вее** [krasív'iyi] *prettier*

After a consonant:

телефо́н [t'il'ifón] *telephone*   **ветерина́р** [v'it'ir'inár] *veterinarian*
мясни́к [m'isn'ík] *butcher*   **ве́чер** [v'éč'ir] *evening*
теа́тр [t'iátr] *theater*   **де́сять** [d'és'it'] *ten*

(*b*) In noun endings, both **я** and **е** are pronounced [ə]. In certains forms of adjective endings (neuter-**ое/-ее**; feminine-**ая/-яя**), unstressed **е** and **я** are pronounced either [yə] or [ə], depending on whether they follow a vowel or a consonant, respectively.

Nouns:

мо́ре [mór'ə] *sea*   **по́ле** [pól'ə] *field*
зда́ние [zdán'iyə] *building*   **ка́пля** [kápl'ə] *drop*
исто́рия [istór'iyə] *history*   **галере́я** [gəl'ir'éyə] *gallery*

Adjectives:

но́вое/но́вая [nóvəyə] *new*   **хоро́шая/хоро́шее** [хʌróšəyə] *good*

Note: When unstressed **е** is preceded by the consonants **ж**, **ш**, or **ц**, it is pronounced like the vowel **ы** [ɨ], e.g., **жена́** [žɨná] *wife*, **щербе́т** [šɨrbét] *sherbet*, **цена́** [cɨná] *price*.

THE CONSONANTS

There are 20 consonants in Russian, 15 of which are paired, that is, they occur in pairs of hard and soft (palatalized) versions.

Paired Consonants: Hard and Soft

б [b] – [b']   **д** [d] – [d']   **л** [l] – [l']   **п** [p] – [p']   **т** [t] – [t']
в [v] – [v']   **з** [z] – [z']   **м** [m] – [m']   **р** [r] – [r']   **ф** [f] – [f']
г [g] – [g']   **к** [k] – [k']   **н** [n] – [n']   **с** [s] – [s']   **х** [x] – [x']

A soft consonant is pronounced the same way as its hard counterpart, except for one important additional feature—the consonant is pronounced with the middle of the tongue raised toward the roof of the mouth, as in the pronunciation of the vowel **и**. As a result, the soft consonant has an [i]-like quality superimposed on it. Soft consonants are represented in transcription as the consonant letter followed by an apostrophe, e.g., a soft **т** is [t']. Also, it is important to remember that a soft consonant is *one* sound, not two. Be careful to avoid pronouncing a soft consonant as a hard consonant with a following [y] sound, that is, avoid pronouncing [t + y], e.g., the Russian word for "aunt" **тётя** is pronounced [t'ót'ə], NOT *[tyótyə].

Since the same consonant letter is used for both the hard and soft consonant, it is only possible to determine which ones are hard and which are soft by what *follows* the consonant in spelling. Remember that hard consonants are those which are followed by one of the hard series vowels **а э о у ы**, or they occur with no vowel following. Soft consonants are those followed by one of the soft series vowels **я е ё ю и**, or they are followed by the soft sign **ь**. For example:

гуля́ть   **г** is hard, **л**, **т** are soft
телефо́н   **т**, **л** are soft, **ф**, **н** are hard
весёлый   **в**, **с** are soft, **л** is hard

изю́ м	з is soft, м is hard
изумру́д	з, м, р, д are hard
зде́сь	*з, д, с are soft

Note: In the last example, **зде́сь**, not only the **д** but also the preceding **з** is soft. This "double softening" affects the consonants **д, т, н, с, з** when they precede a consonant that is softened by a soft series vowel, or a consonant that is *always* soft: **ч** and **щ**, e.g. **ко́нчик** [kón'č'ik] *tip/point*, **же́нщина** [žén'šš'inə] *woman* (see "Unpaired Consonants" below).

The rules for identifying hard and soft paired consonants are summarized in the following chart.

Hard Consonants are followed by:	а	э	о	у	ы	
Soft Consonants are followed by:	я	е	ё	ю	и	ь

Unpaired Consonants

The remaining 5 consonants do not form pairs of hard and soft counterparts. Two consonants are always soft: **ч** and **щ**. Three consonants are always hard: **ш, ж, ц**.

Always Soft	ч щ
Always Hard	ж ш ц

The consonants **ш, ж**, and **ц** remain hard even when they are followed by soft series vowels. In fact, when following these consonants, the stressed soft series vowels **е и** and **ё** are pronounced like their hard series counterparts: **э ы о**. Recall, however, that when unstressed, the combinations **же, ше**, and **це** are pronounced [žɨ], [šɨ], and [cɨ].

ше́ст [šést] *pole*	**шесто́й** [šɨstóy] *sixth*
маши́на [mʌšínə] *car*	**шёлк** [šólk] *silk*
шелкови́стый [šɨlkʌvístɨy] *silky*	**жест** [žést] *gesture*
жесто́кий [žɨstókiy] *cruel*	**жёлтый** [žóltɨy] *yellow*
живо́т [živót] *stomach*	**ци́рк** [cɨrk] *circus*
це́нтр [céntr] *center*	**центра́льный** [cɨntrál'nɨy] *central*

Clusters of Unpaired Consonants

The Clusters **жч, сч,** *and* **зч**

In the consonant cluster **жч**, the unpaired hard consonant **ж** assimilates to the following unpaired soft consonant **ч**, resulting in the pronunciation of the cluster as a long soft [šš'], e.g., **мужчи́на** [mušš'ínə] *man*. In certain words, the clusters **сч** and **зч** are also pronounced [šš'], e.g., **сча́стье** [šš'ás't'yə] *happiness*, **сча́стливо** [šš'ástl'ivə] *happily*, **счёт** [šš'ót] *bill*, **зака́зчик** [zʌkášš'ik] *client/customer*.

The Clusters жж *and* зж

The clusters of unpaired hard consonants **жж** and **зж** are pronounced as a long soft [žž'] in the words **дро́жжи** [dróžž'i] *yeast*, **жжёт** [žž'ót] *burns*, **е́зжу** [yéžž'u] *I travel*, **поезжа́й** [pəyižž'áy] *Go!*, **по́зже** [póžž'i] *later*.

Voiced and Voiceless Consonants

There are six pairs of voiced and voiceless consonants.

Voiced Consonants	б [b]	в [v]	г [g]	д [d]	ж [ž]	з [z]
Voiceless Consonants	п [p]	ф [f]	к [k]	т [t]	ш [š]	с [s]

The remaining consonants are unpaired as to voice: **л**, **р**, **м**, and **н** are voiced; **ц**, **х**, **ч**, and **щ** are voiceless.

Voiced consonants are pronounced with the vocal cords vibrating, whereas voiceless consonants are pronounced without the vibration of the vocal cords. As in English, the opposition of voiced and voiceless consonants can distinguish the meaning of words, e.g., English *bin* and *pin*. Note the following Russian words whose meaning is distinguished solely by the *voiced* or *voiceless member* of a consonant pair:

б́ар	*bar*	па́р	*steam*
до́м	*house*	то́м	*tome*
игра́	*game*	икра́	*caviar*
зу́б	*tooth*	су́п	*soup*

Voicing Rules

Paired consonants may change in pronunciation from their voiced to voiceless counterpart and vice versa, depending on their position in a word. Following are the rules governing the voicing and devoicing of the paired consonants:

1. In word-final position, voiced consonants are pronounced voiceless:

б [b] → [p]	зу́б [zúp]	*tooth*
в [v] → [f]	ле́в [l'éf]	*lion*
г [g] → [k]	до́г [dók]	*Great Dane*
д [d] → [t]	го́д [gót]	*year*
ж [ž] → [š]	но́ж [nóš]	*knife*
з [z] → [s]	га́з [gás]	*gas*

2. In a cluster of two consonants within a word, or at a boundary between two words pronounced rapidly together, the second consonant causes the first consonant to assimilate to it. This rule has two parts:

(*a*) A voiceless consonant is pronounced voiced when followed by a voiced consonant:

тб → [db]	футбо́л [fudból]	*soccer*
сб → [zb]	бейсбо́л [beyzból]	*baseball*
кд → [gd]	как дела́ [kagd'ilá]	*How are you?*
кж → [gž]	та́кже [tágži]	*also*

(*b*)   A voiced consonant is pronounced voiceless when followed by a voiceless consonant:

дк → [tk]	ло́дка [lótkə]	*boat*
вт → [ft]	в теа́тр [ft'iátr]	*to the theater*
жк → [šk]	ло́жка [lóškə]	*spoon*
бк → [pk]	про́бка [própkə]	*cork*
вч → [fč]	вчера́ [fčirá]	*yesterday*
гт → [kt]	ля́гте [l'ákt'i]	*lie down*

Note: There is one exception to rule 2(*a*): The voiced consonant в [v] does not cause a preceding voiceless consonant to be pronounced voiced, e.g., the т in the cluster тв is not pronounced [d], e.g., твой [tvóy] *your.*

SYLLABIFICATION

Words are more easily pronounced when they are divided up into rhythmic parts, called *syllables.* Each syllable in Russian consists of a vowel and, usually, one or more surrounding consonants, e.g., the two syllables in кни́-га *book.* Essentially, there is one basic principle to follow in pronouncing Russian words consisting of more than one syllable: wherever possible, *make the syllable break at a vowel.*

при-ве́т	[pr'i-v'ét]	*Hi*
спа-си́-бо	[spʌ-s'í-bə]	*thank you*
га-зе́-та	[gʌ-z'é-tə]	*newspaper*
пи-сьмо́	[p'i-s'mó]	*letter*
хо-ро-шо́	[xə-rʌ-šó]	*good*

The only exception to this pattern involves words which contain consonant clusters beginning with р, л, м, н, and й. In these words, make the syllable break *after* these consonants.

жур-на́л	[žur-nál]	*magazine*
по́л-ка	[pól-kə]	*shelf*
су́м-ка	[súm-kə]	*handbag*
бан-ке́т	[bʌn-két]	*banquet*
тро́й-ка	[tróy-kə]	*three*

The same general rules that apply for pronouncing words in syllables also apply for hyphenating words that must be divided at the end of a written line. For example, words with various consonant clusters, including clusters of identical consonants, are normally hyphenated between the consonants: ка́с-са *cashier window*, ва́н-на *bathtub.*

SPELLING RULES

Russian, like English, has a few spelling rules. Students learning English, for example, memorize the rule "write *i* before *e* except after *c*" to help them remember to spell correctly words like *relieve*, *believe* vs. *deceive*, *receive*, *conceive*, etc. Russian has three spelling rules that, like this English rule, remind us that certain combinations of letters are not permitted. The Russian rules are important for choosing the correct spelling of endings on nouns, adjectives, and verbs.

Rule 1: Write **и**, *never* **ы**, *after* **к г х** *or* **ж ч ш щ**
Examples: (*a*) In forming plurals of nouns:

руба́шка – руба́шк*и* *shirt–shirts*   **кни́га – кни́г*и*** *book–books*

(*b*) In adjective endings (masculine singular/nominative plural forms):

ру́сск(ий)/ру́сск(ие) *Russian*   **хоро́ш(ий)/хоро́ш(ие)** *good*

Rule 2: Write **а**, *never* **я**,/*Write* **у**, *never* **ю**, *after* **г к х ж ч ш щ ц**
Examples: In the conjugation of verbs (1st pers sg and 3rd pers pl)

Я́ молчу́/Они́ молча́т   *I am/They are silent*
Я́ лежу́/Они́ лежа́т   *I am/They are lying*
Я́ пишу́/Они́ пи́шут   *I/They write*

Rule 3: Write unstressed **е**, *but stressed* **о́**, *after* **ж ч ш щ ц**
Examples:

хоро́шее *good*   **большо́е** *big*
танцева́ть *to dance*   **танцева́льный** *dancing* (adj)
but **танцо́вщик** *(ballet) dancer*

CAPITALIZATION

Russian is similar to English in that it capitalizes proper nouns (**Би́лл, Вашингто́н, Аме́рика, Бори́с, Москва́, Росси́я**), and the first word of a sentence. Russian differs from English in NOT capitalizing:

(*a*) the first person singular pronoun "I" (**я**), unless it is the first word of a sentence.

(*b*) nouns (and adjectives) denoting nationalities (**америка́нец** *American,* **япо́нец** *Japanese,* **ру́сский** *Russian*), as well as cities from which one originates (**москви́ч** *Moscovite,* **петербу́ржец** *Petersburger*).

(*c*) words that follow the first word of a title (**«*Война́ и ми́р*»** *War and Peace*), the name of a holiday (**Но́вый го́д** *New Year*), or an organization (**Акаде́мия нау́к** *Academy of Sciences*).

(*d*) days of the week (**понеде́льник** *Monday,* **вто́рник** *Tuesday*).

(*e*) months of the year (**янва́рь** *January,* **февра́ль** *February,* **ма́рт** *March*).

TRANSLITERATION: ENGLISH TO RUSSIAN

Often it is necessary to represent a word originating in one alphabet with the corresponding letters of another alphabet. This is called *transliteration*. Words commonly transliterated include the names of people and places, as well as loanwords, i.e., those words of foreign origin that are "borrowed" and become part of the vocabulary of the borrowing language. Examples of Russian words transliterated into English are the names Yeltsin, Gorbachev, Chekhov, Tolstoy, Volga, and Vladivostok. English also has a handful of loanwords from Russian, such as sputnik, dacha, borsch, samovar, and more recently, glasnost and perestroika. Russian, in contrast to English, has literally thousands of words that have been borrowed directly, or indirectly, from English, and the influx of English words into Russian has greatly accelerated in the 1990s. In some of these loanwords the English *spelling* of the word determines the way the word is transliterated in Russian, each English letter being replaced by its counterpart in the Cyrillic alphabet, e.g., Robert > **Ро́берт**. In other words the *phonetics* of the English word dictate the choice of Cyrillic letters that most accurately capture the English *pronunciation*, e.g.,

Michael > **Ма́йкл**. Often, a combination of the spelling and the pronunciation of an English word influences the way the word is transliterated. Though there is no one agreed-upon system for transliterating from English to Russian (which may result in variant forms, e.g., David > **Дави́д/Дэ́йвид**, Pamela > **Па́мела/Пэ́мела**), it is very important to be able to pair English letters with their closest phonetic counterparts in the Cyrillic alphabet. In particular, knowing the phonetic correspondences between English and Russian *consonants* will make it much easier to recognize, and make use of, the numerous English words that have been borrowed and assimilated into Russian.

English Consonants and their Cyrillic Counterparts

Most English consonants have one-to-one phonetic counterparts in the Cyrillic alphabet and, consequently, present little difficulty for transliteration.

English Consonants	b c d f g k l m n p r s t v z
Cyrillic Consonants	б к д ф г к л м н п р с т в з

Note: English *c* is sometimes transliterated in Cyrillic as **ц** (e.g., English *Cincinnati* > Russian **Цинцинна́ти**) and rarely as **с** (English *city* > **си́ти**, as in **Джéрси-си́ти** *Jersey City*).

English Consonant Letters Lacking One-to-One Phonetic Equivalents

However, there are five English consonants that have no one-to-one phonetic counterparts in the Cyrillic alphabet. These are *h, j, q, w,* and *x.* The sounds of English *h* and English *w* do not occur in Russian, and the sounds of English *j, q,* and *x* can be approximated in Russian only by Cyrillic letter combinations. It is important to know how these consonants are transliterated, since these letters commonly occur in English loanwords.

1. English *h* is transliterated as Cyrillic **г** or, as in many recent borrowings, **x**.

Examples with **г**:

Harvard	>	**Га́рвард**	Hamburg	>	**Га́мбург**
Henry	>	**Ге́нри/Хе́нри**	Hong Kong	>	**Гонко́нг**

Examples with **x**:

Houston	>	**Хью́стон**	Hillary	>	**Хи́ллари**
hacker	>	**хэ́ккер**	hotdog	>	**хот-до́г**

2. English *j* is transliterated as the Cyrillic letter combination **дж**.

Jeff	>	**Джéф(ф)**	jazz	>	**джа́з**
Jessica	>	**Джéс(с)ика**	jeans	>	**джи́нсы**

English *g,* when equivalent to *j* in pronunciation, is also transliterated as **дж**.

George	>	**Джо́рдж**	image	>	**и́мидж**
manager	>	**мéнеджер**	pager	>	**пéйджер**

3. English *q* is normally transliterated as the Cyrillic letter combination **кв**.

aquarium	>	**аква́риум**	quartet	>	**кварте́т**
aquamarine	>	**аквамари́н**	quart	>	**ква́рта**

4. English *w* is usually transliterated as Cyrillic **у**, occasionally (in earlier loanwords) as **в**. Some words may have variants.

Examples with **у**:

William	>	**Уи́льям/Ви́льям**	walkman	>	**уо́кмен**
weekend	>	**уик-э́нд/вик-е́нд**	show	>	**шо́у**

Examples with **в**:

Washington	>	**Вашингто́н**	whisky	>	**ви́ски**

5. English *x* is usually transliterated in Cyrillic as the letter combination **кс** (rarely as **х**).

Maxine	>	**Макси́н**	fax	>	**фа́кс**
Mexico	>	**Ме́ксика**	taxi	>	**такси́**

But note:

Texas	>	**Теха́с**

English Letter Combinations Transliterated by Single Letters in Cyrillic

Finally, there are a few English letter combinations which are transliterated into Russian by single letters in Cyrillic.

(*a*) English *ch* with the sound value [č] is usually transliterated by Cyrillic **ч**; *ch* with the sound value [š] is transliterated by Cyrillic **ш**.

Examples:

Charles	>	**Ча́рл(ь)з**	Charlotte	>	**Шарло́тт**

But note:

chocolate	>	**шокола́д**

(*b*) English *sh* [š] is transliterated in Cyrillic as **ш**, e.g., Sharon > **Ша́рон**

(*c*) English *ph* [f] is transliterated in Cyrillic as **ф**, e.g., Sophie > **Со́фи**

(*d*) English *th* [θ] does not occur in Russian; therefore, *th* is normally transliterated in English loanwords as Cyrillic **т**, e.g., Cynthia > **Си́нтия**, Theodore > **Тео́дор** (but in this last example, and in a few other words originally from Greek, English *th* may also correspond to **ф**, based on the biblical Greek form of the word, e.g., Theodore > **Фёдор**, and Thaddeus > **Фадде́й**.

RUSSIAN LETTER STYLES

Italic Letters

The Russian letters introduced above in the alphabet chart are given in the ordinary printed block style found in books and other printed texts. These letters can also occur in an italicized form, which in most instances is quite similar to the regular printed style. However, a few of the small italicized letters have a different shape from their printed block style counterparts and therefore must be specially noted. These letters are given in the table below.

Printed Letters	*Italicized* Letters
В в	*В в*
Г г	*Г г*
Д д	*Д д*
И и	*И и*
П п	*П п*
Т т	*Т т*

Cursive Letters

In general, when Russians write by hand, they do not print, but use a cursive script. Like italic, some letters in Cyrillic cursive differ in various ways from their printed block style counterparts. One letter in particular, the small Cyrillic block letter д, has the italicized form *д* (as noted above), but is written in cursive script as *g*. Fortunately, most cursive letters do not differ so dramatically from the printed block or italic styles. Below the three letter styles are listed for comparison, and the most important features of the cursive letters are noted for reference.

Printed	Italics	Cursive Script	Notes on Forming Cursive
А а	*А а*		
Б б	*Б б*		
В в	*В в*		Small letter is as tall as capital.
Г г	*Г г*		Small letter is rounded on top.
Д д	*Д д*		Small *g* looks like English script "*g*."
Е е	*Е е*		
Ё ё	*Ё ё*		The two dots are often omitted.
Ж ж	*Ж ж*		
З з	*З з*		Capital *З* looks like the number 3.
И и	*И и*		
Й й	*Й й*		Note the half circle above the letters.
К к	*К к*		Small letter is half as tall as capital.
Л л	*Л л*		Both letters must begin with a hook.
М м	*М м*		Both letters must begin with a hook.
Н н	*Н н*		
О о	*О о*		
П п	*П п*		
Р р	*Р р*		Small letter is not closed on right.
С с	*С с*		
Т т	*Т т*		Small *т* often has a line across top.
У у	*У у*		Capital *У* does not go below the line.
Ф ф	*Ф ф*		
Х х	*Х х*		
Ц ц	*Ц ц*		Both letters have a short tail.
Ч ч	*Ч ч*		
Ш ш	*Ш ш*		Small *ш* often has a line underneath.

Щ щ	*Щ щ*	*Щ щ*	Both letters have a short tail.
ъ	*ъ*	*ъ*	
ы	*ы*	*ы*	
ь	*ь*	*ь*	
Э э	*Э э*	*Э э*	This letter has a rounded back.
Ю ю	*Ю ю*	*Ю ю*	
Я я	*Я я*	*Я я*	Begins in a hook, like *Л л* and *М м*.

REVIEW

1. Using the Cyrillic equivalents of the English letters, give the Russian name for each of the following states of the U.S. Review the section on "shapes and sounds."

Alabama, Arizona, Vermont, Indiana, Colorado, Illinois, Minnesota, Montana, Nebraska, Nevada, Oregon, Florida

1. _____   7. _____
2. _____   8. _____
3. _____   9. _____
4. _____   10. _____
5. _____   11. _____
6. _____   12. _____

2. Substituting Cyrillic letters for their English counterparts, give the Russian names of the following cities and countries.

America, Canada, Pakistan, Toronto, Boston, London, Berlin, Erevan, Madrid, Panama

1. _____   6. _____
2. _____   7. _____
3. _____   8. _____
4. _____   9. _____
5. _____   10. _____

3. The following words were borrowed into Russian from English. See if you can recognize them, and give their original spelling in English.

студе́нт, профе́ссор, ка́мпус, колле́дж, гамбу́ргер, ке́тчуп, хот-до́г, компа́кт-ди́ск, компью́тер, при́нтер

1. _____   6. _____
2. _____   7. _____
3. _____   8. _____
4. _____   9. _____
5. _____   10. _____

4. Study the list of words below, and identify the soft consonants by writing each word with the soft consonants <u>underlined</u>. Review the sections on "hard series" and "soft series" vowels and on "paired consonants." *Examples:* пере<u>ры́</u>в, про́ру<u>бь</u>

привéт, спасибо, пáмять, письмó, телевизор, сёрфинг, рюкзáк, гóсть, рэ́ппер, дéсять

1. _____   6. _____
2. _____   7. _____
3. _____   8. _____
4. _____   9. _____
5. _____   10. _____

5. Study the following list of words, and in the order in which they appear, write each word that contains the sound [y]. Indicate its location by <u>underlining</u> the appropriate letters in the word. Review the alphabet chart, the sections on "the signs" and the "soft-series" vowels. *Examples:* мо<u>я</u>, стать<u>я</u>

прямóй, пояс, дéнь, едá, сёмга, съёмка, Кáтя, плáтье, Тáня, Татьяна, яблоко, мясо, май, мой, мюзикл, юмор, Ивáн, заём

1. _____   6. _____
2. _____   7. _____
3. _____   8. _____
4. _____   9. _____
5. _____   10. _____

6. Study the list of words below, and in the order in which they appear, write each word that contains the short, lax sound [ʌ] and <u>underline</u> the relevant vowels. Review the section on "vowel reduction." *Examples:* <u>о</u>кнó, хор<u>о</u>шó

дóктор, астронóм, парадóкс, óблоко, таракáн, кóмната, головá, мотóр, над дóмом, молокó, улица, газéта, талáнт, о клáссе

1. _____   6. _____
2. _____   7. _____
3. _____   8. _____
4. _____   9. _____
5. _____   10. _____

7. Study the list of words below, and indicate the location of the sound [ə] by writing the word with the relevant vowels <u>underlined</u>. Review the section on "vowel reduction." *Examples:* лáмп<u>а</u>, <u>ра</u>зговóр

óрган, кóлокол, панарáма, мóре, юмор, мéсто, нóвое, дядя, потолóк, квартира

1. _____   6. _____
2. _____   7. _____
3. _____   8. _____
4. _____   9. _____
5. _____   10. _____

8. Study the list of words below, and identify the location of the sound [i] by writing each word with the relevant vowels <u>underlined</u>. Review the section on "vowel reduction." *Examples:* сви<u>т</u>ер, т<u>я</u>нýть

телефо́н, мясно́й, ве́чер, рестора́н, эко́лог, па́мятник, ветерина́р, река́, эта́ж, сейча́с

1. _____   6. _____
2. _____   7. _____
3. _____   8. _____
4. _____   9. _____
5. _____   10. _____

9. Study the list of words below, and in the order in which they appear, write the words that contain the sound [ɨ] with the relevant vowels underlined. Review the pronunciation of vowels after unpaired hard consonants. *Examples:* ш<u>и</u>на, же<u>ни</u>ть

бы́стро, це́нтр, цеме́нт, жи́вопись, цыплёнок, ци́рк, же́нщина, жена́, жёны, мешо́к, шика́рный, ше́сть, шесто́й, решётка, шербе́т

1. _____   6. _____
2. _____   7. _____
3. _____   8. _____
4. _____   9. _____
5. _____   10. _____

10. Study the list of words below, and in the order in which they appear, write each word that contains the sound [šš']. <u>Underline</u> the consonants or consonant clusters. *Examples:* <u>сч</u>ёт, <u>щ</u>ено́к

щи, уже́, ещё, е́шь, сши́ть, счита́ешь, щека́, мужчи́на, расска́зчик, подпи́счик, исчеза́ть, иска́ть, и́щут, шёл, щёлк

1. _____   6. _____
2. _____   7. _____
3. _____   8. _____
4. _____   9. _____
5. _____   10. _____

11. Study the list of words below, and in the order in which they appear, write the words containing consonants that, due to one of the *voicing* rules, are pronounced different from the way they are spelled. <u>Underline</u> the consonants. *Examples:* са́<u>д</u>, <u>в</u> кино́

глазо́к, гла́с, гла́з, сбо́р, спа́ть, отте́нок, отде́л, кру́жка, круи́з, дро́бь, твёрдо, творо́г, ве́чер, вчера́, апте́ка, абсу́рд, к до́му

1. _____   6. _____
2. _____   7. _____
3. _____   8. _____
4. _____   9. _____
5. _____   10. _____

12. Rewrite each word below, dividing it up into syllables. Review the section on "syllabification." *Examples:* пи́-во, спа-си́-бо

скажи́те, понима́йте, лаборато́рия, дире́ктор, нача́льник, слова́рь, ко́мната, ру́чка, каранда́ш, университе́т

1. _____   6. _____
2. _____   7. _____

3. _____   8. _____
4. _____   9. _____
5. _____   10. _____

13. Give the original English spelling of the following words, all of which are Russian borrowings from English.

ксе́рокс, ко́микс, сэ́ндвич, ма́ркетинг, ме́неджер, ноу-ха́у, диск-пле́йер, фа́кс, компью́тер, хэппи-э́нд

1. _____   6. _____
2. _____   7. _____
3. _____   8. _____
4. _____   9. _____
5. _____   10. _____

14. Give the English equivalents of the following names of famous people.

Ага́та Кри́сти, Дже́к Ло́ндон, Эрне́ст Хе́мингуэй, Ча́рльз Ди́кенс, Уо́лт Дисне́й, Ри́чард Ни́ксон, Джо́н Кви́нси А́дамс, Уи́нстон Че́рчил

1. _____   5. _____
2. _____   6. _____
3. _____   7. _____
4. _____   8. _____

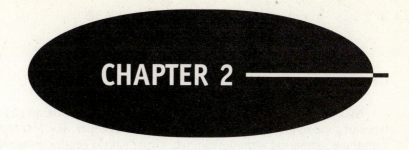

CHAPTER 2

Nouns

A noun is a word that names a person (Sasha, sister, girl), a place (Washington, Russia), a thing (desk, table, lamp), a quality (joy, happiness, sadness), or act (request, rebellion, voting). Nouns are classified into *proper* and *common* nouns. Proper nouns are those which indicate a specific person, place, or thing. For example, the noun "Moscow" is the name of a specific, unique place, whereas "city" is a common noun, i.e., one that refers to a whole class of things. Proper nouns in Russian, as in English, are capitalized. (On differences between Russian and English capitalization, see Chapter 1.)

ARTICLES

Russian, unlike English, has no articles. The meaning of "definite" and "indefinite" conveyed by the English definite article *the* and the indefinite article *a*, respectively, is expressed in Russian through context, by word order, or other means.

NOUN STRUCTURE

Russian nouns (as well as adjectives, pronouns, and verbs) consist of a *stem* followed by an *ending*. The stem always includes a *root*, where the lexical meaning resides. The root may be preceded by a *prefix* and/or followed by a *suffix*, structural elements which contribute additional meanings to a word. Consider, for example, the structure of the Russian noun **сотру́дники** *coworkers*.

STEM	+ ENDING
(prefix) + root + (suffix)	
со + **труд** + **ник**	+ **и**
co + *work* + *er*	+ *s*

Many nouns in English have a similar structure. For example, the English equivalent of the Russian **сотру́дники**, *coworkers* has a stem consisting of the root *work*, the prefix *co-* ("together") and the suffix *-er* ('one who'), followed by the ending *-s* (plural). While many English words share the same *stem + ending* structure of Russian words, *endings* in Russian are far more extensive, and play a far greater role than in English. In particular, the ending on a Russian noun can give information about its **gender**, **number**, and **case**.

19

GENDER

All nouns in Russian belong to one of three genders: *masculine*, *feminine*, or *neuter*. There are two types of gender: grammatical gender and natural gender. The first type, as its name suggests, has to do with the grammatical form of the noun. Grammatical gender is the assignment of gender according to the noun's ending; the meaning of the noun plays no role. For example, the noun **кни́га** *book* is feminine even though it has no relation to female persons; it is grammatically feminine simply because it ends in the vowel **-a**. The vast majority of nouns in Russian are assigned gender in this way. The second type of gender, natural gender, is meaning-based: it is the assignment of masculine or feminine gender based on the *sex* of the person (or animal) denoted by the noun. In most instances, grammatical gender and natural gender coincide, e.g., the noun **ма́ма** *mom* is both grammatically feminine (since it has the ending **-a**), and "naturally" feminine, because its meaning is that of a female person. In a relatively small number of instances, however, grammatical and natural gender do not coincide, e.g., the noun **па́па** *dad* has the *form* of a feminine noun (the ending **-a**), but the *meaning* of a masculine noun. In all such instances, the meaning of the noun, not its form, determines gender.

Grammatical Gender

In most instances, the grammatical gender of a Russian noun is easily determined by its ending in the nominative Singular (the form in which a noun is cited in dictionaries). The following table illustrates grammatical gender.

	Masculine -∅	Feminine -a/-я	Neuter -o/-e (ё)
Hard Stem	дива́н	ла́мпа	кре́сло
Soft Stem	музе́й	ку́хня	зда́ние

Masculine Nouns

In the nominative singular most masculine nouns have *no ending* (or a "zero ending," symbolized by -∅, e.g., **дива́н-∅** *sofa*). Masculine nouns, then, consist only of a stem ending in a consonant, which may be hard or soft. Nouns ending in a hard consonant are characterized as having a *hard stem*, those ending in a soft consonant, a *soft stem*. Specifically, a masculine noun is one whose stem ends in:

(*a*)   a hard paired consonant:
        дива́н *sofa*, **сто́л** *table*, **до́м** *house*, **институ́т** *institute*, **магази́н** *store*

(*b*)   one of the unpaired consonants: hard **ж**, **ш**, or soft **ч**, **щ**:
        но́ж *knife*, **каранда́ш** *pencil*, **вра́ч** *doctor*, **пла́щ** *raincoat*, **бо́рщ** *borsch*

(*c*)   the soft (semi-consonantal) glide **-й**:
        музе́й *museum*, **трамва́й** *trollycar*, **ча́й** *tea*, **кра́й** *edge*, **хокке́й** *hockey*

(*d*)   a soft consonant, which is indicated by a following soft sign **-ь**:
        портфе́ль *briefcase*, **слова́рь** *dictionary*, **ру́бль** *rouble*, **де́нь** *day*, **Кре́мль** *Kremlin*

Feminine Nouns

Feminine nouns have either a hard stem or a soft stem, and this difference correlates with the hard-type or soft-type of vowel ending. Specifically,

(*a*)   Feminine nouns with a hard stem end in the hard-series vowel **-a**:
        ла́мпа *lamp*, **кни́га** *book*, **газе́та** *newspaper*, **ру́чка** *pen*, **гости́ница** *hotel*

(b)   Most feminine nouns with a soft stem end in the soft-series vowel **-я**:
       ку́хня *kitchen*, **дере́вня** *village*, **ле́кция** *lecture*, **земля́** *earth*, **тётя** *aunt*

(c)   Some feminine nouns, just like some masculine nouns, end in the soft sign **-ь**:
       пло́щадь *square*, **тетра́дь** *notebook*, **две́рь** *door*, **крова́ть** *bed*, **ро́ль** *role*

Neuter Nouns

Neuter nouns, like feminine nouns, occur with a hard or soft stem, and it is, again, this difference that accounts for the different endings. Specifically,

(a)   Neuter nouns with a hard stem end in the hard-series vowel **-о**:
       кре́сло *armchair*, **окно́** *window*, **письмо́** *letter*, **сло́во** *word*, **ме́сто** *place*

(b)   Neuter nouns with a soft stem end in the soft-series vowel **-е**, or if the ending is stressed, **-ё**:
       зда́ние *building*, **мо́ре** *sea*, **пла́тье** *dress*, **бельё** *linen*, **ружьё** *gun*

Note: Exceptions to the regular neuter endings **-о**, **-е** (**-ё**) are the few neuter nouns that end in **-мя**. These nouns should be memorized to avoid mistaking them for feminine nouns in **-я**. The most commonly used are:

и́мя *name*, **вре́мя** *time*, **бре́мя** *burden*, **зна́мя** *banner*, **пла́мя** *flame*, **се́мя** *seed*

1.   Give the gender of the following nouns, and then indicate whether the noun stem is hard or soft.

1. письмо́	_____	6. зда́ние	_____
2. газе́та	_____	7. ру́бль	_____
3. трамва́й	_____	8. сто́л	_____
4. магази́н	_____	9. и́мя	_____
5. ле́кция	_____	10. пло́щадь	_____

Why Gender is Important

The gender of a noun is important because it determines the endings of pronouns, adjectives, and the past-tense forms of verbs which must *agree* with, i.e., express the same gender, as the noun they modify or refer to. Following are examples of gender agreement:

Pronoun (Possessive and Third Person) Agreement

The gender of the noun determines both the ending of the modifying possessive pronoun as well as the form of the third person pronoun which can replace it.

Где́ *мо́й* **сто́л**? **Во́т** *о́н*.	*Where is my table? Here it is.*
Где́ *моё* **окно́**? **Во́т** *оно́*.	*Where is my window? Here it is.*
Где́ *моя́* **ла́мпа**? **Во́т** *она́*.	*Where is my lamp? Here it is.*

Adjective Agreement

An adjective must express the same gender as the noun it modifies.

Э́то *но́вый* **сто́л**	*This is a new table.*
Э́то *но́вое* **окно́**	*This is a new window.*
Э́то *но́вая* **ла́мпа**	*This is a new lamp.*

A predicate-adjective must express the same gender as its subject-noun.

Сту́л *за́нят*.	*The chair is occupied.*
Ме́сто *за́нято*.	*The seat is occupied.*
Ко́мната *занята́*.	*The room is occupied.*

Past Tense of Verbs

A predicate-verb in the past tense must agree with the subject-noun it refers to:

Стóл *бы́л* **тáм**.	*The table was there.*
Окнó *бы́ло* **тáм**.	*The window was there.*
Лáмпа *былá* **тáм**.	*The lamp was there.*

2. Supply the form of the personal pronoun **óн, онó** or **онá** required to replace the following nouns.

1. гóрод _____
2. дерéвня _____
3. пятнó _____
4. карандáш _____
5. чáй _____
6. рóль _____
7. журнáл _____
8. врéмя _____
9. рекá _____
10. задáние _____

3. Give the possessive pronoun needed to modify the noun: **мóй, моё, моя́**.

1. _____ дóм
2. _____ мéсто
3. _____ вáза
4. _____ словáрь
5. _____ стýл
6. _____ кóмната
7. _____ кровáть
8. _____ фотогрáфия

GENDER IDENTIFICATION BY NOUN GROUPS

Masculine Nouns of Natural Gender in -a and -я

A small number of masculine nouns have an ending in **-a** and **-я**. These are all nouns which denote male persons. There are three subgroups of these "naturally" masculine nouns:

(*a*) Nouns which are masculine by virtue of their real-world referents:
мужчи́на *man*, **пáпа** *dad*, **дя́дя** *uncle*, **дéдушка** *grandfather*, **ю́ноша** *youth*

(*b*) The full first name of males (very few):
Илья́, Ники́та, Фомá

(*c*) The diminutive forms of male first names. The full name is given in parentheses:

Сáша (Алексáндр)	**Вáся (Васи́лий)**	**Лёня (Леони́д)**
Алёша (Алексéй)	**Ви́тя (Ви́ктор)**	**Ми́ша (Михаи́л)**
Тóля (Анатóлий)	**Жéня (Евгéний)**	**Пáша (Пáвел)**
Бóря (Бори́с)	**Кóля (Николáй)**	**Пéтя (Пётр)**

Masculine Nouns with a Stem Ending in the Soft Sign

A relatively small number of nouns ending in the soft sign **-ь** are masculine. Identifying these nouns as masculine is less straightforward, since the stem of both masculine *and* feminine nouns may end in **-ь**. However, there are some generalizations that help determine the gender of certain groups of these nouns as masculine.

Months of the Year:
янвáрь *January*, **феврáль** *February*, **апрéль** *April*, **ию́нь** *June*, **ию́ль** *July*,
сентя́брь *September*, **октя́брь** *October*, **ноя́брь** *November*, **декáбрь** *December*

Nouns Denoting Male Persons:

кня́зь *prince*, коро́ль *king*, ца́рь *tsar*, па́рень *lad*, зя́ть *son-in-law/brother-in-law*,
те́сть *father-in-law (wife's father)*

*Nouns Ending in the Suffix **-тель*** (cf. the English suffix *-er, -or*) *and **-арь***. Many denote a person,
usually a male (but: слова́рь *dictionary*):

писа́тель *writer*, чита́тель *reader*, води́тель *driver*, учи́тель *teacher (school)*, преподава́тель
teacher (university), покупа́тель *shopper*, зри́тель *spectator*, библиоте́карь *librarian*, пе́карь *baker*,
апте́карь *pharmacist*, врата́рь *goal-keeper*

Feminine Nouns with a Stem Ending in the Soft Sign

A large majority of nouns with a stem ending in the soft sign **-ь** are feminine. As in the case of
masculine soft-sign nouns, there are a few generalizations that help to identify groups of soft-sign
nouns that are feminine.

Nouns Denoting Females (nouns of natural gender):

ма́ть *mother*, до́чь *daughter*, свекро́вь *mother-in-law (husband's mother)*

*Nouns Ending in Soft Sign Preceded by an Unpaired Consonant **-жь**, **-чь**, **-шь**, **-щь***:

молодёжь *young people*, ло́жь *lie*, пе́чь *stove*, но́чь *night*, бро́шь *brooch*, чу́шь *nonsense*, мы́шь
mouse, ве́щь *thing*, о́вощь *vegetable*, по́мощь *help*

*Abstract Nouns Formed with the Suffix **-ость** or **-есть***:

мо́лодость *youth*, гру́бость *rudeness*, ве́жливость *politeness*, но́вость *news*,
ра́дость *joy*, сме́лость *boldness*, зре́лость *maturity*, гла́сность *openness*,
све́жесть *freshness*, тя́жесть *gravity*, неуклю́жесть *clumsiness*

4. Supply the appropriate form of the third person pronoun required to replace the noun.

1.	дя́дя	_____	6.	свекро́вь _____
2.	до́чь	_____	7.	писа́тель _____
3.	коро́ль	_____	8.	но́вость _____
4.	Ми́ша	_____	9.	янва́рь _____
5.	бро́шь	_____	10.	апте́карь _____

NOUNS OF COMMON GENDER

A relatively small number of nouns ending in **-а** and **-я** that denote people are of "common
gender," i.e., they may be either masculine or feminine depending on whether, in a particular context,
they refer to a male or a female, e.g., **Он** *большо́й* **у́мница** *He is a very clever person*, **Она́** *больша́я*
у́мница *She is a very clever person*.

Examples:

у́мница *clever person*, колле́га *colleague*, сирота́ *orphan*, пья́ница *drunkard*,
бродя́га *tramp*, неве́жда *ignoramus*, пла́кса *cry-baby*, рази́ня *scatter-brain*,
неря́ха *sloven*, обжо́ра *glutton*, малю́тка *baby, little one*, одино́чка *lone-person*

GENDER OF NOUNS DENOTING PROFESSIONS

Nouns denoting professions or occupations that were once largely dominated by men are generally of masculine gender. Nevertheless, these nouns are used to refer not only to men, but also to women who have entered these professions, e.g., **Михаи́л био́лог и Мари́на био́лог** *Michael is a biologist and Marina is a biologist.*

Examples:

хиру́рг *surgeon*, **врач** *doctor*, **ветерина́р** *veterinarian*, **профе́ссор** *professor*, **доце́нт** *university lecturer*, **адвока́т** *lawyer*, **педаго́г** *teacher*, **био́лог** *biologist*, **гео́лог** *geologist*, **гео́граф** *geographer*, **карто́граф** *cartographer*, **архите́ктор** *architect*, **космона́вт** *cosmonaut*, **инжене́р** *engineer*, **парикма́хер** *hairdresser*, **строи́тель** *builder*, **секрета́рь** *secretary*

Regarding such nouns, there are two facts to remember about *gender agreement*:

1. Regardless of whether these nouns denote a male or female, a modifying adjective normally agrees with the *masculine* gender of the noun.

Examples:

Она́ *хоро́ший* **врач**.   *She is a good doctor.*
Моя́ сестра́ — *изве́стный* **педаго́г**.   *My sister is a well-known teacher.*

2. When these nouns are used with a predicate adjective, or with a verb in the past tense, the gender form of the adjective or verb is normally determined by the *sex reference* of the noun.

Examples with Predicate Adjective:

Экскурсово́д *бо́лен*.   *The guide (male) is sick.*
Экскурсово́д *больна́*.   *The guide (female) is sick.*

Examples with Verb in the Past Tense:

Профе́ссор Ивано́в *чита́л* **ле́кцию**.   *Professor Ivanov read a lecture.*
Профе́ссор Ивано́ва *чита́ла* **ле́кцию**.   *Professor Ivanova read a lecture.*

Note: The noun **судья́** *judge*, though feminine in form, is masculine in gender. Like the other nouns of profession listed above, it may be used to denote women, but it requires a modifying adjective to have masculine agreement, e.g., **Она́ уважа́емый судья́** *She is a respected judge.*

Note: The noun **челове́к** *person* may refer to both a male or female, but always requires masculine agreement, e.g., **Ле́на** — *о́чень ми́лый* **челове́к** *Lena is a very nice girl.*

5. Choose the appropriate gender form of the word in parentheses.

1. Влади́мир Ива́нович — _____ колле́га. (но́вый/но́вая)
2. Но́вый уче́бник _____ профе́ссор Серге́ева. (написа́л/написа́ла)
3. Э́та же́нщина _____ судья́. (изве́стный/изве́стная)
4. Ири́на Петро́вна _____ инжене́р. (о́пытный/о́пытная)
5. Твой брат _____ неря́ха. (большо́й/больша́я)
6. Врач _____ . Она́ консульти́рует с больны́м. (за́нят/занята́)

GENDER DIFFERENTIATION BY SUFFIX

Nouns Denoting People

A number of masculine nouns denoting profession or occupation have a corresponding feminine form with a suffix indicating the female member of the profession (cf. English *poet/poetess*, *actor/actress*). In fact, males and females may be differentiated by a suffix not only in nouns of occupation, but also in nouns denoting various functions, as well as in those denoting nationality. Below is a representative list of the different suffixes used to distinguish females from males, with examples of commonly used nouns denoting professions, occupations, functions, nationalities, etc. Wherever appropriate, the suffix denoting the female is paired with a suffix denoting the male:

Male	*Female* **-ка**	
журнали́ст	журнали́ст**ка**	*journalist*
арти́ст	арти́ст**ка**	*performing artist*
программи́ст	программи́ст**ка**	*computer programmer*
официа́нт	официа́нт**ка**	*waiter/waitress*

Male	*Female* **иса/-есса**	
актёр	актр**и́са**	*actor/actress*
поэ́т	поэт**е́сса**	*poet/poetess*
при́нц	принц**е́сса**	*prince/princess*

Male	*Female* **-и́ха**	
по́вар	повар**и́ха**	*cook*
сто́рож	сторож**и́ха**	*guard*
портно́й	портн**и́ха**	*tailor/dressmaker*

Male **-ец**	*Female* **-ка**	
вегитариа́**нец**	вегитариа́**нка**	*vegetarian*
америка́**нец**	америка́**нка**	*American*
кана́**дец**	кана́**дка**	*Canadian*
не́**мец**	не́**мка**	*German*

Male **-анин/-янин**	*Female* **-анка/-янка**	
англича́**нин**	англича́**нка**	*Englishman/Englishwoman*
христиа́**нин**	христиа́**нка**	*Christian*
крестья**ни́н**	крестья́**нка**	*peasant*
славя**ни́н**	славя́**нка**	*Slav*

Male **-ин**	*Female* **-ка**	
армя**ни́н**	армя́**нка**	*Armenian*
болга́**рин**	болга́**рка**	*Bulgarian*
грузи́**н**	грузи́**нка**	*Georgian*
россия́**нин**	россия́**нка**	*Russian (citizen)*
тата́**рин**	тата́**рка**	*Tatar*

Male **-ец**	*Female* **-щица**	
прода**ве́ц**	продав**щи́ца**	*salesperson*

Male **-щик**	*Female* **-щица**	
танцо́**вщик**	танцо́**вщица**	*ballet dancer*

| меховщи́к | меховщи́ца | *furrier* |
| гардеро́бщик | гардеро́бщица | *cloakroom attendant* |

Male **-чик**	*Female* **-чица**	
перево́дчик	перево́дчица	*translator*
лётчик	лётчица	*pilot*
буфе́тчик	буфе́тчица	*snackbar attendant*

Male **-ец**	*Female* **-ица**	
певе́ц	певи́ца	*singer*
краса́вец	краса́вица	*attractive person*
счастли́вец	счастли́вица	*lucky person*

Male **-ник**	*Female* **-ница**	
худо́жник	худо́жница	*artist*
рабо́тник	рабо́тница	*helper*
учени́к	учени́ца	*pupil*

Male **-тель**	*Female* **-ница**	
учи́тель	учи́тельница	*(school) teacher*
преподава́тель	преподава́тельница	*(university) instructor*
писа́тель	писа́тельница	*writer*

6. Supply the male or female counterpart of the noun given.

Examples: студе́нт   студе́нтка,   учени́к   учени́ца

1.	певе́ц	_____	8.	худо́жник	_____
2.	_____	счастли́вица	9.	_____	перево́дчица
3.	америка́нец	_____	10.	танцо́вщик	_____
4.	кана́дец	_____	11.	англича́нин	_____
5.	_____	испа́нка	12.	_____	грузи́нка
6.	писа́тель	_____	13.	портно́й	_____
7.	_____	учи́тельница	14.	_____	продавщи́ца

GENDER OF INDECLINABLE NOUNS OF FOREIGN ORIGIN

Thousands of words have been borrowed into Russian from English and other languages. Among these foreign borrowings is a fairly large number of nouns that are indeclinable, that is, their endings do not change for number or case. Nearly all these nouns end in a vowel, but for this group of nouns the vowel ending is often not a reliable indicator of gender. Rather, the gender of indeclinable loanwords is determined by certain categories.

Indeclinable Loanwords Denoting Inanimate Objects are Generally Neuter
Examples:

Моско́вское метро́ *Moscow metro*   **дли́нное резюме́** *long résumé*
удо́бное купе́ *comfortable compartment*   **разнообра́зное меню́** *varied menu*
но́вое кино́ *new cinema*   **ую́тное кафе́** *cosy café*
свобо́дное такси́ *unoccupied taxi*   **интере́сное интервью́** *interesting interview*

Note: But the noun **ко́фе** *coffee* is masculine (**чёрный ко́фе** *black coffee*)

Note: The gender of a few indeclinable loanwords denoting inanimate objects is determined by the gender of the native Russian word that denotes the relevant generic class, e.g., **торна́до** *tornado* is masculine (cf. **ве́тер** *wind*), **саля́ми** *salami* is feminine (cf. **колбаса́** *sausage*), as is **авеньо́** *avenue* (cf. **у́лица** *street*).

Indeclinable Loanwords Denoting People are "Naturally" Masculine or Feminine
Examples:

знамени́тый мае́стро *famous maestro*   **но́вый рефери́** *new referee*
настоя́щая ле́ди *a real lady*   **краси́вая инженю́** *pretty ingénue*

Indeclinable Loanwords Denoting Animals and Birds are Normally Masculine
Examples:

большо́й кенгуру́ *big kangaroo*   **у́мный шимпанзе́** *intelligent chimpanzee*
симпати́чный по́ни *nice pony*   **краси́вый какаду́** *beautiful cockatoo*
ро́зовый флами́нго *pink flamingo*

Indeclinable loanwords denoting *place names* generally have the same gender as the native Russian generic noun that denotes the relevant class. Note the following classes:

Indeclinable Loanwords Denoting Cities are Masculine (cf. **го́род** *city*):

Хе́льсинки	*Helsinki*	**Тбили́си**	*Tbilisi*
То́кио	*Tokyo*	**О́сло**	*Oslo*
Гонолу́лу	*Honolulu*	**Сан-Франци́ско**	*San Francisco*
Ка́лгари	*Calgary*	**Торо́нто**	*Toronto*

Indeclinable Loanwords Denoting Islands are Masculine (cf. **о́стров** *island*):

краси́вый Кюраса́о	*beautiful Curaçao*	**со́лнечный Ко́рфу**	*sunny Corfu*
живопи́сный Анти́гуа	*picturesque Antigua*	**го́рный Ка́при**	*mountainous Capri*

Nouns Denoting Rivers are generally Feminine (cf. **река́** *river*):

Янцзы́	*Yangtze*	**Ко́нго**	*Congo*
Ога́йо	*Ohio*	**Миссиси́пи**	*Mississippi*

The nouns that denote both the river and state of the U.S. are masculine when they refer to the state (cf. **шта́т** *state*), but feminine when they denote the river:

споко́йная Миссиси́пи   *the calm Mississippi*
дли́нная Миссу́ри   *the long Missouri*
бы́страя Колора́до   *the rapid Colorado*

Indeclinable Loanwords Denoting Lakes are Neuter (cf. **о́зеро** *lake*)

свежево́дное Э́ри *freshwater Erie*   **просто́рное Гуро́н** *expansive (Lake) Huron*

7.   Indicate the gender of the following loanwords by writing **ой**, **оно́**, or **она́**.

1.	такси́	_____	7.	Ко́нго	_____
2.	рефери́	_____	8.	ко́фе	_____
3.	меню́	_____	9.	по́ни	_____
4.	авеньо́	_____	10.	Анти́гуа	_____
5.	инженю́	_____	11.	Гонолу́лу	_____
6.	Сан-Франци́ско	_____	12.	Э́ри	_____

NUMBER

Most nouns in Russian, as in English, distinguish singular and plural number. English nouns normally form their plural by adding an ending to the singular form, usually *-s* or *-es* as in *book*, *books*; *box*, *boxes*. In Russian too, nouns are made plural either by *adding* an ending (to the stem of masculine nouns which have no singular ending), or by *changing* the ending of the singular (feminine and neuter nouns). In changing from singular to plural, the (singular) ending that may have indicated the noun's gender is removed; consequently, gender is not expressed in the plural of nouns.

NOMINATIVE PLURAL OF NOUNS

The nominative plural ending of Russian nouns is normally determined by the gender of the noun in the singular, and by whether the noun has a hard or soft stem. Specifically, the nominative plural ending for the majority of masculine and feminine nouns with a hard stem is **-ы**, and with a soft stem, **-и**. The nominative plural ending for neuter nouns with a hard stem is **-а**, and with a soft stem, **-я**. The following table illustrates the way stems and endings combine to form the nominative plural of most nouns.

Gender	Singular	Plural	Ending
Masculine Hard Stem:	дива́н	дива́ны	-ы
Soft Stem:	музе́й	музе́и	-и
	портфе́ль	портфе́ли	
Feminine Hard Stem:	газе́та	газе́ты	-ы
Soft Stem:	ку́хня	ку́хни	-и
	пло́щадь	пло́щади	
Neuter Hard Stem:	кре́сло	кре́сла	-а
Soft Stem:	зда́ние	зда́ния	-я

Note: Some words of foreign origin are indeclinable, that is, they never change their ending, and so they do not form a plural, e.g., **метро́**, **кафе́**, **такси́**, **кино́**. However, such clues as a plural ending on a modifying adjective (**-ые**, **-ие**), or a plural verb ending, can indicate when an indeclinable noun is being used to denote more than one object, e.g. **но́вые такси́** *new taxis*, **В це́нтре бы́ли ую́тные кафе́** *In the center there were cozy cafés.*

Spelling Rule 1 and Nominative Plurals

Russian has a spelling rule which applies, among other places, in forming the nominative plural of certain nouns. This spelling rule (Rule 1, page 11) states that the vowel **-ы** can not occur after the letters **к**, **г**, **х** or **ж**, **ш**, **ч**, **щ**; whenever an "i" vowel is required after one of these letters, it must be spelled **-и**. Therefore, masculine and feminine nouns whose stem ends in one of these consonants must spell their nominative plural ending as **-и**.

Singular		Plural	Singular		Plural
уче́бник	textbook	уче́бники	пля́ж	beach	пля́жи
кни́га	book	кни́ги	ро́ща	grove	ро́щи
стару́ха	old lady	стару́хи	но́чь	night	но́чи

8. Rewrite the following sentences, changing the nouns to the plural. Mark the stress.

Model: Э́то журна́л. *This is a magazine* > Э́то журна́лы. *These are magazines.*

1. Э́то газе́та. *Это газе́ти*
2. Э́то уче́бник. *Это уче́бники*
3. Э́то кни́га. *Это кни́ги*
4. Э́то кре́сло. *Это кре́сла*
5. Э́то ру́чка. *Это ру́чки*
6. Э́то тетра́дь. *Это тетра́ди*
7. Э́то пла́тье. *Это пла́тя*
8. Э́то телефо́н. *Это телефо́ни*
9. Э́то портфе́ль. *Это портфе́ли*
10. Э́то музе́й. *Это музе́й*
11. Э́то ла́мпа. *Это ла́мпи*
12. Э́то студе́нт. *Это студе́нти*
13. Э́то студе́нтка. *Это студе́нтки*
14. Э́то институ́т. *Это институ́ти*
15. Э́то пля́ж. *Это пля́хи*
16. Э́то пло́щадь. *Это пло́щади*

Stress Shifts in Nominative Plurals

In some nouns the change from singular to plural is accompanied by a shift of the stress to a different syllable. Some commonly used nouns undergo a stress shift. Below are examples of such nouns from each gender.

Masculine

In masculine nouns the stress shifts from the final syllable of the stem in the singular to the ending of the plural:

Singular		Plural	Singular		Plural
каранда́ш	pencil	карандаши́	вра́ч	doctor	врачи́
слова́рь	dictionary	словари́	но́ж	knife	ножи́
сто́л	table	столы́	клю́ч	key	ключи́

Neuter

In neuter nouns there is a regular pattern of stress shift that is observed in many two-syllable nouns: the syllable that is unstressed in the singular, gets the stress in the plural:

Singular		Plural	Singular		Plural
сло́во	word	слова́	письмо́	letter	пи́сьма
ме́сто	place	места́	окно́	window	о́кна
мо́ре	sea	моря́	лицо́	face	ли́ца

Feminine

The stress shifts in some feminine nouns from the ending to the stem:

Singular		Plural	Singular		Plural
сестра́	sister	сёстры	рука́	hand	ру́ки
жена́	wife	жёны	нога́	leg	но́ги
звезда́	star	звёзды	голова́	head	го́ловы
страна́	country	стра́ны	гора́	mountain	го́ры

Fleeting Vowels in the Nominative Plural

Some masculine nouns that have the vowel **o**, **e**, or **ë** in the final syllable of the singular, drop this vowel when the Nominative plural (or any other ending) is added. The omission of these "fleeting vowels" occurs in a number of nouns, especially in those that end in the suffixes **-ок**, **ёк**, and **-ец**.

Singular		Plural	Singular		Plural
значо́к	badge	значки́	отец	father	отцы́
кусо́к	piece	куски́	коне́ц	end	концы́
кружо́к	small circle	кружки́	кана́дец	Canadian	кана́дцы
огонёк	small light	огоньки́	америка́нец	American	америка́нцы

9. Rewrite the following sentences, changing the nouns to the plural. Mark the stress.

Model: Где́ письмо́? > Где́ пи́сьма? *Where is the letter?* > *Where are the letters?*

1. Где́ значо́к? *значбки*
2. Где́ но́ж? *ножи*
3. Где́ платоќ? *платоки*
4. Где́ слова́рь? *словаряи*
5. Где́ сестра́? *сестрыбı*
6. Где́ оте́ц? *отцбı*
7. Где́ звезда́? *звездбı*
8. Где́ клю́ч? *качочбı*
9. Где́ окно́? *окна*
10. Где́ жена́? *женбı*

Nominative Plurals in -á (-я)

A small number of masculine nouns form their nominative plural with the stressed ending **-á (-я)**. The following examples occur frequently and should be memorized:

Singular		Plural	Singular		Plural
гла́з	eye	глаза́	но́мер	number	номера́
го́род	city	города́	по́езд	train	поезда́
а́дрес	address	адреса́	па́спорт	passport	паспорта́
до́м	house	дома́	ве́чер	evening	вечера́
го́лос	voice	голоса́	кра́й	edge	края́
профе́ссор	professor	профессора́	учи́тель	teacher	учителя́

IRREGULAR PLURALS

Irregular Nominative Plurals in -ья

A few masculine and neuter nouns form their nominative plural irregularly with the ending **-ья**. These nouns should be memorized:

Masculine			**Neuter**		
Singular		Plural	Singular		Plural
бра́т	brother	бра́тья	де́рево	tree	дере́вья
сту́л	chair	сту́лья	перо́	feather	пе́рья
му́ж	husband	мужья́	крыло́	wing	кры́лья

A few nouns from this group undergo a stem change in the plural:

Singular		Plural
дру́г	*friend*	друзья́
сы́н	*son*	сыновья́

Note: Two nouns augment their stem in the plural by adding the element **-ep-** (as in English mother and daughter) before the ending **-и**:

Singular		Plural	
ма́ть	*mother*	ма́тери	*mothers*
до́чь	*daughter*	до́чери	*daughters*

Irregular Plurals from Different Words

Two nouns use a completely different word for the plural:

Singular		Plural	
ребёнок	*child*	де́ти	*children*
челове́к	*person*	лю́ди	*people*

Plurals of Neuter Nouns in -мя

The small group of neuter nouns in **-мя** undergo a stem change in the plural:

Singular		Plural	Singular		Plural
вре́мя	*time*	времена́	пле́мя	*tribe*	племена́
и́мя	*name*	имена́	бре́мя	*burden*	бремена́
се́мя	*seed*	семена́	зна́мя	*banner*	знамёна

10. Rewrite the sentences, changing all words to the plural. Mark the stress.

> *Model:* Мо́й дру́г профе́ссор. > Мои́ друзья́ профессора́.
> *My friend is a professor.* > *My friends are professors.*

1. Мо́й сы́н учи́тель.   Мои сыновья учителя
2. Моя́ до́чь учи́тельница.   Мои дочери учительницы
3. Мо́й бра́т вра́ч.   Мои братья
4. Моя́ сестра́ студе́нтка.   Мои сестры
5. Мо́й дру́г америка́нец.   Мои друзья американцы

11. Rewrite the sentences, changing the pronoun and the noun to the plural. Mark the stress.
> *Model:* Во́т наш клю́ч. > Во́т на́ши ключи́. *Here is our key.* > *Here are our keys.*

1. Во́т наш ребёнок.   Вот наши дети
2. Во́т наш па́спорт.   Вот наши паспорта
3. Во́т наш сту́л.   Вот наши стулья
4. Во́т наше и́мя.   Вот наши имена   ИМЕНА
5. Во́т наше де́рево.   Вот наши деревья

NOUNS USED ONLY IN THE SINGULAR

Some nouns in Russian, as in English, have only a singular form. These include the names of various materials and substances (e.g. English *gold*, *straw*), abstract nouns denoting various qualities and properties (e.g., English *courage*, *devotion*), as well as *collective* nouns, i.e., those which, while singular in form, denote a collection of people or things viewed as a whole (e.g., English *youth*, *mankind*, *furniture*). In many instances, the same nouns are treated as "singular only" in both English and Russian. There are some nouns, however, which in English are often used in the plural, but whose equivalents in Russian are collective nouns, e.g., English *clothes*, *dishes*, and various nouns denoting fruits and vegetables, e.g., *strawberries*, *potatoes*, *peas*. Below are examples of nouns from various categories used only in the singular. Special note should be taken of those collective nouns which are used with the plural form in English, but in Russian are used only in the singular.

Materials and Substances

де́рево	*wood*	молоко́	*milk*
зо́лото	*gold*	шокола́д	*chocolate*
соло́ма	*straw*	ма́сло	*butter*
желе́зо	*iron*	са́хар	*sugar*
ста́ль	*steel*	ри́с	*rice*

Abstract Nouns Denoting Qualities, Conditions, Sensations, etc.

че́стность	*honesty*	све́тлость	*brightness*
ло́жь	*falsehood*	темнота́	*darkness*
доброта́	*goodness*	гру́сть	*sadness*
го́ре	*grief*	жара́	*heat, hot weather*

Collective Nouns Denoting People and Objects

молодёжь	*young people*	оде́жда	*clothes*
студе́нчество	*the students*	о́бувь	*shoes/footwear*
профессу́ра	*professoriate*	посу́да	*dishes*
детвора́	*children*	бельё	*linen(s)*
родня́	*relatives*	листва́	*leaves/foliage*

Collective Nouns Denoting Fruits and Vegetables

изю́м	*raisins*	морко́вь	*carrots*
виногра́д	*grapes*	горо́х	*peas*
клубни́ка	*strawberries*	капу́ста	*cabbage*
мали́на	*raspberries*	лу́к	*onions*
ежеви́ка	*blackberries*	карто́фель	*potatoes*
ви́шня	*cherries*	крупа́	*groats*

Note that for some of these nouns denoting fruits and vegetables the suffix **-ина** can be added to the noun to express "a raisin," "a grape," etc.: **изю́мина** *a raisin*, **виногра́дина** *a grape*, **горо́шина** *a pea*, **карто́фелина** (or the colloquial noun **карто́шка**) *a potato*. Note also the suffix **-ка** in **морко́вка** *a carrot* (and similarly, **шокола́дка** *a chocolate*). To denote "a strawberry," "a raspberry," one can use the word **я́года** *berry*, e.g., **я́года клубни́ки** *a strawberry*; alternatively, the word **шту́ка** *item* may be used to express one or more individual pieces, e.g., **Да́йте лу́ку**, **три́ шту́ки**, **пожа́луйста** *Give me some onions, three (pieces) please.*

Note also that a collective noun requires singular agreement. For example, a modifying adjective must agree in singular number and in gender (masculine, feminine, and neuter adjective endings are, respectively, **-ый**, **-ая**, **ое**):

Э́то вку́сный виногра́д.	*These are tasty grapes.*
Э́то све́жая клубни́ка.	*These are fresh strawberries.*
Э́то чи́стое бельё.	*These are clean linens.*

Also, a predicate-verb must agree in the singular:

Оде́жда лежи́т на крова́ти.	*The clothes are lying on the bed.*

(The form **лежи́т** is the 3rd person singular, present tense of the verb **лежа́ть** *to lie*)

NOUNS USED ONLY IN THE PLURAL

Some nouns denote objects or processes comprised of at least two essential parts or participants. Often, language reflects this real-world fact grammatically by allowing such nouns to occur generally in the plural, e.g., English *jeans*, *scissors*, *the races*, *negotiations*, etc. The Russian equivalents of these particular nouns also occur only in the plural. In a few instances, however, Russian and English differ in this regard, e.g., the English noun *watch* is a plural-only noun in Russian: **часы́**. Below is a representative list of commonly used nouns that normally occur only in the plural. Take special note of the nouns in the column on the right, which in English are used in the singular, but are plural-only nouns in Russian.

*(a) Plural-only Nouns Ending in **-ы, -и***

часы́	*watch, clock*	де́ньги	*money*
очки́	*eyeglasses*	сли́вки	*cream*
но́жницы	*scissors*	счёты	*abacus*
брю́ки	*trousers*	духи́	*perfume*
джи́нсы	*jeans*	каче́ли	*swing*
шо́рты	*shorts*	са́ни	*sleigh*
трусы́	*underpants*	ша́хматы	*chess*
пла́вки	*swimming trunks*	кани́кулы	*vacation/holidays*
перегово́ры	*negotiations*	ро́ды	*childbirth*
вы́боры	*elections*	по́хороны	*funeral*

*(b) Plural-only Nouns Ending in **-a***

бега́	*trotting races*	пери́ла	*railings*
черни́ла	*ink*	воро́та	*gate*
дрова́	*firewood*	письмена́	*alphabet characters*

12.   For each noun below, supply the correct form of the adjective in the singular or plural.

Model: (столо́вый *table*) бельё	>	столо́**вое** бельё	*table linens*
(но́вый *new*) часы́	>	но́**вые** часы́	*new watch*

1. (ру́сский *Russian*) молодёжь _____
2. (мо́дный *stylish*) оде́жда _____
3. (кра́сный *red*) черни́ла _____
4. (све́жий *fresh*) мали́на _____
5. (желе́зный *iron*) пери́ла _____
6. (чи́стый *clean*) посу́да _____
7. (прия́тный *pleasant*) духи́ _____
8. (сухо́й *dry*) дрова́ _____
9. (но́вый *new*) де́ньги _____
10. (весёлый *cheerful*) детвора́ _____

DECLENSION OF NOUNS

All nouns in Russian (except some of foreign origin, e.g., **ра́дио** *radio*, **меню́** *menu*, **кафе́** *café*) *decline*, that is, change their endings to express a particular *case* in the singular or plural (see Case below). Every declinable noun belongs to one of three declension classes: *first declension*, *second declension*, or *third declension*. The particular declension class a noun belongs to is based on its gender and form in the nominative singular:

First Declension:

- Masculine nouns with a stem ending in a consonant or **-й**
- Masculine nouns with a stem ending in **-ь**
- Neuter nouns ending in **-о**, **-е**, **-ё**

Second Declension:

- Feminine nouns ending in **-а**, **-я**
- Masculine nouns ending in **-а**, **-я**

Third Declension:

- Feminine nouns with a stem ending in **-ь**

The following table illustrates the distribution of nouns into the three declension classes.

Case	First Declension	Second Declension	Third Declension
Nominative	Masculine: **сто́л** **портфе́ль** **музе́й** Neuter: **кре́сло** **зда́ние** **бельё**	Feminine: **маши́на** **ку́хня** Masculine: **па́па** **дя́дя**	Feminine: **пло́щадь**

Most nouns are easily assigned to one of the three declensions. The only nouns whose declension is difficult to determine are those ending in the soft sign (**-ь**). Remember that masculine soft-sign nouns belong to the first declension, while feminine soft-sign nouns are the *only* nouns in the third declension. It is important to know the declension class to which a noun belongs because each declension class has its own set of endings that corresponds to the different cases in Russian.

CASE

The term *case* refers to the function, or type of relation, a noun (or pronoun) has with respect to the other words in a sentence. For example, in the sentence *Mary gave the book to John* the noun *Mary* is the "subject" of the sentence, *book* functions as "direct object" of the verb, and *John* has the function of "indirect object." These three functions normally are fulfilled by nouns in the **nominative**, **accusative**, and **dative** cases, respectively. Similarly, in the phrase *Tanya's brother* the noun *Tanya* functions as the "possessor" in relation to the noun *brother* (what is "possessed"), a relation indicated in English by the ending *-'s*. This "possessor" relation is typically expressed by the **genitive** case. In English these grammatical functions, or relation types, are indicated formally by word order (e.g., the subject is to the left of the verb, the direct object to the verb's right), prepositions (e.g., the preposition *to* in *to John* signals indirect object), or by an ending on the noun (e.g., the possessive ending *-'s* added to the noun *Tanya*). In Russian, certain types of relations, like the English possessive, are indicated by a case ending on the noun. Others, as we shall see in Chapter 3, are expressed by both a preposition and a case ending.

ANIMACY

Some nouns denote living beings, such as people and animals (**оте́ц** *father*, **бра́т** *brother*, **ко́т** *tom-cat*), while others denote various nonliving objects and abstract things (**сто́л** *table*, **сту́л** *chair*, **ра́дость** *joy*). The grammatical terms for these two classes of nouns are *animate* and *inanimate*, respectively. The distinction between animate and inanimate nouns is important in determining which nouns are functioning as "subject" or "object" in Russian. In English, grammatical relations like "subject" and "object" are determined by a fixed subject-verb-object word-order, but in Russian, where word-order is "free," an animate direct object can precede a verb and potentially be mistaken for the subject. This potential ambiguity is generally avoided in Russian by marking masculine animate, but not inanimate, nouns with a special ending when they function as a direct object of the verb in the accusative case. For example, the inanimate masculine noun **сто́л** *table* has the same form whether it functions as subject (**Сто́л та́м** *The table is there*), or object (**Я́ ви́жу сто́л** *I see the table*). But the animate masculine noun **сы́н** *son* adds the ending **-a** when it functions as a direct object in the accusative case, cf. **Я́ ви́дел сы́на** *I saw my son*. Therefore, in the sentence **Оте́ц лю́бит сы́на** *The father loves his son* the direct object is formally distinguished from the subject **оте́ц** *father*, and these roles remain the same even when, for reasons of emphasis, the object precedes the subject, cf. **Сы́на лю́бит оте́ц** *It is the father who loves his son*.

Animate nouns functioning as direct objects in the accusative case have a special ending not only in the singular of first declension masculines; the plurals of animate nouns in all three declensions have an ending which differentiates them from inanimate nouns.

THE CASES OF RUSSIAN

Russian has six cases:

> **Nominative**
> **Accusative**
> **Genitive**
> **Prepositional**
> **Dative**
> **Instrumental**

Nominative Case

Singular and Plural Endings

Below is a table summarizing nominative case endings in both singular and plural.

Gender	Singular	Ending	Plural	Ending
Masculine Hard Stem: Soft Stem:	дива́н музе́й портфе́ль	-∅	дива́ны музе́и портфе́ли	-ы -и
Feminine Hard Stem: Soft Stem:	газе́та ку́хня пло́щадь	-а -я -∅	газе́ты ку́хни пло́щади	-ы -и
Neuter Hard Stem: Soft Stem:	кре́сло зда́ние	-о -е	кре́сла зда́ния	-а -я

The nominative case can be viewed as the basic form of the noun. As previously mentioned, it is the nominative case form in which words are cited in dictionaries, or when they are in other ways removed from context. The nominative case in Russian has several uses.

Uses of The Nominative Case

Nominative as Subject

The nominative case is used for the grammatical subject of the sentence. The noun in the nominative case controls agreement on its predicate: a predicate verb in the present tense must agree with the subject in person and number; in the past tense, a verb in the singular agrees in gender as well. A predicate adjective must also agree with its nominative-case subject in both gender and number.

Профе́ссор **чита́ет ле́кцию.**	*The professor is reading a lecture.*
Студе́нты **слу́шают ле́кцию.**	*The students listen to the lecture.*
Учени́к **за́дал вопро́с.**	*The pupil asked a question.*
Студе́нтка **задала́ вопро́с.**	*The co-ed asked a question.*
Письмо́ **лежи́т на столе́.**	*The letter is (lying) on the table.*
Маши́ны **стоя́т на у́лице.**	*Cars are parked on the street.*

За́л **свобо́ден.**	*The hall is free (available).*
Ме́сто **свобо́дно.**	*The seat is free.*
Ко́мната **свобо́дна.**	*The room is free.*
Места́ **свобо́дны.**	*The seats are free.*

As a Predicate Nominative

A predicate nominative is a noun (pronoun or adjective) which follows a linking verb (stated or implied) and is *equated* with the subject in some way. For example, in the sentence *John is a student* the predicate nominative denotes a class or status—that of "student"—which is attributed to the subject. In Russian, the equivalent of the English linking verb *to be*, **быть**, generally is not used in the present tense, but its meaning is always implied in sentences with predicate nominatives. The implicit "am/is/are" meaning is sometimes indicated in punctuation by a dash.

Ива́н — *студе́нт*.	*Ivan is a student.*
Пу́шкин и Че́хов — *писа́тели*.	*Pushkin and Chekhov are writers.*
Москва́ — *столи́ца Росси́и*.	*Moscow is the capital of Russia.*
Э́то *моя́ сестра́*.	*This is my sister.*
Э́то *мои́ роди́тели*.	*These are my parents.*

Nouns following a past tense form of the verb **быть (бы́л, была́, бы́ли)** may occur as predicates in the nominative case when they denote a permanent property, or one felt to be a defining characteristic of the subject. These include nouns denoting nationalities, kin terms (e.g., **бра́т** *brother*, **сестра́** *sister*), as well as nouns with evaluative meaning (e.g., **добря́к** *good guy*, **краса́вица** *a beauty*, **у́мница** *smart person*).

Мо́й де́душка *был америка́нец*.	*My grandfather was American.*
Моя́ ба́бушка *была́ ру́сская*.	*My grandmother was Russian.*
Ва́ня *был добря́к*.	*Vanya was a good guy.*
Ле́на *была́ у́мница*.	*Lena was a smart person.*

Note: When they occur after the past tense (or other forms) of **быть**, unmodified nouns of occupation, and other nouns denoting function or status, are normally in the instrumental case. See below on the "Uses of the Instrumental Case."

Nominative as Form of Direct Address

The nominative case can be used as a vocative, that is, a form used to call or address someone directly.

Ю́рий Серге́евич! **Мо́жно ва́с?**	*Yuri Sergeevich! Can I see you?*
Са́ша! **Тебя́ к телефо́ну.**	*Sasha! You're wanted on the phone.*
Ва́ня! **Познако́мься с мое́й жено́й.**	*Vanya! I'd like you to meet my wife.*

Note: In colloquial style the informal nouns used as vocatives may lose their final vowel, thus taking on a form different from the nominative: **Са́ш!** *Sash!*, **Ма́м!** *Mom!*, **Ва́нь!** *Vanya!*

As a Noun Title in Apposition

A noun denoting the name or title of something in apposition to the noun denoting its generic class is in the nominative case.

Мы́ чита́ем рома́н «*Война́ и ми́р*».	*We are reading the novel "War and Peace."*
О́н слу́шал о́перу «*Евге́ний Оне́гин*».	*He listened to the opera "Evgenij Onegin."*
Она́ рабо́тает в газе́те «*Пра́вда*».	*She works for the newspaper "Pravda."*

Accusative Case

Singular and Plural

The accusative case endings of first declension *inanimate* masculine, as well as neuter nouns, are identical to the nominative case endings, in both singular and plural.

First Declension

Masculine Inanimate Nouns

Case	Singular Hard Stem	Soft Stem	Plural Hard Stem	Soft Stem
Nom.	**стóл**	**портфéль**	**столы́**	**портфéли**
Acc. = Nom.	**стóл**	**портфéль**	**столы́**	**портфéли**

Neuter Nouns

Case	Singular Hard Stem	Soft Stem	Plural Hard Stem	Soft Stem
Nom.	**окнó**	**здáние**	**óкна**	**здáния**
Acc. = Nom.	**окнó**	**здáние**	**óкна**	**здáния**

The accusative case endings of first declension *animate* masculine nouns in both singular and plural are identical to the genitive case endings (see the section on Animacy).

Animate Masculine Nouns

Case	Singular Hard Stem	Soft Stem	Plural Hard Stem	Soft Stem
Nom.	**студéнт**	**писáтель**	**студéнты**	**писáтели**
Acc. = Gen.	**студéнта**	**писáтеля**	**студéнтов**	**писáтелей**

Second Declension

Second declension feminine nouns ending in **-а/-я**, as well as masculine nouns ending in **-а/-я**, take the ending **-у/-ю** in the accusative singular. Both masculine and feminine *animate* nouns in the plural have an ending in the accusative identical to the genitive plural.

Feminine and Masculine Nouns in -a

Case	Singular Feminine Inanimate	Animate	Masculine Animate	Plural Feminine Inanimate	Animate	Masculine Animate
Nom.	**спáльня**	**бáбушка**	**дéдушка**	**кóмнаты**	**бáбушки**	**дéдушки**
Acc.	**спáльню**	**бáбушку**	**дéдушку**	**кóмнаты**	**бáбушек**	**дéдушек**

Third Declension Nouns

Third declension *inanimate* nouns in the singular and plural have an ending identical to the nominative. Third declension *animate* nouns, of which there are few (e.g., **свекро́вь** *mother-in-law*), have an ending in the accusative plural identical to the genitive plural.

Feminine Nouns in -ь

Case	Singular Inanimate	Animate	Plural Inanimate	Animate
Nom.	**тетра́дь**	**свекро́вь**	**тетра́ди**	**свекро́ви**
Acc.	**тетра́дь**	**свекро́вь**	**тетра́ди**	**свекро́вей**

Uses of the Accusative Case

As the Direct Object of a Transitive Verb

The direct object of a verb is the noun (or pronoun) that often is understood to be the goal of the action, the object affected (or effected) by the action of the verb.

А́втор пи́шет *рома́н.*	*The author is writing a novel.*
Он пи́шет *интере́сные рома́ны.*	*He writes interesting novels.*
Учи́тель откры́л *окно́.*	*The teacher opened the window.*
Профе́ссор спра́шивал *студе́нта.*	*The professor was questioning the student.*
Он ча́сто спра́шивает *студе́нтов.*	*He often questions students.*
Ма́льчик чита́ет *кни́гу.*	*The boy is reading a book.*
Ру́сские лю́бят чита́ть *кни́ги.*	*Russians love to read books.*
Де́вочка лю́бит *ба́бушку и де́душку.*	*The girl loves her grandma and grandpa.*
На́до уважа́ть *ба́бушек и де́душек.*	*One must respect grandmas and grandpas.*

To Express Duration and Repetition of Time

Она́ говори́ла по телефо́ну *це́лый час.*	*She spoke on the phone a whole hour.*
Ба́бушка боле́ла *всю зи́му.*	*Grandma was sick all winter.*
Мы бы́ли в Москве́ *ме́сяц.*	*We were in Moscow a month.*
Ви́ка пи́шет пи́сьма *ка́ждую неде́лю.*	*Vika writes letters every week.*

To Express Extent of Distance, Cost, or Weight

Ка́ждое у́тро он бе́гает *пять киломе́тров.*	*Every morning he runs five kilometers.*
Всю доро́гу **они́ игра́ли в ка́рты.**	*They played cards the whole way.*
Кольцо́ сто́ит *ты́сячу до́лларов.*	*The ring costs a thousand dollars.*
Э́та маши́на ве́сит *то́нну.*	*This car weighs a ton.*

As the Object of Prepositions

Prepositions which require the accusative case are presented in Chapter 3.

13. In each sentence below, identify the case of the underlined word.

		Nominative	Accusative
1.	Профе́ссор чита́л <u>ле́кцию</u>.	_____	_____
2.	Ле́кцию чита́л <u>профе́ссор</u>.	_____	_____
3.	<u>Профе́ссора</u> лю́бят студе́нты.	_____	_____
4.	Э́то моя́ <u>жена́</u>.	_____	_____
5.	Моя́ <u>жена́</u> — программи́ст.	_____	_____
6.	Де́вочка убира́ет <u>ко́мнату</u>.	_____	_____
7.	Мы́ чита́ем <u>журна́л</u> «Та́йм»	_____	_____
8.	Она́ была́ в Росси́и <u>ме́сяц</u>.	_____	_____
9.	Па́па бе́гает ка́ждый <u>де́нь</u>.	_____	_____
10.	Мы́ ви́дели но́вый <u>фи́льм</u>.	_____	_____
11.	<u>Фи́льм</u> шёл в кинотеа́тре «Росси́я»	_____	_____
12.	Како́й интере́сный <u>фи́льм</u>!	_____	_____
13.	<u>Шокола́д</u> сто́ит оди́н до́ллар.	_____	_____
14.	Моя́ сестра́ <u>у́мница</u>.	_____	_____

14. In the sentences that follow, change the underlined nouns to the plural.

1. Па́па чита́ет <u>журна́л</u>. _____
2. Са́ша лю́бит <u>компью́тер</u>. _____
3. Ма́ма пи́шет <u>письмо́</u>. _____
4. Профе́ссор спра́шивает <u>студе́нта</u>. _____
5. Шко́льники покупа́ют <u>тетра́дь</u>. _____
6. Ма́льчик купи́л <u>слова́рь</u>. _____
7. Де́вочка ча́сто но́сит <u>пла́тье</u>. _____
8. Мы́ зна́ем <u>свекро́вь</u>. _____

15. Put the noun into the correct case form.

Model: му́зыка: Она́ слу́шает <u>му́зыку</u>.

1. литерату́ра: Мы́ изуча́ем _____.
2. исто́рия: О́н лю́бит _____.
3. бра́т: Я́ зна́ю _____.
4. соба́ка: Мы́ ви́дели _____.
5. преподава́тель: Студе́нт слу́шает _____.
6. зада́ние: Мы́ де́лаем _____.
7. ра́дио: Ле́на слу́шает _____.
8. матема́тика: Са́ша пло́хо зна́ет _____.
9. ма́ть: Сы́н лю́бит _____.
10. оте́ц: О́н не зна́ет _____.

Genitive Case

Genitive Singular

The endings of the genitive singular for masculine and neuter nouns are:

-а   for nouns with a hard stem
-я   for nouns with a soft stem

Nominative Singular		Genitive Singular
стóл	*table*	**столá**
портфéль	*briefcase*	**портфéля**
брáт	*brother*	**брáта**
гóсть	*guest*	**гóстя**

The endings of the genitive singular for feminine nouns are:

-ы   for nouns with a hard stem
-и   for nouns with a soft stem

Nominative Singular		Genitive Singular
кóмната	*room*	**кóмнаты**
сестрá	*sister*	**сестры́**
кýхня	*kitchen*	**кýхни**

Note: The only exceptions to the above generalizations are those nouns subject to either Spelling Rule 1 or Spelling Rule 2 (see page 11). For example, due to Spelling Rule 1, the genitive singular of feminine nouns whose stem ends in a hard **г, к, х,** or **ж, ш** take the ending **-и** (rather than **-ы**): **кни́га** *book* > **кни́ги, кóшка** *cat* > **кóшки, кóжа** *leather* > **кóжи.** Due to Spelling Rule 2, masculine nouns whose stem ends in the soft consonants **ч** or **щ** take the ending **-а** (rather than **-я**): **врáч** *doctor* > **врачá, плáщ** *raincoat* > **плащá.**

Note: Masculine nouns which end in **-а** or **-я** in the nominative singular (**пáпа, дя́дя**) take the same ending in the genitive case as feminine nouns ending in **-а, -я: Рýчка** *мáмы Mom's pen* — **Рýчка** *пáпы Dad's pen.* Such nouns referring to male persons decline like feminine nouns in all the cases.

Genitive Plural

There are three possible endings in the genitive plural: (1) **-ов (-ев),** (2) **-ей,** and (3) **-∅.** The distribution of these endings is as follows:

The genitive plural ending **-ов:**

(*a*)   Masculine nouns whose stem ends in a hard paired consonant:

Nominative Singular		Genitive Plural
стóл	*table*	**столóв**
дóм	*house*	**домóв**
студéнт	*student*	**студéнтов**

(*b*)   Masculine nouns with the stressed suffix **-éц:**

Nominative Singular		Genitive Plural
отéц	*father*	**отцóв**
певéц	*singer*	**певцóв**

Note: The suffix **-ец** contains a "fleeting vowel" which is omitted when any ending follows this suffix. This is also true of the suffix **-ок: платóк** *shawl* > **платкóв.**

The genitive plural ending **-ев**:

(*a*)   Masculine nouns with the unstressed suffix **-ец**:

Nominative Singular		Genitive Plural
америка́нец	*American*	**америка́нцев**
ме́сяц	*month*	**ме́сяцев**

Note: The spelling of this suffix as **-ев** is due to Spelling Rule 3 (see page 11).

(*b*)   Masculine nouns with a stem ending in **-й**:

Nominative Singular		Genitive Plural
музе́й	*museum*	**музе́ев**
геро́й	*hero*	**геро́ев**
кафете́рий	*cafeteria*	**кафете́риев**

(*c*)   Nouns whose nominative plural is stem-stressed and ends in **-ья**:

Nominative Singular		Nominative Plural	Genitive Plural
бра́т	*brother*	**бра́тья**	**бра́тьев**
сту́л	*chair*	**сту́лья**	**сту́льев**
ли́ст	*leaf*	**ли́стья**	**ли́стьев**
де́рево	*tree*	**дере́вья**	**дере́вьев**

The genitive plural ending **-ей**:

(*a*)   All masculine and feminine nouns whose stem ends in the soft sign **-ь**:

Nominative Singular		Genitive Plural
слова́рь	*dictionary*	**словаре́й**
тетра́дь	*notebook*	**тетра́дей**
писа́тель	*writer*	**писа́телей**

Note: The nouns **ма́ть** *mother* and **до́чь** *daughter* take the genitive plural in **-ей**, but are preceded by the element **-ер-**: **матере́й**, **дочере́й**.

(*b*)   All masculine nouns ending in the unpaired consonants **ж, ч, ш, щ**:

Nominative Singular		Genitive Plural
вра́ч	*doctor*	**враче́й**
но́ж	*knife*	**ноже́й**
каранда́ш	*pencil*	**карандаше́й**
пла́щ	*raincoat*	**плаще́й**

(*c*)   Nouns whose nominative plural ends in stressed **-ья**:

Nominative Singular		Nominative Plural	Genitive Plural
дру́г	*friend*	**друзья́**	**друзе́й**
сы́н	*son*	**сыновья́**	**сынове́й**
му́ж	*husband*	**мужья́**	**муже́й**

(d)   A few nouns form their genitive plural from a different word:

Nominative Singular		Nominative Plural	Genitive Plural
ребёнок	child	дети	детей
челове́к	person	лю́ди	люде́й
го́д	year	го́ды	ле́т

Note: After certain words denoting quantity, e.g., **ско́лько** *how many*, **не́сколько** *several*, and the numerals **пя́ть** *five*, **ше́сть** *six*, and higher, the noun **челове́к** has a genitive plural form that is identical to its nominative singular: **Ско́лько челове́к? Пя́ть челове́к**.

Note: The genitive plural of the noun **го́д** *year* is formed from the noun **ле́то** *summer*, e.g., **Ско́лько ле́т?** *How many years?*

The genitive plural zero ending -∅:

(a)   Most feminine nouns in **-а**, **-я** and neuter nouns in **-о**, **-е** drop this vowel in the genitive plural, leaving only the noun stem (=zero ending):

Nominative Singular		Genitive Plural
кни́га	book	кни́г
газе́та	newspaper	газе́т
де́ло	affair/business	де́л
фами́лия	surname	фами́лий
зда́ние	building	зда́ний
галере́я	gallery	галере́й

Note: Nouns whose nominative singular ends in **ие**, **ия**, or **ея** have a stem ending in **-й**, e.g., **ие**, **ия**, and **ея** is structurally [ий-е], [ий-а], and [ей-а] respectively. Therefore, dropping the final vowel to form the genitive plural results only in a stem in **-й**, i.e., a form with a zero ending.

Note: Three nouns, **тётя** *aunt*, **дя́дя** *uncle*, and **ю́ноша** *youth*, do not take the expected zero ending; instead they form the genitive plural irregularly with the ending **-ей**: **тётей, дя́дей, ю́ношей**.

Note: Two neuter nouns, **мо́ре** *sea*, **по́ле** *field*, do not have the expected zero ending, but instead irregularly form the genitive plural in **-ей**: **море́й, поле́й**. Similarly, the neuter noun **о́блако** *cloud* forms its genitive plural irregularly in **-ов**: **облако́в**.

(b)   Certain nouns with the zero ending in the genitive plural also "insert" the vowel **-о-** or **-е-** in order to break up a consonant cluster at the end of the word:

Nominative Singular		Genitive Plural
студе́нтка	co-ed	студе́нток
ку́хня	kitchen	ку́хонь
дере́вня	village	дереве́нь
балала́йка	balalaika	балала́ек
сестра́	sister	сестёр
окно́	window	о́кон
письмо́	letter	пи́сем

Note: The noun **яйцо́** *egg* has the inserted vowel **-и-** in the genitive plural **яи́ц**.

(*c*) Nouns whose Nominative Singular ends in stressed **-ья** have an inserted vowel **-e-** before a zero ending:

Nominative Singular		Genitive Plural
семья́	*family*	**семе́й**
статья́	*article*	**стате́й**
судья́	*judge*	**суде́й**

Note: These nouns in the singular have a stem ending in **-й**, e.g., **статья́** is comprised of the stem [stat'y-] and the ending [-a]. Therefore, dropping the nominative singular [-a] (and replacing the soft sign **-ь-** with **-e-**) leaves a zero ending in the genitive plural.

(*d*) A few nouns have a genitive plural that is identical to the nominative singular:

Nominative Singular		Genitive Plural
гла́з	*eye*	**гла́з**
ра́з	*time*	**ра́з**
чуло́к	*stocking*	**чуло́к**
солда́т	*soldier*	**солда́т**
челове́к	*person*	**челове́к**

Note: The noun **челове́к** has two genitive plural forms: **челове́к** (only after certain words expressing quantity, as noted above) and **люде́й**.

The following table summarizes the regular genitive case endings of nouns in both singular and plural.

Table of Regular Genitive Singular and Plural Noun Endings

Gender	Nominative Singular	Genitive Singular	Endings	Genitive Plural	Endings
Masculine Hard Stem:	**сто́л**	**стола́**	**-а**	**столо́в**	**-ов**
	студе́нт	**студе́нта**		**студе́нтов**	
Soft Stem:	**музе́й**	**музе́я**	**-я**	**музе́ев**	**-ев**
	портфе́ль	**портфе́ля**		**портфе́лей**	**-ей**
	писа́тель	**писа́теля**		**писа́телей**	
Neuter Hard Stem:	**окно́**	**окна́**	**-а**	**о́кон**	**-∅**
Soft Stem:	**зда́ние**	**зда́ния**	**-я**	**зда́ний**	
Feminine Hard Stem:	**газе́та**	**газе́ты**	**-ы**	**газе́т**	**-∅**
Soft Stem:	**неде́ля**	**неде́ли**	**-и**	**неде́ль**	
	исто́рия	**исто́рии**		**исто́рий**	
	тетра́дь	**тетра́ди**		**тетра́дей**	**-ей**

Uses of the Genitive Case

Genitive after a Noun

The genitive case is used to express various kinds of relationships between two nouns.

To Denote the Possessor of Something

This use of the genitive case in Russian corresponds to the English possessive construction with *'s: the professor's briefcase.* Note, however, that in Russian the possessor follows, rather than precedes, the possessed object.

Э́то портфе́ль *профе́ссора.*	*This is the professor's briefcase.*
Маши́на *отца́* **стои́т в гараже́**.	*My father's car is parked in the garage.*
Где́ слова́рь *сестры́?*	*Where is the sister's dictionary?*
До́м *роди́телей* **на э́той у́лице.**	*The parents' house is on this street.*

To Denote the Person after Whom Something is Named

у́лица *Че́хова*	*Chekhov Street*
пло́щадь *Гага́рина*	*Gagarin Square*
дом-музе́й *Пу́шкина*	*Pushkin Museum*

To Denote the Whole in Relation to the Part

This use of the genitive, and those that follow it, is often expressed in English by the preposition *of.*

переплёт *кни́ги*	*cover of a book*
ру́чка *чемода́на*	*handle of a suitcase*
кры́ша *до́ма*	*roof of a house*
колесо́ *маши́ны*	*wheel of a car*

To Denote the Agent of an Action

выступле́ние *арти́стов*	*performance of the artists*
сме́х *дете́й*	*laughter of children*
объясне́ние *преподава́теля*	*explanation of the teacher*

To Denote the Object of an Action

изуче́ние *языко́в*	*study of languages*
чте́ние *те́кста*	*reading of the text*
откры́тие *вы́ставки*	*opening of the exhibit*

To Denote an Entity to which a Property or Quality is Attributed

красота́ *Кавка́за*	*the beauty of the Caucasus*
теплота́ *со́лнца*	*the warmth of the sun*
доброта́ *челове́ка*	*the goodness of Man*

To Denote a Container or Specific Quantity of an Object

коро́бка *конфе́т*	*a box of candy*
буты́лка *вина́*	*a bottle of wine*
па́чка *сигаре́т*	*a pack of cigarettes*
паке́т *молока́*	*a carton of milk*
ли́тр *во́дки*	*a liter of vodka*

Genitive after Numerals

The previous use of the genitive case after nouns denoting specific quantity is only one example of a more general use of the genitive case to express quantity.

The numerical expression **о́ба/о́бе** *both*, the cardinal numbers **два́/две́** *two*, **три́** *three*, **четы́ре** *four*, and compounds ending in these numbers (e.g., **два́дцать два́** *twenty-two*, **два́дцать три́** *twenty-three*, **три́дцать четы́ре** *thirty-four*), all require the genitive singular of the following noun, when the numerals themselves are in the nominative or (inanimate) accusative case:

два́ *карандаша́*	*two pencils*	**две́** *ру́чки*	*two pens*
три́ *словаря́*	*three dictionaries*	**четы́ре** *студе́нта*	*four students*

The cardinal numbers **пя́ть** *five*, **ше́сть** *six*, **се́мь** *seven*, **во́семь** *eight*, **де́вять** *nine*, **де́сять** *ten*, and higher up to "twenty-one," require the genitive plural on the following noun, when these numbers themselves are in the nominative or accusative case:

пя́ть *студе́нтов*	*five students*	**во́семь** *маши́н*	*eight cars*
ше́сть *столо́в*	*six tables*	**де́вять** *словаре́й*	*nine dictionaries*
се́мь *ру́чек*	*seven pens*	**де́сять** *карандаше́й*	*ten pencils*

Genitive after Adverbial Expressions of Quantity

The genitive case is used after words denoting indefinite quantity, e.g., **ско́лько** *how many/how much*, **сто́лько** *so many/so much*, **мно́го** *many/much*, **немно́го** *not many/not much*, **ма́ло** *few/little*, **не́сколько** *a few*. With nouns denoting objects that can be counted, the genitive plural is used; with abstract nouns or those denoting substances, the genitive singular occurs.

Ско́лько *столо́в?*	*How many tables?*	**Ско́лько** *су́па?*	*How much soup?*
сто́лько *дете́й*	*so many children*	**сто́лько** *шу́ма*	*so much noise*
мно́го *друзе́й*	*many friends*	**мно́го** *вина́*	*a lot of wine*
ма́ло *госте́й*	*few guests*	**ма́ло** *во́дки*	*little vodka*

Note: These adverbial quantifiers require a verb in the past tense to be in the neuter singular: **Та́м бы́ло мно́го кни́г** *There were many books there*. Also, when used with the noun **челове́к** *person*, **ско́лько** and **не́сколько** take the genitive plural **челове́к**, but **мно́го** and **ма́ло** take the genitive plural **люде́й**: **Ско́лько та́м бы́ло челове́к? —Та́м бы́ло мно́го люде́й.** *How many people were there? There were many people there.*

Genitive after Verbs

After Transitive Verbs to Express a "Partitive" Meaning

The genitive case may be used for the object of certain transitive verbs to express a "partitive" sense, that is, to denote a part of the whole, "some" of something.

Да́й, пожа́луйста, *хле́ба*.	*Please give me some bread.*
Она́ вы́пила *вина́*.	*She drank some wine.*
Го́сти пое́ли *пирожко́в*.	*The guests ate some pirozhki.*
Ма́льчик нарва́л *цвето́в*.	*The boy picked some flowers.*

Note: The same object in the accusative case would imply "the whole" of what is referred to, and is often expressed in English by the use of the definite article: **Переда́й, пожа́луйста, *хле́б*.** *Please pass the bread.*

A small number of masculine nouns have two genitive case endings in the singular: the regular genitive ending **-а/-я**, and a second "partitive genitive" ending **-у/-ю**, which may be used to convey the partitive meaning. This partitive genitive **-у** ending is losing ground to the regular genitive case ending, but is still encountered in colloquial Russian: **Она́ попила́ *ча́ю*.** *She drank some tea.* **Ма́льчик пое́л**

су́пу. *The boy ate some soup*. Some common examples of these nouns, many of which denote substances to eat or drink, are given below.

Nominative		*Genitive*	*Partitive Genitive*
су́п	*soup*	**су́па**	**су́пу**
са́хар	*sugar*	**са́хара**	**са́хару**
лу́к	*onion*	**лу́ка**	**лу́ку**
мёд	*honey*	**мёда**	**мёду**
пе́рец	*pepper*	**пе́рца**	**пе́рцу**
сы́р	*cheese*	**сы́ра**	**сы́ру**
ча́й	*tea*	**ча́я**	**ча́ю**
ри́с	*rice*	**ри́са**	**ри́су**
конья́к	*cognac*	**коньяка́**	**коньяку́**
шокола́д	*chocolate*	**шокола́да**	**шокола́ду**

The partitive genitive also occurs after nouns denoting a specific quantity of something, e.g., **буты́лка** *коньяку́* bottle of cognac, **ча́шка** *ча́ю* cup of tea, **таре́лка** *су́пу* plate of soup, **ба́нка** *мёду* jar of honey, **па́чка** *са́хару* package of sugar. When the meaning is one other than quantity, or when these nouns are modified by an adjective, they take the regular genitive ending in **-а**, **-я**: **цена́** *ча́я* price of tea, **стака́н армя́нского** *коньяка́* glass of Armenian cognac.

After Negated Transitive Verbs

When used affirmatively, a transitive verb takes a direct object in the accusative case, or, when a partitive meaning is intended, in the genitive case. Similarly, when transitive verbs are negated, the direct object may be in the accusative or the genitive case: **Де́вочка не чита́ла** *расска́з/расска́за*. *The girl didn't read the story*. Though it is sometimes possible to use either the genitive or accusative case for the direct object of a negated transitive verb, the genitive is strongly preferred when:

1. The object is an abstract noun:

   Вы́ не име́ете *пра́ва* **та́к говори́ть.**   *You don't have the right to talk that way.*
   Не обраща́й *внима́ния* **на э́то.**   *Don't pay any attention to that.*

2. The object is the abstract pronoun **э́то**:

   Я́ *э́того* **не понима́ю.**   *I don't understand that.*
   Мы́ *э́того* **не зна́ли.**   *We didn't know that.*

3. The object is indefinite or nonspecific:

   Мы́ не е́ли *мя́са* **це́лый ме́сяц.**   *We didn't eat (any) meat for a whole month.*
   Она́ не чита́ла *детекти́вов.*   *She didn't read detective stories.*

4. When the object is preceded by an emphatic negative expression with **ни**:

   О́н не сказа́л ни *сло́ва.*   *He didn't say a word.*
   Она́ не чита́ла ни одно́й *страни́цы.*   *She didn't read a single page.*

5. When the object follows a negated verb of perception:

   Она́ не слы́шала *вопро́са.*   *She didn't hear the question.*
   Са́ша не по́нял *объясне́ния.*   *Sasha didn't understand the explanation.*
   Мы́ не ви́дели *таксофо́нов.*   *We didn't see any pay-telephones.*

After Negated Forms of the Verb быть

The genitive case is used to express the "absence" or "nonexistence" of something in locational and possessive sentences with **не́т** *there is no*, **не́ было** *there was/were no*, **не бу́дет** *there will be no*.

Здесь нет *телефона.*	*There is no telephone here.*
Там не было *словаря.*	*There was no dictionary there.*
Дома нет *компьютера.*	*There is no computer at home.*
У меня нет *собаки.*	*I don't have a dog.*
У нас не было *времени.*	*We didn't have time.*
У брата не будет *билета.*	*The brother will not have a ticket.*

After Verbs that Govern the Genitive

There are certain verbs that govern, that is, require the genitive case on their object. The following are common examples:

желать *to wish,* **добиваться** *to strive for,* **достигать** *to achieve,* **бояться** *to be afraid of,* **пугаться** *to be frightened of,* **избегать** *to avoid*

Genitive after Adjectives

After Adjectives that Govern the Genitive

A few adjectives, in both long and short form, govern the genitive case:

полный	*full (of)*	**Там был кувшин, полный** *воды.*
		There was a pitcher full of water.
достойный	*worthy (of)*	**Его труд, достойный** *награды.*
		His work is worthy of an award.
лишённый	*devoid (of)*	**Этот человек лишён** *чувства юмора.*
		This person lacks a sense of humor.

After the Comparative of an Adjective

In a comparative construction, the second term of the comparison may be a noun in the genitive case.

Москва больше *Петербурга.*	*Moscow is bigger than St. Petersburg.*
Волга длиннее *Днепра.*	*The Volga is longer than the Dnieper.*
Мать моложе *отца.*	*The mother is younger than the father.*

Genitive after Prepositions

The genitive case is used for the object of certain prepositions, which are presented in Chapter 3.

REVIEW

16. In each sentence below, identify the case of the underlined nouns by writing them in the appropriate columns.

	Nominative	Accusative	Genitive
1. Она записала номер телефона.	_____	_____	_____
2. Вот фотография жены.	_____	_____	_____
3. Где улица Королёва?	_____	_____	_____
4. Он съел ещё ломтик хлеба.	_____	_____	_____
5. Дочь профессора — студентка.	_____	_____	_____
6. Я знаю брата студента.	_____	_____	_____
7. Мама купила пакет молока.	_____	_____	_____
8. Вопрос учителя был трудный.	_____	_____	_____

9. Я́ откры́л две́рь кварти́ры. _____ _____ _____
10. Откры́тие вы́ставки бы́ло интере́сное. _____ _____ _____
11. Мы́ слы́шали сме́х дете́й. _____ _____ _____
12. На столе́ была́ буты́лка во́дки. _____ _____ _____
13. У меня́ оди́н бра́т и две́ сестры́. _____ _____ _____
14. О́н съе́л таре́лку су́па. _____ _____ _____
15. Студе́нт не слы́шал вопро́са. _____ _____ _____
16. Зде́сь е́сть сто́л, но не́т сту́ла. _____ _____ _____
17. Та́м была́ во́дка, но не́ бы́ло вина́. _____ _____ _____
18. Она́ лю́бит ко́шек, но бои́тся соба́к. _____ _____ _____
19. Ко́мната была́ полна́ дете́й. _____ _____ _____
20. Ма́ма моло́же па́пы. _____ _____ _____

17. Rewrite the two sentences as one sentence with the genitive of possession.

Model: Это Бори́с. А э́то его́ кни́га. > Э́то кни́га Бори́са.
This is Boris. And this is his book. > This is Boris's book.

1. Это профе́ссор. А э́то его́ портфе́ль.   портфель профессора.
2. Это ма́ма. А э́то её су́мка.   сумка мамы
3. Это па́па. А э́то его́ кабине́т.   кабинет папа
4. Это го́сть. А э́то его́ пода́рок.   подарок госте
5. Это сестра́. А э́то её пла́тье. _____
6. Это де́ти. А э́то их игру́шки. _____
7. Это оте́ц. А э́то его́ маши́на. _____
8. Это студе́нты. А э́то и́х уче́бники. _____
9. Это бра́тья. А э́то и́х кварти́ра. _____
10. Это друзья́. А э́то и́х жёны. _____
11. Это студе́нтка. А э́то её бра́т. _____
12. Это писа́тель. А э́то его́ рома́н. _____
13. Это дя́дя. А э́то его́ да́ча. _____
14. Это ба́бушка. А э́то её плато́к. _____
15. Это ребёнок. А э́то его́ крова́ть. _____

18. Name each place after the person mentioned in parentheses.

Model: университе́т (Ломоно́сов) > университе́т Ломоно́сова
Lomonosov University

1. пло́щадь (Пу́шкин) _____
2. у́лица (Королёв) _____
3. бульва́р (Го́голь) _____
4. теа́тр (Мейерхо́льд) _____
5. библиоте́ка (Ге́рцен) _____

19. Below are sentences containing an agent performing an action. After the deverbal noun on the right, put the noun denoting the agent of the action into the genitive singular or plural, as indicated.

Model: Профе́ссор объясни́л пра́вило. > объясне́ние профе́ссора
The professor explained the rule. > explanation of the professor

1. Арти́стка выступа́ла по телеви́зору.   выступле́ние _____
2. Певе́ц пе́л эмоциона́льно.   пе́ние _____
3. Де́ти игра́ли во дворе́.   игра́ _____
4. Ученики́ проси́ли вы́йти из кла́сса.   про́сьба _____
5. Врачи́ до́лго его́ диагнози́ровали.   диа́гноз _____

20. Below are sentences containing an agent performing an action. After the action noun on the right, put the noun denoting the object of the action into the genitive case.

Model: Аспира́нт защити́л диссерта́цию. > защи́та диссерта́ции
The graduate student defended his dissertation. > the defense of the dissertation

1. Оте́ц купи́л маши́ну.   поку́пка _____
2. Ма́ма пригото́вила обе́д.   приготовле́ние _____
3. Учи́тель прове́рил зада́ние.   прове́рка _____
4. Тури́сты посети́ли музе́й.   посеще́ние _____
5. Студе́нт изуча́ет литерату́ру.   изуче́ние _____

21. Below are nouns denoting an object to which some property or quality is ascribed. Put the noun into the genitive singular or plural, as indicated.

Model: тёплый кли́мат > теплота́ кли́мата
warm climate > warmth of the climate

1. тёмная но́чь > темнота́ _____
2. у́мная студе́нтка > у́м _____
3. краси́вое мо́ре > красота́ _____
4. до́брая ма́ть > доброта́ _____
5. бога́тые лю́ди > бога́тство _____
6. све́тлый о́браз > све́тлость _____
7. ще́дрые друзья́ > ще́дрость _____
8. изве́стные писа́тели > изве́стность _____
9. ую́тные гости́ницы > ую́т _____
10. серьёзные оши́бки > серьёзность _____

22. The following sentences assert the existence or availability of some object or person. Negate the sentences so that they *deny the existence* of that object or person. Make all the necessary changes.

Model: Зде́сь е́сть телефо́н. > Зде́сь не́т телефо́на.
There is a telephone here. > There is no telephone here.

1. Зде́сь бу́дет гости́ница.   _____
2. Сего́дня семина́р.   _____
3. Вчера́ в клу́бе бы́л конце́рт.   _____
4. У меня́ сейча́с е́сть вре́мя.   _____
5. У на́с вчера́ была́ ле́кция.   _____
6. Сего́дня в кла́ссе Ви́ктор.   _____
7. Вчера́ Серге́й бы́л до́ма.   _____

8. За́втра бу́дут роди́тели.   _____
9. Сего́дня бу́дет до́ждь.   _____
10. В ка́ссе теа́тра бы́ли биле́ты.   _____

23. Answer the questions, putting the underlined noun into the genitive singular or plural, as required.

Model: —Та́м есть рестора́н?   —Да́, та́м мно́го рестора́нов.
         Is there a restaurant there?   *Yes, there are many restaurants there.*

1. —Та́м есть теа́тр?   —Да́, та́м мно́го _____.
2. —Зде́сь есть музе́й?   —Да́, зде́сь не́сколько _____.
3. —Зде́сь есть библиоте́ка?   —Да́, зде́сь две́ _____.
4. —Та́м бы́ли де́вушки?   —Да́, та́м бы́ло мно́го _____.
5. —Та́м одна́ спа́льня?   —Не́т, та́м две́ _____.
6. —Зде́сь то́лько одно́ письмо́?   —Не́т, зде́сь пя́ть _____.
7. —Та́м то́лько одна́ лаборато́рия? —Не́т, та́м не́сколько _____.
8. —Зде́сь то́лько оди́н каранда́ш?   —Не́т, зде́сь ше́сть _____.
9. —Та́м одна́ ру́чка?   —Не́т, та́м де́сять _____.
10. —Та́м оди́н челове́к?   —Не́т, та́м се́мь _____.

24. Change the underlined direct objects in the following sentences from the accusative to the genitive case, thereby giving the sentence a partitive meaning.

Model: Она́ купи́ла цветы́. > Она́ купи́ла цвето́в.
         She bought flowers. > She bought some flowers.

1. О́н взя́л са́хар.   _____
2. Она́ купи́ла мёд и я́блоки.   _____
3. Переда́й, пожа́луйста, пирожки́.   _____
4. Мы́ пое́ли су́п.   _____
5. Хозя́йка налила́ конья́к.   _____
6. Сы́н проси́л де́ньги.   _____
7. Го́сти пое́ли ри́с и о́вощи.   _____
8. Де́ти попроси́ли фру́кты.   _____
9. Она́ купи́ла грибы́.   _____
10. Мы́ принесли́ сы́р и хле́б.   _____

25. Rewrite the following sentences. Negate the verb and make the necessary change on the verb's object.

Model: Я́ зна́л э́то. > Я́ не зна́л э́того.
         I knew that. > I did not know that.

1. Же́нщины име́ли пра́во го́лоса.   _____
2. Фи́льм произвёл впечатле́ние.   _____
3. Она́ ви́дела авто́бус.   _____
4. О́н пи́л спи́рт.   _____
5. Студе́нт по́нял отве́т.   _____

Prepositional Case

Singular and Plural Endings

The endings of the prepositional singular are:

-е   for most nouns (except those that follow)
-и   for third declension feminine nouns in **-ь**
        for nouns whose nominative singular ends in **-ие**, **-ия**, or **-ий**

The endings of the prepositional plural are:

-ах   for all nouns ending in a hard stem
-ях   for all nouns ending in a soft stem

The following table illustrates the endings of the prepositional case.

Gender	Nominative Singular	Prepositional Singular	Endings	Prepositional Plural	Endings
Masculine Hard Stem:	сто́л	столе́	-е	стола́х	-ах
Soft Stem:	музе́й	музе́е		музе́ях	-ях
	портфе́ль	портфе́ле		портфе́лях	
Stem in **-ий**	кафете́рий	кафете́рии	-и	кафете́риях	
Neuter Hard Stem:	окно́	окне́	-е	о́кнах	-ах
Soft Stem:	мо́ре	мо́ре		моря́х	-ях
Stem in **-ие**	зда́ние	зда́нии	-и	зда́ниях	
Feminine Hard Stem:	газе́та	газе́те	-е	газе́тах	-ах
Soft Stem:	неде́ля	неде́ле		неде́лях	-ях
Stem in **-ия**	аудито́рия	аудито́рии	-и	аудито́риях	
Stem in **-ь**	тетра́дь	тетра́ди	-и	тетра́дях	
	ма́ть	ма́тери		матеря́х	

The prepositional case, as its name might suggest, occurs exclusively with prepositions. All the prepositions that take the prepositional case, and the meanings expressed by these prepositions, are presented in Chapter 3.

It is appropriate to note here, however, that after only two prepositions, **в** *in, at* and **на** *on, at, in*, a small number of masculine nouns take a special prepositional singular case ending in stressed **-ý**, which is sometimes called the "locative," since it is used to denote location, but not other meanings conveyed by other prepositions. Therefore, these nouns may take two prepositional case endings: the regular prepositional case ending for masculine nouns **-е**, and a second prepositional, or "locative" case ending; cf. **о ле́се** *about the forest* and **в лесу́** *in the forest*. The list below contains the most commonly used nouns that take the locative ending in stressed **-ý** after **в** and **на**. The preposition **о/об** governs the prepositional case in the meaning *about, concerning*:

Nominative		Prepositional	Locative
аэропо́рт	airport	об аэропо́рте	в аэропорту́
бе́рег	shore	о бе́реге	на берегу́
гла́з	eye	о гла́зе	в глазу́
До́н	the Don	о До́не	на Дону́
Кры́м	the Crimea	о Кры́ме	в Крыму́
лёд	ice	о льде́	на льду́
ле́с	forest	о ле́се	в лесу́
мо́ст	bridge	о мо́сте	на мосту́
но́с	nose	о но́се	на носу́
по́л	floor	о по́ле	на полу́
по́рт	port	о по́рте	в порту́
ро́т	mouth	о рте́	во рту́
са́д	garden	о са́де	в саду́
сне́г	snow	о сне́ге	в снегу́
у́гол	corner	об угле́	в углу́, на углу́
шка́ф	cupboard	о шка́фе	в шкафу́

Dative Case

Singular and Plural

The following table illustrates the dative case endings of nouns.

Gender	Nominative Singular	Dative Singular	Endings	Dative Plural	Endings
Masculine Hard Stem:	сто́л студе́нт	столу́ студе́нту	-у	стола́м студе́нтам	-ам
Soft Stem:	музе́й писа́тель	музе́ю писа́телю	-ю	музе́ям писа́телям	-ям
Neuter Hard Stem:	окно́	окну́	-у	о́кнам	-ам
Soft Stem:	зда́ние	зда́нию	-ю	зда́ниям	-ям
Feminine Hard Stem:	газе́та	газе́те	-е	газе́там	-ам
Soft Stem:	тётя	тёте		тётям	-ям
Stem in -ия	аудито́рия	аудито́рии	-и	аудито́риям	
Stem in -ь	ма́ть	ма́тери		матеря́м	

The dative singular endings for masculine and neuter nouns are:

-у　　　for nouns with a hard stem
-ю　　　for nouns with a soft stem

The dative singular endings of feminine nouns are:

-е　　　for all nouns in -а and -я
-и　　　for all nouns ending in -ия
　　　　for all third declension feminine nouns in -ь

The dative plural endings are:

-ам   for all nouns with a hard stem
-ям   for all nouns with a soft stem

Uses of the Dative Case

As the Indirect Object of a Verb

The indirect object is normally an animate noun denoting the person *to whom* or *for whom* an action is performed. The indirect object is often understood to be the "addressee," "recipient," or "beneficiary" of an action. Transitive verbs, like those listed below, may take not only a direct object in the accusative case, but also an indirect object in the dative case.

дава́ть	*to give*	**Ма́ша даёт биле́т** *Бори́су.* *Masha is giving the ticket to Boris.*
дари́ть	*to give a gift*	**Оте́ц ча́сто да́рит** *де́тям* **пода́рки.** *Father often gives gifts to the children.*
покупа́ть	*to buy*	**Мы́ покупа́ем сувени́ры** *друзья́м.* *We are buying souvenirs for friends.*
посыла́ть	*to send*	**Она́ посыла́ет письмо́** *подру́ге.* *She is sending a letter to a friend.*
писа́ть	*to write*	**Сы́н ча́сто пи́шет** *отцу́ и ма́тери.* *The son often writes to his father and mother.*
чита́ть	*to read*	**Ба́бушка чита́ла ска́зку** *вну́ку.* *Grandma read a fairy-tale to her grandson.*
говори́ть	*to say, speak*	**О́н не говори́л пра́вду** *роди́телям.* *He did not tell the truth to his parents.*
объясня́ть	*to explain*	**Па́па объясня́ет зада́чу** *до́чери.* *Dad explains the problem to his daughter.*

After Verbs that Govern the Dative

A number of other verbs require their complements to be in the dative case. Several of them can be organized into different groups based on shared elements of meaning. Below are frequently used examples from each group.

1. *Verbs Denoting Assistance or Service*
    помога́ть *to help*, **сове́товать** *to advise*, **служи́ть** *to serve*

2. *Verbs Denoting Harm or Annoyance*
    вреди́ть *to harm*, **меша́ть** *to bother; prevent*, **изменя́ть** *to betray*

3. *Verbs Meaning to Permit or Forbid Someone from Doing Something*
    позволя́ть *to allow/permit*, **разреша́ть** *to allow/permit*, **запреща́ть** *to forbid*

4. *Verbs Denoting Various Emotions*
    удивля́ться *to be surprised at*, **зави́довать** *to envy*, **нра́виться** *to appeal to*

5. *Verbs with the Meaning "to Teach" or "to Learn"*

The verb **учи́ть** in the meaning *to teach*, and the verb **учи́ться** *to study*, govern the dative case on the noun denoting the subject taught or studied.

учи́ть	*to teach*	**Оте́ц у́чит дочере́й** *ру́сскому языку́.*
		The father is teaching his daughters Russian.
учи́ться	*to study*	**Студе́нты у́чатся** *ру́сской интона́ции.*
		The students are studying Russian intonation.

Note: The verb **учи́ть** (**вы́учить**) can be used in the meaning *to study* (*learn*); in this meaning the noun denoting the subject studied is a direct object in the accusative case:

Она́ у́чит *ру́сский язы́к.*   *She is studying the Russian language.*

6. *Verbs with Other Meanings*

| звони́ть | *to call on the phone* | **Бра́т звони́т** *сестре́.* |
| | | *The brother is calling his sister.* |

The verb **отвеча́ть** *to answer* is used with the dative when the complement is a person. When the complement is an inanimate object, this verb takes the preposition **на** and the accusative case.

Профе́ссор отве́тил *студе́нту.*   *The professor answered the student.*
Профе́ссор отве́тил *на вопро́с.*   *The professor answered the question.*

The verb **ве́рить** in the meaning *to believe someone* is used with the dative, but in the meaning *to believe in someone/something* this verb requires the preposition **в** and the accusative case.

Оте́ц ве́рит *сы́ну.*   *The father believes his son.*
Оте́ц ве́рит *в Бо́га.*   *The father believes in God.*

After Adjectives

A few adjectives, in both the long and short form, require the dative case.

благода́рный	*grateful (to)*	**Сы́н благода́рен** *роди́телям.*
		The son is grateful to his parents.
ве́рный	*true, faithful (to)*	**О́н ве́рен** *свои́м при́нципам.*
		He is true to his principles.
подо́бный	*similar (to)*	**На́ш до́м подо́бен** *э́тому до́му.*
		Our house is similar to this house.

The following adjective, which occurs only in the predicate short form, requires the dative.

| ра́д, ра́да, ра́ды | *glad* | **Мы́ о́чень ра́ды** *твоему́ успе́ху.* |
| | | *We are very glad about your success.* |

In Impersonal Constructions

Impersonal constructions, by definition, lack a grammatical subject in the nominative case. However, an impersonal construction may contain a logical (semantic) subject, which is often a noun (or pronoun) in the dative case. When a logical subject is present, it is often interpreted as the "experiencer," that is, the person who experiences some emotional or physical state. The following are different groups of states or conditions that are expressed in impersonal constructions with a dative experiencer.

1. *Expressions of Necessity*

Below are commonly used expressions of necessity. What the subject needs to do is expressed by the infinitive form of the verb.

на́до	*need, must, have to*	Студе́нтам **на́до** занима́ться.
		The students need to study.
ну́жно	*need, must, have to*	Де́тям **ну́жно** убира́ть свою́ ко́мнату.
		The children need to clean up their room.
необходи́мо	*it is essential, must*	А́втору **необходи́мо** ко́нчить кни́гу.
		The author must finish the book.

2. *Expressions of Permission/Prohibition*

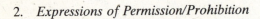

мо́жно	*it is permitted*	Бори́су **мо́жно** сда́ть зада́ние за́втра.
		Boris may turn in the assignment tomorrow.
нельзя́	*it is not permitted*	Де́тям **нельзя́** открыва́ть окно́.
		Children are not allowed to open the window.

The word **нельзя́** has the meaning *is not permitted* only when it is used with an infinitive of the imperfective aspect (**открыва́ть**). When used with an infinitive of the perfective aspect (**откры́ть**), **нельзя́** means *it is not possible*. (See discussion of verbal aspect in Chapter 7.)

нельзя́	*it is not possible*	Де́тям **нельзя́** откры́ть окно́.
		The children are unable to open the window.

Note: The word **мо́жно** may be used in the meaning *it is possible*, but in this meaning it does not normally occur with a logical subject in the dative, e.g., **Где́ зде́сь мо́жно купи́ть газе́ту?** *Where can one buy a newspaper here?* The words **возмо́жно/невозмо́жно** are synonymous with **мо́жно/нельзя́** only in the meanings *it is possible/it is impossible* (not in the meanings *it is permitted/it is not permitted*).

3. *Feelings and Physical States*

These are in the neuter short form of the adjective. Some common expressions in this group include the following.

ве́село	*cheerful*	Ви́ктору **ве́село**.	*Victor feels cheerful.*
гру́стно	*sad*	Сы́ну **гру́стно**.	*The son feels sad.*
оби́дно	*hurt*	Сестре́ **оби́дно**.	*The sister feels hurt.*
жа́лко/жа́ль	*sorry*	Ле́не **жа́лко** ма́му.	*Lena is sorry for her Mom.*
интере́сно	*interesting*	Бра́ту **интере́сно**.	*It's interesting for the brother.*
ску́чно	*boring*	До́чери **ску́чно**.	*The daughter is bored.*
тру́дно	*difficult*	Студе́нту **тру́дно**.	*It's difficult for the student.*
легко́	*easy*	Де́вушке **легко́**.	*It's easy for the girl.*
хо́лодно	*cold*	Ба́бушке **хо́лодно**.	*Grandma feels cold.*
тепло́	*warm*	Де́душке **тепло́**.	*Grandpa feels warm.*

4. *Impersonal Verbs in* **-ся**

In many of the examples with verbs in **-ся** the logical subject is understood to feel either inclined, or disinclined, for some reason to perform the action denoted by the verb. The subject's disposition toward performing the action is felt to be beyond his control. The verb is in the third person singular present tense, or neuter singular past tense.

Cáше хо́чется е́сть.	*Sasha feels like eating.*
Ва́се сего́дня пи́шется легко́.	*Writing is coming easily for Vasya today.*
Серге́ю сего́дня не чита́ется.	*Sergey doesn't feel like reading today.*
Ири́не что́-то не спало́сь.	*Irina for some reason couldn't sleep.*

Expressing Age

The dative case is used to express the age of the person or object denoted by the logical subject.

Ско́лько лет *ва́шим роди́телям?*	*How old are your parents?*
Отцу́ **со́рок ле́т.**	*Father is forty years old.*
Ма́тери **три́дцать три́ го́да.**	*Mother is thirty-three.*
Э́тому де́реву **бо́льше ста́ ле́т.**	*This tree is more than a hundred years old.*

26. Identify the case of the underlined nouns.

		Accusative	Dative
1.	Сы́н пи́шет письмо́ <u>ма́тери</u>.	_____	_____
2.	Мы́ даём пода́рок <u>сестре́</u>.	_____	_____
3.	Ма́ма говори́т <u>до́чери</u> «Здра́вствуй».	_____	_____
4.	Ири́на пока́зывает <u>фотоальбо́м</u> подру́ге.	_____	_____
5.	Сестра́ чита́ет <u>бра́ту</u>.	_____	_____
6.	Сестра́ чита́ет бра́ту <u>ска́зку</u>.	_____	_____
7.	Ученики́ покупа́ют учи́тельнице <u>цветы́</u>.	_____	_____
8.	Оте́ц обеща́л сы́ну <u>соба́ку</u>.	_____	_____
9.	Профе́ссор сове́тует <u>студе́нтам</u>.	_____	_____
10.	Ки́ра да́рит <u>роди́телям</u> ди́ск.	_____	_____

27. Change the underlined nouns from dative singular to dative plural.

1.	Бо́ря покупа́ет пода́рок <u>сестре́</u>.	_____
2.	Ле́на пи́шет письмо́ <u>дру́гу</u>.	_____
3.	Библиоте́карь даёт кни́ги <u>чита́телю</u>.	_____
4.	Хозя́йка пока́зывала <u>го́стю</u> кварти́ру.	_____
5.	Докла́дчик объясня́л свой те́зис <u>слу́шателю</u>.	_____
6.	Ната́ша звони́ла <u>бра́ту</u>.	_____
7.	Де́ти покупа́ли пода́рки <u>ма́тери</u>.	_____
8.	Ма́ть не разреша́ет <u>до́чери</u> кури́ть.	_____
9.	Ба́бушка печёт пироги́ <u>вну́ку</u>.	_____
10.	Студе́нт отвеча́ет <u>профе́ссору</u>.	_____

28. Complete the sentences by putting the underlined noun into the dative case.

Model: Э́то бра́т. Я́ помога́ю <u>бра́ту</u>.
        This is the brother. I help the <u>brother</u>.

1.	Э́то <u>сестра́</u>. Мы́ пи́шем	_____ .
2.	Э́то <u>учи́тель</u>. Учени́к отвеча́ет	_____ .
3.	Э́то <u>до́чь</u>. Ма́ма ве́рит	_____ .
4.	Э́то <u>вну́чка</u>. Ба́бушка чита́ет	_____ .
5.	Э́то <u>вра́ч</u>. Андре́й звони́т	_____ .

6. Это дя́дя. Племя́нник благода́рен _____.
7. Это го́сть. Го́род нра́вится _____.
8. Это де́ти. Игру́шки нра́вятся _____.

29. Rewrite the sentences as impersonal sentences. Replace the adjective **до́лжен, должна́, должны́** *should/must* with the word **на́до**; replace the verb **мо́жет** *can* with the word **мо́жно** or **нельзя́**.

Model: Па́ша до́лжен занима́ться.   > Па́ше на́до занима́ться.
         Pasha should study.   *Pasha needs to study.*
Model: Ива́н мо́жет слу́шать му́зыку.   > Ива́ну мо́жно слу́шать му́зыку.
         Ivan can listen to music.   *Ivan is allowed to listen to music.*
Model: Га́ля не мо́жет кури́ть.   > Га́ле нельзя́ кури́ть.
         Galya can not smoke.   *Galya is not allowed to smoke.*

1. Де́ти должны́ убира́ть ко́мнату.   _____
2. Сестра́ мо́жет отдыха́ть.   _____
3. Серёжа не мо́жет е́сть конфе́ты.   _____
4. Пожилы́е лю́ди мо́гут входи́ть без о́череди. _____
5. Вра́ч до́лжен прописа́ть лека́рство.   _____

30. Rewrite the following sentences as impersonal with a verb in **-ся**. Make all the necessary changes.

Model: Оте́ц не рабо́тает. > Отцу́ не рабо́тается.
         Father isn't working. > *Father doesn't feel like working.*

1. Ма́льчик не чита́ет.   _____
2. До́чка не е́ла.   _____
3. Певи́ца не поёт.   _____
4. Сы́н сего́дня не игра́л.   _____
5. Тётя вчера́ не спала́.   _____

Instrumental Case

Singular and Plural

The instrumental singular endings for masculine and neuter nouns are:
-ом   for nouns with a hard stem
-ем   for nouns with a soft stem when the ending is not stressed;
          for nouns with a stem in **-ж, -ч, -ш, -щ, -ц** that undergo Spelling Rule 3 (page 11)
-ём   for nouns with a soft stem when the ending is stressed

The instrumental singular endings for feminine nouns are:
-ой   for nouns with a hard stem
-ей   for nouns with a soft stem when the ending is not stressed;
          for nouns with a stem in **-ж, -ч, -ш, -щ, -ц** that undergo Spelling Rule 3
-ёй   for nouns with a soft stem when the ending is stressed
-ью   for third declension feminine nouns in **-ь**

The instrumental plural endings are:
-ами for all nouns with a hard stem
-ями for all nouns with a soft stem

The singular and plural endings of nouns in the instrumental case are illustrated in the following table.

Gender	Nominative Singular	Instrumental Singular	Endings	Instrumental Plural	Endings
Masculine Hard Stem: Soft Stem: End-stress:	авто́бус трамва́й секрета́рь	авто́бусом трамва́ем секретарём	-ом -ем -ём	авто́бусами трамва́ями секретаря́ми	-ами -ями
Neuter Hard Stem: Soft Stem:	окно́ по́ле	окно́м по́лем	-ом -ем	о́кнами поля́ми	-ами -ями
Feminine Hard Stem: Soft Stem: End-stress: Stem in -ь	газе́та тётя семья́ ма́ть	газе́той тётей семьёй ма́терью	-ой -ей -ёй -ью	газе́тами тётями се́мьями матеря́ми	-ами -ями

Note: A few nouns have the irregular instrumental plural ending **-ьми́**. For example, the nouns **де́ти** *children* and **лю́ди** *people* have the instrumental plurals **детьми́** and **людьми́**. Also, the nouns **до́чь** *daughter*, **две́рь** *door*, and **ло́шадь** *horse* may form the instrumental plural with the regular ending **-ями**, as well as with the exceptional ending **-ьми́**: **дочеря́ми/дочерьми́**, **дверя́ми/дверьми́**, **лошадя́ми/лошадьми́**.

Uses of the Instrumental Case

To Express the Instrument or Means by which an Action is Performed

Учени́к пи́шет *карандашо́м.*	The student writes with a pencil.
Оте́ц ре́жет хле́б *ножо́м.*	Father cuts bread with a knife.
Мы́ еди́м су́п *ло́жкой.*	We eat soup with a spoon.
Кита́йцы едя́т *па́лочками.*	Chinese eat with chopsticks.
О́н ле́чит себя́ *тра́вами.*	He is treating himself with herbs.

To Denote the Agent of the Action in Passive Sentences

Кни́га была́ надпи́сана *а́втором.*	The book was inscribed by the author.
Тетра́ди бы́ли прове́рены *учи́телем.*	The notebooks were corrected by the teacher.
Клу́б организу́ется *студе́нтами.*	The club is being organized by the students.
Ёлка украша́лась *детьми́.*	The Christmas tree was decorated by the children.

To Denote the Force Responsible for an Action in Impersonal Sentences

Кры́шу сорва́ло *ве́тром.*	The roof was torn off by the wind.
Доро́гу занесло́ *сне́гом.*	The road was covered over by the snow.
Де́рево уда́рило *мо́лнией.*	The tree was struck by lightning.

To Express the Manner or Way an Action is Performed

Она́ говори́ла *шёпотом.*	She spoke in a whisper.
Ребёнок спа́л *кре́пким сно́м.*	The baby slept soundly.

Ма́льчик шёл *бы́стрым ша́гом.*		*The boy walked at a brisk pace.*
Они́ приходи́ли *то́лпами.*		*They came in droves.*
В Росси́и я́йца продаю́т *деся́тками,* **а не** *дю́жинами.*		*In Russia eggs are sold by the tens, and not by the dozen.*

To Denote Similarity

Она́ поёт *соловьём.*	*She sings like a nightingale.*
По́езд лете́л *стрело́й.*	*The train flew like an arrow.*
По́езд ползёт *черепа́хой.*	*The train is moving like a turtle.*

To Express the Means of Travel

Де́ти е́здят в шко́лу *авто́бусом.*	*The children go to school by bus.*
Студе́нты е́хали в Москву́ *по́ездом.*	*The students went to Moscow by train.*
Мы́ лете́ли *самолётом.*	*We went by airplane.*
Оте́ц е́здит на рабо́ту *трамва́ем.*	*Father goes to work by trolley.*

To Denote the Route Taken

Они́ шли́ *ле́сом.*	*They went by way of the woods.*
Маши́на е́хала *бе́регом.*	*The car drove along the shore.*
Де́ти бежа́ли домо́й *по́лем.*	*The children ran home through the field.*
Мы́ шли́ *переу́лками.*	*We went by way of side streets.*
О́н шёл *друго́й доро́гой.*	*He went a different way.*

To Denote the Time When Something Occurs

This use of the instrumental occurs in time expressions that denote:

(a)   *Parts of the Day*

Я́ тебе́ расскажу́ *у́тром.*	*I'll tell you in the morning.*
Сего́дня я́ рабо́таю *днём.*	*Today I'm working in the daytime.*
Мы́ занима́лись *це́лыми дня́ми.*	*We studied for days on end.*
Они́ встреча́ются *вечера́ми.*	*They meet in the evenings.*
Она́ отказа́лась е́хать *но́чью.*	*She refused to go at night.*

(b)   *Seasons of the Year*

Мы́ отдыха́ем *ле́том,* **а они́** *зимо́й.*	*We vacation in summer, but they in winter.*
Уче́бный го́д начина́ется *о́сенью.*	*The school year begins in the fall.*
Они́ е́дут в о́тпуск *весно́й.*	*They are going on vacation in spring.*

After Adjectives

A small number of adjectives, in both the short and long form, govern the instrumental case.

дово́льный	*pleased, satisfied with*	**Оте́ц дово́лен** *но́вой рабо́той.* *Father is pleased with his new job.*
бога́тый	*rich (in)*	**Э́то страна́, бога́тая** *не́фтью.* *This is a country rich in oil.*
изве́стный	*(well) known for*	**О́н изве́стен** *свое́й ще́дростью.* *He is known for his generosity.*
за́нятый	*busy, occupied with*	**Па́па за́нят** *составле́нием докла́да.* *Dad is busy compiling a report.*
бере́менная	*pregnant (with)*	**Она́ бере́менна** *пе́рвым ребёнком.* *She's pregnant with her first child.*
больно́й	*sick (with)*	**Ма́льчик бо́лен** *гри́ппом.* *The boy is sick with the flu.*

After Verbs that Govern the Instrumental

Several verbs require their complement to be in the instrumental case. A number of these verbs can be grouped together according to shared elements of meaning.

(a)   Verbs Denoting the Interests or Attitudes of the Subject

интересова́ться *to be interested in*, **увлека́ться** *to be fascinated with*, **занима́ться** *to be engaged in*; *study*, **наслажда́ться** *to enjoy*, **любова́ться** *to enjoy looking at*, **горди́ться** *to be proud of*, **хва́статься** *to boast of*, **дорожи́ть** *to value*

(b)   Verbs Denoting some Type of Control, Direction, or Use

руководи́ть *to be in charge of, direct*, **владе́ть** *to control, command, own*, **управля́ть** *to govern, rule*; *drive*, **пра́вить** *to govern*; *drive*, **заве́довать** *to manage*, **по́льзоваться** *to use*, **злоупотребля́ть** *to misuse, abuse*

As a Predicate Instrumental

In the English sentence *Viktor was a translator*, the phrase *was a translator* is a compound predicate consisting of the linking verb *was* and the predicate noun *translator*. In Russian, the verb **бы́ть** *to be* may serve as a linking verb, i.e., one which connects a subject with a predicate noun or adjective. When the predicate is a noun it is normally in the instrumental case, especially when the linking verb *to be* is in the infinitive form (**бы́ть**), future tense (**бу́ду, бу́дешь, бу́дет**, etc.), conditional with **бы** (e.g., **бы́л бы, е́сли бы бы́л**), imperative (**бу́дь, бу́дьте**), or gerund (**бу́дучи**).

Она́ хо́чет бы́ть *перево́дчицей.*	*She wants to be a translator.*
О́н бу́дет *профе́ссором.*	*He will be a professor.*
Не бу́дь *дурако́м.*	*Don't be a fool.*
Бу́дучи *инвали́дом,* о́н не мо́г рабо́тать.	*Being handicapped, he wasn't able to work.*
На твоём ме́сте, я была́ бы *актри́сой.*	*If I were you, I would have been an actress.*
А́х! Е́сли бы я бы́л *поэ́том!*	*Oh! If only I were a poet!*

The past-tense forms of the verb *to be* (**бы́л, бы́ло, была́, бы́ли**) may be followed by a predicate either in the nominative (see "Uses of the Nominative Case" above) or instrumental case. The instrumental case of a predicate noun is strongly favored under the following conditions:

1.   The noun denotes an occupation, function, or status.

Моя́ ба́бушка была́ *портни́хой.*	*My grandmother was a dressmaker.*
Мо́й де́душка бы́л *купцо́м.*	*My grandfather was a merchant.*
Бори́с бы́л *председа́телем* клу́ба.	*Boris was the chairman of the club.*
О́н бы́л *секретарём* институ́та.	*He was the secretary of the institute.*

Note: Even in the present tense, when the verb *to be* is not normally used, the predicate noun denoting an occupation or function may be in the instrumental case, e.g., **О́н зде́сь свиде́телем** *He is here as a witness.*

2.   The noun is abstract or deverbal

Ми́ша бы́л *очеви́дцем* происше́ствия.	*Misha was a witness to the accident.*
Э́то бы́ло *причи́ной* его́ успе́ха.	*This was the reason for his success.*
Её *люби́мым заня́тием* бы́ло вяза́ние.	*Her favorite pastime was knitting.*
Му́зыка была́ *выраже́нием* его́ чу́вств.	*Music was an expression of his feelings.*

A number of near-synonyms of **быть** function as linking verbs, and take a predicate noun (or adjective) in the instrumental case.

явля́ться	*to be*	**Украи́на явля́ется** *ро́диной* **Булга́кова**. *Ukraine is the birthplace of Bulgakov.*
станови́ться	*to become*	**Сы́н стано́вится хоро́шим** *музыка́нтом*. *The son is becoming a good musician.*
каза́ться	*to seem to be*	**Она́ мне́ каза́лась** *у́мницей*. *She seemed to me to be a clever person.*
ока́зываться	*to turn out to be*	**О́н всегда́ ока́зывается** *победи́телем*. *He always turns out to be the winner.*
счита́ться	*to be considered*	**Она́ счита́ется** *лу́чшей учи́тельницей*. *She is considered to be the best teacher.*
остава́ться	*to remain as*	**Э́то для́ на́с остаётся** *зага́дкой*. *For us this remains a mystery.*

A few verbs are commonly used instead of **быть** in the sense *work as, serve as, function as*, e.g., **Он рабо́тал (бы́л) учи́телем** *He worked as (was) a teacher*. When used in this sense, these verbs take a predicate noun denoting an occupation, function or status.

рабо́тать	*to work*	**Она́ рабо́тает** *биологом*. *She works as (is) a biologist.*
служи́ть	*to serve*	**О́н слу́жит** *арби́тром*. *He serves as (is) the arbitrator.*
выступа́ть	*appear (publicly)*	**Она́ выступа́ла** *докла́дчиком*. *She appeared as (was) a speaker.*

As the Second Object of a Transitive Verb

Several verbs, when used transitively, take a direct object in the accusative and a second object in the instrumental case. Below are common examples of such verbs.

называ́ть	*to name, call*	**Роди́тели назва́ли ребёнка** *Ми́шей*. *The parents named the child Misha.*
счита́ть	*to consider*	**Учителя́ счита́ют ма́льчика** *ге́нием*. *The teachers consider the boy a genius.*
выбира́ть	*to elect*	**Наро́д выбира́л его́** *президе́нтом*. *The people elected him president.*
нанима́ть	*to hire*	**Мы́ нанима́ем её** *преподава́телем*. *We're hiring her as an instructor.*

31. Put the noun in parentheses into the instrumental case.

1. Учи́тель пи́шет на доске́ (ме́л). _____
2. Студе́нты пи́шут на экза́мене (ру́чки). _____
3. Ма́льчик рису́ет (каранда́ш). _____
4. О́н открыва́ет две́рь (клю́ч). _____
5. Она́ вытира́ет слёзы (плато́к). _____
6. Она́ сде́лала же́ст (рука́). _____
7. Пока́зывать (па́лец) неве́жливо. _____
8. Мы́ э́то ви́дели свои́ми (глаза́). _____
9. Мы́ э́то слы́шали свои́ми (у́ши). _____
10. Она́ э́то сде́лала свои́ми (ру́ки). _____

32. Put the noun in parentheses into the instrumental case.

1. Вре́мя лети́т (мо́лния). _____
2. Де́ти говори́ли (хо́р). _____
3. Они́ е́хали (гру́ппа). _____
4. Сне́г па́дал больши́ми (хло́пья). _____
5. Таки́е сувени́ры продаю́тся (ты́сячи). _____
6. Спортсме́ны лете́ли (самолёт). _____
7. О́н говори́л серьёзным (то́н). _____
8. Мы́ шли́ к це́нтру (у́лица) Го́рького. _____
9. Ли́я е́хала домо́й (трамва́й). _____
10. Ребя́та бежа́ли (бе́рег). _____

33. State when the action occurs, by putting the time expression into the instrumental.

1. Мы́ отдыха́ем (зима́). _____
2. О́н рабо́тает то́лько (вечера́). _____
3. Она́ верну́лась по́здней (но́чь). _____
4. Они́ е́здят в о́тпуск (весна́). _____
5. Оте́ц вста́л ра́но (у́тро). _____
6. Уче́бный го́д начина́ется (о́сень). _____
7. Вра́ч принима́ет (де́нь), до пяти́ часо́в. _____

34. Complete the change from active to passive sentence, by putting the noun denoting the agent of the action into the instrumental case.

Model: Студе́нтка реша́ет зада́чу. > Зада́ча реша́ется студе́нткой.
    The student is solving the problem.   *The problem is being solved by the student.*

1. Журнали́ст пи́шет статью́.   Статья́ пи́шется _____.
2. Студе́нты изуча́ют эконо́мику.   Эконо́мика изуча́ется _____.
3. Ма́ть мо́ет посу́ду.   Посу́да мо́ется _____.
4. Секрета́рь гото́вит докуме́нты.   Докуме́нты гото́вятся _____.
5. Тётя посыла́ет пода́рки.   Пода́рки посыла́ются _____.

35. Complete the change from personal to impersonal sentence, by putting the noun denoting the inanimate "force" responsible for the action into the instrumental case.

Model: Его́ ослепи́ла мо́лния.   Его́ ослепи́ло мо́лнией.
    The lightning blinded him.   *The lightning blinded him.*

1. Ло́дку опроки́нула волна́.   Ло́дку опроки́нуло _____.
2. Его́ ра́нила грана́та.   Его́ ра́нило _____.
3. Ве́тер сорва́л кры́шу.   Кры́шу сорва́ло _____.
4. Све́т зали́л ко́мнату.   Ко́мнату зали́ло _____.
5. Маши́на задави́ла соба́ку.   Соба́ку задави́ло _____.

36. Put the predicate noun in parentheses into the instrumental case.

1. Ра́ньше То́ля бы́л (учи́тель). _____
2. Ви́ка тогда́ была́ (студе́нтка). _____
3. Моя́ до́чка бу́дет (ветерина́р). _____

4. Наш сын хо́чет бы́ть (врач). _____.
5. Оте́ц рабо́тает (программи́ст). _____.
6. Она́ подраба́тывала (перево́дчица). _____.
7. Пу́шкин бы́л вели́ким (поэ́т). _____.
8. Де́вочка мечта́ет бы́ть (балери́на). _____.
9. Ми́ша слу́жит (председа́тель) клу́ба. _____.
10. Та́ня рабо́тает (секрета́рша). _____.
11. Вашингто́н явля́ется (столи́ца) США. _____.
12. Когда́ он пьёт, он стано́вится (дура́к). _____.
13. Она́ мне́ ка́жется хоро́шей (ма́ть). _____.
14. Ма́льчик счита́ется (ге́ний). _____.
15. Для на́с о́н остаётся (геро́й). _____.

37. Put the second object in parentheses into the instrumental case.

1. Мы́ счита́ем её (специали́ст). _____.
2. Рабо́чие вы́брали его́ (ме́неджер). _____.
3. Роди́тели назва́ли де́вочку (Со́ня). _____.
4. Друзья́ устро́или его́ (преподава́тель). _____.
5. Его́ назна́чили (судья́). _____.

38. Put the verb complement in parentheses into the instrumental case.

1. Де́вочки интересу́ются (бале́т). _____.
2. Са́ша увлека́ется (футбо́л). _____.
3. Ири́на занима́ется (гимна́стика). _____.
4. О́н не мо́г не любова́ться её (красота́). _____.
5. Роди́тели гордя́тся (до́чь). _____.
6. Она́ дорожи́т его́ (и́скренность). _____.
7. Ма́ша руководи́т (кружо́к). _____.
8. Они́ владе́ют (кварти́ра). _____.
9. Президе́нт управля́ет (госуда́рство). _____.
10. Сы́н не всегда́ по́льзуется (сове́ты) отца́. _____.

39. Put the complement of the adjective in parentheses into the instrumental.

1. Профе́ссор дово́лен (студе́нты). _____.
2. Ма́ша больна́ (анги́на). _____.
3. Они́ бы́ли недово́льны (еда́) в рестора́не. _____.
4. Сиби́рь бога́та (леса́) и (озёра). _____.
5. Петербу́рг изве́стен свое́й (красота́). _____.
6. Ба́бушка занята́ (шитьё) пла́тья. _____.

PERSONAL NAMES (Part I)

First Names and Patronymics

Russians have three names: a first name (**и́мя**), a middle name, called the patronymic (**о́тчество**), and a family name (**фами́лия**). The patronymic is formed by adding a suffix to the stem of the father's first name: for sons, this suffix is **-ович**, for daughters **-овна**. If the father's first name ends in **-й** (or **-ь**), then these suffixes are spelled **-евич** and **-евна**. The formation of patronymics is illustrated below:

Father's First Name	Patronymic (son of)	Patronymic (daughter of)
Ива́н	Ива́нович	Ива́новна
Серге́й	Серге́евич	Серге́евна
И́горь	И́горьевич	И́горьевна

The combined *first name and patronymic* (e.g., **Михаи́л Серге́евич**) is a polite form of address roughly corresponding to the use of English titles, such as Mr., Mrs., Dr., etc., and a surname (e.g., *Mr. Jones*, *Dr. Smith*). Russian adults use the first name and patronymic in formal situations, such as when first making an acquaintance, and generally when addressing people with whom they are not well acquainted. Students in Russia use this form of address when speaking to their teachers. Foreigners should use the first name and patronymic when addressing Russians in official situations.

Russian first names and patronymics are declined like nouns, as shown below.

	Masculine	*Feminine*
Nom.	Ви́ктор Степа́нович	Татья́на Степа́новна
Acc.	Ви́ктора Степа́новича	Татья́ну Степа́новну
Gen.	Ви́ктора Степа́новича	Татья́ны Степа́новны
Dat.	Ви́ктору Степа́новичу	Татья́не Степа́новне
Prep.	о Ви́кторе Степа́новиче	о Татья́не Степа́новне
Instr.	Ви́ктором Степа́новичем	Татья́ной Степа́новной

Foreign first names follow a different declensional pattern. Foreign first names ending in a consonant are declined as nouns if they denote males, but are indeclinable if they denote females, e.g., **Мы́ слы́шали о Джо́не и о Дже́йн** *We heard about John and Jane*. However, foreign names of females that end in **-а/-я** decline like second-declension feminine nouns, e.g., **Я ви́дел Ли́нду и Си́нтию** *I saw Linda and Cynthia*.

Russian family names either have a mixed noun/adjective declension, or decline completely like adjectives. Family names are discussed in Chapter 5 (page 159).

SUMMARY TABLE OF CASE ENDINGS OF NOUNS IN THE SINGULAR

Case	Masculine Hard Stem/Soft Stem	Neuter Hard Stem/Soft Stem	Feminine Hard Stem/Soft Stem
Nominative	-∅/-∅ (-ь) (-й) (-ий)	-о/-ё -е -ие -мя	-а/-я -ия -∅(-ь)
Accusative *Inanimate* *Animate*	= Nominative = Genitive	= Nominative	-у/-ю -ю -ь
Genitive	-а/-я -я	-а/-я -я -и	-ы/-и -и -и
Prepositional	-е -и	-е -и -и	-е -и -и
Dative	-у/-ю -ю	-у/-ю -ю -и	-е -и -и
Instrumental	-ом/-ём -ем -ем	-ом/-ём -ем -ем	-ой/-ей -ёй -ей -ью

SUMMARY TABLE OF CASE ENDINGS OF NOUNS IN THE PLURAL

Case	Masculine Hard Stem/Soft Stem	Neuter Hard Stem/Soft Stem	Feminine Hard Stem/Soft Stem
Nominative	-ы/-и	-а/-я	-ы/-и
Accusative *Inanimate* *Animate*	=*Nominative* =*Genitive*	=*Nominative* =*Genitive*	=*Nominative* =*Genitive*
Genitive	-ов/-ев -ей	-∅ -ей	-∅ -ей
Prepositional	-ах/-ях	-ах/-ях	-ах/-ях
Dative	-ам/-ям	-ам/-ям	-ам/-ям
Instrumental	-ами/-ями	-ами/-ями	-ами/-ями

CHAPTER 3

Prepositions

Prepositions are words which indicate the relation of a noun (or pronoun) to other words in the sentence. Prepositions can indicate various types of relations between words. For example, they may indicate location (*in* the room), direction (*to* the store), time (*before* dinner), cause (*from* fear), manner (*by* bus), purpose (*for* reading), and many other relations. In general, the meaning of a preposition, and the type of relation it indicates, is dependent on the context. For example, in the sentence **He returned** *from his trip*, the preposition *from* indicates a directional relation, while in the sentence **He is tired** *from his trip*, the same preposition indicates a causal relation, this difference being determined by the lexical meaning of the predicates used. Similarly, changing the object of a preposition may change the type of relation expressed, e.g., *He lived in **Boston*** (location), *He lived in* **luxury** (manner), *He lived in the **Stalin era*** (time).

In English, where case is reflected only in a few personal pronouns, and variation is limited to the choice between the nominative and the accusative cases, all prepositions require their object to be in the accusative case (e.g., nominative *she*, but following a preposition, accusative *her*: at *her*, by *her*, for *her*, in *her*, near *her*, with *her*, etc.). In Russian, by contrast, the noun or pronoun following a preposition can occur in whichever of the six cases is required by the preposition (though the nominative is rare). Therefore, it is important for the student of Russian to learn the case(s) that a given preposition governs. Some prepositions govern only one case, while others may govern two or more cases—and express correspondingly different meanings.

It is also important to keep in mind that close correspondences between English and Russian prepositions are rare. On the one hand, the same preposition in English may be used in several different meanings, which in Russian are each expressed by a different preposition. For example, the English preposition *for* is rendered by six different Russian prepositions in the following phrases: *a gift for Dad* (подáрок **для** пáпы), *closed for repairs* (закрыто **на** ремóнт), **for** *the first time* (**в** пéрвый рáз), *thanks for everything* (спасибо **за** всё), *respect for parents* (уважéние **к** родителям), **for** *this reason* (**по** этой причине). On the other hand, some meanings of English prepositions are not expressed in Russian by a preposition at all, but, as shown in Chapter 2, may be expressed by a Russian case form alone.

PREPOSITIONS GOVERNING THE NOMINATIVE CASE

The nominative case is highly restricted in its use after a preposition. The nominative case occurs only after the following two prepositions.

в
за

B — The nominative plural of animate nouns denoting members of a profession, class, or other group may be used after the preposition **в** in idiomatic expressions, the general meaning of which is *join the ranks of, become a member of* the group indicated.

О́н пошёл *в* солда́ты.	He became a soldier.
О́н не годи́тся *в* офице́ры.	He is not cut out to be an officer.
Она́ пошла́ *в* ня́ньки.	She went to work as a nanny.
Она́ пошла́ *в* го́сти.	She went visiting (as a guest).

За — The preposition **за** is followed by the nominative case in two expressions: (i) the interrogative **Что́ э́то** *за* . . . *What sort/kind of . . . is . . .?* and (ii) the exclamatory expression **Что́** *за* . . .**!** *What (a) . . .!*

Что́ э́то *за* кни́га?	What kind of book is that?
Что́ о́н *за* челове́к?	What sort of person is he?
Что́ *за* пого́да!	What (terrible or wonderful) weather!
Что́ *за* ерунда́!	What nonsense!

PREPOSITIONS GOVERNING THE ACCUSATIVE CASE

The following three prepositions are always followed by the accusative case.

```
про
че́рез
сквозь
```

Про — (*a*) *about* (*Note:* This preposition is characteristic of colloquial Russian.)

О́н рассказа́л *про* тебя́ всё.	He told everything about you.
Ска́зки обы́чно *про* звере́й.	Fairy tales are usually about animals.
Фи́льм бы́л *про* войну́.	The film was about the war.

(*b*) *to* (*Note:* When **про** is followed by **себя́** the phrase means *to oneself*.)

Де́ти чита́ли *про* себя́.	The children read to themselves.
Она́ ду́мала *про* себя́.	She thought to herself.

Че́рез — (*a*) *across, over, through* a place

Мы́ перешли́ *че́рез* у́лицу.	We walked across the street.
Она́ перепры́гнула *че́рез* лу́жу.	She jumped over a puddle.
Они́ вошли́ *че́рез* окно́.	They came in through the window.

(*b*) *through* some means or intermediary

О́н нашёл рабо́ту *че́рез* газе́ту.	He found a job through the newspaper.
Они́ познако́мились *че́рез* дру́га.	They met through a friend.
Мы́ говори́ли *че́рез* перево́дчика.	We spoke through an interpreter.

(*c*) *in* a certain amount of time or space before some action occurs

| Она́ прие́дет *че́рез* неде́лю. | *She will arrive in a week.* |
| Я́ выхожу́ *че́рез* одну́ остано́вку. | *I'm getting off in one stop.* |

(*d*) *every* unit of time or space, at the intervals indicated (*Note:* In this meaning, **че́рез** is followed by the plural form of the pronoun **ка́ждый**.)

| О́н звони́т *че́рез* ка́ждые две́ неде́ли. | *He calls every two weeks.* |
| *Че́рез* ка́ждые три́ строки́ е́сть оши́бка. | *Every three lines there is a mistake.* |

(*e*) *every other* unit of time or space

Она́ занима́ется аэро́бикой *че́рез* де́нь.	*She does aerobics every other day.*
Шко́льники писа́ли *че́рез* стро́чку.	*The students wrote every other line.*
О́н печа́тает статью́ *че́рез* строку́.	*He is typing the article double-spaced.*

Сквозь — *through* (*Note:* **Сквозь** often implies passing *through* some sort of obstruction.)

Они́ пробира́лись *сквозь* толпу́.	*They pushed through the crowd.*
Вода́ протека́ла *сквозь* кры́шу.	*Water was leaking through the roof.*
Тру́дно ви́деть бе́рег *сквозь* тума́н.	*It is difficult to see the shore through the fog.*

1. Fill in the blanks with the required preposition: **в**, **за**, **про**, **че́рез**, **сквозь**

1. Что́ _____ му́зыка!
2. Они́ нашли́ кварти́ру _____ газе́ту.
3. Мы́ пошли́ _____ го́сти.
4. Ма́льчик пры́гнул _____ забо́р.
5. Ученики́ чита́ли не вслу́х, а _____ себя́.
6. Па́па вернётся _____ ме́сяц.
7. А́втор печа́тает ру́копись _____ стро́чку.
8. Они́ расска́зывали _____ пое́здку.
9. Они́ разгляде́ли челове́ка _____ ды́м.
10. Его́ вы́брали _____ нача́льники.

The following three prepositions govern the accusative case when used in the meanings indicated.

| о |
| по |
| с |

О (Об) — *against* in the physical sense of *bump, knock, smash against* something

О́н разби́л буты́лку *о* сто́лб.	*He smashed a bottle against the pole.*
Ло́дка разби́лась *о* ска́лы.	*The boat broke up against the rocks.*
Она́ уда́рилась ного́й *о* сто́л.	*She bumped her leg against the table.*
О́н сту́кнулся голово́й *о* ба́лку.	*He knocked his head against a beam.*
Я́ уда́рился па́льцем ноги́ *о* ка́мень.	*I stubbed my toe on a rock.*

По — (*a*) *up to* and including a certain point in time or space

| У меня́ о́тпуск *по* пя́тое января́. | *I am on vacation up to (and including)* |
| | *the fifth of January.* |

Биле́т действи́телен *по* **суббо́ту.**	*The ticket is valid through Saturday.*
О́н стоя́л *по* **по́яс** в воде́.	*He stood up to his waist in water.*
Они́ в долга́х *пó* **уши.**	*They are in debt up to their ears.*
Я́ сы́т *по* **го́рло.**	*I'm stuffed to the gills.*
	(lit. I'm full up to the throat)

(*b*) *each*, i.e., indicates a distributive meaning when followed by the numerals **два́/две́, три́, четы́ре** (and higher) and a noun in the genitive case: *two . . . each, three . . . each, four . . . each* (*Note:* The preposition **по** governs the dative case when followed by a form of the numeral **оди́н**, i.e., when something is distributed singly to each of multiple recipients: **На́м да́ли** *по* **одному́ жето́ну** *We were given one token each*).

Мы́ вы́пили *по* **два́ стака́на.**	*We drank two glasses each.*
Они́ купи́ли *по* **три́ ру́чки.**	*They bought three pens each.*
Мы́ получи́ли *по* **четы́ре жето́на.**	*We received four tokens each.*

С — *about*, *approximately* with respect to measurement of weight, time, distance, or size

Паке́т ве́сит *с* **килогра́мм.**	*The package weighs about a kilo.*
Я́ поду́мал *с* **мину́ту.**	*I thought for about a minute.*
Мы́ провели́ та́м *с* **неде́лю.**	*We spent about a week there.*
О́н пробежа́л *с* **киломе́тр.**	*He ran about a kilometer.*
Она́ уже́ ро́стом *с* **ма́ть.**	*She's already about as tall as her mother.*

2. Fill in the blanks with the correct accusative preposition: **о, по, с**

1. Ученики́ получи́ли _____ две́ тетра́ди.
2. Вода́ в де́тском бассе́йне _____ коле́но.
3. О́н уже́ ро́стом _____ отца́.
4. Ви́за действи́тельна _____ деся́тое а́вгуста.
5. Она́ уда́рилась _____ две́рцу маши́ны.
6. Мы́ та́м прожи́ли _____ ме́сяц.

PREPOSITIONS GOVERNING EITHER THE ACCUSATIVE OR THE PREPOSITIONAL CASE

When used to indicate a *spatial* relation, the following two prepositions can be used with either the accusative or the prepositional case.

```
в
на
```

Whether these prepositions govern the accusative or the prepositional case is determined by the nature of the verb that occurs with the preposition.

The accusative case is used when the co-occurring verb expresses *direction*, *motion*, or *change in position*. In this context these prepositions answer the question **Куда́?** *Where to?*

The prepositional case is used when the co-occurring verb expresses *location*, *position*, or *motion within a particular location* (e.g., **О́н ходи́л** *в* **па́рке** *He walked in the park*). In this context these prepositions answer the question **Гдé?** *Where?* or *In what place?*

в (accusative) — *to, into, in*	
Она́ идёт *в* шко́лу.	*She is walking to school.*
Она́ вошла́ *в* ко́мнату.	*She walked into the room.*
Óн положи́л письмо́ *в* я́щик.	*He put the letter in(to) the drawer.*
в (prepositional) — *in, at*	
Она́ была́ *в* шко́ле.	*She was in/at school.*
Она́ сиде́ла *в* ко́мнате.	*She sat in the room.*
Письмо́ лежи́т *в* я́щике.	*The letter is in the drawer.*

на (accusative) — *to, into, on (to)*	
Са́ша идёт *на* рабо́ту.	*Sasha is going to work.*
Она́ пошла́ *на* по́чту.	*She went to the post office.*
Па́па положи́л ру́чку *на* сто́л.	*Dad put the pen on(to) the table.*
на (prepositional) — *at, in, on*	
Са́ша бы́л *на* рабо́те.	*Sasha was at work.*
Она́ была́ *на* по́чте.	*She was in/at the post office.*
Ру́чка лежи́т *на* столе́.	*The pen is lying on the table.*

Note: The choice of the preposition **в** or **на** to express location with a given noun is determined in part by the meaning of that noun. (See below, pages 89–92.)

3. Put the object of the preposition in parentheses into the accusative or prepositional case, whichever is required by the context.

1. Она́ положи́ла де́ньги в _____ (су́мка).
2. Óн сиде́л на _____ (дива́н).
3. Они́ пошли́ на _____ (ры́нок).
4. На́ши друзья́ побыва́ли в _____ (музе́й).
5. Дава́й ся́дем на _____ (скаме́йка).
6. Газе́ты лежа́т на _____ (сто́л).
7. Ма́ма поста́вила ча́шки в _____ (шка́ф).
8. За́втра мы́ е́дем на _____ (да́ча).
9. Кни́ги стоя́т на _____ (по́лка).
10. Го́сти сидя́т на _____ (вера́нда).

The prepositions **в** and **на** govern the accusative case in several other meanings.

В — (*a*) at a given hour (*Note:* In telling time, the numeral following the preposition **в** is in the accusative case, but the noun following the numeral is in the genitive case, which is the case governed by the numeral).

Она́ легла́ спа́ть *в* два́ часа́.	*She went to sleep at two o'clock.*
Она́ встаёт *в* се́мь часо́в.	*She gets up at seven o'clock.*
Нача́ло фи́льма *в* по́лдень.	*The film begins at noon.*

(*b*) *at* a given age

Де́ти начина́ют шко́лу *в* пя́ть ле́т.	*Kids begin school at five years of age.*
Она́ вы́шла за́муж *в* два́дцать ле́т.	*She got married at the age of twenty.*

(*c*) *on* a day or a part of the day (*Note:* The preposition **на** is used in the expressions *на* сле́дующий де́нь *on the following day* and *на* друго́й де́нь *on the next day*, but the preposition **в** is used in *в* друго́й де́нь (*on*) *another day*.)

У меня́ семина́р *в* сре́ду.	*I have a seminar on Wednesdsay.*
В пя́тницу я́ е́ду к врачу́.	*On Friday I'm going to the doctor.*
В э́то у́тро я́ узна́л пра́вду.	*On that morning I learned the truth.*
В ту́ но́чь мне́ сни́лся стра́шный со́н.	*That night I had a frightening dream.*

(*d*) *per* unit of time

О́н звони́т два́ ра́за *в* де́нь.	*He calls two times a day.*
У на́с исто́рия три́ ра́за *в* неде́лю.	*We have history three times per week.*
Ско́лько о́н зараба́тывает *в* ме́сяц?	*How much does he earn per month?*

Verbs Governing the Preposition B + Accusative Case

The following verbs govern the preposition **в** followed by the accusative case, when used in the meanings given below.

ве́рить *в* — *to believe in*

Она́ ве́рит *в* чудеса́.	*She believes in miracles.*

вме́шиваться *в* — *to interfere in*

Не вме́шивайся *в* мои́ дела́.	*Do not interfere in my affairs.*

вступа́ть *в* — *to enter (into), join*

Нельзя́ с ни́м вступа́ть *в* разгово́р.	*You shouldn't get into a conversation with him.*
О́н вступа́ет *в* ша́хматный клу́б.	*He is joining the chess club.*

игра́ть *в* — *to play (a sport or game)*

Они́ игра́ют *в* те́ннис.	*They play tennis.*
Де́ти игра́ли *в* каку́ю-то игру́.	*The children were playing some game.*

превраща́ть(ся) *в* — *to turn into*

О́н всё превраща́ет *в* шу́тку.	*He turns everything into a joke.*

На — (*a*) *for* a length of time (*Note:* The preposition **на** + accusative of time is used only with a verb of motion, or one involving a change in position, to indicate how long an action will last, or lasted. When a verb of location occurs, the time expression is in the accusative case, but with no preposition: **Она́ была́ в Москве́ ме́сяц** *She was in Moscow a month*.)

Они́ пое́дут в Москву́ *на* ме́сяц.	*They will go to Moscow for a month.*
Она́ вы́шла *на* пя́ть мину́т.	*She stepped out for five minutes.*
Ма́ша дала́ мне́ кни́гу *на* неде́лю.	*Masha gave me the book for a week.*
Ба́бушка се́ла *на* мину́тку.	*Grandma sat down for a minute.*

(b) *for* a purpose, intended *for*, or (when followed by numeral) sufficient *for*

Музе́й закры́ли *на* **ремо́нт.**　　*They closed the museum for repairs.*
Па́па ко́пит де́ньги *на* **маши́ну.**　*Dad is saving money for a car.*
Мы́ заброни́ровали но́мер *на* **двои́х.**　*We reserved a room for two.*
Она́ гото́вит обе́д *на* **де́сять челове́к.**　*She is making dinner for ten people.*

(c) *by* a certain amount

Мо́й бра́т ста́рше меня́ *на* **го́д.**　*My brother is older than me by a year.*
Она́ похуде́ла *на* **три́ килогра́мма.**　*She lost (got thinner by) three kilos.*
Мы́ опозда́ли *на* **ча́с.**　*We were an hour late/late by an hour.*

Verbs Governing the Preposition На + Accusative Case

The following verbs require the preposition **на** followed by the accusative case, when they are used in the meanings given below.

влия́ть *на* — *to influence, have an affect on*

Приро́да хорошо́ влия́ет *на* **на́с.**　*Nature has a positive effect on us.*

жа́ловаться *на* — *to complain about*

Она́ жа́ловалась мне́ *на* **шу́м.**　*She complained to me about the noise.*

крича́ть *на* — *to shout at*

Сосе́дка крича́ла *на* **дете́й.**　*The neighbor was shouting at the kids.*

наде́яться *на* — *to hope for; rely on*

Она́ наде́ется *на* **по́мощь роди́телей.**　*She relies on help from her parents.*

рассчи́тывать *на* — *to count on, depend on*

Мы́ рассчи́тываем *на* **тебя́.**　*We are counting on you.*

серди́ться *на* — *to be angry at*

О́н се́рдится *на* **дру́га.**　*He is angry at his friend.*

смотре́ть *на* — *to look at*

Она́ смотре́ла *на* **фотогра́фию.**　*She was looking at the photograph.*

Note: The verb **смотре́ть** may be used without a preposition, e.g., **смотре́ть телеви́зор** *to watch television*, **смотре́ть фотоальбо́м** *to look through a photo-album.*

4. Fill in the blank with the preposition **в** or **на**.

1. Музе́й закры́т _____ ремо́нт.
2. Она́ принима́ет табле́тки три ра́за _____ де́нь.
3. Мы́ е́дем в Пари́ж _____ неде́лю.
4. Я́ заказа́л сто́лик _____ трои́х.

5. О́н суеве́рный челове́к, ве́рит _____ приме́ты.
6. Хозя́йка пове́сила пальто́ _____ ве́шалку.
7. Друзья́ приезжа́ют к на́м _____ суббо́ту.
8. О́н научи́лся води́ть маши́ну _____ шестна́дцать ле́т.
9. Я́ моло́же бра́та _____ четы́ре го́да.
10. Моя́ до́чка лю́бит игра́ть _____ ша́хматы.
11. Мы́ обы́чно у́жинаем _____ се́мь часо́в.
12. Она́ о́чень надеётся _____ ва́шу по́мощь.
13. Вода́ при́ кипе́нии превраща́ется _____ па́р.
14. Мы́ жа́ловались официа́нту _____ еду́.
15. О́н, зану́да, всегда́ вме́шивается _____ чужи́е дела́.

PREPOSITIONS GOVERNING EITHER THE ACCUSATIVE OR THE INSTRUMENTAL CASE

When used to indicate a *spatial* relation, the following two prepositions can be followed either by the accusative or the instrumental case.

> **за**
> **под**

Whether these prepositions are followed by the accusative or by the instrumental case depends on the nature of the verb used in the sentence. The same factors that determine the choice of accusative or prepositional case after the prepositions **в** and **на**, also determine the choice of accusative or instrumental case after the prepositions **за** and **под**.

The accusative case is used when the co-occurring verb expresses *motion*, *direction*, or a *change in position*. These prepositions answer the question **Куда́?** *Where to?*

The instrumental case is used when the co-occurring verb expresses *location* or *position*. These prepositions answer the question **Где́?** *Where?* or *In what location?*

за (accusative) — *behind, beyond*

Ма́льчик забежа́л *за* де́рево.	The boy ran behind the tree.
Она́ поста́вила ла́мпу *за* компью́тер.	She put the lamp behind the computer.
О́н се́л *за* сто́л.	He sat down at (lit. behind) the table.
Они́ пое́хали *за* грани́цу.	They went abroad (lit. beyond the border).

за (instrumental) — *behind, beyond*

Ма́льчик пря́чется *за* де́ревом.	The boy is hiding behind the tree.
Ла́мпа стои́т *за* компью́тером.	The lamp is behind the computer.
О́н сиди́т *за* столо́м.	He is sitting at (lit. behind) the table.
Они́ жи́ли *за* грани́цей.	They lived abroad (lit. beyond the border).

под (accusative) — *under*

Ру́чка упа́ла *под* сто́л.　　　　　*The pen fell under the table.*
Мы́ се́ли *под* берёзу.　　　　　*We sat down under a birchtree.*
Óн положи́л чемода́н *под* крова́ть.　*He put the suitcase under the bed.*

под (instrumental) — *under*

Ру́чка лежи́т *под* столо́м.　　　　*The pen is lying under the table.*
Мы́ сиде́ли *под* берёзой.　　　　*We were sitting under a birchtree.*
Чемода́н лежи́т *под* крова́тью.　　*The suitcase is lying under the bed.*

---

5. Put the object of the preposition in parentheses into the accusative or the instrumental case, whichever is required by the context.

1. Маши́на поверну́ла за́ _____ (у́гол).
2. На́ши друзья́ живу́т за _у́голом_ (у́гол). *corner*
3. Кни́га упа́ла за _____ (по́лка).
4. Ребёнок забра́лся под _____ (ла́вка).
5. Письмо́ лежи́т под _кни́гой_ (кни́га).
6. Ла́мпа стои́т за _кре́слом_ (кре́сло).
7. Со́лнце зашло́ за _____ (ту́ча).
8. Это лежи́т пря́мо у него́ под _но́сом_ (но́с).
9. Óн лю́бит пла́вать под _водо́й_ (вода́).
10. Ко́шка залезла под _____ (вера́нда).

The prepositions **за** and **под** govern the accusative case in several other meanings.

За — (*a*) *for* (i.e., *in exchange for*)

Óн получи́л ава́нс *за* кни́гу.　　*He received an advance for his book.*
Ско́лько ты́ заплати́ла *за* ку́клу?　*How much did you pay for the doll?*
Они́ купи́ли биле́т *за* 10 до́лларов.　*They bought a ticket for 10 dollars.*
Большо́е спаси́бо *за* по́мощь.　　*Thank you very much for your help.*

Several verbs occur with the preposition **за** in the meaning *in exchange for.*

благодари́ть *за* — *to thank (someone) for*

Мы́ благодари́ли его́ *за* по́мощь.　*We thanked him for his help.*

хвали́ть *за* — *to praise, compliment (someone) for*

Óн хва́лит на́с *за* хоро́шую рабо́ту.　*He praises us for good work.*

руга́ть *за* — *to scold, criticize (someone) for*

Оте́ц руга́л сы́на *за* гру́бость.　*Father scolded his son for being rude.*

нака́зывать *за* — *to punish (someone) for*

Его́ не ра́з нака́зывали *за* враньё.　*He has often been punished for lying.*

(*b*) *for* someone (i.e., do something on behalf of, in place of someone else)

Сы́н расписа́лся *за* отца́.	*The son signed for his father.*
О́н при́нял пре́мию *за* а́втора.	*He accepted the prize for the author.*
Ми́ша сде́лал э́то *за* дру́га.	*Misha did it in place of his friend*
Она́ сего́дня рабо́тает *за* колле́гу.	*She is working today for a colleague.*

(*c*) *for* someone (i.e., feel something for someone, due to their circumstances)

Мы́ пережива́ем *за* тебя́.	*We feel badly for you.*
Она́ беспоко́ится *за* му́жа.	*She is worried for her husband.*
Ма́ть бои́тся *за* сы́на.	*The mother is afraid for her son.*
Мы́ о́чень ра́ды *за* ва́с.	*We are very glad for you.*

(*d*) *for* someone or something (i.e., do something in support of, in favor of)

Наро́д голосова́л *за* Е́льцина.	*The people voted for Yeltsin.*
Дава́йте вы́пьем *за* дру́жбу.	*Let's drink to our friendship.*
О́н вступи́лся *за* дру́га.	*He stood up for his friend.*
Я́ боле́ю *за* тебя́.	*I am rooting for you.*

(*e*) *in* (*the space of*) (*Note:* The preposition **за** is used here with a verb of the perfective aspect to express the period of time within which an action is *completed*. Compare this meaning with the prepositionless accusative of time, and a verb of the imperfective aspect, to denote the *duration* of the action: **Письмо́ шло́ две́ неде́ли** *The letter was in route for two weeks*.)

Письмо́ дошло́ до на́с *за* две́ неде́ли.	*The letter reached us in two weeks.*
О́н прочита́л ве́сь рома́н *за* три́ дня́.	*He read the entire novel in three days.*
Она́ написа́ла докла́д *за* неде́лю.	*She finished the report in a week.*
О́н сде́лал всю́ рабо́ту *за* пя́тницу.	*He did all the work during Friday.*

(*f*) *after* a certain time, *over* a certain age

Она́ звони́ла уже́ *за* по́лночь.	*She called well after midnight.*
Ему́ уже́ *за* пятьдеся́т.	*He is already over fifty.*

(*g*) *before* an event (*Note:* The preposition **за** + accusative case is used in combination with the preposition **до** + genitive case to express the amount of time that one event precedes another.)

Мы́ прие́хали в аэропо́рт *за* ча́с *до* вы́лета.	*We arrived at the airport an hour before departure.*
О́н вы́шел *за* мину́ту *до* конца́ фи́льма.	*He walked out a minute before the end of the movie.*

(*h*) *at* the distance indicated (*Note:* The preposition **за** + accusative is used in combination with the preposition **от** + genitive case to denote the distance from a place that something occurs; the preposition **в** + prepositional can also be used in this meaning, e.g., **в двух кварта́лах отсю́да** *two blocks from here*.)

Маши́на слома́лась *за* ми́лю *от* его́ до́ма.	*His car broke down a mile from his house.*
За два́ кварта́ла *отсюда* стро́ят бассе́йн.	*Two blocks from here they are building a pool.*

(*i*) *by* with verbs meaning *to lead, take, hold, seize, pull by*

Она́ вела́ ребёнка *за́* руку.	*She led the child by the hand.*
Она́ схвати́ла его́ *за* рука́в.	*She seized him by the sleeve.*
О́н схвати́л ко́шку *за* шки́рку.	*He seized the cat by the scruff of the neck.*

Под — (*a*) *towards*, *approaching* a certain time or age

Мы́ встре́тились *под* **Но́вый го́д.**	*We met on New Year's Eve.*
Она́ пришла́ *под* **ве́чер.**	*She arrived towards evening.*
Ему́ *под* **пятьдеся́т.**	*He is approaching fifty.*

(*b*) *to* the accompaniment of

Они́ танцева́ли *под* **ро́к-му́зыку.**	*They danced to rock music.*
Она́ пе́ла *под* **гита́ру.**	*She sang to (the accompaniment of) the guitar.*

6. Fill in the blanks with the preposition **за** or **под**.

1. Она́ чита́ла докла́д _____ колле́гу.
2. Оте́ц хвали́л сы́на _____ хоро́шую учёбу.
3. Мы́ просну́лись _____ пе́ние пти́ц.
4. Он зако́нчил рабо́ту _____ у́тро.
5. Они́ купи́ли видеомагнитофо́н _____ бесце́нок.
6. Мы́ беспоко́имся _____ дру́га.
7. Бра́т боле́ет _____ сестру́.
8. Я́ засну́л _____ зву́ки ле́са.
9. Он напеча́тал курсову́ю рабо́ту _____ неде́лю.
10. До́мик нахо́дится _____ два́ кварта́ла от бе́рега мо́ря.
11. Сы́н взя́л отца́ _____ ру́ку.
12. Мы́ пришли́ _____ пя́ть мину́т до нача́ла спекта́кля.

PREPOSITIONS GOVERNING THE GENITIVE CASE

Prepositions governing the genitive case are the most numerous. The core prepositions, those most commonly used, are presented below with their principal meanings. All of the prepositions in the following list, except for **с**, are followed only by the genitive case.

Core Prepositions Governing the Genitive Case

без	**ми́мо**
для	**о́коло**
до	**от**
из	**по́сле**
из-за	**про́тив**
из-под	**с**
кро́ме	**у**

Без — (*a*) *without*

Она́ говори́т по-ру́сски *без* **акце́нта.**	*She speaks Russian without a (foreign) accent.*
Нельзя́ выходи́ть зимо́й *без* **ша́пки.**	*One shouldn't go out in winter without a hat.*
Он да́л отве́т *без* **колеба́ния.**	*He answered without hesitation.*

(*b*) in telling time, to indicate the number of minutes until the hour

Сейча́с *без* **пяти́ во́семь.**	*It is now five minutes to eight.*
Бы́ло *без* **че́тверти де́сять.**	*It was a quarter to ten.*

Для — (*a*) *for* the benefit of (*Note:* In the meaning *for the benefit of* the preposition **для** + genitive case has a near-synonym in the prepositionless dative case construction, e.g., **Она́ купи́ла пода́рок** *бра́ту She bought a present for her brother.*)

Она́ купи́ла пода́рок *для* **бра́та**.	*She bought a present for her brother.*
Э́тот а́втор пи́шет кни́ги *для* **дете́й**.	*This author writes books for children.*

    (*b*) *for* the purpose of

Он собира́ет материа́л *для* **докла́да**.	*He is collecting material for a report.*
Он пьёт то́лько *для* **удово́льствия**.	*He drinks only for pleasure.*

До — (*a*) *before*, or *until* a certain time

До **войны́** они́ жи́ли в Москве́.	*Before the war they lived in Moscow.*
Мы рабо́таем *до* **пяти́ часо́в**.	*We work until five o'clock.*

    (*b*) *up to, as far as* a certain place (*Note:* When the preposition **до** is used in this meaning, the co-occurring verb often has the prefix **до-**.)

Она́ досмотре́ла фи́льм *до* **конца́**.	*She watched the film to the end.*
Мы дочита́ли *до* **страни́цы 65**.	*We read up to page 65.*
Они́ дошли́ *до* **Кра́сной пло́щади**.	*They walked as far as Red Square.*

Из — (*a*) *from, out of* when motion or movement is indicated (*Note:* The preposition **из** is used in this meaning only with nouns that require the preposition **в** + accusative case to express motion or movement *in*, *to*, or *into*, e.g., **Мы е́дем** *в* **Москву́** *We are going to Moscow*, **Он положи́л биле́т** *в* **карма́н** *He put the ticket into his pocket.*)

Моя́ подру́га прие́хала *из* **Москвы́**.	*My girlfriend arrived from Moscow.*
Вра́ч вы́шел *из* **кабине́та**.	*The doctor stepped out of his office.*
Па́па вы́нул биле́т *из* **карма́на**.	*Dad took the ticket out of his pocket.*

    (*b*) *from* indicating source of information, place of origin, or material from/of which something is made

Он узна́л *из* **газе́т**.	*He found out from the newspapers.*
Э́то цита́та *из* **Толсто́го**.	*This is a quotation from Tolstoy.*
Он *из* **хоро́шей семьи́**.	*He is from a good family.*
Моя́ ба́бушка *из* **Ми́нска**.	*My grandmother is from Minsk.*
Бензи́н де́лают *из* **не́фти**.	*Gasoline is made from oil.*

    (*c*) *of*, i.e., one or more *out* of a larger group

Оди́н *из* **студе́нтов** вы́рос в Ки́еве.	*One of the students grew up in Kiev.*
Мно́гие *из* **ни́х** учи́лись в Росси́и.	*Many of them have studied in Russia.*
Все́ *из* **ни́х** говоря́т по-ру́сски.	*All of them speak Russian.*

    (*d*) *consisting of, comprised of*

Э́то семья́ *из* **пяти́ челове́к**.	*This is a family of five people.*
Э́то кварти́ра *из* **четырёх ко́мнат**.	*This is an apartment with four rooms.*
Комите́т состои́т *из* **десяти́ чле́нов**.	*The committee is composed of ten members.*

(e) *from, out of* indicating cause or reason

Óн сдéлал всё *из* **любви́ к нéй.**	*He did everything out of love for her.*
Онá э́то сказáла *из* **рéвности.**	*She said it out of jealousy.*
Они́ пришли́ *из* **любопы́тства.**	*They came out of curiosity.*
Мы́ слу́шали егó *из* **вéжливости.**	*We listened to him out of politeness.*

Из-за — (a) *from behind/beyond*

Мáльчик вы́шел *из-за* **дéрева.**	*The boy came out from behind a tree.*
Óн встáл *из-за* **столá.**	*He got up from (behind) the table.*
Они́ верну́лись *из-за* **грани́цы.**	*They returned from abroad*
	(lit. from beyond the border).

(b) *because of* referring to the cause of something undesirable

Из-за дождя́ мы́ не пошли́ в пáрк.	*Because of the rain, we didn't go to the park.*
Мы́ опоздáли *из-за* **авáрии.**	*We were late because of an accident.*

Из-под — (a) *from under*

Из-под дивáна вы́лезла кóшка.	*A cat crawled out from under the sofa.*
Маши́на вы́шла *из-под* **контрóля.**	*The car went out of control.*

(b) to indicate the purpose of a container

бáнка *из-под* **варéнья**	*a jam jar*
буты́лка *из-под* **молокá**	*a milk bottle*
картóнка *из-под* **шля́пы**	*a hat box*
корóбка *из-под* **ту́фель**	*a shoe box*

Крóме — *except, besides, apart from*

Онá съéла всё, *крóме* **колбасы́.**	*She ate everything except the sausage.*
Крóме **меня́, бы́ло ещё трóе гостéй.**	*There were three guests besides me.*
Крóме **тогó, éсть и други́е причи́ны.**	*Apart from that, there are other reasons.*

Ми́мо – *past* (*Note:* The preposition **ми́мо** often occurs after a motion verb with the prefix **про-**.)

Автóбус прохóдит *ми́мо* **э́того мостá.**	*The bus goes past this bridge.*
Óн чáсто хóдит *ми́мо* **нáшего дóма.**	*He often walks past our house.*

Óколо — (a) *near*

Они́ живу́т *óколо* **институ́та.**	*They live near the institute.*
Онá сидéла *óколо* **нáс.**	*She sat near us.*

(b) *around, about (approximately)*

Óн пробежáл *óколо* **пяти́ киломéтров.**	*He ran about five kilometers.*
Мы́ бы́ли тáм *óколо* **трёх часóв.**	*We were there around three hours.*

От — (a) *from* indicating the point of origin of motion, or source of something (*Note:* The preposition **от** + genitive must be used to express motion or movement *from a person.*)

Онá идёт *от* **подру́ги.**	*She is coming from her girlfriend.*
Они́ получи́ли письмó *от* **сы́на.**	*They received a letter from their son.*
Мы́ узнáли нóвость *от* **друзéй.**	*We learned the news from friends.*

(b) *away from* used with a noun denoting the starting-point of motion (*Note:* When used in this meaning, the preposition **от** often occurs with a verb of motion that has the prefix **от-**.)

По́езд отошёл *от* ста́нции.	*The train pulled away from the station.*
Кора́бль отплы́л *от* бе́рега.	*The ship sailed away from the shore.*

Verbs Followed by the Preposition От + Genitive Case

Several commonly used verbs are followed by the preposition **от** and the genitive case. Many of them convey figuratively the sense of movement *away from* something.

защища́ть(ся) *от* — *to defend, protect (oneself) from*

Дере́вья защища́ли до́м *от* ве́тра.	*The trees protected the house from the wind.*
Она́ защища́лась *от* со́лнца зо́нтиком.	*She protected herself from the sun with an umbrella.*

избавля́ть(ся) *от* — *to rid (oneself) of*

То́лько э́то лека́рство избавля́ет меня́ *от* головно́й бо́ли.	*Only this medicine can rid me of a headache.*
О́н избавля́ется *от* дурно́й привы́чки.	*He is getting rid of a bad habit.*

освобожда́ть(ся) *от* — *to free (oneself) of, from*

Сла́бое здоро́вье освобожда́ет челове́ка *от* вое́нной слу́жбы.	*Poor health exempts a person from military service.*
Я́ сего́дня освобожда́юсь *от* рабо́ты в ча́с.	*I get off work today at one o'clock (lit. I free myself from work . . .)*

отка́зываться *от* — *to refuse, decline, turn down*

Она́ всегда́ отка́зывается *от* мои́х приглаше́ний.	*She always turns down my invitations.*

отключа́ться *от* — *to turn off, escape from*

Му́зыка помога́ет мне́ отключа́ться от э́той пробле́мы.	*Music helps me escape from this problem.*

отлича́ться *от* — *to differ from*

Мы́ си́льно отлича́емся дру́г *от* дру́га.	*We are very different from one another.*

пря́таться *от* — *to hide from*

Бра́т пря́чется *от* сестры́.	*The brother is hiding from his sister.*

(c) *from* one place to another (*Note:* In this meaning the preposition **от** + genitive usually combines with the preposition **до** + genitive.)

Она́ зна́ет поэ́му *от* нача́ла *до* конца́.	*She knows the poem from beginning to end.*
В я́слях де́ти *от* трёх *до* пяти́ ле́т.	*In the nursery there are children from three to five years of age.*
Мно́гие лю́ди живу́т *от* зарпла́ты *до* зарпла́ты.	*Many people live from paycheck to paycheck.*

(d) *from* i.e., the distance from a point (*Note:* The distance may be expressed either by **за** + accusative or **в** + prepositional case, as shown in the first two examples below.)

Аэропо́рт нахо́дится за де́сять киломе́тров *от* го́рода.	*The airport is located ten kilometers from the city.*
О́н жи́л в дву́х кварта́лах *от* Кремля́.	*He lived two blocks from the Kremlin.*
Их да́ча располо́жена далеко́ *от* го́рода.	*Their dacha is located far from the city.*

(e) indicates the purpose for which an object is intended

клю́ч *от* маши́ны	*the key to the car*
кры́шка *от* ба́нки	*the lid to the jar*
пу́говица *от* руба́шки	*a shirt button*

(f) indicates something to counter or protect against (*Note:* This meaning is sometimes expressed by the preposition **про́тив** + genitive, as indicated below.)

страхова́ние *от* пожа́ра и кра́ж	*insurance against fire and theft*
лека́рство *от* ка́шля	*cough medicine*
табле́тки *от* бо́ли	*pain pills*

(g) indicates the cause of some physical or emotional state (*Note:* In colloquial style this meaning is often expressed by the preposition **с** + genitive, as shown below.)

Не́которые пью́т *от* ску́ки.	*Some people drink from boredom.*
Она́ дрожи́т *от* хо́лода.	*She is shivering from the cold.*
Де́ти закрича́ли *от* испу́га.	*The children screamed with fright.*
Они́ запла́кали *от* ра́дости.	*They cried with joy.*

По́сле — *after*

Мы́ встре́тились *по́сле* заня́тий.	*We met after class.*
По́сле дождя́ вы́глянуло со́лнце.	*After the rain the sun came out.*

Про́тив — (a) *against*

О́н голосова́л *про́тив* нало́гов.	*He voted against taxes.*
Мы́ шли́ *про́тив* ве́тра.	*We were walking against the wind.*
Я́ ничего́ не име́ю *про́тив* э́того.	*I have nothing against this.*
Ему́ сде́лали уко́л *про́тив* ти́фа.	*He was inoculated against typhus.*

(b) *opposite*

О́н поста́вил га́лочку *про́тив* фами́лии.	*He put a check mark opposite the name.*
Мы́ сиде́ли дру́г *про́тив* дру́га.	*We sat opposite each other.*

С — (a) *from* a place (*Note:* The preposition **с** + genitive is used to indicate place of origin or motion from a place, when the noun denoting the place requires the preposition **на** + accusative to express motion *to*, *in* (*to*), *on* (*to*) and **на** + prepositional to express location *in*, *on*, or *at*.)

Она́ *с* Кавка́за.	*She is from the Caucasus.*
Ма́ма верну́лась *с* рабо́ты.	*Mom has returned from work.*
Мы́ шли́ пешко́м *с* по́чты.	*We walked from the post office.*

(b) *off* the surface of, *down* from something

Кни́га упа́ла *с* по́лки.	*The book fell off the shelf.*
О́н сня́л часы́ *со* стены́.	*He took the clock down from the wall.*
Официа́нтка убрала́ посу́ду *со* стола́.	*The waitress cleared the dishes off the table.*
Маши́на сверну́ла *с* доро́ги.	*The car turned off the road.*

(c) *from, out of, with* in a causal sense (*Note:* The preposition **с** + genitive to express the cause of an action is a colloquial synonym of **от** + genitive. Note the prepositional object in the first two examples has the genitive case ending **-y**, also characteristic of colloquial style.)

Она́ закрича́ла *с* испу́гу.	*She cried with fright.*
Ма́льчик убежа́л *со* стра́ху.	*The boy ran away out of fear.*
О́н позвони́л е́й *с* отча́яния.	*He called her out of despair.*
Она́ запры́гала *с* ра́дости.	*She began jumping for joy.*

(d) *since, from* in a temporal sense (*Note:* To express time *from . . . to . . .* the preposition **с** + genitive is used with **до** + genitive.)

Мы́ живём зде́сь *с* а́вгуста.	*We've been living here since August.*
О́н говори́л по-ру́сски *с* де́тства.	*He spoke Russian from childhood.*
У на́с заня́тия *с* девяти́ часо́в.	*We have classes from nine o'clock.*
Переры́в на обе́д *с* ча́са *до* дву́х.	*Lunch break is from one to two.*

У — (a) *by, at* a place

Мы́ жи́ли на да́че *у* реки́.	*We lived in a dacha by the river.*
Учи́тель стоя́л *у* доски́.	*The teacher stood at the blackboard.*

(b) *at* someone's place (*Note:* The preposition **у** + genitive case of a noun denoting a person may function like French *chez*.)

Она́ была́ *у* подру́ги.	*She was at her girlfriend's (place).*
Вчера́ о́н бы́л *у* врача́.	*Yesterday he was at the doctor's.*
Мы́ останови́лись *у* дру́га.	*We stayed with a friend (at a friend's).*
У на́с пого́да всегда́ жа́ркая.	*In our area the weather is always hot.*

(c) used with a noun or personal pronoun to express a relation of possession (*Note:* The preposition **у** + genitive case normally expresses possession by a person or animal, and corresponds to the English verb *to have*.)

У бра́та е́сть но́вый компью́тер.	*My brother has a new computer.*
У его́ сестры́ краси́вые глаза́.	*His sister has pretty eyes.*
У меня́ к ва́м вопро́с.	*I have a question for you.*

Verbs Followed by the Preposition У + Genitive Case

Several verbs in combination with the preposition **у** and an animate noun indicate the source of something, especially the person from whom something is obtained.

бра́ть *у* — *to take, borrow from*

Я́ бра́л кни́гу *у* колле́ги.	*I borrowed the book from a colleague.*

занима́ть *у* — *to borrow from*

О́н занима́ет де́ньги *у* друзе́й.	*He borrows money from friends.*

отнима́ть *у* — *to take away*

Э́то отнима́ет *у меня́* часа́ два́.   *This takes me about two hours.*

спра́шивать *у* — *to ask (information)*

О́н спра́шивал *у на́с* доро́гу.   *He asked us the way.*

проси́ть *у* — *to ask, request*

О́н проси́л *у меня́* по́мощь.   *He asked me for help.*

покупа́ть *у* — *to buy from*

Мы́ покупа́ем *у него́* о́вощи.   *We buy vegetables from him.*

7. Supply the most appropriate genitive preposition from the following list: **без, для, из-за, из-под, кро́ме, ми́мо, о́коло, по́сле, про́тив**

1. _____ ле́кции профе́ссор отвеча́л на вопро́сы слу́шателей.
2. На́ш до́м нахо́дится пря́мо _____ па́рка.
3. Авто́бус проезжа́ет _____ на́шего до́ма.
4. Мы́ жи́ли в Москве́ _____ шести́ ме́сяцев.
5. О́н пьёт ко́фе чёрный _____ са́хара.
6. О́н вста́л _____ стола́ и предложи́л то́ст.
7. На ку́хне е́сть насте́нный шка́ф _____ посу́ды.
8. Ребёнок съе́л всё, что бы́ло на таре́лке, _____ зелёного горо́шка.
9. На столе́ стоя́ла буты́лка _____ молока́.
10. Ко́шка вы́лезла _____ дива́на.
11. Уо́лт Дисне́й со́здал прекра́сные фи́льмы _____ дете́й.
12. Но́вые дома́ расту́т бы́стро, как грибы́ _____ дождя́.
13. Э́та доро́га прохо́дит где́-то _____ о́зера.
14. Самолёты не могли́ вы́лететь _____ тума́на.
15. Делега́ты выступа́ли _____ предложе́ния президе́нта.

8. Supply the most approprate genitive preposition from the following list: **до, из, от, с, у**

1. В я́сли принима́ют дете́й _____ пяти́ ле́т.
2. Она́ вы́нула па́спорт _____ су́мки.
3. О́н взя́л кни́гу _____ ве́рхней по́лки.
4. Мы́ получи́ли письмо́ _____ дру́га.
5. О́н проси́л де́ньги _____ роди́телей.
6. Мы́ узна́ли об э́том _____ газе́ты.
7. Ло́дка отплыла́ _____ бе́рега.
8. Э́ти ло́жки сде́ланы _____ серебра́.
9. О́н до́лго стоя́л на моро́зе и дрожа́л _____ хо́лода.
10. Она́ устро́ила сканда́л _____ ре́вности.
11. О́н бы́л _____ врача́, ему́ сде́лали уко́л _____ гри́ппа.
12. Ма́ма _____ Росси́и, а па́па _____ Украи́ны.
13. Сего́дня я́ дое́хал _____ университе́та за 30 мину́т.
14. Мы́ занима́емся _____ девяти́ _____ двух часо́в.
15. Где́ клю́ч _____ кварти́ры?
16. Дава́й смотре́ть фи́льм, _____ на́с е́сть но́вый ви́дик.

17. Óн не мóг избáвиться _____ мы́сли, что онá встрегáется с другúм пáрнем.
18. Не покупáй матрёшки _____ у́личных торгóвцев, э́ти матрёшки нúзкого кáчества.

Other Prepositions Governing the Genitive Case

A number of other prepositions govern the genitive case. Many are structurally more complex than those presented in the first group. Some of them are derived from nouns, e.g., **вмéсто** *instead of*, *in place of* is an amalgam of the more basic preposition **в** *in* and the noun **мéсто** *place*. Others, formed from adverbs, may function both as adverbs and prepositions, e.g., **позадú** is used as an adverb in **Онú остáвили всё** *позадú They left everything behind*, but as an adjective in **Дéти игрáют** *позадú* **нáшего дóма** *The children play behind our house*. Since many of the prepositions in this next group are more characteristic of written style, familiarity with these prepositions will contribute to greater proficiency in reading Russian.

блúз	врóде
вблизú	мéжду
ввиду́	напрóтив
вдóль	повéрх
вмéсто	позадú
внé	посредú
внутрú	путём
внýтрь	рáди
вóзле	свéрх
вокрýг	сзáди
впередú	средú

Блúз — *near*, *close to* (*Note:* The preposition **блúз** is characteristic of poetic style.)

Дóм стоя́л *блúз* мóря.   *The house stood near the sea.*

Вблизú — *not far from*, *near*, *close to* (*Note:* The preposition **вблизú**, a synonym of **блúз**, is stylistically neutral.)

Дóм находúлся *вблизú* мóря.   *The house was located near the sea.*

Ввиду́ — *in view of*

Ввиду́ э́тих обстоя́тельств, мы́   *In view of these circumstances, we*
реши́ли отложи́ть заседáние.   *decided to postpone the meeting.*

Вдóль — *along* a line or the length of something

Посадúли дерéвья *вдóль* дорóги.   *They planted trees along the road.*
Дельфúны плы́ли *вдóль* бéрега.   *Dolphins swam along the shore.*
Мы́ шлú *вдóль* нáбережной.   *We walked along the embankment.*
Вдóль у́лицы стоя́ли мáшины.   *Cars were parked along the street.*

Вмéсто — *instead of*, *in place of*

Вмéсто вóдки лýчше пúть винó.   *Instead of vodka, it is better to drink wine.*
Онá пошлá тудá *вмéсто* мýжа.   *She went there in place of her husband.*

Вне — *outside, out of, beyond*

Кури́ть мо́жно, но то́лько *вне* до́ма.	*You may smoke, but only outside the house.*
На́м нельзя́ де́йствовать *вне́* зако́на.	*We cannot act outside the law.*
Ребёнок роди́лся *вне́* бра́ка.	*The child was born out of wedlock.*
Э́то *вне́* вся́кого сомне́ния.	*This is beyond any doubt.*

Внутри́ — *inside* indicates the position or location in which something is found

Мы́ не́ были *внутри́* дворца́.	*We haven't been inside the palace.*
Медве́дь бы́л *внутри́* пеще́ры.	*The bear was inside the cave.*

Вну́трь — *inside* indicates motion or direction inward (*Note*: This preposition also occurs in the form **вовну́трь** which is used in colloquial style.)

Тури́сты вошли́ *внутрь* дворца́.	*The tourists went inside the palace.*
Де́ти загляну́ли *вовну́трь* пеще́ры.	*The kids glanced inside the cave.*

Во́зле — *near, very close to* (*Note*: In comparison with **вблизи́**, **бли́з**, and **о́коло**, the preposition **во́зле** denotes closer proximity to something.)

Они́ живу́т *во́зле* на́с.	*They live very close to us.*
На́ш до́м *во́зле* са́мой реки́.	*Our house is right near the river.*

Вокру́г — *round, around*

Мы́ сиде́ли *вокру́г* костра́.	*We sat round the campfire.*
Земля́ враща́ется *вокру́г* со́лнца.	*The earth revolves around the sun.*
Вокру́г него́ собрала́сь толпа́.	*A crowd gathered around him.*

Впереди́ — *in front of, ahead of*

Ги́д шёл *впереди́* гру́ппы тури́стов.	*The guide walked in front of the tourist group.*
Мили́ция е́хала *впереди́* автоколо́нны.	*The police rode ahead of the motorcade.*

Вро́де — *like*

У ни́х е́сть дива́н *вро́де* на́шего.	*They have a sofa like ours.*
О́н что́-то *вро́де* консульта́нта.	*He's something like a consultant.*
	(He's a consultant of sorts).

Ме́жду — *between* (*Note*: The preposition **ме́жду** + genitive case occurs quite rarely. It is found in a few idiomatic expressions, and always when the objects involved are of the same type. More often, **ме́жду** is followed by the instrumental case.)

О́н оказа́лся *ме́жду* дву́х огне́й.	*He found himself between two fires.*
	(i.e., between two unpleasant alternatives)
О́н сиди́т *ме́жду* дву́х сту́льев.	*He is sitting between two chairs.*
	(i.e., trying to please both sides in a dispute)
На́до чита́ть *ме́жду* стро́к.	*One must read between the lines.*

Напро́тив — *opposite, across from*

Они́ живу́т *напро́тив* па́рка.	*They live opposite the park.*
Напро́тив на́шего до́ма е́сть кафе́.	*Across from our house is a café.*

Пове́рх — *over, above, on top of* a physical surface

Она́ постели́ла про́стыню *пове́рх* матра́са.	She lay the sheet over the mattress.
О́н смотре́л *пове́рх* очко́в.	He looked over the top of his glasses.

Позади́ — *behind*

Позади́ на́шего до́ма е́сть огоро́д.	Behind our house there is a vegetable garden.

Посреди́ — *in the middle of* (in a spatial sense only)

Посреди́ пло́щади стоя́л кио́ск.	In the middle of the square was a kiosk.

Путём — *by means of*

Вопро́с реши́ли *путём* перегово́ров.	The question was decided by means of negotiations.

Ра́ди — *for the sake of* someone or something

Они́ помири́лись *ра́ди* дете́й.	They reconciled for the sake of the children.
О́н де́лал всё *ра́ди* на́шей дру́жбы.	He did everything for the sake of our friendship.

Све́рх — *on top of, in excess of, beyond* in an abstract sense

О́н получи́л пре́мию *све́рх* зарпла́ты.	He received a bonus on top of his salary.
Его́ прие́зд бы́л *све́рх* мои́х ожида́ний.	His arrival was beyond my expectations.

Сза́ди — *behind*

Сза́ди до́ма была́ ре́чка.	Behind the house was a stream.
Сза́ди на́с разда́лся кри́к.	A shout was heard behind us.

Среди́ — (*a*) *in the middle of* (in a spatial or temporal sense)

Село́ затеря́лось *среди́* лесо́в.	The village was lost in the middle of the woods.
Она́ просну́лась *среди́* но́чи.	She woke up in the middle of the night.
Его́ огра́били *среди́* бе́ла дня́.	He was robbed in broad daylight.

(*b*) *among*

О́н выделя́лся умо́м *среди́* все́х.	He stood out among everyone for his intelligence.
Мы́ нашли́ письмо́ *среди́* ста́рых бума́г.	We found the letter among the old papers.
Да́ча стоя́ла *среди́* дере́вьев.	The dacha stood among the trees.

9. Supply the most appropriate genitive preposition from the following list: **ввиду́, вме́сто, вне́, вро́де, путём, ра́ди, све́рх**

   1. О́н э́того доби́лся _____ больши́х уси́лий.
   2. О́н поменя́л рабо́ту _____ семьи́.
   3. Ему́ предложи́ли зарпла́ту_____ его́ ожида́ний.
   4. Мы́ реши́ли заказа́ть ры́бу _____ мя́са.
   5. _____ вспы́шки холе́ры в э́той стране́ мы́ не пое́хали туда́.
   6. Его́ спосо́бности к языка́м _____ спо́ра.
   7. О́н купи́л костю́м _____ моего́.

10. Supply the most appropriate genitive preposition from the following list: **вблизи́, вдо́ль, внутри́, вну́трь, во́зле, вокру́г, впереди́, ме́жду, напро́тив, пове́рх, посреди́, сза́ди, среди́**

  1. Óн живёт в до́ме _____ са́мого вокза́ла.
  2. Они́ путеше́ствовали _____ све́та.
  3. Мы́ шли́ _____ бе́рега, собира́я раку́шки.
  4. И́х до́м нахо́дится _____ мо́ря.
  5. Óн заглянýл _____ шкафа́.
  6. Соба́ка бежа́ла _____ хозя́ина.
  7. Мы́ не́ были _____ э́того музе́я, его́ закры́ли на ремо́нт.
  8. _____ домо́в ду́л си́льный ве́тер.
  9. _____ руба́шки, о́н наде́л ку́ртку.
 10. Она́ сиде́ла _____ него́ и массажи́ровала ему́ пле́чи.
 11. _____ рове́сников, о́н выделя́лся больши́м ро́стом.
 12. _____ па́рка, в са́мом его́ це́нтре, бы́л фонта́н.
 13. Ка́к ра́з _____ на́шего до́ма была́ це́рковь.

PREPOSITIONS GOVERNING THE PREPOSITIONAL OR LOCATIVE CASE

The following preposition is followed only by the prepositional case.

> при

При — (a) *under/during (the reign of)*, *in the time of*

Санкт-Петербу́рг бы́л постро́ен *при* Петре́ Пе́рвом.	*St. Petersburg was built during the reign of Peter the First.*
Проце́сс демократиза́ции в Росси́и начался́ *при* Горбачёве.	*The process of democratization in Russia began under Gorbachev.*

(b) *affiliated with*, *attached to* (*Note:* In this use the preposition **при** indicates that something is closely connected with, or is administered by, an institution. In this meaning the preposition itself may not be translated.)

Она́ обе́дает в столо́вой *при* университе́те.	*She has lunch at the university cafeteria.*
При заво́де е́сть я́сли.	*The factory has a day care center.*
При до́ме е́сть небольшо́й огоро́д.	*The house has a small vegetable garden on the grounds.*

(c) *in the presence of*

Мы́ не говори́м об э́том *при* де́тях.	*We don't talk about that in front of the children.*
Э́ти докуме́нты на́до подписа́ть *при* свиде́телях.	*These documents must be signed in the presence of witnesses.*

(d) *given*, *with* indicating a certain condition or property

При жела́нии о́н мо́г бы всего́ доби́ться.	*Given the desire, he could accomplish anything.*
При таки́х тала́нтах о́н непреме́нно найдёт хоро́шую рабо́ту.	*With such talent, he will surely find a good job.*

The following prepositions govern the prepositional case when used in the meanings indicated.

```
в
на
о
по
```

В — (*a*) *in, at* indicating position or location (*Note:* The preposition **в** governs the accusative case when motion or directionality is expressed or implied.)

Они́ живу́т *в* дере́вне.	*They live in the country.*
Мы́ бы́ли *в* теа́тре.	*We were at the theater.*

(*b*) *in* certain articles of clothing, i.e., indicating what someone is/was wearing

Я́ бу́ду *в* джи́нсах и кроссо́вках.	*I'll be in jeans and tennis shoes.*
Она́ была́ *в* бе́лом сви́тере.	*She was wearing a white sweater.*

(*c*) *in* certain periods of time, i.e., indicating the time when an event occurred, when the unit of time is a month, semester, year, century, various life periods, and ages.

Она́ родила́сь *в* ма́рте.	*She was born in March.*
Они́ поже́нятся *в* бу́дущем году́.	*They will get married next year.*
Она́ умерла́ *в* девятна́дцатом ве́ке.	*She died in the nineteenth century.*
В мо́лодости она́ мечта́ла ста́ть балери́ной.	*In her youth she dreamed of becoming a ballerina.*

(*d*) *at* half past the hour, when telling time (*Note:* This is an exception to the rule that, when telling time, the preposition **в** is used with the accusative case; see above.)

Она́ встаёт *в* полови́не седьмо́го.	*She gets up at half past seven.*

(*e*) indicates the distance *at* which something is located from another point (expressed by the preposition **от** + genitive case.)

Метро́ нахо́дится *в* киломе́тре от на́шего до́ма.	*The metro is located a kilometer from our house.*
О́н жи́л *в* пяти́ мину́тах ходьбы́ от на́с.	*He lived a five-minute walk from us.*

Verbs Governing the Preposition В + Prepositional Case

A number of verbs govern the preposition **в** and the prepositional case. Some of the most commonly used among these verbs are given below.

нужда́ться *в* — *to be in need of*

О́н нужда́ется *в* на́шей по́мощи.	*He needs our help.*

обвиня́ть *в* — *to accuse (someone) of*

Его́ не ра́з обвиня́ли *в* кра́же.	*More than once he's been accused of theft.*

отка́зывать *в* — *to refuse, deny (someone) something*

    Она́ отка́зывала на́м *в* **про́сьбах.**   *She has refused our requests.*

подозрева́ть *в* — *to suspect (someone) of*

    Его́ подозрева́ют *в* **преступле́нии.**   *He is suspected of a crime.*

разбира́ться *в* — *to be proficient in, have an understanding of*

    Она́ пло́хо разбира́ется *в* **му́зыке.**   *She doesn't understand music.*

сомнева́ться *в* — *to doubt*

    Я́ не сомнева́юсь *в* **её и́скренности.**   *I don't doubt her sincerity.*

убежда́ть(ся) *в* — *to convince/be convinced of*

    Мы́ убежда́ли его́ *в* **пра́вде.**   *We tried to convince him of the truth.*

уверя́ть *в* — *to assure of*

    О́н уверя́л её *в* **свое́й ве́рности.**   *He tried to assure her of his faithfulness.*

уча́ствовать *в* — *to participate in*

    Она́ уча́ствует *в* **конце́рте.**   *She is participating in the concert.*

На — (*a*) *on* the surface of a physical object, i.e., indicating the position or location where something or someone is found (*Note:* The preposition **на** governs the accusative case when motion or direction *to* a place is expressed.)

Кни́ги стоя́т *на* **по́лке.**	*The books are (standing) on the shelf.*
Журна́лы лежа́т *на* **столе́.**	*The magazines are (lying) on the table.*
Мы́ сиде́ли *на* **дива́не.**	*We sat on the sofa.*

    (*b*) *in*, *at*, *on* indicating location in a place that typically has an activity or event associated with it. Since learning the particular types of nouns that must be used with the preposition **на** typically presents some difficulty for the student, a special section is devoted to this problem.

Nouns Requiring the Preposition На to Express Location

    The preposition **на**, not the preposition **в**, must be used with a number of nouns to express location. Many of the nouns which require **на** denote places that involve an open area, and/or one where people tend to gather for various activities, e.g., **на де́тской площа́дке** *on the playground*, **на ко́ртах** *on the tennis courts*. Some of these nouns in combination with **на** refer to buildings, but the reference may also be to the surrounding grounds, e.g., **на вокза́ле** *at the railroad station (i.e., the terminal building, along with the tracks and platforms outside)*. Other nouns may not seem to fit this general description and must simply be memorized. Below are some commonly used nouns that require **на**, grouped into a few broad categories.

Places Associated with Activities of Students and Teachers

заня́тие	*university class*	*на* **заня́тии**
ка́федра	*department (university)*	*на* **ка́федре**

ку́рс	course	на ку́рсе
ле́кция	lecture	на ле́кции
пра́ктика	practical training	на пра́ктике
семина́р	seminar	на семина́ре
уро́к	lesson	на уро́ке
факульте́т	faculty, department	на факульте́те
экза́мен	examination	на экза́мене

Places for Social Gatherings, Relaxation, and Various Types of Entertainment

бале́т	ballet	на бале́те
ве́чер	party (formal)	на ве́чере
вечери́нка	evening get-together	на вечери́нке
вы́ставка	exhibition	на вы́ставке
да́ча	summer cottage	на да́че
конце́рт	concert	на конце́рте
ко́рты	(tennis) courts	на ко́ртах
куро́рт	resort	на куро́рте
ку́хня	kitchen	на ку́хне
ма́тч	sporting match	на ма́тче
о́пера	opera	на о́пере
пье́са	play	на пье́се
приём	reception	на приёме
сва́дьба	wedding	на сва́дьбе
спекта́кль	performance	на спекта́кле
стадио́н	stadium	на стадио́не

Note: The nouns **бале́т**, **о́пера**, **пье́са**, **спекта́кль** occur with the preposition **на** when reference is made to attendance at an event: **Вчера́ мы́ бы́ли** *на* **бале́те** *Yesterday we were at the ballet*. These same nouns, however, may occur with the preposition **в** when reference is made to an artist's participation in a particular performance, or to the content of the ballet, opera, etc.: *В* **э́том бале́те танцева́л Бары́шников** *Baryshnikov danced in this ballet*, *В* **э́том бале́те прекра́сная му́зыка** *There is wonderful music in this ballet*.

Places Associated with the Conduct of Work, Trade and Types of Meetings

база́р	market, bazaar	на база́ре
би́ржа	stock exchange	на би́рже
вокза́л	railway station	на вокза́ле
заво́д	factory	на заво́де
заседа́ние	meeting (of key personnel)	на заседа́нии
конфере́нция	conference	на конфере́нции
по́чта	post office	на по́чте
предприя́тие	enterprise	на предприя́тии
рабо́та	work	на рабо́те
ры́нок	market	на ры́нке
собра́ние	meeting	на собра́нии
ста́нция	station	на ста́нции
съе́зд	congress	на съе́зде
фа́брика	factory	на фа́брике
фе́рма	farm	на фе́рме
я́рмарка	fair	на я́рмарке

Geographic Places

(i) *Points of the Compass*

восто́к	*east*	*на* **восто́ке**
за́пад	*west*	*на* **за́паде**
се́вер	*north*	*на* **се́вере**
юг	*south*	*на* **ю́ге**

(ii) *Natural Formations*

бе́рег	*shore*	*на* **берегу́**
лу́г	*meadow*	*на* **лугу́**
мо́ре	*sea*	*на* **мо́ре**
о́зеро	*lake*	*на* **о́зере**
океа́н	*ocean*	*на* **океа́не**
о́стров	*island*	*на* **о́строве**
пля́ж	*beach*	*на* **пля́же**
побере́жье	*coast*	*на* **побере́жье**
полуо́стров	*peninsula*	*на* **полуо́строве**
равни́на	*plain*	*на* **равни́не**
река́	*river*	*на* **реке́**

Note: The nouns denoting bodies of water occur with the preposition **на** when the intended meaning is location "on the surface" or "on the shores of": **Мы́ провели́ де́нь** *на* **о́зере, купа́лись, загора́ли на пля́же** *We spent the day at the lake, we swam, sunbathed on the beach.* However, the same nouns may occur with the preposition **в** when the intended meaning is location "beneath the surface": *В* **э́том о́зере о́чень чи́стая вода́** *The water in this lake is very pure.*

(iii) *Place Names (of specific islands, lakes, mountain ranges, peninsulas, etc.)*

Аля́ска	*Alaska*	*на* **Аля́ске**
Байка́л	*(lake) Baikal*	*на* **Байка́ле**
Балка́ны	*the Balkans*	*на* **Балка́нах**
Бли́жний Восто́к	*Middle East*	*на* **Бли́жнем Восто́ке**
Да́льний Восто́к	*Far East*	*на* **Да́льнем Восто́ке**
Гава́йи	*Hawaii*	*на* **Гава́йях**
		на **Гава́йских острава́х**
Кавка́з	*Caucasus*	*на* **Кавка́зе**
Ку́ба	*Cuba*	*на* **Ку́бе**
Украи́на	*Ukraine*	*на* **Украи́не**
Ура́л	*Urals*	*на* **Ура́ле**

(iv) *Cityscape: streets, roads, squares, etc.*

бульва́р	*avenue, boulevard*	*на* **бульва́ре**
дво́р	*yard*	*на* **дворе́**
доро́га	*road*	*на* **доро́ге**
мо́ст	*bridge*	*на* **мосту́**
окра́ина	*outskirts*	*на* **окра́ине**
пло́щадь	*square*	*на* **пло́щади**

проспе́кт	avenue	на проспе́кте
стоя́нка	parking lot	на стоя́нке
у́гол	(street) corner	на углу́
у́лица	street	на у́лице

Note: A few nouns in the group above may occur with the preposition **в**, but the resulting phrase will have a different meaning, e.g., **у́гол:** *на* **углу́** *on the corner (of the street)/ в* **углу́** *in the corner (of something)* and **дво́р:** *на* **дворе́** *outside/в* **дворе́** *in a yard (enclosed by a fence or surrounded by buildings).*

Conditions of Nature, Weather

во́здух	air	на све́жем/откры́том во́здухе
		in the fresh/open air
восхо́д (со́лнца)	sunrise	на восхо́де со́лнца
зака́т	sunset	на зака́те
моро́з	frost, intense cold	на моро́зе
рассве́т	dawn	на рассве́те
со́лнце	sun	на со́лнце

    (*c*) used with nouns denoting vehicles and other forms of transportation to indicate the means by which one travels. This construction is synonymous with the use of the instrumental case of the noun to express "the means of travel" (see Chapter 2, page 60).

Мы́ е́хали на рабо́ту *на* **авто́бусе.**	*We went to work by bus.*
До́чка лю́бит е́здить *на* **велосипе́де.**	*The daughter likes to ride her bicycle.*
Они́ прие́хали к на́м *на* **трамва́е.**	*They came to our place by tram.*

Note: The preposition **в** is used with nouns denoting types of transportation when reference is made to an activity that takes place inside the vehicle, e.g., **Она́ сиде́ла и чита́ла** *в* **авто́бусе** *She sat and read in the bus.*

    (*d*) indicates time when with "weeks"

На **про́шлой неде́ле она́ была́ больна́.**	*Last week she was sick.*
На **э́той неде́ле о́н идёт к врачу́.**	*This week he is going to the doctor.*
На **бу́дущей неде́ле мы́ е́дем в о́тпуск.**	*Next week we are going on vacation.*

Verbs Followed by the Preposition Ha + Prepositional Case

    A few common verbs are followed by the preposition **на** and the prepositional case.

жени́ться *на — to marry (of men)*

    Бори́с жени́лся *на* **Та́не.**   *Boris married Tanya.*

игра́ть *на — to play (instrument)*

    Са́ша хорошо́ игра́ет **на гита́ре.**   *Sasha plays the guitar well.*

ката́ться *на — to go for a ride on*

    Ле́на ката́ется *на* **велосипе́де.**   *Lena is out riding her bicycle.*

наста́ивать *на — to insist on*

> **О́н наста́ивает** *на* **то́чности.**   *He insists on accuracy.*

осно́вываться *на — to be based on*

> **Э́ти вы́воды осно́вываются** *на* **фа́ктах.**   *These conclusions are based on facts.*

О (Об, Обо) — *about, concerning* (*Note:* The preposition **о** + prepositional case is synonymous with the colloquial preposition **про** + accusative. It is written **об** when the following noun begins with the vowels **а, э, и, о,** or **у**: *об* **А́нне** *about Anna, об* **э́том** *about that, об* **Ива́не** *about Ivan, об* **окне́** *about the window, об* **уро́ке** *about the lesson.* The form **обо** occurs only with pronoun objects in the expressions *обо* **мне́** *about me, обо* **всём** *about everything, обо* **все́х** *about everyone.*)

> **Мы́ ду́маем** *о* **де́тях.**   *We think about the children.*
> **О́н ча́сто говори́т** *о* **рабо́те.**   *He often talks about work.*
> **Она́ мечта́ет** *о* **любви́.**   *She dreams about love.*

По — *after, on, upon* (*Note:* The preposition **по** + prepositional case is characteristic of formal, written Russian and is used primarily with deverbal nouns.)

> *По* **оконча́нии университе́та,**   *Upon graduating from the university,*
>   **о́н реши́л, что пора́ жени́ться.**   *he decided it was time to get married.*
> *По* **прие́зде домо́й она́**   *Upon her arrival home, she called her*
>   **позвони́ла му́жу.**   *husband.*

11. Supply the most appropriate preposition followed in these sentences by the prepositional case: **при, в, на, о, по**

1. Она́ была́ _____ ле́кции _____ Кита́е.
2. _____ де́тстве о́н игра́л _____ балала́йке.
3. _____ капитали́зме це́ны зави́сят от спро́са и предложе́ния.
4. _____ оконча́нии шко́лы о́н поступи́л на вое́нную слу́жбу.
5. _____ жела́нии всего́ мо́жно доби́ться.
6. Ка́к меня́ узна́ть? Я́ бу́ду _____ джи́нсах и пуло́вере.
7. О́н е́здит _____ рабо́ту _____ метро́.
8. О́н роди́лся _____ ма́е.
9. Я́ ча́сто ду́маю _____ на́шей встре́че в Петербу́рге.
10. Го́сти сиде́ли _____ дива́не.
11. О́н жени́лся _____ во́зрасте тридцати́ ле́т.
12. Нельзя́ руга́ться _____ де́тях.
13. Институ́т нахо́дится _____ двадцати́ мину́тах езды́ отсю́да.
14. _____ заво́де е́сть де́тский ла́герь.
15. Америка́нские пиани́сты уча́ствовали _____ э́том ко́нкурсе.
16. Я́ пло́хо разбира́юсь _____ матема́тике.
17. _____ её красоте́ она́ могла́ бы ста́ть и манеке́нщицей.
18. Зде́сь зимо́й всё де́ти ката́ются _____ конька́х.
19. _____ про́шлой неде́ле мы́ бы́ли _____ Москве́.
20. Мы́ не сомнева́емся _____ его́ спосо́бностях.

PREPOSITIONS GOVERNING THE DATIVE CASE

The following prepositions are followed only by the dative case.

> благодаря́
> вопреки́
> к
> навстре́чу
> согла́сно

Благодаря́ — *thanks to* indicating cause of an action that usually has a desirable result

Они́ вы́жили то́лько *благодаря́* твое́й по́мощи.	*They survived only thanks to your help.*

Вопреки́ — *contrary to, despite*

Вопреки́ сове́ту врача́, о́н ещё ку́рит.	*Contrary to the advice of his doctor, he still smokes.*

К — (*a*) *towards, up to* a point (in a spatial sense)

Де́ти бегу́т *к* о́зеру.	*The children are running towards the lake.*
Маши́на подъе́хала *к* до́му.	*The car drove up to the house.*

(*b*) *towards, by* a point in time

Она́ пришла́ домо́й *к* ве́черу.	*She arrived home towards evening.*
Я́ зако́нчу докла́д *к* пя́тнице.	*I will finish the report by Friday.*
Мы́ придём домо́й *к* ча́су.	*We will be home by one o'clock.*

(*c*) to a person (*Note:* After a verb of motion, the preposition **к** + the dative case must be used when the destination is a person. The general sense is going *to someone's place, home, office,* etc. The translation may be going *to see* someone.)

Сего́дня мы́ идём *к* врачу́.	*Today we are going to the doctor's.*
Вчера́ мы е́здили *к* роди́телям.	*Yesterday we went to our parents'.*
Она́ зашла́ *к* подру́ге.	*She dropped by to see a friend.*

(*d*) after certain nouns to indicate feelings or attitude *toward* something or someone

дове́рие *к*	trust/faith in	У меня́ нет дове́рия *к* нему́.
		I have no faith in him.
интере́с *к*	interest in	У него́ большо́й интере́с *к* му́зыке.
		He has a strong interest in music.
любо́вь *к*	love for	О́н э́то сде́лал из любви́ *к* де́тям.
		He did it out of love for his children.
сла́бость *к*	weakness for	У меня́ сла́бость *к* шокола́ду.
		I have a weakness for chocolate.
стра́сть *к*	passion for	Она́ име́ет стра́сть *к* чте́нию.
		She has a passion for reading.
уваже́ние *к*	respect for	О́н пое́хал туда́ из уваже́ния *к* отцу́.
		He went there out of respect for his father.

(*e*) with noun objects denoting certain emotions

к **сожале́нию**	*unfortunately*
к **сча́стью**	*fortunately*
к **моему́ удивле́нию**	*to my surprise*

Verbs Followed by the Preposition K + Dative Case

A number of verbs govern the preposition **к** and the dative case. Several have the prefix **при-** and denote approach or attachment to something.

гото́виться *к — to prepare for*

> Студе́нты гото́вятся *к* экза́мену.   *The students are preparing for an examination.*

обраща́ться *к — to turn to*

> Когда́ ему́ нужны́ де́ньги, о́н   *When he needs money, he turns to*
> обраща́ется *к* отцу́.   *his father.*

относи́ться *к — to relate to*

> Э́тот профе́ссор хорошо́ отно́сится *к*   *This professor relates well to*
> студе́нтам.   *students.*

подходи́ть *к — to approach*

> По́езд подхо́дит *к* ста́нции.   *The train is approaching the station.*

приближа́ться *к — to approach, draw near to*

> Мы́ приближа́емся *к* Эрмита́жу.   *We are approaching the Hermitage.*

привыка́ть *к — to get used to, grow accustomed to*

> Она́ ещё привыка́ет *к* кли́мату.   *She is still getting used to the climate.*

прикле́ивать *к — to glue/paste to, affix to*

> О́н прикле́ивает ма́рки *к* конве́ртам.   *He is gluing the stamps onto the envelopes.*

прилипа́ть *к — to stick/adhere to (intransitive)*

> Иногда́ таре́лки прилипа́ют *к* столу́.   *Sometimes plates stick to the table.*

принадлежа́ть *к — to belong to, be a member of*

> О́н принадлежи́т *к* ша́хматному клу́бу.   *He belongs to the chess club.*

пришива́ть *к — to sew on*

> Она́ пришива́ет пу́говицу *к* руба́шке.   *She is sewing a button on the shirt.*

Навстре́чу *— towards, to meet*

> Я́ вы́шел *навстре́чу* гостя́м.   *I came out to meet the guests.*
> Я́ пошёл ему́ *навстре́чу.*   *I met him half-way* (figurative).

Согла́сно — *in accordance with*

    Мы́ поступи́ли *согла́сно* **реше́нию**   *We acted in accordance with the*
       комите́та.   *decision of the committee.*

The following preposition is followed by the dative case when used in the meanings indicated.

$$\boxed{\text{по}}$$

По — (*a*) *along*, *down* a line (*Note:* This use of **по** + dative is synonymous with the use of the instrumental case to express the route taken, cf. **Де́ти бежа́ли бе́регом.**)

    Де́ти бежа́ли *по* **бе́регу.**   *The children ran along the shore.*
    Мы́ шли́ *по* **у́лице Че́хова.**   *We walked down Chekhov Street.*

    (*b*) *round*, *throughout* indicating movement in various directions

    Чита́я ле́кцию, профе́ссор   *While lecturing, the professor*
       ходи́л *по* **ко́мнате.**   *walked round the room.*
    Но́вость бы́стро разнесла́сь *по*   *The news quickly spread throughout*
       всему́ го́роду.   *the whole city.*
    Они́ бе́гали *по* **всем магази́нам.**   *They ran round to all the stores.*

    (*c*) *on* the surface (*Note:* This meaning occurs with verbs meaning *to hit*, *strike*, *bang*, etc.)

    До́ждь стуча́л *по* **о́кнам.**   *The rain was pattering on the windows.*
    О́н тра́хнул кулако́м *по́* **столу.**   *He banged on the table with his fist.*
    О́н хло́пнул дру́га *по* **спине́.**   *He slapped his friend on the back.*

    (*d*) *according to*, *by*

    Поезда́ хо́дят то́чно *по* **расписа́нию.**   *The trains run precisely according to schedule.*
    О́н де́лает всё *по* **пра́вилам.**   *He does everything by the rules.*
    Кни́ги расста́влены *по* **те́мам.**   *The books are arranged by subject.*

    (*e*) *by* a certain means of communication

    Това́ры доста́вили *по* **желе́зной доро́ге.** *The goods were delivered by rail.*
    Они́ посла́ли посы́лку *по* **по́чте.**   *They sent the package by mail.*
    Мы́ говори́ли *по* **телефо́ну.**   *We spoke by telephone.*
    Она́ слы́шала но́вость *по* **ра́дио.**   *She heard the news over the radio.*

    (*f*) *in* (the field of), *on* (the subject of), *by* (= with respect to)

    О́н специали́ст *по* **компью́терам.**   *He is a specialist in computers.*
    О́н чита́л ле́кцию *по* **фина́нсам.**   *He gave a lecture on finance.*
    По **профе́ссии она́ бухга́лтер.**   *She is an accountant by profession.*
    О́н гре́к *по* **происхожде́нию.**   *He is Greek by descent.*

    (*g*) *on*, *in* indicating days and other time periods when an action recurs

    О́н посеща́ет ку́рсы води́телей *по* **сре́дам.** *He has driver education classes on Wednesdays.*
    Ба́нки закрыва́ют *по* **пра́здникам.**   *The banks are closed on holidays.*
    Она́ рабо́тает *по* **вечера́м.**   *She works in the evenings.*

(*h*) *one* (*thousand*, *million*) *each* indicating distribution of objects by ones (*Note:* With the numerals two, three and four, the preposition **по** takes the accusative case: **Они получи́ли** *по* **два/три я́блока** *They received two/three apples each*. With other numerals, the dative or the accusative may be used).

Они́ получи́ли *по* **одному́ я́блоку.**	They received one apple each.
Она́ дала́ де́тям *по* **биле́ту.**	She gave the children one ticket each.
Ма́льчикам да́ли *по* **ты́сяче рубле́й.**	The boys were given one thousand rubles each.

(*i*) *for*, *out of*, *due to* indicating the cause of an action

По **како́й причи́не?**	For what reason?
Он э́то сде́лал *по* **глу́пости.**	He did it out of stupidity.
Он ра́но вы́шел на пе́нсию *по* **боле́зни.**	He retired early due to illness.
Она́ сде́лала оши́бку *по* **нео́пытности.**	She made the mistake out of inexperience.

12. Supply the most appropriate dative preposition: **благодаря́**, **вопреки́**, **к**, **навстре́чу**, **по**, **согла́сно**

1. Ру́ки прилипа́ют _____ кра́ске.
2. Нам да́ли _____ одному́ жето́ну.
3. Вчера́ в институ́те была́ ле́кция _____ марке́тингу.
4. Он прие́хал сюда́ неда́вно и ещё с трудо́м привыка́ет _____ э́той культу́ре.
5. _____ ва́шей подде́ржке, мы доби́лись на́шей це́ли.
6. _____ предупрежде́ниям, он реши́л пое́хать в э́ту страну́.
7. У неё сла́бость _____ сла́достям.
8. _____ постановле́нию президе́нта ограни́чилась прода́жа спи́рта.
9. Соба́ка побежа́ла нам _____ .
10. Он ча́сто бе́гает _____ э́тому па́рку.
11. За́втра мы идём _____ на́шим друзья́м.
12. Ма́льчик разби́л ва́зу _____ неосторо́жности.
13. Ле́том молоды́е па́ры лю́бят гуля́ть _____ на́бережной.

PREPOSITIONS GOVERNING THE INSTRUMENTAL CASE

The following prepositions are followed only by the instrumental case.

```
над
пе́ред
```

Над — (*a*) *over*, *above*

Ла́мпа виси́т *над* **столо́м.**	The lamp is hanging over the table.
Самолёт лете́л *над* **облака́ми.**	The airplane flew above the clouds.

(*b*) used figuratively after certain verbs:

ду́мать *над*	think over	**Мне на́до поду́мать** *над* **э́тим.**	
		I need to think this over.	
издева́ться *над*	to tease	**Де́ти издева́лись** *над* **то́лстым ма́льчиком.**	
		The children teased the fat boy.	

работать *над*	*to work on*	**Она́ рабо́тает** *над* **докла́дом.**
		She is working on a report.
смея́ться *над*	*to laugh at*	**Все́ смея́лись** *над* **его́ нело́вкостью.**
		Everyone laughed at his clumsiness.

Пе́ред — (*a*) *in front of, before* in a spatial sense

Авто́бус стои́т *пе́ред* **музе́ем.**	*The bus is parked in front of the museum.*
Она́ стоя́ла *пе́ред* **зе́ркалом.**	*She stood in front of the mirror.*
О́н предста́л *пе́ред* **судо́м.**	*He appeared before the court.*

(*b*) *before* in a temporal sense (*Note:* In contrast to the preposition **до** + genitive case which may also denote time *before*, **пе́ред** + instrumental usually denotes time *immediately or shortly before.*)

Она́ всегда́ чита́ет *пе́ред* **сно́м.**	*She always reads before going to bed.*
О́н погаси́л све́т *пе́ред* **ухо́дом.**	*He turned out the light before leaving.*
Мы́ вы́шли *пе́ред* **са́мым**	*We walked out just before the end*
концо́м спекта́кля.	*of the performance.*

The following prepositions are followed by the instrumental case when used in the meanings indicated.

```
за
ме́жду
под
с
```

За — (*a*) *behind, beyond* when location is indicated (*Note:* When the preposition **за** follows a verb expressing motion or direction, this preposition governs the accusative case.)

| *За* **на́шим до́мом** — **ле́с.** | *Behind our house are woods.* |
| *За* **ле́сом** — **доро́га.** | *Beyond the woods is a road.* |

(*b*) *during, at, over*

| *За* **за́втраком па́па чита́ет газе́ту.** | *During breakfast Dad reads the newspaper.* |
| *За* **обе́дом мы́ бу́дем говори́ть обо всём.** | *At lunch we'll talk about everything.* |

(*c*) after a verb of motion to indicate the object that is the goal of the motion

| **О́н пошёл в библиоте́ку** *за* **кни́гой.** | *He went to the library for a book.* |
| **Она́ побежа́ла в магази́н** *за* **хле́бом.** | *She ran to the store for bread.* |

Verbs Followed by the Preposition За + Instrumental Case

A few common verbs are followed by the preposition **за** + instrumental.

наблюда́ть *за — to keep an eye on, observe*

Врачи́ наблюда́ют *за* **новорождёнными.**	*The doctors are observing the newborn babies.*

сле́довать *за* — *to follow*

Тури́сты сле́дуют *за* **ги́дом.**	*The tourists are following the guide.*

следи́ть *за* — *to keep up with*; *to look after*

Он следи́т *за* **теку́щими собы́тиями.**	*He keeps up with current events.*
Ба́бушка следи́т *за* **свои́м здоро́вьем.**	*Grandma looks after her health.*

Ме́жду — *between, among* (*Note:* Though a few idiomatic expressions show an older use of **ме́жду** followed by the genitive case, in contemporary Russian the preposition **ме́жду** is normally followed by the instrumental case.)

Ме́жду **столо́м и стено́й стои́т ла́мпа.**	*Between the table and the wall is a lamp.*
Ме́жду **до́мом и ле́сом течёт ре́чка.**	*Between the house and the woods is a stream.*
Пу́сть э́то бу́дет *ме́жду* **на́ми.**	*Let's keep that (just) between us.*

Под — (*a*) *below, beneath, under* indicating literal or figurative location (*Note:* When motion or direction is expressed, the preposition **под** is followed by the accusative case.)

Гео́логов интересу́ет, что́ лежи́т *подо* **льдо́м Антаркти́ды.**	*Geologists are interested in what lies beneath the ice of the Antarctic.*
Он пря́чется *под* **крова́тью.**	*He is hiding under the bed.*
Она́ нашла́ серёжку *под* **поду́шкой.**	*She found an earring under the pillow.*
Он нахо́дится *под* **её влия́нием.**	*He is under her influence.*
Он пи́шет *под* **псевдони́мом.**	*He writes under a pseudonym.*
Го́род *под* **угро́зой сне́жной бу́ри.**	*The city is under threat of a snow storm.*

    (*b*) *with* indicating foods prepared with (i.e., under) a dressing or sauce

Она́ заказа́ла ры́бу *под* **бе́лым со́усом.**	*She ordered fish with white sauce.*

    (*c*) *in the environs of, near*

Он живёт *под* **Москво́й.**	*He lives in the environs of Moscow.*

С — (*a*) *with* in the sense of *together with, along with, accompanied by*

Она́ ча́сто говори́т *с* **подру́гой.**	*She often talks with her girlfriend.*
Он пошёл на вы́ставку *с* **жено́й.**	*He went to the exhibit with his wife.*
Мы́ пьём ча́й *с* **лимо́ном и са́харом.**	*We drink tea with lemon and sugar.*

    (*b*) indicates an accompanying characteristic or attribute of something or someone

Мы́ сня́ли кварти́ру *с* **балко́ном.**	*We rented a flat with a balcony.*
Э́то де́вушка *с* **краси́выми глаза́ми.**	*This is a girl with beautiful eyes.*
Он челове́к *с* **вы́сшим образова́нием.**	*He is a person with a higher education.*

    (*c*) indicates manner

Он говори́т по-ру́сски *с* **акце́нтом.**	*He speaks Russian with an accent.*
Я́ слу́шал *с* **больши́м интере́сом.**	*I listened with great interest.*
Мы́ *с* **удово́льствием при́няли и́х приглаше́ние.**	*We accepted their invitation with pleasure.*

(*d*) used in expressions of congratulations after the verb **поздравля́ть** *to congratulate*, which is often omitted

Поздравля́ем ва́с *с* **пра́здником!**	*Happy Holidays!*
С **Но́вым го́дом!**	*Happy New Year!*
Поздравля́ем *с* **рожде́нием ребёнка!**	*Congratulations on the birth of your child.*

Verbs Followed by the Preposition C + Instrumental Case

Several verbs are followed by the preposition **c** + instrumental case. Following is a partial list of these verbs.

встреча́ться *с — to meet with*

Она́ ча́сто встреча́ется *с* **дру́гом.**	*She often meets with her friend.*

знако́миться *с — to become acquainted with*

Ему́ легко́ знако́миться *с* **людьми́.**	*It is easy for him to meet people.*

расстава́ться *с — to part with, leave*

Жа́лко, что ты́ расстаёшься *с* **не́й.**	*It's a pity you are parting with her.*

сове́товаться *с — to consult with*

О́н ча́сто сове́туется *с* **ме́неджером.**	*He often consults with the manager.*

13. Fill in the blanks with the appropriate instrumental preposition: **над**, **пе́ред**, **за**, **ме́жду**, **под**, **с**

1. Она́ пошла́ на по́чту _____ ма́рками и конве́ртами.
2. На́до мы́ть ру́ки _____ едо́й.
3. О́н _____ ра́достью согласи́лся на́м помо́чь.
4. Доро́га идёт _____ ци́рком и университе́том.
5. Пти́цы лете́ли _____ ле́сом.
6. Зри́тели входи́ли в кинотеа́тр дру́г _____ дру́гом.
7. Вы́ в э́том де́ле игра́ете _____ огнём.
8. Такси́ останови́лось _____ на́шим до́мом.
9. Конце́рт бы́л в па́рке _____ откры́тым не́бом.
10. Мы́ ещё ду́маем _____ э́тим вопро́сом.
11. Де́ти жда́ли кани́кул _____ нетерпе́нием.
12. Ма́ма пошла́ в де́тский са́д _____ до́чкой.
13. _____ бе́регом реки́ и доро́гой шла́ у́зкая тропи́нка.
14. О́н челове́к высо́кого ро́ста и _____ бородо́й.
15. Она́ рабо́тает _____ статьёй.
16. Па́русная ло́дка шла́ _____ мосто́м.
17. Посети́тели рестора́на сле́довали _____ официа́нтом к столу́.
18. Она́ челове́к _____ твёрдыми убежде́ниями.

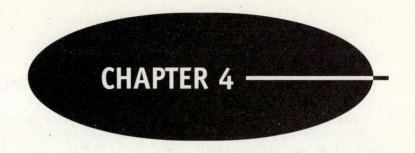

CHAPTER 4

Pronouns

A pronoun is a word used in place of a noun or another pronoun. Pronouns are classified according to their function.

PERSONAL PRONOUNS

Nominative Case

Person	Singular		Plural	
First	я	*I*	мы́	*we*
Second	ты́	*you*	вы́	*you*
Third	о́н	*he/it*	они́	*they*
	оно́	*it*		
	она́	*she/it*		

First Person

The first person (**я, мы́**) is used to indicate the speaker or writer.

Second Person

The second person (**ты́, вы́**) is used to indicate the addressee, i.e., the person or persons to whom one is speaking. The two second-person pronouns distinguish not only singular and plural, but may also convey different degrees of formality.

The singular pronoun **ты́** is the "familiar" *you*. Within a family the pronoun **ты́** is used by all family members, regardless of age. Outside the family context, the pronoun **ты́** is normally used between friends, professional peers of similar age, by an adult addressing a child, by a child to another child, or when addressing a pet.

The pronoun **вы́** must be used when addressing two or more people, but when addressing one person, it also serves as the "formal" *you*. The second-person **вы́** is used when addressing a person in authority (e.g., student to teacher, employee to supervisor) or a person higher in status or years (e.g., child to nonrelated adult). It is also customary for adults to use the formal form of address when they first meet. It is important that foreigners, in particular, address adult Russians using the formal **вы́**; use of the informal **ты́** should normally be initiated by the Russian. Generally speaking, **вы́** is the appropriate form of address to use when the speaker wishes to show respect. In letter writing, this pronoun is often capitalized.

The informal/formal difference signaled by the two second-person pronouns **ты/вы** in the singular is also conveyed by two different forms of the word for "Hello": informal **Здравствуй!** and formal (with added **-те**) **Здравствуйте!**

> **Здравствуй, Саша. Как** *ты* **живёшь?**
> *Hello, Sasha. How are you doing?*

> **Здравствуйте!** *Вы* **профессор Волков?**
> *Hello! Are you Professor Volkov?*

Third Person

The third person (**он**, **оно**, **она**, **они**) indicates the person(s) or object(s) spoken about. In the singular, a third-person pronoun must reflect the gender of its antecedent, i.e., the noun mentioned earlier to which the pronoun refers. When the antecedent is a male or female person, the pronouns **он** and **она** mean *he* and *she*, respectively. When these same pronouns refer to an inanimate object, they, like the neuter pronoun **оно**, are translated into English as *it*.

The third-person plural pronoun **они** *they* may refer both to people and things. The plural pronoun, like the plural form of the noun in Russian, does not distinguish between masculine, neuter, and feminine gender.

— **Где Борис?**	*Where is Boris?*
— *Он* **дома.**	*He is at home.*
— **Где карандаш?**	*Where is the pencil?*
— *Он* **на столе.**	*It is on the table.*
— **Где мама?**	*Where is Mom?*
— *Она* **на кухне.**	*She is in the kitchen.*
— **Где ручка?**	*Where is the pen?*
— *Она* **на полке.**	*It is on the shelf.*
— **Где брат и сестра?**	*Where are the brother and sister?*
— *Они* **в школе.**	*They are in school.*

1. Fill in the blanks with the correct personal pronouns in the nominative case.

1. — Мама, _____ не знаешь, где моя тетрадь?
   — Да, знаю. _____ тут на столе.
2. — Здравствуйте! _____ профессор Смирнов?
   — Да, _____ Смирнов.
3. — Я дома и Лена тоже.
   — Что _____ делаете?
   — _____ слушаем музыку.
4. — Где мама и папа?
   — _____ на работе.
5. — Мам, где мои новые джинсы?
   — _____ лежат на стуле.
6. — Лена, посмотри на новое кольцо.
   — Ой, _____ такое красивое!
7. — Знаешь, Сергей провёл целый семестр в Америке.
   — Интересно. _____ наверно говорит хорошо по-английски.

Accusative Case

Person	Singular		Plural	
First	меня́	me	на́с	us
Second	тебя́	you	ва́с	you
Third	его́ (на него́)	him/it	и́х (на ни́х)	them
	его́ (на него́)	it		
	её (на неё)	her/it		

Note: In the masculine and neuter third-person accusative pronoun **его́**, the consonant **г** is pronounced [v], e.g., **его́** is pronounced [yivó]. The preposition **на** is only one of several prepositions that may take the accusative case.

The accusative case of the personal pronouns are used when they occur as the direct object of the verb or as the object of a preposition which governs the accusative case. When the third-person pronouns **о́н, оно́, она́** are the object of a preposition, they must occur in the accusative case with an initial **н**, as shown in the table above. The third-person pronouns take this initial **н** not only in the accusative case after a preposition, but after most prepositions governing any of the cases (except the nominative).

The accusative case of the personal pronouns can be illustrated with the verb **зва́ть** *to call* and the construction used in Russian to ask and give someone's name. The question **Ка́к зову́т . . .?** literally means *How do they call . . .?* and the person referred to is grammatically the direct object of the verb in the accusative case. So, *Меня́* **зову́т Джи́м** literally means "Me they call Jim," but in English is translated as *My name is Jim.*

Note: The direct object pronoun in this construction occurs before the verb, whereas the direct object noun follows the verb. This is due to a general principle of Russian word order according to which "old information" (i.e., previously mentioned or present in the context) normally precedes "new information" (i.e., newly introduced into the discourse). For example, the direct object pronoun in the second sentence below is "old information," since its antecedent is mentioned in the previous sentence: **Э́то мо́й бра́т**. *Его́* **зову́т Серёжа** *This is my brother. His name is Seryozha.*

— Ка́к *тебя́* зову́т?　　　　　　　　　*What is your name?*
— *Меня́* зову́т Са́ша. А *тебя́*?　　　　　*My name is Sasha. And yours?*
— Ле́на.　　　　　　　　　　　　　　　*Lena.*

— Ка́к *ва́с* зову́т?　　　　　　　　　　*What is your name?*
— *Меня́* зову́т Никола́й. А *ва́с*?　　　　*My name is Nikolaj. And yours?*
— Татья́на.　　　　　　　　　　　　　*Tatyana.*
— О́чень прия́тно.　　　　　　　　　　*Pleased to meet you.*

— Ка́к зову́т *ва́шего бра́та*?　　　　　　*What is your brother's name?*
— *Его́* зову́т Па́вел.　　　　　　　　　*His name is Pavel.*

— Ка́к зову́т *ва́шу сестру́*?　　　　　　*What is your sister's name?*
— *Её* зову́т Та́ня.　　　　　　　　　　*Her name is Tanya.*

— Ка́к зову́т *ва́ших друзе́й*?　　　　　　*What are the names of your friends?*
— *И́х* зову́т Ди́ма и Пе́тя.　　　　　　　*Their names are Dima and Petya.*

Below are examples of the accusative case of the personal pronouns functioning as objects of a preposition.

— Óн хоро́ший дру́г.		*He is a good friend.*
— Да́, на *него́* мо́жно наде́яться.		*Yes, we can count on him.*

— Они́ хоро́шие друзья́.		*They are good friends.*
— Да́, на *ни́х* мо́жно наде́яться.		*Yes, we can count on them.*

— Э́тот слова́рь мне́ о́чень ну́жен.		*I really need this dictionary.*
— Спаси́бо за *него́.*		*Thank you for it.*
— Пожа́луйста.		*You're welcome.*

2. Fill in the blanks with personal pronouns in the accusative case.

1. — Бори́с пи́шет докла́д? — Да́, о́н _____ пи́шет.
2. — Сы́н пло́хо у́чится в шко́ле. Ма́ть беспоко́ится за _____ .
3. — Ири́на отве́тила на письмо́? — Да́, она́ на _____ отве́тила.
4. — Ты́ ви́дела ма́му? — Не́т, я _____ не ви́дела.
5. — Зна́ешь, Га́ля получи́ла при́з! — Да́, мы́ ра́ды за _____ .
6. — Вы́ зна́ете Све́ту и Бо́рю? — Да́, мы́ _____ зна́ем.
7. — Вы́ смотре́ли на мой рису́нки? — Да́, мы́ на _____ смотре́ли.
8. — Ка́к зову́т твоего́ бра́та? — _____ зову́т Ди́ма.
9. — Ка́к зову́т твою́ подру́гу? — _____ зову́т Ма́ша.
10. — Э́та кни́га мне́ о́чень нужна́. Большо́е спаси́бо за _____ .
11. — Учи́тель за́дал вопро́с, но учени́к не мо́г отве́тить на _____ .
12. — Мы́ ви́дели на́ших друзе́й, но они́ не ви́дели _____ .
13. — Я́ говори́л по-ру́сски, но _____ не понима́ли.
14. — Ми́ша, мы́ вчера́ ви́дели _____ , когда́ ты́ шёл домо́й.
15. — Мы́ вы́играли лотере́ю! — Ка́к здо́рово! Я́ ра́д за _____ .

Genitive Case

Person	Singular		Plural	
First	меня́	*me*	на́с	*us*
Second	тебя́	*you*	ва́с	*you*
Third	его́ (у него́)	*him/it*	и́х (у ни́х)	*them*
	его́ (у него́)	*it*		
	её (у неё)	*her/it*		

Note: The third-person personal pronouns in the genitive case **его́, её, и́х** also serve as possessive pronouns with the meaning *his, her, their.* When used as possessives, these forms do not have the initial **н** which is added to the object forms after most prepositions. Compare the genitive case object in the first sentence with the possessive pronoun in the second: **У него́ е́сть сестра́** *He has a sister* (literally "By him is a sister"), but **У его́ сестры́ краси́вые глаза́** *His sister has pretty eyes* (literally "By his sister [are] pretty eyes").

The personal pronouns in the genitive case are identical in form to the accusative case. The genitive case of the personal pronouns is used after verbs that govern the genitive (e.g., **боя́ться** *to be afraid of*, **избега́ть** *to avoid*) and after prepositions that govern the genitive case (e.g., **у** *by*, **для** *for the benefit of*, **от** *from*).

Я́ давно́ тебя́ не ви́дел. Ты́ что́, избега́ешь *меня́*?
I haven't seen you for a long time. What are you doing, avoiding me?

Ты́ мне́ та́к помо́г, хочу́ купи́ть для *тебя́* пода́рок.
You helped me so much, I want to buy a present for you.

О́н тако́й зло́бный челове́к. Де́ти *его́* боя́тся.
He is such a mean person. The children are afraid of him.

О́н ре́дко пи́шет, но то́лько сего́дня я́ получи́л от *него́* письмо́.
He rarely writes, but just today I received a letter from him.

Она́ зло́бная же́нщина. Мы́ *её* избега́ем.
She is a mean woman. We avoid her.

Она́ на́м о́чень нужна́, без *неё* про́сто нельзя́ обойти́сь.
She is really important to us, it's simply impossible to manage without her.

Мы́ купи́ли но́вые ди́ски. У *на́с* больша́я колле́кция ди́сков.
We bought new compact disks. We have a big collection of CDs.

Они́ зде́сь бы́ли го́д наза́д, но́ с те́х по́р мы́ не слы́шали от *ни́х*.
They were here a year ago, but since then we haven't heard from them.

3. Supply the genitive case form of the underlined personal pronoun.

1. <u>Я́</u> иду́ в университе́т. У _____ заня́тия.
2. Я слы́шал, <u>ты́</u> сего́дня бы́л в институ́те. У _____ что́, экза́мен бы́л?
3. <u>О́н</u> о́чень стро́гий учи́тель, ученики́ _____ боя́тся.
4. <u>О́н</u> бы́л на рабо́те. У _____ бы́ло собра́ние.
5. <u>Она́</u> давно́ не писа́ла, ни одного́ письма́ от _____ мы́ не получи́ли.
6. <u>Мы́</u> идём в университе́т. У _____ сего́дня ле́кция.
7. Когда́ <u>вы</u> та́к кричи́те на дете́й, они́ _____ боя́тся.
8. Заче́м <u>они́</u> купи́ли ещё ру́чки, у _____ уже́ мно́го ру́чек.

Prepositional Case

Person	Singular		Plural	
First	**обо мне́**	*about me*	**о на́с**	*about us*
Second	**о тебе́**	*about you*	**о ва́с**	*about you*
Third	**о нём**	*about him/it*	**о ни́х**	*about them*
	о нём	*about it*		
	о не́й	*about her/it*		

The prepositional case of the personal pronouns is used only after prepositions that govern the prepositional case (e.g., **в** *in*, **на** *on*, **о/об/обо** *about*).

— **Во́т институ́т фи́зики.** — Here is the physics institute.
— **В *нём* у́чится моя́ сестра́.** — My sister studies in it.

— **Во́т но́вая шко́ла би́знеса.** — Here is the new school of business.
— **В *не́й* гото́вятся ме́неджеры.** — Managers are trained in it.

— **Ты́ ду́мал о Бори́се?** — Were you thinking about Boris?
— **Да́, я ду́мал о *нём*.** — Yes, I was thinking about him.

— **Ты́ писа́ла об Ири́не?** — Did you write about Irina?
— **Да́, я писа́ла о *не́й*.** — Yes, I wrote about her.

| — Вы́ беспоко́итесь об экза́менах? | Are you anxious about the exams? |
| — Не́т, мы́ не беспоко́имся о *ни́х*. | No, we're not anxious about them. |

— А, вот и ты́!	Oh, here you are!
— Мы́ ка́к ра́з спра́шивали о *тебе́*.	We were just asking about you.
— Обо *мне́*?	About me?
— Да́, о *тебе́*.	Yes, about you.

4. Supply the prepositional case form of the underlined pronoun.

1. О́н неда́вно зде́сь. Я́ ма́ло зна́ю о _____ .
2. Я́ неда́вно прие́хал. Вы́ наве́рно не слы́шали обо _____ .
3. Она́ отли́чная студе́нтка. О _____ говори́л на́ш профе́ссор.
4. Вы́ зде́сь но́вый, и о _____ ма́ло зна́ют.
5. Они́ побежда́ли в соревнова́ниях. Всё о _____ говоря́т.
6. Э́то ты́ вы́играл лотере́ю. О _____ говори́т ве́сь го́род!

5. Rewrite the following sentences, replacing the italicized noun phrases with the appropriate form of the personal pronouns.

1. Мы́ мно́го слы́шали о *но́вом преподава́теле*.
2. Де́ти говори́ли о *роди́телях*.
3. О́н ча́сто ду́мает о *жене́*.
4. Она́ не забы́ла о *дя́де*.
5. Они́ спра́шивали о *на́ших де́тях*.

Dative Case

Person	Singular		Plural	
First	мне́	to/for me	на́м	to/for us
Second	тебе́	to/for you	ва́м	to/for you
Third	ему́ (к нему́)	to/for him		
	ему́ (к нему́)	to/for it	и́м (к ни́м)	to/for them
	ей (к ней)	to/for her		

The dative forms of the personal pronouns are used when they are the indirect object of verbs, the object of verbs that govern the dative case (e.g., **звони́ть** *to call*, **помога́ть** *to help*, **меша́ть** *to bother*, *prevent*, **сове́товать** *to advise*), or the object of prepositions that govern the dative (e.g., **к** *to*, *toward*, **по** *along*).

— Ма́ма, что́ ты́ купи́ла *мне́*?	Mom, what did you buy for me?
— Я́ купи́ла *тебе́* игру́шку.	I bought a toy for you.
— Ты́ всё рассказа́ла па́пе?	Did you tell Dad everything?
— Да́, я *ему́* всё рассказа́ла.	Yes, I told him everything.
— Ты́ посла́л Све́те письмо́?	Did you send the letter to Sveta?
— Да́, я посла́л *ей* письмо́.	Yes, I sent her the letter.

— Вы́ помогли́ сосе́дям?	*Did you help the neighbors?*
— Да́, мы́ *им* помогли́.	*Yes, we helped them.*
— Де́ти *ва́м* меша́ют?	*Are the children bothering you?*
— Не́т, они́ *на́м* не меша́ют.	*No, they are not bothering us.*
— Ты́ звони́ла сестре́?	*Did you call your sister?*
— Да́, я *ей* звони́ла.	*Yes, I called her.*
— Ты́ е́здила к роди́телям?	*Did you go to (see) your parents?*
— Да́, я́ к *ни́м* е́здила.	*Yes, I went to (see) them.*
— А ты́ вчера́ ходи́л к сестре́?	*Did you go to your sister's yesterday?*
— Да́, я́ к *не́й* ходи́л.	*Yes, I went to her (place).*
— Куда́ ты́ идёшь?	*Where are you going?*
— К бра́ту, я́ к *нему́* давно́ не ходи́л.	*To my brother's, I haven't been to see him in a long time.*

6. Supply the dative case of the underlined personal pronoun.

1. <u>О́н</u> на́ш хоро́ший дру́г. Мы́ покупа́ем _____ пода́рок.
2. <u>Они́</u> до́лго не писа́ли. Я́ _____ позвоню́.
3. <u>Она́</u> проси́ла у на́с по́мощь, и мы́ _____ помогли́.
4. <u>Ты́</u> собира́ешь ма́рки, поэ́тому я́ да́м _____ э́ту краси́вую ма́рку.
5. <u>Я́</u> хоте́л пи́ть, и они́ да́ли _____ воды́.

7. Rewrite the following, replacing the italicized nouns with the appropriate forms of the dative personal pronouns.

1. Мы́ купи́ли *сы́ну* велосипе́д.
2. Она́ подари́ла *ма́ме* ша́рф.
3. О́н пошёл к *нача́льнику*.
4. Мы́ ча́сто ходи́ли в го́сти к *друзья́м*.
5. О́н придёт к *сестре́*.
6. Мы́ ча́сто ходи́ли по *Не́вскому Проспе́кту*.

Instrumental Case

Person	Singular		Plural	
First	**мно́й**	*with me*	**на́ми**	*with us*
Second	**тобо́й**	*with you*	**ва́ми**	*with you*
Third	**и́м (с ни́м)**	*with him/it*		
	и́м (с ни́м)	*with it*	**и́ми (с ни́ми)**	*with them*
	е́й (с не́й)	*with her*		

Note: The forms **мно́й**, **тобо́й**, **е́й** have the alternative forms **мно́ю**, **тобо́ю**, **е́ю** which may occur in poetic as well as in colloquial style.

Note: The meaning *with* given in the table above is appropriate for several uses of the instrumental case, including its most basic use as "instrument" of the action, as well as in combination with the preposition **с** in the meaning *along with, together with*. However, the instrumental case has several other uses following verbs and other prepositions where this meaning does not apply, as shown below.

The instrumental personal pronouns are used when they are the object of a verb which governs the instrumental case (e.g., **занима́ться** *to involve oneself with*, **увлека́ться** *to be fascinated with*, **любова́ться** *to admire*, **по́льзоваться** *to use*), an adjective that governs the instrumental (e.g., **дово́лен** *pleased with*, **недово́лен** *displeased with*), or the object of a preposition (e.g., **за** *behind*, **ме́жду** *between*, **над** *above*, **пе́ред** *in front of*, **под** *below*, **с** *with*), or a verb followed by a preposition which governs the instrumental case (e.g., **знако́миться с** *to become acquainted with*, **встреча́ться с** *to meet with*, **рабо́тать над** *to work on*, **следи́ть за** *to look after*).

The instrumental forms of the personal pronouns may occur after the preposition **с** in an idiomatic construction involving a plural subject. The following are common examples:

(Я́ и ты́)	Мы́ с *тобо́й*	*You (fam.) and I*
(Я́ и вы́)	Мы́ с *ва́ми*	*You (formal) and I*
(Я́ и о́н)	Мы́ с *ни́м*	*He and I*
(Я́ и она́)	Мы́ с *не́й*	*She and I*
(Я́ и они́)	Мы́ с *ни́ми*	*They and I*
(Вы́ и о́н)	Вы́ с *ни́м*	*You and he*
(Вы́ и она́)	Вы́ с *не́й*	*You and she*

Note: This instrumental case construction is also used when the subject consists of a personal pronoun and a noun, e.g., **Мы́ с жено́й** *My wife and I*, **Мы́ с друзья́ми** *My friends and I*, **Вы́ с бра́том** *You and your brother*, or when two nouns are conjoined, e.g., **Са́ша с Ната́шей** *Sasha and Natasha*.

— О́н увлека́ется спо́ртом?	*Is he taken with sports?*
— Да́, о́н *и́м* о́чень увлека́ется.	*Yes, he is really fascinated with them.*
— Она́ уже́ по́льзуется косме́тикой?	*Does she already use make-up?*
— Не́т, она́ пока́ *е́ю* не по́льзуется.	*No, she doesn't use it yet.*
— Каки́е краси́вые го́ры!	*What beautiful mountains!*
— Да́, я са́м ча́сто любу́юсь *и́ми*.	*Yes, I myself often admire them.*
— Ты́ давно́ встреча́ешься с Ми́шей?	*Have you been dating Misha long?*
— Да́, я с *ни́м* встреча́юсь уже́ го́д.	*Yes, I've been dating him for a year already.*
— Ты́ написа́л отли́чный докла́д!	*You wrote an excellent report!*
— Спаси́бо, я са́м дово́лен *и́м*.	*Thanks, I myself am pleased with it.*
— Вы́ зна́ете Ма́шу Воло́дину?	*Do you know Masha Volodina?*
— Да́, мы́ с *не́й* знако́мы.	*Yes, we are acquainted with her.*
— Зна́ешь, Пе́тя бы́л на ле́кции.	*You know, Petya went to the lecture.*
— Зна́ю, мы́ сиде́ли пря́мо за *ни́м*.	*I know, we sat right behind him.*

8. Supply the appropriate personal pronoun in the instrumental case.

1. Ты́ хорошо́ у́чишься. Мы́ о́чень дово́льны _____.
2. Я́ была́ в кинотеа́тре и передо _____ сиде́л Бо́ря Петро́в!
3. Мы́ ви́дели большо́е де́рево и реши́ли отдыха́ть под _____.
4. Мы́ шли́ по по́лю и вдру́г над _____ пролете́л самолёт.
5. Де́тям нельзя́ остава́ться одни́м. Кто́-то до́лжен следи́ть за _____.
6. Докла́д ещё не гото́в. На́до порабо́тать ещё немно́го над _____.
7. Ты́ зна́ешь Ле́ну Смирно́ву? Я́ вчера́ ходи́л с _____ в кино́.

8. Э́то хоро́ший уче́бник. Мы ＿＿＿＿＿＿＿＿＿ по́льзовались на ку́рсах.
9. В па́рке расту́т больши́е берёзы. Ме́жду ＿＿＿＿＿＿＿＿＿ стои́т скаме́йка.
10. Йра получи́ла плоху́ю отме́тку. Учи́тель недово́ден ＿＿＿＿＿＿＿＿＿ .

THE REFLEXIVE PERSONAL PRONOUN Себя́

The reflexive personal pronoun **себя́** *oneself* refers to the subject of the clause in which it is located. This pronoun occurs in five of the six cases, each indicating different ways the action of the subject is reflected back to it. Since this pronoun reflects the action of the subject, it can not *itself* occur as subject in the nominative case. The reflexive personal pronoun has the same form for all persons, i.e., it does not change for gender or number.

Nom.	＿＿
Acc./Gen.	себя́
Prep./Dat.	себе́
Instr.	собо́й

Accusative Case

Я смотре́л на *себя́* в зе́ркало.	*I looked at myself in the mirror.*
Ты представля́ешь *себя́* отцо́м?	*Do you imagine yourself as a father?*
Она́ счита́ет *себя́* актри́сой.	*She considers herself an actress.*
Вам на́до ве́рить в *себя́.*	*You must believe in yourself.*

Note: The direct object pronoun **себя́** gives reflexive meaning to transitive verbs that are not normally used as reflexives. True reflexive verbs, which typically involve a subject performing an action that directly affects himself, normally do not occur with direct object **себя́**, but instead are used intransitively with post-verbal **-ся**, e.g., **Она́ одева́ется** *She is dressing (herself)*, **Он мо́ется** *He is washing (himself)*. See "Verbs in -ся" in Chapter 7.

Genitive Case

Я посмотре́л вокру́г *себя́.*	*I looked around myself.*
Ты купи́л пода́рок для *себя́?*	*Did you buy a present for yourself?*
Он был вне́ *себя́* от гне́ва.	*He was beside himself with rage.*

Prepositional Case

Ты ду́маешь то́лько о *себе́.*	*You think only of yourself.*
Он всегда́ име́ет при *себе́* де́ньги.	*He always has money on him.*
Она́ уве́рена в *себе́.*	*She has confidence in herself.*

Dative Case

Я купи́л *себе́* кни́гу.	*I bought a book for myself.*
Ты о́чень тре́бователен к *себе́.*	*You are very demanding of yourself.*

Instrumental Case

Мы разложи́ли пе́ред *собо́й* пла́н го́рода.	*We spread the city map before us (ourselves).*
Он не мо́г владе́ть *собо́й.*	*He could not control himself.*
Она́ дово́льна *собо́й.*	*She is pleased with herself.*
Они́ спо́рили ме́жду *собо́й.*	*They argued among themselves.*

Idiomatic Uses of себя

Several verbs combine with a form of the reflexive personal pronoun in fixed expressions, where the reflexive meaning of **себя** is more abstract, or may not be felt at all.

бра́ть с собо́й — *to take along* (lit. *with oneself*)

    О́н всегда́ берёт с *собо́й* **портфе́ль.**   *He always takes his briefcase along.*

вести́ себя́ — *to behave* (*conduct oneself*)

    Ты́ ведёшь *себя́* **ка́к ребёнок.**   *You are behaving like a child.*

представля́ть себе́ — *to imagine* (*represent to oneself*)

    Ра́ньше о́н представля́л *себе́* **Аме́рику как ра́й.**   *Earlier he imagined America as paradise.*

чу́вствовать себя́ — *to feel*

    Я́ чу́вствую *себя́* **хорошо́.**   *I feel well.*

The pronoun **себя** is used in a number of other idiomatic expressions.

Я́ поду́мал про *себя́.*	*I thought to myself.*
Она́ о́чень хороша́ *собо́ю.*	*She is very good-looking.*
О́н вы́шел из *себя́.*	*He lost his temper.*
Ему́ ка́к-то не по *себе́.*	*He is somehow not himself.*
Э́то само́ *собо́й* **разуме́ется.**	*That goes without saying.*
Профе́ссор Орло́в у *себя́?*	*Is Professor Orlov in (his office)?*
Она́ пошла́ к *себе́* **домо́й.**	*She went home (to her own place).*

9. Supply the required form of the reflexive personal pronoun **себя́.**

   1. О́н тако́й эго́ист, о́н всегда́ ду́мает то́лько о _____ .
   2. Она́ провали́лась на экза́мене и о́чень недово́льна _____ .
   3. О́н уве́ренный в _____ челове́к, о́н всегда́ наде́ется на _____ .
   4. У него́ ро́вный хара́ктер, о́н никогда́ не выхо́дит из _____ .
   5. Я́ купи́л пода́рки не то́лько для жены́ и дете́й, но и для _____ .
   6. Она́ положи́ла пе́ред _____ меню́ и поду́мала, что́ заказа́ть на обе́д.
   7. О́н вошёл в ко́мнату и закры́л за _____ две́рь.
   8. О́н сде́ржанный челове́к, о́н ре́дко говори́т о _____ .
   9. Она́ скро́мная де́вушка, она́ не лю́бит привлека́ть к _____ внима́ние.
 10. У него́ хоро́шее чу́вство ю́мора, о́н мо́жет смея́ться и на́д _____ .
 11. Прочита́й письмо́ вслу́х, а не про _____ .
 12. Ма́льчик не ходи́л вчера́ в шко́лу, о́н пло́хо чу́вствовал _____ .
 13. Сы́н попроси́л па́пу: — Возьми́ меня́ с _____ .
 14. Мы́ пригласи́ли к _____ в го́сти но́вую колле́гу.
 15. Ма́ма так ра́да, что де́ти веду́т _____ хорошо́.

THE RECIPROCAL PRONOUN Дру́г дру́га

The reciprocal pronoun **дру́г дру́га** *each other* is comprised of two parts, the first of which is not declined, while the second part declines like an animate masculine noun (i.e., Acc. = Gen.). The declined form takes the case required by the governing verb, adjective, or preposition. When a preposition occurs, it is placed between undeclined **дру́г** and the declined form. Like the reflexive personal pronoun **себя́**, the reciprocal pronoun **дру́г дру́га** *each other* does not occur in the nominative case. The declension of the reciprocal pronoun is presented in the table below.

Nom.	————
Acc.	дру́г дру́га
	дру́г на дру́га
Gen.	дру́г дру́га
	дру́г у дру́га
Prep.	дру́г о дру́ге
Dat.	дру́г дру́гу
	дру́г к дру́гу
Instr.	дру́г дру́гом
	дру́г с дру́гом

Note: The pronoun **дру́г дру́га** adds reciprocal meaning to verbs that are not typically understood to express a reciprocal action. Verbs which do have an inherently reciprocal meaning, such as *embrace, kiss, meet,* etc., normally do not occur with the pronoun **дру́г дру́га**; instead, they incorporate the post-verbal particle **-ся**, e.g., **При встре́че, они́ всегда́ обнима́ются и целу́ются** *Upon meeting, they always embrace and kiss (each other).* On verbs with reciprocal meaning, see Chapter 7.

Accusative Case

Ми́ша и Та́ня лю́бят *дру́г дру́га.*   *Misha and Tanya love each other.*
Они́ полага́ются *дру́г на дру́а.*   *They rely on each other.*
Мы́ ве́рим *дру́г в дру́га.*   *We believe in each other.*

Genitive Case

Они́ боя́тся *дру́г дру́га.*   *They are afraid of each other.*
Мы́ ча́сто быва́ем *дру́г у дру́га.*   *We often visit each other.*
Они́ не мо́гут жи́ть *дру́г без дру́га.*   *They can't live without each other.*

Prepositional Case

Они́ ду́мают *дру́г о дру́ге.*   *They think about each other.*
Мы́ забо́тимся *дру́г о дру́ге.*   *We take care of each other.*

Dative Case

Они́ посыла́ют пи́сьма *дру́г дру́гу.*   *They send letters to each other.*
Они́ помога́ют *дру́г дру́гу.*   *They help each other.*
Они́ верны́ *дру́г дру́гу.*   *They are faithful to each other.*
Мы́ привыка́ем *дру́г к дру́гу.*   *We are getting used to each other.*

Instrumental Case

Они́ интересу́ются *дру́г дру́гом.*   *They are interested in each other.*
Мы́ ча́сто спо́рим *дру́г с дру́гом.*   *We often argue with each other.*
Они́ посмея́лись *дру́г над дру́гом.*   *They played a joke on each other.*

10. Supply the correct form of the reciprocal pronoun, with a preposition, if required.

    1. Э́ти де́вушки ча́сто говоря́т по телефо́ну _____ (with each other).
    2. Са́ша и Та́ня поздра́вили _____ (each other) с Но́вым го́дом.
    3. Они́ всегда́ покупа́ют пода́рки _____ (for each other).

4. Они́ не мо́гут обойти́сь _____ (without each other).
5. Они́ молодожёны, и ещё привыка́ют _____ (to each other).
6. Они́ хоро́шие друзья́, они́ всегда́ наде́ются _____ (on each other).
7. Нас критикова́ли, но мы́ заступа́лись _____ (for each other).
8. Му́ж и жена́ не всегда́ живу́т в ладу́, иногда́ они́ се́рдятся _____ (at each other).
9. Хотя́ они́ похо́жи по вне́шности, по хара́ктеру э́ти близнецы́ си́льно отлнча́ются _____ (from each other).
10. Когда́ мои́ сыновья́ бы́ли детьми́, они́ ча́сто спо́рили, но тепе́рь, ста́в взро́слыми, они́ хорошо́ отно́сятся _____ (toward each other).

INTERROGATIVE PRONOUNS: Кто́, Что́

Nom.	кто́	что́
Acc.	кого́	что́
Gen.	кого́	чего́
Prep.	о ко́м	о чём
Dat.	кому́	чему́
Instr.	ке́м	чём

The Pronoun Кто́

The pronoun **кто́** *who* requires its predicate to agree in the singular:

Кто́ идёт в кино́?   *Who is going to the movies?*
Кто́ говори́т по-ру́сски?   *Who speaks Russian?*

Кто́ requires its predicate to agree in the masculine gender:

Кто́ вы́шел?   *Who stepped out?*
Кто́ гото́в?   *Who is ready?*

Masculine agreement is required by **кто́** even in instances when reference is clearly made to females; for example, the subject of the phrase **вы́йти за́муж** *to get married* can only be a woman:

Кто́ из твои́х подру́г вы́шел за́муж?   *Who of your girlfriends got married?*
Кто́ гото́в вы́йти за́муж?   *Who is ready to get married?*

Кто́ *who* is used in Russian to refer to people, even in certain instances where native speakers of English would use the pronoun *what*:

Кто́ у ни́х роди́лся, ма́льчик?   *What did they have, a boy?*
Кто́ она́ по профе́ссии?   *What is she by profession?*
Ке́м о́н рабо́тает, инжене́ром?   *What does he work as, an engineer?*
Кто́ о́н по происхожде́нию, Шве́д?   *What is he by descent, a Swede?*

When asking about someone whose name s/he does not know, the speaker may ask the question **Кто́ э́то?** *Who is that?* The pronoun **кто́** also has a wider application than its English equivalent, in that it may be used to refer to animals as well as people.

— *Кто́* э́то?	*Who is that?*
— Э́то мо́й бра́т, Ми́ша.	*That's my brother, Misha.*
— **А** *кто́* э́то?	*And who is that?*
— Э́то моя́ ко́шка.	*That is my cat.*

When the speaker already knows someone's name, but wishes to learn more about the person's identity, the appropriate question is **Кто́ о́н?** *Who is he?* **Кто́ она́?** *Who is she?* Alternatively, one may ask **Кто́ о́н тако́й?** or **Кто́ тако́й** ... followed by the person's name (for a female **Кто́ она́ така́я?/Кто́ така́я** ...).

— Ребя́та, *кто́* э́то?	*Guys, who is that?*
— Э́то Мари́я Во́лкова.	*That's Maria Volkova.*
— *Кто́* она́ (**така́я**)?	*Who is she?*
— Она́ но́вая аспира́нтка.	*She is a new graduate student.*

— *Кто́* э́то?	*Who is that?*
— Э́то Васи́лий Аксёнов.	*That is Vasilij Aksyonov.*
— *Кто́ тако́й* Васи́лий Аксёнов?	*Who is Vasilij Aksyonov?*
— Аксёнов — э́то ру́сский писа́тель.	*Aksyonov is a Russian writer.*

The pronoun **кто́** occurs in both direct questions (*Кто́* **э́та де́вушка?** *Who is that girl?*) and indirect questions (**О́н меня́ спроси́л,** *кто́* **э́та де́вушка?** *He asked me who that girl was*). This pronoun may occur in any of the six Russian cases.

Кто́ сказа́л тебе́ об э́том?	*Who told you about this?*
Кого́ ты́ ви́дел на ле́кции?	*Whom did you see at the lecture?*
У *кого́* ты́ взя́л э́ту кни́гу?	*From whom did you get this book?*
О *ко́м* вы́ говори́те?	*Who are you talking about?*
Кому́ ты́ да́л мо́й а́дрес?	*To whom did you give my address?*
С *ке́м* она́ идёт в кино́?	*With whom is she going to the movie?*

11. Supply the correct form of the interrogative personal pronoun **кто́**.

1. Я́ не зна́ю, о _____ ты́ говори́шь.
2. Она́ меня́ спроси́ла, с _____ я́ встреча́юсь.
3. На _____ ты́ наде́ешься?
4. _____ вы́ там ви́дели?
5. Они́ на́с спроси́ли, _____ мы́ бои́мся.
6. _____ ты́ покупа́ешь пода́рки?
7. Учи́тель спроси́л, _____ в кла́ссе не́т.
8. _____ па́па недово́лен, мно́й, и́ли тобо́й?
9. За _____ ты́ беспоко́ишься, за сы́на?
10. Мы́ её спроси́ли, у _____ она́ была́.

The Pronoun Что́

The interrogative pronoun **что́** *what* requires its predicate to agree in the neuter gender and singular number.

| *Что́* случи́лось? | *What happened?* |
| *Что́* бы́ло на семина́ре? | *What went on at the seminar?* |

Что́ is used to ask about the identity of an inanimate object, an abstract notion, or about a verbal action. When asking about the identity of some object, the speaker normally asks **Что́ э́то?** *What is that?* or **Что́ э́то тако́е?** *What is that?* If the name of something is known, but more information is desired, one may ask **Что́ тако́е . . .** followed by the name of the thing in question.

— Что́ э́то?	*What is that?*
— Э́то диск-пле́йер.	*That is a CD player.*
— А *что́* э́то тако́е?	*And what is that?*
— Э́то компа́кт-ди́ск.	*That is a compact disk.*
— Что́ тако́е «хот-до́г»?	*What is a "hotdog"?*
— «Хот-до́г» — э́то соси́ска.	*A hotdog is a sausage.*

The interrogative pronoun **что́** may occur in any of the six cases, in both independent clauses (**Что́ э́то?** *What is that?*), as well as dependent clauses (**Я зна́ю,** *что́* э́то *I know what that is*).

Что́ с тобо́й?	*What is (the matter) with you?*
Что́ ты́ зна́ешь об э́том?	*What do you know about this?*
Чего́ вы́ бои́тесь?	*What are you afraid of?*
О *чём* ты́ говори́шь?	*What are you talking about?*
К *чему́* она́ гото́вится?	*What is she preparing for?*
Я́ зна́ю, с *ке́м* она́ знако́ма.	*I know with whom she is acquainted.*

12.   Supply the correct form of the interrogative pronoun **что́**.

1. Над _____ ты́ рабо́таешь?
2. На _____ он смо́трит?
3. Для _____ э́тот футля́р?
4. _____ вы́ об э́том ду́маете?
5. От _____ э́тот клю́ч?
6. Во _____ ты́ ве́ришь? В астроло́гию?
7. За _____ мы́ вы́пьем? За твоё здоро́вье!
8. _____ она́ бои́тся, экза́мена?
9. _____ ты́ пи́шешь, ру́чкой или карандашо́м?
10. С _____ ты́ пьёшь чай, с са́харом или с мёдом?

POSSESSIVE PRONOUNS

Russian has a possessive pronoun corresponding to each of the personal pronouns, and an interrogative possessive pronoun corresponding to the interrogative pronoun **кто́**.

кто́ *who?*	я́	ты́	о́н оно́	она́	мы́	вы́	они́
чей *whose?*	мо́й	тво́й	его́	её	на́ш	ва́ш	и́х

The Possessive Pronouns Чей? Мо́й, Тво́й, На́ш, Ва́ш

The interrogative possessive **чей** *whose* and the possessive pronouns **мо́й** *my/mine*, **тво́й** *your/yours*, **на́ш** *our/ours*, **ва́ш** *your/yours* must agree in gender, number and case with the noun they modify. The tables below give the complete declensions for these pronouns.

Case	Masculine,	Neuter	Feminine	Plural
Nom.	чей	чьё	чья	чьи
Acc.	чей/чьего	чьё	чью	чьи/чьих
Gen.	чьего		чьей	чьих
Prep.	о чьём		о чьей	о чьих
Dat.	чьему		чьей	чьим
Instr.	чьим		чьей	чьими

Note: In the declension of **чей**, and that of all the other possessive pronouns which change for agreement, when the noun modified is singular, masculine *inanimate*, the accusative case is identical to the nominative; when the noun modified is singular, masculine *animate*, the accusative case is identical to the genitive. The rule "inanimate accusative = nominative/animate accusative = genitive," which affects only masculine nouns and their modifiers in the singular, applies to all three genders in the plural.

Case	Masculine,	Neuter	Feminine	Plural
Nom.	мой	моё	моя	мои
Acc.	мой/моего	моё	мою	мои/моих
Gen.	моего		моей	моих
Prep.	о моём		о моей	о моих
Dat.	моему		моей	моим
Instr.	моим		моей	моими

Case	Masculine,	Neuter	Feminine	Plural
Nom.	наш	наше	наша	наши
Acc.	наш/нашего	наше	нашу	наши/наших
Gen.	нашего		нашей	наших
Prep.	о нашем		о нашей	о наших
Dat.	нашему		нашей	нашим
Instr.	нашим		нашей	нашими

Note: The declension of **твой** is identical to **мой**, and the declension of **ваш** is identical to **наш**.

— Чей э́то слова́рь, *твой*?
— Да́, э́то *мой* слова́рь.

Whose dictionary is this, yours?
Yes, this is my dictionary.

— Чья́ э́то кни́га, *твоя́*?
— Да́, *моя́*.

Whose book is this, yours?
Yes, mine.

— Чей чемода́н взя́л швейца́р?
— О́н взя́л *ваш* чемода́н.

Whose suitcase did the porter take?
He took your suitcase.

— Чьего́ ребёнка вы́ ви́дели?
— Мы́ ви́дели *вашего* ребёнка.

Whose child did you see?
We saw your child.

— Чью́ кни́гу вы́ чита́ете?	*Whose book are you reading?*
— Я́ чита́ю *ва́шу* кни́гу.	*I'm reading your book.*
— О чье́й подру́ге о́н спра́шивал?	*About whose girlfriend did he ask?*
— О *ва́шей* подру́ге.	*About yours.*
— Во́т *на́ш* сы́н и *на́ша* до́чь.	*Here is our son and our daughter.*
— Я́ уже́ знако́м с *ва́шим* сы́ном	*I'm already acquainted with your son*
и *ва́шей* до́черью.	*and your daughter.*
— Познако́мьтесь, э́то *на́ши* друзья́.	*I'd like you to meet our friends.*
— Мы́ с *ва́шими* друзья́ми уже́ знако́мы.	*We are already acquainted with your friends.*

13. Supply the appropriate pronoun **че́й, мо́й, тво́й, на́ш, ва́ш** in the required form.

1. Во́т идёт мо́й бра́т. Ты́ зна́ешь _____ бра́та?
2. Во́т на́ши сосе́ди. Вы́ знако́мы с _____ сосе́дями?
3. Ты́ неда́вно бы́л за грани́цей. Расскажи́ на́м о _____ пое́здке!
4. Вы́ мно́го сде́лали для на́с. Мы́ о́чень благада́рны за _____ по́мощь.
5. _____ э́то кни́га? Мо́жет бы́ть, э́то кни́га Ви́ктора?
6. Вы́ не зна́ете, _____ э́то письмо́? Э́то не Са́шино письмо́?
7. Во́н та́м стои́т моя́ сестра́. По-мо́ему, ты́ не знако́м с _____ сестро́й.
8. О́н расска́зывал мне́ о статья́х мно́гих а́второв. Но я́ не по́мню, о _____ статье́ он расска́зывал с бо́льшим интере́сом.
9. Я́ оста́вил ключи́ у кого́-то до́ма, но я забы́л в _____ до́ме э́то бы́ло.
10. Мы́ хоте́ли тебе́ позвони́ть, но мы́ не зна́ли но́мер _____ телефо́на.
11. У на́с в университе́те е́сть теа́тр. В _____ теа́тре быва́ют хоро́шие конце́рты.
12. В _____ ко́мнате по́лный беспоря́док. Тебе́ на́до её убра́ть.

The Possessive Pronouns Его́, Её, Их

The third-person possessive pronouns **его́** *his*, **её** *her/hers*, **и́х** *their/theirs* are invariable, that is, they do not change according to the gender, number, or case of the noun they qualify.

Во́т *его́* бра́т и *его́* сестра́.	*Here is his brother and his sister.*
Я́ зна́ю *его́* бра́та и *его́* сестру́.	*I know his brother and his sister.*
Я́ слы́шал о *его́* бра́те и о *его́* сестре́.	*I heard about his brother and sister.*
Мы́ знако́мы с *его́* роди́телями.	*We are acquainted with his parents.*
Во́т *её* ма́ма и *её* па́па.	*Here are her mom and dad.*
Мы́ уже́ ви́дели *её* ма́му и *её* па́пу.	*We already saw her mom and dad.*
И́х до́м ря́дом с на́шим.	*Their house is next to ours.*
Мы́ ча́сто быва́ем в *и́х* до́ме.	*We often visit in their house.*

The pronouns **его́, её,** and **и́х** never refer to the subject of the clause in which they occur; the noun or pronoun they refer to must be outside of their clause.

Ми́ша не́ сказа́л Анто́ну, но о́н сказа́л *его́* дру́гу.	*Misha didn't tell Anton, but he told his (Anton's) friend.*

Note: The third-person possessive pronouns are identical in form to the genitive case of the third-person personal pronouns **о́н** *he*, **она́** *she*, **они́** *they*. Unlike the personal pronouns, however, the third-person possessive pronouns never have an initial **н-** affixed when they follow a preposition; cf. **пода́рок для** *него́* (personal pronoun) *a gift for him* and **пода́рок для** *его́* **жены́** (possessive pronoun) *a gift for his wife.*

The Reflexive Possessive Pronoun Свой

Russian has a reflexive possessive pronoun **свой** *one's own*, which declines exactly like **мой** (and **твой**). Unlike **мой**, however, **свой** normally does not modify the nominative subject of the clause, but refers back to, and gets its meaning from, the subject.

Я́ урони́л *свой* **каранда́ш.**	*I dropped **my** pencil.*
Ты́ урони́л *свой* **каранда́ш.**	*You dropped **your** pencil.*
Она́ урони́ла *свой* **каранда́ш.**	*She dropped **her** pencil.*

In clauses with a subject in the first or second person, **свой** may be used as an *optional alternative* to the corresponding first- and second-person possessive pronouns **мой**, **твой**, **наш**, and **ваш**.

Я́ забы́л *мой/свой* **зо́нтик.**	*I forgot my umbrella.*
Ты́ забы́л *твой/свой* **зо́нтик.**	*You forgot your umbrella.*
Мы́ забы́ли *наш/свой* **зо́нтик.**	*We forgot our umbrella.*
Вы́ забы́ли *ваш/свой* **зо́нтик.**	*You forgot your umbrella.*

In clauses where the subject is a noun or a third-person pronoun, however, the reflexive **свой** is *obligatory* when the subject and possessor are the same. Replacing **свой** with one of the third-person possessive pronouns **его́**, **её**, and **и́х** changes the meaning of the sentence, such that the possessor is someone other than the subject.

Ми́ша ви́дел *свою́* **сестру́.**	*Misha saw his (own) sister.*
Ми́ша ви́дел *его́* **сестру́.**	*Misha saw his (someone else's) sister.*
Она́ звони́ла *своему́* **дру́гу.**	*She called her (own) friend.*
Она́ звони́ла *её* **дру́гу.**	*She called her (someone else's) friend.*
Они́ рассказа́ли о *свое́й* **пое́здке.**	*They told about their (own) trip.*
Они́ рассказа́ли об *и́х* **пое́здке.**	*They told about their (others') trip.*

Note: When the subject and the possessor are conjoined in a noun phrase, and therefore are both in the same case, **свой** is not allowed: **Óн и его́** [*свой*] **дру́г бы́ли у на́с** *He and his friend were at our place.*

The reflexive possessive **свой** can only be used when the possessor and subject are in the same clause. Thus, in a complex sentence where the possessor in the subordinate clause refers to the subject in the main clause, **свой** is not allowed, as indicated below by the asterisk *.

Пе́тя сказа́л, что *его́* **бра́т ушёл.**	*Pete said that his brother left.*
Пе́тя сказа́л, что *свой* ...	
Ле́на ду́мает, что *её* **подру́га больна́.**	*Lena thinks that her friend is sick.*
Ле́на ду́мает, что *своя́* ...	
Они́ говоря́т, что *и́х* **де́ти у́мные.**	*They say that their children are smart.*
Они́ говоря́т, что *свой* ...	

When **свой** does occur in a subordinate clause, it must refer back to the subject of that clause.

Бóря сказáл, что *егó* **дрýг**	*Borya said that his friend*
потеря́л *свою́* **кни́гу.**	*lost his book.*

Note that while the English translation of this sentence is ambiguous with regard to whether it was Borya's or his friend's book that was lost, use of **свой** in the Russian sentence eliminates any ambiguity: the book can only be understood to belong to the friend.

In impersonal sentences which have no overt subject, only **свой** can be used to express possession.

Вáжно знáть кóрни *своéй* **семьи́.**	*It is important to know the roots of one's family.*

Finally, as noted above, **свой** does not normally occur in the nominative case. However, in a few Russian proverbs, and in a small number of other idiomatic expressions, **свой** can be found in the nominative case.

Свóй **свояка́ ви́дит издалека́.**	*Birds of a feather flock together.*
Свóй **дурáк дорóже чужóго ýмника.**	*Blood is thicker than water.*
Своя́ **рубáшка бли́же к тéлу.**	*Charity begins at home.*
У нáс *своя́* **маши́на.**	*We have our own car.*
Óн бы́л сáм не *свóй.*	*He was not himself.*
Онá самá не *своя́.*	*She is not herself.*

14. Fill in the appropriate pronoun **егó, её, и́х,** or **свой** in the required form.

1. У Дáши оди́н брáт и однá сестрá. Онá чáсто говори́т о _____ (her) брáте и о _____ (her) сестрé. _____ (her) брáт и сестрá живýт далекó от дáши.
2. Пéтя пошёл в гóсти к _____ (his) дрýгу. _____ (his) дрýг живёт в цéнтре.
3. Кáтя лю́бит _____ (her) мýжа. Онá чáсто говори́т о _____ (her) мýже.
4. Рýсские лю́бят _____ (their) дáчи. _____ (their) дáчи — это возмóжность уедини́ться.
5. Лéна недáвно éздила в Пари́ж. Онá рассказáла всéм о _____ (her) поéздке.
6. Это дóчь Сергéя. _____ (his) дóчь приéхала вчерá из Москвы́. Сергéй óчень рáд ви́деть _____ (his) дóчь.
7. Петербýрг роднóй гóрод моегó дéдушки. Дéдушка хорошó пóмнит _____ (his) роднóй гóрод. _____ (his) гóрод нахóдится на рекé Невé. Óн мнóго знáет об истóрии _____ (his) роднóго гóрода.
8. У бáбушки óчень симпати́чная сосéдка. Бáбушка чáсто хóдит к _____ (her) сосéдке.
9. Мóй знакóмый пьёт, кýрит, и не занимáется спóртом. Óн плóхо забóтится о _____ (his) здорóвье.
10. Нáши друзья́ живýт хорошó. У ни́х ужé _____ (their own) маши́на.
11. У Свéты родилáсь дéвочка. Свéта лю́бит _____ (her) дéвочку. Онá дýмает, что _____ (her) дéвочка óчень ýмная и краси́вая.
12. Когдá кóнчился урóк, всé ученики́ взя́ли _____ (their) вéщи и ушли́ домóй.
13. _____ (her) друзья́ купи́ли дáчу. Онá рáда за _____ (her) друзéй.
14. Óчень вáжно знáть истóрию _____ (one's own) страны́. Ведь, это при́знак образóванного человéка.

DEMONSTRATIVE PRONOUNS

The Demonstrative Pronouns Э́тот and То́т

The demonstrative pronouns **э́тот** *this* (or *that*) and **то́т** *that* are used to point out a particular object or person. These pronouns are modifiers, and agree in gender, number, and case with the modified noun. The complete declensions of these pronouns are given in the tables below.

Case	Masculine,	Neuter	Feminine	Plural
Nom.	э́тот	э́то	э́та	э́ти
Acc.	э́тот/э́того	э́то	э́ту	э́ти/э́тих
Gen.	э́того		э́той	э́тих
Prep.	об э́том		э́той	э́тих
Dat.	э́тому		э́той	э́тим
Instr.	э́тим		э́той	э́тими

Case	Masculine,	Neuter	Feminine	Plural
Nom.	то́т	то́	та́	те́
Acc.	то́т/того́	то́	ту́	те́/те́х
Gen.	того́		то́й	те́х
Prep.	о то́м		то́й	те́х
Dat.	тому́		то́й	те́м
Instr.	те́м		то́й	те́ми

Note: Observe in the tables above that the stem-final **т** in both pronouns changes from hard to soft in the masculine and neuter of the instrumental singular, and throughout the plural.

Of the two pronouns **э́тот** and **то́т**, the former is more general in meaning. For example, the singular forms of **э́тот** may be translated into English as either *this* or *that*, the plural forms as either *these* or *those*, depending on the context.

Э́тот рестора́н дорого́й.	*This/that restaurant is expensive.*
Э́то окно́ бы́ло откры́то.	*This/that window was open.*
Э́та кни́га интере́сная.	*This/that book is interesting.*
Э́ти ключи́ не мой.	*These/those keys are not mine.*

The forms of **то́т** are normally translated as *that* (and plural *those*) and are frequently used to contrast with forms of **э́тот**. When contrasted in this way, **э́тот** may be understood to refer to that which is nearer to the speaker, and **то́т** to that which is more remote from the speaker.

Э́тот га́лстук мо́дный, а *то́т* не́т.	*This tie is stylish, but that one isn't.*
Э́та кни́га моя́, а *та́* его́.	*This book is mine, and that one his.*
Я возьму́ *э́ту* блу́зку, а не *ту́.*	*I'll take this blouse, but not that one.*
Я куплю́ *э́ти* джи́нсы, а не *те́.*	*I'll buy these jeans, but not those.*
О́н живёт в *э́том* до́ме, а она́ живёт в *то́м* до́ме.	*He lives in this house, and she lives in that house.*
Я дово́лен *э́тим* результа́том, но не *те́м.*	*I'm satisfied with this result, but not with that one.*

The pronoun **тóт** may also be used when no explicit contrast is made with a form of **э́тот**, although such a contrast is implied. Note that in the following examples, **тóт** conveys the sense of a more remote *that*, in contrast to an implied, nearer *this*.

На́ш до́м на *то́й* стороне́ у́лицы.	Our house is on that side of the street.
О́н рабо́тает во́н та́м, в *то́м* большо́м но́вом зда́нии.	He works over there, in that big new building.

There are several other important uses of **тóт**, all of which imply a contrast of some kind. Below are some common expressions with this important pronoun.

(a) **не тóт** *the wrong (one)*

Negated forms of **тóт** (**не тóт, не тó, не тá, не тé**) may express the idea, "the wrong one," in contrast to an implied "right one."

Я́ набра́л *не то́т* но́мер.	I dialed the wrong telephone number.
Официа́нт принёс на́м *не то́* блю́до.	The waiter brought us the wrong dish.
О́н взя́л с по́лки *не ту́* кни́гу.	He took the wrong book off the shelf.
На́м да́ли *не те́* биле́ты.	We were given the wrong tickets.

(b) **тóт же (са́мый)** *the (very) same*

Forms of **тóт** followed by the emphatic particle **же (са́мый)** express the idea "the (very) same." The pronoun **тóт (же)** may occur in the main clause of a complex sentence as a modifier of the antecedent to the relative pronoun **кото́рый** *that/who* in the subordinate clause, e.g., **тóт же ..., кото́рый** *the same ... that*

О́н наде́л *то́т же са́мый* костю́м, в кото́ром о́н бы́л на ве́чере.	He put on the very same suit that he was wearing at the party.
Мы́ жи́ли в *то́й же* гости́нице, в кото́рой и вы́ жи́ли.	We lived in the same hotel that you lived in.
О́н говори́л с *те́м же* челове́ком, с кото́рым о́н говори́л вчера́.	He spoke with the same person with whom he spoke yesterday.

(c) **и тóт и друго́й** *both*

Forms of **тóт** conjoined with forms of **друго́й** *other* have the meaning *both*, i.e., *that one and the other*. This phrase is used when the two entities referred to differ in some way. When the two things differ in gender or number, the neuter form **и тó и друго́е** must be used, as in the first example below.

— Что́ ты́ возьмёшь с собо́й, пла́щ или ку́ртку?	What will you take with you, a raincoat or a jacket?
— Я́ возьму́ *и то́ и друго́е*.	I'll take both.
— Како́й га́лстук тебе́ нра́вится, э́тот кра́сный, и́ли то́т зелёный?	Which tie do you like, this red one or that green one?
— Мне́ нра́вятся *и то́т и друго́й*.	I like both.
— Каки́е брю́ки мне́ купи́ть, чёрные в поло́ску, и́ли се́рые в кле́тку?	Which pants should I buy, the black striped or the grey plaid?
— Купи́ *и те́ и други́е*.	Buy both.

15. Supply the required form of the pronouns **э́тот** and **то́т**.

1. Она́ жила́ не на _____ у́лице, а на _____ у́лице.
2. На́ша гру́ппа чита́ла _____ расска́зы, а _____ мы́ не чита́ли.
3. Иностра́нцы живу́т в _____ общежи́тии, а ру́сские живу́т в _____.
4. Мы́ заказа́ли _____ блю́до, а не _____.
5. _____ кварти́ра больша́я, а _____ кварти́ра ещё бо́льше.
6. Мы́ посла́ли приглаше́ния _____ лю́дям, а _____ не посла́ли.
7. _____ си́ний костю́м мне́ нра́вится, а _____ се́рый мне́ не нра́вится.
8. Я́ знако́м с _____ студе́нтами, а с _____ я́ не знако́м.
9. Мы́ да́ли наш зака́з _____ официа́нту, а не _____.
10. Да́й мне́, пожа́луйста, _____ меню́, а держи́ _____ себе́.

16. Supply the correct form of the pronoun **то́т**.

1. Я́ не могу́ откры́ть две́рь. Мо́жет бы́ть, у меня́ не _____ клю́ч.
2. Э́то _____ же кроссо́вки, в кото́рых я вы́играл соревнова́ние.
3. Она́ не могла́ реши́ть, каки́е ту́фли купи́ть. Поэ́тому, она́ купи́ла и _____ и други́е.
4. Э́ти брю́ки мне́ не подхо́дят. Мне́ ка́жется, э́то не _____ разме́р.
5. На э́то интервью́ я наде́л _____ же га́лстук, кото́рый мне́ всегда́ приноси́л уда́чу.
6. Э́то _____ же маши́на, кото́рая была́ у меня́ 5 ле́т наза́д.

The Indeclinable Pronoun Э́то

The "Identifying" Э́то

Russian has an invariable pronoun **э́то** *this/that is, these/those are*, which may be used both to question and give the identify of an object or person (*Что́ э́то? Э́то часы́. What's that? That's a watch*). It is identical to the neuter singular form of the demonstrative pronoun **э́тот**, but unlike the latter, "identifying" **э́то** does not modify the following noun; rather, it serves as the sentence subject, and the following noun is the predicate in the nominative case.

— Что́ та́м лежи́т?	*What is that lying there?*
— Э́то пе́йджер.	*That is a pager.*
— Кто́ э́ти молоды́е лю́ди?	*Who are those young people?*
— Э́то мои́ студе́нты.	*Those are my students.*

In sentences with identifying **э́то**, an accompanying verb agrees with the predicate nominative, not with **э́то**.

— Кто́ приходи́л?	*Who came by?*
— Э́то бы́л мо́й бра́т.	*That was my brother.*
— Кто́ звони́л?	*Who called?*
— Э́то была́ моя́ жена́.	*That was my wife.*
— Кто́ бы́л у ва́с ве́чером?	*Who was at your place last night?*
— Э́то бы́ли мои́ друзья́.	*Those were my friends.*

The "Characterizing" **Э́то**

The pronoun **э́то** can also be used as the subject of a sentence which refers to, and characterizes, a *situation* described in a preceding statement.

— **Ка́тя Воло́дина вы́шла за́муж.**	*Katya Volodina got married.*
— *Э́то* **интере́сно.**	*That's interesting.*
— **Са́ша обеща́л мне́ помо́чь.**	*Sasha promised to help me.*
— *Э́то* **хорошо́.**	*That's good.*

When a verb occurs with **э́то** in this characterizing function, it agrees in the neuter singular past tense with **э́то**, the subject; if a predicate noun follows, it is normally (if abstract) in the instrumental case.

В про́шлом году́ у Та́ни родила́сь де́вочка.	*Last year Tanya gave birth to a girl.*
Э́то **бы́ло большо́й ра́достью для на́с.**	*This was a great joy for us.*
Вчера́ зашла́ ко мне́ Ви́ка. *Э́то* **бы́ло**	*Yesterday Vika dropped by my place.*
по́лной неожи́данностью для меня́.	*This was a complete surprise for me.*

---

17. Determine whether the sentence involves "identifying" or "characterizing" **э́то**, and choose the correct past-tense form of the verb **бы́ть**: **бы́л, бы́ло, была́, бы́ли.**

   1. Вчера́ на у́лице ла́яла кака́я-то жёлтая соба́ка. По-мо́ему, э́то _____ англи́йский лабрадо́р.
   2. Она́ пришла́ на рабо́ту в ми́ни-ю́бке. Э́то _____ для все́х шо́ком.
   3. Мы́ расста́лись. О́н мне́ позвони́л го́д спустя́. Э́то _____ для меня́ большо́й неожи́данностью.
   4. — Кто́ заходи́л? — Э́то _____ подру́га до́чери.
   5. Мы́ уви́дели впереди́ све́т. Э́то _____ огни́ го́рода.
   6. Когда́ ты́ позвони́л, э́то _____ тако́й сюрпри́з.

The Demonstrative Pronoun Тако́й

The demonstrative pronoun **тако́й** *such a/like that* declines like a hard-stem adjective (see page 141, Chapter 5), and in the plural is subject to Spelling Rule 1 (page 11). The declension of **тако́й** is given in the following table.

	Masculine,	*Neuter*	*Feminine*	*Plural*
Nom.	**тако́й**	**тако́е**	**така́я**	**таки́е**
Acc.	**тако́й/тако́го**	**тако́е**	**таку́ю**	**таки́е/таки́х**
Gen.	**тако́го**		**тако́й**	**таки́х**
Prep.	**о тако́м**		**о тако́й**	**о таки́х**
Dat.	**тако́му**		**тако́й**	**таки́м**
Instr.	**таки́м**		**тако́й**	**таки́ми**

In the examples below, **такóй** points to a property or quality of the noun it modifies.

Э́то спокóйная, лáсковая собáка. Мнé нужнá *такáя* **собáка.**
This is a calm, affectionate dog. I need a dog like that.
Ми́ша надёжный, вéрный дрýг. *Такóго* **дрýга трýдно найти́.**
Misha is a reliable, loyal friend. Such a friend is difficult to find.
Óн извéстный и уважáемый профéссор. Я́ бы хотéл учи́ться у *такóго* **профéссора.**
He is a famous and respected professor. I would like to study with such a professor.
Óн высокомéрный и догмати́чный. Трýдно рабóтать с *таки́м* **человéком.**
He is arrogant and dogmatic. It's difficult to work with such a man.

When an adjective follows, the pronoun **такóй** functions as an intensifier, and may be rendered into English as *such a* or *so*.

Онá *такáя* **ýмная дéвочка.**	*She is such a clever little girl.*
Онá *такáя* **ми́лая.**	*She is so nice.*
Óн *такóй* **серьёзный человéк.**	*He is such a serious person.*
Э́ти цветы́ *таки́е* **краси́вые.**	*These flowers are so beautiful.*

The demonstrative pronoun **такóй** can modify the noun antecedent of the relative pronoun **какóй**, e.g., **Óн купи́л** *такóй* (же) **костю́м,** *какóй* **и я́ купи́л** *He bought the (same) kind of suit that I bought.* This construction is illustrated in greater detail in the section on relative pronouns.

18. Supply the correct form of the pronoun **такóй**.

1. Едá в э́том ресторáне _____ вкýсная.
2. Экзáмен бы́л _____ трýдный, что мнóгие студéнты провали́лись на нём.
3. У ни́х большáя, свéтлая кварти́ра. Мы́ хоти́м снять _____ кварти́ру.
4. И́х дóм похóж на дворéц. Мы́ никогдá не ви́дели _____ большóго дóма.
5. Э́то не моя́ сýмка. Э́та сýмка бéлая, мáленькая. Моя́ сýмка не _____. Онá чёрная, большáя, и чéрез плечó.
6. Вéтер бы́л _____ си́льный, что мы́ не могли́ идти́.

DETERMINATIVE PRONOUNS

The Emphatic Pronoun Сáм

The pronoun **сáм** adds emphasis to a particular noun or pronoun in the sentence. It corresponds to the English "intensive" pronoun ending in -*self*, as in "He *himself* is to blame," "She said so *herself*," "We blame only *ourselves*." The Russian emphatic pronoun must agree in gender, number, and case with the noun it modifies. This pronoun declines like the demonstrative pronoun **э́тот**; note, however, that except for the nominative and accusative (inanimate) plural, the pronoun **сáм** is *stressed on the ending* throughout.

The declension of the emphatic pronoun **са́м** is presented in the following table.

	Masculine,	*Neuter*	*Feminine*	*Plural*
Nom.	са́м	само́	сама́	са́ми
Acc.	са́м/самого́	само́	саму́	са́ми/сами́х
Gen.	самого́		само́й	сами́х
Prep.	о само́м		о само́й	о сами́х
Dat.	самому́		само́й	сами́м
Instr.	сами́м		само́й	сами́ми

The pronoun **са́м** may refer to a noun functioning as subject or object. When it refers to an animate subject, it emphasizes that the subject performs the action independently, with no help from others.

> **Е́й никто́ не помога́ет, она́ де́лает всё** *сама́.*
> *No one helps her; she does everything herself.*

> **Не объясня́й ему́. Пу́сть о́н** *са́м* **поймёт.**
> *Don't explain it to him. Let him figure it out himself.*

Similarly, when the subject is inanimate, the pronoun **са́м** may be used to emphasize that the action of the subject-referent occurs by itself, without the assistance of a human agent.

> **Никто́ не откры́л две́рь, она́ откры́лась** *сама́.*
> *No one opened the door; it opened by itself.*

> **Я́ не вы́ключил компью́тер, о́н** *са́м* **отключи́лся.**
> *I didn't turn off the computer; it shut off by itself.*

The pronoun **са́м** may also be used to emphasize that a particular person, and not some other, is involved in the action.

> **Она́** *сама́* **винова́та.**   *She herself is to blame.*
> **За э́то предложе́ние вы́ступил**   *The president himself came out*
> ** *са́м* президе́нт.**   *   in favor of this proposal.*

The pronoun **са́м** is also used to lend emphasis to the reflexive pronoun **себя́**.

> **Я́ виню́ то́лько** *самого́* **себя́.**   *I blame only myself.*
> **Вчера́ во сне́ ты́ разгова́ривал**   *Last night in your sleep you were*
> ** *са́м* с собо́й.**   *   talking to yourself.*

19. Supply the required form of the emphatic pronoun **са́м.**

1. Ма́льчик у́меет всё де́лать _____ .
2. Окно́ _____ откры́лось.
3. Мы́ _____ удиви́лись э́тому.
4. На́м на́до ви́деть её _____, а не её подру́гу.
5. У него́ _____ не́т вре́мени.

6. Я не чита́л _____ статьи́, но я слы́шал о не́й.
7. У на́с не́т _____ докуме́нтов; у на́с е́сть то́лько ксероко́пии.
8. Она́ передала́ докла́д _____ нача́льнику.
9. Скажи́ об э́том не её сестре́, а е́й _____.
10. Они́ встре́тились не на у́лице, а в _____ теа́тре.
11. Мы́ не говори́ли с _____ дека́ном, мы́ говори́ли с его́ ассисте́нтом.
12. Они́ живу́т не под Москво́й, а в _____ Москве́.
13. На́ша кварти́ра нахо́дится не в при́городе, а в _____ це́нтре го́рода.
14. Ва́м на́до спроси́ть об э́том не на́с, а _____ себя́.

The Pronoun Са́мый

The pronoun **са́мый** *the very* expresses a precise point in space or time. It is sometimes easy to confuse this pronoun with the emphatic pronoun **са́м**, as shown in the following pair of sentences.

Она́ живёт в *са́мом* **це́нтре го́рода.**   *She lives in the very center of the city.*
Она́ живёт в *само́м* **це́нтре го́рода.**   *She lives in the city center itself.*

Although similar in form and meaning, the pronouns **са́мый** and **са́м** differ in their declensions: **са́м**, as discussed above, declines like a pronoun with the stress falling largely on the endings, while **са́мый** declines like a hard-stem adjective (see Chapter 5, page 141) with *the stress on the stem*. The following sentences further illustrate this use of **са́мый**.

Она́ живёт на *са́мом* **конце́ у́лицы.**   *She lives at the very end of the street.*
Дава́йте начнём с *са́мого* **нача́ла.**   *Let's start from the very beginning.*
Э́тот авто́бус идёт до *са́мой* **Я́лты.**   *This bus goes all the way to Yalta.*
Мя́ч попа́л ему́ в *са́мый* **гла́з.**   *The ball hit him right in the eye.*
Проходи́те в *са́мый* **коне́ц трамва́я.**   *Go to the very back of the trolley.*

The pronoun **са́мый**, as discussed above in the section on demonstrative pronouns, may be used after the pronoun **то́т (же)**, e.g., **то́т (же) са́мый, то́ са́мое, та́ са́мая**, in the meaning *the (very) same*: **Э́то то́т са́мый челове́к, кото́рый бы́л зде́сь ра́ньше** *This is the same person who was here before.*

The pronoun **са́мый** is also used to form the compound superlative of adjectives. This use of **са́мый** will be presented in Chapter 5.

20. Supply the required form of the pronoun **са́мый**.

1. Сне́г шёл с _____ утра́.
2. Не на́до жда́ть до _____ зимы́, на́до загота́вливать дрова́ ле́том.
3. О́н стоя́л на _____ краю́ про́пасти.
4. Мы́ дошли́ до _____ конца́ доро́ги.
5. Они́ шли́ по _____ краю́ обры́ва.

The Pronoun Ве́сь

The English translation of the pronoun **ве́сь** differs, depending on whether it is used as a modifier or whether it stands alone as a subject or object. When it is used to modify a noun, in the singular it normally translates as *the whole* (**ве́сь го́род** *the whole city*), while in the plural it means *all* (**все́ студе́нты** *all (the) students*). When it stands alone as a subject or object of the sentence, the neuter singular form means *everything* (**Всё решено́** *Everything is decided*; **О́н ду́мает, что всё зна́ет** *He thinks he knows everything*), while the plural means *everyone/everybody*. Note that unlike the English

pronoun *everyone* which is grammatically singular, Russian **всé** is plural and requires plural agreement:
Всé знáют об э́том *Everyone knows about this.*

The declension of the pronoun **вéсь** is given in the following table.

	Masculine,	Neuter	Feminine	Plural
Nom.	вéсь	всё	вся	всé
Acc.	вéсь/всегó	всё	всю	всé/всéх
Gen.		всегó	всéй	всé
Prep.	обо	всём	обо всéй	обо всéх
Dat.		всемý	всéй	всéм
Instr.		всéм	всéй	всéми

Note: The preposition **о** *about* takes the form **обо** with the prepositional case forms of this pronoun.

Following are examples of the pronoun **вéсь**, first in its use as a modifier, then as a noun-like subject or object of the sentence.

The Pronoun **Вéсь** *as Modifier*

Всё студéнчество волнýется о стóимости обучéния.	The whole student body is concerned about the cost of tuition.
Вся странá ждёт разрешéния кри́зиса.	The whole country is waiting for a resolution to the crisis.
Всé рабóтники получáют óтпуск по болéзни.	All workers are given sick-leave.
Óн рассказáл нáм *всю* истóрию.	He told us the whole story.
Óн достáл билéты для *всéй* грýппы.	He got tickets for the whole group.
Мы́ говори́ли обо *всём* плáне.	We talked about the whole plan.
Онá одинáково забóтится о *всéх* свои́х дéтях.	She cares equally for all of her children.
Нóвость разнеслáсь по *всемý* гóроду.	The news spread throughout the whole city.
Óн éздил по *всéй* странé.	He has traveled throughout the whole country.
Óн знакóм со *всéми* гостя́ми.	He is acquainted with all the guests.

The Pronoun **Вéсь** *as Subject*

Всё в поря́дке.	Everything is okay (lit. *in order*).
Всé здесь имéют прáво гóлоса.	Everyone here has the right to vote.

The Pronoun **Вéсь** *as Object*

Мы́ благодáрны вáм за *всё*.	We are grateful to you for everything.
Загрязнéния вóздуха волнýет *всéх*.	Pollution of the air concerns everyone.
Óн рассказáл нáм *обо всём*.	He told us about everything.
Óн вы́болтал её секрéт при *всéх*.	He blurted out her secret in front of everyone.
Ко *всемý* мóжно привы́кнуть.	One can get used to anything.
Онá всегдá помогáет *всéм*.	She is always helping everyone.
Онá довóльна *всéм*.	She is satisfied with everything.
Óн ужé познакóмился со *всéми*.	He has already met everyone.

21. Supply the required form of the determinative pronoun **весь**.

1. _____ лю́ди хотя́т сча́стья.
2. _____ меня́ется в э́том ми́ре.
3. Он побыва́л во _____ уголка́х земно́го ша́ра.
4. Когда́ оте́ц спроси́л дочь, почему́ она́ но́сит три серёжки, она́ отве́тила «_____ так де́лают».
5. Он справедли́вый челове́к, он отно́сится ко _____ одина́ково.
6. Как сказа́ли в кни́ге «Три Мушкетёра», оди́н за _____, _____ за одного́.
7. Во _____ ми́ре зна́ют и́мя ру́сского космона́вта, Юрия Гага́рина.
8. Он э́того добьётся _____ пра́вдами и непра́вдами.
9. Тури́сты спра́шивали ги́да обо _____ карти́нах в галере́е.
10. Он большо́й экспе́рт, и зна́ет _____ то́нкости пробле́мы.

RELATIVE PRONOUNS

The Relative Pronoun Кото́рый

A relative pronoun refers back to a noun or pronoun in the main clause of a complex sentence — its antecedent — and it introduces a subordinate clause which *relates* to that antecedent. Relative pronouns in English include *who* ("The girl *who* called was Russian"), *which* ("The book *which* you gave me is interesting"), and *that* ("The food *that* they served was delicious"). The most commonly used relative pronoun in Russian is **кото́рый**, and this one pronoun, depending on whether its antecedent is animate or inanimate, may be rendered by English *who*, *that*, or *which*.

The relative pronoun **кото́рый** is used with a noun antecedent. **Кото́рый** must have the same gender and number as its antecedent, but its case is determined by its function within the relative clause. Thus, if this pronoun is the grammatical subject of the relative clause, it will be in the nominative case; if it is the direct object of a verb within the relative clause, the pronoun will be in the accusative case; and if it is the object of a preposition, or the complement of a case-assigning verb, it must be in whichever case is governed by the preposition or verb.

The pronoun **кото́рый** declines like a hard-stem adjective. The complete declension of this pronoun is given in the table below.

	Masculine,	Neuter	Feminine	Plural
Nom.	кото́рый	кото́рое	кото́рая	кото́рые
Acc.	кото́рый/ кото́рого	кото́рое	кото́рую	кото́рые/ кото́рых
Gen.	кото́рого		кото́рой	кото́рых
Prep.	о кото́ром		о кото́рой	о кото́рых
Dat.	кото́рому		кото́рой	кото́рым
Instr.	кото́рым		кото́рой	кото́рыми

Unlike the English relative pronouns which may be "dropped" in relaxed speech, the Russian relative pronoun **кото́рый** may not be omitted, e.g., *The movie (that) I saw was interesting* **Фи́льм, кото́рый я ви́дел, был интере́сный**. Note, also, that in Russian the relative clause is always set off by commas. Following are examples of **кото́рый** in each of the cases.

Nominative Case

The relative pronoun in each of the following examples is in the nominative case because it functions as the subject of the relative clause.

Э́то мо́й дру́г, *кото́рый* **учи́лся в Ки́еве.**	*This is my friend who studied in Kiev.*
Где́ письмо́, *кото́рое* **пришло́ сего́дня?**	*Where is the letter which came today?*
Э́то моя́ сестра́, *кото́рая* **вы́шла за́муж.**	*This is my sister who got married.*
Во́т джи́нсы, *кото́рые* **мне́ нра́вятся.**	*Here are the jeans that I like.*

22. Combine each pair of sentences into a complex sentence with a relative clause introduced by **кото́рый**. Note that **кото́рый** will be in the same *case* as the word it *replaces*.

Model: Э́то мо́й дру́г Ви́ктор. *Ви́ктор* ра́ньше жи́л в Москве́.
Э́то мо́й дру́г Ви́ктор, *кото́рый* ра́ньше жи́л в Москве́.

1. Ка́к зову́т э́ту де́вушку? Де́вушка прие́хала неда́вно из Новосиби́рска.
_____

2. О́н живёт в до́ме. До́м нахо́дится в це́нтре го́рода.
_____

3. Во́т иду́т ма́льчики. Ма́льчики у́чатся в шко́ле вме́сте с на́шим сы́ном.
_____

Accusative Case

The relative pronoun in each of the following examples is in the accusative case because it is either the direct object of the verb, or the object of a preposition which governs the accusative case. When it functions as direct object, the relative pronoun is identical to the nominative case when the noun it refers to is masculine inanimate singular, or inanimate plural; when the noun it refers to is masculine animate singular, or animate plural, the form of the relative pronoun in the accusative is identical to the genitive.

Э́то фи́льм, *кото́рый* **я́ ви́дел вчера́.**	*This is the movie that I saw yesterday.*
Э́то дру́г, *кото́рого* **я́ встре́тил вчера́.**	*This is the friend whom I met yesterday.*
Где́ статья́, *кото́рую* **ты́ прочита́л?**	*Where is the article that you read?*
Э́то усло́вия, на *кото́рые* **вы́ согласи́лись.**	*These are the conditions to which you agreed.*
Во́т но́вые ту́фли, *кото́рые* **я́ купи́л.**	*Here are the new shoes that I bought.*
Э́то лю́ди, *кото́рых* **мы́ уважа́ем.**	*These are people whom we respect.*

23. Combine each pair of sentences into a complex sentence with a relative clause introduced by **кото́рый** in the accusative case.

Model: Я́ уже́ получи́л письмо́. Ты́ посла́л мне́ э́то *письмо́* вчера́.
Я́ уже́ получи́л письмо́, *кото́рое* ты́ мне́ посла́л вчера́.

1. Я́ чита́л статью́. Профе́ссор рекомендова́л э́ту статью́.
_____

2. Ка́к называ́ется университе́т? Ты́ око́нчил э́тот университе́т.
_____

3. Я́ зна́ю одного́ бизнесме́на. Бизнесме́на зову́т Влади́мир Соро́кин.
_____

4. На́ши сосе́ди нашли́ де́ньги. Ты́ потеря́л э́ти де́ньги.
_____

5. Вчера́ к на́м прие́хали друзья́. Мы́ давно́ не ви́дели э́тих друзе́й.
_____

Genitive Case

As shown in the first three examples below, the English meaning *whose* is expressed by the relative pronoun in the genitive case. The genitive case of the pronoun immediately follows the noun denoting the possessed object or person. As always, the pronoun **кото́рый** takes its gender and number from the noun it refers to, which in these examples is the noun denoting the possessor.

As the last two examples show, the relative pronoun is also in the genitive case when it is the object of a preposition or verb that governs the genitive.

Э́то дру́г, маши́ну *кото́рого* укра́ли.	*This is my friend whose car was stolen.*
Э́то де́вушка, оте́ц *кото́рой* откры́л сво́й би́знес.	*This is the girl whose father opened his own business.*
Э́то друзья́, до́чь *кото́рых* неда́вно вы́шла за́муж.	*These are the friends whose daughter recently got married.*
Э́то та́ де́вушка, для *кото́рой* мы́ купи́ли пода́рок.	*That's the girl for whom we bought the gift.*
То́т ма́льчик, *кото́рого* боя́лся на́ш сы́н, бы́л аресто́ван за дра́ку.	*That boy who our son was afraid of, was arrested for fighting.*

24. Combine the two simple sentences into a complex sentence with a relative clause introduced by **кото́рый** in the genitive case.

Model: У меня́ хоро́шая подру́га. У *подру́ги* неда́вно роди́лся ребёнок.
У меня́ хоро́шая подру́га, у *кото́рой* неда́вно роди́лся ребёнок.

1. Я́ позвони́л дру́гу. От дру́га я́ давно́ не получа́л письма́.
   _____

2. На́с помести́ли в све́тлую ко́мнату. О́кна ко́мнаты смо́трят на пля́ж.
   _____

3. О́н рабо́тает в институ́те. О́коло институ́та стро́ят гости́ницу.
   _____

4. Ка́к фами́лия студе́нтки? Роди́тели студе́нтки живу́т в Росто́ве.
   _____

5. О́н подари́л е́й духи́. За́пах духо́в е́й о́чень понра́вился.
   _____

Prepositional Case

The relative pronoun is in the prepositional case when it is the object of a preposition that governs this case. Note that whenever it is the object of a preposition, **кото́рый** immediately follows that preposition which must be at the *beginning of the clause*. This is an important difference between Russian and English: English allows prepositions to "dangle" at the end of a sentence (see the English translations below), but Russian does not permit a preposition to be moved out of the phrase it heads.

Э́то до́м, в *кото́ром* мы́ жи́ли ра́ньше.	*This is the house which we used to live in.*
Во́т де́вушка, о *кото́рой* я́ тебе́ говори́л.	*Here is the girl who I told you about.*
Э́то фотогра́фии гости́ниц, в *кото́рых* мы́ остана́вливались.	*These are photographs of the hotels which we stayed in.*

25. Combine each pair of sentences into a single complex sentence with a relative clause introduced by **кото́рый** in the prepositional case.

Model: Óн написа́л письмо́. В *письме́* о́н на́м всё объясни́л.
Óн написа́л письмо́, в *кото́ром* о́н на́м всё объясни́л.

1. Ты́ чита́л кни́гу? Я́ тебе́ говори́л о кни́ге.
_____

2. Мы́ бы́ли на спекта́кле. В спекта́кле уча́ствовала на́ша до́чь.
_____

3. Сего́дня ко мне́ прие́дет дру́г. Я́ расска́зывал тебе́ о дру́ге.
_____

4. Че́рез воро́та Кремля́ прое́хал лимузи́н. В лимузи́не е́хал президе́нт.
_____

5. Та́м стро́ят общежи́тия. В общежи́тиях бу́дут жи́ть студе́нты.
_____

Dative Case

The relative pronoun is in the dative case when it functions as an indirect object, or when it is the complement of a preposition, adjective, or verb that governs the dative case.

Э́то сы́н, *кото́рому* я́ посла́л письмо́.	*This is the son to whom I sent a letter.*
Э́то на́ш ста́рый дру́г, *кото́рому* мы́ всегда́ бу́дем благода́рны.	*This is our old friend to whom we will always be grateful.*
Э́то сосе́дка, *кото́рой* мы́ помогли́.	*This is the neighbor whom we helped.*
Э́то друзья́, к *кото́рым* мы́ е́здили.	*These are the friends we went to see.*
Она́ живёт те́м о́бразом жи́зни, к *кото́рому* она́ привы́кла.	*She is living the lifestyle to which she has become accustomed.*

26. Combine each pair of sentences into a single complex sentence with a relative clause introduced by **кото́рый** in the dative case.

Model: На́с поблагодари́л дру́г. Мы́ помогли́ *дру́гу*.
На́с поблагодари́л дру́г, *кото́рому* мы́ помогли́.

1. Они́ вы́шли из ле́са и уви́дели о́зеро. Они́ направля́лись к о́зеру.
_____

2. Ка́к зову́т де́вушку? Я́ до́лжен переда́ть письмо́ де́вушке.
_____

3. Во́т бе́рег. Мы́ бе́гаем по бе́регу ка́ждое у́тро.
_____

4. Вчера́ я́ сдава́ла экза́мен. Я́ до́лго гото́вилась к экза́мену.
_____

5. За́втра к на́м прие́дут друзья́. Мы́ е́здим к друзья́м ча́сто.
_____

Instrumental Case

The relative pronoun is in the instrumental case when it is the object of a preposition, adjective, or verb which governs the instrumental case, or when it expresses one of the many uses of this case: "the instrument or means of the action," the "route taken," etc.

Э́то же́нщина, с *кото́рой* я́ рабо́таю.	*This is a woman with whom I work.*
Э́то де́ти, за *кото́рыми* она́ следи́т.	*These are the children she looks after.*

Та́м лежи́т ру́чка, *кото́рой* о́н подписа́л   *There is the pen with which he signed*
докуме́нты.   *the documents.*
Докла́дчик освети́л вопро́сы, *кото́рыми*   *The speaker shed light on questions*
интересова́лись слу́шатели.   *in which the audience was interested.*
Это доро́жка, *кото́рой* я́ хожу́ домо́й.   *This is the path that I take to go home.*

27. Combine each pair of sentences into a complex sentence with a relative clause introduced by **кото́рый** in the instrumental case.

Model: Профе́ссор зако́нчил уче́бник. О́н до́лго рабо́тал на́д *уче́бником.*
Профе́ссор зако́нчил уче́бник, на́д *кото́рым* о́н до́лго рабо́тал.

1. Я́ хочу́ познако́мить тебя́ с де́вушкой. Я́ рабо́таю с де́вушкой в институ́те.
_____

2. Вдали́ мы́ уви́дели го́ры. Ме́жду гора́ми вила́сь доро́га.
_____

3. Студе́нт подошёл к столу́. За столо́м сиде́л экзамена́тор.
_____

4. Мы́ подошли́ к теа́тру. Пе́ред теа́тром тяну́лась дли́нная о́чередь.
_____

5. Она́ вчера́ узна́ла результа́ты экспериме́нта. Она́ о́чень дово́льна результа́тами.
_____

The Relative Pronoun Како́й

The pronoun **како́й** (declined like **тако́й**, see p. 122) may be used both as an interrogative as well as a relative pronoun. When used as a relative pronoun, **како́й** has a noun antecedent which, for emphasis, may be modified by the demonstrative pronoun **тако́й**. Like **кото́рый**, the pronoun **како́й** takes its gender and number from its antecedent, but its case is determined by its function in its own clause.

The construction **тако́й (же)** ..., **како́й** may be rendered into English as *the (same) kind of* ... *that* .... Following are several examples of this construction.

Это *така́я* маши́на, *кака́я* е́сть у Пе́ти.
This is the kind of car that Petya has.

Это то́чно *така́я же* зада́ча, *кака́я* была́ у на́с на экза́мене.
This is exactly the same kind of problem we had in the exam.

О́н слу́шает *таку́ю* му́зыку, *каку́ю* слу́шают мно́гие лю́ди его́ во́зраста.
He listens to the kind of music that many people his age listen to.

Мы́ жи́ли в *тако́й* кварти́ре, в *како́й* и вы́ жи́ли.
We lived in an apartment like the one that you lived in.

Таки́х де́вушек, на *како́й* ты́ жени́лся, нечасто встреча́ешь.
Girls of the kind that you married don't come along very often.

Ю́ра совсе́м не измени́лся, о́н оста́лся *таки́м, каки́м* и бы́л.
Yura has not changed at all, he has stayed just as he was.

28. Supply the required form of the relative pronoun **како́й**.

1. Мне́ ну́жен тако́й слова́рь, _____ у тебя́ е́сть.
2. Я да́же никогда́ не слы́шал о тако́м о́воще, о _____ ты говори́шь.
3. Таки́х специали́стов, _____ вы и́щете, тру́дно найти́.
4. Я хочу́ то́чно тако́й же мотоци́кл, _____ у него́ е́сть.
5. А́х, е́сли бы у меня́ была́ така́я фигу́ра, _____ у тебя́!
6. О́н живёт в тако́м до́ме, в _____ живу́т то́лько бога́тые лю́ди.
7. О́н уже́ не получа́ет таки́е больши́е де́ньги, к _____ он привы́к.
8. Продаве́ц показа́л ему́ таки́е кроссо́вки, _____ о́н и иска́л.

The Relative Pronouns Кто́ and Что́

The words **кто́** and **что́** may be used not only as interrogative pronouns, but also as relative pronouns. Unlike **кото́рый** and **како́й** which take a noun antecedent, **кто́** and **что́** normally take a pronoun antecedent. Typical antecedents include forms of the demonstrative pronoun **то́т** (**то́т, кто́** *he who*, **те́, кто́** *those who*, **то́, что́** *that which*), forms of the pronoun **ве́сь** *all* (**всё, кто́** *all/everyone who*, **всё, что́** *everything that*), and the pronouns **ка́ждый** *each (one)* and **любо́й** *any (one)* (**ка́ждый, кто́** *each one who*, **любо́й, кто́** *anyone who*).

When its antecedent is plural, as in **те́, кто́** *those who* and **всё, кто́** *everyone who*, the pronoun **кто́** may take either singular (masculine) or plural agreement. This option is indicated by the parentheses in two examples below.

Те́, кто́ **чита́л(и) докла́д, бы́ли дово́льны и́м.**
Those who read the report were pleased with it.

Всё, кто́ **бы́л(и) на ве́чере, пото́м собрали́сь на дискоте́ке.**
Everyone who was at the party, gathered afterwards at the dance club.

Ка́ждый, кто́ **подходи́л к нему́, поздравля́л его́.**
Each person who approached, congratulated him.

Любо́й, кто́ **хоте́л, мо́г задава́ть вопро́сы.**
Anyone who wanted to, was able to ask questions.

The construction **то́т, кто́** *he who/one who* is usually used in general statements such as those characteristic of proverbs. The two pronouns in these constructions may be contiguous, or they may be separated, as shown in the following two Russian proverbs.

Хорошо́ смеётся *то́т, кто́* **смеётся после́дним.**
He laughs best who laughs last.

Кто́ **мно́го грози́т,** *то́т* **ма́ло вреди́т.**
He who has a loud bark, seldom has a sharp bite.

In constructions containing the relative pronouns **кто́** and **что́**, as in other relative clause constructions, the case of the relative pronoun, as well as the case of its pronoun antecedent, is determined by the function of each pronoun within its own clause.

The following examples demonstrate how the case of the relative pronoun **что́** changes according to its grammatical function within the relative clause.

Произошло то,	*что* **нас о́чень обра́довало.**
Something occurred	*that* (Nom.) *made us very happy.*
	что **мы́ давно́ ожида́ли.**
	that (Acc.) *we had long expected.*
	чего́ **мы́ все́ боя́лись.**
	that (Gen.) *we had all been afraid of.*
	о чём **мы́ бу́дем вспомина́ть до́лго.**
	that (Prep.) *we will think about a long time.*
	чему́ **удиви́лись все́.**
	that (Dat.) *everyone was surprised at.*
	чём **мы́ до си́х по́р восхища́емся.**
	that (Instr.) *we are delighted with to this day.*

The following examples illustrate how the case of the demonstrative pronoun **то́т** is determined by its grammatical function within the main clause. Note that while Russian grammar requires that the various case forms of the word **то́т** occur (except for the accusative direct object **то́**, which may be omitted), this word is not translated into English.

На́с обра́довало *то́,*	**что́ он сде́лал.**
We were gladdened by (Nom.)	*what he did.*
Мы́ понима́ем (*то́***),**	
We understand (Acc.)	
Мы́ испуга́лись *того́,*	
We were frightened by (Gen.)	
Мы́ беспоко́имся о *то́м,*	
We are worried about (Prep.)	
Мы́ не́ были гото́вы к *тому́,*	
We were not prepared for (Dat.)	
Мы́ о́чень дово́льны *те́м,*	
We are very pleased with (Instr.)	

29. Fill in the required form of the missing pronoun in the construction **то́, что́**.

1. _____, что́ о́н сде́лал, на́м о́чень помогло́.
2. Она́ расска́зывала о _____, чём она́ занима́ется.
3. Мы́ о́чень дово́льны _____, чего́ ты́ доби́лся.
4. Она́ бои́тся того́, над _____ о́н рабо́тает.
5. Роди́тели удиви́лись тому́, _____ увлека́ется сы́н.
6. Она́ не согла́сна с _____, что он де́лает.
7. У меня́ сомне́ния в _____, что они́ предлага́ют.
8. Я́ о́чень интересу́юсь _____, над чём вы́ рабо́таете.
9. На́м ну́жно и́менно то́, к _____ они́ стремя́тся.
10. Она́ не пове́рила _____, что ей рассказа́ли.

30. Fill in the required form of the missing pronoun in the construction **то́т, кто́**.

1. Сча́стлив то́т, у _____ мно́го друзе́й.
2. Хорошо́ тому́, _____ занима́ется интере́сной рабо́той.
3. Для э́той рабо́ты нам ну́жен _____, кто́ име́ет большо́й о́пыт.
4. Кто́ ра́но встаёт, _____ уда́ча ждёт.
5. Кому́ везёт в ка́ртах, _____ не везёт в любви́.

INDEFINITE PRONOUNS

The Pronouns Кто́-то/Кто́-нибудь, Что́-то/Что́-нибудь, Како́й-то/Како́й-нибудь, Чей-то/Чей-нибудь

The unstressed particles -то and -нибудь can be attached to the interrogative pronouns кто́, что́, како́й, and чей (and to certain adverbs, see Chapter 5) to create indefinite pronouns with the meaning *someone*, *anyone*, etc. However, as the table below indicates, the particles -то and -нибудь do not directly correspond to English *some* and *any*, respectively: while the forms with the particle -то are normally rendered by English pronouns beginning with *some*, it must be noted that indefinite pronouns with -нибудь can be translated into English by either *any-* or *some-*.

кто́ *who*	кто́-то *someone*	кто́-нибудь *anyone, someone*
что́ *what*	что́-то *something*	что́-нибудь *anything, something*
како́й *what (sort of)*	како́й-то *some (sort of)*	како́й-нибудь *any (sort of), some (sort of)*
чей *whose*	чей-то *someone's someone else's*	чей-нибудь *anyone's somebody else's*

The indefinite pronouns in -то and -нибудь decline just like the interrogative pronouns (кто́-то, кого́-то, кому́-то . . .; что́-нибудь, о чём-нибудь, чём-нибудь . . .).

Meaning and Uses of the Particle -то

A form with -то is used when the speaker has a definite person or thing in mind, but which s/he does not mention by name, either because (*a*) s/he does not know it (s/he may have known, but has forgotten), or (*b*) s/he may know it, but simply chooses for some reason not to mention it. Forms with the particle -то are limited primarily to *statements* expressed in the *past tense* and the *present tense*, unless the action or state denoted by the verb is repeated or habitual.

Note: In the *future tense*, forms with -то are possible, but occur more rarely: they are used only when the speaker refers to a particular person or thing which s/he does not wish to identify, e.g., **Я приведу́** *кого́-то* **на ве́чер, но я́ не скажу́ тебе́, кто́ э́то. Э́то бу́дет мо́й сюрпри́з для тебя́** *I'm going to bring someone to the party, but I won't tell you who. This will be my surprise for you.*

Past Tense

Кто́-то звони́л, но я́ забы́л кто́.	*Someone called, but I forget who.*
О́н *что́-то* сказа́л, но я́ не по́нял.	*He said something, but I didn't understand.*
К тебе́ заходи́ла *кака́я-то* де́вушка, но она́ не сказа́ла своё и́мя.	*Some girl came by to see you, but she didn't say what her name was.*
Я́ по оши́бке взя́л *чей-то* зо́нтик.	*I took somebody's umbrella by mistake.*

Present Tense

Кто́-то стучи́т в две́рь.	*Someone is knocking at the door.*
Мо́й бо́сс в плохо́м настрое́нии, о́н я́вно *чём-то* недово́лен.	*My boss is in a bad mood, he is obviously unhappy with something.*
Сего́дня идёт *како́й-то* но́вый фи́льм, не по́мню, ка́к называ́ется.	*Some new movie is playing today, I don't remember what it is called.*
Зде́сь лежи́т *чья́-то* су́мка, но не зна́ю, чья́.	*Somebody's handbag is lying here, but I don't know whose.*

Meaning and Uses of the Particle **-нибудь**

Unlike **-то**, the particle **-нибудь** is used when the speaker has no particular person or object in mind, but refers instead to someone or something indefinite, and whose very identity is still unknown. As a general rule, pronouns with **-нибудь** are used in *questions*, after *commands*, in statements expressed in the *future tense*, as well as with *repeated actions in the present tense*.

Questions

Кто́-*нибудь* **звони́л?**	*Did anyone call?*
Ты́ *что́-нибудь* **зна́ешь об э́том?**	*Do you know anything about this?*
Ты́ с *ке́м-нибудь* **говори́л об э́том?**	*Did you talk with anyone about this?*
Та́м продаю́т *каки́е-нибудь* **сувени́ры?**	*Do they sell any souvenirs there?*
Вы́ ви́дели та́м *чью́-нибудь* **маши́ну?**	*Did you see anyone's car there?*

Commands

Спроси́те *кого́-нибудь* **из его́ друзе́й.**	*Ask one of his friends.*
Возьми́ *что́-нибудь* **почита́ть.**	*Take something to read.*
Спо́й на́м *каку́ю-нибудь* **пе́сню.**	*Sing us a song (any one at all).*
Не покупа́йте но́вый рюкза́к на **сво́й пе́рвый похо́д. Попроси́те** *чей-нибудь* **на вре́мя.**	*Don't buy a new backpack for your first hike. Ask (to borrow) someone else's for a time.*

Future Tense

Я́ спрошу́ *кого́-нибудь* **об э́том.**	*I'll ask someone (or other) about this.*
Ма́ма пригото́вит *что́-нибудь* **на обе́д.**	*Mom will make something for lunch.*
Я́ куплю́ себе́ *каки́е-нибудь* **санда́лии,** **когда́ я́ прие́ду на мо́ре.**	*I will buy myself some sandals when I get to the seashore.*
Когда́ авто́буса не́т, я́ е́ду на по́чту **на** *чьём-нибудь* **велосипе́де.**	*When there is no bus, I go to the post office on somebody's bicycle.*

Present Tense (Repeated Actions)

Когда́ ему́ тру́дно, о́н всегда́ **про́сит у** *кого́-нибудь* **по́мощь.**	*When he is having trouble, he always asks someone for help.*
Она́ ча́сто покупа́ет *что́-нибудь* **на э́том ры́нке.**	*She often buys something at this market.*
О́н всегда́ чита́ет *како́й-нибудь* **детекти́в.**	*He is always reading some detective story.*
По́сле ле́кции в большо́й аудито́рии, **всегда́ остаю́тся** *чьи́-нибудь* **ве́щи.**	*After a lecture in a large classroom, someone's things are always left (behind).*

It is important to note that in contrast to the English pronouns *anything*, *anyone*, etc., which can occur in both positive and negative sentences, the Russian indefinite pronouns with the particles **-то** and **-нибудь** can not be used in negative sentences; in a negative sentence the English pronouns beginning in *any-* are expressed in Russian by forms of the negative pronouns in **ни-** (**никто́**, **ничто́**), as shown in the following:

— **Ты́** *что́-нибудь* **купи́л?**	*Did you buy anything?*
— **Не́т, я́** *ничего́* **не купи́л.**	*No, I didn't buy anything.*
— **Вы́** *кого́-нибудь* **та́м ви́дели?**	*Did you see anyone there?*
— **Не́т, я́** *никого́* **не ви́дел.**	*No, I didn't see anyone.*

31. Fill in the blanks with the appropriate indefinite pronoun in the required form.

1. — Мне́ _____ звони́л?
   — Да́. _____ звони́л, но не сказа́л своё и́мя.

2. — Что́ же мне́ тепе́рь де́лать с э́тими биле́тами?!
   — Отда́й их _____ студе́нтам.

3. — Где́ вчера́ бы́л Па́ша?
   — О́н ходи́л к _____ из свои́х друзе́й, но я́ не зна́ю к кому́.

4. — Ко мне́ _____ приходи́л?
   — Да́. Приходи́ла Ната́ша и ещё _____ па́рень, но о́н не предста́вился.

5. — Вы́ чита́ли _____ кни́ги э́того писа́теля?
   — Да́, я давно́ чита́ла _____ его́ кни́гу, но не по́мню её назва́ние.

6. — Ка́к узна́ть, бу́дет ли за́втра экза́мен?
   — Позвони́ _____ из на́шей гру́ппы.

7. — Отку́да ты́ зна́ешь но́мер её телефо́на?
   — Я́ _____ спроси́л.

8. — Пе́тя, когда́ сего́дня футбо́льный ма́тч?
   — Я́ не зна́ю, я́ _____ спрошу́.

9. — Сего́дня де́нь рожде́ния Та́ни. Что́ ей подари́ть?
   — Подари́ ей _____ прия́тное для неё, ... цветы́, духи́.

10. — Что́ чита́ет Ма́ша?
    — Она́ чита́ет _____ из Бу́нина, ка́жется _____ расска́з.

11. — За́втра я́ е́ду в командиро́вку, но у меня́ не́т ма́ленького чемода́на.
    — Ну́, возьми́ _____ .

12. — Ой, э́то не моя́ ру́чка. Ка́жется, я́ по оши́бке взя́л _____ ру́чку.

NEGATIVE PRONOUNS

Negative Pronouns in Ни-: Никто́, Ничто́, Никако́й, Ниче́й

Russian has a series of negative pronouns (and adverbs, see Chapter 5) which are formed from the pronouns **кто́, что́, како́й**, and **че́й** by means of the prefix **ни-**. These negative pronouns are declined like **кто́, что́**, etc., except that **ничто́** in the accusative case always takes the form of the genitive: **ничего́**. When a preposition occurs, it is placed between the **ни-** and the pronoun, which takes the case governed by the preposition, e.g., **ни о ко́м** *not about anyone*, **ни с че́м** *not with anything*, **ни для кого́** *not for anyone*.

кто́	who	никто́	(ни...кто́)	no one	
что́	what	ничто́	(ни...что́)	nothing, not anything	
како́й	what kind	никако́й	(ни...како́й)	no (kind), not any (kind)	
че́й	whose	ниче́й	(ни...че́й)	no one's, not any one's	

The predicate of this type of negative pronoun must always be negated with **не**, which results in a "double negative" (**ни-**...**не**...), e.g., *Никто́ не звони́л* No one called. Note that in these negative sentences the pronouns in **ни-** are the Russian equivalent of English pronouns in *any-* (*anyone, anything,* etc.). However, in positive sentences, as noted in the preceding section, English *any-* is expressed in Russian by the indefinite pronouns in **-нибудь**.

    — **Ты́ кому́-нибудь звони́л?**   *Did you call anyone?*
    — **Не́т, я *никому́* не звони́л.**   *No, I didn't call anyone.*

The following examples further illustrate the use of the negative pronouns in **ни-**.

— Кто́ пришёл?	*Who came?*
— *Никто́* не пришёл.	*No one came.*
— Вы́ кого́-нибудь та́м ви́дели?	*Did you see anyone there?*
— Не́т, мы́ *никого́* та́м не ви́дели.	*No, we didn't see anyone there.*
— У кого́ е́сть слова́рь?	*Who has a dictionary?*
— *Ни* у *кого́* не́т словаря́.	*No one has a dictionary.*
— О ко́м ты ду́маешь?	*Who are you thinking about?*
— Я́ *ни* о *ко́м* не ду́маю.	*I'm not thinking about anyone.*
— Кому́ нра́вится э́та му́зыка?	*Who likes this music?*
— *Никому́* не нра́вится.	*No one likes it.*
— О́н с ке́м-нибудь говори́л об э́том?	*Did he speak with anyone about this?*
— Не́т, о́н *ни* с *ке́м* не говори́л.	*No, he did not speak with anyone.*
— Каки́е у ва́с е́сть вопро́сы?	*What questions do you have?*
— У на́с не́т *никаки́х* вопро́сов.	*We do not have any questions.*
— О како́й кни́ге о́н спра́шивал?	*What book was he asking about?*
— О́н не спра́шивал *ни* о *како́й* кни́ге.	*He wasn't asking about any book.*
— Что́ тебя́ беспоко́ит?	*What is bothering you?*
— *Ничто́* меня́ не беспоко́ит.	*Nothing is bothering me.*
— О́н че́м-нибудь за́нят?	*Is he busy with something?*
— Не́т, о́н *ниче́м* не за́нят.	*No, he is not busy with anything.*
— Че́й рису́нок тебе́ понра́вился?	*Whose drawing did you like?*
— Мне́ *ниче́й* рису́нок не понра́вился.	*I didn't like anybody's drawing.*

32. Answer the questions negatively, using a negative pronoun in the required form.

1. Кто́ тебе́ нра́вится? _____
2. Что́ его́ интересу́ет? _____
3. Что́ ты́ де́лаешь? _____
4. К кому́ ты́ идёшь? _____
5. О ко́м ты́ мечта́ешь? _____
6. Че́м она́ занима́ется? _____
7. С ке́м о́н встре́тился? _____
8. У кого́ ты́ была́? _____
9. Чего́ о́н бои́тся? _____
10. К чему́ ты́ гото́вишься? _____
11. На каки́е усту́пки они́ согласи́лись? _____
12. Чьи́ сове́ты она́ слу́шала? _____
13. Каки́е вопро́сы ва́с интересу́ют? _____
14. Чью́ маши́ну ты́ води́л? _____
15. На кого́ ты́ наде́ешься? _____

Negative Pronouns in Не́-: Не́кого, Не́чего

The negative pronouns **не́кого** *there is no one* and **не́чего** *there is nothing* are formed from the interrogative pronouns **кто́** and **что́** by means of the stressed negative prefix **не́-**. These pronouns are declined like **кто́** and **что́**, except that (*a*) they do not occur in the nominative case and (*b*) the prepositionless accusative of the pronoun based on **что́** has the same form as the genitive: **не́чего**. When a preposition occurs, it is placed between **не́** and the pronoun. The declension of these pronouns is given in the following table.

	не́кого *there is no one*	**не́чего** *there is nothing*
Nom.	_____	_____
Acc.	не́кого (не́ . . . кого́)	не́чего (не́ . . . что́)
Gen.	не́кого (не́ . . . кого́)	не́чего (не́ . . . чего́)
Prep.	не́ . . . ком	не́ . . . чем
Dat.	не́кому (не́ . . . кому́)	не́чему (не́ . . . чему́)
Instr.	не́кем (не́ . . . кем)	не́чем (не́ . . . чем)

Note: Nominative case forms with the prefix **не́-** do occur, but in a different meaning: **не́кто** *someone, a certain* (**Не́кто Смирно́в** *a certain Smirnov*), **не́что** *something* (**не́что невероя́тное** *something unbelievable*).

Note: When a preposition occurs, the three elements of the negative pronoun are written separately, but they are pronounced as one word, and with only one stress on **не́**: **не́ у кого** [n'éukəvə], **не́ за что** [n'ézəštə].

The negative pronouns in **не́-** are typically used in impersonal (subjectless) constructions with the infinitive form of the verb. The case of the pronoun is determined either by the infinitive or by a co-occurring preposition.

Не́кого **спроси́ть.**	*There is no one to ask.*
Не́ с кем **говори́ть.**	*There is no one to talk with.*
Не́чего **боя́ться.**	*There is nothing to be afraid of.*
Не́ о чем **беспоко́иться.**	*There is nothing to worry about.*

A noun or pronoun denoting the performer of the action must be in the dative case.

Бра́ту *не́ к кому́* **обрати́ться.**	*My brother has no one to turn to.*
Мне́ *не́кого* **боя́ться.**	*I have no one to fear.*
Не́кому **пойти́ за вино́м.**	*There is no one to go for the wine.*

The past and future tenses are expressed by **бы́ло** *was* and **бу́дет** *will be.*

Мне́ *не́кому* **бы́ло звони́ть.**	*There was no one for me to call.*
Тебе́ *не́ с кем* **бу́дет говори́ть.**	*There will be no one for you to talk to.*

33. Fill in the blanks with the required form of **не́кого** or **не́чего**, with the appropriate preposition, when necessary.

1. — Кого́ тут мо́жно спроси́ть? — Тут _____ спроси́ть.
2. — На что́ он бу́дет жа́ловаться? — Ему́ _____ жа́ловаться.
3. — Что́ бы нам сде́лать? — Нам _____ де́лать.
4. — Чем ты́ бу́дешь писа́ть? — Мне́ _____ писа́ть.
5. — Кому́ она́ бу́дет звони́ть? — Ей звони́ть бу́дет _____ .

6.   — С ке́м вы́ бу́дете говори́ть? — Мне́ бу́дет _____ говори́ть.
7.   — К кому́ он пойдёт? — Ему́ _____ пойти́.
8.   — Кто́ пойдёт за хле́бом? — _____ пойти́ за хле́бом.
9.   — О чём вы́ бу́дете говори́ть? — На́м _____ говори́ть.
10. — За что́ его́ благодари́ть? — Его́ благодари́ть _____ .

CHAPTER 5

Adjectives and Adverbs

ADJECTIVES

Qualitative and Relational Adjectives

Most adjectives in Russian are *qualitative,* i.e., they denote a quality or property of the noun or pronoun they modify. A qualitative adjective may denote size (*big*, *small*, *tall*), color (*red*, *green*, *blue*), taste (*sweet*, *sour*, *salty*), temperature (*hot*, *cold*, *warm*), and various other qualities of people and things (*intelligent*, *happy*, *sad*, *interesting*). Russian qualitative adjectives have a number of important grammatical properties:

(*a*) They may be used in both a *long* form (expressing gender, number, and case) and a *short* (caseless) form.

(*b*) The long form may be used *attributively*, usually preceding the noun it modifies (The *new* teacher arrived), or *predicatively*, usually after a form of the link verb *be* (This teacher is *new*). The short form, however, is used *only* predicatively.

(*c*) They form comparatives (*quicker*, *more interesting*) and superlatives (*quickest*, *most interesting*).

(*d*) They form derived adverbs (*quickly*, *interestingly*).

A smaller number of adjectives in Russian are *relational*, i.e., they express a relationship, indicating that the noun modified is of, from, or connected in some way with something or someone else. For example, a relational adjective may denote a property of the modified noun that relates to people (*де́тские* **кни́ги** *children's books*), to animals (*ко́нский* **база́р** *horse bazaar*), to an inanimate object (*мото́рная* **ло́дка** *motor-boat*), to the material from which it is made (*деревя́нный* **дом** *wooden house*), to a place (*городска́я* **библиоте́ка** *city library*), to time (*ле́тние* **кани́кулы** *summer vacation*), and to various other categories. Compared with qualitative adjectives, relational adjectives are more restricted in usage:

(*a*) They have only an attributive long form.

(*b*) They do not have comparatives or superlatives.

(*c*) They do not form derived adverbs.

140

THE LONG FORM OF ADJECTIVES

Attributive and Predicative

In Russian, as in English, an attributive adjective normally precedes, but may immediately follow, the noun it modifies.

Э́то *надёжная* **маши́на.**	*This is a reliable car.*
Маши́ну, *надёжную* **ка́к э́та,**	*A car, reliable like this (one),*
легко́ содержа́ть.	*is easy to maintain.*

Qualitative adjectives may also occur predicatively, as a "predicate adjective," usually after the verb **бы́ть** *to be*, which in the present tense is not stated, but is implied.

Э́та маши́на *надёжная.*	*This car is reliable.*
Э́ти маши́ны *надёжные.*	*These cars are reliable.*

Adjective Structure

As the different endings on the adjective above demonstrate, the long form of the adjective, in both its attributive and predicative use, must agree with the noun it modifies in gender, number, and case. Like nouns and pronouns, adjectives consist of a stem followed by an ending. Taking the adjective above as an example, the stem of the adjective **надёжн-** is constant, but the ending changes to reflect the change in case from nominative to accusative, and in number from singular to plural.

STEM + ENDING
надёжн + *ая* (feminine, singular, nominative)
надёжн + *ую* (feminine, singular, accusative)
надёжн + *ые* (plural, nominative)

Declension of Adjectives

The spelling of the adjective's declensional endings is influenced by the phonetic nature of its stem-final consonant. Adjectives with the following types of stems occur:

- stem ending in a hard consonant (**но́вый** *new*, **молодо́й** *young*)
- stem ending in a soft consonant (**си́ний** *blue*, **ле́тний** *summer*, **пти́чий** *bird*)
- stem ending in the consonants **-г, -к, -х** (**до́лгий** *long*, **ру́сский** *Russian*, **ти́хий** *quiet*)
- stem ending in the unpaired consonants **-ж, -ш, -ч, -щ** (**хоро́ший** *good*, **све́жий** *fresh*)

Adjectives whose Stem Ends in a Hard Consonant

Adjectives with a stem ending in a hard consonant take endings that begin with a hard-series vowel (**ы, о, а,** or **у**). Hard-stem adjectives may have the stress on the stem (**но́в-ый** *new*) or on the ending (**молод-о́й** *young*). The declensional endings are the same for both stem-stressed and end-stressed adjectives, except in the nominative and accusative inanimate masculine singular (**-ый** vs. **-о́й**). The following table shows the declension of the hard-stem adjective **но́вый** *new*.

	Masculine,	Neuter	Feminine	Plural
Nom.	**но́вый**	**но́вое**	**но́вая**	**но́вые**
Acc. Inan./Anim.	**но́вый/но́вого**	**но́вое**	**но́вую**	**но́вые/но́вых**
Gen.	**но́вого**		**но́вой**	**но́вых**
Prep.	**о но́вом**		**но́вой**	**о но́вых**
Dat.	**но́вому**		**но́вой**	**но́вым**
Instr.	**но́вым**		**но́вой**	**но́выми**

Note: The **г** is pronounced [v] in the genitive case of the adjective ending **-ого**: [әvә].

Note: It is important to remember the "animate accusative rule": the accusative singular of an *animate masculine* noun—and its modifying adjective or pronoun—is identical to the genitive: **Он ви́дел но́вого студе́нта** *He saw the new student.* In the plural, the animate accusative rule applies to *animate nouns of all genders*: **Он ви́дел но́вых студе́нтов и студе́нток** *He saw the new male and female students.* In the masculine singular and the plural of all genders, *inanimate* nouns in the accusative are identical to the nominative: **Он купи́л но́вый стол и но́вые сту́лья** *He bought a new table and new chairs.*

Note: An adjective (or pronoun) modifying a "naturally masculine" second declension noun (**де́душка** *grandfather,* **мужчи́на** *man,* **дя́дя** *uncle*) must show *masculine* agreement, but the noun declines like a feminine noun in **-а, -я**: **Она́ встре́тила симпати́чного мужчи́ну** *She met a nice-looking man.*

The following are some common adjectives with a stem ending in a hard consonant.

аккура́тный	neat	молодо́й	young
бе́лый	white	молчали́вый	taciturn
бы́стрый	fast	неопря́тный	sloppy
ве́жливый	polite	некраси́вый	ugly
весёлый	cheerful	но́вый	new
глу́пый	stupid	разгово́рчивый	talkative
гру́бый	rude	све́тлый	light
гру́стный	sad	серьёзный	serious
гря́зный	dirty	ску́чный	boring
до́брый	kind	смешно́й	funny
зло́бный	mean	ста́рый	old
интере́сный	interesting	тёмный	dark
краси́вый	pretty	трудолюби́вый	industrious
лени́вый	lazy	у́мный	smart
ме́дленный	slow	чи́стый	clean
		чёрный	black

1. Choose the antonym of the italicized adjective from the list above, and insert it in the sentence in the required form.

1. Та́ня *трудолюби́вая* де́вушка, а её подру́га Ле́на ЛЕНИВАЯ.
2. Мы живём в *но́вой* кварти́ре, а они́ живу́т в СТАРОЙ кварти́ре.
3. Хотя́ он *у́мный* челове́к, он за́дал ГЛУПЫЙ вопро́с.
4. Он лю́бит носи́ть *чёрную* ша́пку, а она́ обы́чно но́сит БЕЛУЮ ша́пку.
5. Ты обы́чно тако́й *весёлый*, почему́ у тебя́ сего́дня тако́й ГРУСТНЫЙ вид?
6. В го́роде движе́ние *ме́дленное*, а за́ городом движе́ние БЫСТРОЕ.
7. Ма́льчик *ве́жливый* с прия́телями, но ГРУБЫЙ с ро́дственниками.
8. Она́ *до́брый* челове́к, но её муж челове́к ЗЛОБНЫЙ.
9. Он *интере́сный* челове́к, но СКУЧНЫЙ собесе́дник.
10. Э́ти бра́тья си́льно отлича́ются: оди́н *разгово́рчивый*, а друго́й МОЛЧАЛИВЫЙ.
11. Она́ лю́бит *смешны́е* фи́льмы, а он бо́льше лю́бит СЕРЬЁЗНЫЕ фи́льмы.
12. Она́ со *све́тлыми* волоса́ми, а её сестра́ с ТЁМНЫМИ волоса́ми.
13. У э́той *молодо́й* де́вушки СТАРЫЙ муж.
14. У неё *краси́вая* причёска, а у её подру́ги причёска НЕКРАСИВАЯ.
15. Э́тот шкаф для *чи́стой* оде́жды, а э́тот для ГРЯЗНОЙ оде́жды.
16. У него́ на рабо́те *аккура́тный* вид, а до́ма вид у него́ НЕОПРЯТНЫЙ.

Adjectives whose Stem Ends in a Soft -н

A small number of adjectives have a stem ending in a soft **-н**. These soft-stem adjectives take endings beginning with a soft-series vowel (**и, е, я,** or **ю**). The declension of the soft-stem adjective **си́ний** *blue* is given in the following table.

	Masculine,	Neuter	Feminine	Plural
Nom.	си́ний	си́нее	си́няя	си́ние
Acc. Inan./Anim.	си́ний/си́него		си́нюю	си́ние/си́них
Gen.	си́него		си́ней	си́них
Prep.	о си́нем		о си́ней	о си́них
Dat.	си́нему		си́ней	си́ним
Instr.	си́ним		си́ней	си́ними

The following are some common adjectives with a stem ending in soft **-н**. The majority of these adjectives denote either "time" or "place":

Time

весе́нний	spring	вече́рний	evening
зи́мний	winter	у́тренний	morning
ле́тний	summer	ны́нешний	present-day
осе́нний	autumn	тепе́решний	present-day
вчера́шний	yesterday's	тогда́шний	of that time
за́втрашний	tomorrow's	неда́вний	recent
сего́дняшний	today's	да́вний	old, long-standing
ра́нний	early	дре́вний	ancient
по́здний	late	пре́жний	former

Place

ве́рхний	upper, top	бли́жний	near
ни́жний	lower, bottom	да́льний	far
пере́дний	front	вну́тренний	internal
сре́дний	middle	вне́шний	external
за́дний	back, rear	дома́шний	home, domestic
зде́шний	local	сосе́дний	neighboring

Miscellaneous

и́скренний	sincere	ли́шний	spare, unnecessary
си́ний	blue	посторо́нний	outside, extraneous
после́дний	last		

2. Complete the sentences by inserting the soft-stem adjectives in parentheses into the required case form.

1. О́н рабо́тал над докла́дом с _____(ра́нний) утра́ до _____(по́здний) ве́чера.
2. Ко мне́ подошли́ и спроси́ли: "У ва́с не́т _____ (ли́шний) биле́та".
3. В _____ (сосе́дний) кварти́ре живёт америка́нский бизнесме́н.
4. Студе́нты гото́вятся к _____ (после́дний) экза́мену.
5. Мо́й оте́ц чита́ет «Пра́вду» и «_____ (Вече́рняя) Москву́»

6. Она́ сама́, без по́мощи му́жа, занима́ется все́ми _____ (дома́шний) дела́ми.
7. Мы́ бы́ли с детьми́ в ку́кольном теа́тре на _____ (у́тренний) спекта́кле.
8. Я́ узна́л э́ту но́вость из _____ (сего́дняшний) газе́ты.
9. Пассажи́р положи́л свои́ ве́щи на _____ (ве́рхний) по́лку.
10. У _____ (зде́шний) люде́й надо́лго оста́нется в па́мяти э́то землетрясе́ние.

Adjectives whose Stem Ends in -г, -к, -х

Adjectives with a stem ending in the consonants **-г**, **-к**, or **-х** undergo Spelling Rule 1 (after **г**, **к**, **х** write **-и**, never **-ы**) in the plural of all the cases, and in certain forms of the singular. Adjectives with a stem in one of these consonants usually have stress on the stem (**ру́сский** *Russian*), but may also occur with stress on the ending (**дорого́й** *expensive*). The declension of stem-stressed **ру́сский** is presented in the following table.

	Masculine, Neuter	Feminine	Plural
Nom.	ру́сский ру́сское	ру́сская	ру́сские
Acc. Inan./Anim.	ру́сский/ру́сского	ру́сскую	ру́сские/ру́сских
Gen.	ру́сского	ру́сской	ру́сских
Prep.	о ру́сском	о ру́сской	о ру́сских
Dat.	ру́сскому	ру́сской	ру́сским
Instr.	ру́сским	ру́сской	ру́сскими

Note: The interrogative pronoun **како́й** *what sort of, which?* and the demonstrative pronoun **тако́й** *such a* decline like the end-stressed adjective **дорого́й**.

The following are some commonly used adjectives with a stem in **г**, **к**, **х**.

Stem-stressed

бли́зкий	close	лёгкий	easy
высо́кий	tall	мя́гкий	soft
вели́кий	great	сла́дкий	sweet
ги́бкий	flexible	стро́гий	severe
гро́мкий	loud	ти́хий	quiet
жа́ркий	hot	то́нкий	thin
далёкий	distant	у́зкий	narrow
до́лгий	long	широ́кий	wide
жа́ркий	hot	я́ркий	bright

End-stressed

дорого́й	dear, expensive	плохо́й	bad
городско́й	city	глухо́й	deaf
мужско́й	masculine, male	сухо́й	dry

3. Complete the sentences, filling in the blanks with the required form of the adjective in parentheses.

1. В _____ (жа́ркий) дни́ лю́ди ча́сто приезжа́ют на э́то го́рное о́зеро.
2. Са́мым _____ (вели́кий) поэ́том в Росси́и счита́ется Алекса́ндр Пу́шкин.
3. Всё бо́льше и бо́льше автомоби́лей е́здят по _____ (широ́кий) у́лицам Москвы́.

4. В _____ (такóй) _____ (дорогóй) ресторáнах обéдают тóлько богáтые лю́ди.
5. Смотрéть без тёмных очкóв на _____ (я́ркий) сóлнце врéдно для глáз.
6. Нью-Йóрк извéстен своúми óчень _____ (высóкий) домáми.
7. Отéц ругáл сы́на за _____ (плохóй) отмéтки.
8. Дéти лю́бят _____ (слáдкий) пúщу.
9. Он об э́том говорúл тóлько с _____ (блúзкий) друзья́ми.
10. Всé турúсты устáли пóсле _____ (дóлгий) экскýрсии.

Adjectives whose Stem Ends in -ж, -ч, -ш, -щ

Like adjectives with a stem in **-г**, **-к**, **-х**, adjectives whose stem ends in one of the unpaired consonants **-ж**, **-ч**, **-ш**, **-щ** undergo Spelling Rule 1 and therefore have several endings beginning with **-и** (e.g., the plural endings **-ие**, **-их**, **-им**, **-ими**). In addition, adjectives in one of these unpaired consonants undergo Spelling Rule 3 (page 11): after the unpaired consonants write unstressed **e**, but stressed **ó**. The declension of both stem-stressed **хорóший** *good* and end-stressed **большóй** *big* is presented in the table below.

	Masculine, Neuter	Feminine	Plural
Nom.	хорóший хорóшее большóй большóе	хорóшая большáя	хорóшие большúе
Acc.	*Inan. = Nom.* *Anim. = Gen.*	хорóшую большýю	*Inan. = Nom.* *Anim. = Gen.*
Gen.	хорóшего большóго	хорóшей большóй	хорóших большúх
Prep.	о хорóшем о большóм	о хорóшей о большóй	о хорóших о большúх
Dat.	хорóшему большóму	хорóшей большóй	хорóшим большúм
Instr.	хорóшим большúм	хорóшей большóй	хорóшими большúми

Following are some common adjectives with a stem ending in **-ж**, **-ч**, **-ш**, **-щ**.

бýдущий	*future*	óбщий	*common*
бы́вший	*former*	ры́жий	*red-haired*
везýчий	*lucky*	рабóчий	*working*
горя́чий	*hot*	свéжий	*fresh*
млáдший	*younger*	стáрший	*older*
неуклю́жий	*clumsy*	хорóший	*good*
настоя́щий	*real, genuine*	чужóй	*someone else's*

4. Complete the sentences, filling in the blanks with the adjective in parentheses in the required form.

1. Не су́йте сво́й но́с в (чужо́й) _____ дела́.
2. Земля́ покры́лась (све́жий) _____ сне́гом.
3. Осторо́жно! Не тро́гай блю́до, оно́ (горя́чий) _____ .
4. На́м повезло́ с (хоро́ший) _____ пого́дой.
5. У неё с му́жем мно́го (о́бщий) _____ интере́сов.
6. Авто́бус останови́лся пе́ред (большо́й) _____ зда́нием.
7. Роди́тели осо́бенно забо́тятся о (мла́дший) _____ сы́не.
8. Я́ всегда́ легко́ узнаю́ свою́ до́чь по её (ры́жий) _____ голове́.
9. Она́ мечта́ет о (настоя́щий) _____ любви́.
10. По (рабо́чий) _____ дня́м магази́ны откры́ты до девяти́.
11. Она́ уже́ сейча́с гото́вится к своему́ (бу́дущий) _____ ребёнку.
12. Преподава́тель получи́л письмо́ от (бы́вший) _____ студе́нта.

THE SHORT FORM OF ADJECTIVES

Most qualitative adjectives can occur in a short form, used only predicatively. Relational adjectives, including all adjectives with the suffix **-ск-** (e.g., **де́тский** *children's*) and **-ян-** (e.g., **деревя́нный** *wooden*) do not have short forms.

The short form of the adjective is derived from the long form. The masculine short form is equal to the adjective stem, minus the long-form ending. The feminine, neuter, and plural forms are comprised of the stem, plus the first vowel of the long-form ending: feminine **-а**, neuter **-о**, and plural **-ы** (or **-и**). Compare the long and short forms of the adjectives **краси́вый** *pretty* and **высо́кий** *tall*:

	Long form	*Short form*	*Long form*	*Short form*
Masculine	**краси́в-**ый	**краси́в**	**высо́к-**ий	**высо́к**
Feminine	**краси́в-**ая	**краси́в-**а	**высо́к-**ая	**высок-**а́
Neuter	**краси́в-**ое	**краси́в-**о	**высо́к-**ое	**высок-**о́
Plural	**краси́в-**ые	**краси́в-**ы	**высо́к-**ие	**высок-**и́

Adjectives whose stem ends in a cluster of two or more consonants normally have a vowel inserted between the final two consonants in the *masculine* form. For adjectives which have a consonant cluster with a final **-н**, the inserted vowel is usually **-е-**; for clusters with a final **-к**, the inserted vowel is usually **-о-**.

Following are some common adjectives that have a consonant cluster ending in **-н** with an inserted **-е-** in the masculine short form:

Stems with cluster in **-н-**		*Short forms*
бе́дный	*poor*	**бе́ден** (бедна́, бе́дно, бедны́)
ва́жный	*important*	**ва́жен** (важна́, ва́жно, важны́)
голо́дный	*hungry*	**го́лоден** (голодна́, голодно́, голодны́)
гря́зный	*dirty*	**гря́зен** (грязна́, гря́зно, грязны́)
дли́нный	*long*	**дли́нен**, (длинна́, дли́нно, длинны́)
дру́жный	*amicable*	**дру́жен** (дружна́, дру́жно, дружны́)
жела́тельный	*desirable*	**жела́телен** (-льна, -льно, -льны)
заба́вный	*amusing*	**заба́вен** (заба́вна, заба́вно, заба́вны)
интере́сный	*interesting*	**интере́сен** (-сна, -сно, -сны)
кра́сный	*red*	**кра́сен** (красна́, красно́, красны́)
ло́жный	*false*	**ло́жен** (ло́жна, ло́жно, ло́жны)
мо́дный	*fashionable*	**мо́ден** (модна́, мо́дно, мо́дны)

ну́жный	*necessary*	ну́жен (нужна́, нужно́, нужны́)
поле́зный	*useful, helpful*	поле́зен (поле́зна, поле́зно, поле́зны)
ра́вный	*equal*	ра́вен (равна́, равно́, равны́)
серьёзный	*serious*	серьёзен (серьёзна, серьёзно, серьёзны)
тру́дный	*difficult*	тру́ден (трудна́, тру́дно, трудны́)
у́мный	*smart*	умён (умна́, умно́, умны́)
я́сный	*clear*	я́сен (ясна́, я́сно, ясны́)

Note: Two adjectives with a consonant cluster ending in **-н** have an inserted **-о-** in the masculine short form: **по́лный** *full* (**по́лон**) and **смешно́й** *funny* (**смешо́н**).

Following are a few common adjectives with a consonant cluster ending in **-к** that have an inserted **-о-** in the masculine short form.

Stems with a cluster in **-к**		*Short forms*
бли́зкий	*near*	бли́зок (близка́, бли́зко, близки́)
коро́ткий	*short, brief*	коро́ток (коротка́, ко́ротко, коротки́)
кре́пкий	*strong*	кре́пок (крепка́, кре́пко, крепки́)
лёгкий	*easy, light*	лёгок (легка́, легко́, легки́)
ни́зкий	*low*	ни́зок (низка́, ни́зко, низки́)
сла́дкий	*sweet*	сла́док (сладка́, сла́дко, сладки́)
у́зкий	*narrow*	у́зок (узка́, у́зко, узки́)

The following two adjectives have special short forms:

большо́й	*big*	вели́к, велика́, велико́, велики́
ма́ленький	*small*	ма́л, мала́, мало́, малы́

Note: Alongside the short-form adjective **вели́к** *(too) big* is a long-form adjective with the same root, but with a different meaning **вели́кий** *great*, e.g., **Пётр Вели́кий** *Peter the Great*, **Екатери́на Вели́кая** *Catherine the Great*.

Use of Short-Form Adjectives

Short-form adjectives can only be used predicatively after a linking verb, usually **бы́ть** *to be*. Short-form adjectives agree in gender and number with the subject, but they are not inflected for case.

In the present tense the linking verb **бы́ть** is omitted before a predicate adjective.

Фи́льм *интере́сен.*	*The movie is interesting.*
Кни́га *интере́сна.*	*The book is interesting.*
Письмо́ *интере́сно.*	*The letter is interesting.*
Заня́тия *интере́сны.*	*The classes are interesting.*

In the past tense one of the forms **бы́л, была́, бы́ло, бы́ли** is used, whichever agrees with the gender and number of the subject.

Ча́й **бы́л** *кре́пок.*	*The tea was strong.*
Во́дка **была́** *крепка́.*	*The vodka was strong.*
Вино́ **бы́ло** *вку́сно.*	*The wine was tasty.*
Блины́ **бы́ли** *вкусны́.*	*The pancakes were tasty.*

In the future tense either **бу́дет** or **бу́дут** is used, depending on whether the subject is singular or plural.

Зада́ча бу́дет *трудна́.*	*The problem will be difficult.*
Экза́мены бу́дут *трудны́.*	*The exams will be difficult.*

5. Rewrite the following sentences, replacing the attributive long form of the adjective with a predicative short form.

> *Model:* Э́то *тру́дный* вопро́с.   >   Вопро́с *тру́ден.*
> *This is a difficult question.*   *The question is difficult.*

1. Э́то кре́пкий ча́й.   > Ча́й _____.
2. Э́то поле́зный сове́т.   > Сове́т _____.
3. Э́то серьёзная пробле́ма.   > Пробле́ма _____.
4. Э́то прекра́сный де́нь.   > Де́нь _____.
5. Э́то коро́ткий пиджа́к.   > Пиджа́к _____.
6. Э́то бе́дный стари́к.   > Стари́к _____.
7. Э́то ну́жный слова́рь.   > Слова́рь _____.
8. Э́то ни́зкий за́работок.   > За́работок _____.
9. Э́то лёгкий зачёт.   > Зачёт _____.
10. Э́то сла́дкий апельси́н.   > Апельси́н _____.
11. Э́то у́мный ребёнок.   > Ребёнок _____.
12. Э́то по́лный зал.   > За́л _____.
13. Э́то ра́вные по́рции.   > По́рции _____.
14. Э́то свобо́дные места́.   > Места́ _____.
15. Э́то лёгкая су́мка.   > Су́мка _____.

Choosing the Short Form or Long Form in the Predicate

Many adjectives have both a long form and a short form that can occur predicatively.

Э́та кни́га *интере́сная.*	*This book is interesting.*
Э́та кни́га *интере́сна.*	*This book is interesting.*
Вода́ была́ *тёплая.*	*The water was warm.*
Вода́ была́ *тепла́.*	*The water was warm.*
Ча́й бу́дет *кре́пкий.*	*The tea will be strong.*
Ча́й бу́дет *кре́пок.*	*The tea will be strong.*

The choice between the short form and long (nominative case) form of the adjective in predicative position is determined by several factors. Following are some often-noted distinctions between the short and long forms:

(i) For many adjectives, the choice between the predicative short form and long form is essentially one of style. The short form indicates a more formal style characteristic of written Russian; the long form indicates a more informal style typical of spoken Russian.

Она́ *у́мная.*	*She is smart.* (informal)
Она́ *умна́.*	*She is smart.* (formal)
Он *лени́вый.*	*He is lazy.* (informal)
Он *лени́в.*	*He is lazy.* (formal)

(ii) For some adjectives, the predicative short form in certain contexts may denote a temporary property or state of the subject; the long form, by contrast, indicates a property that is permanently or inherently associated with the subject. Following are a few common adjectives which may show this distinction.

больно́й	*(chronically) ill*	бо́лен	*ill, sick (at a particular time)*
занято́й	*(a) busy (person)*	за́нят	*busy (at a particular time)*
здоро́вый	*healthy (in general)*	здоро́в	*healthy (not now ill)*
споко́йный	*calm (by nature)*	споко́ен	*calm (at the moment)*

Де́душка *больно́й.*	*Grandfather is (chronically) ill.*
Де́душка сего́дня *бо́лен.*	*Grandfather is ill today.*
О́н *занято́й.*	*He is (a) busy (man).*
О́н сейча́с *за́нят.*	*He is busy now.*
О́н тако́й *здоро́вый.*	*He is so healthy (strong).*
О́н бы́л бо́лен, но тепе́рь о́н *здоро́в.*	*He was sick, but now he is well.*
Э́та река́ *споко́йная.*	*This river is (a) calm (one).*
Река́ сего́дня *споко́йна.*	*The river today is calm.*

6. Complete the sentence with the appropriate long or short form of the adjective.

   здоро́вый/здоро́в
   1. Она́ спортсме́нка. Она́ всегда́ така́я _____. Но сего́дня она́ не _____. Она́ простуди́лась.

   занято́й/за́нят
   2. Мо́й му́ж дире́ктор иностра́нной компа́нии. О́н тако́й _____. Но сего́дня он не _____, потому́ что в стране́ его́ компа́нии пра́здник.

   больно́й/бо́лен
   3. Ба́бушка _____. Она́ до́лго страда́ет а́стмой.
   4. Моя́ до́чь не пошла́ сего́дня в шко́лу. Она́ _____.

   споко́йный/споко́ен
   5. Чёрное мо́ре _____. Но сейча́с оно́ не _____ из-за се́верных ветро́в.

(iii) A small number of adjectives that denote certain gradable properties like size and age (e.g., "big," "small," "young," "old") have a predicative short form indicating that the given property is excessive ("too . . .") with respect to the needs of a particular person or circumstance. The predicative long form of the same adjective, by contrast, wholly identifies this property with the subject. Following are common adjectives that may show this distinction.

большо́й	*big*	вели́к	*too big*
ма́ленький	*small*	ма́л	*too small*
дли́нный	*long*	дли́нен	*too long*
коро́ткий	*short*	коро́ток	*too short*
у́зкий	*narrow*	у́зок	*too narrow*
широ́кий	*wide*	широ́к	*too wide*
молодо́й	*young*	мо́лод	*too young*
ста́рый	*old*	ста́р	*too old*

Э́та шля́па *больша́я*.	*This hat is big (compared to others).*
Э́та шля́па *велика́*.	*This hat is too big (for someone).*
Э́ти де́тские ту́фли таки́е *ма́ленькие*.	*These children's shoes are so small.*
Э́ти ту́фли мне́ *малы́*.	*These shoes are too small for me.*
Её ю́бки всегда́ *дли́нные*.	*Her skirts are always long (ones).*
Э́та ю́бка е́й *длинна́*.	*This skirt is too long for her.*
Я́ уже́ *ста́рый*.	*I'm already (an) old (man).*
Я́ *ста́р* для неё.	*I am too old for her.*
О́н *молодо́й*.	*He is (a) young (man).*
О́н *мо́лод* для э́той рабо́ты.	*He is too young for this work.*

7. Complete the sentence with the appropriate long or short form of the adjective.

ма́ленький/ма́л
1. Э́та кварти́ра _____ для на́шей семьи́.
2. На́ша кварти́ра _____ , но ую́тная.

ста́рый/ста́р
3. Дома́ в э́том райо́не _____ , но больши́е.
4. Хотя́ э́тот мужчи́на не _____ , но он _____ для э́той рабо́ты.

широ́кий/широ́к
5. По-мо́ему, э́ти мо́дные штаны́ тебе́ не иду́т, они́ _____ тебе́.
6. Штаны́ у него́ всегда́ дли́нные и _____ , как у кло́уна в ци́рке.

у́зкий/у́зок
7. Э́та ю́бка о́чень _____ . Та́ ю́бка е́й то́же о́чень _____ .

дли́нный/дли́нен
8. Э́ти чёрные брю́ки не _____ , но ему́ они́ _____ .

молодо́й/мо́лод
9. Она́ не _____ выходи́ть за́муж, но име́ть дете́й она́ ещё _____ .

большо́й/вели́к
10. Э́то пальто́ не_____ , но оно́ _____ для меня́.

(iv) The short and long form of some adjectives may differ in meaning; that is, in certain adjectives that have more than one sense, one of those senses may predominate in the short form of the adjective. The following are a few examples of adjectives of this type.

живо́й	*lively (full of energy)*	жи́в	*alive*
пра́вый	*right (just)*	пра́в	*right (correct)*
смешно́й	*funny*	смешо́н	*ridiculous*
ужа́сный	*horrible (very bad)*	ужа́сен	*horrifying (evoking horror)*

Ребёнок о́чень *живо́й*.	*The child is very lively.*
Ры́ба ещё *жива́*.	*The fish is still alive.*
На́ше де́ло *пра́вое*.	*Our cause is just.*
Вы́ соверше́нно *пра́вы*.	*You are absolutely right.*
Его́ анекдо́ты о́чень *смешны́е*.	*His jokes are very funny.*
О́н *смешо́н*.	*He is (being) ridiculous.*
Пого́да была́ *ужа́сная*.	*The weather was horrible.*
Его́ ви́д бы́л *ужа́сен*.	*His appearance was horrifying.*

8. Complete the sentences with the appropriate long or short form of the adjective.

живо́й/жив

1. И́х до́чка така́я _____. Она́ всегда́ бе́гает и весели́тся.
2. Мо́й дру́г попа́л в большу́ю ава́рию, но о́н оста́лся _____.

непра́вый/непра́в

3. Э́то реше́ние бы́ло _____. На́до пода́ть на апелля́цию.
4. На э́тот раз она́ была́ _____.

смешно́й/смешо́н

5. О́н тако́й _____. Он всегда́ заставля́ет на́с смея́ться на уро́ке.
6. Э́то утвержде́ние _____. Никто́ не пове́рит э́тому.

ужа́сный/ужа́сен

7. Когда́ о́н посмоте́л на меня́, его́ глаза́ бы́ли _____.
8. Де́нь у меня́ бы́л _____. Я́ не сда́л экза́мен и опозда́л на по́езд.

(v) If the grammatical subject is one of a small number of pronouns, e.g., **э́то** *this/that*, *it*, **всё** *everything*, or **что́** *what*, a predicate adjective must be in the neuter short form.

Всё *хорошо́.*	*Everything is good.*
Всё *норма́льно.*	*Everything is okay* (lit. *normal*).
Э́то о́чень *интере́сно.*	*That is very interesting.*
Э́то бы́ло про́сто *смешно́.*	*That was simply ridiculous.*
Э́то бу́дет *тру́дно.*	*It will be difficult.*
Что́ *непоня́тно?*	*What is not understood?*
Всё *я́сно.*	*Everything is clear (understood).*

(vi) A predicate adjective followed by a complement must be in the short form. Below are several adjectives commonly found in the predicative short form followed by various complements.

Note: All the short forms below, except **до́лжен** *supposed to* and **рад** *glad (to)*, have a corresponding long form.

Followed by an Infinitive

гото́в   *ready to*
Мы́ *гото́вы* **е́хать в аэропо́рт.**   *We are ready to go to the airport.*

до́лжен   *supposed to, must*
Она́ *должна́* **позвони́ть на́м.**   *She is supposed to call us.*

наме́рен   *intend to*
Я́ *наме́рен* **голосова́ть за него́.**   *I intend to vote for him.*

ра́д   *glad to*
Мы́ о́чень *ра́ды* **ви́деть тебя́.**   *We are very glad to see you.*

свобо́ден   *free to*
Ты́ *свобо́дна* **де́лать как хо́чешь.**   *You are free to do as you wish.*

спосо́бен   *capable of*
О́н не *спосо́бен* **поня́ть э́то.**   *He is incapable of understanding that.*

скло́нен   *inclined to*
Я́ *скло́нен* **согласи́ться с ва́ми.**   *I am inclined to agree with you.*

Followed by a Prepositional Phrase

бли́зок с (+ Instr.)	*close to; intimate with*
Óн óчень *бли́зок с* отцо́м.	*He is very close to his father.*
Она́ была́ *близка́ с* ни́м.	*She was intimate with him.*

винова́т в (+ Prep.); **пе́ред** (+ Instr.)	*at fault, to blame for; guilty before*
Я́ *винова́т во* всём.	*I'm to blame for everything.*
Óн *винова́т в* то́м, что она́ ушла́.	*It is his fault that she left.*
Óн *винова́т пе́ред* жено́й.	*He did his wife wrong.*

гото́в к (+ Dat.); **на** (+ Acc.)	*prepared for, ready for*
Она́ *гото́ва к* экза́мену.	*She is prepared for the exam.*
Óн *гото́в на* всё.	*He is ready for anything.*
	(i.e., ready to resort to any measure)

знако́м с (+ Instr.)	*acquainted with*
Я́ хорошо́ *знако́м с* его́ рабо́той.	*I am well acquainted with his work.*

похо́ж на (+ Acc.)	*similar to*
Она́ óчень *похо́жа на* ма́му.	*She is very much like her mom.*

равноду́шен к (+ Dat.)	*indifferent to*
Óн *равноду́шен к* поли́тике.	*He is indifferent to politics.*

серди́т на (+ Acc.)	*angry at*
Она́ *серди́та на* меня́.	*She is angry at me.*

силён в (+ Prep.)	*strong in, good at*
Óн *силён в* иностра́нных языка́х.	*He is good at foreign languages.*

согла́сен с (+ Instr.); **на** (+ Acc.)	*agree with; agree to*
Я́ *согла́сен с* э́той иде́ей.	*I agree with this idea.*
Я́ не *согла́сен на* э́то.	*I do not agree to that.*

Followed by a Noun/Pronoun in an Oblique Case

благода́рен (+ Dat.)	*grateful to*
Мы́ óчень *благода́рны* ва́м.	*We are very grateful to you*

бога́т (+ Instr.)	*rich in*
Росси́я *бога́та* ре́ками и óзёрами.	*Russia is rich in rivers and lakes.*

дово́лен (+ Instr.)	*satisfied/pleased with*
Дире́ктор *дово́лен* на́шей рабо́той.	*The director is pleased with our work.*

досто́ин (+ Gen.)	*worthy of, deserves*
Она́ *досто́йна* награ́ды.	*She deserves an award.*

по́лон (+ Gen.)	*full of*
У́лицы бы́ли *полны́* наро́ду.	*The streets were full of people.*

пре́дан (+ Dat.)	*devoted to*
Óн *пре́дан* свои́м де́тям.	*He is devoted to his children.*

9. Complete the sentence by supplying the required long or short form of the adjective.

тру́дный/тру́ден

1. Э́то не _____ зада́ча, но для него́ она́ бу́дет _____ .

богáтый/богáт

2. У негó нéт мнóго дéнег, но óн _____ душóй.

довóльный/довóлен

3. Мóй дя́дя вéчно не_____ , но моя́ тётя всегдá _____ всéм.

достóйный/достóин

4. Óн _____ похвалы́.

5. Онá _____ жéнщина.

прéданный/прéдан

6. Óн добúлся мнóгого в жúзни, потомý что бы́л _____ своемý дéлу.

7. Онá лю́бящая мáть и _____ женá.

пóлный/пóлон

8. У нáс сейчáс _____ дóм. Приéхали всé рóдственники на прáздник.

9. У меня́ дóм _____ гостéй.

свобóдный/свобóден

10. Онá не _____ пойтú на концéрт сейчáс.

11. Мы́ живём в _____ странé.

блúзкий/блúзок

12. Мой дéти óчень _____ друг с дрýгом.

13. Онú _____ друзья́ и хорошó поддéрживают друг дрýга.

виновáтый/виновáт

14. Óн сознáлся, что _____ в э́том.

15. Собáка посмотрéла на меня́ _____ глазáми.

спосóбный/спосóбен

16. Я́ _____ программúст, но я не _____ решúть э́ту задáчу.

склóнный/склóнен

17. Я́ _____ повéрить емý.

18. Лю́дям, _____ к депрéссии, не рекомендýется смотрéть э́тот фúльм.

готóвый/готóв

19. Стройтели сдаю́т дéсять _____ домóв в концé мéсяца, а жúтели _____ въéхать ужé сейчáс.

знакóмый/знакóм

20. Я́ шёл по óчень _____ ýлице, но лю́ди мнé бы́ли ужé не _____ .

похóжий/похóж

21. Э́ти дéвочки двойня́шки, но онú не óчень _____ друг на дрýга.

22. У Лéны с мáмой óчень _____ голосá, и úх чáсто пýтают по телефóну.

сúльный/силён

23. Онá отлúчная пловчúха, и онá тáкже _____ в гимнáстике.

24. В э́той комáнде éсть и _____ и слáбые игрокú.

равнодýшный/равнодýшен

25. Óн преслéдует её, но онá _____ к немý.

26. Онú _____ лю́ди, и поэ́тому у нúх нéт друзéй.

нормáльный/нормáлен

27. Кáк делá? Всё _____ ?

28. У нúх _____ , стабúльные отношéния.

непоня́тный/непоня́тен

29. Мóжет бы́ть, э́то современно и авангáрдно, но мнé э́то _____ .

30. Для меня́ э́то такóй _____ предмéт.

Use of Какой vs. Каков and Такой vs. Таков

Corresponding to the long and short forms of adjectives are two different interrogative pronouns, respectively **какой** and **каков** (**какова́**, **каково́**, **каковы́**) *what (sort of)*. The pronoun **какой** agrees in gender, number, and case with the noun it modifies; the pronoun **каков** is a short (caseless) form used only predicatively.

— *Какой* **он студе́нт?**	*What kind of student is he?*
— **Он** *у́мный* **студе́нт.**	*He is a smart student.*
— *Каков* **он?**	*What is he like?*
— **Он** *умён.*	*He is smart.*
— *Како́е* **у ва́с впечатле́ние?**	*What impression do you have?*
— **У меня́** *хоро́шее* **впечатле́ние.**	*I have a good impression.*
— *Каково́* **ва́ше мне́ние о нём?**	*What is your opinion of him?*
— **По-мо́ему, он** *спосо́бный* **челове́к.**	*I think he is a capable person.*
Кака́я **сего́дня пого́да?**	*What is the weather like today?*
Какова́ **це́ль э́того пла́на?**	*What is the goal of this plan?*
Каки́е **у ва́с пла́ны?**	*What plans do you have?*
Каковы́ **ва́ши пла́ны?**	*What are your plans?*

Note: Both **какой** and **каков** function not only as interrogatives but also as relative pronouns (see Chapter 4); they also occur in exclamations, e.g., **Како́й у неё го́лос!** *What a voice she has!* **Какова́ та́м приро́да!** *What (beautiful) nature there is there!*

Similarly, there are two different demonstrative pronouns, **такой** and **таков** (**такова́**, **таково́**, **таковы́**) *so, such*, corresponding to the long and short form of adjectives. The pronoun **такой**, like the long-form adjective it qualifies, can be used both attributively and predicatively. The short demonstrative **таков**, however, is used only predicatively, and may precede the noun.

Он *такой* **челове́к, какой нам ну́жен.**	*He is just the kind of person we need.*
Така́я **ша́пка мне́ и нужна́.**	*I need a hat just like that.*
Я хочу́ прожи́ть *таку́ю* **жи́знь.**	*I want to live such a life.*
Моё пальто́ не *тако́е.*	*My coat is not like that one.*
Он *тако́в,* **ка́к ты его́ и опи́сывал.**	*He is just as you described him.*
Такова́ **жи́знь.**	*Such is life.*
Таково́ **моё мне́ние.**	*Such is my opinion.*
Таковы́ **на́ши впечатле́ния.**	*Such are our impressions.*

Use of Такой vs. Та́к and Какой vs. Ка́к

The pronoun **такой** may also be used to intensify the property or state denoted by the long form of the adjective, with which it agrees in gender, number, and case. The same intensifying function with the short form of adjectives (and adverbs) is carried by the adverb **та́к**.

Ва́ша до́чь *така́я* **краси́вая.**	*Your daughter is such a pretty girl.*
Она́ *та́к* **краси́ва в э́том пла́тье.**	*She is so pretty in that dress.*
Ты́ *тако́й* **до́брый.**	*You are such a kind man.*
Ты́ *та́к* **до́бр к на́м.**	*You are so kind to us.*

Расска́зы *таки́е* **интере́сные.**	*The stories are such interesting ones.*
Расска́зы *та́к* **интере́сны.**	*The stories are so interesting.*
Óн *та́к* **интере́сно расска́зывает.**	*He tells stories so interestingly.*

In exclamatory sentences the pronoun **како́й** *what* modifies the long form of the adjective, while the adverb **ка́к** *how* modifies the short form:

Кака́я **она́ у́мная!**	*What a smart girl she is!*
Ка́к **она́ умна́!**	*How smart she is!*
Како́й **о́н молодо́й!**	*What a young man he is!*
Ка́к **о́н мо́лод!**	*How young he is!*
Каки́е **они́ глу́пые.**	*How foolish they are.*
Ка́к **они́ глупы́.**	*How stupid they are!*
Ка́к **э́то до́рого!**	*How expensive this is!*
Ка́к **э́то хорошо́!**	*How good this is!*

10. Complete the sentences, supplying the appropriate form of one of the following: **како́й**, **тако́й**, **та́к**, **ка́к како́в**, **тако́в**.

1. (What) _____ ва́ши наме́рения?
2. (What) _____ у ва́с пла́ны на бу́дущее?
3. (Such) _____ челове́ка на́до уважа́ть.
4. Óн (so) _____ умён.
5. (What) _____ же о́н идио́т!
6. О́н ника́к не спра́вится с э́тим. (Such) _____ моё мне́ние.
7. Сего́дня бы́ло голосова́ние. (What) _____ результа́т?
8. О́н (such) _____ любе́зный челове́к.
9. (What) _____ она́ краси́ва!

ADJECTIVES USED AS NOUNS

Russian has a number of adjectives that can also function as nouns, e.g., **ру́сский** *a Russian*. Typically, these "adjectival nouns" arise from the omission of a "modified" noun, which, though absent, still determines their gender and number, e.g., **ру́сский** (челове́к *person*). Though they function as nouns, these words decline like any long-form adjective, e.g., **Она́ вы́шла за́муж за ру́сского** [Acc. Anim.] *She married a Russian.*

Following are some commonly used adjectival nouns grouped according to their omitted, but understood, noun. Among the adjectives that refer to people, some have both a masculine and feminine form, while others occur only in the masculine; all adjectives referring to people can occur in the plural (e.g., **ру́сские** *Russians*).

Note: Some adjectival nouns can be used as an adjective or a noun (**Зде́сь живёт** *ру́сская* **семья́** *A Russian family lives here*, **Зде́сь живёт** *ру́сская* *A Russian (f.) lives here*); others have lost the ability to function as an adjective, and are used only as a noun (**портно́й** *tailor*).

Note: A large number of participles, which decline like adjectives, may also be used as nouns denoting people and things, e.g., **куря́щий** *a smoker*, **люби́мый** *loved one*, **ископа́емые** *minerals*, **отдыха́ющий** *vacationer*.

(мужчи́на *man*/же́нщина *woman*)
больно́й/больна́я *ill person* (*m./f.*), **взро́слый/взро́слая** *grownup, adult* (*m./f.*), **знако́мый/знако́мая** *acquaintance* (*m./f.*), **ру́сский/ру́сская** *Russian* (*m./f.*)

(челове́к *person*)
вое́нный *soldier*, **портно́й** *tailor*, **рабо́чий** *worker*, **учёный** *scientist*

(ко́мната *room*)
ва́нная *bathroom*, **гости́ная** *living room*, **де́тская** *nursery, children's room*, **операцио́нная** *operating room*, **приёмная** *reception room*, **прихо́жая** *entrance hall*, **убо́рная** *half-bath*, **столо́вая** *dining room*

(ла́вка *shop*)
бу́лочная *bread store*, **бутербро́дная** *sandwich shop*, **заку́сочная** *snack-bar*, **конди́терская** *confectioner's shop*, **моло́чная** *dairy shop*, **парикма́херская** *hair salon*, **пивна́я** *alehouse, pub*, **шашлы́чная** *shish kebab house*

(существо́ *being*)
живо́тное *(domestic) animal*, **насеко́мое** *insect*

(блю́до *dish*)
пе́рвое *first course*, **второ́е** *second course/entrée*, **тре́тье** *third course/dessert*, **жарко́е** *roasted meat dish*, **сла́дкое** *dessert*

(вино́ *wine*)
шампа́нское *champagne*

(молоко́ *milk*)
моро́женое *ice cream*

(вре́мя *time*)
настоя́щее *the present*, **про́шлое** *the past*, **бу́дущее** *the future*

(де́ньги *money*)
нали́чные *cash*, **сверхуро́чные** *overtime*, **чаевы́е** *gratuities, tip*

11. Put the adjectival noun in parentheses into the required form.

1. На́м ну́жен хле́б. Я́ сбе́гаю в (бу́лочная) _____.
2. Мы́ встре́тились с дру́гом в (пивна́я) _____.
3. Всё э́то тепе́рь в (про́шлое) _____.
4. Мо́й дру́г до́лго жи́л в Росси́и и жени́лся на (ру́сская) _____.
5. Э́тот вра́ч всегда́ забо́тится о свои́х (больно́й) _____.
6. В Росси́и за поку́пки не пла́тят че́ками, а то́лько (нали́чные) _____.
7. Я́ уважа́ю рабо́ты э́того (учёный) _____.
8. Мои́ де́ти лю́бят ча́й с (моро́женое) _____.
9. На столе́ стоя́ла буты́лка (шампа́нское) _____.
10. У э́той де́вочки е́сть и ко́шка и соба́ка. Она́ лю́бит (живо́тное) _____.
11. Э́ти общежи́тия то́лько для (вое́нный) _____.
12. В э́тот па́рк с аттракцио́нами дете́й впуска́ют то́лько со (взро́слый) _____.

Neuter Singular Adjectives Used as Nouns

A number of Russian adjectives can be used as nouns with abstract meaning. Unlike the adjectival nouns discussed above, these are not related to some deleted, but still implicit, noun; rather, these occur in the neuter singular long form of the adjective with a very general, abstract meaning (**но́вое** *the new*, **ста́рое** *the old*, **мо́дное** *the stylish*, **совреме́нное** *the contemporary*): **Она́** лю́бит всё *мо́дное и совреме́нное* She loves everything stylish and contemporary.

These neuter adjectival nouns often occur in the genitive case after words expressing quantity, such as **мно́го** *much*, **ма́ло** *little*, **ничего́** *nothing*, and others when used in a "partitive" sense, e.g., **что́** *what (of)*, **что́-нубудь** *something (of)*.

Что́ *но́вого?*	*What's new?*
Ничего́ *но́вого.*	*Nothing's new.*
Он сде́лал мно́го *хоро́шего.*	*He has done much good.*
Та́м бы́ло ма́ло *интере́сного.*	*There was little of interest.*
Хо́чется что́-нибудь съе́сть *сла́денького.*	*I feel like eating something sweet.*

Note: These abstract neuter adjectival nouns can also be of participle origin, e.g., the verb **забы́ть** *to forget* > **забы́тый** *forgotten* (passive participle and adjective) > **забы́тое** *what is forgotten* (adjectival noun), as in **Мне́ ну́жно вспо́мнить** *забы́тое I need to remember what I have forgotten*. Some other examples of departicipial adjectival nouns in **-ое**: **зарабо́танное** *what is earned*, **поте́рянное** *what is lost*, **укра́денное** *what is stolen* (cf. **кра́деное** *stolen goods*, which functions only as a noun).

12. Complete the sentences with an abstract adjectival noun in the required form.

1. В Москве́ мно́го (ста́рый) _____ и (но́вый) _____.
2. Все́ де́ти лю́бят (сла́дкий) _____.
3. Он но́сит всё (дорого́й) _____.
4. Мне́ (ста́рый) _____ надое́ло.
5. Он пропи́л всё (зарабо́танный) _____.
6. В э́том не́т ничего́ (смешно́й) _____.
7. Хо́чется чего́-нибудь съе́сть (о́стренький) _____.
8. У меня́ от (о́стрый) _____ живо́т боли́т.
9. Мне́ ну́жно вы́пить чего́-нибудь (горя́чий) _____.
10. Альпини́сты взя́ли с собо́й то́лько (необходи́мый) _____.

POSSESSIVE ADJECTIVES

Possessive Adjectives of the Type Пти́чий

A number of adjectives derived from nouns denoting animals, birds, and other living things have a possessive-relational meaning: **во́лк** *wolf*/**во́лчий** *wolf's*, **коро́ва** *cow*/**коро́вий** *cow's*, **лиса́** *fox*/**ли́сий** *fox's*, **медве́дь** *bear*/**медве́жий** *bear's*, **пти́ца** *bird*/**пти́чий** *bird's*, **соба́ка** *dog*/**соба́чий** *dog's*. Several of these possessive adjectives occur in idiomatic colloquial phrases, e.g., *во́лчий* **аппети́т** *voracious appetite*, *медве́жий* **у́гол** *God-forsaken place*, *соба́чий* **хо́лод** *intense cold*. Possessive adjectives of this type follow the declensional pattern of **пти́чий** given in the table below.

	Masculine,	Neuter	Feminine	Plural
Nom.	пти́чий	пти́чье	пти́чья	пти́чьи
Acc. Inan. = Nom.	пти́чий	пти́чье	пти́чью	пти́чьи/
Anim. = Gen.	пти́чьего			пти́чьих
Gen.	пти́чьего		пти́чьей	пти́чьих
Prep.	о пти́чьем		о пти́чьей	о пти́чьих
Dat.	пти́чьему		пти́чьей	пти́чьим
Instr.	пти́чьим		пти́чьей	пти́чьими

Note: The ordinal adjective **тре́тий** *third* declines like **пти́чий** (see Chapter 6, page 194).

Possessive Adjectives in the Suffix -ин

Russian has a possessive adjective used in informal, colloquial style that is formed by adding the suffix **-ин** to the stem of nouns ending in **-а/-я**, most of which fall into two groups:

(*a*) family kin terms

ма́ма *mom*	**ма́мин** *mom's*	**ба́бушка** *grandma*	**ба́бушкин** *grandma's*
па́па *dad*	**па́пин** *dad's*	**де́душка** *grandpa*	**де́душкин** *grandpa's*
дя́дя *uncle*	**дя́дин** *uncle's*	**тётя** *aunt*	**тётин** *aunt's*

(*b*) familiar first names

Алёша	**Алёшин** *Alyosha's*	**Ми́ша**	**Ми́шин** *Masha's*
Ва́ля	**Ва́лин** *Valya's*	**Ната́ша**	**Ната́шин** *Natasha's*
Ко́ля	**Ко́лин** *Kolya's*	**Са́ша**	**Са́шин** *Sasha's*
Ма́ша	**Ма́шин** *Masha's*	**Та́ня**	**Та́нин** *Tanya's*

Note: This familiar possessive adjective may also be based on nouns denoting pets and other animals, e.g., **ко́шка** *cat*, **соба́ка** *dog* (cf. also the pejorative **су́кин сы́н** *son of a bitch* from the possessive adjective based on the noun **су́ка** *bitch*).

The possessives in **-ин** agree in gender, number, and case with the modified noun. In the nominative case they have the endings of the short-form adjective:

Masculine -∅	Neuter -o	Feminine -a	Plural -ы
Са́шин до́м	**Са́шино письмо́**	**Са́шина кни́га**	**Са́шины ту́фли**
Sasha's house	*Sasha's letter*	*Sasha's book*	*Sasha's shoes*

However, the endings in the other cases reflect a mixed noun/adjective declension. The complete declension of the possessive adjective **Са́шин** is presented in the following table.

	Masculine,	Neuter	Feminine	Plural
Nom.	**Са́шин**	**Са́шино**	**Са́шина**	**Са́шины**
Acc. Inan. = Nom.	**Са́шин/**	**Са́шино**	**Са́шину**	**Са́шины/**
Anim. = Gen.	**Са́шиного**			**Са́шиных**
Gen.	**Са́шиного**		**Са́шиной**	**Са́шиных**
Prep.	**о Са́шином**		**о Са́шиной**	**о Са́шиных**
Dat.	**Са́шиному**		**Са́шиной**	**Са́шиным**
Instr.	**Са́шиным**		**Са́шиной**	**Са́шиными**

Note: A few of these possessive adjectives denoting animals have acquired the endings of the long-form adjective in all forms, e.g., **ле́бедь** *swan* > **лебеди́ный** *swan's* («**Лебеди́ное о́зеро**» *Swan Lake*).

Я́ ви́дел *ма́мину* **подру́гу.**	*I saw Mom's girlfriend.*
Портфе́ль лежи́т в *па́пином* **кабине́те.**	*The briefcase is in Dad's study.*
Мы́ лю́бим *ба́бушкины* **пирожки́.**	*We love Grandma's pirozhki.*
Она́ ушла́ бе́з *дя́диного* **а́дреса.**	*She left without her uncle's address.*
Я́ да́л письмо́ *тётиной* **сосе́дке.**	*I gave the letter to my aunt's neighbor.*

13. Complete the sentences with the possessive form of the noun in parentheses.

1. Я́ взя́л э́ти де́ньги и́з (ма́ма) _____ су́мки.
2. Письмо́ лежи́т на (па́па) _____ столе́.
3. Я́ не могу́ найти́ (соба́чка) _____ игру́шку.
4. Сего́дня мы́ встре́тили (Та́ня) _____ дру́га.

PERSONAL NAMES (Part II)

Family Names in -ин and -ов, -ев, -ёв

Russian family names in **-ин**, **-ов**, **-ев/-ёв** (**Пу́шкин**, **Че́хов**, **Турге́нев**) originally had a possessive meaning similar to that of the possessive adjectives of the type **Са́шин** described above. Family names formed with one of these suffixes, like the possessive adjectives in **-ин**, have a mixed declension: some case forms are noun endings, while others are adjective endings. The following table gives the complete declension of the family name **Аксёнов**.

	Masculine	Feminine	Plural
Nom.	Аксёнов	Аксёнова	Аксёновы
Acc. (Anim.)	Аксёнова	Аксёнову	Аксёновых
Gen.	Аксёнова	Аксёновой	Аксёновых
Dat.	Аксёнову	Аксёновой	Аксёновым
Prep.	об Аксёнове	об Аксёновой	об Аксёновых
Instr.	Аксёновым	Аксёновой	Аксёновыми

Family Names in -ий and -ой

Russian family names in **-ий** and **-ой** (**Го́рький**, **Чайко́вский**, **Толсто́й**) are declined like regular adjectives, e.g., **Я́ люблю́ му́зыку *Чайко́вского*** *I love Tchaikovsky's music.* **Э́та кни́га о *Чайко́вском*** *This book is about Tchaikovsky.*

Foreign family names follow the same pattern as foreign first names (page 65): family names ending in a consonant decline like first-declension nouns if they denote males (e.g., **стихи́ *Ба́льмонта*** *Balmont's poetry*), but do not decline if they denote females (e.g., **биогра́фия Э́леонор *Ру́звельт*** *biography of Eleanor Roosevelt*). Foreign family names of both males and females that end in unstressed **-а**, **-я** normally do decline, especially if they are well known (**автопортре́т *Го́йи*** *self-portrait of Goya*, **пе́сни *Фра́нка Сина́тры*** *songs by Frank Sinatra*).

COMPARISON OF ADJECTIVES AND ADVERBS

The Degrees of Comparison

Adjectives can be used to compare the qualities of the nouns or pronouns they modify. Similarly, adverbs can be used to compare the manner in which verbal actions occur. Russian, like English, has three degrees of comparison: positive, comparative, and superlative.

The positive degree denotes the basic (uncompared) quality of a person or thing. Adjectives and adverbs are cited in the dictionary in the positive degree (*new*, *old*, *smart*, *quickly*, *slowly*, *interestingly*).

The comparative degree *compares* the qualities of two persons, things, or actions. In English, comparatives are formed in one of two ways: (i) by adding to the positive degree the ending -*er* (e.g., *newer*, *smarter*, *faster*, *slower*), or (ii) by combining the word *more* with the adjective or adverb (e.g., *more interesting*, *more interestingly*).

The superlative is used to indicate that, compared to several others, one person or thing possesses a quality to the *highest* degree or to a very great degree. The English superlative, like the comparative, is formed either by adding an ending (-*est*) to the positive degree (*newest*, *smartest*, *fastest*, *slowest*), or by combining the word *most* with the adjective or adverb (*most interesting*, *most interestingly*).

The methods of forming comparatives and superlatives in Russian are similar to those in English: they can be formed either by adding an ending to the adjective/adverb stem, producing a "simple comparative" and "simple superlative"; or they can be formed with the Russian equivalent of English *more* and *most*, combined with the positive degree of the adjective. This method results in the "compound comparative" and "compound superlative," respectively.

Russian Comparatives

Formation of the Compound Comparative

The compound comparative consists of two words, the indeclinable adverb **бо́лее** *more* (or **ме́нее** *less*) and the long form of the adjective, which agrees with the modified noun:

Positive Degree		*Compound Comparative*	
но́вый	new	бо́лее но́вый дом	*newer house*
		бо́лее но́вое зда́ние	*newer building*
		бо́лее но́вая маши́на	*newer car*
		бо́лее но́вые райо́ны	*newer neighborhoods*
дорого́й	expensive	ме́нее дорого́й костю́м	*less expensive suit*
		ме́нее дорого́е кольцо́	*less expensive ring*
		ме́нее дорога́я кни́га	*less expensive book*
		ме́нее дороги́е джи́нсы	*less expensive jeans*

The compound comparative can be formed from almost any adjective. A few adjectives, however, do not form a comparative with **бо́лее**. The following four adjectives, for example, do not form a compound comparative, but they do have a related adjective with comparative meaning:

большо́й	big	бо́льший	*bigger*
ма́ленький	small	ме́ньший	*smaller*
плохо́й	bad	ху́дший	*worse* (or *worst*)
хоро́ший	good	лу́чший	*better* (or *best*)

Они́ живу́т в *бо́льшем* до́ме.	*They live in a bigger house.*
Мы сня́ли *ме́ньшую* кварти́ру.	*We rented a smaller apartment.*
Кто́ из ни́х *лу́чший* писа́тель?	*Which of them is the better/best writer?*

A few other adjectives form a regular compound comparative with **бо́лее**, and in addition have a special comparative (or superlative) adjective with a different sense:

молодо́й	young	бо́лее молодо́й	*younger* (in age)
		мла́дший	*junior* (in rank)
			younger/youngest (in one's family)
ста́рый	old	бо́лее ста́рый	*older* (in age)
		ста́рший	*senior* (in rank)
			older/eldest (in one's family)

Óн *мла́дший* **нау́чный сотру́дник.**	*He is a junior research associate.*
Это́ моя́ *мла́дшая* **сестра́.**	*This is my younger/youngest sister.*
Она́ *ста́рший* **преподава́тель.**	*She is a senior instructor.*
Это́ мо́й *ста́рший* **бра́т.**	*This is my older/eldest brother.*

высо́кий	*high, tall*	**бо́лее высо́кий**	*higher, taller (in size)*
		вы́сший	*higher (in status)*
ни́зкий	*low*	**бо́лее ни́зкий**	*lower (in size)*
		ни́зший	*lower (in status)*

Это́ *бо́лее высо́кая* **гора́.**	*This is a higher mountain.*
Институ́т — это́ *вы́сшее* **уче́бное заведе́ние.**	*An institute is a higher educational institution.*
Для дро́в испо́льзуйте *ни́зшие* **сорта́ де́рева.**	*For firewood use inferior kinds of wood.*

Use of the Compound Comparative

The compound comparative with **бо́лее** is used primarily in *attributive* position, that is, preceding the noun, with which it agrees in gender, number, and case.

Для мое́й спины́ ну́жен *бо́лее твёрдый* **матра́с.**
For my back I need a firmer mattress.

Я́ предпочита́ю *бо́лее мя́гкий* **кли́мат.**
I prefer a milder climate.

Это́т костю́м сши́т для *бо́лее кру́пного* **мужчи́ны.**
This suit is tailored for a larger man.

Мы́ живём в *бо́лее но́вом* **райо́не.**
We live in a newer area.

Она́ зави́дует *бо́лее молоды́м* **же́нщинам.**
She envies younger women.

Она́ занима́ется с *бо́лее о́пытным* **тре́нером.**
She practices with a more experienced trainer.

14. Complete the sentences with the correct form of the comparative in Russian.

1. На э́тот ра́з преподава́тель да́л на́м (less difficult) _____ зада́чу.
2. Я́ никогда́ не встреча́л (a more interesting) _____ челове́ка.
3. Мы́ останови́лись в (more expensive) _____ гости́нице.
4. Моя́ сестра́ лю́бит (higher) _____ матема́тику.
5. Это́ оди́н из (newer) _____ микрорайо́нов.
6. Мы́ говори́м о (more serious) _____ дела́х.
7. Я́ познако́млю тебя́ с мои́м (older) _____ бра́том.
8. Óн предпочита́ет (older) _____ ви́на.
9. Тру́дно сказа́ть, кто́ из ни́х (better) _____ гитари́ст, они́ оба́ та́к хорошо́ игра́ют.
10. Что́бы уви́деть мо́ре, на́м на́до взойти́ на (higher) _____ го́ру.
11. Ра́ньше мы́ жи́ли в (smaller) _____ кварти́ре.
12. Для э́той рабо́ты нужны́ (younger) _____ и си́льные ру́ки.

Formation of the Simple Comparative

The simple comparative consists of only one word, to which a comparative ending is added. The comparative forms of most Russian adjectives and adverbs have the ending **-ee** (**-ей** in poetic or colloquial style). For adjectives whose stem in the positive degree consists of two or more syllables, the stress normally remains on the same syllable in the comparative.

Adjective		Adverb	Comparative
интере́сн-ый	interesting	интере́сн-о	интере́сн-ее
краси́в-ый	beautiful	краси́в-о	краси́в-ее
ме́дленн-ый	slow	ме́дленн-о	ме́дленн-ее
осторо́жн-ый	careful	осторо́жн-о	осторо́жн-ее
поле́зн-ый	useful, of benefit	поле́зн-о	поле́зн-ее
серьёзн-ый	serious	серьёзн-о	серьёзн-ее
споко́йн-ый	calm	споко́йн-о	споко́йн-ее
удо́бн-ый	convenient	удо́бн-о	удо́бн-ее

Adverbs of manner are derived from qualitative adjectives by adding to their stems the ending **-о** (**-е** to a few soft stems): **серьёзн-ый** serious/**серьёзн-о** seriously, **и́скренн-ий** sincere/**и́скренн-е** seriously. These adverbs are usually identical to the neuter short form of the adjective.

If the stem of the adjective has only one syllable, or if the feminine short form is stressed, then the comparative ending is stressed **-ée**, as shown in the following table.

Long-form Adjective		Adverb	Short-form Fem.	Comparative
бы́стр-ый	fast	бы́стр-о	быстр-а́	быстр-е́е
весёл-ый	cheerful	ве́сел-о	весел-а́	весел-е́е
дли́нн-ый	long	дли́нн-о	длинн-а́	длинн-е́е
мо́дн-ый	stylish	мо́дн-о	мод-на́	модн-е́е
но́в-ый	new	но́в-о	нов-а́	нов-е́е
тёпл-ый	warm	тепл-о́	тепл-а́	тепл-е́е
тру́дн-ый	hard	тру́дн-о	трудн-а́	трудн-е́е
у́мн-ый	smart	умн-о́	умн-а́	умн-е́е
холо́дн-ый	cold	хо́лодн-о	холодн-а́	холодн-е́е

A small number of adjectives form their comparatives using the ending **-е**, with the stress invariably on the syllable preceding this ending. All of these undergo some modification in the final consonant of the adjective/adverb stem. Certain changes to the stem-final consonant are regular and predictable. Among these regular changes are:

- stems ending in **-г, -к, -х** change to **-ж, -ч,** and **-ш**

Long-form Adjective		Adverb	Comparative
дорог-о́й	dear/expensive	до́рог-о	доро́ж-е
жа́рк-ий	hot	жа́рк-о	жа́рч-е
стро́г-ий	strict	стро́г-о	стро́ж-е
гро́мк-ий	loud	гро́мк-о	гро́мч-е
мя́гк-ий	soft	мя́гк-о	мя́гч-е
ти́х-ий	quiet	ти́х-о	ти́ш-е

- stems ending in the cluster **-ст** change to **-щ**

прост-о́й	simple	про́ст-о	про́щ-е
то́лст-ый	thick	то́лст-о	то́лщ-е
ча́ст-ый	frequent	ча́ст-о	ча́щ-е
чи́ст-ый	clean	чи́ст-о	чи́щ-е

The formation of some comparatives in **-e** entails other changes to the adjective/adverb stem that are irregular. These comparatives must be memorized.

бли́зк-ий	close	бли́зк-о	бли́ж-е
бога́т-ый	rich	бога́т-о	бога́ч-е
высо́к-ий	tall	высок-о́	вы́ш-е
глубо́к-ий	deep	глубок-о́	глу́бж-е
далёк-ий	far	далек-о́	да́льш-е
дешёв-ый	inexpensive	дёшев-о	деше́вл-е
до́лг-ий	long	до́лг-о	до́льш-е
коро́тк-ий	short	ко́ротк-о	коро́ч-е
лёгк-ий	easy	легк-о́	ле́гч-е
молод-о́й	young	мо́лод-о	моло́ж-е (or мла́дше)
по́здн-ый	late	по́здн-о	по́зж-е (or поздне́е)
ра́нн-ий	early	ра́н-о	ра́ньш-е
ре́дк-ий	rare	ре́дк-о	ре́ж-е
сла́дк-ий	sweet	сла́дк-о	сла́щ-е
ста́р-ый	old	—	ста́рше (comparing people)
			старе́е (comparing things)
широ́к-ий	wide	широк-о́	ши́р-е

Finally, a few adjectives have a simple comparative in **-e** that is a different word from the positive degree or the associated adverb:

хоро́ш-ий	good	хорош-о́	лу́чш-е
плох-о́й	bad	пло́х-о	ху́ж-е
больш-о́й	big	мно́г-о	бо́льш-е
ма́леньк-ий	small	ма́л-о	ме́ньш-е

Use of the Simple Comparative

The simple comparative is almost always used predicatively after a link verb. Simple comparatives are invariable, i.e., their form is constant regardless of the gender or number of the subject.

О́н вы́глядит *моло́же.*	He looks younger.
Она́ вы́глядит *моло́же.*	She looks younger.
Они́ вы́глядят *моло́же.*	They look younger.
Бы́ло жа́рко, но ста́ло *жа́рче.*	It was hot, but it became hotter.
Дни стано́вятся *длинне́е.*	The days are getting longer.
Э́тот ча́й *кре́пче.*	This tea is stronger.
О́н чу́вствует себя́ *лу́чше.*	He feels better.
Поезда́ тепе́рь хо́дят *ча́ще.*	The trains now run more often.

Note: In conversational Russian the simple comparative can also be used with attributive meaning. In this usage the comparative invariably follows the noun, and it generally occurs with the prefix **по-,** which adds the meaning "a little, slightly": **Покажи́те мне́ брю́ки *подеше́вле*** *Show me some slightly cheaper pants.*

Adverbs Used with Comparatives

Comparatives are often preceded by one of the following adverbs:

(*a*)   **ещё** *still (even more)*

Она́ у́мная, но её подру́га *ещё умне́е.*
She is smart, but her friend is even smarter.

(*b*)   **гора́здо**, **намно́го** *much*

На э́той рабо́те вы́ бу́дете получа́ть *гора́здо бо́льше.*
In this job you will receive much more (money).

Вчера́ бы́ло жа́рко, но сего́дня *намно́го жа́рче.*
Yesterday it was hot, but today it is much hotter.

(*c*)   **всё** preceding a comparative means *more and more.* For greater emphasis the comparative may be repeated (as in the English translation).

Дни́ стано́вятся *всё коро́че.*
The days are becoming shorter and shorter.

На́ш сы́н пи́шет на́м *всё ре́же и ре́же.*
Our son writes to us more and more rarely.

15.   Supply the comparative of the italicized adjective or adverb.

1.   В магази́не це́ны на фру́кты *высо́кие*, а на ры́нке они́ ещё _____.
2.   О́н зараба́тывает *мно́го*, а его́ дру́г гора́здо _____.
3.   Проду́кты бы́ли уже́ и та́к *дороги́е*, но неда́вно ста́ли ещё _____.
4.   О́н *ча́сто* е́здит в Петербу́рг, а в Москву́ _____.
5.   И́горь *симпати́чный*, а Вади́м ещё _____.
6.   Ра́ньше ты́ *хорошо́* говори́л по-ру́сски, а тепе́рь ты́ говори́шь ещё _____.
7.   Э́тот до́м *высо́кий*, а то́т намно́го _____.
8.   Пе́рвая зада́ча *лёгкая*, а втора́я зада́ча гора́здо _____.
9.   О́н е́здит *бы́стро*, а его́ бра́т е́здит ещё _____.
10. У меня́ действи́тельно по́черк *плохо́й*, но у моего́ отца́ ещё _____.

Expressing the Second Term of a Comparison

In comparisons where the two terms being compared are explicitly stated, such as in *Viktor is smarter than Vadim, He speaks Russian better than he speaks German, It's warmer in Moscow than in St. Petersburg,* the Russian equivalent of English *than* is rendered in one of two ways:

1.   In most instances, the conjunction **чём** is used (preceded by a comma). A construction with **чём** is *obligatory* when:

(*a*)   the compound comparative is used

Та́ня бо́лее серьёзная студе́нтка, *чём* **Ма́ша.**
Tanya is a more serious student than Masha.

Это бо́лее мо́дный га́лстук, *чём то́т.*
This is a more stylish tie than that (tie).

Note: When, as in the two examples above, what follows **чём** is a noun or pronoun, the word must be in the *nominative* case.

(b)   the second term of the comparison is an indeclinable expression, such as an adverb, infinitive, a prepositional phrase, or a clause:

Adverb

Мне́ прия́тнее ходи́ть в кино́ вдвоём, *чём одному́.*
It's more enjoyable to go to the movies with someone than alone.

Infinitive

Я́ люблю́ бо́льше ходи́ть, *чём бе́гать.*
I like to walk more than to run.

Prepositional Phrase

Мне́ прия́тнее на мо́ре, *чём в гора́х.*
It is more pleasant for me at the seashore than in the mountains.

Clause

Э́то доро́же, *чём я ду́мал.*
This is more expensive than I thought.

2.   If the second term of the comparison is a declinable noun or pronoun, it may *optionally* be followed by **чём**; otherwise, it must be in the *genitive* case.

(a)   When **чём** is used, the nouns or pronouns being compared must be in the same case:

Óн **зараба́тывает бо́льше, чём** *я́.*
He earns more than I do.

Даю́т бо́льше *тебе́,* **чём** *мне́.*
They give more to you than to me.

У *него́* **бо́лее тёмные во́лосы, чём у** *неё.*
He has darker hair than she has.

(b)   The *genitive* case can be used only after a simple predicative comparative, and only when the first term of the comparison is in the *nominative* case.

Ви́ктор **умне́е** *Вади́ма.*	*Viktor is smarter than Vadim.*
Ле́на **вы́ше** *Та́ни.*	*Lena is taller than Tanya.*
Тво́й **костю́м модне́е** *моего́.*	*Your suit is more stylish than mine.*
Му́ж **ста́рше** *жены́.*	*The husband is older than the wife.*
Э́та **маши́на старе́е** *то́й.*	*This car is older than that one.*

16. Answer the question, using the genitive of comparison where possible; otherwise use the construction with **чём**.

Model: Что́ бо́льше, деся́ток и́ли дю́жина? <u>Дю́жина бо́льше деся́тка.</u>

1.   Кака́я страна́ бо́льше, Росси́я и́ли Кита́й?
2.   Где́ холодне́е, в Торо́нто и́ли в Новосиби́рске?
3.   Како́й ме́сяц коро́че, октя́брь и́ли ноя́брь?
4.   Когда́ зде́сь тепле́е, в декабре́ и́ли в ма́е?
5.   Кто́ вы́ше, кенгуру́ и́ли жира́ф?
6.   Что́ да́льше от США́, Пари́ж и́ли Ки́ев?
7.   Како́й шта́т ме́ньше, Нью-Йо́рк и́ли Теха́с?
8.   Како́й го́род старе́е, Санкт-Петербу́рг или Москва́?

9. Кака́я маши́на доро́же, «Мерседе́с» и́ли «Москви́ч»?
10. Како́е о́зеро глу́бже, Мичига́н или Байка́л?
11. Что́ сла́ще, мёд или со́к?
12. Что́ кре́пче, конья́к и́ли шампа́нское?
13. Что́ удобне́е, печа́тать на компью́тере и́ли на пи́шущей маши́нке?
14. Что́ поле́знее, пи́ть ко́ка-ко́лу и́ли е́сть фру́кты?
15. Кака́я река́ длинне́е, Дне́пр или Во́лга?
16. Что́ ва́м ле́гче, говори́ть по-ру́сски или чита́ть по-ру́сски?
17. Где́ веселе́е, на ле́кции и́ли на дискоте́ке?
18. На чём е́здить быстре́е, на трамва́е и́ли на автобу́се?

Other Expressions with Comparatives

The following are three common expressions containing comparatives.

1. **ка́к мо́жно . . .**   *as . . . as possible*

   Я́ приду́ домо́й *ка́к мо́жно скоре́е.*   *I will come home as soon as possible.*
   О́н бежа́л *ка́к мо́жно быстре́е.*   *He ran as fast as possible.*
   Сде́лай э́то *ка́к мо́жно лу́чше.*   *Do it as well as possible.*

2. **че́м . . ., те́м . . .**   *the . . . er, the -. . . er*

   Че́м бо́льше ты́ занима́ешься, *те́м лу́чше* **твои́ успе́хи.**
   The more you study, the better your progress.

   Че́м скоре́е ты́ уберёшь ко́мнату, *те́м скоре́е* **ты́ пойдёшь гуля́ть.**
   The sooner you clean up your room, the sooner you can go have a good time.

   Че́м ста́рше мы́ стано́вимся, *те́м лу́чше* **мы́ понима́ем дру́г дру́га.**
   The older we become, the better we understand each other.

3. **бо́льше всего́** *most of all (more than anything else)*
   бо́льше все́х *most of all (more than anyone else)*

   These phrases are used as superlative adverbs. Similarly used are **лу́чше всего́** *best of all (better than all other things)*, **лу́чше все́х** *best of all (better than all other people)*.

   Мо́й сы́н лю́бит все́ жа́нры му́зыки: джа́з, ка́нтри, блю́з, но *бо́льше всего́* **он лю́бит рок-му́зыку.**
   My son likes all types of music: jazz, country, blues, but most of all he likes rock music.

   Мно́гие ребя́та хорошо́ игра́ют на гита́ре, но Са́ша игра́ет *лу́чше все́х.*
   Many of the guys play guitar well, but Sasha plays best of all.

The Compound Superlative: Form and Use

The compound superlative consists of two words, the adjective **са́мый** *most* and the long form of the adjective that is being compared. Both adjectives decline, agreeing in gender, number, and case with the modified noun.

Positive Degree	*Compound Superlative*	
краси́вый	*са́мый* **краси́вый го́род**	*the most beautiful city*
	са́мое **краси́вое о́зеро**	*the most beautiful lake*
	са́мая **краси́вая маши́на**	*the most beautiful car*
	са́мые **краси́вые го́ры**	*the most beautiful mountains*

Росси́я — са́мая больша́я страна́ в ми́ре.
Russia is the biggest country in the world.

Кавка́зские го́ры — э́то *са́мые высо́кие* **го́ры в Росси́и.**
The Caucasus Mountains are the highest mountains in Russia.

Сан Дие́го — оди́н из *са́мых краси́вых* **городо́в в США.**
San Diego is one of the most beautiful cities in the U.S.A.

Note that sentences with the compound superlative often contain a phrase which defines the context within which someone or something, compared to others, is *the most* . . ., e.g., in the sentences above: **в ми́ре** *in the world,* **в Росси́и** *in Russia,* **в США** *in the U.S.A.*

Another phrase, **из всех** (. . .) *of all* . . ., indicates the group of people or things out of which someone or something is distinguished as *the most* . . ..

Из всех но́вых гости́ниц, э́то са́мая роско́шная.
Of all the new hotels, this is the most luxurious.

Ро́ллс Ро́йс — э́то *са́мая дорога́я маши́на из всех.*
Rolls-Royce is the most expensive car of all.

17. Complete the sentence with the required form of the compound superlative.

1. О́зеро Байка́л — э́то (deepest) _____ о́зеро ми́ра.
2. Река́ Миссу́ри — э́то (the longest) _____ река́ в США.
3. Сели́н Дио́н одна́ из (most popular) _____ певи́ц в на́шей стране́.
4. Учи́тель расска́зывал об Аля́ске, (the biggest) _____ шта́те США.
5. Я счита́ю его́ мои́м (closest) _____ дру́гом.

The Simple Superlative: Form and Use

The simple superlative is sometimes called the superlative of "high degree," since it often is used in the meaning *a most* (e.g., *a most important matter*). It is formed by adding the suffix **-ейш-** (and the soft ending **-ий**) to the stem of the long adjective:

Positive Degree		Simple Superlative
ва́жн-ый	*important*	**важн-е́йший**
вку́сн-ый	*tasty*	**вксн-е́йший**
глу́п-ый	*stupid*	**глуп-е́йший**
но́в-ый	*new*	**нов-е́йший**
у́мн-ый	*smart*	**умн-е́йший**
интере́сн-ый	*interesting*	**интере́сн-ейший**
тру́дн-ый	*difficult*	**трудн-е́йший**

The suffix **-айш-** (and the ending **-ий**) is added to adjectives whose stem ends in the consonants **г, к, х,** and **ст** which then change to **ж, ч, ш,** and **щ.**

стро́г-ий	*strict*	**строж-а́йший**
вели́кий	*great*	**велич-а́йший**
высо́к-ий	*tall*	**высоч-а́йший**
кре́пк-ий	*strong*	**крепч-а́йший**
ти́х-ий	*quiet*	**тиш-а́йший**

The simple superlative is common in scientific and literary Russian; however, the same form is also used in colloquial Russian to express the speaker's personal impressions (*интере́снейшая кни́га* *a most interesting book*, *вкусне́йший бо́рщ* *a very tasty borsch*).

The following two sentences illustrate the difference in meaning between the compound superlative (*the most . . .*) and the simple superlative, when the latter has the force of "high degree."

Би́лл Ге́йтс — *са́мый бога́тый* **челове́к в ми́ре.**
Bill Gates is the richest man in the world.

О́н *богате́йший* **челове́к.**
He is an extremely rich man.

A few other examples of the simple comparative:

«Преступле́ние и наказа́ние» — *серьёзнейший* **рома́н.**
"Crime and Punishment" is a most serious novel.

Пу́шкин — *велича́йший* **ру́сский писа́тель.**
Pushkin is a very great Russian writer.

Во́дка — *крепча́йший* **напи́ток.**
Vodka is a very strong drink.

18. Rewrite the sentence, changing the compound superlative to a simple superlative.

Model: У Вади́ма бы́л *са́мый интере́сный* докла́д.
 У Вади́ма бы́л *интере́снейший* докла́д.

1. Нью-Йо́рк — э́то *са́мый кру́пный* морско́й по́рт.
2. В э́том рестора́не подаю́т *са́мые вку́сные* пельме́ни.
3. Сибиряки́ счита́ются *са́мыми здоро́выми* людьми́.
4. Гора́ Эвере́ст — э́то *са́мая высо́кая* гора́.
5. Влади́мир Петро́в — *са́мый стро́гий* учи́тель.

ADVERBS

Adverbs are indeclinable words that can modify a verb, adjective, noun, or another adverb. Note the following examples:

(*a*)   a verb:

писа́ть *хорошо́* to write well, **чита́ть** *вслу́х* to read aloud, **рабо́тать** *вме́сте* to work together, **говори́ть** *шёпотом* to speak in a whisper, **идти́** *пешко́м* to go on foot

(*b*)   an adjective:

удиви́тельно **хоро́ший** surprisingly good, *невероя́тно* **у́мный** incredibly smart

(*c*)   a noun:

ша́г *вперёд* a step forward, **езда́** *верхо́м* riding horseback

(*d*)   another adverb:

о́чень **хорошо́** very well, *соверше́нно* **ве́рно** quite right, *кра́йне* **интере́сно** extremely interesting

Adverbs can be classified according to their meaning. For example, the primary semantic groups of Russian adverbs are those referring to manner, time, place, and measure or degree.

Adverbs of Manner

Adverbs of manner answer the question **ка́к?** *how?* They are formed from adjectives of various types, as well as from nouns.

(*a*) One type of manner adverb is identical to the neuter short form of a qualitative adjective (some of these originated as past passive participles, e.g., **взволно́ванно** *excitedly*); most of these manner adverbs have the ending **-o**.

аккура́тно	*neatly*	осторо́жно	*carefully*
интере́сно	*interestingly*	серьёзно	*seriously*
ме́дленно	*slowly*	хорошо́	*well*
мо́дно	*stylishly*	умно́	*intelligently*

(*b*) Adverbs of manner are also formed from present active participles, or the adjectives derived from them, by adding the ending **-e** to the participle/adjective stem, e.g., **понима́ющ-ий** *understanding* → **понима́ющ-е** *understandingly*. These adverbs often correspond to English manner adverbs ending in *-ingly*.

бодря́ще	*invigoratingly*	раздража́юще	*irritatingly*
одобря́юще	*approvingly*	угрожа́юще	*threateningly*
осужда́юще	*condemningly*	умоля́юще	*imploringly*

(*c*) Adjectives with the suffix **-ск-** and **-цк-**, which do not have short forms, can derive adverbs by adding **-и** to the adjective stem, e.g., **дру́жеск-ий** *amicable* → **дру́жеск-и** *amicably*. Sometimes these adverbs occur with the hyphenated prefix **по-** in virtually the same meaning: **по-дру́жески** *like a friend*.

бра́тски/по-бра́тски	*brotherly/like a brother*
де́тски/по-де́тски	*childish/like a child*
дура́цки/по-дура́цки	*foolishly/like a fool*
челове́чески/по-челове́чески	*humanly/like a human being*

(*d*) Adverbs prefixed in **по-** and ending in **-и** are derived from adjectives with the suffix **-ск-** that denote nationality, e.g., **ру́сск-ий** → **по-ру́сски** *in Russian* or *in the Russian style*.

по-англи́йски	*in English*
по-кита́йски	*in Chinese*
по-францу́зски	*in French*

(*e*) Adverbs of manner are formed from the dative case of the masculine/neuter form of certain adjectives prefixed in **по-**, e.g., **но́вый** *new* → **по-но́вому** *in a new way*.

по-друго́му	*in a different way, otherwise*
по-пре́жнему	*as before*
по-ра́зному	*in various ways*

(*f*) The following are a few examples of manner adverbs derived from nouns:

верхо́м	*on horseback*
босико́м	*barefoot*
пешко́м	*on foot*
вслу́х	*aloud*

19.   Complete the sentence with the Russian equivalent of the given manner adverb.

1. Она́ всегда́ о́чень _____ одева́ется.   *fashionably*
2. Он выполня́ет рабо́ту _____.   *neatly*
3. Моя́ до́чь у́чится е́здить _____.   *on horseback*
4. Он обня́л меня́ _____.   *like a brother*
5. Я бы отве́тил на э́тот вопро́с _____.   *in a different way*
6. Ка́ждый из нас прореаги́ровал _____.   *in different ways*
7. Он кивну́л _____.   *understandingly*
8. Па́па _____ смотре́л на сы́на.   *approvingly*
9. Он ел своё блю́до па́лочками, _____.   *in the Chinese style*
10. Учени́к чита́л поэ́му _____.   *aloud*
11. Вы ко мне всегда́ относи́лись _____.   *like a human being*
12. Он _____ помаха́л мне кулако́м.   *threateningly*
13. Ничего́ не измени́лось, мы живём _____.   *as before*
14. На у́лице ско́льзко, на́до идти́ _____.   *carefully*
15. Он о́чень _____ расска́зывал о пое́здке.   *interestingly*
16. Ребёнок _____ смотре́л на ма́му.   *imploringly*
17. Де́ти бе́гали _____ по двору́.   *barefoot*
18. Он вёл себя́ _____.   *like a fool*
19. Му́зыка звуча́ла _____ гро́мко.   *irritatingly*
20. Э́тот моро́з тако́й _____ -освежа́ющий.   *invigoratingly*

Adverbs of Time

Adverbs of time answer questions such as **когда́?** *when*, **ско́лько вре́мени** *how long*, **на ско́лько вре́мени**, or **как ча́сто?** *how often?* Some of the most common adverbs of time are listed below.

Adverbs answering the question **когда́?**

сего́дня	*today*	**неда́вно**	*recently*
за́втра	*tomorrow*	**ско́ро**	*soon*
послеза́втра	*day after tomorrow*	**наконе́ц**	*finally*
вчера́	*yesterday*	**сра́зу**	*immediately*
позавчера́	*day before yesterday*	**сейча́с**	*now, at the moment*
снача́ла	*(at) first*	**тепе́рь**	*now, nowadays*
пото́м	*then (afterwards)*	**ра́но**	*early*
тогда́	*then (at that time)*	**по́здно**	*late*
давно́	*a long time ago*	**во́-время**	*on time*

ПОРА *it's time*

The following adverbs referring to periods of the day, and the seasons, are all formed from the instrumental case of a noun, e.g., **у́тро** *morning* → **у́тром** *in the morning*, **весна́** *spring* → **весно́й** *in the spring*.

у́тром	*in the morning*	**ле́том**	*in the summer*
днём	*during the day*	**весно́й**	*in the spring*
ве́чером	*in the evening*	**зимо́й**	*in the winter*
но́чью	*in the night*	**о́сенью**	*in the fall*

20. Complete the sentence with the appropriate adverb.

1. Я обы́чно пью ко́фе то́лько ___у́тром___.　　　　*in the morning*
2. Моя́ ба́бушка __давно́__ иммигри́ровала в Аме́рику.　　*a long time ago*
3. Она́ __тогда́__ рабо́тала портни́хой.　　　　*at that time*
4. Мы уезжа́ем в о́тпуск __послезавтра__.　　　*day after tomorrow*
5. Па́па прие́хал из командиро́вки __позавчера́__.　　*day before yesterday*
6. __Снача́ла__ мы пошли́ в кино́, а __пото́м__ в кафе́.　*first, afterwards*
7. В Аме́рике _____ почти́ у ка́ждого есть ви́дик.　　*now* сейча́с, тепе́рь
8. Ма́ма _____ на ку́хне, бесе́дует с подру́гой.　　*now*
9. Мы отдыха́ем __ле́том__, когда́ пого́да тёплая.　　*in the summer*
10. А́втор три го́да писа́л кни́гу, и __наконе́ц__ ко́нчил её.　*finally*
11. __Днём__ на́ша дочь хо́дит в де́тский са́д.　　*during the day*
12. На́м о́чень нужна́ твоя́ по́мощь, ты __ско́ро__ придёшь?　*soon*
13. Приро́да у на́с __весно́й__ про́сто прекра́сная.　　*in the spring*
14. Лу́чше __по́здно__, чём никогда́.　　　　*late*
15. Па́па та́к уста́л, что лёг на дива́н и __сра́зу__ засну́л.　*immediately*
16. О́н не опа́здывает на рабо́ту, о́н всегда́ прихо́дит __во́-время__.　*on time*
17. Кто́ __ра́но__ ложи́тся и __ра́но__ встаёт, здоро́вье, богатство и у́м наживёт.　*early, early*

Adverbs answering the question **ско́лько вре́мени?**

до́лго	*(for) a long time*
давно́	*for a long time (and continuing up to a defined point)*

Adverbs answering the question **на ско́лько вре́мени?**

надо́лго	*for a long time (following the completion of an action)*
навсегда́	*forever*

21. Complete the sentence with the appropriate adverb.

1. Она́ влюби́лась __навсегда́__　　　　　*forever*
2. Мы́ _____ его́ жда́ли, и наконе́ц-то о́н пришёл.　*a long time*
3. Моя́ до́чка лю́бит _____ мы́ться в ва́нне.　*a long time*
4. Мы́ уже́ _____ живём в Вашингто́не.　　*a long time*
5. О́н к на́м прие́хал __давно́__, наве́рное на го́д.　*for a long time*

Adverbs answering the question **ка́к ча́сто?**

всегда́	*always*
иногда́	*sometimes*
обы́чно	*usually*
ре́дко	*rarely*

22.   Complete the sentence with the required adverb.

1.   Мы _всегда_ ра́ды тебя́ ви́деть.   *always*
2.   Мы _ре́дко_ обе́даем в рестора́не, сли́шком до́рого.   *rarely*
3.   Я _обы́чно_ бе́гаю в спортза́ле.   *usually*
4.   Он лю́бит джа́з, но _иногда_ он слу́шает и рок-му́зыку.   *sometimes*

Note also the following important temporal adverbs:

уже́	*already/as early as*
уже́ не/бо́льше не	*no longer*
ещё (всё ещё)	*still*
ещё не	*not yet*

23.   Complete the sentence with the required adverb.

1.   Мо́жете меня́ поздра́вить, я _____ курю́.   *no longer*
2.   К сожале́нию, мой му́ж _____ бо́лен.   *still*
3.   Ей всего́ 18 ле́т, а она́ _____ выхо́дит за́муж.   *already*
4.   Он до́лго реша́ет зада́чу, но _ещё не_ реши́л.   *not yet*
5.   Она́ _уже_ вчера́ зако́нчила писа́ть письмо́.   *as early as*

Adverbs of Place

Adverbs of place are divided into those that indicate location and answer the question **где?** *where?*, and those that indicate direction and answer the questions **куда́** *where to?* or **отку́да?** *from where?* The choice of adverb, therefore, normally depends on whether a sentence contains a verb of location or a verb of motion/direction.

The following list contains many of the most commonly used adverbs of place expressing either location or direction.

Location		*Direction (To)*		*Direction (From)*	
где?	*where*	куда́	*where to?*	отку́да	*from where?*
здесь	*here*	сюда́	*here*	отсю́да	*from here*
та́м	*there*	туда́	*there*	отту́да	*from there*
везде́, всю́ду	*everywhere*	—		отовсю́ду	*from everywhere*
до́ма	*at home*	домо́й	*home*	—	
сле́ва	*on the left*	нале́во	*to the left*	—	
спра́ва	*on the right*	напра́во	*to the right*	—	
впереди́	*in front, ahead*	вперёд	*forward, ahead*	—	
позади́, сза́ди	*behind*	наза́д	*back(ward)*	—	
наверху́	*above*	наве́рх	*up(ward)*	све́рху	*from above*
внизу́	*below*	вни́з	*down(ward)*	сни́зу	*from below*
внутри́	*inside*	вну́трь	*inside*	изнутри́	*from inside*
снару́жи	*outside*	нару́жу	*outside*	снару́жи	*from outside*

24.   Complete the sentence with the appropriate adverb of location or direction.

1.   Вчера́ я бы́л бо́лен и оста́лся _____ .   *at home*
2.   Води́тель повора́чивал маши́ну _____ и _____ .   *to the left, to the right*
3.   Я спроси́л де́вушку, _____ она́.   *where from*

4. Мы́ подошли́ к кра́ю скалы́ и посмотре́ли _____ . *down*
5. Пришла́ весна́ и _____ зацвели́ цветы́. *everywhere*
6. Э́то окно́ открыва́ется _____ . *to the outside*
7. _____ на́ша да́ча покра́шена в си́ний цве́т. *on the outside*
8. На съе́зд прие́хали учёные _____ . *from everywhere*
9. Мы́ подняли́сь _____ по ле́стнице. *up*
10. Ма́льчик за́пер две́рь _____ . *from inside*
11. О́н спусти́лся на ли́фте _____ на пе́рвый эта́ж. *down*
12. Нельзя́ смотре́ть _____ , на́до смотре́ть _____ . *back/forward*
13. Мы́ подняли́сь на́ гору и _____ уви́дели о́зеро. *from above*
14. Охо́тники нашли́ пеще́ру и загляну́ли _____ . *inside*
15. Я́ положи́л журна́лы _____ на по́лку. *here*
16. О́н рабо́тает _____ , _____ я рабо́тал ра́ньше. *there, where*
17. Когда́ о́н е́здит в маши́не, он во́зит дете́й _____ . *behind*
18. У меня́ _____ ещё мно́го рабо́ты. *ahead*
19. По́сле рабо́ты я пошёл пря́мо _____ . *home*
20. У э́той маши́ны зеркала́ за́днего ви́да _____ и _____ . *on the left/on the right*

Adverbs of Measure or Degree

Adverbs of measure or degree answer questions such as **ско́лько?** *how much/many?*, **в како́й сте́пени** *to what degree?* Some of the most common of these adverbs are listed below.

о́чень	*very, very much*	**слегка́**	*slightly*
та́к	*so*	**доста́то́чно**	*sufficiently*
мно́го	*a lot, very much*	**совсе́м**	*quite*
ма́ло	*little*	**соверше́нно**	*absolutely*
немно́го	*a little*	**сли́шком**	*too*
чу́ть (чу́ть-чу́ть)	*a tiny bit*	**почти́**	*almost, nearly*

Note: One must be careful in choosing the correct adverb to express English *much*, *a lot*, or *very much*, which can be rendered in Russian both by **о́чень** and **мно́го**. These two adverbs, however, are not interchangeable: when used to modify a verb **о́чень** refers to the intensity of an action (answering the question **в како́й сте́пени?**), whereas **мно́го** refers to quantity (answering the question **ско́лько?** **Он о́чень лю́бит её и** *мно́го* **де́лает для неё** *He loves her very much and does (very) much for her*.

25. Complete the sentence with the appropriate adverb.

1. Я́ бы́л _____ за́нят, что не успе́л пообе́дать. *so*
2. Э́та студе́нтка пи́шет по-ру́сски _____ аккура́тно. *very*
3. Мо́й оте́ц дире́ктор компа́нии и _____ рабо́тает. *a lot*
4. Ты́ _____ гото́ва? На́м пора́ идти́ в теа́тр. *almost*
5. Я́ удиви́лся, что за всё э́ти го́ды о́н та́к _____ измени́лся. *little*
6. Я́ _____ бою́сь, что Са́ше не понра́вится но́вая шко́ла. *a little*
7. Я́ согла́сен с ва́ми, вы́ _____ пра́вы! *absolutely*
8. Пиро́г тако́й вку́сный! Да́й мне́ _____ побо́льше. *a tiny bit*
9. Вчера́ о́н бы́л бо́лен, а сего́дня о́н _____ здоро́в. *quite*
10. Она́ _____ умна́, что́бы э́то поня́ть. *sufficiently*
11. Не покупа́й э́тот костю́м, о́н _____ до́рого сто́ит. *too*
12. Жа́лко! Э́то мя́со _____ пережа́рено. *slightly*

Indefinite Adverbs

Adverbs of place, time, manner, and others can occur with the particles **-то** and **-нибудь** to form indefinite adverbs.

Adverbs of Place

Location
где? *where?*   **где-то** *somewhere*   **где-нибудь** *somewhere*

Direction
куда *where*   **куда-то** *somewhere*   **куда-нибудь** *somewhere*

Adverbs of Time
когда *when?*   **когда-то** *once, at one time*   **когда-нибудь** *ever, at any time*

Adverbs of Manner
как *how?*   **как-то** *somehow*   **как-нибудь** *somehow (or other)*

Adverbs of Cause
почему? *why*   **почему-то** *for some reason*   **почему-нибудь** *for any reason*

The meanings that the particles **-то** and **-нибудь** give to adverbs are the same as those given to indefinite pronouns (**кто-то** *someone*, **кто-нибудь** *someone/anyone*, etc.) described in Chapter 4 (page 134). Also, the contexts for use of adverbs and pronouns in **-то** and **-нибудь** are the same. To review those contexts briefly, forms in **-то** are used primarily in statements in the past tense, and in sentences with nonrepeated actions in the present tense; forms in **-нибудь** are used in many more sentence types: in questions, after imperatives, in sentences expressed in the future tense, as well as in those expressing repeated actions in the present tense.

— **Они** *где-нибудь* **отдыхали прошлым летом?**
— *Did they vacation anywhere last summer?*
— **Да, они** *где-то* **отдыхали, но я не помню где.**
— *They vacationed somewhere, but I don't remember where.*

— **Лена** *куда-нибудь* **едет на каникулы?**
— *Is Lena going anywhere for the holidays?*
— **Я не знаю, едет ли она** *куда-нибудь*.
— *I don't know if she is going anywhere.*

— **Вы** *когда-нибудь* **были в Нью-Йорке?**
— *Have you ever been to New York?*
— **Да, я** *когда-то* **был в Нью-Йорке с родителями.**
— *Yes, I was once in New York with my parents.*

26. Complete the sentence with the correct indefinite adverb.

1. Ты должен завтра _____ поехать?   *somewhere*
2. В детстве бабушка жила _____ на Украине.   *somewhere*
3. Нам _____ удастся это сделать.   *somehow*
4. Если ты _____ не сможешь прийти, то позвони.   *for any reason*
5. Положи свои вещи _____.   *anywhere*
6. Пойдём _____ погуляем.   *somewhere*
7. Он приезжал к нам _____ давно.   *once*
8. Она _____ не пришла на работу.   *for some reason*

9. Óн _____ спрáвился с трýдной ситуáцией.   *somehow*
10. Мы́ э́то кýпим _____ в слéдующем годý.   *sometime*

Negative Adverbs

There are two types of negative adverbs, those with the prefix **ни-** (**никогдá** *never*) and those with the stressed prefix **нé-** (**нéкогда** *there is no time*).

1. Negative adverbs may be formed by prefixing **ни-** to certain interrogative adverbs, as shown below:

Adverb		*Negative Adverb*	
гдé	*where?*	**нигдé**	*nowhere*
кудá	*where (to)?*	**никудá**	*(to) nowhere*
когдá	*when?*	**никогдá**	*never*
кáк	*how?*	**никáк**	*nohow, in no way*
скóлько	*how much*	**нискóлько**	*not at all*

Negative adverbs in **ни-** are used in personal sentences, that is, with a subject in the nominative case. A sentence with a negative adverb of this type requires a finite verb form preceded by the negative particle **не**, which results in a construction with a "double negative" (see negative pronouns **никтó**, **ничтó**, in Chapter 4, page 136):

Óн *нигдé не* **рабóтает.**	*He doesn't work anywhere.*
Мы́ *никудá не* **ходи́ли.**	*We didn't go anywhere.*
Онá тáм *никогдá не* **былá.**	*She has never been there.*
Я́ *нискóлько не* **устáл.**	*I'm not at all tired.*

2. Negative adverbs with the prefix **нé-** are formed from some of the same adverbs, as shown below:

гдé?	*where*	**нéгде**	*there is no place*
кудá	*where*	**нéкуда**	*there is no place (to go)*
когдá	*when*	**нéкогда**	*there is no time*
зачéм	*what for*	**нéзачем**	*there is no point*

Adverbs in **нé-** are used just like pronouns in **нé-** (e.g., **нéкого** *there is no one*, see page 137): they occur in impersonal sentences which either have no subject, or which have a logical subject in the dative case; the verb is in the infinitive form, and past and future tense is expressed by **бы́ло** and **бýдет**, respectively:

Нéкуда **бы́ло сéсть.**	*There was no place to sit down.*
Нéгде **бýдет спáть.**	*There will be no place to sleep.*
Мнé *нéкогда* **писáть.**	*There is no time for me to write.*
Тебé *нéзачем* **идти́ тудá.**	*There is no need for you to go there.*

27. Answer the following questions using a sentence with the appropriate negative adverb.

Model: — Когдá ты́ читáл э́тот ромáн?   — Я́ никогдá не читáл э́тот ромáн.
— Когдá нáм встрéтиться с ни́м?   — Вáм нéкогда встрéтиться с ни́м.

1. — Куда́ мне́ пойти́ сего́дня ве́чером? _____
2. — Куда́ ты́ пойдёшь по́сле семина́ра? _____
3. — Где́ же на́м рабо́тать? _____
4. — Где́ мы́ бу́дем рабо́тать? _____
5. — Заче́м ему́ чита́ть э́ту кни́гу? _____
6. — Ка́к о́н спра́вится с э́тим? _____

CHAPTER 6

Numbers, Dates, Time

NUMBERS

There are three classes of numbers in Russian: cardinal, collective, and ordinal. All three classes decline.

Cardinal Numbers

Cardinal numbers, such as 1, 20, or 500, are used in counting, and in general to indicate quantity. The nominative case forms of the cardinal numbers are as follows.

0 но́ль/ну́ль	16 шестна́дцать	300 три́ста
1 оди́н, одно́, одна́, одни́	17 семна́дцать	400 четы́реста
2 два́/две́	18 восемна́дцать	500 пятьсо́т
3 три́	19 девятна́дцать	600 шестьсо́т
4 четы́ре	20 два́дцать	700 семьсо́т
5 пя́ть	21 два́дцать оди́н	800 восемьсо́т
6 ше́сть	30 три́дцать	900 девятьсо́т
7 се́мь	40 со́рок	1 000 ты́сяча
8 во́семь	50 пятьдеся́т	1 001 ты́сяча оди́н
9 де́вять	60 шестьдеся́т	2 000 две́ ты́сячи
10 де́сять	70 се́мьдесят	5 000 пя́ть ты́сяч
11 оди́ннадцать	80 во́семьдесят	1 000 000 миллио́н
12 двена́дцать	90 девяно́сто	2 000 000 два́ миллио́на
13 трина́дцать	100 сто́	5 000 000 пя́ть миллио́нов
14 четы́рнадцать	101 сто́ оди́н	1 000 000 000 миллиа́рд/биллио́н
15 пятна́дцать	200 две́сти	2 000 000 000 два́ миллиа́рда

Note: Several numbers are an amalgam of two or more individual elements. The numbers 11–19 are derived forms that consist of three elements: a number 1–9, e.g., **оди́н-** *one*, **-на-** *on*, and **-дцать** (a contraction of **де́сять** *ten*): **оди́н-на-дцать** *eleven* is literally "one-on-ten"; the numbers 20 and 30 are derived from the two elements **два́-дцать**, **три́-дцать**, that is, "two tens," "three tens." And the numbers 300 and 400 are an amalgam of **три́** *three* or **четы́ре** *four* and **ста** (the genitive singular of

стó *hundred*): **трúста**, **четы́реста**; similarly formed are 500, 600, 700, 800, 900, e.g., **пятьсóт** (**пять** + **сот**, the genitive plural of **стó**).

Note: The numbers 5–20 and 30 all end in the soft sign **-ь** (**пять**, **шéсть**, **двáдцать**, **трúдцать**); the numbers 50, 60, 70, 80, and 500, 600, 700, 800, 900 all have the soft sign in the middle of the word, separating its component parts (**пятьдеся́т**, **шестьдеся́т**, **пятьсóт**, **шестьсóт** . . . **девятьсóт**).

Note: Any numbers higher than 20 ending in 1–9, e.g., 21, 33, 45, 79, 101, 542, etc., are compounds formed by two or more words written separately: **двáдцать одúн** *twenty-one*, **трúдцать трú** *thirty-three*, **сóрок пя́ть** *forty-five*, **стó одúн** *hundred and one*, **пятьсóт сóрок двá** *five hundred and forty-two.*

Use of Нóль/Ну́ль 0

The masculine nouns **нóль** and **ну́ль** *nought, nil, zero,* are end-stressed (e.g., **Нáм пришлóсь начáть с** *нуля́* We had to start from zero/scratch) and they are followed by the genitive case (e.g., **В э́той óбласти у негó** *нóль* **знáний** *He has zero knowledge in this field*). Though synonymous, these nouns tend to have their own spheres of use: **ну́ль** is used, for example, to express temperature at *zero* degrees, while **нóль** is used to indicate *zero* in telephone numbers, in game scores, and in expressing the time of an event at a precise hour using the 24-hour clock.

Температу́ра упáла нúже *нуля́.*
The temperature fell below zero.

Мóй телефóн: 251-03-05 (двéсти пятьдеся́т одúн *нóль* **трú** *нóль* **пя́ть)**
My telephone number is 251-03-05.

Игрá кóнчилась со счётом 7:0 (сéмь: *нóль***)**
The game ended with a score of 7 to nothing.

Пóезд отхóдит в пятнáдцать *нóль-нóль.*
The train departs at fifteen hundred (15:00).

Declension and Use of 1

The number **одúн** *one* takes the same endings as the demonstrative pronoun **э́тот** (page 119). The complete declension of **одúн** is presented in the following table.

	Masculine,	Neuter	Feminine	Plural
Nom.	одúн	однó	однá	однú
Acc. Inam.	одúн/	однó	однý	однú/
Anim.	одногó			однúх
Gen.	одногó		однóй	однúх
Prep.	об однóм		об однóй	об однúх
Dat.	одномý		однóй	однúм
Instr.	однúм		однóй	однúми

Note: The medial vowel **-и-** which occurs in the masculine nominative/accusative inanimate singular (**одúн**) is omitted in all other forms.

Note: When counting up from one, Russians use the word **рáз** instead of **одúн**, e.g., **рáз**, **двá**, **трú** . . . *one, two, three . . . .*

The number "one" is a modifier, which changes its form to agree with the masculine, feminine, or neuter gender, as well as number, and case, of the modified noun.

У нас в семье *один сын, одна дочка и одно домашнее животное.*
In our family we have one son, one daughter, and one pet.

В киоске он купил *один конверт и одну марку.*
At the kiosk he bought one envelope and one stamp.

Дети учатся считать от *одного* **до двадцати.**
The children learn to count from one to twenty.

In compound numbers ending in "one" (e.g., 21, 31, 41), agreement is normally in the singular (but see below on uses of "one" in the plural).

В этой группе двадцать *один* **студент.**
There are twenty-one students in this group.

Я заказал для студентов двадцать *одну* **книгу.**
I ordered twenty-one books for the students.

Other Meanings of Один

In addition to its basic meaning *one*, **один** may also be used in the following meanings:

(a) a, a certain

У меня есть *один* **знакомый, который**   *I have a friend who used to live in Siberia.*
раньше жил в Сибири.

(b) alone, by oneself

Она живёт *одна.*   *She lives alone.*
Ему трудно жить *одному.*   *It is difficult for him to live alone.*
Нельзя оставлять ребёнка *одного.*   *One can't leave a baby alone.*

(c) the same

Мы учились в *одной* **школе.**   *We studied in the same school.*
Мы сидели за *одним* **столом.**   *We sat at the same table.*

(d) only

Один **Бог знает.**   *God only knows.*

Use of Один in the Plural

It is important to note that in all of its meanings, **один** may be used in the plural. For example, when used to modify a noun that occurs only in the plural (**часы** *watch*), the plural form of "one" is required:

У меня только *одни* **часы.**   *I have only one watch.*
На столе были *одни* **ножницы.**   *There was one pair of scissors on the table.*

Note the following example of the plural of **один** in the meaning *only (nothing but ...)*:

На тарелке остались *одни* **крошки.**   *Nothing but crumbs remained on the plate.*

Also, **оди́н** occurs in the expression **оди́н** . . . **друго́й** . . . *one . . . the other*, and in the plural form of this expression: **одни́** . . . **други́е** . . . *some . . . others* . . . .

> **У ни́х два́ сы́на,** *оди́н* **журнали́ст, а** *друго́й* **бизнесме́н.**
> *They have two sons, one is a journalist, and the other is a businessman.*

> **Одни́ студе́нты живу́т в общежи́тиях, а** *други́е* **живу́т до́ма у роди́телей.**
> *Some students live in dormitories, while others live at home with their parents.*

1. Supply the correct form of **оди́н**.

1. То́лько о́н _____ мо́жет реши́ть, что́ де́лать.
2. Ко дню́ рожде́ния до́чери ма́ма купи́ла то́рт и два́дцать _____ свечу́.
3. Мы́ заказа́ли ра́зные блю́да, _____ мясны́е, а други́е вегетариа́нские.
4. Мы́ бы́ли в Москве́ то́лько _____ неде́лю.
5. Ты́ молоде́ц! В дикта́нте ты́ не сде́лал ни _____ оши́бки.
6. Бы́ло те́сно, но мы́ все́ помести́лись в _____ маши́не.
7. У меня́ две́ сестры́, _____ рабо́тает врачо́м, а друга́я учи́тельницей.
8. У него́ в ко́мнате бы́ли _____ кни́ги, они́ бы́ли везде́, да́же на полу́.
9. Я́ слы́шал об _____ челове́ке, кото́рый излечи́лся от э́той боле́зни.
10. Мы́ с Вади́мом из _____ го́рода.

Declension and Use of 2, 3, and 4

The number *two* has two gender forms: **два́** when followed by a masculine or neuter noun, and **две́** when followed by a feminine noun. The numbers *three* **три́** and *four* **четы́ре** (and higher) have only one form for all genders. The full declensions for *two*, *three*, and *four* are given in the following table.

	2	3	4
Nom.	два́ *(m/n)* две́ *(f.)*	три́	четы́ре
Acc. Inam. = Nom.	два́, две́/	три́/	четы́ре/
Anim. = Gen.	дву́х	трёх	четырёх
Gen.	дву́х	трёх	четырёх
Prep.	о дву́х	о трёх	о четырёх
Dat.	дву́м	трём	четырём
Instr.	двумя́	тремя́	четырьмя́

Use of the Numbers 2, 3, and 4 Followed by a Noun

(a) In the Nominative and Inanimate Accusative

The numbers **два́/две́**, **три́**, and **четы́ре** (including compounds ending in these numbers) take the genitive singular of the following noun, *when the numbers themselves are either in the nominative or inanimate accusative.*

У меня́ *два́ бра́та* **и** *две́ сестры́.*	*I have two brothers and two sisters.*
В э́той гру́ппе *два́дцать два́ челове́ка.*	*In this group there are twenty-two people.*
В э́том авто́бусе помеща́ется *три́дцать три́ пассажи́ра.*	*This bus holds thirty-three passengers.*
Мы́ ви́дели *три́ авто́буса и четы́ре маши́ны.*	*We saw three buses and four cars.*

(b)   In the Oblique Cases

When the numbers 2, 3, and 4 modify a noun phrase in an "oblique" case (i.e., genitive, prepositional, dative, or instrumental), the number must be in the same case as the modified noun, which is in the *plural*.

Genitive

> **Она́ прожила́ в Москве́ о́коло** *четырёх ме́сяцев.*
> *She lived in Moscow about four months.*

Prepositional

> **Я́ говорю́ об э́тих** *двух но́вых студе́нтах.*
> *I'm talking about these two new students.*

Dative

> **Они́ подошли́ к** *трём де́вушкам.*
> *They walked up to the three girls.*

Instrumental

> **Она́ владе́ет** *тремя́ языка́ми.*
> *She has command of three languages.*

(c)   In the Animate Accusative

When **два/две́**, **три́**, **четы́ре** modify an *animate* noun in the accusative case, the "animate accusative" rule applies, i.e., the accusative of both the number and the noun takes the form of the genitive, with the modified noun in the *plural*.

> **Мы́ ви́дели** *двух ма́льчиков* **и** *трёх де́вочек.*
> *We saw two boys and three girls.*

However, in compound numbers ending in **два/две́**, **три́**, **четы́ре** the "animate accusative" rule does *not* apply: the number is in the form of the accusative that is identical to the nominative, and the animate noun following the number is in the *genitive singular*.

> **На де́нь рожде́ния мы́ пригласи́ли** *два́дцать два́ малыша́.*
> *We invited twenty-two kids to the birthday party.*

2.   Put the number and noun in parentheses into the required form.

> *Model:* Она́ живёт с (2, подру́га) _____ . Она́ живёт с <u>двумя́ подру́гами.</u>

1.   Мы́ ча́сто звони́м на́шим (2, сы́н) _____ .
2.   Когда́ мы́ бы́ли в Росси́и, мы́ побыва́ли в (3, го́род) _____ .
3.   В аудито́рии бы́ло (34, студе́нт), _____ но то́лько (32, ме́сто) _____ .
4.   На рабо́ту в рестора́н взя́ли (2, мужчи́на) _____ и (3, же́нщина) _____ .
5.   На э́тот ку́рс преподава́тель принима́ет то́лько (22, студе́нт) _____ .
6.   У на́с в университе́те (2, библиоте́ка) _____ .
7.   И́х маши́на слома́лась в (4, киломе́тр) _____ от на́шего до́ма.
8.   У э́тих (3, де́вушка) _____ не́т биле́тов.
9.   Оте́ц о́чень горди́тся свои́ми (3, до́чка) _____ .
10.   Я́ написа́л пи́сьма (3, дру́г) _____ .

Use of the Numbers 2, 3, and 4 Followed by an Adjective + Noun

(a) In the Nominative and Inanimate Accusative

When the numbers **два/две**, **три**, **четыре** are themselves in the nominative or inanimate accusative case, they take the *genitive plural* of a following adjective that is modifying a masculine or neuter noun, and usually the *nominative plural* of an adjective modifying a feminine noun; the noun, however, is in the genitive singular.

На по́лке бы́ло *два́ ру́сских словаря́.*
There were two Russian dictionaries on the shelf.

Он купи́л *две́ но́вые кни́ги.*
He bought two new books.

В э́той ко́мнате *три больши́х окна́.*
There are three big windows in this room.

Note: Adjectival nouns (page 155) after 2, 3, and 4, like regular adjectives, are in the genitive plural (due to an implicit masculine head noun) or nominative plural (with implicit feminine head noun): **два́ учёных** *two scientists,* **четы́ре взро́слых** *four adults,* **две́ бу́лочные** *two bread shops,* **три́ столо́вые** *three cafeterias.* In fractions (page 195), however, an ordinal adjective after 2, 3, and 4 is in the *genitive plural,* even though it is modifying the implied feminine noun **ча́сть** *part:* $\frac{2}{5}$ is read as **две́ пя́тых** (**ча́сти**).

Note: Adjectives (and pronouns) that precede a number are normally in the nominative or accusative plural: *Э́ти пе́рвые* **два́ дня́ прошли́ бы́стро** *These first two days passed quickly.* **В часы́ пи́к поезда́ хо́дят** *ка́ждые* **три́ мину́ты** *During rush-hour trains run every three minutes.*

3. Change the adjective + noun phrase in parentheses from the nominative singular to the required form.

Model: Студе́нт реши́л 3 (тру́дная зада́ча) _____ .
Студе́нт реши́л 3 <u>тру́дные зада́чи.</u>

1. На э́той у́лице откры́ли 2 (но́вый рестора́н) _____ .
2. К на́м на обме́н прие́хали 3 (ру́сский учёный) _____ .
3. В Москве́ неда́вно постро́или 3 (больша́я гости́ница) _____ .
4. В пе́рвом ряду́ бы́ло 2 (свобо́дное ме́сто) _____ .
5. У на́с в общежи́тии живёт 4 (иностра́нный студе́нт) _____ .
6. В на́шем университе́те 2 (студе́нческая столо́вая) _____ .

(b) In the Oblique Cases and Animate Accusative

In the oblique cases, as well as in the animate accusative, **два/две**, **три**, **четы́ре** and the following adjective are in the same case as the modified noun, and the adjective and noun are in the *plural*:

Animate Accusative

Мы́ встре́тили *дву́х но́вых студе́нтов.*
We met the two new students.

Genitive

Мы́ купи́ли пода́рки для *дву́х ма́леньких де́вочек.*
We bought presents for two little girls.

Prepositional

Лéкции прохо́дят в *трёх больши́х аудито́риях.*
Lectures are held in three large lecture halls.

Dative

Мы́ да́ли тало́ны на пита́ние *двум иностра́нным студе́нтам.*
We gave meal tickets to the two foreign students.

Instrumental

Они́ о́чень дово́льны э́тими *четырьмя́ но́выми компью́терами.*
They are very pleased with these four new computers.

4. Put the number and following adjective + noun phrase into the required form.

   Model: Профе́ссор говори́л с (3, но́вый студе́нт) _____ .
   Профе́ссор говори́л с <u>тремя́ но́выми студе́нтами</u>.

   1. В боло́те мы́ ви́дели (2, живо́й крокоди́л) _____ .
   2. Мы́ позвони́ли (2, но́вая студе́нтка) _____ .
   3. На́м не хвата́ет (3, ча́йная ло́жка) _____ .
   4. На́ш сы́н игра́ет с (2, ру́сский ма́льчик) _____ .
   5. Уча́стники конфере́нции жи́ли в (4, университе́тское общежи́тие) _____ .

Declension of 5–20 and 30

The numbers 5–20 and 30 end in the soft sign **-ь**, and they decline exactly like feminine nouns of the third declension (e.g., **две́рь** *door*). The following table shows the declension of the numbers 5–10, 20, and 30 which all have the stress shifting from the stem in the nominative/accusative to the ending in the other cases.

	5	6	7	8	9	10	20 and 30
Nom. Acc.	пя́ть	ше́сть	се́мь	во́семь	де́вять	де́сять	два́дцать/ три́дцать
Gen. Prep. Dat.	пяти́	шести́	семи́	восьми́	девяти́	десяти́	двадцати́/ тридцати́
Instr.	пятью́	шестью́	семью́	восьмью́	девятью́	десятью́	двадцатью́ тридцатью́

Note: The vowel **-e-** in the nominative/accusative of **во́семь** is replaced by **-ь-** in the oblique cases. However, the instrumental case **восьмью́** has a variant form, **восемью́**, sometimes found in more formal, written styles.

Note: The numbers 11–19 have the same endings as those in the table above, but have the stress fixed on the same syllable of the stem: Nom./Acc. **оди́ннадцать**, Gen./Prep./Dat. **оди́ннадцати**, Instr. **оди́ннадцатью**.

Declension of 50, 60, 70, and 80

The numbers **пятьдеся́т**, **шестьдеся́т**, **се́мьдесят**, and **во́семьдесят** consist of two parts, both of which decline like third-declension nouns, except that the nominative/accusative does not end in the soft sign.

	50	60	70	80
Nom. Acc.	пятьдеся́т	шестьдеся́т	се́мьдесят	во́семьдесят
Gen. Prep. Dat.	пяти́десяти	шести́десяти	семи́десяти	восьми́десяти
Instr.	пятью́десятью	шестью́десятью	семью́десятью	восьмью́десятью

Declension of 40, 90, and 100

The numbers **со́рок**, **девяно́сто**, and **сто́** have a very simple declension, with only one oblique case ending: **-а**.

	40	90	100
Nom./Acc.	со́рок	девяно́сто	сто́
Gen./Prep./Dat./Instr.	сорока́	девяно́ста	ста́

Declension of 200, 300, 400

There are two parts to the numbers **две́сти**, **три́ста**, and **четы́реста** and both parts decline: the first part declines just like **две́**, **три́**, **четы́ре** and the second part, **сто́**, declines like a noun following the numbers 2, 3, and 4, i.e., it either has the form of the genitive singular **-ста** (except for **-сти** in **две́сти**, an old "dual" form), or it is in the genitive, prepositional, dative, or instrumental plural (**-со́т**, **-ста́х**, **-ста́м**, **-ста́ми**).

	200	300	400
Nom./Acc.	две́сти	три́ста	четы́реста
Gen.	двухсо́т	трёхсо́т	четырёхсо́т
Prep.	двухста́х	трёхста́х	четырёхста́х
Dat.	двумста́м	трёмста́м	четырёмста́м
Instr.	двумяста́ми	тремяста́ми	четырмяста́ми

Declension of 500, 600, 700, 800, and 900

Like the numbers 200, 300, and 400, the numbers **пятьсо́т**, **шестьсо́т**, **семьсо́т**, **восемьсо́т**, and **девятьсо́т** consist of two declined parts: the first part declines like the numbers **пя́ть–де́вять**, and the second part, **сто́**, declines like a noun in the plural of the oblique cases.

	500	600	700	800	900
Nom./Acc.	пятьсо́т	шестьсо́т	семьсо́т	восемьсо́т	девятьсо́т
Gen.	пятисо́т	шестисо́т	семисо́т	восьмисо́т	девятисо́т
Prep.	пятиста́х	шестиста́х	семиста́х	восьмиста́х	девятиста́х
Dat.	пятиста́м	шестиста́м	семиста́м	восьмиста́м	девятиста́м
Instr.	пятьюста́ми	шестьюста́ми	семьюста́ми	восьмьюста́ми	девятьюста́ми

Use of Cardinal Numbers 5–999

(a)   In the Nominative and Accusative

When the numbers 5–999 are themselves in the nominative or accusative case, both adjectives and nouns follow in the *genitive plural*.

> **К на́м на обме́н приезжа́ют** *пя́ть ру́сских студе́нтов.*
> *Five Russian students are coming to us on an exchange.*

> **На э́той у́лице стро́ят** *шесть больши́х домо́в.*
> *They are building five big houses on this street.*

> **Мы́ посмотре́ли** *де́сять иностра́нных фи́льмов.*
> *We saw ten foreign films.*

> **В э́той гости́нице** *две́сти два́дцать во́семь просто́рных номеро́в.*
> *There are two hundred and twenty-eight spacious rooms in this hotel.*

The numbers 5 and above do not undergo the "animate accusative" rule, i.e., the accusative case form of the number is identical to the nominative, whether the modified noun is animate or inanimate.

> **В зоопа́рке мы́ ви́дели** *пя́ть ти́гров и шесть льво́в.*
> *At the zoo we saw five tigers and six lions.*

> **Э́тот конце́ртный за́л вмеща́ет** *восемьсо́т пятьдеся́т зри́телей.*
> *This concert hall holds eight hundred and fifty spectators.*

Note: Compound numbers higher than 5 whose last component is 1 follow the pattern of agreement discussed above for **оди́н** (e.g., **два́дцать** *оди́н конве́рт* twenty-one envelopes, **три́дцать** *одна́ ма́рка* twenty-one stamps); compounds ending in 2, 3, and 4 (e.g., 22, 34, 53) when in the nominative/accusative case follow the rules given above for these numbers: they take the genitive singular of the following noun: **два́дцать** *два́ карандаша́* twenty-two pencils, **три́дцать** *четы́ре биле́та* thirty-four tickets.

(b)　In the Oblique Cases

In the oblique cases the numbers 5 and higher function as modifiers, agreeing in case with the modified noun (and any modifying adjective) in the *plural*.

Мы́ побыва́ли в *пяти́ изве́стных музе́ях.*
We visited five famous museums.

Я́ посла́л откры́тки *семи́ хоро́шим друзья́м.*
I sent postcards to seven good friends.

Что́ де́лать с *десятью́ рубля́ми?*
What can one do with ten rubles?

In the oblique cases each part of a compound number declines:

На конфере́нцию прие́хали учёные из *девяно́ста дву́х стра́н.*
Scholars from ninety-two countries came to the conference.

Спортсме́нов размести́ли в *тридцати́ трёх номера́х.*
The athletes were placed in thirty-three rooms.

В его́ колле́кции бо́льше *двухсо́т шести́десяти пяти́ ру́сских ма́рок.*
In his collection there are more than two hundred and sixty-five Russian stamps.

5.　Put the number, adjective, and noun in parentheses into the required form.

Model: У на́ших сосе́дей (5, ма́ленький ребёнок) ＿＿＿＿＿＿ .
　　　　 У на́ших сосе́дей <u>пя́ть ма́леньких дете́й.</u>

1.　Мы́ познако́мились с (6, ру́сский тури́ст) ＿＿＿＿＿ .
2.　Студе́нт реши́л (7, тру́дная зада́ча) ＿＿＿＿＿ .
3.　Учи́тельница дала́ карандаши́ (10, но́вый учени́к) ＿＿＿＿＿ .
4.　В Вашингто́не (5, ча́стный университе́т) ＿＿＿＿＿ .
5.　Э́та стару́ха живёт с (20, ста́рая ко́шка) ＿＿＿＿＿ .
6.　Мы́ посла́ли приглаше́ния (35, хоро́ший дру́г) ＿＿＿＿＿ .
7.　Санкт-Петербу́рг бы́л постро́ен на (100, небольшо́й о́стров) ＿＿＿＿＿ .
8.　В э́том университе́те преподаю́т бо́льше (350, о́пытный профе́ссор) ＿＿＿＿＿ .
9.　Говоря́т, что в Петербу́рге о́коло (215, дождли́вый де́нь) ＿＿＿＿＿ в году́.
10.　В э́том ма́леньком городке́ ме́ньше (540, постоя́нный жи́тель) ＿＿＿＿＿ .

Declension and Use of Ты́сяча

The word **ты́сяча** *thousand* is declined like the second declension noun **встре́ча** *meeting*, except that in the instrumental singular it has the form **ты́сячью**, which in most contexts has replaced the expected **ты́сячей** (the latter form, however, is still used when preceded by **одно́й**: **с одно́й ты́сячей** *with one thousand*).

	Singular	*Plural*
Nom.	ты́сяча	ты́сячи
Acc.	ты́сячу	ты́сячи
Gen.	ты́сячи	ты́сяч
Prep.	ты́сяче	ты́сячах
Dat.	ты́сяче	ты́сячам
Instr.	ты́сячью/ты́сячей	ты́сячами

As a noun, **ты́сяча** can itself be quantified like any other noun. For example, when preceded by **две́**, **три́**, and **четы́ре** in the nominative or inanimate accusative, **ты́сяча** is in the genitive singular (**две́ ты́сячи** *two thousand*, **три́ ты́сячи** *three thousand*, **четы́ре ты́сячи** *four thousand*). Similarly, when preceded by the nominative and accusative of the numbers **пя́ть**, **ше́сть**, and higher, **ты́сяча** is in the genitive plural (**пя́ть ты́сяч** *five thousand*, **два́дцать ты́сяч** *twenty thousand*).

The noun **ты́сяча** is normally followed by the genitive plural, regardless of its own case in a given context:

На съе́зд собрала́сь *одна́ ты́сяча делега́тов.*
One thousand delegates gathered at the congress.

Ка́ждый ме́сяц о́н прино́сит домо́й *одну́ ты́сячу до́лларов.*
Each month he brings home one thousand dollars.

В забасто́вке уча́ствовали бо́льше *пятидесяти ты́сяч шахтёров.*
More than fifty thousand coal-miners participated in the strike.

На́до почини́ть брако́ванный водопрово́д в *одно́й ты́сяче но́вых домо́в.*
Faulty water-pipes have to be repaired in one thousand new homes.

Прави́тельство пошло́ на усту́пки *пятиста́м ты́сячам забасто́вщиков.*
The government made concessions to fifty thousand strikers.

Мы́ не смо́жем обойти́сь *пятью́ ты́сячами рубле́й.*
We can not manage with five thousand rubles.

Note: When unmodified in an oblique case, **ты́сяча** may also be treated as a number. It then behaves just like the numbers **пя́ть** and above, i.e., it is followed by a plural noun in the same oblique case, e.g., **Он уе́хал с** *ты́сячью рубля́ми He left with a thousand rubles*. This usage is characteristic of colloquial style.

Declension and Use of Миллио́н and Миллиа́рд/Биллио́н

The numbers **миллио́н** *million* and **миллиа́рд** *milliard* (= **биллио́н** *billion*) are declined as regular hard-stem masculine nouns. Like **ты́сяча**, these nouns can themselves be quantified (**два́ миллио́на** *two million*, **се́мь миллио́нов** *seven million*, **три́ миллиа́рда** *three milliard*, **де́сять миллиа́рдов** *ten milliard*), and they govern the genitive plural of following nouns and adjectives.

Населе́ние Росси́и — *сто́ пятьдеся́т миллио́нов челове́к.*
The population of Russia is one hundred and fifty million people.

Би́лл Ге́йтс — **миллиарде́р. У него́ бо́льше** *сорока́ миллиа́рдов до́лларов.*
Bill Gates is a billionaire. He is worth more than forty billion dollars.

Representing Thousands and Millions in Figures

When using figures to write numbers in the thousands and higher, Russian requires either a period or a space, where English has a comma, e.g., **ты́сяча** 1.000/1 000 (= English 1,000), **сто́ ты́сяч** 100.000/100 000 (= English 100,000), **два́ миллио́на** 2.000.000/2 000 000 (= English 2,000,000).

6. Write out the number and noun in parentheses, putting them into the required form.

1. На́м придётся ограни́читься (10 000, ру́бль) _____ .
2. На вы́ставку прие́хали о́коло (15 000, посети́тель) _____ .
3. В на́шем университе́те у́чатся (24 000, студе́нт) _____ .

4. Студе́нты и аспира́нты живу́т в (10 000, ко́мната) _____ университе́тских общежи́тий.

5. Граби́тели ба́нка скры́лись, прихвати́в с собо́й бо́льше (150 000, до́ллар) _____ .

6. Во Второ́й мирово́й войне́ поги́бло бо́льше (20 000 000, сове́тский граждани́н) _____ .

7. Специали́сты предска́зывают дефици́т в (5.000.000.000, до́ллар) _____ в госбюдже́те США.

Money and Prices

The two monetary units in Russia are the **ру́бль** *ruble* and the **копе́йка** *kopeck* (1/100 ruble). As a result of intermittent periods of rapid inflation that have characterized post-Soviet Russia's shift to a market economy, the value of the ruble has fluctuated greatly, and continues to be unstable. As of October 1998, the rate of exchange was approximately $1 = 10 rubles.

The following table illustrates the case forms of the nouns **ру́бль** and **копе́йка** after numbers.

1 (оди́н) **ру́бль**	2 (два́), 3, 4 **рубля́**	5, 6, 7, . . . **рубле́й**
1 (одна́) **копе́йка**	2 (две́), 3, 4 **копе́йки**	5, 6, 7, . . . **копе́ек**

— **Ско́лько де́нег вы́ зараба́тываете в ме́сяц?**
— *How much money do you earn a month?*
— **Я́ зараба́тываю** *ты́сячу пятьсо́т рубле́й* **в ме́сяц.**
— *I earn 1500 rubles a month.*

— **Ско́лько сто́ит компа́кт-ди́ск?**
— *How much does a CD cost?*
— **Компа́кт-ди́ск сто́ит** *90 рубле́й 52 копе́йки.*
— *A compact disk costs 90 rubles 52 kopecks.*

7. The following are only approximate costs of various items in rubles and kopecks. Write out the numbers in words, and put the nouns for rubles and kopecks in the correct form.

1. Буты́лка вина́ (60 р 20 к)   _____
2. Деся́ток яи́ц (12 р 22 к)   _____
3. Па́чка ко́фе (30 р 41 к)   _____
4. Паке́т молока́ (11 р 43 к)   _____
5. Коро́бка конфе́т (72 р)   _____
6. Ви́дик (3 000 р)   _____

Telephone Numbers

In large Russian cities such as Moscow and St. Petersburg, telephone numbers, like those in America, consist of 7 digits. However, unlike English, where telephone numbers are normally read and spoken one digit at a time, telephone numbers in Russian are divided into three separate units: an initial 3-digit number in the "hundreds," followed by two 2-digit numbers in the "tens," e.g., 350-21-44 is read as **три́ста пятьдеся́т-два́дцать оди́н-со́рок четы́ре**). A true zero 0, one that is not part of a larger number, is rendered by **но́ль**, e.g., -10- is «**де́сять**», but -01- is «**но́ль оди́н**», -00- is «**но́ль но́ль**» (or «**два́ ноля́**»).

8. Write the following telephone numbers as they would be read and spoken in Russian.

1. 742-00-66   _____
2. 239-12-10   _____
3. 444-87-09   _____
4. 993-03-30   _____
5. 521-55-77   _____

Numerical Nouns Formed from Cardinal Numbers

The following nouns with numerical meaning are derived from the cardinal numbers.

едини́ца	*one*	**шестёрка**	*six*
дво́йка	*two*	**семёрка**	*seven*
тро́йка	*three*	**восьмёрка**	*eight*
четвёрка	*four*	**девя́тка**	*nine*
пятёрка	*five*	**деся́тка**	*ten*

In addition to being the names of the corresponding figures (e.g., **семёрка** *the figure 7*), these nouns have several special uses. For example, they are used to indicate:

University and School Grades

In the Russian educational system, the first five nouns refer to grades given for academic work: **едини́ца** (**пло́хо** *bad*/F), **дво́йка** (**неудовлетвори́тельно** *unsatisfactory*/D), **тро́йка** (**удовлетвори́тельно** *satisfactory*/C), **четвёрка** (**хорошо́** *good*/B) and **пятёрка** (**отли́чно** *excellent*/A).

> **Бо́ря мно́го занима́лся и получи́л** *пятёрку* **на экза́мене.**
> *Borya studied hard and got an A on the exam.*

> **Пе́тя пло́хо написа́л экза́мен и получи́л** *дво́йку.*
> *Pete wrote poorly on the exam and got a D.*

Playing Cards

The nouns **дво́йка** through **деся́тка** also denote playing cards of a suit:

дво́йка бубён	*two of diamonds*	**восьмёрка черве́й**	*eight of hearts*
пятёрка пи́к	*five of spades*	**деся́тка треф**	*ten of clubs*

> **О́н сда́л мне́** *семёрку* **треф.**
> *He dealt me the seven of clubs.*

Numbers of Buses and Trolleys

In colloquial Russian, nouns in the list above (and a few others, e.g., **двадца́тка** *20*, **тридца́тка** *30*) can be used to refer to the numbers of buses and trolleys.

> **Мо́жно дое́хать до университе́та на** *восьмёрке.*
> *You can get to the university on (bus or trolley) 8.*

> **Я́ прие́хал домо́й на** *пятёрке.*
> *I came home on (bus or trolley) 5.*

Groups of People and Objects Comprised of Several Units

Several of these nouns are used to refer to groups of people, or objects consisting of several units, for example:

тро́йка	*three-person commission; a team of three horses, three-piece suit, etc.*
четвёрка	*team of four horses; a four-oar boat*
пятёрка	*five-ruble note*
семёрка	*group of seven people*
деся́тка	*ten-ruble note*

Он пришёл на рабо́ту в *тро́йке.*
He came to work in a three-piece (suit).

Similarly, the nouns **пято́к** and **деся́ток** are used colloquially to refer, respectively, to groups of *five* and *ten* (usually similar objects), e.g., **пято́к огурцо́в** *five cucumbers*, **деся́ток яи́ц** *a ten of eggs*.

В Росси́и я́йца продаю́тся *деся́тками,* **а не дю́жинами.**
In Russia eggs are sold in tens, not in dozens.

Note: The noun **со́тня** *a hundred* is used in a similar way, typically when money is implied, e.g., **Он проси́л у меня́** *со́тню He asked me for a hundred (rubles).*

9. Complete the sentence with the correct form of the numerical noun.

1. За хоро́шее сочине́ние учи́тель поста́вил ей (5) _____ .
2. У меня́ при себе́ нет де́нег. Ты не да́шь мне (10-ruble note) _____ ?
3. Ле́на была́ на ры́нке и купи́ла (a 10) _____ све́жих яи́ц.
4. Что́бы дое́хать до гости́ницы «Мир», на́до се́сть на ((bus) No. 6) _____ .
5. Что́бы вы́играть па́ртию, мне нужна́ была́ (7) _____ бубён.
6. Он вообще́ не занима́лся и получи́л (2) _____ на экза́мене.

Collective Numbers

Collective numbers indicate the quantity of people, animals, or things in a group, and present them as a *single unit*. The collective numbers include **о́ба/о́бе** *both*, along with the series **дво́е** *two* to **де́сятеро** *ten*:

о́ба/о́бе	*both*	**ше́стеро**	*six*
дво́е	*two*	**се́меро**	*seven*
тро́е	*three*	**во́сьмеро**	*eight*
че́тверо	*four*	**де́вятеро**	*nine*
пя́теро	*five*	**де́сятеро**	*ten*

The Collective Number **Оба/Обе**

Like the cardinal number **два́/две́** *two*, the collective number **о́ба/о́бе** *both* has two gender forms: one for masculine and neuter nouns, the other for feminine nouns. However, unlike **два́/две́**, which distinguishes gender only in the nominative/accusative case, the collective **о́ба/о́бе** distinguishes gender (via the stem vowel **-о-** vs. **-е-**) throughout the entire declension. **Оба/о́бе** in the oblique cases takes soft-stem plural adjective endings.

	Masculine and Neuter	Feminine
Nom.	**о́ба**	**о́бе**
Acc. Inam. = Nom.	**о́ба**	**о́бе**
Anim. = Gen.	**обо́их**	**обе́их**
Gen.	**обо́их**	**обе́их**
Prep.	**об обо́их**	**об обе́их**
Dat.	**обо́им**	**обе́им**
Instr.	**обо́ими**	**обе́ими**

The case of nouns and adjectives after **о́ба/о́бе** follows the same pattern as **два́/две́**: when the number itself is in the nominative or inanimate accusative, the noun following is in the *genitive singular*, and the adjective is in the *genitive plural* (for masculines and neuters), or the *nominative plural* (for feminines). **О́ба/о́бе** is used when *both* of the things referred to are of the same kind.

> *О́ба но́вых рестора́на* **нахо́дятся на Не́вском проспе́кте**.
> *Both new restaurants are located on Nevsky Prospekt.*

> *О́бе но́вые гости́ницы* **откры́лись весно́й**.
> *Both new hotels opened in the spring.*

In an oblique case, **о́ба/о́бе** agrees in case with the following *plural* noun and adjective.

> **На́ши друзья́ останови́лись в** *обе́их гости́ницах*.
> *Our friends have stayed in both hotels.*

> **Держи́сь за ру́ль** *обе́ими рука́ми*.
> *Hold the steering wheel with both hands.*

The Collective Number Series **Дво́е, Тро́е,** ...

The declension of the collective numbers **дво́е** and **че́тверо** is presented in the table below. The declension of **тро́е** is like that of **дво́е**, and **пя́теро**, **ше́стеро**, **се́меро**, etc., are declined like **че́тверо**.

Nom.	**дво́е**	**че́тверо**
Acc. Inam. = Nom.	**дво́е**	**че́тверо**
Anim. = Gen.	**двои́х**	**четверы́х**
Gen.	**двои́х**	**четверы́х**
Prep.	**о двои́х**	**о четверы́х**
Dat.	**двои́м**	**четверы́м**
Instr.	**двои́ми**	**четверы́ми**

The collective numbers in this series are followed by the genitive plural of adjectives, nouns, and pronouns, when the numbers themselves are in the nominative/inanimate accusative. In all other cases, collective numbers are followed by the required plural case form of the (usually animate) noun: **Она́ ма́ть** *двои́х* **краси́вых дете́й** *She is the mother of two beautiful children.*

Collective numbers have the following uses:

(i)   Collective numbers must be used with nouns that have only a plural form (see page 33):

двóе **нóвых джи́нсов**   *two new pairs of jeans*
трóе **швейца́рских часо́в**   *three Swiss watches*
че́тверо **су́ток**   *four days*

Collective numbers may also be used with nouns denoting things that come in "pairs," e.g., *socks*, *gloves*, *shoes*, *skis*. However, with such nouns the same meaning can also be expressed by a cardinal number combined with the noun **па́ра** *pair*:

дво́е носко́в/две́ па́ры носко́в   *two pairs of socks*
тро́е лы́ж/три́ па́ры лы́ж   *three pairs of skis*

(ii) with nouns denoting male persons:

дво́е ма́льчиков   *two boys*   **пя́теро холостяко́в**   *five bachelors*
тро́е мужчи́н   *three men*   **ше́стеро женихо́в**   *six bridegrooms*
че́тверо ю́ношей   *four youths*   **се́меро студе́нтов**   *seven students*

Cardinal numbers are also possible with nouns denoting males (**два́ ма́льчика** *two boys*, **три́ мужчи́ны** *three men*, **четы́ре студе́нта** *four students*). The cardinal presents the people in a group as *individuals*, whereas the collective presents a group of people as a *whole*. With nouns denoting female persons, only a cardinal number is possible (**две́ де́вушки** *two girls*, but *not* *дво́е де́вушек).

(iii) with *pronouns* denoting a group of males, females, or a group of mixed gender:

На́с *трóе.*   *There are three of us.*
На́м *трои́м* **нужны́ биле́ты.**   *The three of us need tickets.*
Их бы́ло *че́тверо:* **две́ же́нщины**   *There were four of them: two women*
    и дво́е мужчи́н.   *and two men.*

(iv) independently, without an accompanying noun or pronoun:

Пришло́ *дво́е.*   *Two people came.*
Óн е́ст за *трои́х.*   *He eats (enough) for three people.*
Я́ заказа́л сто́лик на *четверы́х.*   *I ordered a table for four.*

(v) with the plural nouns **лю́ди** *people*, **де́ти** *children*, **близнецы́** *twins*, **ребя́та** *kids*

За столо́м сиде́ло *тро́е* **людéй.**   *Three people sat at the table.*
У на́с *дво́е* **детéй.**   *We have two children.*
У неё роди́ло́сь *че́тверо* **близнецо́в.**   *She gave birth to quadruplets.*

(vi) with nouns denoting young animals:

У неё *дво́е* **котя́т.**   *She has two kittens.*
В зоомагази́не мы́ ви́дели *трои́х* **щеня́т.**   *We saw three puppies at the pet shop.*

10. Complete the sentence using a collective number in the required form.

    1. (Both) _____ сестры́ вы́шли за́муж.
    2. Я́ зна́ю (both) _____ бра́тьев и (both) _____ сестёр.
    3. Мы́ провели́ на да́че (3) _____ су́ток.

4. Она́ купи́ла (2) _____ но́жниц.
5. Мы́ заброни́ровали но́мер на (4) _____ .
6. У него́ большо́й аппети́т. Он мо́жет е́сть за (2) _____ .
7. На углу́ стоя́ло (3) _____ ма́льчиков.
8. Они́ все́ (4) _____ ушли́ ра́но с ле́кции.
9. Неда́вно в Аме́рике у одно́й же́нщины роди́ло́сь (7) _____ близнецо́в.
10. Ка́к же она́ бу́дет расти́ть (7) _____ дете́й?

Ordinal Numbers

An ordinal number indicates the relative position or rank in a series, e.g., *first*, *third*, *fifth*. Ordinal numbers, with the exception of **пе́рвый** *first* and **второ́й** *second*, are derived from correlated cardinal numbers, e.g., **пя́тый** (<**пя́ть**), **шесто́й** (<**ше́сть**).

1st	пе́рвый	40th	сороково́й
2nd	второ́й	50th	пятидеся́тый
3rd	тре́тий	60th	шестидеся́тый
4th	четвёртый	70th	семидеся́тый
5th	пя́тый	80th	восьмидеся́тый
6th	шесто́й	90th	девяно́стый
7th	седьмо́й	100th	со́тый
8th	восьмо́й	200th	двухсо́тый
9th	девя́тый	300th	трёхсо́тый
10th	деся́тый	400th	четырёхсо́тый
11th	оди́ннадцатый	500th	пятисо́тый
12th	двена́дцатый	600th	шестисо́тый
13th	трина́дцатый	700th	семисо́тый
14th	четы́рнадцатый	800th	восьмисо́тый
15th	пятна́дцатый	900th	девятисо́тый
16th	шестна́дцатый	1000th	ты́сячный
17th	семна́дцатый	1001st	ты́сяча пе́рвый
18th	восемна́дцатый	2000th	двухты́сячный
19th	девятна́дцатый	3000th	трёхты́сячный
20th	двадца́тый	5000th	пятиты́сячный
21st	два́дцать пе́рвый	1 000 000th	миллио́нный
30th	тридца́тый	1 000 000 000th	миллиа́рдный

Note: The final soft sign **-ь** of a cardinal number is omitted before the adjective ending of the ordinal: де́сять → деся́т-ый. Also, the **-ь-** in the middle of the cardinal numbers 50, 60, 70, 80, and 500, 600, 700, 800, 900 is replaced by **-и-** in the corresponding ordinal: пятьдеся́т 50 → пятидеся́тый *50th*, семьсо́т *700* → семисо́тый *700th*.

Note: In compounds the initial element is an undeclined *cardinal* number and the final element is a declined *ordinal*, e.g., **три́дцать** *восьмо́й* **авто́бус** *bus thirty-eight* (literally *thirty-eighth bus*).

Ordinal numbers decline like hard-stem adjectives (see page 141), except for **тре́тий** *third*, which has the special declension shown in the following table.

	Masculine,	Neuter	Feminine	Plural
Nom.	**тре́тий**	**тре́тье**	**тре́тья**	**тре́тьи**
Acc. Inam. = Nom.	**тре́тий**	**тре́тье**	**тре́тью**	**тре́тьи**
Anim. = Gen.	**тре́тьего**			**тре́тьих**
Gen.	**тре́тьего**		**тре́тьей**	**тре́тьих**
Prep.	**тре́тьем**		**тре́тьей**	**тре́тьих**
Dat.	**тре́тьему**		**тре́тьей**	**тре́тьим**
Instr.	**тре́тьим**		**тре́тьей**	**тре́тьими**

Since ordinal numbers are adjectives, they agree in gender, number, and case with the noun they modify.

Мы́ приближа́емся к *два́дцать пе́рвому* **ве́ку.**   *We are approaching the twenty-first century.*

Мо́й о́фис нахо́дится на *второ́м* **этаже́.**   *My office is located on the second floor.*

О́н за́нял *тре́тье* **ме́сто.**   *He took third place.*

Они́ сиде́ли в *тре́тьем* **ряду́.**   *They sat in the third row.*

11. Complete the following sentences with the ordinal number in the correct form.

1. Моя́ до́чка у́чится в (1st) _____ кла́ссе.
2. Э́тот студе́нт на (2nd) _____ ку́рсе.
3. Мы́ выхо́дим на (3rd) _____ остано́вке.
4. Мы́ останови́лись у (5th) _____ подъе́зда.
5. Она́ была́ на (7th) _____ не́бе.
6. Я́ люблю́ (9th) _____ симфо́нию Бетхо́вена.

Use of Russian Ordinals for English Cardinals

Ordinal numbers are often used in Russian, where English typically uses a cardinal, for example, to indicate hotel rooms, buses and trolleys, seat numbers, TV and radio channels, pages, chapters, and volumes of books. Note the English translations of the following Russian examples:

Мы́ жи́ли в *три́ста шесто́м* **но́мере.**   *We stayed in room 306.*

Она́ ждёт *со́рок пе́рвый* **авто́бус.**   *She is waiting for bus No. 41.*

О́н сиде́л на *два́дцать второ́м* **ме́сте.**   *He was sitting in seat 22.*

Что́ по *тре́тьей* **програ́мме?**   *What is on Channel 3?*

Я́ дочита́л до *пятьдеся́т пя́той* **страни́цы.**   *I read up to page 55.*

Я́ тепе́рь пишу́ *шесту́ю* **главу́.**   *I am now writing Chapter 6.*

12. Write the Russian equivalents of the following.

1. Chapter 32   _____
2. Volume 17   _____

3. Row 56 _____
4. Channel 3 _____
5. Bus No. 67 _____
6. Seat 125 _____

Fractions

Fractions denote part of a whole number. They are comprised of both a cardinal and an ordinal number. The numerator of a fraction is denoted by the cardinal number in the *nominative* case. The denominator is denoted by an ordinal number, which is in one of two forms:

1. If the numerator of the fraction is the number 1 (**одна́**), the denominator is in the *nominative* case, and (like the numerator) takes the *feminine* form (to agree with the understood feminine noun **ча́сть** *part*).

$\frac{1}{5}$	одна́ пя́тая	one fifth
$\frac{1}{6}$	одна́ шеста́я	one sixth
$\frac{1}{7}$	одна́ седьма́я	one seventh
$\frac{1}{8}$	одна́ восьма́я	one eighth
$\frac{1}{9}$	одна́ девя́тая	one ninth
$\frac{1}{10}$	одна́ деся́тая	one tenth
$\frac{1}{100}$	одна́ со́тая	one one hundredth
$\frac{1}{1000}$	одна́ ты́сячная	one one thousandth

2. If the numerator of the fraction is 2 (**две́**) 3, 4 (or a higher number), the ordinal denoting the denominator is in the *genitive plural* (not the nominative plural usually found after 2, 3, and 4 when the modified noun is feminine; see page 182).

$\frac{2}{5}$	две́ пя́тых	two fifths
$\frac{3}{10}$	три́ деся́тых	three tenths
$\frac{5}{8}$	пя́ть восьмы́х	five eighths

Both the numerator and denominator of a fraction decline, as shown in the following table.

	$\frac{1}{10}$	$\frac{2}{5}$
Nom.	одна́ деся́тая	две́ пя́тых
Acc.	одну́ деся́тую	две́ пя́тых
Gen.	одно́й деся́той	дву́х пя́тых
Prep.	одно́й деся́той	дву́х пя́тых
Dat.	одно́й деся́той	дву́м пя́тым
Instr.	одно́й деся́той	двумя́ пя́тыми

Regardless of the case of the fraction itself, a noun following a fraction is always in the *genitive* case.

У него́ температу́ра подняла́сь всего́ на *одну́ деся́тую гра́дуса.*
His temperature went up by only one tenth of a degree.

В го́нке о́н бы́л быстре́е на *две́ со́тых секу́нды.*
He was faster in the race by two hundredths of a second.

О́коло *двух пя́тых жи́телей го́рода* **име́ют маши́ны.**
About two fifths of the residents of the city have cars.

If a fraction follows a whole number, the adjective **це́лый** *whole* is sometimes used after the cardinal denoting the whole number. Note how such fractions are read or spoken:

$1\frac{3}{6}$ одна́ це́лая и три́ шесты́х
$2\frac{5}{8}$ две́ це́лых и пя́ть восьмы́х
$7\frac{1}{5}$ се́мь це́лых и одна́ пя́тая

Colloquial Forms of "Quarter," "Third," "Half"

In colloquial Russian, fractions involving *quarters* ($\frac{1}{4}$, $\frac{3}{4}$), *thirds* ($\frac{1}{3}$, $\frac{2}{3}$), and a *half* ($\frac{1}{2}$) are normally expressed by special nouns which are used instead of the regular form of the denominator.

Fraction	Formal	Informal/Colloquial
$\frac{1}{4}$	одна́ четвёртая	(одна́) че́тверть
$\frac{1}{3}$	одна́ тре́тья	(одна́) тре́ть
$\frac{1}{2}$	одна́ втора́я	полови́на/пол

These special nouns, like regular fractions, take the genitive case of a following noun:

$\frac{2}{3}$ *две тре́ти* **доро́ги**   *two thirds of the way*
$\frac{3}{4}$ *три че́тверти* **го́рода**   *three quarters of the city*

The noun **полови́на** *half* is normally followed by a noun that denotes something other than a unit of measure.

О́н уже́ истра́тил *полови́ну* **де́нег.**   *He already spent half of the money.*
О́н подписа́л *полови́ну* **докуме́нтов.**   *He signed half the documents.*

The truncated form **пол** (**ови́на**) is often combined with nouns denoting measurement. When the compound form with **пол** is used in the nominative or accusative case, the noun denoting measure takes a genitive ending.

Полме́сяца **прошло́ бы́стро.**   *Half a month passed quickly.*
Мы́ говори́ли *полчаса́.*   *We spoke for half an hour.*
О́н прожи́л в Москве́ *полго́да.*   *He lived in Moscow half a year.*
Она́ вы́пила *полстака́на.*   *She drank half a glass.*

In the oblique cases, both parts of the compound normally decline: **пол** changes to **полу**, and the measure-noun takes the oblique case ending required in the context.

Мы́ жда́ли о́коло *получа́са.*   *We waited about a half an hour.*
О́н живёт в *получа́се* **езды́ отсю́да.**   *He lives a half hour's drive from here.*

Note: In informal, colloquial speech **пол** may not change to **полу** in some nouns, e.g., **О́н вы́пил бо́лее** *полстака́на* *He drank more than a half a glass*. **Пол** remains constant in certain phrases, e.g., **на полста́вки** *at half-pay/part-time*: **О́н рабо́тает на** *полста́вки* *He works part-time (and receives half-pay)*.

The Expression $1\frac{1}{2}$: **Полтора́/Полторы́**

Russian has a special number *one and a half*, which has the simple declension presented in the following table.

	Masculine Neuter	*Feminine*
Nom./Acc.	**полтора́**	**полторы́**
Gen./Prep./Dat./Instr.	**полу́тора**	

The choice of nominative and accusative case forms **полтора́** or **полторы́** is determined by the gender of the following noun: the former is used with masculine and neuter nouns, the latter with feminine nouns. The forms **полтора́/полторы́** govern the genitive singular of the following noun.

На столе́ лежа́ло *полтора́ бато́на* **хле́ба.**
One and a half loaves of (white) bread lay on the table.

Она́ вы́пила *полторы́ ча́шки* **ча́я.**
She drank one and a half cups of tea.

A third form, **полу́тора**, is used for each of the remaining cases. The noun following **полу́тора** is in the *plural* of the case required in the given context.

На́м на́до ограни́читься *полу́тора ты́сячами* **до́лларов.**
We have to limit ourselves to one and a half thousand dollars.

Other Numbers with "Half"

To express "$\frac{1}{2}$" with other numbers, the phrase **с полови́ной** *with a half* can be used after the number, e.g., $2\frac{1}{2}$ **два́ с полови́ной**, $3\frac{1}{2}$ **три́ с полови́ной**. This is an informal way of expressing **три́ це́лых и пя́ть деся́тых** *three wholes and five tenths*.

13.   Write the number and the noun in parentheses in the correct form.

    1. О́н съе́л ($1\frac{1}{2}$ пирожо́к) _____ .
    2. Мы́ поговори́ли то́лько ($1\frac{1}{2}$ мину́та) _____ .
    3. Она́ не смо́жет обойти́сь бе́з ($1\frac{1}{2}$ ты́сяча) _____ .
    4. О́н не мо́г не ду́мать о ($1\frac{1}{2}$ миллио́н) _____ .
    5. Она́ вернётся че́рез ($1\frac{1}{2}$ ча́с) _____ .

Decimal Fractions

In expressing percentages, weight, volume, and other forms of measurement, a comma is used in Russian, where English uses a decimal point. The following table gives a few examples of how decimal fractions are read aloud.

	Russian	English
0,1	но́ль це́лых, одна́ деся́тая	0.1 or $\frac{1}{10}$
1,75	одна́ це́лая, се́мьдесят пя́ть со́тых	1.75
2,4	две́ це́лых, четы́ре деся́тых	2.4
3,5	три́ це́лых, пя́ть деся́тых	3.5

Note that when the word **це́лый** is used, the word **и** is usually omitted. Alternatively, the word **це́лый** may be omitted, and **и** used in its place, for example:

7,5% (се́мь и пя́ть деся́тых *проце́нта***)**   *7.5% (seven point five percent)*

14. Write out the following fractions in words, as they would be read aloud in Russian.

1. $\frac{3}{8}$ _____
2. 0,7   _____
3. $2\frac{3}{5}$ _____
4. $4\frac{1}{8}$ _____
5. $\frac{1}{4}$ _____
6. $\frac{2}{3}$ _____
7. 4,05   _____

Decimal Fractions in Colloquial Style

In informal conversation Russians often simplify decimal fractions, omitting both the words **це́лый** and **и**, as well as the declined forms of **деся́тый** *tenth* and **со́тый** *hundredth*.

О́н вы́пил небольшу́ю буты́лку пи́ва   *He drank a small, .33 (liter) size,*
ёмкостью но́ль три́дцать три́ (0,33).   *bottle of beer.*

The metric system of measurement is used in Russia. The following examples present a few approximate equivalents between the units of measure in the different systems used in America and Russia. Note the simplification of the decimal fractions.

— **Ско́лько оди́н фу́нт в килогра́ммах?**
— *How much is one pound in kilograms?*
— **Оди́н фунт — но́ль со́рок пя́ть (0,45) килогра́мма.**
— *One pound is .45 kilograms.*

— **Ско́лько одна́ пи́нта в ли́трах?**
— *How much is one pint in liters?*
— **Одна́ пи́нта — но́ль пя́ть (0,5) ли́тра/пол-ли́тра.**
— *One pint is point five liters (half a liter).*

— **Ско́лько одна́ ми́ля в киломе́трах?**
— *How much is one mile in kilometers?*
— **Одна́ ми́ля — оди́н и ше́сть (1,6) киломе́тра.**
— *One mile is one point six kilometers.*

Note: Nouns following a decimal fraction, like those in the examples above, are in the genitive singular: 2,5% **два́ и пя́ть деся́тых** *проце́нта.*

15. The following are beverages and fruit in quantities that one might find on a typical menu in a Russian restaurant. Write the decimal fractions in words, as they would be read or spoken informally.

1. Минера́льная вода́ 0,25 л   _____
2. Ко́ка-Ко́ла 0,33 л   _____
3. Во́дка 0,5 л   _____
4. Шампа́нское 0,75 л   _____
5. Со́к 1,0 л   _____
6. Апельси́ны 0,5 кг   _____

DATES

Days of the Week

The days of the week in Russian are not capitalized.

понеде́льник	*Monday*
вто́рник	*Tuesday*
среда́	*Wednesday*
четве́рг	*Thursday*
пя́тница	*Friday*
суббо́та	*Saturday*
воскресе́нье	*Sunday*

Note: The names for Tuesday, Thursday, and Friday are formed from ordinal numbers: **вто́рник** (<вто́рой) is the "second" day, **четве́рг** (<четвёртый) is the "fourth" day, and **пя́тница** (<пя́тый) is the "fifth" day of the week, respectively.

To indicate what day it *is*, *was*, or *will be*, the noun denoting the day is in the *nominative* case.

— **Како́й сего́дня де́нь?**   — *What day is today?*
— **Сего́дня** *пя́тница.*   — *Today is Friday.*

— **Како́й вчера́ бы́л де́нь?**   — *What day was yesterday?*
— **Вчера́ был** *четве́рг.*   — *Yesterday was Thursday.*

— **Како́й за́втра бу́дет де́нь?**   — *What day will it be tomorrow?*
— **За́втра бу́дет** *суббо́та.*   — *Tomorrow it will be Saturday.*

To express time *on* a particular day (*on Wednesday, on next Tuesday, on that day*), use the preposition **в** followed by the name of the day in the *accusative* case.

в понеде́льник	*on Monday*
во вто́рник	*on Tuesday*
в сре́ду	*on Wednesday*
в четве́рг	*on Thursday*
в пя́тницу	*on Friday*
в суббо́ту	*on Saturday*
в воскресе́нье	*on Sunday*

— Когда́ у тебя́ экза́мен?	— When do you have an exam?
— У меня́ экза́мен *в сре́ду.*	— I have an exam on Wednesday.
— В како́й де́нь вы́ прие́дете домо́й?	— On what day will you come home?
— Мы́ прие́дем *в суббо́ту.*	— We'll arrive on Saturday.
— В каки́е дни́ о́н рабо́тает?	— On what days does he work?
— О́н рабо́тает *во вто́рник* и *в четве́рг.*	— He works on Tuesday and Thursday.
В э́тот де́нь мы́ перее́хали в Москву́.	On that day we moved to Moscow.

To express "this," "last," and "next" referring to days (as well as weeks, months, seasons, years, and centuries) the noun is preceded by the modifiers **э́тот**, **про́шлый**, and **бу́дущий** (or **сле́дующий**) respectively.

в э́тот понеде́льник	*this Monday*
в про́шлую сре́ду	*last Wednesday*
в бу́дущий/сле́дующий вто́рник	*next Tuesday*

To express repeated occurrence *on* a day of the week (*on Mondays, on Fridays*), use the preposition **по** followed by the name of the day in the *dative plural*.

Она́ рабо́тает до́ма *по сре́дам.*	She works at home on Wednesdays.
По пя́тницам она́ покупа́ет проду́кты.	On Fridays she buys groceries.
По суббо́там мы́ е́здим на да́чу.	On Saturdays we go to the dacha.

Expressing Parts of a Day

Parts of a day (**у́тро** *morning,* **ве́чер** *evening,* **но́чь** *night*) preceded by a demonstrative pronoun (*that morning, that evening*) are expressed by the preposition **в** followed by the *accusative* case.

В э́то у́тро мы́ ра́но вста́ли.	On that morning we got up early.
В ту́ но́чь мне́ не спало́сь.	That night I couldn't sleep.

Otherwise, use the *instrumental* case of the noun *with no preceding preposition*:

у́тром	*in the morning*	**ве́чером**	*in the evening*
днём	*in the daytime*	**но́чью**	*in the night*

Note: English *in the afternoon* can be rendered in Russian either as **днём** or as **во второ́й полови́не дня́** (lit. *in the second half of the day*).

Note: English *this* referring to parts of the day (e.g., *this morning*) is expressed by the adverb **сего́дня** *today*: **сего́дня у́тром** *this morning,* **сего́дня днём** *this afternoon,* **сего́дня ве́чером** *this evening* (*tonight*). With other units of time, *this* is normally expressed by a form of the demonstrative pronoun **э́тот**.

Weeks

To express time with weeks, use the preposition **на** followed by the *prepositional* case of the noun **неде́ля**. Note the following common expressions:

на э́той неде́ле	*this week*
на про́шлой неде́ле	*last week*
на бу́дущей/сле́дующей неде́ле	*next week*

Months

All names of months are masculine and, unlike English, the names of the months are not capitalized.

янва́рь	*January*	ию́ль	*July*
февра́ль	*February*	а́вгуст	*August*
ма́рт	*March*	сентя́брь	*September*
апре́ль	*April*	октя́брь	*October*
ма́й	*May*	ноя́брь	*November*
ию́нь	*June*	дека́брь	*December*

To express *in* a particular month, use the preposition **в** followed by the name of the month, or the noun **ме́сяц** *month*, in the *prepositional* case. The months from **сентя́брь** through **февра́ль** have stress on the ending, e.g., **в сентябре́** *in September*, **в октябре́** *in October*, **в ноябре́** *in November*. The other names of the months have fixed stress.

Она́ вы́шла за́муж *в а́вгусте.*	She got married in August.
О́н око́нчит шко́лу *в ию́не.*	He will graduate from school in June.
Она́ ожида́ет ребёнка *в э́том ме́сяце.*	She is expecting a baby this month.
О́н бы́л в Ло́ндоне *в про́шлом ме́сяце.*	He was in London last month.
Мы́ е́дем в о́тпуск *в бу́дущем ме́сяце.*	We are going on vacation next month.

English expressions such as "this June," "last August," "next September" are rendered in Russian as **в ию́не э́того го́да** *in June of this year*, **в а́вгусте про́шлого го́да** *in August of last year*, **в сентябре́ бу́дущего го́да** *in September of next year*.

Они́ поже́нятся *в ию́ле бу́дущего го́да.*	They will get married next July.
О́н вы́шел на пе́нсию *в ма́рте* *про́шлого го́да.*	He retired last March.

Seasons

Following are the nouns denoting the seasons, as well as their *instrumental* case forms, which denote *in* the respective season.

весна́	*spring*	весно́й	*in the spring*
ле́то	*summer*	ле́том	*in the summer*
зима́	*winter*	зимо́й	*in the winter*
о́сень	*fall*	о́сенью	*in the fall*

Мы́ отдыха́ем *ле́том.*	We vacation in the summer.
Зде́сь *зимо́й* о́чень хо́лодно.	It is very cold here in the winter.
Уче́бный го́д начина́ется *о́сенью.*	The school year begins in the fall.

Expressions with "this/next/last" and the seasons are usually rendered by the *instrumental* case of the modifier + noun phrase, e.g., **э́той весно́й** *this spring*, **бу́дущим ле́том** *next summer*, **про́шлой зимо́й** *last winter*.

Years and Centuries

To express *in* a year or *in* a century, use the preposition **в** followed by the *prepositional* case of the noun **го́д** *year* or **ве́к/столе́тие** *century*. The following are commonly used expressions with years and centuries.

в э́том году́	*this year*	**в э́том ве́ке/столе́тии**	*in this century*
в про́шлом году́	*last year*	**в про́шлом ве́ке**	*in the last century*
в бу́дущем году́	*next year*	**в бу́дущем ве́ке**	*in the next century*

16. Write the Russian equivalents of the following time expressions.

1.	on Friday	_____	9.	next December	_____
2.	next week	_____	10.	this week	_____
3.	last Wednesday	_____	11.	last month	_____
4.	that evening	_____	12.	in the afternoon	_____
5.	in the spring	_____	13.	next Saturday	_____
6.	in June	_____	14.	in the summer	_____
7.	this year	_____	15.	in the last century	_____
8.	this March	_____	16.	last winter	_____

Dates with Months and Years

To simply state the date of the month (e.g., *Today is the 7th of June, Yesterday was the 6th*), use the neuter singular *nominative* case form of an ordinal number (the noun **число́** *number* is understood). The name of the month, if mentioned, is in the *genitive* case.

— **Како́е сего́дня число́?**	— *What is the date today?*
— **Сего́дня** *пе́рвое* **ма́я.**	— *Today is the first of May.*
— **Како́е вчера́ бы́ло число́?**	— *What was the date yesterday?*
— **Вчера́ бы́ло** *тридца́тое* **ию́ня.**	— *Yesterday was the thirtieth of June.*

To express *on* a particular date of the month, the ordinal number (along with the month) is in the *genitive* case, with *no preceding preposition*.

— **Како́го числа́ ты́ уезжа́ешь?**	— *On what date are you leaving?*
— **Я́ уезжа́ю** *деся́того* **а́вгуста.**	— *I'm leaving on the tenth of August.*
— **Когда́ у тебя́ де́нь рожде́ния?**	— *When is your birthday?*
— *Два́дцать второ́го* **ию́ня.**	— *On June twenty-second.*

Unlike English, where the number expressing the date can either precede or follow the month (He was born *on the fifth of June/on June fifth*), in Russian dates the ordinal number must *precede* the month.

Use of Prepositions with Dates

To express *from . . .* (a certain date), or *since . . .* (a certain time) use the preposition **c** followed by the time expression in the *genitive* case.

    Мы́ бу́дем в о́тпуске *с седьмо́го июля.*   *We'll be on vacation from July 7th on.*
    Он здесь рабо́тает *с пе́рвого ию́ня.*   *He's been working here since June 1st.*

To express *from . . . to . . .* with dates (and other time expressions), use the prepositions **c . . . до . . .** (or **от . . . до . . .**), each of which is followed by the *genitive* case.

    Я́ бу́ду в Москве́ *с тре́тьего до*   *I'll be in Moscow from the third to*
      деся́того **января́**.   *the tenth of January.*
    Он занима́лся *с утра́ до ве́чера.*   *He studied from morning until night.*

The prepositions **c** + *genitive* case and **по** + *accusative* case are used to express dates inclusively: *from . . . through . . . .*

    Мы́ бу́дем в Пари́же *с второ́го по*   *We will be in Paris from the 2nd*
      шесто́е **ма́рта**.   *through the 6th of March.*

Dates in Years

Dates in years, like months, are expressed by ordinal numbers. For example, unlike in English, where the year 1998 is read or spoken as "nineteen ninety-eight," in Russian one says: "the one thousand nine hundred ninety-eighth year." Note that the last number is a declined ordinal number, agreeing with the noun **го́д** *year*.

    Ты́сяча девятьсо́т девяно́сто *восьмо́й* **го́д**.
    The year 1998.

When answering the question **в како́м году́** *in what year* (or **когда́** *when*), the year date, like the question phrase, is expressed by the preposition **в** followed by the *prepositional* case of the ordinal and the word *year* in the "locative" form, **году́**.

    — **Когда́ основа́ли го́род Са́нкт-Петербу́рг?**
    — *When was the city of St. Petersburg founded?*
    — **Са́нкт-Петербу́рг основа́ли** *в ты́сяча семьсо́т тре́тьем году́.*
    — *St. Petersburg was founded in 1703.*

    — **В како́м году́ роди́лся Бори́с Пастерна́к?**
    — *In what year was Boris Pasternak born?*
    — **Пастерна́к роди́лся** *в ты́сяча восемьсо́т девяно́стом году́.*
    — *Pasternak was born in 1890.*

    — **В како́м году́ у́мер Ле́в Толсто́й?**
    — *In what year did Leo Tolstoy die?*
    — **Толсто́й у́мер** *в ты́сяча девятьсо́т деся́том году́.*
    — *Tolstoy died in 1910.*

To indicate a more specific time of the year (*in August 1945*, *on September 21 1998*), the ordinal and the word **год** must be in the *genitive* case.

Моя́ до́чь ко́нчит шко́лу в ию́не две́ ты́сячи *восьмо́го го́да.*
My daughter will graduate from high school in June of 2008.

Мы́ поженились два́дцать второ́го ма́я ты́сяча девятьсо́т во́семьдесят *тре́тьего го́да.*
We got married on May 22, 1983.

In Russian, as in English, when the century referred to is obvious in the context, the date may be reduced in conversational style to just the ordinal number and the required form of the word **год**.

Он ко́нчил шко́лу *в шестьдеся́т седьмо́м году́.*
He graduated high school in '67.

To indicate decades, as in for example *the sixties*, *the nineties*, the preposition **в** is followed by the *accusative or* the *prepositional* case of the ordinal number in the plural:

Он бы́л студе́нтом *в шестидеся́тые го́ды/в шестидеся́тых года́х.*
He was a student in the sixties.

Note: The Russian equivalents of the abbreviations B.C. and A.D. are respectively, **до на́шей э́ры (до н.э.)** *before our era* and **на́шей э́ры (н.э.)**, e.g., **Он жи́л** *до на́шей э́ры* **в пе́рвом ве́ке** *He lived in the first century B.C.*

Order of Numbers in Dates

In Russian, unlike in English, the first number in a date given in figures indicates the day, the second indicates the month (often in Roman numerals), followed by the year. Each number is separated either by a period or a forward slash: 7.VI.98 or 7/VI/98 (English 6/7/98 or June 7, 1998). This is the standard form for dates used in the headings of letters, on Russian visa applications, and other documents.

Да́та рожде́ния: *22.VI.49*   *Date of Birth: 6/22/49*
Да́та прибы́тия в Росси́ю: *10.III.98*   *Date of Arrival in Russia: 3/10/98*

17. Write the dates in parentheses in Russian.

1. Сего́дня (is June 7, 1998) _____.
2. Са́ша родила́сь (on February 6, 1990) _____.
3. А́нна Ахма́това умерла́ (in 1966) _____.
4. Ру́сский алфа́вит со́здали (in 860 A.D.) _____.
5. Мы́ бу́дем в о́тпуске (from the 5th to the 12th) _____.
6. Вчера́ бы́ло (21st of April) _____.
7. Да́та прибы́тия в Росси́ю (5/VII/99) _____.
8. Она́ здесь живёт (since the 15th of September) _____.

Expressing Age

To express age in Russian the person (or thing) whose age is indicated is in the *dative* case, and the number of years (or months) is typically rendered by a cardinal number and the required case form of the noun *year* (1, 21, 31 **год**/ 2, 3, 4, 22, ... **го́да**/ 5, 6, 7 ... **лет**). One may ask **Ско́лько ва́м (ему́,**

ей, etc.) **лет?** *How old are you* (*is he, she*, etc.)? or about an infant, **Сколько ему (ей) месяцев?** to which one may answer:

Ребёнку *три месяца.*	*The child is three months.*
Девочке *год и семь месяцев.*	*The little girl is a year and seven months.*
Ей *двадцать один год.*	*She is twenty-one.*
Мне *тридцать два года.*	*I am thirty-two.*
Отцу *сорок шесть лет.*	*My father is forty-six.*

To indicate an approaching birthday, the ordinal number may be used with the present or past tense of the verb **идти.**

Ему идёт *восьмой год.*	*He is going on eight.*
Ей тогда шёл *десятый год.*	*At that time she was going on ten.*

To ask *at what age* the preposition **в** + the *prepositional* case is used: **В каком возрасте?** This question may be answered either by **в возрасте** + the *genitive* case of the number, or simply by **в** + the *accusative* case of the number.

— **В каком возрасте она вышла замуж?**	*At what age did she get married?*
— **В** *восемнадцать лет.*	*At eighteen.*

18. Express the following in Russian.

1. She is twenty-one.
2. He is forty-five.
3. How old is the baby?
4. How old is the mother?
5. The baby is a year and 3 months.
6. He is going on sixteen.
7. At what age did he die?
8. He died at the age of 71.

TIME

Both cardinal and ordinal numbers are used in answering the questions: **Который час?** or the more colloquial **Сколько (сейчас) времени?** *What time is it* (*now*)? There are two methods for telling time in Russian: a conversational way of telling time by the clock, and the 24-hour system used for official purposes.

Conversational Clock Time

In the conversational method of telling time by the clock, the time can fall *on the hour*, within *the first half of the hour*, or within *the second half of the hour*. Time on the hour is expressed by a cardinal number and the appropriate case/number form of the noun **час** *o'clock* (lit. *hour*).

On the Hour		
1.00	час	1:00
2.00	два часа	2:00
3.00	три часа	3:00
4.00	четыре часа	4:00
5.00	пять часов	5:00
8.00	восемь часов	8:00
12.00	двенадцать часов	12:00

Note: Russian uses a period instead of a colon to separate hours and minutes.

Note: 12:00 *noon* is **по́лдень** and 12:00 *midnight* is **по́лночь**.

Time that falls between the hour and the first half-hour is expressed by both a cardinal and an ordinal number: the cardinal is used to state the number of minutes elapsed of the *following* hour, expressed by the ordinal number, e.g., 1:10 is understood as "ten minutes (elapsed) of the *second* hour": **де́сять мину́т второ́го**.

In the First Half of the Hour		
12.01	одна́ мину́та пе́рвого	12:01
1.02	две́ мину́ты второ́го	1:02
2.05	пя́ть мину́т тре́тьего	2:05
3.15	пятна́дцать мину́т четвёртого	3:15
	че́тверть четвёртого	
4.30	полови́на пя́того	4:30
	полпя́того	

Note: In colloquial speech, **че́тверть** *quarter* is used instead of **пятна́дцать мину́т** *fifteen minutes*, and **полови́на** *half* may be shortened to **пол** and prefixed to the ordinal, e.g., **полшесто́го** *half past five*.

The ordinal number denotes the 60-minute period between hours: **пе́рвый ча́с** (the period between 12:00 and 1:00), **второ́й ча́с** (the period between 1:00 and 2:00), **тре́тий ча́с** (the period between 2:00 and 3:00), etc. Thus, when one says in Russian «**в пе́рвом часу́**», it is comparable to saying in English *after twelve o'clock*.

Сейча́с *шесто́й* **ча́с.**	*It's now after five.*
Она́ позвони́ла *в восьмо́м часу́.*	*She called after seven.*
О́н прие́хал *в нача́ле деся́того.*	*He arrived shortly after nine.*

In the second half of the hour, the approaching hour is expressed by a cardinal number "less the number of minutes remaining" before the hour strikes, e.g., 2:55, expressed in English as *Five minutes until three*, is expressed in Russian as "without five minutes three": **без пяти́ (мину́т) три́**, where the preposition **без** *without* is followed by the genitive case of the cardinal number and (optionally) the genitive case of **мину́та**.

In the Second Half of the Hour		
4.31	без двадцати́ девяти́ (мину́т) пя́ть	4:31
6.40	без двадцати́ (мину́т) се́мь	6:40
8.45	без че́тверти де́вять	8:45
10.57	без трёх (мину́т) оди́ннадцать	10:57
11.59	без одно́й (мину́ты) двена́дцать	11:59
12.50	без десяти́ (мину́т) ча́с	12:50

One distinguishes A.M. and P.M., for example, 7:00 A.M. and 7:00 P.M., or 2:00 A.M. and 2:00 P.M., by using one of the following nouns in the genitive case:

у́тро	(5:00–12:00 A.M.)	се́мь часо́в *утра́*	*seven o'clock in the morning*
де́нь	(12:00–5:00 P.M.)	два́ часа́ *дня́*	*two o'clock in the afternoon*
ве́чер	(5:00–12:00 P.M.)	се́мь часо́в *ве́чера*	*seven o'clock in the evening*
но́чь	(12:00–5:00 A.M.)	два́ часа́ *но́чи*	*two o'clock in the morning*

Expressing "At What Time?"

To ask *at what time?* use the phrase **В кото́ром часу́?** or the more colloquial **Во ско́лько вре́мени?** The construction used to respond to either of these phrases (or to the question **Когда́** *When*) depends on the clock time:

(i) on the hour, and up to the first half-hour, use the preposition **в** + the *accusative* case:

в ча́с дня́	*at one o'clock in the afternoon*
в одну́ мину́ту второ́го	*at one minute past one*
в пя́ть мину́т тре́тьего	*at five past two*
в че́тверть восьмо́го	*at a quarter past seven*

(ii) in the second half of the hour, **в** is omitted before the preposition **без**:

без че́тверти де́вять	*at quarter to nine*
без дву́х мину́т двена́дцать	*at two minutes to twelve*

(iii) at the half-hour, use the preposition **в** + the *prepositional* case of **полови́на**:

в полови́не второ́го	*at one thirty*

Also, to express non-specific time "between hours," e.g., *after five*, use **в** + *prepositional* case:

в шесто́м часу́	*after five/between five and six*
в нача́ле восьмо́го	*shortly after seven*

19. Write the following in Russian, using words for the numbers.

1. It is now 7:00 A.M.
2. It is now after two.
3. 6:00 P.M.
4. 8:15
5. at 9:30 in the evening
6. at 12:00 midnight
7. at 3:00 in the morning
8. at 12:45
9. It is now 1:00 in the afternoon.
10. 3:57
11. at 9:59
12. 12:00 noon

Official Time: 24-hour System

Official time in Russia is expressed according to the 24-hour clock. This is the system used for schedules at railroad stations and airports, for newspaper listings of radio and television programming, as well as for movies, concerts, performances, and other official schedules.

In the 24-hour system, the declined forms of the words **ча́с** and **мину́та** may be omitted. A *zero* is usually expressed by **но́ль**. Official time is read as in the table below.

7.30	сéмь (часóв) трúдцать (минýт)	7:30 A.M.
8.45	вóсемь (часóв) сóрок пя́ть (минýт)	8:45 A.M.
11.15	одúннадцать (часóв) пятнáдцать (минýт)	11:15 A.M.
12.00	двенáдцать нóль нóль	Noon
13.05	тринáдцать (часóв) пя́ть (минýт)	1:05 P.M.
	тринáдцать нóль пя́ть	
18.00	восемнáдцать нóль нóль	6:00 P.M.
21.10	двáдцать одúн (чáс) дéсять (минýт)	9:10 P.M.
0.00	нóль часóв (нóль нóль минýт)	Midnight
0.10	нóль (часóв) дéсять (минýт)	12:10 A.M.
1.00	чáс нóль нóль	1:00 A.M.
3.03	трú (часá) трú (минýты)	3:03 A.M.
	трú нóль трú	

To express *at a certain time* use the preposition **в** + the *accusative case.*

Пóезд отправля́ется в *пя́ть сóрок.*	*The train departs at 5:40* A.M.
Самолёт вылетáет в *вóсемь нóль трú.*	*The plane takes off at 8:03* A.M.

20. Write the times in Russian, according to the 24-hour clock.

1.	6:40 A.M.	6.	6:05 P.M.
2.	8:35 A.M.	7.	8:10 P.M.
3.	10:20 A.M.	8.	11:40 P.M.
4.	1:00 P.M.	9.	Midnight
5.	3:15 P.M.	10.	12:50 A.M.

Approximation

Approximation with numbers indicating time, quantity, age, distance, weight, etc., can be expressed in several ways:

(*a*)   by reversing the order of the number and the noun, e.g.,

двá мéсяца/мéсяца двá	*two months/about two months*
емý сóрок лéт/емý лéт сóрок	*he is 40 years old/he is about 40 years old*

A preposition in a time expression invariably stands before the number, e.g.,

в двá часá/часá в двá	*at two o'clock/at about two o'clock*
чéрез трú гóда/гóда чéрез трú	*in three years/in about three years*

(*b*)   with **óколо** *about* followed by the number in the genitive case, e.g.,

óколо двýх мéсяцев	*about two months*
óколо пятú мéтров	*about five meters*

(*c*)   with the adverbs **примéрно** *roughly*, or **приблизúтельно** *approximately*, e.g.,

примéрно стó человéк	*roughly a hundred people*
приблизúтельно в чáс	*at approximately one o'clock*

CHAPTER 7

Verbs

OVERVIEW OF VERBS

In Russian, as in English, verbs are words which express an action (*run*, *shout*), a process (*blush*, *melt*), or a state (*be*, *know*).

Transitive and Intransitive Verbs

Russian verbs, like English verbs, fall into two fundamental categories—*transitive verbs* and *intransitive verbs*. Transitivity is related to the notion of "direct object." A verb is transitive if it can take a direct object. A direct object is the noun or pronoun that usually follows the verb (with no preceding preposition), and denotes something (or someone) that is directly affected by the action of the verb. In the sentence *He opens the door* the noun *door* is the direct object of the verb *open*. Similarly, in *She loves him* the pronoun *him* is the direct object of the verb *love*. In both English and Russian, the direct object answers the question *what?* or *whom?*: *Чтó* **он открыва́ет?** *What* (Acc.) *does he open? Когó* **она́ лю́бит** *Whom* (Acc.) *does she love?* The direct object in Russian is normally in the accusative case (but a direct object of a negated transitive verb may be in the genitive case, see Chapter 2, page 47).

An intransitive verb is one that can not (normally) occur with a direct object, for example, the verbs *snore* and *nap*. In the sentences *He snores* and *Grandpa often naps*, a direct object is impossible. A verb that is transitive in English may be intransitive in Russian, e.g., the verb *envy* is transitive in English (*I envy him* (direct object)), but its Russian equivalent, **зави́довать**, is not transitive, since it takes an object in the dative case (**Я́ зави́дую** *емý* (dative object)). Russian verbs which end in the particle **-ся/-сь** are intransitive (see page 212).

Personal Endings

In English one says *I know*, but *s/he knows*, adding an *-s* to the verb when the subject is in the *third person*, and *singular* in *number*. Russian verbs also have endings to indicate the person and number of the verb's subject, but in Russian there are six such *personal endings*, one for each subject in the *first*, *second*, and *third persons, singular and plural*. Changing the personal endings of the verb so that they agree with the subject is called *conjugation*. In Russian there are two conjugation patterns, or sets of verb endings, called the *first conjugation* and the *second conjugation*. All regular verbs belong to one of these two conjugations.

Forms of Address: Informal and Formal

Russian has two forms for the English pronoun *you*—**ты** and **вы**. The pronoun **ты** is a familiar singular form, used when addressing a pet, child, relative, friend, or a colleague who is of similar age or professional status. The pronoun **вы** has two functions: it is the formal *you*, used both when addressing one individual, or several individuals, who are strangers or casual acquaintances; **вы** also functions simply as the plural *you* when addressing any two (or more) individuals. Even when it is used to address one person formally, **вы** requires the verb to agree in the *plural* (see also page 101).

Verb Tenses

In Russian, as in English, verbs have *tense*. Tense relates the time of the action or state denoted by the verb to some other time, usually to the present moment. Russian verbs distinguish three tenses: the present (now), the past (prior to now), and the future (subsequent to now). English verbs, by contrast, distinguish not only the present, past, and future, but make a number of other distinctions that are described in English grammar as "progressive" and "perfect" tenses, for example, the "present progressive" (*He is writing*), the "present perfect progressive" (*He has been writing*), the "past progressive" (*He was writing*), the "past perfect" (*He had written*), the "future perfect" (*He will have written*), and several others. While Russian lacks equivalents to these English verb forms, the meanings associated with them can be approximated in Russian through a combination of tense, and a second temporal property of the verb, that of *aspect*.

Verb Aspects

Nearly all Russian verbs are either *imperfective* or *perfective* in *aspect*. While tense indicates the time *when* an action occurs, aspect refers to different ways of viewing *how* the action occurs in time. For example, *imperfective* verbs are used to describe: (*a*) an action in progress without reference to its completion or result (*She is/was/will be working*); (*b*) an action that is habitual or repeated (*She works/used to work/will be working—every day*); (*c*) an action viewed in general terms, without reference to its performance on any specific occasion (*She works hard; He speaks Russian well*). *Perfective* verbs are used to describe an action that has been, or will be, carried through to completion, and whose result may be expressed in the context (*He wrote/will write the letter. He will send it tomorrow (result)*).

Verbs of the imperfective aspect have the three tenses: present, past, and future. However, perfective verbs have only the past and future tense, since the meaning of the perfective aspect—"completed action"—is incompatible with the present tense meaning of an action "in progress at the present moment."

Verb Moods

Verbs in Russian, as in English, have *mood*, that is, a way of indicating the speaker's attitude toward the factuality or likelihood of the stated action. Verbs in Russian distinguish four moods: the *indicative*, the *imperative*, the *conditional*, and the *subjunctive*.

The *indicative* mood is used to make factual statements. This is the most commonly used mood, and the only one which expresses tense (John *studies* Russian, Sasha *went* to Moscow, Mary *will buy* the wine).

The *imperative* mood is used to make commands or to give advice (*Read* this article! *Don't buy* that book!)

The *conditional* mood expresses hypothetical and contrary-to-fact statements. These refer to conditional statements which are not likely to be realized (hypothetical) or were not realized (contrary-to-fact). Compare the following statements:

(*a*)   If you *invite* me, I *will* go.

(*b*)   If you *invited* me, I *would go*.

(*c*)   If you *had invited* me, I *would have gone*.

The situation described in (a) *may* in fact occur, and is expressed in the indicative mood. The situation described in (b) is *hypothetical*; statements of this type imply that the situation is doubtful or unlikely (It's unlikely that you will invite me, and unlikely that I will go). The situation in (c) is *contrary-to-fact*; statements of this type imply that the situation described was not realized, i.e., the facts are the opposite (You did not invite me and I did not go). In Russian, statements like those in (b) and (c) are expressed by the particle **бы** + the past tense of the verb in the conditional clause, as well as in the consequence clause (see page 260).

The *subjunctive* mood is used to refer to actions that have yet to be, and may not be, realized, since they are wishes (I wish you *were* here), desires (We asked that he *might* bring some wine), or even fears (I am afraid that he *could* tell her). Like the conditional mood, the subjunctive in Russian is expressed by the particle **бы** or the conjunction **чтóбы** (an amalgam of **чтó** + **бы**) followed by the past tense form of the verb (see page 262).

CONJUGATION

The Infinitive

The infinitive of the verb (e.g., *to read*) is the form used to cite Russian verbs in dictionaries. It is also the form of the verb that often follows another verb (I love *to read*, He wants *to go*). Most Russian verbs have the infinitive ending **-ть** (читáть *to read*), less common are **-ти** (нести *to carry*) and **-чь** (мóчь *to be able*).

The Past Tense

The past tense of a verb in Russian agrees in gender and number with its subject. The past tense of most verbs can be obtained by removing the infinitive ending and replacing it with **-л** (masc./sing.), **-ло** (neut./sing.), **-ла** (fem./sing.) or **-ли** (plural): читá-ть: **Óн** читáл, **Онó** читáло, **Онá** читáла, **Они** читáли.

Russian has only one past tense, formed from both imperfective and perfective verbs. An imperfective verb in the past tense corresponds to several forms of the English past, e.g., English "She *read*," "She *was reading*," "She *used to read*," can all be rendered by the Russian past tense imperfective **Онá** *читáла*, while English "She *read (to completion)*," "She *had read*," by the past tense perfective **Онá** *прочитáла* (**журнáл**).

The Present Tense

Russian has only *one* present tense form corresponding to numerous forms of the English present; for example, English "She *reads*," "She *is reading*," "She *has been reading*" can all be rendered, in the appropriate context, by Russian **Онá** *читáет*.

First and Second Conjugation Endings

The present tense of a verb has six endings, one each to denote the six possible subjects in the first, second, and third persons singular (*I, you, he/she/it*) and plural (*we, you, they*). These endings (except in the first singular and third plural) begin with a vowel which signals present (or future perfective) tense and indicates the verb's conjugation class: **-e-** (or stressed **-ë**) indicates *first* (*I*) conjugation, while **-и-** indicates *second* (*II*) conjugation.

Person	Conjugation I	Conjugation II
Singular		
1st **я**	**-ю (-у)**	**-ю (-у)**
2nd **ты́**	**-ешь/-ёшь**	**-ишь**
3rd **óн/онá/онó**	**-ет/-ёт**	**-ит**
Plural		
1st **мы́**	**-ем/-ём**	**-им**
2nd **вы́**	**-ете/-ёте**	**-ите**
3rd **они́**	**-ют (-ут)**	**-ят (-ат)**

Note: In first conjugation verbs with stressed endings, the vowel **e** is spelled **ё**.

Note: The spelling of the first-person singular ending as **-ю** or **-у**, and the third-person plural endings as **-ют** or **-ут** (conjugation I), **-ят** or **-ат** (conjugation II), is determined by (1) whether the preceding consonant is soft or hard, respectively, and (2) the spelling rule that requires the unpaired consonants **ж**, **ч**, **щ**, **ш** to be followed only by the vowels **a** and **y**, never **я** and **ю** (see Spelling Rule 2, page 11).

These two sets of endings can be called the *non-past* endings, since "past" is the one tense they do *not* indicate; they indicate the *present* tense of an imperfective verb, and the *future* tense of a perfective verb. For example, **прочитáть** *to read* (pfv), when conjugated, has the meaning of the future tense: **Я́ прочитáю** *I will read*, **ты́ прочитáешь** *you will read*, etc.

The following table shows the fully conjugated forms of the first conjugation verbs **читáть** *to read*, **писáть** *to write*, **имéть** *to have*, and the second conjugation verbs **говори́ть** *to speak*, **ви́деть** *to see*.

	читáть *to read*	**писáть** *to write*	**имéть** *to have*	**говори́ть** *to speak*	**ви́деть** *to see*
я́	читáю	пишу́	имéю	говорю́	ви́жу
ты́	читáешь	пи́шешь	имéешь	говори́шь	ви́дишь
óн/онá	читáет	пи́шет	имéет	говори́т	ви́дит
мы́	читáем	пи́шем	имéем	говори́м	ви́дим
вы́	читáете	пи́шете	имéете	говори́те	ви́дите
они́	читáют	пи́шут	имéют	говоря́т	ви́дят

Verbs can also occur with the particle **-ся/-сь** following the verbal endings. This particle, which signals intransitivity, is spelled **-ся** after a consonant, and **-сь** after a vowel, e.g., the verb **занимáться** *to study*:

Non-Past				*Past Tense*	
я́	занимáюсь	**мы́**	занимáемся	**óн**	занимáлся
ты́	занимáешься	**вы́**	занимáетесь	**онá**	занимáлась
óн/онá	занимáется	**они́**	занимáются	**они́**	занимáлись

Stress Patterns in the Non-Past

The verbs presented above illustrate the three regular stress patterns for verbs in the non-past:

1. *Stem* stress. All forms are stressed on the same syllable of the stem, e.g., in **читáть**, **имéть**, and **вúдеть**.

2. *End* stress. All forms are stressed on the same syllable of the ending, e.g., in **говорúть**.

3. *Shifting stress*. The first person singular is stressed, but the stress *shifts* back one syllable in all the other forms, e.g., in **писáть**.

Consonant Alternations in Conjugation

In a number of verbs the final consonant of the stem alternates with another consonant in certain forms. In first conjugation verbs that have a consonant alternation, the change takes place in all forms of the non-past, e.g., **с → ш** in писáть: пишý, пúшешь, пúшет, пúшете, пúшут. In second conjugation verbs that have a consonant alternation, the change takes place *only in the first person singular*, e.g., **д → ж** in вúдеть: вúжу, вúдишь, вúдит, etc. These consonant alternations are not random; they follow a regular pattern (see below, pages 221 and 226).

In order to conjugate a Russian verb, then, one must know three essential facts:

1. Whether the verb belongs to the first or second conjugation.

2. Whether the verb has fixed or shifting stress.

3. Whether the stem-final consonant alternates with another consonant in conjugation.

However, these facts can *not* be determined from the infinitive form of the verb: while both **читáть** and **писáть**, two verbs with an infinitive in **-ать**, belong to the first conjugation, the conjugation patterns of these verbs are very different. Similarly, while both **имéть** and **вúдеть** have an infinitive in **-еть**, these verbs differ with respect to two of the above essential facts, namely, (1) and (3).

Since the information needed to conjugate a verb is *not* predictable from the infinitive, one approach to learning the conjugation of verbs is to memorize at least three key forms of each verb: the *infinitive*, and the *first and second person singular*. The remaining forms of the verb are predictable from these three forms.

Infinitive	**писáть**
1st person sing.	**пишý**
2nd person sing.	**пúшешь**

Knowing the three key forms above, one can correctly conjugate any regular verb. However, a more general approach is possible, one which groups hundreds, even thousands, of verbs into a small number of *types*, based on similar endings, stress patterns, and consonant alternation properties. Obviously, knowing a verb's type will greatly simplify the task of learning the conjugation of Russian verbs. The key to this approach is knowing which verbal *suffix* is found at the end of the verb's *basic stem*. It is the particular suffix (or the shape of a *nonsuffixed* stem) which classifies the verb as belonging to one of the verb types.

Verbal Stem Structure: (Prefix) + Root + (Suffix)

The Basic Stem: Suffixed and Nonsuffixed

Russian verbs, like nouns and adjectives, have the structure *stem + ending*. All verb stems contain a *root*, the segment where the basic meaning resides, e.g., **чит** *read*. In addition, the verb root may be preceded by a *prefix* and/or followed by a *suffix*. A prefix normally adds some element of meaning to the initial verb (and may change its aspect), for example, when added to the verb **читáть**, the prefix **пере-** has the meaning *re-*, and produces the new (perfective) verb, **перечита́ть** *to re-read*. While prefixes like **пере-** greatly enrich the meanings of verbs, they have no affect on a verb's conjugation.

A suffix, on the other hand, is the element of the stem which specifies the way the verb conjugates. The vast majority of Russian verb stems end in a suffix. However, due to modifications that occur when endings are added to the stem, the suffix may not be visible in all forms of the verb: the suffix may appear in a "truncated" (reduced) form, or if it consists of only a single vowel, it may not appear at all.

Below are the basic stems of the verbs introduced in the table above. Note how the verb's suffix changes in form, or even disappears, in the third-person plural non-past, in the infinitive, and past tense.

Basic Stem	Third-person Plural	Infinitive	Past Tense
чит-**АЙ**	чита́ют (читай-ут)	чита́ть	чита́л
пис-**А**	пи́шут	писа́ть	писа́л
им-**ЕЙ**	име́ют (имей-ут)	име́ть	име́л
вид-**Е**	ви́дят	ви́деть	ви́дел
говор-**И**	говоря́т	говори́ть	говори́л

Rules for Combining Basic Stem + Endings

These changes in the appearance of the verb suffix are governed by two simple rules that apply at the juncture where endings are added to the basic stem. The rules concern what happens to consonants and vowels when they come together. Verb stems may end in a vowel (V) or a consonant (C), and verb endings may begin with a vowel or a consonant. The rules for combining stems and endings are:

- When combining "unlikes," i.e., vowel + consonant, or consonant + vowel, simply *add* them together:

  V + C = VC
  C + V = CV

- When adding "likes," i.e., vowel + vowel, or consonant + consonant, *truncate* (drop) the first element:

  $V^1 + V^2 = V^2$
  $C^1 + C^2 = C^2$

Applying these rules of combination to **чит-ай** and **говор-и**:

C + V	чит-ай-	+ ут	= чита́ют (читай-ут)
$C^1 + C^2$	чит-ай-	+ ть	= чита́ть
	чит-ай-	+ л	= чита́л
$V^1 + V^2$	говор-и-	+ ят	= говоря́т
V + C	говор-и-	+ ть	= говори́ть
	говор-и-	+ л	= говори́л

Note: Whenever a stem ending in **й**, such as **чит-ай-** (or **им-ей-**), is combined with vowel endings, the rule C + V applies regularly: the **й** remains at the end of the stem, but is "hidden" by the Cyrillic spelling of the sequence "vowel + soft series vowel." Recall that when they follow a vowel, the soft series vowel letters **я, е, ё,** and **ю** indicate the presence of [у] **й** between the two vowel letters. Therefore, the boundary line between stem and ending runs through these letters, i.e., **чита́ют** has the stem + ending structure **читай-** + **ут** (and **име́ют** has the structure **имей-** + **ут**).

A relatively small number of verbs have a basic stem that does not contain a suffix, e.g., the verb жи́ть *to live*, has the basic stem **жив-**. All verbs with a nonsuffixed basic stem belong to the first conjugation. The same rules for adding endings to stems apply to nonsuffixed stems:

$$C + V = CV \qquad \text{жив-} + \text{ут} \quad = \quad \text{живу́т}$$
$$C^1 + C^2 = C^2 \qquad \text{жив-} + \text{ть} \quad = \quad \text{жи́ть}$$
$$ \qquad \text{жив-} + \text{л} \quad = \quad \text{жи́л}$$

Stems with a Suffix

Suffixes that Build First Conjugation Verbs

A small number of suffixes build first conjugation verbs, and each one of these suffixes distinguishes a verb type or class. These verb classes are either *productive* or *nonproductive*. The productive classes are those on which new verbs entering the language are modeled. The nonproductive classes are remnants from earlier periods, which no longer serve as a model for new verbs.

The following seven suffixes are used to form first conjugation verbs: (1) **АЙ**, (2) **ЕЙ**, (3) **ОВА/УЙ**, (4) **НУ**, (5) **А**, (6) **А-ВАЙ**, and (7) **О**.

(1) Stems in **АЙ**

чита́ть (чита́й-) *to read*					
Non-Past				*Past*	
я	чита́**ю**	мы́	чита́**ем**	о́н	чита́**л**
ты́	чита́**ешь**	вы́	чита́**ете**	она́	чита́**ла**
о́н/она́	чита́**ет**	они́	чита́**ют**	они́	чита́**ли**

Characteristics:

Verbs with a stem in **ай** *have fixed stress and no consonant alternations.*

This productive class contains thousands of verbs. In some verbs, such as **гуля́ть** *to take a stroll*, the suffix **ай** is spelled **яй**, to indicate a preceding soft consonant. In other verbs the suffix **ай** occurs within a larger suffix such as **вай** (наде-**ва́й-**/ **надева́ть** *to put on*) or **ывай/ивай** (расска́з-**ывай-** /**расска́зывать** *to tell*, спра́шивай/**спра́шивать** *to ask*), but these verbs conjugate exactly like the verbs with a stem containing the simple suffix **ай**.

The following is a list of some commonly used verbs with a stem in **ай**.

бе́гать	*to run, jog*	объясня́ть	*to explain*
вспомина́ть	*to recall*	опа́здывать	*to be late*
встреча́ть	*to meet*	отвеча́ть	*to answer*
выступа́ть	*to perform*	отдыха́ть	*to rest, relax*
гуля́ть	*to take a stroll*	повторя́ть	*to repeat*
де́лать	*to do, make*	покупа́ть	*to buy*
ду́мать	*to think*	помога́ть	*to help*
за́втракать	*to have breakfast*	понима́ть	*to understand*
занима́ться	*to study*	посыла́ть	*to send*
зна́ть	*to know*	рабо́тать	*to work*
игра́ть	*to play*	реша́ть	*to decide, solve*
конча́ть	*to finish*	слу́шать	*to listen*
мечта́ть	*to dream*	собира́ть	*to collect*
начина́ть	*to begin*	спра́шивать	*to ask*
обе́дать	*to have lunch*	у́жинать	*to have dinner*
обсужда́ть	*to discuss*	чита́ть	*to read*

1. Complete the following with the appropriate forms of the present tense of the indicated verbs.

1. Óн часто _____ му́зыку.   *слу́шать*
2. Я _____ ма́рки.   *собира́ть*
3. Она́ _____ тру́дную зада́чу.   *реша́ть*
4. Мы обы́чно _____ до́ма.   *за́втракать*
5. Что́ ты _____ ?   *де́лать*
6. Óн _____ о любви́.   *мечта́ть*
7. Она́ _____ фру́кты на ры́нке.   *покупа́ть*
8. Óн хорошо́ _____ на гита́ре.   *игра́ть*
9. Они́ ре́дко _____ в рестора́не.   *обе́дать*
10. Мы ча́сто _____ э́то вре́мя.   *вспомина́ть*
11. Ка́ждое у́тро он _____ в па́рке.   *гуля́ть*
12. Сего́дня _____ хоро́ший пиани́ст.   *выступа́ть*
13. Мы обы́чно_____ на мо́ре.   *отдыха́ть*
14. Óн _____ программи́стом.   *рабо́тать*
15. Та́ня ча́сто _____ на ле́кции.   *опа́здывать*
16. Она́ _____ марке́тингом.   *занима́ться*
17. Я _____ интере́сную кни́гу.   *чита́ть*
18. Они́ _____ семе́йный бюдже́т.   *обсужда́ть*
19. Мы ча́сто_____ пи́сьма от сы́на.   *получа́ть*
20. Учи́тель _____ уро́к ученика́м.   *объясня́ть*
21. Вы _____ по-ру́сски?   *понима́ть*
22. Профе́ссор _____ ле́кцию в де́вять часо́в. *начина́ть*
23. Ма́ма _____ рабо́ту в пя́ть часо́в.   *конча́ть*
24. Мо́й дру́г ча́сто _____ анекдо́ты.   *расска́зывать*
25. Ребёнок тако́й "почему́чка", всегда́ _____ «почему́»? *спра́шивать*

(2) Stems in **ЕЙ**

име́ть (име́й-) *to have*		
Non-Past		*Past*
я име́ю мы име́ем		óн име́л
ты име́ешь вы име́ете		она́ име́ла
óн/она́ име́ет они́ име́ют		они́ име́ли

Characteristics:

Verbs with a stem in **ей** *have fixed stress on the suffix. There are no consonant alternations.*

This productive verb type includes hundreds of verbs, many of which are formed from adjectives in the meaning "to become the property denoted" (e.g., **кра́сный** *red* > **красне́ть** *to become red, to blush*, **пусто́й** *empty* > **пусте́ть** *to become empty*). The majority of the verbs in this group are intransitive.

The following is a list of some commonly used verbs with a stem in **ей**.

бедне́ть	*to grow poor*	**неме́ть**	*to grow numb*
беле́ть	*to become, show white*	**полне́ть**	*to become stout*
бледне́ть	*to grow pale*	**пусте́ть**	*to become empty*
богате́ть	*to get rich*	**пьяне́ть**	*to get drunk*

боле́ть	to be ill	реде́ть	to thin out
веселе́ть	to become cheerful	робе́ть	to be timid
владе́ть	to own	слабе́ть	to become weak
голубе́ть	to turn blue	сме́ть	to dare
гре́ть	to warm	старе́ть	to grow old, to age
жале́ть	to be sorry, to regret	тепле́ть	to become warm
желте́ть	to turn yellow	уме́ть	to know how
здорове́ть	to become healthy	успе́ть	to have time (to do . . .)
име́ть	to have	худе́ть	to become thin, lose weight
красне́ть	to turn red, to blush	ясне́ть	to clear up
лысе́ть	to grow bald		

2. Complete the following with the appropriate forms of the present tense of the verb.

1. Он всегда́ _____ , когда́ ему́ де́лают уко́л.   *бледне́ть*
2. Она́ с де́тства _____ а́стмой.   *боле́ть*
3. Когда́ он се́рдится, лицо́ у него́ _____ .   *красне́ть*
4. Моя́ нога́ _____ , когда́ я сижу́ на не́й.   *неме́ть*
5. Зимо́й со́лнце све́тит, но не _____ .   *гре́ть*
6. О́сенью ли́стья на дере́вьях _____ .   *желте́ть*
7. Он вы́глядит ста́рше свои́х ле́т потому́ что _____ .   *лысе́ть*
8. Ка́к ты _____ сказа́ть тако́е?   *сме́ть*
9. За оди́н де́нь мы не _____ сде́лать всё.   *успе́ть*
10. Она́ то́лько неда́вно се́ла на дие́ту и уже́ _____ .   *худе́ть*
11. Ба́бушка _____ от боле́зни.   *слабе́ть*
12. Что ты _____ ? Тебе́ не́чего боя́ться.   *робе́ть*
13. Во́лосы у меня́ уже́ _____ .   *седе́ть*
14. Мно́гие лю́ди в Аме́рике _____ дома́ми.   *владе́ть*
15. Не́бо _____ по́сле дождя́.   *голубе́ть*
16. Он до́лго боле́л, но тепе́рь он _____ .   *здорове́ть*
17. Па́рус _____ на гаризо́нте.   *беле́ть*
18. У́лицы _____ по́сле полу́ночи.   *пусте́ть*
19. Она́ _____ от одно́й рю́мки.   *пьяне́ть*
20. Я _____ , что не смо́гу прийти́ на ве́чер.   *жале́ть*
21. Ма́льчик _____ от перееда́ния.   *полне́ть*
22. Ребёнок всегда́ _____ при ви́де отца́.   *веселе́ть*
23. Вы не _____ пра́ва так к на́м относи́ться.   *име́ть*
24. Во́лосы у него́ на голове́ _____ .   *реде́ть*
25. В э́той стране́ прави́тели _____ , а наро́д _____ . *богате́ть/бедне́ть*

(3) Stems in **ОВА/УЙ**

рискова́ть (рискова-) *to risk*	
Non-Past	*Past*
я́ риску́ю мы́ риску́ем	он́ рискова́л
ты́ риску́ешь вы́ риску́ете	она́ рискова́ла
он/она́ риску́ет они́ риску́ют	они́ рискова́ли

Characteristics:

Verbs with a stem in **ова** *(spelled* **ева** *after a soft consonant and the unpaired* **ж, ц, ч, ш, щ**) *replace this suffix in the non-past with* **уй**, *to which the personal endings are added (* **риск-у́й-** + **у** *is spelled* **риску́ю** *and* **риск-у́й-** + **ешь** *is spelled* **риску́ешь**, *etc.).*

The stress is fixed either on the root or on the suffix; if the stress in the infinitive falls on the second vowel of the suffix **ова́**, *in the non-past it will fall on* **у́й**.

There are thousands of verbs with a stem in **ОВА**, most of which contain roots borrowed from English, French, or German. This is a very productive class which is steadily growing. In many verbs **ОВА** is contained within a larger suffix, such as **из-ова-** (легал-**из-ова́**-ть *to legalize*) or **-(из)-ир-ова-** (приват-**из-и́р-ова**-ть *to privatize*, имит-**и́р-ова**-ть *to imitate*).

The following list contains some commonly used verbs with a stem in **ОВА**.

анализи́ровать	*to analyze*	практикова́ться	*to practice*
арестова́ть	*to arrest*	приватизи́ровать	*to privatize*
волнова́ться	*to be nervous*	про́бовать	*to test, try*
гаранти́ровать	*to guarantee*	путеше́ствовать	*to travel*
горева́ть	*to grieve*	ра́довать	*to gladden*
де́йствовать	*to function, work*	реклами́ровать	*to advertise*
жа́ловаться	*to complain*	рекомендова́ть	*to recommend*
импорти́ровать	*to import*	ремонти́ровать	*to repair*
интересова́ться	*to be interested in*	рисова́ть	*to draw*
комбини́ровать	*to combine*	сле́довать	*to follow*
копи́ровать	*to copy*	танцева́ть	*to dance*
легализова́ть	*to legalize*	тре́бовать	*to demand*
организова́ть	*to organize*	уча́ствовать	*to take part in*
ночева́ть	*to spend the night*	чу́вствовать	*to feel*
пакова́ть	*to pack*	фотографи́ровать	*to photograph*
паркова́ть	*to park*	экспорти́ровать	*to export*

3. Complete the following with the appropriate forms of the present tense of the verb.

1. Студе́нты _____ ша́хматный клу́б.   *организова́ть*
2. Вы _____ мно́го от ва́ших студе́нтов.   *тре́бовать*
3. Росси́я _____ пшени́цу из Аме́рики.   *импорти́ровать*
4. Мы _____ маши́ну на э́той стоя́нке.   *паркова́ть*
5. Я _____ вам посмотре́ть э́тот фи́льм.   *сове́товать*
6. Э́та де́вушка _____ в ко́нкурсе красоты́.   *уча́ствовать*
7. Твои́ пи́сьма нас всегда́ _____ .   *ра́довать*
8. Э́тот худо́жник _____ карикату́ры.   *рисова́ть*
9. Япо́ния _____ автомоби́ли в Аме́рику.   *экспорти́ровать*
10. Вы _____ ру́сской литерату́рой?   *интересова́ться*
11. Хотя́ он ча́сто боле́ет, он никогда́ не _____ .   *жа́ловаться*
12. Он ка́ждый де́нь _____ в игре́ на гита́ре.   *практикова́ться*
13. Мы _____ на́шу кварти́ру.   *ремонти́ровать*
14. Прави́тельство _____ промы́шленность.   *приватизи́ровать*
15. Тури́сты _____ все́ истори́ческие па́мятники.   *фотографи́ровать*
16. Ли́фт не _____ , подни́мемся по ле́стнице.   *де́йствовать*
17. Э́тот худо́жник уника́льно _____ цвета́.   *комбини́ровать*
18. Э́та фи́рма ча́сто _____ свои́ това́ры.   *реклами́ровать*

19. Я́ бы́л бо́лен, но я́ _____ себя́ лу́чше.　　　　*чу́вствовать*

20. Они́ сейча́с в о́тпуске и _____ по Евро́пе.　　　*путеше́ствовать*

21. Её му́ж у́мер го́д наза́д, но она́ о нём ещё _____ .　　*горева́ть*

22. По суббо́там они́ ча́сто _____ на дискоте́ке.　　　*танцева́ть*

23. О́н всегда́ _____ сове́ту отца́.　　　　　　　　　*сле́довать*

24. Э́та ксе́рокс- маши́на хорошо́ _____ .　　　　　*копи́ровать*

25. Я́ _____ э́тот рестора́н, у ни́х отли́чное меню́.　　*рекомендова́ть*

(4) Stems in НУ

Verbs of this type fall into two subgroups: (*a*) the suffix **ну** remains in the past tense (**кри́кнуть** *give a shout*, **О́н кри́кнул** *He gave a shout*), and (*b*) the suffix (**ну**) disappears in the past tense (**исче́знуть** *to disappear*, **О́н исче́з** *He disappeared*).

(*a*)　the suffix **ну** remains in the past tense

кри́кнуть (крик**ну-**) *to give a shout*		
Non-Past		*Past*
я́　　кри́к**ну**　　мы́　кри́к**нем**		о́н　кри́к**нул**
ты́　кри́к**нешь**　вы́　кри́к**нете**		она́　кри́к**нула**
он/она́ кри́к**нет**　они́　кри́к**нут**		они́　кри́к**нули**

Characteristics:

　In all but three verbs, the stress is fixed, either on the root or the suffix/non-past endings. The three verbs with shifting stress are:

тону́ть	*to drown* (я́ **тону́**, ты́ **то́нешь**)
тяну́ть	*to pull* (я́ **тяну́**, ты́ **тя́нешь**)
помяну́ть	*to mention* (я́ **помяну́**, ты́ **помя́нешь**)

　This is a productive class with hundreds of verbs, most of which are perfective in aspect. Many of the perfective verbs in this group denote an instantaneous action performed once, e.g., **кри́кнуть** *to give a shout*, **пры́гнуть** *to make a jump*, **толкну́ть** *to give a push*. The few imperfective verbs in this group include **гну́ть** *to bend*, and the two shifting stress verbs noted above, **тону́ть**, **тяну́ть**.

　The following list contains some common verbs with a stem in **ну**.

верну́ться	*to return*	**ло́пнуть**	*to burst, to split*
взгляну́ть	*to cast a glance*	**отдохну́ть**	*to rest*
вздохну́ть	*to sigh; take a breath*	**просну́ться**	*to wake up*
вы́кинуть	*to throw out*	**пры́гнуть**	*to jump*
вы́нуть	*to take out*	**рискну́ть**	*to risk (once)*
дёрнуть	*to pull*	**ру́хнуть**	*to collapse*
засну́ть	*to fall asleep*	**улыбну́ться**	*to smile*
кри́кнуть	*to shout*	**шагну́ть**	*to step*

(*b*) the suffix (**ну**) disappears in the past tense

исчéзнуть (исчéз(**ну**)-) *to disappear*		
Non-Past		*Past*
я исчéзну мы́ исчéзн**ем**		óн исчéз
ты́ исчéзн**ешь** вы́ исчéзн**ете**		онá исчéзла
óн/онá исчéзн**ет** они́ исчéзн**ут**		они́ исчéзли

Characteristics:

*The stress is fixed on the root. The suffix (**ну**) is normally dropped in the past tense. When the suffix is dropped, the masculine singular form also loses the characteristic past tense marker **л**, though this marker does occur in the other past tense forms.*

This is a nonproductive group with about 60 verbs, most of which are intransitive. The simple (prefixless) verbs are imperfective, while the prefixed verbs are perfective.

Below are some common verbs which lose the suffix (**ну**) in the past tense.

блёкнуть	to fade; to wither	крéпнуть	to grow stronger
гáснуть	to be extinguished	мёрзнуть	to be cold, to freeze
ги́бнуть	to perish	мóкнуть	to get wet, soaked
глóхнуть	to go deaf	пáхнуть	to smell
дости́гнуть	to reach; achieve	привы́кнуть	to get used to
замóлкнуть	to fall silent	слéпнуть	to go blind
ки́снуть	to turn sour	сóхнуть	to become dry

4. Complete the sentences with the correct non-past forms of the indicated verbs.

1. Паровóз _____ сéмь вагóнов.   *тяну́ть*
2. На ку́хне _____ чéм-то вку́сным.   *пáхнуть*
3. Я устáл, давáйте _____.   *отдохну́ть*
4. У́личные фонари́ автомати́чески _____ на рассвéте.   *гáснуть*
5. В таку́ю жáркую погóду урожáй бы́стро _____.   *сóхнуть*
6. Ребёнок скóро _____ и захóчет éсть.   *просну́ться*
7. Онá подойдёт к крáю бассéйна и _____ в вóду.   *пры́гнуть*
8. Жди́ меня́, я _____ через пя́ть мину́т.   *верну́ться*
9. Éсли ты́ не уберёшь свои́ вéщи, мáма и́х _____.   *вы́кинуть*
10. Давáйте _____!   *вздохну́ть*
11. Зимóй такáя трубá _____ от морóза.   *лóпнуть*
12. Водá в óзере холóдная, но вы́ к нéй _____.   *привы́кнуть*
13. Молокó бы́стро_____ в теплé.   *ки́снуть*
14. Я не вы́ношу хóлода, зимóй я чáсто _____.   *мёрзнуть*
15. Óн занимáется на тренажёрах и _____ с кáждым днём.   *крéпнуть*

5. Change the italicized verbs from the present (or future perfective) to the past tense.

1. Цветы́ *поги́бнут* от морóза.
2. Цветá *поблёкнут* от сóлнца.

3. Он скоро *достигнет* больши́х успе́хов в свое́й рабо́те.
4. Де́ти но́вых иммигра́нтов бы́стро *привы́кнут* к но́вому языку́.
5. Ребёнок *заснёт* и зву́ки из де́тской *замо́лкнут*.
6. Наступи́ла зима́, о́зеро ско́ро *замёрзнет*.
7. Она́ глубоко́ *вздохнёт* пе́ред прыжко́м в во́ду.
8. Костёр *га́снет*.
9. Самолёт ско́ро *исче́знет* за облака́ми.
10. От него́ ча́сто *па́хнет* табако́м.
11. Она́ с ка́ждым днём *кре́пнет* от лека́рства.
12. Секрета́рь вы́шел, но он ско́ро *вернётся*.
13. Кры́ша *ру́хнет* под тя́жестью сне́га.
14. Он *рискнёт* на э́тот ра́з.

(5) Stems in **А (Я)**

Verbs with a basic stem ending in the suffix **-a** fall into three subgroups: (*a*) those which are preceded by a vocalic root and whose root-final consonant alternates (**пис-/пиш-/писа́ть** *to write*); (*b*) those with a vocalic root ending in **й**, and so the suffix is spelled **я (й + а)** (**надея-ся/наде́яться** *to hope*), and (*c*) those which are preceded by a nonvocalic root (**жд-/жда́ть** *to wait*).

(*a*) vocalic root followed by **a**

писа́ть (писа-) *to write*			
Non-Past			*Past*
я пишу́	мы пи́шем		он писа́л
ты пи́шешь	вы пи́шете		она́ писа́ла
он/она́ пи́шет	они́ пи́шут		они́ писа́ли

Characteristics:

The suffix **a** *is truncated and the preceding (root-final) consonant undergoes an alternation throughout the non-past.*

If, in the infinitive, the stress falls on the suffix **a**, *then the non-past forms generally will have the shifting stress pattern: stressed on the ending of the first-person singular, and shifting to the stem in all other forms. (Two exceptions are:* **посла́ть** *to send* — **пошлю́, пошлёшь . . . пошлю́т**, *and* **колеба́ться** *to shake to and fro, to hesitate* — **коле́блюсь, коле́блешься . . . коле́блются**.)

If the stress in the infinitive falls on the root, it is normally fixed (**ре́зать** *to cut* — **ре́жу, ре́жешь . . . ре́жут**).

This is a nonproductive class which contains about 60 verbs. Below are some common verbs of this type. The root-final alternations are shown on the right.

Infinitive		*Non-Past*	*Alternation*
писа́ть	*to write*	**пишу́, пи́шешь . . . пи́шут**	**с → ш**
маха́ть	*to wave*	**машу́, ма́шешь . . . ма́шут**	**х → ш**
ре́зать	*to cut*	**ре́жу, ре́жешь . . . ре́жут**	**з → ж**
сказа́ть	*to say*	**скажу́, ска́жешь . . . ска́жут**	**з → ж**
пла́кать	*to cry*	**пла́чу, пла́чешь . . . пла́чут**	**к → ч**
пря́тать	*to hide*	**пря́чу, пря́чешь . . . пря́чут**	**т → ч**
шепта́ть	*to whisper*	**шепчу́, ше́пчешь . . . ше́пчут**	**т → ч**

щекота́ть	to tickle	щекочу́, щеко́чет . . . щеко́чут	т → ч
свиста́ть	to whistle	свищу́, сви́щешь . . . сви́щут	ст → щ
иска́ть	to look for	ищу́, и́щешь . . . и́щут	ск → щ
сы́пать	to strew	сы́плю, сы́плешь . . . сы́плют	п → пл
колеба́ть	to shake	коле́блю, коле́блешь, коле́блют	б → бл
дрема́ть	to doze	дремлю́, дре́млешь . . . дре́млют	м → мл

Note: Other prefixed perfective verbs with the root **-каз-** follow the same pattern as **сказа́ть**: **рассказа́ть** *to tell*, **показа́ть** *to show*, **заказа́ть** *to order*, etc.

Note: All perfective verbs prefixed with **вы-** have fixed stress on this prefix in all forms:

вы́писать *to write out* — вы́пишу, вы́пишешь . . . вы́пишут.

вы́сказать *to state* — вы́скажу, вы́скажешь . . . вы́скажут.

6. Complete the sentences with the correct forms of the present or future perfective.

1. Ма́ма _____ письмо́ сы́ну.   *писа́ть*
2. Я́ всегда́ _____ клю́ч на́д две́рью.   *пря́тать*
3. Он ко́нчил шко́лу и тепе́рь он _____ рабо́ту.   *иска́ть*
4. Де́ти _____ бума́гу но́жницами.   *ре́зать*
5. Вы́ не _____, где́ остано́вка авто́буса?   *сказа́ть*
6. Он сиди́т в кла́ссе и _____ ей на́ ухо.   *шепта́ть*
7. Ма́льчик _____ потому́ что его́ поруга́л оте́ц.   *пла́кать*
8. Ве́тер _____.   *свиста́ть*
9. Он _____ в своём реше́нии.   *колеба́ться*
10. У меня́ в го́рле _____.   *щекота́ть*
11. Де́душка _____ в кре́сле по́сле обе́да.   *дрема́ть*
12. Мину́точку, я́ сейча́с _____ ва́м квита́нцию.   *вы́писать*
13. Она́ бои́тся, что нача́льник _____ ей в про́сьбе.   *отказа́ть*
14. Он сиди́т на скаме́йке и споко́йно _____ ко́рм голубя́м. *сы́пать*

(*b*) root-final **й** + **а** (spelled **я**)

надéяться (надея-ся) *to hope for*				
Non-Past			*Past*	
я́	надéюсь	мы́ надéемся	о́н	надéялся
ты́	надéешься	вы́ надéетесь	она́	надéялась
о́н/она́	надéется	они́ надéются	они́	надéялись

Characteristics:

The suffix is truncated throughout the present tense, but no alternation occurs.
There are 12 verbs of this type, of which the following are most common:

Infinitive		*Non-Past*
се́ять	*to sow*	**се́ю, се́ешь . . . се́ют**

наде́яться	*to hope*	наде́юсь, наде́ешься ... наде́ются
смея́ться	*to laugh*	смею́сь, смеёшься ... смею́тся
ла́ять	*to bark*	ла́ю, ла́ешь ... ла́ют
та́ять	*to melt*	та́ю, та́ешь ... та́ют

7. Complete the sentences with the correct present-tense forms of the verbs.

1. Соба́ка _____, когда́ стуча́т в две́рь.   *ла́ять*
2. Сего́дня тепло́, и снег _____.   *та́ять*
3. Я всегда́ _____ на́д его́ шу́тками.   *смея́ться*
4. Мы _____, что тебе́ уда́стся прие́хать к на́м.   *наде́яться*
5. Де́душка _____ пшени́цу в по́ле.   *се́ять*

(*c*) nonvocalic root followed by **a**

<table>
<tr><td colspan="3">жда́ть (жда-) to wait</td></tr>
<tr><td colspan="2">Non-Past</td><td>Past</td></tr>
<tr><td>я   жду́</td><td>мы   ждём</td><td>он   жда́л</td></tr>
<tr><td>ты   ждёшь</td><td>вы   ждёте</td><td>она́   ждала́</td></tr>
<tr><td>он/она́ ждёт</td><td>они́   жду́т</td><td>они́   жда́ли</td></tr>
</table>

Characteristics:

All verbs with a nonvocalic root and the suffix **a** *have fixed stress on the endings in the non-past. In the past, the stress shifts from the stem in the masculine, neuter, and plural forms to the ending in the feminine.*

There are about 12 verbs of this type, the most common of which appear below.

Infinitive		*Non-Past*	*Past*
вра́ть	*to lie* (coll.)	вру́, врёшь ... вру́т	вра́л, врала́, вра́ли
жда́ть	*to wait*	жду́, ждёшь ... жду́т	жда́л, ждала́, жда́ли
жра́ть	*to guzzle*	жру́, жрёшь ... жру́т	жра́л, жрала́, жра́ли
лга́ть	*to lie*	лгу́, лжёшь ... лгу́т	лга́л, лгала́, лга́ли
рва́ть	*to tear*	рву́, рвёшь ... рву́т	рва́л, рвала́, рва́ли
ржа́ть	*to neigh*	ржу́, ржёшь ... ржу́т	ржа́л, ржала́, ржа́ли

Three verbs in this group have an inserted root vowel in the non-past:

бра́ть	*to take*	беру́, берёшь ... беру́т	бра́л, брала́, бра́ли
дра́ть	*to tear*	деру́, дерёшь ... деру́т	дра́л, драла́, дра́ли
зва́ть	*to call*	зову́, зовёшь ... зову́т	зва́л, звала́, зва́ли

Note: Two verbs with a root vowel conjugate like those with no root vowel: **соса́ть** *to suck* (**сосу́**, **сосёшь** ... **сосу́т**) and **стона́ть** *to groan* (**стону́**, **сто́нешь** ... **сто́нут**).

Note: Two verbs with a nonvocalic root followed by the suffix **a** belong to the second conjugation: **спа́ть** *to sleep* (**сплю́**, **спи́шь** ... **спя́т**) and **гна́ть** *to chase* (**гоню́**, **го́нишь** ... **го́нят**).

8. Complete the sentences with the correct form of the present tense of the given verb.

1. Я _____ ча́стные уро́ки ру́сского языка́.   *брать*
2. Ло́шади _____ при ви́де хозя́ина.   *ржа́ть*
3. Он _____ на ка́ждом шагу́ и поэ́тому ему́ никто́ не ве́рит.   *врать*
4. Мы _____ наш о́тпуск с больши́м нетерпе́нием.   *ждать*
5. Ма́льчик сиди́т на полу́ и _____ бума́гу на кусо́чки.   *рвать*
6. Почему́ ты _____ и не говори́шь пра́вду?   *лгать*
7. Пора́ домо́й, ма́ма _____ нас на обе́д.   *звать*
8. Он так _____ как бу́дто он це́лый ме́сяц не е́л.   *жрать*
9. Они́ _____ кору́ с пру́тьев и де́лают из пру́тьев корзи́ны.   *драть*

(6) Stems in **А-ВАЙ**

давáть (да-вай-) *to give*				
Non-Past			*Past*	
я	даю́	мы	даём	он	дава́л
ты	даёшь	вы	даёте	она́	дава́ла
он/она́	даёт	они́	даю́т	они́	дава́ли

Characteristics:

The **ва** *part of the stem is omitted in the non-past, leaving the stem in* **ай**. *The non-past has fixed stress on the endings.*

The verbs in this nonproductive group are formed from one of three roots ending in the vowel **а** — **-да-** *give*, **-зна-** *know*, **-ста-** *stand* — to which the suffix **-вай-** is added. All the verbs in this group are imperfective, and all but **дава́ть** are prefixed.

Some common verbs in this group are listed below according to the underlying root.

(a)   Verbs with the root **-да-**

отдава́ть	*to give back, return; to give (up), devote*
передава́ть	*to pass; convey; broadcast*
подава́ть	*to serve*
преподава́ть	*to teach*
продава́ть	*to sell*
раздава́ться	*to be heard, resound*

(b)   Verbs with the root **-зна-**

признава́ть	*to admit, acknowledge*
сознава́ть	*to be conscious of, realize*
узнава́ть	*to recognize; to find out*

(c)   Verbs with the root **-ста-**

встава́ть	*to get up, stand up*
остава́ться	*to remain, stay, be left*
отстава́ть	*to fall/lag behind*
перестава́ть	*to stop (something in progress)*
устава́ть	*to grow tired*

9. Complete the sentences with the correct present-tense form of the given verbs.

1. Óн всегда́ _____ на́м от тебя́ приве́т.	*передава́ть*
2. Торго́вцы _____ вся́кие сувени́ры на у́лице.	*продава́ть*
3. Óн расстро́ен, потому́ что _____ в свое́й рабо́те.	*отстава́ть*
4. В э́том рестора́не _____ вкусне́йшие шашлыки́.	*подава́ть*
5. Ма́льчик _____ свою́ оши́бку.	*признава́ть*
6. Она́ _____ англи́йский как иностра́нный.	*преподава́ть*
7. Да́, я _____ мою́ вину́ и я извиню́сь.	*сознава́ть*
8. Óн всегда́ _____ долги́ во́-время.	*отдава́ть*
9. Я обы́чно _____ его́ по похо́дке.	*узнава́ть*
10. Óн спи́т днём то́лько, когда́ он о́чень _____ .	*устава́ть*
11. Я сра́зу _____ , когда́ _____ звоно́к буди́льника.	*встава́ть/* *раздава́ться*
12. По́сле ле́кции о́н ча́сто _____ в аудито́рии, что́бы поговори́ть с преподава́телем.	*остава́ться*

(7) Stems in **O**

боро́ться (бор**о**-) *to struggle*	
Non-Past	*Past*
я боркю́сь мы́ бо́ремся ты́ бо́решься вы́ бо́ретесь о́н/она́ бо́рется они́ бо́рются	о́н боро́лся она́ боро́лась они́ боро́лись

Characteristics:

The suffix **о** *is truncated before the vowel endings of the non-past, and the root-final* **р** *(or* **л**) *becomes soft. These verbs have shifting stress.*

There are only 5 verbs in this group, and each has a stem ending in **оло** or **оро**. In one verb, **моло́ть** *to grind*, the root vowel **о** becomes **е** in the non-past (**мелю́, ме́лешь . . . ме́лют**).

боро́ться	*to struggle*
коло́ть	*to chop, split; prick*
моло́ть	*to grind*
поло́ть	*to weed*
поро́ть	*to undo, rip at the seams*

10. Complete the sentences with the correct present-tense form of the indicated verb.

1. Óн _____ дрова́ во дворе́.	*коло́ть*
2. Мы́ _____ за охра́ну приро́ды.	*боро́ться*
3. Она́ всегда́ _____ ко́фе в кофемо́лке.	*моло́ть*
4. Они́ _____ в огоро́де.	*поло́ть*
5. Портно́й _____ брю́ки.	*поро́ть*

Suffixes that Build Second Conjugation Verbs

There are only three suffixes that build second conjugation verbs, bringing the total number of verb suffixes to ten: (8) **И**, (9) **Е**, and (10) **А** (represented here as **жа**, since it is normally preceded by ж, ч, ш, щ, e.g., лежа́ть/лежа- *to lie*).

(8) Stems in **И**

проси́ть (проси-) *to ask, make a request*					
Non-Past				*Past*	
я	прошу́	мы́	про́сим	о́н	проси́л
ты́	про́сишь	вы́	про́сите	она́	проси́ла
о́н/она́	про́сит	они́	про́сят	они́	проси́ли

Characteristics:

Root-final л, р, *or* н *are soft throughout, i.e., in the first-person singular and third-person plural non-past they are followed by the endings* -ю *and* -ят *(e.g., я* говорю́, они́ говоря́т*). Verbs with a root ending in* д, з, с, т, ст *or one of the labial consonants (*б, в, м, п, ф*) undergo a consonant alternation in the first-person singular only.*

*Some of these verbs have fixed stress (*говорю́, говори́шь . . . говоря́т*), while others have shifting stress (*прошу́, про́сишь . . . про́сят*).*

This class contains thousands of verbs. Below are some common verbs of this type that undergo a consonant alternation in the first-person singular, indicated on the right.

Infinitive		*Non-Past*	*Alternation*
ходи́ть	*to walk*	хожу́, хо́дишь . . . хо́дят	д → ж
вози́ть	*to transport*	вожу́, во́зишь . . . во́зят	з → ж
носи́ть	*to carry*	ношу́, но́сишь . . . но́сят	с → ш
плати́ть	*to pay*	плачу́, пла́тишь . . . пла́тят	т → ч
чи́стить	*to clean*	чи́щу, чи́стишь . . . чи́стят	ст → щ
люби́ть	*to like, love*	люблю́, лю́бишь . . . лю́бят	б → бл
гото́вить	*to prepare*	гото́влю, гото́вишь . . . гото́вят	в → вл
лови́ть	*to catch*	ловлю́, ло́вишь . . . ло́вят	,,
ста́вить	*to put (upright)*	ста́влю, ста́вишь . . . ста́вят	,,
корми́ть	*to feed*	кормлю́, ко́рмишь . . . ко́рмят	м → мл
купи́ть	*to buy*	куплю́, ку́пишь . . . ку́пят	п → пл

Following are some common verbs whose root-final consonant does not alternate:

варй́ть	*to boil*	варю́, ва́ришь . . . ва́рят
говори́ть	*to speak*	говорю́, говори́шь . . . говоря́т
жени́ться	*to get married*	женю́сь, же́нишься . . . же́нятся
кури́ть	*to smoke*	курю́, ку́ришь . . . ку́рят
учи́ть	*to teach; study*	учу́, у́чишь . . . у́чат
хвали́ть	*to praise*	хвалю́, хва́лишь . . . хва́лят

11. Complete the sentences with the correct non-past form of the indicated verbs.

1. Э́та учи́тельница всегда́ _____ свои́х ученико́в.   *хвали́ть*
2. Меня́ удивля́ет, что ты́ ещё _____ .   *кури́ть*
3. Ка́ждое у́тро я _____ по па́рку.   *ходи́ть*
4. Профессора́ ча́сто _____ на заня́тия портфе́ли.   *носи́ть*
5. Я́ ча́сто _____ свои́х дете́й в шко́лу.   *вози́ть*
6. Э́ти студе́нты хорошо́ _____ по-ру́сски.   *говори́ть*
7. Оте́ц _____ свою́ до́чь води́ть маши́ну.   *учи́ть*
8. Я́ не _____ , когда́ де́ти _____ соба́ку объе́дками.   *люби́ть/корми́ть*
9. Мо́й дру́г _____ на о́чень ми́лой и у́мной де́вушке.   *жени́ться*
10. Ба́бушка _____ карто́шку.   *вари́ть*
11. Я́ всегда́ _____ са́м за себя́.   *плати́ть*
12. Му́ж _____ ры́бу, а я её _____ .   *лови́ть/чи́стить*

(9) Stems in **E**

сиде́ть (сид**е**-) *to sit*		
Non-Past		*Past*
я сижу́ мы́ сиди́м		о́н сиде́л
ты́ сиди́шь вы́ сиди́те		она́ сиде́ла
о́н/она́ сиди́т они́ сидя́т		они́ сиде́ли

Characteristics:

Most of the verbs in this class have fixed stress, though the stress in a few common verbs is shifting (e.g., **смотре́ть** *to watch*).

Like verbs with the suffix **и**, *verbs with the suffix* **е** *undergo an alternation if the root-final consonant is one that alternates; otherwise, the root-final consonant is soft throughout the non-past, as indicated by the spelling of the personal endings* (e.g., я смотрю́, они́ смо́трят).

This is a non-productive class containing about 50 verbs. Some commonly used verbs of this type that have an alternation in the first person singular are listed below.

Infinitive		*Non-Past*	*Alternation*
ви́деть	*to see*	**ви́жу, ви́дишь … ви́дят**	д → ж
висе́ть	*to hang* (intr.)	**вишу́, виси́шь … вися́т**	с → ш
зави́сеть	*to depend*	**зави́шу, зави́сишь … зави́сят**	,,
лете́ть	*to fly*	**лечу́, лети́шь … летя́т**	т → ч
свисте́ть	*to whistle*	**свищу́, свисти́шь … свистя́т**	ст → щ
терпе́ть	*to tolerate*	**терплю́, те́рпишь … те́рпят**	п → пл
храпе́ть	*to snore*	**храплю́, храпи́шь … храпя́т**	,,
шуме́ть	*to make noise*	**шумлю́, шуми́шь … шумя́т**	м → мл

Following are a few common verbs in this class whose root-final consonant does not alternate in the first-person singular.

боле́ть	*to ache*	*3rd person only:* **боли́т, боля́т**
горе́ть	*to burn*	**горю́, гори́шь … горя́т**
смотре́ть	*to look, watch*	**смотрю́, смо́тришь … смо́трят**

12. Complete the sentence with the correct present-tense form of the given verb.

1. Я _____ от твое́й по́мощи.   *зави́сеть*
2. Она́ не лю́бит, а то́лько _____ своего́ му́жа.   *терпе́ть*
3. Я _____ в Москву́, а куда́ ты _____?   *лете́ть*
4. Óн _____ жела́нием пое́хать в Пари́ж.   *горе́ть*
5. Спа́ть с ни́м невозмо́жно: о́н та́к гро́мко _____ .   *храпе́ть*
6. Я гро́мко _____ и соба́ка бежи́т ко мне́.   *свисте́ть*
7. Его́ судьба́ _____ на волоске́.   *висе́ть*
8. Сосе́ди не лю́бят, когда́ на́ши де́ти _____ .   *шуме́ть*
9. Я пло́хо _____ без очко́в.   *ви́деть*
10. Я везу́ сы́на к зубно́му врачу́, у него́ _____ зу́б.   *боле́ть*

(10) Stems in ЖА

This class is a historically related subgroup of the verbs in **e**: in an early period the suffix **e** changed to **a** after "palatalizing" a root-final velar consonant, e.g., **к → ч** in the verb **крича́ть** *to shout* (*крик-е-ть → крич-а-ть*, unlike the perfective **кри́кнуть** which preserves the original form of the root, **крик**). Since the suffix **a** is almost always preceded by one of the unpaired palatal consonants **ж, ч, ш, щ**, the stem of these verbs is represented as **ЖА**. This representation also serves to differentiate this group from the first conjugation verbs with a stem in **A** (e.g., писа-, but крича-).

лежа́ть (лежа-) *to lie*			
Non-Past		*Past*	
я лежу́	мы́ лежи́м	о́н лежа́л	
ты́ лежи́шь	вы́ лежи́те	она́ лежа́ла	
о́н/она́ лежи́т	они́ лежа́т	они́ лежа́ли	

Characteristics:

The suffix **a** *in these verbs is normally preceded by* **ж, ч, ш, щ**, *but in two verbs it is preceded by* **й** (**йа** *spelled* **я**): **стоя́ть** *to stand*, **боя́ться** *to be afraid*.

Most verbs in this group have stress fixed on the endings.

Some of the more common verbs in this group are the following:

Infinitive		*Non-Past*
боя́ться	*to be afraid of*	**бою́сь, бои́шься ... боя́тся**
держа́ть	*to hold, keep*	**держу́, де́ржишь ... де́ржат**
дрожа́ть	*to tremble*	**дрожу́, дрожи́шь ... дрожа́т**
дыша́ть	*to breathe*	**дышу́, ды́шишь ... ды́шат**
звуча́ть	*to sound*	**звучу́, звучи́шь ... звуча́т**
крича́ть	*to shout*	**кричу́, кричи́шь ... крича́т**
молча́ть	*to be silent*	**молчу́, молчи́шь ... молча́т**
слы́шать	*to hear*	**слы́шу, слы́шишь ... слы́шат**
стоя́ть	*to stand*	**стою́, стои́шь ... стоя́т**
стуча́ть	*to knock*	**стучу́, стучи́шь ... стуча́т**

Note: Not all verbs whose infinitive ends in **-жать, -чать, -шать**, and **-щать** are second conjugation **лежа́ть**-type verbs with a stem in **ЖА**; there are also first conjugation verbs whose basic stem consists of an unpaired consonant preceding the suffix **-АЙ** (**чита́ть** type), e.g., **сажа́ть** *to seat*, **получа́ть** *to receive*, **слу́шать** *to listen*, **посеща́ть** *to visit*.

13. Supply the correct present-tense forms of the indicated verbs.

1. Кто́-то _____ в две́рь.   *стуча́ть*
2. Говори́те гро́мче, я пло́хо _____ .   *слы́шать*
3. О́н ничего́ не говори́т, он _____ .   *молча́ть*
4. Переходя́ у́лицу, я всегда́ _____ до́чку за ру́ку.   *держа́ть*
5. Ты́ _____ от хо́лода, погре́йся у огня́.   *дрожа́ть*
6. Заче́м ты́ _____? Мо́жно без кри́ка обойти́сь.   *крича́ть*
7. На столе́ _____ча́шки и блю́дца.   *стоя́ть*
8. Го́лос у неё сего́дня _____ прекра́сно.   *звуча́ть*
9. О́н _____ со́бственной те́ни.   *боя́ться*
10. По́сле у́жина па́па обы́чно _____ на дива́не.   *лежа́ть*

Irregular Verbs of Mixed Conjugation

There are very few irregular verbs in Russian. The following 2 irregular verbs are very common and should be memorized: **хоте́ть** *to want*, **бежа́ть** *to run*.

хоте́ть *to want*		
Present Tense		*Past Tense*
я́ хочу́	мы́ хоти́м	о́н хоте́л
ты́ хо́чешь	вы́ хоти́те	она́ хоте́ла
о́н/она́ хо́чет	они́ хотя́т	они́ хоте́ли

Irregular characteristics:

(*a*)   *First conjugation endings in the singular, second conjugation endings in the plural.*

(*b*)   *Irregular stress pattern.*

(*c*)   *Alternation of root-final* **т → ч** *in the singular, but not in the plural.*

бежа́ть *to run*		
Present Tense		*Past Tense*
я́ бегу́	мы́ бежи́м	о́н бежа́л
ты́ бежи́шь	вы́ бежи́те	она́ бежа́ла
о́н/она́ бежи́т	они́ бегу́т	они́ бежа́ли

Irregular characteristics:

Endings of the second conjugation, except the third-person plural ending **-ут**.

14. Translate with the required past or non-past form of the verbs *хотéть* or *бежáть*.

1. Онá (wants) _____ слýшать мýзыку, а они́ (want) _____ пойти́ в кино́.
2. — Что́ вы (want) _____ на обéд, мя́со, или ры́бу? — Я́ (want) _____ ры́бу.
3. Когдá онá былá молодóй, онá (wanted) _____ бы́ть балери́ной.
4. — Кудá ты́ (are running) _____ ? — Я́ (am running) _____ на заня́тие.
5. Дéти сейчáс (are running) _____ по бéрегу реки́.
6. Мы́ (are running) _____ в теáтр, мы́ не (want) _____ опоздáть.

Summary Table

Conjugation I and II Verbs Classified by Basic Stem with a Suffix

First Conjugation Verbs

Suffix	Infinitive	Basic Stem	3rd Pl. Non-Past
(1) АЙ	читáть	чит-ай	читáют
(2) ЕЙ	имéть	им-ей	имéют
(3) ОВА/УЙ	рисковáть	риск-ова	рискýют
(4) НУ	кри́кнуть	крик-ну	кри́кнут
(НУ)	исчéзнуть	исчез-(ну)-	исчéзнут
(5) А	(*a*) писáть	пис-а	пи́шут
	(*b*) надéяться	наде-я-ся	надéются
	(*c*) ждáть	жд-а-	жду́т
(6) А-ВАЙ	давáть	да-вай	даю́т
(7) О	борóться	бор-о-ся	бóрются

Second Conjugation Verbs

Suffix	Infinitive	Basic Stem	3rd Pl. Non-Past
(8) И	говори́ть	говор-и	говоря́т
(9) Е	сидéть	сид-е	сидя́т
(10) ЖА	лежáть	леж-а	лежáт

Irregular Verbs of Mixed Conjugation

хотéть		хотя́т
бежáть		бегýт

Nonsuffixed Stems

Verbs with nonsuffixed stems all belong to the first conjugation. The stems of these verbs are equal to the root (or prefix + root). Verbs with no suffix are classified according to the final consonant of the stem/root. This consonant will be one of two types:

1. Resonants: **в, й, м, н, р**.
2. Obstruents: **б, п, д, т, з, с, г, к, х**.

Since all of the nonsuffixed stems end in a consonant, this consonant will be truncated before the consonant endings of the past tense and infinitive, as specified by the rules for combining stems and endings (page 214).

Resonant Stems

(1) Stems in **В**

жи́ть (жив-) *to live*					
Non-Past				*Past*	
я́	живу́	мы́	живём	о́н	жи́л
ты́	живёшь	вы́	живёте	она́	жила́
о́н/она́	живёт	они́	живу́т	они́	жи́ли

Characteristics:

The consonant **в** *is retained throughout the non-past. The stress shifts to the ending in the feminine past tense.*

There are only 3 verbs of this type:

Infinitive		*Non-Past*	*Past*
жи́ть	*to live*	**живу́, живёшь . . . живу́т**	**жи́л, жила́**
плы́ть	*to swim*	**плыву́, плывёшь . . . плыву́т**	**плы́л, плыла́**
слы́ть	*to be reputed, to be*	**слыву́, слывёшь . . . слыву́т**	**слы́л, слыла́**

15. Change the italicized verbs from past to present tense.

1. Мы́ *жи́ли* в кварти́ре 10, а моя́ тётя *жила́* в кварти́ре 15.
2. Я́ *плы́л* к ло́дке, а она́ *плыла́* к бе́регу.
3. О́н *слы́л* знатоко́м в э́той о́бласти.

(2) Stems in **Н**

ста́ть (стан-) *to become; to begin*					
Non-Past				*Past*	
я	ста́ну	мы́	ста́нем	о́н	ста́л
ты́	ста́нешь	вы́	ста́нете	она́	ста́ла
о́н/она́	ста́нет	они́	ста́нут	они́	ста́ли

Characteristics:

The consonant **н** *is retained throughout the non-past. Stress is fixed on the stem.*

There are only a few verbs, mostly prefixed forms of **ста́ть** and **де́ть** *to put*:

Infinitive		*Non-Past*
вста́ть	*to stand up*	**вста́ну, вста́нешь . . . вста́нут**
де́ть	*to put, do with*	**де́ну, де́нешь . . . де́нут**
наде́ть	*to put on*	**наде́ну, наде́нешь . . . наде́нут**
оде́ться	*to get dressed*	**оде́нусь, оде́нешься . . . оде́нутся**
разде́ться	*to get undressed*	**разде́нусь, разде́нешься . . . разде́нутся**

16. Complete the sentence with the required non-past form of the verb.

1. Что ты сегодня _____, джинсы или юбку?   *надеть*
2. Он любит животных, наверное он _____ ветеринаром.   *стать*
3. Завтра утром я _____ в шесть часов.   *встать*
4. Он сказал, что _____ и сразу пойдёт спать.   *раздеться*
5. Сейчас мы _____ и быстро позавтракаем.   *одеться*

(3) Stems in **ОЙ**

открыть (открой-) *to open*	
Non-Past	*Past*
я открою мы открбем ты открбешь вы открбете он/она открбет они открбют	он открыл она открыла они открыли

Characteristics:

The vowel **о → ы** *before consonantal endings. The stress is fixed on the stem.*
There are only a few verbs of this type, the more common of which are:

Infinitive		*Non-Past*	*Past*
открыть	*to open*	**открою, открбешь . . . открбют**	**открыл, открыла**
закрыть	*to close*	**закрою, закрбешь . . . закрбют**	**закрыл, закрыла**
мыть	*to wash*	**мою, мбешь . . . мбют**	**мыл, мыла**
ныть	*to ache*	**нбю, нбешь . . . нбют**	**ныл, ныла**
рыть	*to dig*	**рбю, рбешь . . . рбют**	**рыл, рыла**

17. Complete the sentence with the appropriate non-past form of the indicated verbs.

1. Мама _____ посуду, а папа вытирает.   *мыть*
2. Здесь душно, я _____ окно.   *открыть*
3. Собака _____ яму во дворе и прячет в ней еду.   *рыть*
4. Когда вы сегодня _____ магазин?   *закрыть*
5. У меня мышцы _____ от усталости.   *ныть*

(4) Stems in **ИЙ**

пить (пий-) *to drink*	
Non-Past	*Past*
я пью мы пьём ты пьёшь вы пьёте он/она пьёт они пьют	он пил она пила они пили

Characteristics:

*The vowel **и** is dropped throughout the non-past and is replaced by **ь**. The consonant **й** is truncated before the consonantal endings of the past tense and infinitive. The stress shifts to the ending of the feminine past tense.*

There are a total of 5 unprefixed verbs which conjugate exactly like **пить**.

Infinitive		Non-Past	Past
бить	*to beat*	**бью, бьёшь ... бьют**	**бил, била**
вить	*to twist*	**вью, вьёшь ... вьют**	**вил, вила**
лить	*to pour*	**лью, льёшь ... льют**	**лил, лила**
пить	*to drink*	**пью, пьёшь ... пьют**	**пил, пила**
шить	*to sew*	**шью, шьёшь .., шьют**	**шил, шила**

18. Complete the sentence with the appropriate present-tense form of the given verbs.

1. Я сама́ _____ свои пла́тья. — *шить*
2. Ну и пого́да! Дождь сего́дня _____ как из ведра́. — *лить*
3. Она́ из него́ верёвки _____. — *вить*
4. Вечера́ми мы обы́чно _____ чай. — *пить*
5. Когда́ он се́рдится, он _____ кулако́м по столу́. — *бить*

Miscellaneous Stems in **Й**

A few isolated verbs have one or another vowel preceding root-final **й**:

Infinitive		Non-Past	Past
ду́ть (дуй-)	*to blow*	**ду́ю, ду́ешь ... ду́ют**	**ду́л, ду́ла**
гни́ть (гний-)	*to rot*	**гнию́, гниёшь ... гнию́т**	**гни́л, гни́ла**

Two very commonly used verbs have one vowel in the infinitive and past tense, and a different vowel in the non-past.

Infinitive		Non-Past	Past
(е → о)петь	*to sing*	**пою́, поёшь ... пою́т**	**пел, пе́ла**
(и → е)брить	*to shave*	**бре́ю, бре́ешь ... бре́ют**	**брил, бри́ла**

19. Complete the sentence with the appropriate non-past form of the indicated verb.

1. Э́та певи́ца прекра́сно _____. — *петь*
2. Па́па _____ на суп, потому́ что он горя́чий. — *дуть*
3. Э́тот актёр ча́сто _____ себе́ го́лову. — *брить*
4. Де́рево _____ от сы́рости. — *гнить*

(5) Stems in **М** *or* **Н**

There are two groups of verbs with a stem in **м** or **н**:

(*a*) In the verbs of this group root-final **м** or **н** changes to the vowel **а** when followed by the consonantal endings of the infinitive and past tense. The consonant preceding **а** is normally soft (so **а** is spelled **я**, unless preceded by **ч** or **ж**). In two verbs (**взять** *to take*, **нача́ть** *to begin*) the stress shifts from the stem to the ending in the feminine past.

There are 6 verbs in this group.

Root	Infinitive		Non-Past	Past
-ьм-	**взя́ть**	*to take*	возьму́, возьмёшь . . . возьму́т	взя́л, взяла́
-жм-	**жа́ть**	*to press, squeeze*	жму, жмёшь . . . жмут	жа́л, жа́ла
-жн-	**жа́ть**	*to reap*	жну, жнёшь . . . жнут	жа́л, жа́ла
-мн-	**мя́ть**	*to crumple*	мну, мнёшь . . . мнут	мя́л, мя́ла
-чн-	**нача́ть**	*to begin*	начну́, начнёшь . . . начну́т	на́чал, начала́
-пн-	**распя́ть**	*to crucify*	распну́, распнёшь . . . распну́т	распя́л, распя́ла

(*b*) The verbs in this group have a non-past stem in **-йм-** or **-ним-**, which both change to **ня** before the consonantal endings of the infinitive and past tense; the stem **-йм-** follows prefixes ending in a vowel, while **-ним-** follows prefixes ending in a consonant. Verbs in the former group have shifting stress (to the feminine ending) in the past, while those in the latter group have shifting stress in both the non-past and past tenses. All these verbs are prefixed and perfective in aspect.

Following are some common verbs in **-нять** with the non-past in **-йм-**:

Infinitive		Non-Past	Past
заня́ть	*to borrow*	займу́, займёшь . . . займу́т	за́нял, заняла́
наня́ть	*to hire*	найму́, наймёшь . . . найму́т	на́нял, наняла́
поня́ть	*to understand*	пойму́, поймёшь . . . пойму́т	по́нял, поняла́

Following are some common verbs in **-нять** with the non-past in **-ним-**:

Infinitive		Non-Past	Past
обня́ть	*to embrace*	обниму́, обни́мешь . . . обни́мут	о́бнял, обняла́
отня́ть	*to take away*	отниму́, отни́мешь . . . отни́мут	о́тнял, отняла́
подня́ть	*to raise, lift*	подниму́, подни́мешь . . . -и́мут	по́днял, подняла́
сня́ть	*to take off*	сниму́, сни́мешь . . . сни́мут	сня́л, сняла́

One verb, **приня́ть**, has a prefix ending in a vowel, and has **-М-** in the non-past:

приня́ть	*to accept*	приму́, при́мешь . . . при́мут	при́нял, приняла́

20. Replace the past tense of the italicized verb with the non-past.

1. Она́ пра́вильно *поняла́* тебя́.
2. Я́ *взя́л* с собо́й схе́му ста́нций метро́.
3. Я́ ду́маю, что она́ *приняла́* его́ приглаше́ние.
4. Э́то де́ло *о́тняло* у на́с мно́го вре́мени.
5. О́н *за́нял* 5 ты́сяч до́лларов в ба́нке.
6. Мы́ *на́няли* на рабо́ту о́пытного программи́ста.
7. Она́ *начала́* рабо́тать в 9 часо́в утра́.
8. Ма́ма *жа́ла* со́к из апельси́нов.
9. Фе́рмеры *жа́ли* пшени́цу серпо́м.
10. Учени́к бы́стро *по́днял* ру́ку.
11. О́н *мя́л* цветы́ от волне́ния.
12. Я́ *сня́л* ку́ртку.

(6) Stems in **Р**

Stems in **р** are found in a few verbs which contain the roots **мр**, **пр**, and **тр**. The verbs with these roots have the following characteristics:

(a)　　**р → ере** before the infinitive ending **ть** (**у-мере́-ть** *to die*).

(b)　　**р → ер** before other consonants (**у-мер-ла́** *(She) died*).

(c)　　**л** is dropped in the masculine past tense (**Он у́мер** *He died*).

The verbs with these roots are often prefixed, therefore perfective in aspect:

Infinitive		Non-Past	Past
тере́ть	*to rub, grate*	**тру́, трёшь … тру́т**	**тёр, тёрла**
вы́тереть	*to rub (dry)*	**вы́тру, вы́трешь …**	**вы́тер, вы́терла**
стере́ть	*to erase*	**сотру́, сотрёшь … сотру́т**	**стёр, стёрла**
запере́ть	*to lock*	**запру́, запрёшь … запру́т**	**за́пер, заперла́**
отпере́ть	*to unlock*	**отопру́, отопрёшь …**	**о́тпер, отперла́**
умере́ть	*to die*	**умру́, умрёшь … умру́т**	**у́мер, умерла́**

21.　Change the italicized verb from the past tense to non-past.

1.　Э́ти ту́фли *тёрли* мои́ но́ги.
2.　Я́ бы́стро *вы́тер* ру́ки.
3.　Учи́тельница *стёрла* упражне́ние с доски́.
4.　Она́ *заперла́* две́рь на замо́к.
5.　О́н бы́стро *о́тпер* сейф.
6.　Ба́бушка *умерла́* от ста́рости.

Obstruent Stems

(7) Stems in **З** *and* **С**

The verbs with a stem ending in **з** or **с** drop the **л** in the masculine past tense. The most common verbs in this group are:

Infinitive		Non-Past	Past
везти́	*to transport*	**везу́, везёшь … везу́т**	**вёз, везла́**
ле́зть	*to climb*	**ле́зу, ле́зешь … ле́зут**	**лез, ле́зла**
ползти́	*to crawl*	**ползу́, ползёшь … ползу́т**	**по́лз, ползла́**
нести́	*to carry*	**несу́, несёшь … несу́т**	**нёс, несла́**
спасти́	*to save, rescue*	**спасу́, спасёшь … спасу́т**	**спа́с, спасла́**
трясти́	*to shake*	**трясу́, трясёшь … трясу́т**	**тря́с, трясла́**

(8) Stems in **Д** *and* **Т**

The stem-final **д** and **т** changes to **с** before the infinitive ending. The **д** and **т** are dropped before the **л** in each past-tense form.

Following are common verbs with stem-final **д**:

Infinitive		Non-Past	Past
брести́	*to wander*	**бреду́, бредёшь … бреду́т**	**брёл, брела́**
вести́	*to lead*	**веду́, ведёшь … веду́т**	**вёл, вела́**
кла́сть	*to put*	**кладу́, кладёшь … кладу́т**	**кла́л, кла́ла**
кра́сть	*to steal*	**краду́, крадёшь … краду́т**	**кра́л, кра́ла**
упа́сть	*to fall*	**упаду́, упадёшь … упаду́т**	**упа́л, упа́ла**

In one verb in this group the vowel **е** in the infinitive and past tense changes to **я** in the non-past:

се́сть	*to sit down*	**ся́ду, ся́дешь … ся́дут**	**се́л, се́ла**

The following are some common verbs with a stem-final **т**:

Infinitive		Non-Past	Past
мести́	*to sweep*	**мету́, метёшь … мету́т**	**мёл, мела́**
плести́	*to weave*	**плету́, плетёшь … плету́т**	**плёл, плела́**
приобрести́	*to acquire*	**приобрету́, приобретёшь …**	**приобрёл, -ла́**
цвести́	*to bloom*	**цвету́, цветёшь … цвету́т**	**цвёл, цвела́**

The verb **прочесть** has the nonvocalic root **чт**, which gets an inserted vowel **е** or **ё** before the nonvocalic ending of the infinitive and masculine past tense.

проче́сть	*to read*	**прочту́, прочтёшь … прочту́т**	**прочёл, прочла́**

(9) Stems in Б

The stem-final **б** changes to **с** in the infinitive. The past-tense marker **л** is dropped in the masculine singular. There are only two verbs of this type.

Infinitive		Non-Past	Past
грести́	*to rake; row*	**гребу́, гребёшь … гребу́т**	**грёб, гребла́, гребли́**
скрести́	*to scrape*	**скребу́, скребёшь … скребу́т**	**скрёб, скребла́, скребли́**

22. Change the tense of the italicized verb from past to non-past or vice versa.

1. О́н *се́л* на дива́н ря́дом с не́й.
2. Ко́шка *скребла́* кре́сло когтя́ми.
3. О́н *приобрёл* но́вых друзе́й.
4. Студе́нты *несу́т* на заня́тия словари́.
5. Ты́ всегда́ *кла́л* клю́ч под ко́врик?
6. Дво́рник *метёт* тротуа́р.
7. Тюльпа́ны *цвели́* в саду́.
8. Пау́к *плетёт* паути́ну.
9. О́н *гребёт* де́ньги лопа́той.
10. В часы́ пи́к маши́ны е́ле *ползу́т*.
11. Ко́шка *ле́зет* на де́рево.
12. Ма́льчики *трясли́* я́блоню.
13. Э́то лека́рство *спасёт* мне́ жи́знь.
14. Ма́ма *везёт* ребёнка на коля́ске.
15. Она́ *вела́* дете́й в шко́лу.
16. Температу́ра *упа́ла* ни́же нуля́.

(10) Stems in Г and К

Verbs with a stem in **г** and **к** have an infinitive ending in **-чь**. These consonants also alternate in the non-past: **г → ж** and **к → ч** before the vowel **е/ё** (i.e., in all forms except the first singular and third plural). The past-tense marker **л** is omitted in the masculine singular only.

Following are some common verbs with stem-final **г**:

Infinitive		Non-Past	Past
бере́чь	*to guard*	**берегу́, бережёшь … берегу́т**	**берёг, берегла́**
стри́чь	*to cut (hair)*	**стригу́, стрижёшь … стригу́т**	**стри́г, стри́гла**
мо́чь	*to be able*	**могу́, мо́жешь … мо́гут**	**мо́г, могла́**
помо́чь	*to help*	**помогу́, помо́жешь … помо́гут**	**помо́г, помогла́**

In one verb from this group the vowel **e/ё** in the infinitive/past tense changes to **я** in the non-past:

ле́чь	*to lie down*	**ля́гу, ля́жешь . . . ля́гут**	**лёг, легла́**

The verb **же́чь** has the nonvocalic root **жг**, which gets the inserted vowel **e** or **ё** before the nonvocalic endings of the infinitive and masculine past tense.

же́чь	*to burn*	**жгу́, жгёшь . . . жгу́т**	**жёг, жгла́**

Following are some common verbs with stem-final **к**:

пе́чь	*to bake*	**пеку́, печёшь . . . пеку́т**	**пёк, пекла́**
отвле́чь	*to distract*	**отвлеку́, отвлечёшь . . . отвлеку́т**	**отвлёк, отвлекла́**
привле́чь	*to attract*	**привлеку́, привлечёшь . . .**	**привлёк, -влекла́**
те́чь	*to flow*	**теку́, течёшь . . . теку́т**	**тёк, текла́**

23. Change the tense of the italicized verb from past tense to non-past.

1. О́н *лёг* спа́ть в де́сять часо́в.
2. Она́ не *берегла́* своё здоро́вье.
3. О́н *мо́г* купи́ть биле́ты в теа́тр.
4. Ма́ма ча́сто *пекла́* вку́сные пироги́.
5. Мы́ *помогли́* ему́ сня́ть кварти́ру

6. О́тдых на мо́ре *отвлёк* его́ от забо́т.
7. Парикма́хер *стри́г* клие́нта.
8. О́н *обжёг* па́льцы спи́чкой.
9. Вре́мя *текло́* бы́стро.
10. Э́тот фи́льм *привлёк* большо́е внима́ние.

Irregular Verbs with Nonsuffixed Stem

The following verbs depart in various ways from the regular patterns of the verb types presented above. These verbs should be memorized.

Infinitive		*Non-Past*	*Past Tense*
бы́ть	*to be*	**бу́ду, бу́дешь . . . бу́дут**	**бы́л, была́, бы́ли**
да́ть	*to give*	**да́м, да́шь, да́ст, дади́м, дади́те, даду́т**	**да́л, дала́, да́ли**
е́сть	*to eat*	**е́м, е́шь, е́ст, еди́м, еди́те, едя́т**	**е́л, е́ла, е́ли**
е́хать	*to go by vehicle*	**е́ду, е́дешь . . . е́дут**	**е́хал, е́хала, е́хали**
идти́	*to go on foot*	**иду́, идёшь . . . иду́т**	**шёл, шла́, шли́**
расти́	*to grow*	**расту́, растёшь . . . расту́т**	**ро́с, росла́, росли́**

Summary Table

First Conjugation Verbs with Nonsuffixed Stem Classified by Stem-Final Consonant

Classifier	*Infinitive*	*Basic stem*	*3rd Pl. Non-Past*
		Resonant Stems	
(1) В	**жи́ть**	**жив-**	**живу́т**
(2) Н	**ста́ть**	**стан-**	**ста́нут**
(3) ОЙ	**откры́ть**	**от-крой-**	**откро́ют**
(4) ИЙ	**пи́ть**	**пий-**	**пью́т**
(5) М or Н	**нача́ть**	**на-чн-**	**начну́т**
	поня́ть	**по-йм-**	**пойму́т**
	сня́ть	**с-ним-**	**сни́мут**
(6) Р	**умере́ть**	**у-м/р-**	**умру́т**

Obstruent Stems

(7) З or С	везти́	вез-	везу́т
	нести́	нес-	несу́т
(8) Д or Т	вести́	вед-	веду́т
	мести́	мет-	мету́т
(9) Б	грести́	греб-	гребу́т
(10) Г or К	мо́чь	мог-	мо́гут
	пе́чь	пек-	пеку́т

VERB TENSES: FORMATION

Present Tense

The present tense is formed only from imperfective verbs. Conjugating an imperfective verb in the non-past gives the present tense. Numerous examples of the present tense for all types of first and second conjugation verbs were presented in the above classification of verbs with suffixed and nonsuffixed basic stems.

Past Tense

Russian has but one past-tense form, obtained from both imperfective and perfective verbs. The past tense is obtained by attaching to the verbal stem the ending **-л**, followed by the appropriate gender/number marker to agree with the subject: **-∅** (zero ending), **-а**, **-о**, **-и**. In most instances, the rule of "likes" and "unlikes" for combining stems and endings applies as expected:

(*a*)   If a basic stem ends in a vowel, simply add the consonantal ending of the past tense:

Verb Stem		Past		Gender/Number		Example
				∅	(Masc. subject)	о́н писа́л
писа	+	л	+	а	(Fem. subject)	она́ писа́ла
				о	(Neut. subject)	оно́ писа́ло
				и	(Plural)	они́ писа́ли

(*b*)   If the basic stem ends in a consonant, truncate that consonant before the consonant л:

чита́й	+	л	=	чита́л, чита́ла, чита́ло, чита́ли
жив	+	л	=	жи́л, жила́, жило́, жи́ли
стан	+	л	=	ста́л, ста́ла, ста́ло, ста́ли
вед	+	л	=	вёл, вела́, вело́, вели́
мет	+	л	=	мёл, мела́, мело́, мели́

However, nonsuffixed stems in **з**, **с**, **б**, **р**, **г**, and **к** are exceptions to the rule that the first of two "likes" truncates: here the stem-final consonant is retained in all past-tense forms, and it is the past-tense marker **л** that is dropped, *but only in the masculine*.

вез	+	л	=	вёз, везла́, везло́, везли́
нес	+	л	=	нёс, несла́, несло́, несли́
греб	+	л	=	грёб, гребла́, гребло́, гребли́
мог	+	л	=	мо́г, могла́, могло́, могли́
пек	+	л	=	пёк, пекла́, пеко́, пекли́
ум/р	+	л	=	у́мер, умерла́, у́мерло, у́мерли

Finally, verbs which lose the suffix **ну** in the past tense, also lose the past-tense marker **л** in the masculine:

дости́г(ну)ть	*to achieve*	дости́г, дости́гла, дости́гло, дости́гли
замёрз(ну)ть	*to freeze*	замёрз, замёрзла, замёрзло, замёрзли
мо́к(ну)ть	*to get wet*	мо́к, мо́кла, мо́кло, мо́кли

Future Tense

The future tense is formed from both imperfective and perfective verbs.

Imperfective Future

The future tense of an imperfective verb is formed from the appropriate conjugated form of the auxiliary verb **бы́ть** *to be* (**я́ бу́ду, ты́ бу́дешь ... они́ бу́дут**) followed by the infinitive of the imperfective verb, e.g., the future tense of the imperfective verb **писа́ть** *to write*.

я́	бу́ду писа́ть
ты́	бу́дешь писа́ть
о́н/а́/о́	бу́дет писа́ть
мы́	бу́дем писа́ть
вы́	бу́дете писа́ть
они́	бу́дут писа́ть
will write, will be writing	

Perfective Future

The future of any perfective verb is obtained simply by conjugating that verb. The endings of the perfective future are identical to those of the imperfective present tense. This is why the first and second conjugation endings of any verb are called "non-past": when an imperfective verb is conjugated, these endings indicate the present tense, but when a perfective verb is conjugated, these same endings indicate the perfective future.

The forms and distribution of the present, past, and future tenses are illustrated in the table below with the imperfective/perfective verb pair, **чита́ть/прочита́ть** *to read*.

Imperfective **чита́ть**		
Past Tense	*Present Tense*	*Future Tense*
о́н　чита́л	я́　чита́ю	я́　бу́ду чита́ть
она́　чита́ла	ты́　чита́ешь	ты́　бу́дешь чита́ть
оно́　чита́ло	о́н/а́/о́　чита́ет	о́н/а́/о́　бу́дет чита́ть
они́　чита́ли	мы́　чита́ем	мы́　бу́дем чита́ть
	вы́　чита́ете	вы́　бу́дете чита́ть
	они́　чита́ют	они́　бу́дут чита́ть
Perfective **прочита́ть**		
Past Tense	*Present Tense*	*Future Tense*
о́н　прочита́л	———————	я́　прочита́ю
она́　прочита́ла		ты́　прочита́ешь
оно́　причита́ло		о́н/а́/о́　прочита́ет
они́　прочита́ли		мы́　прочита́ем
		вы́　прочита́ете
		они́　прочита́ют

24. Complete the sentence with the future tense of the imperfective verbs on the right.

1. Что́ вы _____ _____ за́втра ве́чером?   *де́лать*
2. За́втра мы _____ _____ фи́льм.   *смотре́ть*
3. Ты́ сего́дня _____ _____ упражне́ния?   *писа́ть*
4. Сего́дня я _____ _____ на компью́тере.   *рабо́тать*
5. Она́ ско́ро _____ _____ ру́сский язы́к.   *изуча́ть*
6. По́сле ле́кции студе́нты _____ _____ зада́чи.   *реша́ть*

VERB ASPECTS: FORMATION

Most Russian verbs occur in aspectual pairs: an imperfective form and a perfective form. In general, the members of an aspectual pair are similar in appearance, and practically identical in meaning, but are differentiated by (1) prefixation, (2) suffixation, or rarely (3) suppletion (which means that the members of the pair are different words, as in **бра́ть — взя́ть** *to take*).

(1) Prefixation

The perfective is formed from the imperfective verb by adding a particular prefix. The prefix changes the aspect of the verb, but it does not change its meaning or conjugation. It is important to learn which prefixes perfectivize particular unprefixed imperfective verbs. Below are examples of common imperfective verbs and their prefixed perfective partners.

IMPERFECTIVE	PERFECTIVE	
	Prefix **вы́-**	
пи́ть (пий-)	**вы́пить** (вы́пий-)	*to drink*
учи́ть (учи-)	**вы́учить** (вы́учи-)	*to learn*
	Prefix **за-**	
плати́ть (плати-)	**заплати́ть** (заплати-)	*to pay*
хоте́ть (irreg.)	**захоте́ть** (irreg.)	*to want*
	Prefix **ис-**	
пе́чь (пек-)	**испе́чь** (испек-)	*to bake*
	Prefix **на-**	
печа́тать (печатай-)	**напеча́тать** (напечатай-)	*to print, type*
писа́ть (писа-)	**написа́ть** (написа-)	*to write*
рисова́ть (рисова-)	**нарисова́ть** (нарисова)	*to draw*
	Prefix **по-**	
звони́ть (звони-)	**позвони́ть** (позвони-)	*to ring, telephone*
смотре́ть (смотре-)	**посмотре́ть** (посмотре-)	*to look, watch*
стро́ить (строи-)	**постро́ить** (построи-)	*to build*
	Prefixes **при-, про-, раз-**	
гото́вить (готови-)	**пригото́вить** (приготови-)	*to prepare*
чита́ть (читай-)	**прочита́ть** (прочитай-)	*to read*
буди́ть (буди-)	**разбуди́ть** (разбуди-)	*to awaken*
	Prefix **с-**	
де́лать (делай-)	**сде́лать** (сделай-)	*to do, make*
е́сть (irreg.)	**съе́сть** (irreg.)	*to eat*
игра́ть (играй-)	**сыгра́ть** (сыграй-)	*to play*

пе́ть (irreg.)	**спе́ть** (irreg.)	*to sing*
мо́чь (мог-)	**смо́чь** (смог-)	*to be able*
	Prefix **у-**	
ви́деть (виде-)	**уви́деть** (увиде-)	*to see*
слы́шать (слыша-)	**услы́шать** (услыша-)	*to hear*

(2) Suffixation

A. The imperfective and perfective partners have different suffixes and, therefore, different conjugation patterns.

IMPERFECTIVE	PERFECTIVE	
изуча́ть (изучай-)	**изучи́ть** (изучи-)	*to study*
конча́ть (кончай-)	**ко́нчить** (кончи-)	*to finish*
покупа́ть (покупай-)	**купи́ть** (купи-)	*to finish*
реша́ть (решай-)	**реши́ть** (реши-)	*to decide, solve*
крича́ть (крич-а-)	**кри́кнуть** (крикну-)	*to shout*
отдыха́ть (отдыхай-)	**отдохну́ть** (отдохну-)	*to rest*
узнава́ть (узнавай-)	**узна́ть** (узнай-)	*to find out, recognize*
дава́ть (давай-)	**да́ть** (irreg.)	*to give*
переводи́ть (переводи-)	**перевести́** (перевед-)	*to translate*

Note: The aspectual pair **покупа́ть/купи́ть** *to buy* is the only one where the imperfective is prefixed (**по-**), and not the perfective.

In a few instances, there is also an alternation in the root vowel (**o → a**) and/or in the stem-final consonant:

спра́шивать (спрашивай-)	спроси́ть (спроси-)	*to ask*
отвеча́ть (отвечай-)	отве́тить (ответи-)	*to answer*

B. Certain prefixes added to an imperfective verb change not only the aspect, but also the *meaning* of the verb. The following table shows how the meaning of the imperfective verb **писа́ть** *to write* may be altered by some commonly used prefixes. The meaning given for each prefix, in most instances, is only one of several possible meanings associated with that prefix.

BASIC IMPERFECTIVE	PREFIXED PERFECTIVE (with new meaning)	
писа́ть *to write*	**в**писа́ть	*to write **in***
	вы́писать	*to write **out***
	дописа́ть	*to **finish** writing*
	записа́ть	*to write **down***
	надписа́ть	*to write **on the surface***
	описа ть	*to describe*
	переписа́ть	*to **re**-write*
	подписа́ть	*to sign*
	приписа́ть	*to add (to something written)*
	прописа́ть	*to prescribe*
	списа́ть	*to copy*

New *derived imperfective* partners for such prefixed perfectives are formed with one of three suffixes: **-ывай-/ивай-**, **-вай-**, or **-ай-**.

IMPERFECTIVE		PREFIXED PERFECTIVE		DERIVED IMPFV.
писа́ть	*to write*	записа́ть	*to write down*	запи́сывать (ывай)
чита́ть	*to read*	дочита́ть	*to finish reading*	дочи́тывать (ывай)
кры́ть	*to cover*	закры́ть	*to close*	закрыва́ть (вай)
мы́ть	*to wash*	умы́ть	*to wash up*	умыва́ть (вай)
де́ть	*to put*	наде́ть	*to put on*	надева́ть (вай)
бра́ть	*to take*	собра́ть	*to collect*	собира́ть (ай)
зва́ть	*to call*	вы́звать	*to summon*	вызыва́ть (ай)

(3) Suppletion

Verbs in suppletive pairs are completely different words. There are very few pairs of this type.

IMPERFECTIVE	PERFECTIVE	
бра́ть	взя́ть	*to take*
говори́ть	сказа́ть	*to speak, say/tell*
иска́ть	найти́	*to look for/to find*
кла́сть	положи́ть	*to put in a lying position*
лови́ть	пойма́ть	*to try to catch/to catch*

25. Replace the present tense of the italicized imperfective verb with the past tense of its perfective partner.

Model: Óн *пи́шет* письмо́. > Óн <u>написа́л</u> письмо́.

1. Ма́льчик *пьёт* молоко́.
2. Ма́ма *гото́вит* обе́д.
3. Студе́нты *реша́ют* зада́чу.
4. Худо́жник *рису́ет* портре́т.
5. Актёр *у́чит* свою́ ро́ль.
6. Мы́ *покупа́ем* проду́кты.
7. Она́ *пла́тит* за себя́.
8. Óн *отдыха́ет* под де́ревом.
9. Студе́нт *спра́шивает* преподава́теля.
10. Преподава́тель *отвеча́ет* на вопро́сы студе́нтов.

26. Replace the past tense of the italicized perfective verb with its imperfective partner in the present tense.

Model: Óн *наде́л* джи́нсы. > Óн <u>надева́ет</u> джи́нсы.

1. Óн *собра́л* цветы́.
2. Она́ *записа́ла* но́мер телефо́на.
3. Мы́ *вы́звали* врача́.
4. Óн *положи́л* клю́ч под ко́врик.
5. Она́ *взяла́* кни́ги в библиоте́ке.
6. Óн *сказа́л* пра́вду.
7. Она́ *закры́ла* окно́.
8. Ма́ма *умы́ла* ребёнка.
9. Óн *нашёл* свои́ очки́.
10. Мы́ *пойма́ли* ры́бу.

VERB ASPECTS: MEANINGS AND USES

Of the two aspects, the perfective is the more specific in meaning and limited in use. Available in the past and future (but not in the present) tense, a perfective verb presents the action as a *total event*, one with a beginning and an end. Typically, the perfective focuses on the end of the event, indicating that the action was, or will be, *completed*, often with an attendant *result*.

The imperfective aspect, available in the three tenses—present, past, and future—has a very general, nonspecific meaning: the imperfective merely indicates the occurrence of an action, without referring to its completion or result. The imperfective may be used in a wide range of contexts, and must be used in those contexts that are incompatible with the perfective meaning of "one-time completed action" (e.g., actions in progress, or actions that are indefinitely repeated).

Aspect Choice and Context

Perfective verbs do not occur in the present tense; therefore, any action in the present tense will be expressed by an *imperfective* verb form. However, since both perfective and imperfective verbs occur in the past and future tenses, when describing an action in the past or future, one must choose the correct aspect form of the verb. The choice of perfective or imperfective aspect is very often determined by context. Below are several contexts in the past and future where *only one or the other* aspect is possible.

Aspect in the Past and Future

Contexts for Using Perfective Verbs

(a) Completion with Attendant Result

The meaning of result may be expressed in the context by another clause.

Она́ *прочита́ла* **письмо́ и тепе́рь** **она́ всё понима́ет.**	*She has read the letter and now she understands everything.*
Она́ *сда́ст* **экза́мен и** *полу́чит* **стипе́ндию в сле́дующем семе́стре.**	*She will pass the exam and receive a stipend for the next semester.*

A resultative nuance is also conveyed when the object of the verb denotes a definite quantity of items affected by the action of the verb.

Он *написа́л* **де́сять упражне́ний.**	*He wrote ten exercises.*
Она́ *реши́т* **все зада́чи.**	*She will solve all the problems.*

The perfective form of the verb tends to co-occur with certain words which imply the completion of the action, e.g., the conjunction **как то́лько** *as soon as*, and with adverbs that signal the completion, suddenness, or immediacy of the action, e.g., **наконе́ц** *finally*, **вдру́г** *suddenly*, **сра́зу/сейча́с же** *immediately*, **сейча́с** *right now*.

Я *позвони́л* **тебе́, как то́лько я** *узна́л* **но́вость.**	*I called you as soon as I learned the news.*
По́сле конце́рта, мы́ сра́зу *пошли́* **домо́й.**	*After the concert, we immediately started for home.*

(b) Achievement of Intended Result

Some verbs fall into aspectual pairs where the imperfective indicates *trying* to do something (a process), while the *perfective* signals that the subject has achieved (or failed to achieve) the *intended result*. These meanings can be clearly illustrated with both verbs occurring in the same sentence.

Я́ всё у́тро *вспомина́л* **его́ и́мя, и наконе́ц** *вспо́мнил.*	*I was trying to recall his name all morning and finally I remembered it.*
Он *поступа́л* **в университе́т, но не** *поступи́л.*	*He applied to the university, but didn't get in.*

Some other common imperfective/perfective aspectual pairs that can fit into sentences of this type are:

привыка́ть/привы́кнуть	*try to get used to/become accustomed*
реша́ть/реши́ть	*to work on, try to solve/solve*
сдава́ть/сда́ть	*to take/pass (an exam)*
угова́ривать/уговори́ть	*to try to persuade/talk into*
учи́ть/вы́учить	*to study/memorize* (+ Acc.)
учи́ться/научи́ться	*to study/learn* (+ Infinitive)

(c) Sequential Actions

When a single action follows another in sequence, the two actions are expressed by *perfective* verbs.

О́н *встал и предложил* **то́ст.**	*He stood up and proposed a toast.*
Я́ *откро́ю* **буты́лку** *и* **вы́пью вина́.**	*I'll open a bottle and drink some wine.*

(d) Actions Completed in a Specific Amount of Time (expressed by **за** *+ Accusative)*

A perfective verb must be used with the preposition **за** + *accusative of time* to express the length of time it took to *complete an action*. To elicit this information one asks, **За ско́лько вре́мени** …?

За ско́лько вре́мени ты́ *решил* **зада́чу?**	*How long did it take you to solve the problem?*
О́н *прочитал* **э́тот рома́н** *за* **неде́лю.**	*He read this novel in a week.*
Э́то зда́ние *построили за пять лет.*	*This building was built in five years.*

(e) Actions of Limited Duration

A perfective verb with the prefix **по-** may be used to express that an action lasted (or will last) a short while. A perfective verb with the prefix **про-** may indicate an action of a comparatively longer duration. The verbs that take these prefixes in the meaning of "limited duration" are either intransitive, or they may be transitive verbs that are being used intransitively.

Мы́ *посиде́ли и поговори́ли.*	*We sat for a while and had a talk.*
Мы́ *посиди́м и поду́маем.*	*We will sit a while and think a bit.*
Я́ *почита́л,* а пото́м *пописа́л.*	*I read a while, and then I wrote a bit.*
О́н немно́го *поспа́л.*	*He took a little nap.*
Мы́ до́лго *простоя́ли* в о́череди.	*We stood in line for a long time.*
Они́ *прожи́ли* два́ го́да в Москве́.	*They lived in Moscow for two years.*

(f) Instantaneous Actions

Instantaneous one-time actions are expressed by *perfective* verbs. Perfectives which denote an action that *begins and ends instantaneously* are formed with the suffix **ну**, e.g., **кри́кнуть** *to give a shout*, **пры́гнуть** *to jump once*, **толкну́ть** *to give a shove*.

О́н *пры́гнул* в во́ду.	*He jumped into the water.*
Она́ *кри́кнула.*	*She gave a shout.*

Another group of perfective verbs denote only the *starting point of the action*. These verbs are typically formed with various prefixes, for example, **за-** (**заболе́ть** *to fall ill*, **засмея́ться** *to begin to* *laugh*, **заинтересова́ться** *to become interested*), **по-** (**пойти́** *to begin walking*, **полюби́ть** *to fall in love*), **рас-** (**рассерди́ться** *to get angry*), and **у-** (**уви́деть** *to catch sight of*, **услы́шать** *to hear*).

Сы́н *увидел* **отца́** и *побежа́л* **к нему́.**	*The son saw his father and started running toward him.*
Она́ *прочита́ла* **письмо́** и *засмея́лась.*	*She read the letter and began to laugh.*

Contexts for Using Imperfective Verbs

(a) Action in Progress

The imperfective is obligatory when an action is ongoing or lasts for some time. This durative meaning may be reinforced by temporal adverbs and time expressions such as **до́лго** *a long time*, **недо́лго** *for a short while*, **ве́сь де́нь** *all day*, **всё у́тро** *all morning*, **це́лый ме́сяц** *the whole month*.

Мы́ до́лго *жи́ли* в **Москве́.**	*We lived in Moscow a long time.*
Она́ ве́сь ве́чер *бу́дет рабо́тать.*	*She will be working all evening.*
О́н це́лый де́нь *смотре́л* **телеви́зор.**	*He watched television the whole day.*

Note that the durational (prepositionless) accusative contrasts with **за** + accusative, when describing how long an action was *in process*. To elicit this information one asks, **Ско́лько вре́мени ...?** or **Ка́к до́лго ...?**

— **Ско́лько вре́мени** о́н *писа́л* **кни́гу?**	*How long was he writing the book?*
— **О́н** *писа́л* **кни́гу** оди́н го́д.	*He was writing the book for a year.*

(b) Simultaneous Actions

Two actions occurring at the same time are normally expressed by two *imperfective* verbs.

Мы́ *сиде́ли* и *вспомина́ли* **про́шлое.**	*We were sitting and recalling the past.*
Ма́ма *гото́вила* **обе́д** и *слу́шала* **ра́дио.**	*Mom was preparing dinner while she listened to the radio.*

However, when an action in progress is *interrupted* by another action, the former (background) action is *imperfective*, while the latter (interrupting) action is *perfective*.

Я́ спокойно *чита́л*, когда́ вдру́г *постуча́ли* в две́рь.	*I was reading quietly when suddenly there was a knock at the door.*

(c) Repeated (Habitual) Actions

The imperfective aspect of the verb is used to present an action as recurring on a regular (or irregular) basis. The meaning of repetition is often reinforced by accompanying temporal adverbs and time expressions such as, for example, **всегда́** *always*, **ка́ждый де́нь** *everyday*, **ча́сто** *often*, **обы́чно** *usually*, **иногда́** *sometimes*, **ре́дко** *rarely*.

О́н всегда́ *за́втракал* **до́ма.**	*He always had breakfast at home.*
Они́ ча́сто *звоня́т* **дру́г дру́гу.**	*They often call each other.*
Я́ бу́ду *занима́ться* **ка́ждый де́нь.**	*I will study every day.*

(d) Annulled (Reversed) Actions

An *imperfective* verb is used to indicate an action that was carried out and then *reversed*, so that the result of the action is no longer in force at the moment of speaking. This situation can arise only with verbs denoting *reversible* actions, i.e., those that can be done and then undone (or *annulled*). The verbs that can express an annulled action typically involve movement or change in position, e.g., get up/lie down, take/return, open/close, put on/take off, turn on/turn off. The perfective verb in such a pair signals that the result of the action is still in force. Compare the use of the aspects below:

Заче́м ты́ ве́чером *встава́л* с посте́ли?	*Why were you out of bed last night?*
Ты́ бо́лен и до́лжен лежа́ть.	*You are sick and should stay in bed.*
Заче́м ты́ *вста́л* с посте́ли?	*Why have you gotten out of bed?*
Ложи́сь сейча́с же в посте́ль.	*Get back in bed right now.*
— Где́ ку́ртка, в кото́рой ты́ бы́л вчера́?	*Where's the jacket you were wearing yesterday?*
— Э́то была́ не моя́ ку́ртка, я *бра́л* её у дру́га.	*That was not my jacket, I took (borrowed) it from a friend.*
— Отку́да у тебя́ э́та ку́ртка?	*Where did you get that jacket from?*
— Я́ *взя́л* у дру́га. Тебе́ нра́вится?	*I took it from a friend. Do you like it?*

Below are a few verb pairs where the imperfective may indicate an annulled action:

бра́ть/взя́ть	*to take*
встава́ть/вста́ть	*to get up*
включа́ть/включи́ть	*to turn on*
отдава́ть/отда́ть	*to give back, return*
открыва́ть/откры́ть	*to open*
поднима́ться/подня́ться	*to ascend*
приноси́ть/принести́	*to bring*

(e) Denial of Intent to Perform an Action

A *negated imperfective* is used in the past tense to indicate not only that an action did not take place, but that the action was *not intended* or *not expected* to take place.

— Ты́ *взя́л* мою́ гребёнку?	*Did you take my comb?*
— Не́т, я́ не *бра́л*.	*No, I didn't take it!*

Compare the two responses below, where the perfective indicates the speaker had expected the letter, while the imperfective indicates the letter was never expected.

	— Вы́ *получи́ли* моё письмо́?	*Did you receive my letter?*
(*a*)	— Не́т, мы́ ещё не *получи́ли*.	*No, we still haven't received it.*
(*b*)	— Не́т, мы́ никако́го письма́ не *получа́ли*.	*No, we didn't receive any letter.*

Aspect in Questions

Imperfective Past: Did an Action Take Place?/What Action Took Place?

When a speaker is interested in finding out merely if an action has taken place, the question must be posed with the *imperfective past*. In such questions the completion or result of the action is not of interest to the questioner. The *imperfective* is also used in the answer to these questions as a mere *statement of fact* that the action did (or did not) take place.

— Вы́ *чита́ли* «А́нну Каре́нину»?	*Did you ever read "Anna Karenina"?*
— Да́, *чита́л*./Не́т, не *чита́л*.	*Yes, I read it./No, I did not read it.*

Similarly, to ask general questions like "What did you do yesterday?" or "What went on at the meeting?" the question (and the answer) will employ the *imperfective*, since the focus of the question is on *activities engaged in*, not results.

| — Что́ ты́ *де́лал* вчера́? | What did you do yesterday? |
| — Я́ *гото́вился* к экза́мену. | I was preparing for an exam. |

Perfective Past: Was an Expected Action Completed?

The notion of "intent" or "expectation" regarding the performance of an action is important in the choice of aspect in questions. When the speaker has reason to expect that the listener was to perform a given action, s/he will ask if that action *has been accomplished*. In this case, both the question and the answer will employ the *perfective*. For example, in the following exchange the questioner knows that the listener intended to see a particular play, and therefore the perfective form is used:

— Ты́ *посмотре́л* пье́су «Ча́йка»?	Did you see the play "The Seagull"?
У тебя́, ка́жется, бы́ли биле́ты на неё.	It seems to me you had tickets for it.
— Да́, *посмотре́л.*	Yes, I saw it.

However, if the person asking the question has no such expectation, but instead is simply inquiring if the listener has ever seen the play, then the *imperfective* is required.

| — Ты́ *смотре́л* э́ту пье́су? | Have you seen this play? |
| — Да́, *смотре́л.*/Не́т, не *смотре́л.* | Yes, I did./No, I didn't. |

27. Fill in the blanks with the correct aspectual form of the verb in the past tense. Determine whether the context calls for an *imperfective* denoting *process*, or a *perfective* denoting *result*.

1. Мы́ це́лый го́д _____ к жи́зни в э́том ма́леньком городке́, но та́к и не _____ .   *привыка́ть/привы́кнуть*
2. Я́ до́лго _____ его́ позвони́ть е́й, но о́н не соглаша́лся. Но в конце́ концо́в я́ его́ _____ .   *угова́ривать/уговори́ть*
3. Она́ вчера́ _____ экза́мен, но не _____ . Она́ пло́хо подгото́вилась.   *сдава́ть/сда́ть*
4. Мо́й дру́г ве́сь де́нь проводи́л на о́зере. О́н та́м _____ ры́бу. В конце́ дня́ о́н _____ щу́ку.   *лови́ть/пойма́ть*
5. Оте́ц не мо́г пойти́ с на́ми в па́рк, потому́ что о́н _____ докла́д.   *гото́вить/пригото́вить*
6. Мо́й клю́ч куда́-то исче́з. Я́ _____ его́, но не _____ .   *иска́ть/найти́*
7. Ма́ма до́лго _____ сы́на, но та́к и не _____ его́.   *буди́ть/разбуди́ть*

28. Complete the sentence with the appropriate aspectual form in the past tense. Determine whether the action is *ongoing* or of *limited duration*.

1. Мы́ _____ немно́го, отдохну́ли, и пошли́ да́льше.   *(по)сиде́ть*
2. Она́ была́ больна́ и всю́ суббо́ту _____ до́ма.   *(по)сиде́ть*
3. У́тром по́сле за́втрака они́ до́лго _____ по го́роду.   *(по)гуля́ть*
4. Я́ _____ полчаса́ и лёг спа́ть.   *(по)рабо́тать*
5. О́н ве́сь ве́чер _____ на компью́тере.   *(по)рабо́тать*
6. Я́ до́лго _____ об э́том. Наконе́ц я́ при́нял реше́ние.   *(по)ду́мать*
7. Учени́к _____ мину́тку и отве́тил на вопро́с учи́теля.   *(по)ду́мать*

29. Complete the sentence with the appropriate aspectual form of the verb. Determine whether the context indicates an *action in progress* or the *beginning of an action*.

1. Когда́ де́вочка узна́ла о сме́рти ба́бушки, она́ _____. (за)пла́кала
2. Де́вочка _____ це́лый де́нь. (за)пла́кала
3. Мы́ попроща́лись с ни́м на платфо́рме и о́н _____ к ваго́ну. (по)шёл
4. Всё у́тро _____ до́ждь. (по)шёл
5. Мы́ бы́ли в Изма́йлово на верниса́же, когда́ вдру́г _____ си́льный до́ждь. (по)шёл
6. Когда́ на́м сказа́ли э́ту но́вость, мы́ _____ от ра́дости. (за)пры́гали
7. Мы́ смотре́ли, как де́ти _____ на одно́й ноге́. (за)пры́гали
8. Когда́ до́чь пришла́ домо́й по́здно, ма́ма _____. (рас)серди́лась
9. Мы́ споко́йно гуля́ли в па́рке, когда́ вдру́г _____ кри́к. (у)слы́шали
10. Когда́ мы́ сиде́ли на скаме́йке, мы́ _____, ка́к пти́цы пе́ли. (у)слы́шали

30. Choose the appropriate aspectual form of the verbs in the past tense. Determine whether the context expresses a *repeated action* or a *one-time completed action*.

1. О́н вчера́ _____ по́здно, в де́сять часо́в. вставáл/встáл
   Ле́том о́н всегда́ _____ ра́но, в се́мь часо́в.
2. Вчера́ ма́ма _____ сы́ну дли́нное письмо́. писáла/написáла
   Ка́ждую неде́лю ма́ма _____ сы́ну пи́сьма.
3. Сего́дня мы́ _____ письмо́ от на́ших друзе́й. получáли/получи́ли
   Ра́ньше мы́ _____ пи́сьма от ни́х ра́з в ме́сяц.
4. Она́ _____ рабо́ту в 3 часа́ и пошла́ домо́й. кончáла/кóнчила
   Ка́ждый де́нь она́ _____ рабо́ту в 3 часа́.
5. Вчера́ ма́ма _____ о́чень вку́сный пиро́г. пеклá/испеклá
   По воскресе́ньям ма́ма ча́сто _____ пироги́.

31. Complete the sentence with the correct aspectual form in the future tense. Determine whether the action will be *in progress*, will be *repeated*, or will be a *one-time completed action*.

1. На ка́ждом уро́ке я́ _____ ва́м грамма́тику. бýду объяснять/
   Я́ сейча́с _____ ва́м ва́жное пра́вило. объясню́
2. Сего́дня я́ _____ твою́ статью́ и отда́м её тебе́. бýду читáть/
   Когда́ я́ бу́ду в Испа́нии, я́ _____ испа́нские газе́ты. прочитáю
3. О́н сказа́л, что _____ на́м ча́сто. бýдет писáть/
   О́н сказа́л, что _____ письмо́ и сра́зу пошлёт. напи́шет
4. Она́ обеща́ла, что _____ и ска́жет на́м сво́й отве́т. бýдет звони́ть/
   Она́ обеща́ла, что _____ на́м ка́ждую неде́лю. позвони́т
5. Сего́дня на уро́ке мы́ _____ все́ упражне́ния. бýдем дéлать/
   Я́ не зна́ю, что́ мы́ _____ сего́дня на уро́ке. сдéлаем

32. Supply the correct aspectual form of the verbs in the past tense. Determine whether the result of the action is *still in force* or has been *annulled*.

1. (*a*) Мы́ _____ на верши́ну горы́. Бо́льше мы́ никогда́ не поднимáться
     вернёмся в те́ живопи́сные места́. подняться
   (*b*) Мы́ _____ на верши́ну горы́. Тепе́рь мы́ мо́жем
     отдохну́ть в ла́гере альпини́стов.

2. (*a*) Я _____ тебé твóй компáкт-дѝск, вóт óн.   *приносúть*
   (*b*) Вчерá я _____ тебé твóй компáкт-дѝск, но тебя́   *принестú*
        нé было дóма.
3. (*a*) — Сáша, ты́ вчерá _____ телевѝзор?   *включáть*
        — Дá, _____. А что́?   *включúть*
        — Óн сегóдня почемý-то не рабóтает.
   (*b*) — Гдé пáпа?
        — Óн _____ телевѝзор и смóтрит какóй-то фѝльм.
4. (*a*) — Гдé магнитофóн?   *отдавáть*
        — Не знáю. Я́ егó _____ в ремóнт, нó вчерá я его́ принёс   *отдáть*
        и óн дóлжен бы́ть гдé-то дóма.
   (*b*) — Гдé магнитофóн?
        — Я́ его́ _____ в ремóнт. Егó нéт дóма.
5. (*a*) — Я́ _____ нóвую рубáшку и пошёл на тáнцы.   *надевáть*
   (*b*) — Почемý ты́ не нóсишь свою́ нóвую рубáшку?   *надéть*
        — Я́ её вчерá _____.

33. Complete the sentence with the correct aspectual form of the verbs in the past tense. Determine which sentences focus on how long the *action was in progress*, and which sentences are concerned with the time needed to *accomplish the action*.

1. Мы́ _____ на мóре двé недéли. За э́то врéмя   *отдыхáть/*
   мы́ хорошó _____.   *отдохнýть*
2. Áвтор нéсколько мéсяцев _____ материáл для кнѝги.   *собирáть/*
   За э́ти мéсяцы он _____ отлѝчный материáл.   *собрáть*
3. Óн óчень дóлго _____ э́тот тéкст, но его́ сестрá   *переводúть/*
   _____ такóй же тéкст бы́стро.   *перевестú*
4. Аспирáнт _____ диссертáцию цéлые двá гóда.   *писáть/*
   Нó за э́то врéмя óн _____ тóлько половѝну.   *написáть*
5. — За скóлько врéмени ты́ _____ э́ту задáчу?   *решáть/*
   — Я́ её _____ всегó за нéсколько минýт.   *решúть*

34. Indicate whether the sentences below express actions that are *simultaneous*, *sequential*, or "*interrupted*."

1. Когдá мáма *мы́ла* посýду, пáпа *отдыхáл* в своём любѝмом крéсле.
2. Мы́ *ýжинали*, когдá *позвонѝл* телефóн.
3. Мы́ бы́стро *поужѝнали* и *пошлѝ* на концéрт.
4. Когдá мы *отдыхáли* на мóре, сы́н *заболéл*.
5. Когдá худóжник *рисовáл* мóй портрéт, я́ *сидéла* совершéнно неподвѝжно.
6. Когдá худóжник *нарисовáл* мóй портрéт, óн *дáл* его́ мнé.
7. Когдá Лéна *сдавáла* экзáмен, онá *нéрвничала*.
8. Когдá Лéна *сдалá* экзáмен, онá *пошлá* с подрýгами в кафé.

35. Complete the sentence with the appropriate aspectual form of the verbs. Determine from the context whether the questioner is asking merely if an *action ever took place*, or if the question implies an expectation that an *intended action was done*.

1. (*a*) — Ты́ _____ нóвый ромáн Аксёнова?   *читáл/прочитáл*
        Я́ знáю, что ты́ давнó хотéл э́то сдéлать.
        — Дá, _____. Ромáн о "нóвых рýсских".

      (*b*)   — Тебя интересует русская литература. Ты _____
             Василия Аксёнова?

             — Да, _____. По-моему, он хороший писатель.

2. (*a*)   — Таня, ты _____ новые джинсы?   *покупала/купила*
             Ты ведь собиралась это сделать.

             — Да, _____. Я их уже надевала.

      (*b*)   — Таня, ты когда-нибудь _____ духи «Эсте»?

             — Нет, не _____. Они слишком дорого стоят.

3. (*a*)   — Маша _____ тебе фотографии своей свадьбы?   *показывала/*
             — Да, _____. Очень хорошие фотографии.   *показала*

      (*b*)   — Маша уже _____ фотографии своей свадьбы?
             Она ведь хотела, чтобы ты их посмотрела.

36. Supply the appropriate aspect of the italicized verbs in the past tense. In one context the speaker indicates that he had *no intention* to perform the action, while in the other context the speaker has *failed to carry out an intended action*.

    1.   — Кто *сказал*, что завтра не будет экзамена?

        — Не знаю, я не _____.

    2.   — Ты *поздравил* Мишу с днём рождения?

        — Нет, ещё не _____.

    3.   — Это ты *открыл* окно?

        — Нет, я не _____.

    4.   — Кто *включил* телевизор?

        — Не знаю, я не _____.

    5.   — Что ты с ним *сделал*? Почему он плачет?

        — Я ничего ему не _____!

Aspect in the Infinitive

    The uses of the imperfective and perfective aspects in the infinitive fall within the same parameters as those in the past and future tenses.

    The imperfective infinitive may indicate a *continuous process* or *repeated action*:

Continuous Process:

Вечером я должен *писать* **письма друзьям.**   *This evening I have to write letters to friends.*

Repeated Action:

Моя подруга просила меня *писать* **ей чаще.**   *My girlfriend asked me to write her more often.*

    The perfective infinitive indicates a *result* to be achieved.

Я должен *написать* **письмо другу**   *I have to write a letter to a*
и сразу послать его.   *friend and send it right away.*

    In general, after modal words (**хотеть** *to want*, **мочь** *to be able*, **надо/нужно** *it is necessary, one must*, **должен** *one should, one is supposed to*) the choice of imperfective or perfective infinitive depends on the meaning of the verb, and what the speaker intends to communicate. If the action is *specific and occurs on one occasion only*, then the *perfective* infinitive is used, while actions that are *recurring* will be expressed by an *imperfective* infinitive.

Мне́ ну́жно *приня́ть* **аспири́н.**	*I need to take a dose of aspirin.*
Мне́ ну́жно *принима́ть* **аспири́н.**	*I need to take aspirin (regularly).*

Verbs Followed Only by Imperfective Infinitives

The following verbs, in either aspect, require that an accompanying infinitive be *imperfective*. Several of these verbs express the beginning, continuation, or the end of an action; others refer to habitual processes, or desirable/undesirable activities.

начина́ть/нача́ть	*to begin*
ста́ть	*to begin*
конча́ть/ко́нчить	*to finish*
перестава́ть/переста́ть	*to cease*
броса́ть/бро́сить	*to quit*
продолжа́ть/продо́лжить	*to continue*
устава́ть/уста́ть	*to grow tired*
надоеда́ть/надое́сть	*to be fed up with*
привыка́ть/привы́кнуть	*to become accustomed*
отвыка́ть/отвы́кнуть	*to get out of the habit*
учи́ться/научи́ться	*to learn how*
разучи́ться	*to forget how*
нра́виться/понра́виться	*to like*

О́н *на́чал вставáть* **ра́но.**	*He has started getting up early.*
Она́ *ко́нчила печа́тать* **докла́д.**	*She has finished typing the report.*
О́н *наконе́ц бро́сил курйть.*	*He finally quit smoking.*
Она́ *переста́ла рабо́тать.*	*She has stopped working.*
Я́ *уста́л говори́ть* **об э́том.**	*I'm tired of talking about this.*
Ему́ *надое́ло реша́ть* **зада́чи.**	*He's fed up with solving problems.*
Е́й *нра́вится игра́ть* **в те́ннис.**	*She likes to play tennis.*
О́н *у́чится води́ть* **маши́ну.**	*He is learning to drive a car.*

Verbs Followed Only by Perfective Infinitives

The following *perfective* verbs are followed only by *perfective infinitives*.

забы́ть	*to forget*
успе́ть	*to manage, have time*
уда́ться	*to manage, succeed*

Я́ *забы́л купи́ть* **пода́рок Са́ше.**	*I forgot to buy a present for Sasha.*
Ты́ *успе́ешь посмотре́ть* **Эрмита́ж?**	*Will you manage to see the Hermitage?*
О́н *не успе́л позáвтракать.*	*He didn't have time to eat breakfast.*
Мне́ *не удало́сь купи́ть* **биле́ты на концéрт, всé биле́ты бы́ли про́даны.**	*I was unable to buy tickets for the concert, all the tickets were sold.*

37. Circle the imperfective or perfective infinitive, as required.

1. Сего́дня профе́ссор на́чал (объясня́ть/объясни́ть) ви́ды глаго́ла.
2. Когда́ де́ти ко́нчили (обе́дать/пообе́дать), ма́ма убрала́ со стола́.
3. Я́ у́тром та́к торопи́лся, что не успе́л (за́втракать/поза́втракать).
4. Ма́ма, извини́, я́ была́ та́к занята́, что забы́ла тебе́ (звони́ть/позвони́ть).
5. О́н ко́нчил университе́т, но продолжа́л (изуча́ть/изучи́ть) ру́сский язы́к.
6. Мы́ ра́ды, что на́м удало́сь (посеща́ть/посети́ть) э́тот интере́сный го́род.
7. Ви́ка переста́ла (встреча́ться/встре́титься) с э́тим па́рнем.
8. Роди́тели уста́ли (отвеча́ть/отве́тить) на бесконе́чные вопро́сы ребёнка.
9. У кого́ ты́ та́к хорошо́ научи́лся (игра́ть/сыгра́ть) в ша́хматы?
10. Мне́ надое́ло (реша́ть/реши́ть) э́ти тру́дные зада́чи.
11. Когда́ она́ жила́ в дере́вне, она́ привы́кла (встава́ть/вста́ть) ра́но.
12. Врачи́ ему́ сове́товали бро́сить (пи́ть/вы́пить).

Negation and Imperfective Infinitives

There is a strong correlation between negation and the imperfective aspect. This was evident in the use of the negated imperfective past tense to signal the speaker's denial of involvement in an action and/or his lack of intention to carry it out. Negation is also tied to the use of the imperfective aspect in the infinitive.

Не + Imperfective Infinitives

A *negated infinitive* normally occurs in the *imperfective* aspect after verbs which express exhortation or intention to perform an action, for example, after the following verbs:

обеща́ть/пообеща́ть	to promise
проси́ть/попроси́ть	to ask (request)
реша́ть/реши́ть	to decide
сове́товать/посове́товать	to advise
угова́ривать/уговори́ть	to persuade

Compare the aspect of the infinitives when preceded and when not preceded by the negative particle **не**.

О́н посове́товал мне́ *купи́ть* **слова́рь.**
He advised me to buy a dictionary.

Он посове́товал мне́ *не покупа́ть* **слова́рь.**
He advised me not to buy a dictionary.

Она́ уговори́ла его́ *наде́ть* **ку́ртку.**
She persuaded him to put on a jacket.

Она́ уговори́ла его́ *не надева́ть* **ку́ртку.**
She persuaded him not to put on a jacket.

38. Complete the answers to the questions, changing the aspect of the verb, as in the model.

Model: — Ма́ма *пригото́вила* обе́д?
— Не́т, она́ реши́ла *не гото́вить* обе́д.

1. — Серге́й *рассказа́л* об э́том? — Не́т, о́н реши́л не _____.
2. — Ната́ша *позвони́ла* свое́й ма́тери? — Не́т, она́ реши́ла не _____.
3. — Она́ *встре́тилась* с э́тим па́рнем? — Не́т, она́ обеща́ла не _____.
4. — О́н *посмотре́л* э́тот фильм? — Не́т, мы́ посове́товали ему́ не _____.
5. — О́н *поста́вил* маши́ну на у́лице? — Не́т, я уговори́л его́ не _____.
6. — Йра *сказа́ла* ему́ что случи́лось? — Не́т, мы́ проси́ли её не _____.

Absence of Necessity (Не На́до) + Imperfective Infinitives

Only *imperfective* infinitives occur after modal expressions that denote lack of necessity, or inadvisability, such as, for example, **не на́до/не ну́жно** *it is not necessary*, **не обяза́тельно** *one doesn't have to*, **не сто́ит** *it is not worth/it doesn't make sense*.

Compare the aspect of the infinitives in the sentences that express the necessity or advisability of doing something, with those that express the *absence of necessity* to carry out those actions.

Ва́м *на́до отве́тить* **на письмо́.**	*You have to answer the letter.*
Ва́м *не на́до отвеча́ть* **на письмо́.**	*You do not have to answer the letter.*
На́м *ну́жно купи́ть* **э́ту кни́гу.**	*We need to buy this book.*
На́м *не ну́жно покупа́ть* **э́ту кни́гу.**	*We don't need to buy this book.*
Э́тот фи́льм *сто́ит посмотре́ть.*	*This movie is worth seeing.*
Э́тот фи́льм *не сто́ит смотре́ть.*	*This movie is not worth seeing.*

39. Complete the sentence in the dialog with the infinitive in the required aspect.

1. — Ну́жно *объясни́ть* ему́, ка́к прие́хать к на́м.
    — Не ну́жно _____, я ему́ уже́ объясни́л.
2. — На́до *узна́ть* а́дрес э́того магази́на.
    — Не на́до _____, я уже́ узна́л.
3. — На́до *взя́ть* э́ту кни́гу в библиоте́ку.
    — Не на́до _____, я уже́ взя́л.
4. — Ну́жно *вы́звать* эле́ктрика.
    — Не ну́жно _____, я уже́ вы́звал.
5. — На́до *заказа́ть* биле́ты на конце́рт.
    — Не сто́ит _____. Я зна́ю, биле́ты уже́ распро́даны.
6. — На́до *спроси́ть* Бори́са, о чём э́та статья́?
    — Не сто́ит его́ _____. О́н са́м не чита́л.

Нельзя́ and Aspect in the Infinitive

The modal word **нельзя́** has two potential meanings: *it is not possible*, and *it is not allowed/one should not*. When **нельзя́** is followed by a *perfective* infinitive, it expresses *impossibility* of performing the action. However, when **нельзя́** is followed by an *imperfective* infinitive, it expresses *prohibition* (*it is not allowed*).

Э́ту ба́нку ко́фе *нельзя́ откры́ть:* **у на́с не́т открыва́лки.**	*This can of coffee can not be opened: we don't have an opener.*
Э́ту ба́нку ко́фе *нельзя́ открыва́ть:* **э́то пода́рок дру́гу.**	*This can of coffee is not to be opened: it is a gift for a friend.*

The modal word **мо́жно**, like **нельзя́**, has two possible interpretations relating to *possibility* and *permission*, namely, *one can* and *one may* (in questions *can I?*, *may I?*). Compare the two answers to the following question:

	— **Мо́жно** *включи́ть* **телеви́зор?**	*Can I turn on the television?*
(*a*)	— **Не́т, его́ нельзя́** *включи́ть.*	*No, it won't turn on.*
	О́н не рабо́тает.	*It is not working.*
(*b*)	— **Не́т, его́ нельзя́** *включа́ть.*	*No, you may not turn on the TV.*
	Тебе́ на́до занима́ться.	*You have to study.*

40. Complete the sentence with the infinitive in the correct aspect. Determine from the context whether the action is *not possible* or *not allowed/not advisable*.

1. Реце́пт врача́ нельзя́ (чита́ть/прочита́ть), о́н напи́сан неразбо́рчиво.
2. Э́то письмо́ нельзя́ (чита́ть/прочита́ть), оно́ не тебе́.
3. В аудито́риях нельзя́ (е́сть/съе́сть), э́то пра́вило университе́та.
4. Его́ нельзя́ (буди́ть/разбуди́ть), о́н та́к кре́пко спи́т.
5. Его́ нельзя́ (буди́ть/разбуди́ть), о́н бо́лен и до́лжен спа́ть.
6. Э́ту кни́гу нельзя́ (бра́ть/взя́ть), о́н её ещё чита́ет.
7. У пожа́рного кра́на нельзя́ (оставля́ть/оста́вить) маши́ну, та́м штрафу́ют.
8. На ле́кции нельзя́ (опа́здывать/опозда́ть), на́до приходи́ть во́время.
9. В общежи́тии нельзя́ (отдыха́ть/отдохну́ть), та́м о́чень шу́мно.
10. О́н говори́т с таки́м си́льным акце́нтом, что его́ нельзя́ (понима́ть/поня́ть).
11. Отсю́да нельзя́ (звони́ть/позвони́ть), зде́сь не́т телефо́на.
12. Де́тям до 14 ле́т нельзя́ (смотре́ть/посмотре́ть) э́тот фи́льм.
13. В э́том о́зере нельзя́ (лови́ть/пойма́ть) ры́бу, не разреша́ется.
14. Нельзя́ (продава́ть/прода́ть) спи́рт по воскресе́ньям, э́то зако́н шта́та.
15. Нельзя́ как сле́дует (учи́ть/вы́учить) иностра́нный язы́к, не побыва́в в стране́ языка́.

IMPERATIVES

The imperative is used to give commands or make requests. There are three types of imperative in Russian: a second-person imperative (*Cut* the cake, *Sit* next to me), a first-person imperative (*Let's buy* wine, *Let's write* to him), and a third-person imperative (*Let* Sasha buy the wine, *Let* Katya make dinner). Of the three types, the most commonly used is the second-person imperative.

Second-Person Imperative: Formation

The second-person imperative is formed easily from the verb's basic stem. There are two possibilities, depending on where the stress falls in conjugation: (1) if the first-person singular of the verb is stressed, then the stressed ending **-й (те)** is added to the basic stem (**те** is added to the ending for the formal and/or plural *you*); (2) if the stress falls only on the stem of a verb, then no vowel is added, and the final vowel of the basic stem, if there is one, drops.

Examples of Imperative Formation

I. Stress on first-person singular **-у́/-ю́**: imperative in stressed **-й**

INFINITIVE		BASIC STEM	1st SG.	IMPERATIVE
говори́ть	*to speak*	говори-	**говорю́**	**говори́(те)**
учи́ться	*to study*	учи-ся	**учу́сь**	**учи́сь/учи́тесь**
плати́ть	*to pay*	плати-	**плачу́**	**плати́(те)**

купи́ть	to buy	купи-	куплю́	купи́(те)
писа́ть	to write	писа-	пишу́	пиши́(те)
сказа́ть	to tell	сказа-	скажу́	скажи́(те)
жда́ть	to wait	жда-	жду́	жди́(те)
лежа́ть	to lie	лежа-	лежу́	лежи́(те)
сиде́ть	to sit	сиде-	сижу́	сиди́(те)
нести́	to carry	нес-	несу́	неси́(те)

The rules which apply when combining stems and endings in conjugation (i.e., addition and truncation) also apply in the formation of the imperative. Therefore, when the imperative vowel ending **-й** is added to a nonsuffixed consonant stem, it is a matter of simple addition (нес- + й → неси́). When the vowel **-й** is added to a basic stem ending in **-и**, **-а**, or **-е**, the first of these two "likes" is truncated (e.g., говори- + й → говори́, жда- + й → жди́, сиде- + й → сиди́). Also, if a verb undergoes a consonant alternation *throughout* the non-past, as do verbs with a stem in **-а**, then the same alternation occurs in the imperative (писа́-: пишу́, пи́шешь/пиши́ and сказа-: скажу́, ска́жешь/скажи́). However, a verb that undergoes a consonant alternation in the *first-person singular only*, will *not* have that alternation in the imperative (купи́, плати́, сиди́).

II.　Stress on the stem

Stem-stressed verbs can be divided into two main subgroups:

(*a*) Verbs with stem-final **-й**: no ending is added, the imperative is identical to the shape of the basic stem. Verbs with a stem in **-а-вай**, though end-stressed in the non-past, also belong in this group, e.g., да-ва́й-: даю́, даёшь, даю́т/дава́й(те).

INFINITIVE		BASIC STEM	IMPERATIVE
чита́ть	to read	читай-	чита́й(те)
занима́ться	to study	занимай-ся	занима́йся/занима́йтесь
надева́ть	to put on	надевай-	надева́й(те)
расска́зывать	to tell	расска́зывай-	расска́зывай(те)
открыва́ть	to open (I)	открывай-	открыва́й(те)
откры́ть	to open (P)	открой-	откро́й(те)
сове́товать	to advise	сове́това-/уй	сове́туй(те)
дава́ть	to give (I)	да-вай-	дава́й(те)
встава́ть	to get up	вста-вай-	встава́й(те)
узнава́ть	to find out (I)	узна-вай-	узнава́й(те)
узна́ть	to find out (P)	узнай-	узна́й(те)
да́ть	to give (P)	(irreg.)	да́й(те)

(*b*) Other stem-stressed verbs: no ending is added, and if there is a stem-final suffix, it is dropped; the imperative is spelled with **-ь** (even if the preceding consonant is one that is always hard, e.g., **ре́зать** *to cut*: **ре́жь**).

гото́вить	to prepare	готови-	гото́вь(те)
отве́тить	to answer	отве́ти-	отве́ть(те)
вста́ть	to get up (P)	встан-	вста́нь(те)
наде́ть	to put on (P)	наден-	наде́нь(те)

The vowel **-и** is never dropped after a cluster of two consonants.

| ко́нчить | to finish | кончи- | ко́нчи(те) |
| по́мнить | to remember | помни- | по́мни(те) |

Irregular Second-Person Imperatives

The following verbs have imperatives that are irregular:

е́сть	*to eat*	**е́шь(те)**
да́ть	*to give*	**да́й(те)**
(по)е́хать	*to go by vehicle*	**поезжа́й(те)**
ле́чь	*to lie down*	**ля́г(те)**
пе́ть	*to sing*	**по́й(те)**
пи́ть	*to drink*	**пе́й(те)**

Note: There are 5 verbs of the **пи́ть** type, all of which form their imperative the same way, e.g., **би́ть/бе́й(те)** *beat*, **ви́ть/ве́й(те)** *twist*, **ли́ть/ле́й(те)** *pour*, **ши́ть/ше́й(те)** *sew*.

Aspect and the Second-Person Imperative

The choice of aspect in the imperative is generally dictated by the same contexts already enumerated for aspect use in the past and future tenses, as well as the infinitive. Imperatives can be affirmative (*Do …*) or negated (*Do not …*).

Affirmative Imperatives

Use of the Perfective Imperative

The primary use of the perfective aspect in affirmative commands is to request that a concrete action be performed on one occasion. A transitive perfective verb must be used with its direct object (stated or implied), which draws attention to a result.

Запиши́те **мо́й телефо́н.**	*Write down my telephone number.*
Ты́ идёшь на по́чту. *Купи́* **мне́ ма́рки.**	*You are going to the post office. Buy me some stamps.*
Закро́йте, **пожа́луйста, окно́.**	*Close the window please.*
Позвони́те **мне́ в се́мь часо́в.**	*Call me at seven o'clock.*

Uses of the Imperfective Imperative

The *imperfective* imperative is used in a wide range of contexts, including:

(*a*)   Requests for a *repeated action* or when giving *general advice*.

Пиши́ **на́м ча́ще.**	*Write to us more often.*
Покупа́йте **о́вощи на э́том ры́нке.**	*Buy vegetables at this market.*
Береги́те **здоро́вье.**	*Look after your health.*

(*b*)   Requests to *modify an action in progress* (used with an adverb of manner).

Говори́те **гро́мче.**	*Speak louder.*
Пиши́ **аккура́тнее.**	*Write more carefully.*

(*c*)   *Prompting* the addressee to *begin an action* that had already been requested (with the perfective imperative), but not yet implemented. By repeating the request with the imperfective partner of the verb, the speaker may convey a sense of *urgency* to perform the action.

— *Расскажи́,* **что́ случи́лось. Что́ же ты́ молчи́шь?** *Расска́зывай!*	*Tell me what happened. Why are you keeping silent? Go ahead, tell me!*
— *Возьми́* **э́ти де́ньги. Они́ тебе́ бу́дут нужны́. Ну, чего́ ты́ ждёшь?** *Бери́!*	*Take this money. You will need it. Well, what are you waiting for? Take it.*

(d) Imperfective imperatives are used to convey *polite invitations* in social situations. For example, a host(ess) will say to guests:

Входи́те.	*Come in.*
Раздева́йтесь, пожа́луйста.	*Please take off your coat.*
Сади́тесь, пожа́луйста.	*Please sit down.*
Бери́те!	*Take one/some.*

Negated Imperatives

Use of the Negated Imperfective

When requesting that an action *not* be performed, normally the *imperfective* imperative is used, even when the action is a specific one-time action. In other words, in these negated imperatives, one uses the imperfective partner of the perfective verbs that would be used in affirmative imperatives.

Закро́йте, пожа́луйста, окно́.	*Please close the window.*
Не закрыва́йте, пожа́луйста, окно́.	*Please don't close the window*
Посмотри́те э́тот фи́льм.	*See this movie.*
Не смотри́те э́тот фи́льм.	*Don't see this movie.*
Спроси́те его́ об э́том.	*Ask him about it.*
Не спра́шивайте его́ об э́том.	*Don't ask him about it.*

Use of the Negated Perfective

The negated perfective is used only when the speaker is expressing a *warning* against an action that might be performed *inadvertently*, and with undesirable results. The sense of warning is sometimes emphasized by the words **смотри́/смотри́те** *See (to it you don't)* or **осторо́жно** *Careful*. The verbs used in the negated perfective usually denote actions that have obvious negative consequences, e.g., **упа́сть** *to fall*, **обже́чься** *to burn oneself*, **простуди́ться** *to catch cold*, **опозда́ть** *to be late*, **потеря́ть** *to lose*, **забы́ть** *to forget*.

Не упади́те, зде́сь ско́льзко.	*Don't fall, it's slippery here.*
Не обожги́сь, вода́ горя́чая.	*Don't burn yourself, the water is hot.*
Смотри́, *не опозда́й.*	*See to it that you are not late.*
Осторо́жно, *не урони́ э́ту ва́зу.*	*Be careful, don't drop that vase.*

41. Answer the question, telling the person "Alright," go ahead with the given action.

Model: — Мо́жно *записа́ть* телефо́н? — Хорошо́, *запиши́те.*

1. — Мо́жно тебя́ *подожда́ть?* — Хорошо́, _____.
2. — Мо́жно *включи́ть* телеви́зор? — Хорошо́, _____.
3. — Мо́жно *нали́ть* вино́? — Хорошо́, _____.
4. — Мо́жно *наре́зать* хле́б? — Хорошо́, _____.
5. — Мо́жно *спе́ть* ва́м пе́сню? — Хорошо́, _____.
6. — Мо́жно *наде́ть* га́лстук? — Хорошо́, _____.
7. — Мо́жно *откры́ть* окно́? — Хорошо́, _____.
8. — Мо́жно *заплати́ть* за э́то? — Хорошо́, _____.
9. — Мо́жно *вы́пить* ча́шку ча́я? — Хорошо́, _____.
10. — Мо́жно *танцева́ть?* — Хорошо́, _____.
11. — Мо́жно *отве́тить* на его́ письмо́? Хорошо́, _____.
12. — Мо́жно *пригото́вить* обе́д? Хорошо́, _____.

42. Complete the sentence with the required imperative of the indicated verbs.

писа́ть/написа́ть
1. — _____ а́дрес. Ну, _____ аккура́тнее, а то бу́дет неразбо́рчив.

говори́ть/сказа́ть
2. — _____, ка́к та́м пого́да? Что́? Что́? _____ гро́мче, ва́с пло́хо слы́шно.

расска́зывать/рассказа́ть
3. — _____ о пое́здке. Пожа́луйста, _____ подро́бнее. На́м ведь всё о́чень интере́сно.

чита́ть/прочита́ть
4. — _____ те́кст вслу́х. Ну, _____ ме́дленее, что́бы всем бы́ло поня́тно.

43. Disagree with the affirmative request made with the perfective imperative. Using the imperfective imperative, request that the action not be performed (it isn't necessary).

Model: — *Подожди́те* его́.   — Не́т, *не жди́те*. Не на́до.

1. — *Включи́те* телеви́зор.   — Не́т, _____ .
2. — *Покажи́те* ему́ ва́шу рабо́ту.   — Не́т, _____ .
3. — *Переведи́те* э́тот те́кст.   — Не́т, _____ .
4. — *Расскажи́те* ей о командиро́вке.   — Не́т, _____ .
5. — *Да́йте* ему́ сове́т.   — Не́т, _____ .
6. — *Узна́й* об э́том.   — Не́т, _____ .
7. — *Закро́йте* окно́.   — Не́т, _____ .
8. — *Съе́шь* ещё оди́н пирожо́к.   — Не́т, _____ .

44. Object to someone's request to perform an action. Using the negated imperfective, indicate that there is no need for the action, since it has already been done.

Model: — Мы́ хоти́м *заплати́ть* за обе́д.   — *Не плати́*те, я́ уже́ заплати́л.

1. — Я́ хочу́ *позвони́ть* Ми́ше.   — _____, я́ ему́ уже́ позвони́л.
2. — Мы́ хоти́м *помо́чь* сосе́дке.   — _____, я́ ей уже́ помо́г.
3. — Я́ хочу́ *сказа́ть* ей об э́том.   — _____ ей. Ей уже́ сказа́ли.
4. — Мы́ хоти́м *купи́ть* ребёнку шокола́д. — _____, я́ уже́ купи́ла.
5. — Я́ хочу́ *пригото́вить* за́втрак.   — _____, И́ра уже́ пригото́вила.

45. Express a *warning* against performing the indicated action.

1. По́езд отхо́дит ро́вно в се́мь утра́. Не _____ .   (*опа́здывай/опозда́й*)
2. Сего́дня бу́дет до́ждь. Не _____ зо́нтик.   (*забыва́й/забу́дь*)
3. В де́тской спи́т ребёнок. Смотри́, не _____ .   (*буди́/разбуди́*)
4. Осторо́жно, не _____ э́ту ва́зу, она́ о́чень дорога́я.   (*роня́й/урони́*)
5. Не _____ со́к, пя́тна от э́того со́ка не смыва́ются.   (*пролива́й/проле́й*)
6. Не _____ по оши́бке мою́ су́мку.   (*бери́те/возьми́те*)

First-Person Imperative

The first-person imperative is used to suggest an action which will be performed together with the speaker, e.g., *Let's go, Let's play*. This imperative is formed in one of two ways, depending on the nature of the action:

(1) **Давáй/Давáйте + IMPERFECTIVE INFINITIVE**

This form of the imperative is used when the action to be performed will be continuous or repeated. The form **давáй** is used when addressing one person informally, while **давáйте** is the formal and/or plural form of address.

<blockquote>

Давáй говорúть **на ты.**   Let's speak using the informal "you."
Давáйте читáть **тóлько по-рýсски.**   Let's read only in Russian.

</blockquote>

Давáй(те) + imperfective infinitive is also used to make a negative suggestion (*Let's not . . .*). In negative suggestions, however, the first-person plural form **бýдем** must precede the infinitive, creating the imperfective future tense.

<blockquote>

Давáй не бýдем спóрить **об э́том.**   Let's not argue about this.
Давáй не бýдем смотрéть **телевúзор.**   Let's not watch television.

</blockquote>

To make an alternative suggestion to do something *instead*, the word **лýчше** is used between **давáй(те)** and the verb.

<blockquote>

Давáй не бýдем рабóтать. *Давáй*   Let's not work. Let's listen to the
лýчше слýшать **нóвый компáкт-дúск.**   new CD instead.

</blockquote>

(2) **Давáй(те) + PERFECTIVE FIRST-PERSON PLURAL**

This form of the imperative is used when the speaker is suggesting a specific, one-time action. The perfective **мы-** form of the verb is used *without* the pronoun subject.

<blockquote>

Давáй напúшем **письмó.**   Let's write a letter.
Давáй позвонúм **родúтелям.**   Let's make a call to our parents.
Давáй встрéтимся **в двá часá.**   Let's meet at two o'clock.

</blockquote>

46. The speaker wishes to perform an action, and he invites others to join him.

> Model: Я́ хочý *купúть* морóженое. *Давáй кýпим* морóженое.
>   Я́ хочý *смотрéть* телевúзор. *Давáй смотрéть* телевúзор.

1. Я́ хочý *вы́пить* за Сáшу.
2. Я́ хочý *отдохнýть.*
3. Я́ хочý *взя́ть* таксú.
4. Я́ хочý *заказáть* ры́бу.
5. Я́ хочý *подождáть* брáта.
6. Я́ хочý *потанцевáть.*
7. Я́ хочý *рабóтать* ýтром.
8. Я́ хочý *погуля́ть* в пáрке.
9. Я́ хочý *сидéть* и *говорúть.*
10. Я́ хочý *игрáть* в тéннис.
11. Я́ хочý *поéхать* в Москвý.
12. Я́ хочý *съéсть* кусóк пирогá.

47. Reject the speaker's invitation to join him in some activity. Be contrary, suggest that you and the speaker *not* perform the suggested action.

> Model: — *Давáй подýмаем* об э́том. Нéт, *давáй не бýдем дýмать* об э́том.

1. — *Давáй уберём* кóмнату.   — Нéт, _____.
2. — *Давáй испечём* тóрт.   — Нéт, _____.
3. — *Давáй вы́трем* посýду.   — Нéт, _____.
4. — *Давáй пообéдаем.*   — Нéт, _____.

Third-Person Imperative

The third-person imperative conveys a command or request to be given to a third person or persons (*Let Petya* buy wine/*Have them* call Misha). This imperative is formed with the word **пусть** *let/allow* (or the more colloquial **пускай**). The person who is to perform the action is the grammatical subject in the *nominative* case, and the verb is perfective or imperfective, depending on the nature of the action (e.g., *single specific* action or *continuous*).

Пусть **Лéна испечёт тóрт.**	*Let Lena bake a cake.*
Пусть **Мúша уберёт кóмнату.**	*Have Misha clean up his room.*
Пусть **дéти игрáют.**	*Let the children play.*

48. Refuse to participate in the action suggested by the speaker. You suggest that someone else perform the action.

   Model: — Давáй напúшем Вúте письмó.   — Нéт, *пусть Серёжа напúшет.*

   1. — Давáй помóем посýду.   — Нéт, _____.
   2. — Давáй заплáтим за обéд.   — Нéт, _____.
   3. — Давáй ся́дем ря́дом с мáмой.   — Нет, _____.
   4. — Давáй открóем бытьíлку винá.   — Нéт, _____.
   5. — Давáй споём пéсню.   — Нéт, _____.

THE CONDITIONAL

Real and Unreal Conditionals

There are two types of conditional statements: (1) *real* conditionals, i.e., those that present the action as likely to occur, and (2) *unreal* conditionals, i.e., those that present the action either as unlikely to occur (*hypothetical*), or as having failed to occur (*contrary-to-fact*).

Real Conditional

   Éсли **óн позвонúт, (тó) я́ тебé скажý.**
   If he calls (will call), (then) I will tell you.

Unreal Conditional

   Éсли бы **óн позвонúл, (тó) я́ бы тебé сказáл.**
   If he were to call, (then) I would tell you. (Hypothetical)
   If he had called, (then) I would have told you. (Contrary to Fact)

The first sentence (the real conditional) presents the situation as likely to occur and is expressed in the *indicative mood*, i.e., it presents the condition as an objective fact. Thus, it is a fact that the condition, if met, *will have* the indicated consequence. In Russian, as in English, real conditional sentences consist of two clauses: a subordinate clause (containing the condition) usually introduced by the conjunction **éсли** *if*, and the main clause (containing the consequence) which may be introduced by the conjunction **тó** (or **тогдá**) *then*. This word, as in English, is often omitted.

   Éсли ..., (тó) ...   *If ..., (then) ...*

Real conditionals in Russian differ from those in English in one important respect: when the verb in the *If*-clause refers to a *future* action, Russian grammar requires the verb to be in the future tense (the above example has **позвони́т** (pfv) *will call*), whereas English uses the present tense (*If he calls*).

The second sentence above (the unreal conditional) describes the situation as doubtful (or impossible) and is expressed in the *conditional mood*. Unreal conditions in Russian consist of a condition clause and a consequence clause, each of which must contain the unstressed particle **бы** + *past tense form* of the verb:

Condition clause: **Éсли бы** + past-tense form of the verb
Consequence clause: (**то́**) + past-tense form of verb + **бы**

In an unreal conditional the past tense of the verb is past in *form only*, it is *not* necessarily past in meaning. The tense form in an unreal conditional construction may, depending on context, relate to present, past, or future time. For example, in the following two sentences it is the adverbs **за́втра** *tomorrow* and **вчера́** *yesterday* that relate the time of the situation to the future (*If I were to receive* ...) and the past (*If I had received* ...), respectively.

Éсли **за́втра я** *получи́л бы* **де́ньги, я** *бы купи́л* **пле́йер.**
If I were to receive the money tomorrow, I would buy a CD-player.

Éсли **вчера́ я** *получи́л бы* **де́ньги, я** *бы купи́л* **пле́йер.**
If I had received the money yesterday, I would have bought a CD-player.

49. Combine the two sentences into one complex sentence introduced by a *Éсли*-clause of real condition, as in the model.

Model: За́втра бу́дет хоро́шая пого́да. Мы́ пойдём купа́ться.
    Éсли за́втра бу́дет хоро́шая пого́да, (то́) мы́ пойдём купа́ться.

1. За́втра бу́дет до́ждь. Мы́ обяза́тельно бу́дем сиде́ть до́ма.
2. Ты́ не оде́нешься быстре́е. Мы́ опозда́ем на конце́рт.
3. Ты́ и́м позвони́шь. Они́ бу́дут о́чень ра́ды.
4. Вы́ придёте к на́м. Я́ пригото́влю ва́м вку́сный обе́д.
5. У меня́ бу́дет вре́мя. Я́ тебе́ помогу́.
6. У на́с бу́дут де́ньги. Мы́ ку́пим но́вую маши́ну.

50. Rewrite the sentences, changing the mood from the indicative (it is a fact that the action *did not occur*) to the conditional mood (hypothetical or contrary to fact).

Model: О́н не да́л на́м сво́й а́дрес, и мы́ не написа́ли ему́.
    Éсли бы о́н да́л на́м сво́й а́дрес, (то́) мы́ бы написа́ли ему́.

1. Она́ не пришла́, и я́ не поговори́л с не́й.
2. На́ши друзья́ не позвони́ли, и мы́ не пригласи́ли и́х в го́сти.
3. О́н не захоте́л смотре́ть фи́льм, и мы́ не пошли́ в кино́.
4. Мы́ не пригласи́ли его́, и о́н не пришёл на вечери́нку.
5. Ты́ не проси́л меня́, и я́ не купи́л буты́лку вина́.

51. Rewrite the sentences, changing the real conditions to unreal conditions.

Model: Éсли ты́ прие́дешь в Петербу́рг, я́ покажу́ тебе́ Эрмита́ж.
    Éсли бы ты́ прие́хал в Петербу́рг, я́ бы показа́л тебе́ Эрмита́ж.

1. Éсли фильм кóнчится в дéвять часóв, мы́ встрéтимся с вáми.
2. Éсли óн попрóсит, я́ обязáтельно помогý емý.
3. Éсли мы́ успéем купи́ть билéты, мы́ пойдём смотрéть концéрт.
4. Éсли вы́ скáжете нáм дорóгу, мы́ поéдем тудá.
5. Éсли óн сдéлает всё упражнéния, óн смóжет пойти́ в кинó.
6. Éсли у меня́ бýдет врéмя, я́ позвоню́ вáм.

THE SUBJUNCTIVE

While the conditional mood is used in expressing hypothetical and contrary-to-fact conditional statements, the *subjunctive* mood is used in referring to other situations that are uncertain, tentative, unlikely, hypothetical, or contrary to fact. In particular, the subjunctive is used to express advice, wishes, hopes, desires, requests, and commands that may or may not be (or may not have been) realized. The grammatical means for expressing the subjunctive mood, like the conditional mood, is the unstressed particle **бы** and the *past-tense form* of the verb. The subjunctive mood may also be expressed in certain subordinate clauses introduced by the conjunction **чтóбы** (**чтó + бы**). In the subjunctive, as in the conditional mood, the past-tense form of the verb used with **бы** or **чтóбы** does *not* necessarily signal past-tense *meaning*. The time of the situation expressed by the verb in the subjunctive mood is determined by the context.

The Subjunctive with бы + Past Tense

The following are the most common uses of the subjunctive mood expressed by **бы** and the past-tense form of the verb. Depending on the meaning of the verb and context, this construction may convey mild advice, polite requests, or wishes.

Expressing Polite Advice

The particle **бы** combined with the past-tense form of the verbs **совéтовать** *to advise* and **рекомендовáть** *to recommend* are commonly used to express polite, mild advice.

Я́ *бы* **тебé** *посовéтовал* **позвони́ть éй.**	*I would advise you to call her.*

Я́ *бы* **вáм** *рекомендовáл* **прочитáть**
    э́ту кни́гу.
	I would recommend that you read
	    this book.

The particle **бы** may be combined with verbs of other meanings, which results in nuances ranging from mild advice and recommendations to polite requests. This construction is milder than commands of the second-person imperative, and is more common in informal, colloquial style.

Вáня, *пошёл бы* **ты́ купáться.**	*Vanya, why don't you go for a swim.*
Свéта, *поговори́ла бы* **ты́ с ни́м.**	*Sveta, you ought to talk with him.*
Пáпа, *лёг бы* **ты́ отдохнýть.**	*Dad, why don't you lie down and rest.*
Сóня, *помоглá бы* **ты́ емý.**	*Sonya, why don't you help him!*

Expressing a Wish

The speaker may use the particle **бы** + past tense of the verb **хотéть** *to want* to express a mild wish or desire to perform an action, e.g., **Я́ хотéл бы** ... *I would like to* ... This construction is less categorical than saying **Я́ хочý** ... *I want* ...

Я́ *хотéл бы* **поспáть.**	*I would like to take a nap.*
Онá *хотéла бы* **пойти́ в кинó.**	*She would like to go to a movie.*

The particle **бы** may be combined with other verbs to express a wish. This construction is used in informal, colloquial style.

Э́х, *поспа́л бы* **я́ часо́к!**　　　　　　　*Boy, I wish I could take an hour's nap!*
О́х, *пое́л бы* **я́ сейча́с что́-нибудь!**　　*Boy, I could eat something right now!*
О́х, *вы́пил бы* **я́ сейча́с пи́ва.**　　　　*Boy, I sure could drink some beer!*

The speaker may also use the subjunctive mood to express a wish that someone else do something, or that some situation were different.

То́лько *бы* **о́н** *позвони́л!*　　　　　*If only he would call (had called)!*
Е́сли *бы* **о́н бо́льше** *занима́лся!*　　*If only he would study (had studied) more!*
Пришла́ бы **она́ пора́ньше.**　　　　　*If only she could (have) come a little earlier.*
Бы́ло бы **у меня́ вре́мя!**　　　　　　*If only I had (had) the time!*
Хорошо́ *(бы́ло) бы* **име́ть маши́ну.**　*It would be good to have a car.*

The Subjunctive with Что́бы + Past Tense

The subjunctive mood may also be used in a complex sentence with a subordinate clause introduced by the conjunction **что́бы**. There are two types of sentences that require the subjunctive mood: (1) those in which the predicate of the main clause has the meaning of *desire*, *wish*, *advice*, *command*, or *necessity*, and (2) those in which the **что́бы-** clause expresses the *purpose* of the action expressed by the verb in the main clause.

Wishes, Desires, and Commands Expressed by One Person to Another

The subjunctive mood is used in the Russian translation of English sentences of the type indicated by (*b*), but not those of the type indicated by sentence (*a*).

(*a*)　*I want to see this movie.*

(*b*)　**I** want **her** to see this movie.

In sentence (*a*) there is only one subject, the subject of the verb *want* is also understood to be the subject of the infinitive *to see*, that is, the person expressing the wish is the same person who is to see the movie. In sentences like (*a*) the English infinitive is rendered by an infinitive in Russian: **Я́ хочу́** *посмотре́ть* э́тот фи́льм.

In sentence (*b*), by contrast, there are two subjects: the subject of the verb *want* is different from the subject of the infinitive *to see*. In sentences like (*b*), the so-called "direct object + infinitive" construction of English must be rendered in Russian by the subjunctive with **что́бы** + past-tense form of the verb. In the Russian translation of this construction, the English direct object becomes the *nominative subject* (*her* becomes **она́** *she*).

Я́ хочу́, *что́бы* **она́** *посмотре́ла* э́тот фи́льм.

Following are some common verbs with the meaning of desire, wish, or command that may be used as predicates in the main clause of complex sentences of the type illustrated by sentence (*b*) and its Russian equivalent: **хоте́ть/захоте́ть** *to want*, **проси́ть/попроси́ть** *to ask*, **веле́ть** *to order*, **сказа́ть** *to tell (someone to do something)*, **тре́бовать/потре́бовать** *to demand*.

Жена́ *проси́ла, что́бы* **я́ е́й** *позвони́л.*　　*My wife asked me to call her.*
Ма́ть *сказа́ла, что́бы* **сы́н**　　　　　　　*The mother told her son to*
　　убра́л **ко́мнату.**　　　　　　　　　　　*clean up his room.*
Вра́ч *веле́л, что́бы* **о́н** *лежа́л* **в посте́ли.**　*The doctor ordered him to stay in bed.*
Она́ *тре́бует, что́бы* **о́н** *извини́лся.*　　　*She is demanding that he apologize.*

A few verbs, for example, **проси́ть/попроси́ть**, **сове́товать/посове́товать**, may be followed *either* by an infinitive *or* by **что́бы** + past tense.

Она́ *попроси́ла* **меня́** *позвони́ть* **ей.**   She asked me to call her.
Она́ *попроси́ла*, **что́бы я** *позвони́л* **ей.**   She asked me to call her.

Вра́ч *посове́товал* **ему́ похуде́ть.**   The doctor advised him to lose weight.
Вра́ч *посове́товал*, **что́бы о́н** *похуде́л*.   The doctor advised him to lose weight.

In addition to the verbs listed above, there are also modal words with the meaning of desire or necessity that may serve as the predicate in the main clause of such sentences, e.g., **жела́тельно** *it is desirable*, **ва́жно** *it is important*, **на́до/ну́жно** *it is necessary*.

Жела́тельно, что́бы **вы́** *бы́ли* **на собра́нии.**   It is desirable that you be at the meeting.
Ва́жно, что́бы **о́н** *сда́л* **экза́мен.**   It is important that he pass the exam.
На́до, что́бы **все́** *голосова́ли*.   It is necessary that everyone vote.

Subjunctive in Purpose Clauses

Analogous to the two sentence types expressing desires, wishes, and commands noted above in (*a*) and (*b*), *purpose* clauses introduced by **что́бы** have two possible forms:

1. **что́бы** + *infinitive*, when the subject of the purpose clause is the same as the subject in the main clause:

Са́ша включи́л телеви́зор, *что́бы смотре́ть* **но́вости.**   Sasha turned on the TV (in order) to watch the news.

The conjunction **что́бы** may be omitted, especially when it follows a verb of motion:

Она́ *пошла́* **на по́чту** *купи́ть* **ма́рки.**   She went to the post office to buy stamps.

2. **что́бы** + *past tense* (the subjunctive mood), when the two clauses have different subjects:

Са́ша включи́л телеви́зор, *что́бы* **па́па** *смотре́л* **но́вости.**   Sasha turned on the TV so that his dad could watch the news.

Ле́на оста́вила запи́ску, *что́бы* **мы́** *зна́ли*, **куда́ она́** *пошла́*.   Lena left a note so that we might know where she went.

52. Rewrite the sentence, adding the particle **бы** and putting the italicized verb in the form of the past tense, as in the model. The wish or advice you've expressed is now less categorical and more polite.

Model: Я́ *сове́тую* ва́м посети́ть Ру́сский музе́й.
        Я́ *бы посове́товал* ва́м посети́ть Ру́сский музе́й.

1. Я́ *хочу́* чита́ть но́вый рома́н Аксёнова.
2. Я́ *рекоменду́ю* ва́м сходи́ть на э́ту вы́ставку.
3. Я́ *сове́тую* ва́м поговори́ть с нача́льником.
4. Что́ вы́ *хоти́те* посмотре́ть по телеви́зору?
5. Како́й слова́рь ты́ *сове́туешь* мне́ купи́ть?

53. Rewrite the sentence, removing the verb **хочу́** and adding the particle **бы** and the past-tense form of the italicized verb, as in the model. The wish you've expressed is now less categorical and more conversational in style.

Model: Я́ хочу́ *поигра́ть* в те́ннис.　　　　　　　Я́ *бы поигра́л* в те́ннис.

1. Я́ хочу́ *вы́пить* стака́н холо́дного пи́ва.
2. Я́ хочу́ *поспа́ть* немно́го.
3. Я́ хочу́ *послу́шать* хоро́шую рок-му́зыку.
4. Я́ хочу́ *пое́сть* сала́т "Столи́чный".
5. Я́ хочу́ *пое́хать* на мо́ре.

54. Rewrite the sentences, replacing the imperative with a more mild, polite form of request. Follow the model.

Model: *Покажи́* ему́ свои́ карти́ны.　　　　　*Показа́л бы* ты́ ему́ свои́ карти́ны.

1. *Помоги́* е́й реши́ть зада́чу.
2. *Посмотри́* э́тот но́вый францу́зский фи́льм.
3. *Убери́* свою́ ко́мнату.
4. *Послу́шай* мо́й но́вый ди́ск.
5. *Поговори́* с ни́м об э́том.

55. Rewrite the sentences, changing the infinitive to the subjunctive construction with **что́бы** + past tense of the verb. Follow the model.

Model: Студе́нт попроси́л преподава́теля *объясни́ть* ему́ зада́чу.
　　　　　Студе́нт попроси́л преподава́теля, *что́бы* о́н *объясни́л* ему́ зада́чу.

1. Я́ посове́товал дру́гу *бро́сить* кури́ть.
2. Ми́ша попроси́л меня́ *купи́ть* ему́ газе́ту.
3. Мы́ угова́ривали дру́га *пое́хать* отдыха́ть на мо́ре.
4. Я́ попрошу́ бра́та *помо́чь* мне́.
5. Учи́тель посове́товал ученика́м *слу́шать* внима́тельнее.

56. Complete the purpose clauses, putting the verb in parentheses into the correct form, i.e., either the unchanged infinitive or the past-tense form of the verb.

1. Я́ взя́л слова́рь, что́бы _____ (перевести́) поэ́му.
2. Я́ взя́л слова́рь, что́бы Бори́с _____ (перевести́) те́кст.
3. Она́ принесла́ фотогра́фии, что́бы мы́ _____ (посмотре́ть) и́х.
4. Я́ принёс докла́д, что́бы _____ (показа́ть) его́ нача́льнику.
5. О́н вста́л, что́бы _____ (поздоро́ваться) с друзья́ми.
6. О́н вста́л, что́бы же́нщина _____ (мо́чь) се́сть.

57. Translate into Russian, using the subjunctive mood.

1. It would be good to vacation in Europe.　_____
2. It is important that you finish the report.　_____
3. It is necessary that he answer the letter.　_____
4. If only he would find work.　_____
5. If only I had more time.　_____

TRANSITIVE AND INTRANSITIVE VERBS

Verbs in Russian, as in English, are either transitive or intransitive. Transitive verbs in Russian may take a direct object in the accusative case. Transitive verbs do not have any grammatical form to signal their transitivity. However, a useful diagnostic for whether a verb is transitive or not is if it can be questioned with **Что?** or **Кого?**, the accusative case forms of the pronouns *What? Whom?* For example, the verbs **читать** *to read* and **слушать** *to listen to* are transitive:

— *Что́ ты́ чита́ешь?*	*What are you reading?*
— *Я́ чита́ю поэ́му.*	*I'm reading a poem.*
— *Кого́ ты́ слу́шаешь?*	*Whom are you listening to?*
— *Я́ слу́шаю профе́ссора.*	*I'm listening to the professor.*

Many transitive verbs can be used intransitively, though a direct object is implied, e.g., **Он лю́бит чита́ть** *He likes to read* (*novels*, *stories*, etc.).

Intransitive verbs can *not* take a direct object; nor, therefore, can they be questioned with the pronouns **Что?**, **Кого?** For example, verbs such as **спа́ть** *to sleep*, **идти́** *to go*, **улыба́ться** *to smile* are intransitive. Unlike transitive verbs which have no marker indicating their transitivity, a great number of intransitive verbs do have a grammatical form which marks them as intransitive: these are verbs with the particle **-ся**.

VERBS WITH THE PARTICLE -СЯ (-СЬ)

All verbs with the particle **-ся** (spelled **-ся** after a consonant, **-сь** after a vowel) are intransitive, though some of them may take an object in a case other than the accusative.

боя́ться *to be afraid of, to fear*	
Она́ бои́тся соба́ки.	*She is afraid of the dog.* [genitive case]
занима́ться *to study*	
Он занима́ется би́знесом.	*He is studying business.* [instrumental case]
учи́ться *to study*	
Он у́чится му́зыке.	*He is studying music.* [dative case]

Principal Groups of Verbs in -СЯ

A great number of Russian verbs exist in pairs of transitive verb/intransitive verb in **-ся**. This is because transitive verbs can have the particle **-ся** added to them to derive an intransitive counterpart in **-ся**. When this happens, the verb, in addition to becoming intransitive, often acquires an additional meaning. In fact, it is possible to divide verbs in **-ся** into a small number of groups according to these meanings. The following are the principal meanings associated with verbs in **-ся**.

Reflexive Meaning

Certain verbs to which **-ся** is added acquire a *reflexive* meaning, that is, the action of the verb is performed by the subject upon himself. The verbs in this group typically denote physical actions that are characteristically reflexive.

мы́ть(ся)/помы́ть(ся)	*to wash (oneself)*
вытира́ть(ся)/вы́тереть(ся)	*to dry (oneself)*
бри́ть(ся)/побри́ть(ся)	*to shave (oneself)*
причёсывать(ся)/причеса́ть(ся)	*to comb one's hair*
одева́ть(ся)/оде́ть(ся)	*to dress (oneself)*

Note the contrast in the following pairs of sentences:

Жена́ *мо́ет* **посу́ду.**	*The wife washes the dishes.*
Она́ *мо́ется* **холо́дной водо́й.**	*She washes (herself) with cold water.*
Му́ж *вытира́ет* **посу́ду.**	*The husband dries the dishes.*
Он *вытира́ется* **полоте́нцем.**	*He is drying himself with a towel.*

Characteristically reflexive verbs normally do not occur transitively with the direct object pronoun **себя́** *oneself*. However, transitive verbs which are not usually conceived of as reflexive may be used in a reflexive construction with **себя́**, e.g., **Она́ хорошо́** *понима́ет* **себя́** *She understands herself well,* **Он не** *лю́бит* **себя́** *He doesn't like himself.*

Reciprocal Meaning

Certain verbs to which **-ся** is added acquire a *reciprocal* meaning, that is, they denote actions that involve more than one subject, each performing the action upon the other. The verbs in this group typically involve two participants and the action is characteristically a mutual one. One of the participants may be expressed in the instrumental case after the preposition **с** *with*.

встреча́ть(ся)/встре́тить(ся)	*to meet (each other)*
ви́деть(ся)/уви́деть(ся)	*to see (each other)*
знако́мить(ся)/познако́мить(ся)	*to meet (each other)*
обнима́ть(ся)/обня́ть(ся)	*to embrace (each other)*
целова́ть(ся)/поцелова́ть(ся)	*to kiss (each other)*

Compare the transitive and intransitive use of the verbs.

Я́ *встре́тил* **его́ по́сле ле́кции.**	*I met him after the lecture.*
Мы́ *встре́тились* **по́сле ле́кции.**	*We met (each other) after the lecture.*
Я́ *о́бнял и поцелова́л* **её.**	*I hugged and kissed her.*
Мы́ *обняли́сь и поцелова́лись.*	*We hugged and kissed (each other).*
Хо́чешь, я́ тебя́ *познако́млю* **с не́й.**	*If you want, I'll introduce you to her.*
Он *познако́мился* **с не́й в шко́ле.**	*He met her in school.*

Verbs which characteristically denote reciprocal actions normally do not occur with the reciprocal pronoun **дру́г дру́га** *one another*. However, this pronoun is used to provide a reciprocal meaning to verbs which do not inherently have this meaning, e.g., **Они́** *уважа́ют* **дру́г дру́га.** *They respect one another.*

Verbs Denoting Emotion

Several common verbs denoting emotions and attitudes may be used transitively with an *animate* direct object. When such verbs are used intransitively with **-ся**, the animate direct object appears as the subject in the nominative case, and the noun denoting the source of the emotion appears in an oblique case, with or without a preposition.

The following are some common emotion verbs of this type.

Transitive	*Intransitive in* **-ся** *+ Instrumental*
интересова́ть/за- *to interest*	**интересова́ться/за-** *to be interested in*
увлека́ть/увле́чь *to fascinate*	**увлека́ться/увле́чься** *to be fascinated by*

Transitive	*Intransitive in* **-ся** *+ Dative*
ра́довать/обра́довать *to make glad*	**ра́доваться/обра́доваться** *to be glad for*
удивля́ть/удиви́ть *to surprise*	**удивля́ться/удиви́ться** *to be surprised at*

Transitive	*Intransitive in* **-ся** + *Genitive*
пуга́ть/испуга́ть *to frighten, scare*	пуга́ться/испуга́ться *to be frightened of*

Transitive	*Intransitive in* **-ся** (**на** + *Accusative*)
серди́ть/рассерди́ть *to anger*	серди́ться/рассерди́ться *to be angry at*
обижа́ть/оби́деть *to offend*	обижа́ться/оби́деться *to be offended by*

Transitive	*Intransitive in* **-ся** (**о** + *Prepositional*)
беспоко́ить/о- *to worry, bother*	беспоко́иться/о- *to be worried about*
волнова́ть/вз- *to worry, disturb*	волнова́ться/вз- *to be nervous about*

Compare the transitive and intransitive use of these verbs:

Меня́ *интересу́ет* му́зыка.	*Music interests me.*
Я *интересу́юсь* му́зыкой.	*I'm interested in music.*

На́с *удиви́ла* его́ ще́дрость.	*His generosity surprised us.*
Мы́ *удиви́лись* его́ ще́дрости.	*We were surprised at his generosity.*

Э́то *беспоко́ит* его́.	*This worries him.*
О́н *беспоко́ится* об э́том.	*He is worried about this.*

Verbs that Occur Only in **-ся**

A relatively small number of verbs occur only intransitively with the particle **-ся**, i.e., they have no transitive counterpart. Several of these also express some emotion. Some common verbs in this group include **боя́ться** *to be afraid of* [+ Gen.], **смея́ться** *to laugh* [**над** + Instr.], **улыба́ться** *to smile*, **наде́яться** *to hope* [**на** + Acc.], **нра́виться/по-** *to like* [+ Dat. of the person who "likes" and Nom. for what/who is liked].

Она́ всегда́ *смеётся* над его́ шу́тками.	*She always laughs at his jokes.*
О́н *улыба́ется* при ви́де отца́.	*He smiles when he sees his father.*
Мне́ *нра́вится* твоя́ но́вая ша́пка.	*I like your new hat.*

58. Complete the sentences with the transitive or intransitive verb in the required form.

1. Ка́ждое у́тро Ва́ня _____ в ду́ше. (мы́ть — мы́ться)
2. Ка́ждую неде́лю он _____ свою́ маши́ну. (мы́ть — мы́ться)
3. До́чка сейча́с _____ сама́ в ва́нне. (мы́ть — мы́ться)
4. Ма́ть бы́стро _____ и пошла́ на рабо́ту. (оде́ть — оде́ться)
5. До́чка до́лго _____ ку́клы. (одева́ть — одева́ться)
6. Ма́ма о́чень тепло́ _____ ребёнка и повела́ его́ на като́к. (оде́ть — оде́ться)
7. В Сиби́ри зимо́й на́до всегда́ _____ тепло́. (одева́ть — одева́ться)
8. Де́вочка ча́сто _____ свои́ во́лосы. (причёсывать — причёсываться)
9. Де́вочка сиде́ла пе́ред зе́ркалом и _____ . (причёсывать — причёсываться)
10. Сестра́ _____ мла́дшего бра́та. (причёсывать — причёсываться)

59. Complete the sentences with the transitive or intransitive verb in the required form.

1. Друзья́ до́лго не _____ . (ви́деть — ви́деться)
2. О́н не _____ свою́ подру́гу уже́ три го́да. (ви́деть — ви́деться)
3. Я наде́юсь, что мы́ ско́ро _____ . (уви́деть — уви́деться)
4. Мне́ каза́лось, что мы́ с ни́м где́-то _____ . (встреча́ть — встреча́ться)
5. По доро́ге домо́й я́ _____ дру́га. (встре́тить — встре́титься)

6. Ми́ша _____ с сестро́й. (поцелова́ть — поцелова́ться)
7. До́чь _____ отца́. (поцелова́ть — поцелова́ться)
8. Оте́ц с сы́ном _____ . (обня́ть — обня́ться)
9. Кто́ ва́с _____ с э́той де́вушкой? (познако́мить — познако́миться)
10. Мы́ _____ на заня́тиях в институ́те. (познако́мить — познако́миться)

60. Complete the sentence with the verb in the correct form.

1. Твоё письмо́ на́с о́чень _____ (обра́довать — обра́доваться)
2. Мы́ _____ твое́й хоро́шей но́вости. (обра́довать — обра́доваться)
3. Меня́ о́чень _____ здоро́вье отца́. (беспоко́ить — беспоко́иться)
4. О́н о́чень _____ об отце́. (беспоко́ить — беспоко́иться)
5. Каки́е писа́тели ва́с _____? (интересова́ть — интересова́ться)
6. О́н _____ ру́сскими писа́телями. (интересова́ть — интересова́ться)
7. Я́ о́чень _____ (волнова́ть — волнова́ться), сы́н ещё не пришёл из шко́лы.
8. Экономи́ческая ситуа́ция в стране́ _____ все́х. (волнова́ть — волнова́ться)
9. Она́ _____ на него́: о́н не пришёл и не позвони́л. (серди́ть — серди́ться)
10. Его́ поведе́ние о́чень _____ жену́. (серди́ть — серди́ться)
11. На́с _____ хоро́шие отме́тки сы́на. (удиви́ть — удиви́ться)
12. Роди́тели _____ успе́хам сы́на. (удиви́ть — удиви́ться)

Voice and the Particle -СЯ

Active Voice

The term "voice" refers to the relationship between the verbal action, the Agent (the conscious initiator of the action), and the Patient (the entity which undergoes the action). Normally, the Agent of the action is the grammatical subject of the sentence and in Russian is in the nominative case, while the Patient is the direct object in the accusative case. This arrangement, which presents the action as emanating from the Agent to the Patient, is called the *active* voice. Sentences presented in the active voice are transitive constructions, since the verb is followed by a direct object.

Active Voice

Nominative subject/Agent — Transitive Verb — Accusative direct object/Patient

Студе́нты — организу́ют — клу́б.
The students — are organizing — a club.

Passive Voice

The active voice is not the only way to represent the relationship of the Agent and Patient to the verbal action. For example, the speaker may wish to present the action in the *passive* voice, that is, from the perspective of the object that undergoes the action (the Patient). In the passive voice the Patient is made prominent and the Agent is deemphasized. This is accomplished by removing the Agent from the subject position, and replacing it with the direct object Patient. In forming the Russian passive, two things happen when the direct object is made the grammatical subject: (1) the particle **-ся** is added to the (imperfective) verb, and (2), the Agent, if mentioned, is put in the instrumental case.

Passive Voice

Nominative subject/Patient — Intransitive Verb in **-ся** — (Instrumental Agent)

Клу́б — организу́ется — студе́нтами.
A club — is being organized — by the students.

Though the action in a passive construction is always understood to involve an Agent, the Agent may not be mentioned if his identity is either unknown or unimportant.

Програ́мма «Вре́мя» *передаётся* ка́ждый ве́чер.	The program "Vremya" is aired every evening.
В э́том кинотеа́тре *пока́зываются* иностра́нные фи́льмы.	Foreign films are shown in this movie theater.

In more informal style, the so-called "indefinite personal" construction may be used as an alternative to the passive construction with the verb in **-ся**. The indefinite personal uses a transitive verb in the third-person plural and an accusative direct object. There is no overt subject Agent, but the personal form of the verb implies an indefinite subject "they." This construction may be translated into English either in the passive voice (as above), or in the active voice, as shown below.

Програ́мму «Вре́мя» *передаю́т* ка́ждый ве́чер.	They show the program "Vremya" every evening.
В э́том кинотеа́тре *пока́зывают* иностра́нные фи́льмы.	They show foreign films in this movie theater.

Middle Voice

Another way to present the action from the perspective of the Patient is to make the direct object the subject, and completely eliminate reference to an Agent. This *middle voice* construction is formed the same way as the passive, except that in the passive the Agent is only *deemphasized* and may occur in the instrumental, while in a middle construction there can be *no mention of an Agent*. Both imperfective and perfective verbs form middles in **-ся**.

The following are examples of the middle voice in which the situations involve phenomena of nature, and therefore exclude the possibility of an Agent's participation.

Со́лнце *поднима́ется.*	The sun rises/is rising.
Ве́тер *уси́лился.*	The wind strengthened.
Температу́ра *повы́силась.*	The temperature rose.

A middle construction may also be used when the real-world situation is one which may involve an Agent, but the speaker chooses to present the action as occurring autonomously. The following middle sentences can not occur with an instrumental Agent.

Две́рь *откры́лась.*	The door opened.
Компью́тер *отключи́лся.*	The computer shut down.
Маши́на *останови́лась.*	The car stopped.
Ле́кция *начала́сь* в де́вять часо́в.	The lecture began at nine o'clock.

61. Rewrite the sentences, changing them from active voice to passive voice.

Model: Экономи́сты *обсужда́ют* э́ти вопро́сы.
Э́ти вопро́сы *обсужда́ются* экономи́стами.

1. Студе́нты в э́той гру́ппе *реша́ют* тру́дные зада́чи.
2. Социо́логи в э́том институ́те *прово́дят* опро́с.
3. Тури́сты *покупа́ют* матрёшки.
4. Преподава́тели *проверя́ют* контро́льные рабо́ты.
5. У́личные торго́вцы *продаю́т* вся́кие ве́щи.

62. Rewrite the sentences, changing them from the "indefinite personal" to the passive construction in **-ся**. Follow the model.

Model: Лабораторию *закрывают* в шесть часов.
Лаборатория *закрывается* в шесть часов.

1. На этой кафедре *изучают* методику преподавания.
2. В городе *открывают* новую картинную галерею.
3. Сводку погоды *передают* по Второй программе в 21.00.
4. В этом журнале *публикуют* работу этого автора впервые.
5. В России книги Аксёнова *читают* с большим интересом.

VERBAL GOVERNMENT

Besides transitive verbs that may be followed by a direct object in the accusative case, there are other verbs (and prepositions) in Russian that govern, or require, one of the so-called oblique cases—dative, genitive, or instrumental—on their objects. Since the particular oblique case required by these verbs is largely unpredictable, the case-governing properties of these verbs must be memorized. For example, the verbs **звонить** *to ring, telephone*, **помогать** *to help*, **советовать** *to advise* govern the dative case; **бояться** *to be afraid of*, **достигать** *to attain*, **избегать** *to avoid* govern the genitive; and **владеть** *to command*, **пользоваться** *to use*, **руководить** *to direct* govern the instrumental. A more complete listing of the verbs that govern one of the oblique cases is given in Chapter 2, where each case is discussed.

Other verbs in Russian govern a preposition + case, for example, **верить в** (+ Acc.) *to believe in*, **рассчитывать на** (+ Acc.) *to rely on*, **благодарить за** (+ Acc.) *to thank for*, **отличаться от** (+ Gen.) *to differ from*, **участвовать в** (+ Prep.) *to participate in*, **настаивать на** (+ Prep.) *to insist on*, **готовиться к** (+ Dat.) *to prepare for*, **следить за** (+ Instr.) *to keep up with, look after*. A more complete listing of verbs that govern a particular preposition + case is given in Chapter 3, where each of the prepositions is presented.

VERBS OF MOTION

Unidirectional and Multidirectional Verbs

The vast majority of Russian verbs have only one imperfective. However, there is one special group of paired unprefixed verbs denoting various types of movement (*walking*, *driving*, *running*, *swimming*, *flying*, *taking*, etc.) called the *verbs of motion*, that have *two imperfectives*.

1. The *unidirectional* (or *determinate*) imperfective normally refers to continuous motion in one direction toward a stated (or implied) goal.

Мы *идём* **в парк.**	*We are walking to the park.*
Мы *шли* **домой из парка.**	*We were walking home from the park.*

2. The *multidirectional* (or *indeterminate*) imperfective has several uses. Specifically, it may be used to denote (*a*) motion that is random, or in more than one direction, (*b*) motion that is habitual (when a return trip is implied), (c) motion spoken of in general terms, (*d*) roundtrip motion in the past (went and returned).

(*a*)	**Он** *ходит* **по комнате.**	*He walks around the room.*
(*b*)	**Он часто** *ходит* **на работу.**	*He often walks to work.*
(*c*)	**Наша девочка уже** *ходит*.	*Our little girl already walks.*
(*d*)	**Вчера я** *ходил* **в библиотеку.**	*Yesterday I went to the library.*

Among the motion verbs, some are transitive, while others are intransitive. Below are the five most important pairs of intransitive verbs of motion, listed with the unidirectional imperfective preceding the multidirectional imperfective.

Intransitive Verbs of Motion

(1) *to walk, go on foot*

Infinitive	*Non-Past*	*Past*	*Imperative*
идти́ (U)	иду́, идёшь, иду́т	шёл, шла́, шли́	иди́(те)
ходи́ть (M)	хожу́, хо́дишь, хо́дят	ходи́л, ходи́ла, ходи́ли	ходи́(те)

(2) *to ride, go by vehicle*

е́хать (U)	е́ду, е́дешь, е́дут	е́хал, е́хала, е́хали	поезжа́й(те)
е́здить (M)	е́зжу, е́здишь, е́здят	е́здил, е́здила, е́здили	е́зди(те)

(3) *to run*

бежа́ть (U)	бегу́, бежи́шь, бежи́т, бежи́м, бежи́те, бегу́т	бежа́л, бежа́ла, бежа́ли	беги́(те)
бе́гать (M)	бе́гаю, бе́гаешь, бе́гают	бе́гал, бе́гала, бе́гали	бе́гай(те)

(4) *to fly*

лете́ть (U)	лечу́, лети́шь, летя́т	лете́л, лете́ла, лете́ли	лети́(те)
лета́ть (M)	лета́ю, лета́ешь, лета́ют	лета́л, лета́ла, лета́ли	лета́й(те)

(5) *to swim; to sail*

плы́ть (U)	плыву́, плывёшь, плыву́т	плы́л, плыла́, плы́ли	плыви́(те)
пла́вать (M)	пла́ваю, пла́ваешь, -ают	пла́вал, пла́вала, пла́вали	пла́вай(те)

Principal Uses of Unidirectional Verbs

The following are the most important uses of the unidirectional verbs.

1. To denote motion in progress in one direction in the present, past, or future. A goal or destination is expressed by the prepositions **в** or **на** + accusative (of nouns denoting places), or **к** + dative (of nouns denoting people). Otherwise, a goal is expressed by directional adverbs, e.g., **домо́й** *home(ward)*, **сюда́** *here*, **туда́** *there*.

Куда́ вы́ *идёте*, **домо́й**?	*Where are you going, home?*
Я́ *иду́* **на ле́кцию.**	*I am going (walking) to a lecture.*
Мы́ *е́дем* **к дру́гу.**	*We are going to our friend's place.*
О́н *е́дет* **в Москву́.**	*He is going (traveling) to Moscow.*
Она́ *лети́т* **к бра́ту в Пари́ж.**	*She is flying to her brother in Paris.*

In the past and future tenses the unidirectional verb of motion is normally used to provide a background against which some other action occurs. Thus, the motion verb is in one clause of a complex sentence, while the verb in the other clause, if imperfective, denotes a simultaneous action, but if perfective, denotes one that was/will be completed during the time the motion was/will be in progress.

Когда́ я́ *лете́л* **в самолёте,** я́ *чита́л* **детекти́в.**	*When I was flying in the airplane, I was reading a detective novel.*
Когда́ мы́ *е́хали* **в маши́не,** у на́с *ко́нчился* **бензи́н.**	*When we were riding in the car, we ran out of gas.*
Когда́ ты́ *бу́дешь идти́* **ми́мо кио́ска,** *купи́* **мне́** *газе́ту.*	*When you are walking past the newsstand, buy me a newspaper.*

2. A unidirectional verb in the present tense may be used to denote an action that is intended for the near future, just as in English.

Сего́дня ве́чером я́ *иду́* в кино́.	*Tonight I'm going to the movies.*
За́втра мы́ *е́дем* на да́чу.	*Tomorrow we're going to the dacha.*

3. When the focus is on some circumstance or characteristic of one-way motion, e.g., the speed, manner, or means of travel.

Письмо́ *шло́* к на́м неде́лю.	*The letter reached us in a week.*
Я́ *е́ду* на рабо́ту ча́с.	*It takes me an hour to drive to work.*
О́н *е́хал* домо́й сего́дня на метро́.	*He went home today by metro.*
Она́ *шла́* в кинотеа́тр одна́.	*She went to the movie theater alone.*

4. Only the unidirectional is used to indicate figurative motion in certain idiomatic expressions. The multidirectional can not occur here, even when the motion is repeated. This is because the subject in these idioms is understood to move in only one direction.

Ка́к *лети́т* вре́мя!	*How time flies!*
Сего́дня *шёл* до́ждь.	*It rained today.*
Ле́том здесь ча́сто *иду́т* дожди́.	*It often rains here in the summer.*
Что́ *идёт* в кинотеа́тре?	*What's playing at the movie theater?*

Principal Uses of Multidirectional Verbs

The following are the most important uses of the multidirectional verbs.

1. To indicate random motion, i.e., motion in no specific direction or in several directions. The meaning of motion "around" or "about" is often expressed by the preposition **по** + dative case, but nondirected motion may also occur "in a place" expressed by **в/на** + prepositional.

Мы́ *ходи́ли* по па́рку.	*We walked around the park.*
Са́ша ве́сь де́нь *е́здил* по го́роду.	*Sasha drove around town all day.*
Соба́ка *бе́гает* во дворе́.	*The dog is running about in the yard.*

2. Motion that is repeated or habitual (implying *two* opposite directions, "there and back").

Он ка́ждый де́нь *хо́дит* в институ́т.	*Everyday he goes to the institute.*
	(He goes there and then returns.)
Мы́ *е́здим* на да́чу по суббо́там.	*We go to the dacha on Saturdays.*

3. Motion spoken of in general terms, for example, when characterizing one's ability or propensity for the action. Thus, a multidirectional verb is often used with qualitative adverbs, and after verbs such as **уме́ть** *to know how*, **люби́ть** *to love/like*, **нра́виться** *to like*, and **боя́ться** *to be afraid*.

О́н не уме́ет *пла́вать*.	*He doesn't know how to swim.*
Она́ бы́стро *бе́гает*.	*She runs fast (is a fast runner).*
Моя́ жена́ бои́тся *лета́ть*.	*My wife is afraid to fly.*
Э́тот ребёнок ещё не *хо́дит*.	*This child can not walk yet.*

4. To denote a single "round-trip" in the past. This use of the multidirectional verb implies that the subject "was" somewhere and has returned. Therefore, questions that ask where one *was* (**Где́ ты́ бы́л …?**) can be answered with the past tense of the multidirectional verb (a round-trip was completed).

— Где́ ты́ *была́* вчера́?	*Where were you yesterday?*
— Я́ *ходи́ла* к сестре́.	*I went to my sister's (place).*
— Где́ вы́ *бы́ли* в суббо́ту?	*Where were you on Saturday?*
— Мы́ *е́здили* на да́чу.	*We went to the dacha.*

63. Circle the appropriate form of the unidirectional or multidirectional imperfective.

1. Мы сейча́с (идём/хо́дим) в магази́н. Мы (идём/хо́дим) туда́ ча́сто.
2. Когда́ мы (шли/ходи́ли) домо́й, мы встре́тили ста́рого дру́га.
3. За́втра па́па (идёт/хо́дит) к врачу́. Он (идёт/хо́дит) к врачу́ ра́з в ме́сяц.
4. Я сего́дня (е́ду/е́зжу) в командиро́вку в Ки́ев. Я туда́ ча́сто (е́ду/е́зжу).
5. — Куда́ ты та́к бы́стро (бежи́шь/бе́гаешь)? — Я (бегу́/бе́гаю) на экза́мен.
6. — Ты (бежи́шь/бе́гаешь) на стадио́не? — Нет, я (бегу́/бе́гаю) в па́рке.
7. Вчера́ мы (шли/ходи́ли) в теа́тр. На́м о́чень понра́вился конце́рт.
8. Она́ не лю́бит (бежа́ть/бе́гать), она́ предпочита́ет (идти́/ходи́ть).
9. Моя́ до́чка хорошо́ (плывёт/пла́вает), она́ (плывёт/пла́вает) ка́ждый де́нь.
10. Про́шлым ле́том мы (е́хали/е́здили) в о́тпуск на мо́ре.
11. Куда́ (плывёт/пла́вает) э́тот кора́бль? Он (плывёт/пла́вает) из Та́ллина в Санкт-Петербу́рг.
12. — Где бы́л Са́ша на про́шлой неде́ле? — Он (лете́л/лета́л) в Москву́.
13. Я сего́дня (лечу́/лета́ю) в Нью-Йо́рк. А куда́ ты (лети́шь/лета́ешь)?
14. — Где ты бы́л вчера́? — Я (е́хал/е́здил) за го́род к сестре́.
15. Когда́ я (е́хал/е́здил) к сестре́, я ду́мал о то́м, ка́к я скуча́ю по ней.
16. Каки́е фи́льмы сейча́с (иду́т/хо́дят) в кинотеа́тре «Росси́я»?
17. В э́том теа́тре ча́сто (иду́т/хо́дят) америка́нские фи́льмы.
18. Зимо́й в Москве́ ча́сто (идёт/хо́дит) сне́г.

Transitive Verbs of Motion

The following are the three most commonly used transitive verbs of motion, listed with the unidirectional followed by the multidirectional imperfective.

(1)   *to carry* (*while walking*)

Infinitive	Non-Past	Past	Imperative
нести́ (U)	несу́, несёшь, несу́т	нёс, несла́, несли́	неси́(те)
носи́ть (M)	ношу́, но́сишь, но́сят	носи́л, носи́ла, носи́ли	носи́(те)

(2)   *to transport, to take by vehicle*

везти́ (U)	везу́, везёшь, везу́т	вёз, везла́, везли́	вези́(те)
вози́ть (M)	вожу́, во́зишь, во́зят	вози́л, вози́ла, вози́ли	вози́(те)

(3)   *to lead on foot*

вести́ (U)	веду́, ведёшь, веду́т	вёл, вела́, вели́	веди́(те)
води́ть (M)	вожу́, во́дишь, во́дят	води́л, води́ла, води́ли	води́(те)

Transitive motion verbs have the same uses outlined above for intransitive motion verbs. The following examples illustrate these uses for transitive verbs of unidirectional and multidirectional motion.

Transitive Verbs of Unidirectional Motion

Я сейча́с *несу́* письмо́ на по́чту.	*I am taking a letter to the post office.*
Ма́ть *ведёт* до́чь в шко́лу.	*The mother is taking (walking) her daughter to school.*
Когда́ она́ *вела́* де́вочку в па́рк, пошёл до́ждь.	*When she was taking the little girl to the park, it began to rain.*
Грузови́к *везёт* фру́кты на ры́нок.	*The truck is taking fruit to the market.*

Transitive Verbs of Multidirectional Motion

Я́ всегда́ *ношу́* **с собо́й фотогра́фии свои́х дете́й.**	*I always carry with me photos of my children.*
Почтальо́н *но́сит* **пи́сьма, газе́ты, и журна́лы.**	*The mail carrier carries letters, newspapers, and magazines.*
Она́ рабо́тает ги́дом и *во́дит* **тури́стов по музе́ю.**	*She works as a guide and takes tourists around the museum.*
Вчера́ мы́ *вози́ли* **дете́й на о́зеро.**	*Yesterday we took the children to the lake (and back).*

Transitive Motion Verbs in Idiomatic Expressions

Transitive motion verbs, like intransitive motion verbs, can be used figuratively.

• The multidirectional verb **носи́ть** can be used in the meaning *to wear* (*regularly*).

Я́ ча́сто *ношу́* **джи́нсы.**	*I often wear jeans.*
Она́ *но́сит* **очки́.**	*She wears glasses.*

• The pair **води́ть/вести́** may take the object **маши́ну** in the meaning *to drive a car*.

Она́ у́чится *води́ть* **маши́ну.**	*She is learning to drive a car.*
Кто́ *вёл* **маши́ну, когда́ произошла́ ава́рия?**	*Who was driving the car when the accident occurred?*

Correlating Transitive and Intransitive Motion Verbs

When transitive and intransitive motion verbs are used in the same context, they must correlate in two respects: they must both be unidirectional or multidirectional, and normally they must both express motion "on foot" or "by vehicle."

Она́ *идёт* **на по́чту,** *несёт* **туда́ письмо́.**	*She is walking to the post office, she's taking (carrying) a letter there.*
Я́ *иду́* **в па́рк с соба́кой,** *веду́* **её гуля́ть.**	*I'm going to the park with the dog, I'm taking it for a walk.*
Ги́д *е́дет* **на авто́бусе с тури́стами, о́н** *везёт* **и́х в музе́й.**	*The guide is riding the bus with tourists, he's taking them to a museum.*
Ма́ть ча́сто *хо́дит* **в па́рк и** *во́дит* **туда́ дете́й.**	*The mother often walks to the park and takes the children there.*

64. Complete the sentence with the appropriate present-tense form of the transitive verb of motion: **нести́**, **вести́**, ог **везти́**.

1. По у́лице иду́т шко́льники и _____ кни́ги.
2. По у́лице е́дут грузовики́ и _____ фру́кты и о́вощи.
3. Де́ти иду́т из са́да и _____ цветы́.
4. Ма́ть идёт и _____ до́чь в шко́лу.
5. Во́т идёт почтальо́н, о́н _____ на́м пи́сьма.
6. Авто́бусы е́дут к теа́тру, они́ _____ зри́телей.
7. Студе́нт идёт на ле́кцию и _____ портфе́ль.
8. Самолёт лети́т на Кари́бские острова́ и _____ тури́стов.
9. Ребя́та иду́т из ле́са и _____ грибы́.
10. Оте́ц е́дет домо́й из командиро́вки и _____ де́тям пода́рки.

65. Complete the sentence with the required present- or past-tense form of the transitive verb of motion: **носи́ть/нести́**, **води́ть/вести́**, or **вози́ть/везти́**.

1. Ми́ша рабо́тает води́телем авто́буса. Он _____ пассажи́ров по го́роду.
2. По доро́ге е́хали маши́ны. Они́ _____ пассажи́ров в аэропо́рт.
3. Моя́ сестра́ рабо́тает экскурсово́дом. Она́ _____ тури́стов по музе́ю.
4. Ги́д шёл с гру́ппой тури́стов, он _____ их в гардеро́б.
5. Он рабо́тает носи́льщиком и _____ бага́ж прожива́ющих в гости́нице.
6. Вот идёт почтальо́н. Он _____ нам посы́лку.
7. Он учи́лся на ку́рсах води́телей и тепе́рь он хорошо́ _____ маши́ну.
8. Оле́г _____ маши́ну, когда́ вдруг ко́нчился бензи́н.
9. У него́ плохо́е зре́ние, поэ́тому он _____ очки́.
10. Я ненави́жу шо́рты и никогда́ не _____ их.

Prefixed Verbs of Motion

Unidirectional Verbs with the Prefix по-

Unidirectional imperfectives become perfective when formed with the prefix **по-**.

Unidirectional Imperfective	Prefixed Perfective
идти́	пойти́
е́хать	пое́хать
бежа́ть	побежа́ть
лете́ть	полете́ть
плы́ть	поплы́ть
нести́	понести́
везти́	повезти́
вести́	повести́

Note: When **по-** (or any other prefix) is added to **идти́**, the shape of the infinitive changes to **-йти**, and the shape of the root in the non-past changes from **ид-** to **йд-**: **пойду́, пойдёшь, пойду́т** (the only exception is **прийти́**: **приду́, придёшь, приду́т**).

The perfective motion verb with the prefix **по-** may express:

1. The onset or beginning of movement in one direction:

Когда́ ко́нчился фи́льм, мы встали и *пошли́* **к вы́ходу.**	*When the movie ended, we got up and began walking toward the exit.*
Де́вочка уви́дела отца́ и *побежа́ла* **к нему́.**	*The little girl saw her father and started running toward him.*
Когда́ на светофо́ре загоре́лся зелёный све́т, маши́на *пое́хала.*	*When the traffic light turned green, the car took off.*

2. The beginning of a new direction, or change in the speed of the movement:

Снача́ла мы шли пря́мо, пото́м *пошли́* **напра́во.**	*First we walked straight, then we started walking to the right.*
Я шёл ме́дленно, пото́м посмотре́л на часы́ и *пошёл* **быстре́е.**	*I was walking slowly, then I looked at my watch and began to walk faster.*

3.   The beginning of one-time unidirectional movement in the future. The form in **по-** may indicate an action *to occur* (in the infinitive), one that *will begin* (in future perfective), or it may be used to indicate a suggestion by the speaker for joint action (first-person imperative).

За́втра я хочу́ *пойти́* в кино́.	*Tomorrow I want to go to the movies.*
Когда́ я ко́нчу зада́ния, я *пойду́* к тебе́.	*When I finish my homework, I'll come to your place.*
Пое́дем на вы́ставку.	*Let's go to the exhibit.*

4.   The beginning of movement in the past. The past-tense form in **по-** indicates that the subject *has gone* or *has set out* for some destination, but says nothing about whether or not the subject has reached the intended destination.

Ле́ны здесь нет. Она́ *пошла́* домо́й.	*Lena is not here. She has gone home.*
Ва́ни нет до́ма. Он *пое́хал* на рабо́ту.	*Vanya is not home. He left for work.*
– Где Ири́на?	*Where is Irina?*
– Она́ *понесла́* ребёнка в де́тскую.	*She carried the baby to the nursery.*
– Где па́па?	*Where is Dad?*
– Он *повёз* дру́га на вокза́л.	*He drove his friend to the station.*

Multidirectional Verbs in the Prefix по-

The prefix **по-** makes a multidirectional verb perfective and denotes that the given movement occurs *for a while*, e.g., **походи́ть** *to walk around for a while*, **пое́здить** *to drive around for a while*, **побе́гать** *to run around for a while*. This meaning may be reinforced by the adverb **немно́го** *a little* or by a time expression indicating short duration.

Мы *походи́ли* немно́го по Арба́ту.	*We walked awhile around the Arbat.*
Они́ *пое́здили* немно́го по го́роду.	*They drove awhile around the city.*
Самолёт *полета́л* не́сколько мину́т над аэропо́ртом и приземли́лся.	*The airplane flew several minutes above the airport and landed.*

66.   Choose the appropriate motion verb, the unidirectional imperfective, or the same verb "perfectivized" with the prefix **по-**.

(е́хала/пое́хала)

1.   Маши́на _____ бы́стро, а на перекрёстке _____ ме́дленнее.
2.   Маши́на _____ по у́лице, вдруг сде́лала разворо́т и _____ в другу́ю сто́рону.
3.   Я се́ла в такси́ и _____ в аэропо́рт.

(шли/пошли́)

4.   Они́ _____ по у́лице, останови́лись поздоро́ваться с на́ми и _____ да́льше.
5.   Мы до́лго _____ по лесно́й тропи́нке. Наконе́ц уви́дели ре́чку и _____ к ней.

(плыл/поплы́л)

6.   Снача́ла Ми́ша _____ во́льным сти́лем, а пото́м _____ на спине́.
7.   Кора́бль _____ на за́пад, измени́л курс и _____ на восто́к.

(нёс/понёс)

8.   Носи́льщик по́днял чемода́ны и _____ их к такси́.
9.   На́ши чемода́ны бы́ли тяжёлые и он _____ их с трудо́м.

67. Choose the appropriate perfective motion verb with the prefix **по-**.

(попла́вали/поплы́ли)
1. У́тки _____ у бе́рега и _____ в другу́ю сто́рону.

(полета́ли/полете́ли)
2. Пти́цы немно́го _____ над на́ми, а пото́м _____ на большо́е де́рево.

(походи́ли/пошли́)
3. Мы _____ ча́с по го́роду, уста́ли и _____ домо́й.

(побе́гали/побежа́ли)
4. Де́ти _____ полчаса́ по па́рку, проголода́лись и _____ домо́й обе́дать.

Directional Prefixes

Certain prefixes give verbs of motion a specific *directional* meaning. The following are some common prefixes and the basic meanings they have when used with verbs of motion.

Directional Prefixes	Basic Meanings
при-	*come, arrive*
у-	*leave, depart*
в-	*into, enter into*
вы-	*out, exit*
под-	*come up to, approach*
от-	*away from*
пере-	*across*
про-	*past; through*
за-	*drop in; behind*

A new aspect pair is formed when a directional prefix is added to an unprefixed pair of unidirectional and multidirectional imperfectives. Specifically, when a unidirectional imperfective is prefixed, it becomes *perfective*; however, when a directional prefix is added to a multidirectional verb, it remains *imperfective*.

ходи́ть (*Multi/Impfv*)	**идти́** (*Uni/Impfv*)	*to go (on foot)*
Imperfective	*Perfective*	*New Meanings*
приходи́ть	**прийти́**	*to come, arrive*
уходи́ть	**уйти́**	*to leave, depart*
входи́ть	**войти́**	*to go into, enter*
выходи́ть	**вы́йти**	*to go out, exit*
подходи́ть	**подойти́**	*to go up to, approach*
отходи́ть	**отойти́**	*to go away from*
переходи́ть	**перейти́**	*to go across*
проходи́ть	**пройти́**	*to go past, go through*
заходи́ть	**зайти́**	*to drop in; go behind*

Note: The table above uses **ходи́ть/идти́** to illustrate the effect of adding the various prefixes to create new prefixed imperfective/perfective pairs with new meaning. These prefixes, however, can be used with any of the intransitive or transitive verbs of motion, e.g., **приноси́ть/принести́** *to bring* (*on foot*), **привози́ть/привезти́** *to bring* (*by vehicle*), **уводи́ть/увести́** *to lead away*.

Note the following modifications that result from prefixation:

- After a prefix **идти́** changes to **-йти** (**прийти́**, **уйти́**).
- The vowel **о** is inserted after prefixes ending in a consonant (**в-**, **от-**, **под-**) before **-йти** (**в-ходи́ть/во-йти́**, **от-ходи́ть/ото-йти́**, **под-ходи́ть/подо-йти́**).
- A hard sign **ъ** is inserted when the same consonantal prefixes **в-**, **от-**, **под-** are added to **е́хать** and **е́здить** (**въе́хать**, **отъе́хать**, **подъе́хать**).
- The stem of two multidirectional verbs is modified by a *directional* prefix: **е́здить** changes to **-езжа́ть** (**подъезжа́ть**, **приезжа́ть**, **уезжа́ть**), and the stem of **пла́вать** *to swim* changes to **-плыва́ть**, e.g., **переплыва́ть**, **уплыва́ть**).
- The stress on the stem of **бе́гать** changes to **-бега́ть** (**прибега́ть**).

Aspectual Usage of Prefixed Motion Verbs

The prefixed motion verbs follow the same general guidelines for choosing the imperfective or perfective aspect of other verbs: the perfective is used primarily to denote a single completed action, while the imperfective may denote actions that are ongoing, repeated, habitual, etc.

Prefixed Imperfective and Annulled (Round-trip) Action

One important contrast between the perfective and imperfective aspect applies uniquely to verbs expressing movement, and particularly to motion verbs: the perfective in the past tense denotes an action whose "result remains in effect," while the imperfective past tense may denote an action whose effect has been "annulled" or reversed. Such annulled actions are identical to what was characterized as the "round-trip" meaning of unprefixed multidirectional imperfectives (see page 273).

Compare the following examples:

> **Вчера́ ко мне́** *прие́хал* **дру́г. Сего́дня я́ тебя́ с ни́м познако́млю.**
> *Yesterday my friend came to visit me. Today I'll introduce you to him.*
> **Вчера́ ко мне́** *приезжа́л* **дру́г. Я́ попроща́лся с ни́м уже́ сего́дня у́тром.**
> *Yesterday my friend came to visit me. I already said goodbye to him this morning.*

> **К тебе́** *зашёл* **Серге́й. О́н ждёт тебя́ на ку́хне.**
> *Sergey has dropped by to see you. He is waiting in the kitchen.*
> **К тебе́** *заходи́л* **Серге́й. О́н сказа́л, что вернётся че́рез ча́с.**
> *Sergey dropped by to see you. He said he would come back in an hour.*

> **Ма́ша** *принесла́* **ва́м пода́рок. О́н лежи́т та́м на столе́.**
> *Masha brought you a present. It is lying there on the table.*
> **Ма́ша** *приноси́ла* **ва́м пода́рок, но не оста́вила. Она́ хо́тела да́ть сама́.**
> *Masha brought you a present, but didn't leave it. She wanted to give it in person.*

As the above examples indicate, the past tense of the prefixed imperfective may denote an action carried out in two directions: *came and left*, *brought and took away*. The following is a partial list of prefixed imperfective motion verbs that, in the past tense, may be used to denote an annulled (round-trip) action:

```
┌─────────────────────────────────────────────────┐
│  Prefixed Imperfectives Denoting Annulled Action  │
├─────────────────────────────────────────────────┤
│                                                   │
│         приходи́л = пришёл и ушёл                  │
│          уходи́л = ушёл и пришёл                   │
│       приезжа́л = прие́хал и уе́хал                 │
│         уезжа́л = уе́хал и прие́хал                  │
│       приноси́л = принёс и унёс                    │
│         уноси́л = унёс и принёс                    │
│       подходи́л = подошёл и отошёл                 │
│        отходи́ть = отошёл и подошёл                │
│                                                   │
└─────────────────────────────────────────────────┘
```

68.   Complete the sentences with the prefixed motion verb of the correct aspect.

1.   — Мы́ вчера́ ва́м звони́ли, но ва́с не́ было до́ма.
      — Да́, мы́ _____ (уходи́ли/ушли́) в кино́.
2.   — Где́ сейча́с Ва́ня?
      — Его́ не́т. Он _____ (уходи́л/ушёл) к дру́гу.
3.   — Приве́т Ви́тя. Я́ тебя́ давно́ не ви́дел.
      — Я́ _____ (уезжа́л/уе́хал) в командиро́вку в Росто́в.
4.   — А где́ же Ва́ля? Я́ не ви́дел её уже́ неде́лю.
      — Она́ _____ (уе́зжала/уе́хала) в Москву́ и прие́дет домо́й за́втра.
5.   — Кто́ к тебе́ _____ (подходи́л/подошёл) по́сле ле́кции?
      — Э́то бы́л бра́т Вале́ры.
6.   — Кто́ э́то _____ (подходи́л/подошёл) к Ко́ле? С ке́м о́н разгова́ривает?
      — Э́то его́ дру́г Ми́ша.

VERBAL ADJECTIVES (PARTICIPLES)

A participle combines characteristics of both a verb and an adjective. Like verbs, participles may be transitive or intransitive, perfective or imperfective in aspect, present or past (but not future) in tense, and in the active or passive voice. A participle governs the same case (or preposition + case) as the verb from which it is derived. On the other hand, participles are like adjectives in that they take adjective endings and they agree in gender, number, and case with the noun they modify.

Participles are used primarily in the written language, especially in journalistic, academic, and scientific writing. A participle is sometimes used in place of a relative clause. For example, the English present participle *reading* in "The boy *reading* the book" is equivalent to the relative clause *who is reading* in "The boy *who is reading* the book." There are two kinds of participles in Russian: active and passive. Each kind of participle can be present or past.

Active Participles

Active participles can be used in place of a relative clause introduced by the pronoun **кото́рый** *who*, *which*, *that*, if **кото́рый** is the subject of the clause in the *nominative* case. A *present* active participle can replace a clause with **кото́рый** in the nominative case and a verb in the *present* tense, while a *past* active participle replaces such a clause with a verb in the *past* tense.

Present Active Participles

Present active participles are formed from *imperfective* verbs by adding **-ущий/-ющий** to the basic stem of a first conjugation verb, or **-ащий/-ящий** to the stem of a second conjugation verb. Active participles formed from verbs in **-ся** simply add **-ся** (never **-сь**) after the participle ending. The general rule for combining stems and endings (truncate the first of two "likes," add two "unlikes") applies in the formation of participles:

First conj.:	**читай- + ущий**	**чита́ющий**	*who is reading*
	занима́й- + ущий-ся	**занима́ющийся**	*who is studying*
	жив- + ущий	**живу́щий**	*who is living*
Second conj.:	**говори- + ящий**	**говоря́щий**	*who is speaking*
	сиде- + ящий	**сидя́щий**	*who/which is sitting*
	лежа- + ащий	**лежа́щий**	*who/which is lying*

Note: In verbs with a basic stem in **-ова-**, this suffix alternates with **-уй-** in forming the present active participle: **рисова-/уй- + ущий → рису́ющий** *who is drawing*.

Compare the following synonymous pairs of sentences. Note that a relative clause introduced by **кото́рый** in the *nominative* case and containing a verb in the present tense, can be replaced by a present active participle.

Ма́льчик, *кото́рый чита́ет* **кни́гу, мо́й сы́н.**
Ма́льчик, *чита́ющий* **кни́гу, мо́й сы́н.**
The boy (who is) reading the book is my son.

Де́вочка, *кото́рая сиди́т* **за столо́м, моя́ до́чь.**
Де́вочка, *сидя́щая* **за столо́м, моя́ до́чь.**
The little girl (who is) sitting at the table is my daughter.

Па́рни, *кото́рые говоря́т* **по-ру́сски, мои́ студе́нты.**
Па́рни, *говоря́щие* **по-ру́сски, мои́ студе́нты.**
The guys (who are) speaking Russian are my students.

69. Replace the present active participle with a relative clause introduced by **кото́рый**.

1. Де́вушка, *живу́щая* в кварти́ре 7, у́чится в МГУ.
2. Кни́ги, *лежа́щие* на столе́, не мои́.
3. Молодо́й челове́к, *занима́ющийся* марке́тингом, хо́чет нача́ть своё де́ло.
4. Профе́ссор, *чита́ющий* ле́кцию, неда́вно прие́хал из Москвы́.
5. Студе́нты, *реша́ющие* э́ту зада́чу, о́чень у́мные.

Past Active Participles

Past active participles are formed from both perfective and imperfective verbs by adding either **-ший** or **-вший** to the basic stem. Those verbs used with the particle **-ся** take a final **-ся**, never **-сь**.

- Stems ending in **д, т, г, к, б, п, р, с, з,** and **(ну)** add **-ший**.
- All other stems add **-вший**.

привы́к(ну)- + ший	**привы́кший**	*who got used to*
помо́г- + ший	**помо́гший**	*who helped*
вы́рос- + ший	**вы́росший**	*who grew up*
переве́д- + ший	**переве́дший**	*who translated*
сиде- + вший	**сиде́вший**	*who was sitting*
написа + вший	**написа́вший**	*who wrote*
роди- + вший- ся	**роди́вшийся**	*who was born*

Note: Past active participles of the irregular motion verb **идти́** *to go* and its prefixed perfectives (e.g., **прийти́**, **уйти́**, **вы́йти**) are formed from the root **шед-**: **ше́дший** *who was walking*, **прише́дший** *who arrived*, **уше́дший** *who left*.

Compare the following synonymous pairs of sentences. Note that a relative clause introduced by **кото́рый** in the *nominative* case that contains a verb in the past tense, can be replaced by a past active participle.

> **Де́вушка,** *кото́рая сиде́ла* **ря́дом со мно́й, моя́ сестра́.**
> **Де́вушка,** *сиде́вшая* **ря́дом со мно́й, моя́ сестра́.**
> *The girl who was sitting next to me is my sister.*

> **Челове́к,** *кото́рый принёс* **журна́л, колле́га моего́ отца́.**
> **Челове́к,** *принёсший* **журна́л, колле́га моего́ отца́.**
> *The person who brought the magazine is a colleague of my father.*

> **Я зна́ю челове́ка,** *кото́рый роди́лся* **в э́том селе́.**
> **Я зна́ю челове́ка,** *роди́вшегося* **в э́том селе́.**
> *I know a person who was born in this village.*

70. Replace the past active participle with a relative clause introduced by **кото́рый.**

1. А́втор, *написа́вший* э́ту кни́гу, получи́л пре́мию.
2. Ма́льчик, *помо́гший* тебе́, мо́й мла́дший бра́т.
3. Челове́к, *переве́дший* э́ту кни́гу, отли́чный перево́дчик.
4. Я́ сего́дня познако́мился с челове́ком, *вы́росшим* в моём родно́м го́роде.
5. Учени́к, *уше́дший* ра́но с уро́ка, пло́хо себя́ чу́вствовал.

Passive Participles

Passive participles can be used in place of a relative clause introduced by the pronoun **кото́рый**, if this pronoun is in the *accusative* case. A *present* passive participle replaces the accusative of **кото́рый** and the *present*-tense verb in the clause it introduces, while a *past* passive participle replaces such a clause with a verb in the *past* tense.

Present Passive Participle

Present passive participles are formed from a limited number of *imperfective transitive* verbs. First conjugation verbs form present passive participles by adding **-емый** to the basic stem, while second conjugation verbs add **-имый**.

First conj.:	**чита́й-** + **емый**	**чита́емый**	*which is being read*
	издава́й- + **емый**	**издава́емый**	*which is published*
Second conj.:	**люби-** + **имый**	**люби́мый**	*who/which is loved*
	цени- + **имый**	**цени́мый**	*who/which is valued*

Note: First conjugation verbs with a basic stem in **-ова-**, alternate with **-уй-** in forming the present passive participle: **публикова-/уй** + **емый → публику́емый** *that is published*.

Note: For many conjugation I and II verbs, this participle is equivalent to the **мы-** form of the verb + adjective endings.

Compare the following synonymous pairs of sentences. Note that a relative clause introduced by **кото́рый** in the *accusative* case and containing a verb in the present tense, can be replaced by a present passive participle. If the relative clause contains a subject/agent in the nominative case, then the corresponding participle phrase will have the agent in the instrumental case.

Пробле́ма, *кото́рую изуча́ют* **специали́сты, о́чень важна́.**
Пробле́ма, *изуча́емая* **специали́стами, о́чень важна́.**
The problem being studied by specialists is very important.

Я́ получа́ю журна́л «Огонёк», *кото́рый издаю́т* **в Москве́.**
Я́ получа́ю журна́л «Огонёк», *издава́емый* **в Москве́.**
I receive the magazine "Ogonyok" which is published in Moscow.

71. Replace the present passive participle with a relative clause introduced by **кото́рый**.

1. Зада́ча, *реша́емая* студе́нтом, тру́дная.
2. Учи́тель, *люби́мый* все́ми, вы́шел на пе́нсию.
3. Собы́тия, *опи́сываемые* в э́той статье́, происходи́ли давно́.
4. Това́ры, *производи́мые* на э́том заво́де, высо́кого ка́чества.
5. Ве́чер, *организу́емый* студе́нтами, бу́дет о́чень интере́сный.

Past Passive Participles

Past passive participles are formed from perfective transitive verbs by adding one of three endings to the verb's basic stem: **-тый**, **-енный**, or **-нный**.

- After suffixed stems in **-ну-** and **-о-**, and after nonsuffixed stems in **р**, **м**, **н**, **й**, and **в**, add **-тый**.

заверну- + тый	**завёрнутый**	*wrapped*
выпий- + тый	**вы́питый**	*drunk*
запер- + тый	**за́пертый**	*locked*
оден- + тый	**оде́тый**	*dressed*

- After suffixed stems in **-и-** and after nonsuffixed stems in **б**, **д**, **г**, **к**, **п**, and **т**, add **-енный**. Verbs with a stem in **-и** undergo the same consonant alternation as in the first-person singular non-past.

с → ш	**броси- + енный**	**бро́шенный**	*thrown*
п → пл	**купи- + енный**	**ку́пленный**	*bought*
	получи- + енный	**полу́ченный**	*received*
	построи- + енный	**постро́енный**	*built*
	перевед- + енный	**переведённый**	*translated*
	испек- + енный	**испечённый**	*baked*

- After all other stems, add **-нный**.

написа- + нный	**напи́санный**	*written*
прочитай- + нный	**прочи́танный**	*read*
уви́де- + нный	**уви́денный**	*seen*
нарисова- + нный	**нарисо́ванный**	*painted*

Compare the following pairs of synonymous sentences. Note that a relative clause introduced by **кото́рый** in the *accusative* case and containing a verb in the past tense, can be replaced by a past passive participle. If the relative clause contains a subject/agent in the nominative case, then the corresponding participle phrase will have the agent in the instrumental case.

Шампа́нское, *кото́рое купи́л* **Вади́м, о́чень дорого́е.**
Шампа́нское, *ку́пленное* **Вади́мом, о́чень дорого́е.**
The champagne bought by Vadim is very expensive.

Пироги́, *кото́рые испекла́* **ба́бушка, бы́ли вку́сные.**
Пироги́, *испечённые* **ба́бушкой, бы́ли вку́сные.**
The pies baked by grandma were tasty.

72. Replace the past passive participle with a relative clause introduced by **кото́рый**.

1. Я́ чита́л интере́сную кни́гу, *напи́санную* э́тим журнали́стом.
2. В э́той кни́ге мно́го краси́вых фотогра́фий, *сде́ланных* а́втором.
3. Я́ ви́дел фотогра́фию портре́та, *нарисо́ванного* э́тим худо́жником.
4. Э́тот музе́й нахо́дится в зда́нии, *постро́енном* в девятна́дцатом ве́ке.
5. Я́ рассказа́л ему́ о письме́, *полу́ченном* на́ми вчера́.
6. В аудито́рии мы́ нашли́ *забы́тую* ке́м-то су́мку.

Short Past Passive Participles

Past passive participles may occur in a short form when they are used predicatively, that is, after the verb *to be*. The short-form passive participles are very common in both written and conversational Russian. They are easily formed from their long-form counterparts by dropping the attributive adjective ending (and reducing the **-нн** suffix to one **-н**). The short passive participles express gender and number, but not case.

Long Form		Short Form
подпи́санный	*signed*	подпи́сан, подпи́сана, подпи́сано, подпи́саны
постро́енный	*built*	постро́ен, постро́ена, постро́ено, постро́ены
сде́ланный	*done*	сде́лан, сде́лана, сде́лано, сде́ланы
полу́ченный	*received*	полу́чен, полу́чена, полу́чено, полу́чены
забы́тый	*forgotten*	забы́т, забы́та, забы́то, забы́ты
за́пертый	*locked*	за́перт, заперта́, за́перто, за́перты
закры́тый	*closed*	закры́т, закры́та, закры́то, закры́ты
откры́тый	*open(ed)*	откры́т, откры́та, откры́то, откры́ты

The short participle agrees with its subject in gender and number. Tense is expressed by the past and future forms of **бы́ть**.

The short past passive participle may be used to denote:

(*a*) a completed action undergone by the subject:

Докуме́нты *подпи́саны.*	*The documents have been signed.*
Окно́ бы́ло *откры́то* **ке́м-то.**	*The window had been opened by someone.*
За́втра магази́н бу́дет *закры́т.*	*Tomorrow the store will be closed.*
Я́ посети́л дворе́ц, кото́рый бы́л *постро́ен* **в XVIII ве́ке.**	*I visited a palace which was built in the 18th century.*

(*b*) a state of the subject:

Две́рь *заперта́.*	*The door is locked.*
Окно́ *закры́то.*	*The window is closed.*
Све́т *включён.*	*The light is (turned) on.*

73. Rewrite the sentence, making the subject the direct object, and replacing the short-form past passive participle with the third-person plural past tense of the same (subjectless) verb. The result is a synonymous sentence with passive meaning.

Model: Э́та ва́за *была́ сде́лана* из фарфо́ра. > Э́ту ва́зу *сде́лали* из фарфо́ра.

1. Э́та исто́рия *была́ забы́та* давно́.
2. Телегра́мма *была́ полу́чена* в суббо́ту.
3. Вы́ставка *была́ откры́та* на про́шлой неде́ле.
4. Рабо́та *была́ сде́лана* хорошо́.
5. До́м *бы́л постро́ен* в про́шлом ве́ке.

VERBAL ADVERBS (GERUNDS)

Verbal adverbs, also called gerunds, express an action accompanying the action of the main verb and performed by the same subject. Verbal adverbs combine characteristics of both verbs and adverbs. Like verbs, verbal adverbs can be imperfective or perfective, transitive or intransitive, depending on the verb from which they are derived. Similarly, they govern the same case, or preposition + case, as their underlying verb.

On the other hand, a verbal adverb is like an adverb in that it is indeclinable, and modifies the verb in the main clause. It indicates, depending on context, the manner, time, reason, or condition under which the action of the main verb takes place. Found primarily in written Russian, verbal adverbs can be used in place of subordinate clauses introduced by conjunctions such as *when*, *since*, *because*, *if*. Russian verbal adverbs have English equivalents in *-ing*. For example, the English *-ing* form in the following sentence would be translated by a (imperfective) verbal adverb: "You will strain your eyes *reading* [i.e., if you read] in bed."

Russian verbal adverbs are divided into two basic types: *imperfective* verbal adverbs (formed from imperfective verbs), and *perfective* verbal adverbs (formed from perfective verbs).

Imperfective Verbal Adverbs

Imperfective verbal adverbs are formed from the verb's basic stem by adding the suffix **-а/-я**. If the verb ends in **-ся**, then a final **-сь** is added to the vowel suffix.

Infinitive	*Stem*	*Verbal Adverb*	
чита́ть	читай-	чита́я	*reading*
занима́ться	занимай- ся	занима́ясь	*studying*
име́ть	имей-	име́я	*having*
волнова́ться	волнова/уй-ся	волну́ясь	*being nervous*
боя́ться	боя-ся	боя́сь	*fearing*
встава́ть	вставай-	встава́я	*getting up*
жи́ть	жив-	живя́	*living*
идти́	ид-	идя́	*going/walking*
говори́ть	говори-	говоря́	*speaking*
смотре́ть	смотре-	смотря́	*looking*
слы́шать	слыша-	слы́ша	*hearing*

Note: Some verbs have no imperfective verbal adverb, for example the irregular verbs **бежа́ть** *to run*, **éхать** *to go by vehicle*, **éсть** *to eat*, **мо́чь** *to be able*, **спа́ть** *to sleep*. The irregular verb **хоте́ть** *to want* has no imperfective verbal adverb (the form **хотя́** already serves as a conjunction with the meaning *although*), but the one formed from its synonym **жела́ть** *to wish* can be used in its place: **жела́я** *wishing*, *wanting*.

Imperfective verbal adverbs denote an attendant action which occurs simultaneously with that of the verb in the main clause. The verbal adverb by itself does not express tense; its tense coincides with the present, past, or future tense of the main verb.

Óн занима́ется, *слу́шая му́зыку.*   *He studies while listening to music.*
Óн занима́лся, *слу́шая му́зыку.*   *He studied while listening to music.*
Óн бу́дет занима́ться, *слу́шая му́зыку.*   *He will study while listening to music.*

Verbal adverbs indicate the time, reason, condition, or manner of the action expressed by the main verb. They can be used as an alternative to a subordinate clause, where these meanings are expressed explicitly by conjunctions such as **когда́** *when, while,* **пока́** *while,* **та́к как** *since, because,* **потому́ что** *because,* **е́сли** *if.*

Чита́я те́кст, о́н подчёркивает незнако́мые слова́.
(When) reading a text, he underlines the unfamiliar words.
Когда́ о́н чита́ет те́кст, . . .
When he reads a text, he . . .

Гуля́я по па́рку, я́ встре́тил дру́га.
(While) walking in the park, I met a friend.
Пока́ я́ гуля́л по па́рку, . . .
While I was walking in the park, . . .

Не *зна́я* её но́мер телефо́на, я́ не мо́г е́й позвони́ть.
Not knowing her telephone number, I was not able to call her.
Та́к как я́ не зна́л её но́мер телефо́на, . . .
Since I did not know her telephone number, . . .

Занима́ясь бе́гом, о́н бу́дет снима́ть стре́сс.
By running, he will reduce stress.
Е́сли о́н занима́ется бе́гом, . . .
If he runs, . . .

74. Replace the imperfective verbal adverb phrase by a subordinate clause introduced by **когда́** *when, while.* Be sure to put the verb in the same tense as the verb in the main clause. Follow the model.

Model: Убира́я ко́мнату, Све́та *нашла́* поте́рянную серёжку.
        Когда́ она́ убира́ла ко́мнату, . . .

1. *Занима́ясь* аэро́бикой, она́ улучша́ет своё здоро́вье.
2. *Возвраща́ясь* домо́й из кинотеа́тра, друзья́ разгова́ривали о фи́льме.
3. *Выходя́* из аудито́рии, студе́нты говори́ли об экза́мене.
4. *Рабо́тая* на компью́тере, о́н де́лает бо́льше.
5. *Живя́* в Москве́, мы́ ча́сто ходи́ли в теа́тр.

75. Replace the verbal adverb phrase by a subordinate clause introduced by **та́к как** *since, because,* as in the model. The tense must be the same as that of the main verb.

Model: Боя́сь опозда́ть, о́н *взя́л* такси́.
        Та́к как о́н боя́лся опозда́ть, . . .

1. *Желáя* чтó-нибудь éсть, они́ зашли́ в заку́сочную.
2. Мы́ ходи́ли по стоя́нке, *надéясь* найти́ потéрянную су́мку.
3. Не *понимáя* по-ру́сски, я́ не могу́ обща́ться с ни́м.
4. Не *имéя* дéнег, я́ не смóг купи́ть билéты.
5. *Вставáя* рáно, он успевáл сдéлать бóльше.

76. Replace the imperfective verbal adverb phrase with a subordinate clause introduced by **Éсли** *If*. Keep the same tense as that of the main verb. Follow the model.

Model: *Гуля́я* по чáсу в дéнь, вы́ намнóго укрепи́те своё здорóвье.
      Éсли вы́ бу́дете гуля́ть по чáсу в дéнь, . . .

1. *Тáк волну́ясь*, ты́ расшатáешь своё здорóвье.
2. *Изучáя* инострáнные языки́, вы́ смóжете хорошó познакóмиться с рáзными культу́рами.
3. *Путешéствуя* по рáзным стрáнам, вы́ смóжете расши́рить свóй кругозóр.
4. *Занимáясь* му́зыкой, вы́ смóжете обогати́ть себя́.

Perfective Verbal Adverbs

The perfective verbal adverb of most verbs is formed by adding the suffix **-в** to the verb's basic stem:

Infinitive	*Stem*	*Verbal Adverb*	
прочитáть	прочитáй-	прочитáв	*having read*
написáть	написа-	написáв	*having written*
отвéтить	ответи-	отвéтив	*having answered*
закóнчить	закончи-	закóнчив	*having finished*

For perfective verbs with the particle **-ся**, add **-вшись**:

верну́ться	верну-ся	верну́вшись	*having returned*
прости́ться	прости-ся	прости́вшись	*after saying goodbye*
умы́ться	умóй-ся	умы́вшись	*having washed*

Some perfective verbs that lose **-л** in the masculine past tense are found with the suffix **-ши** added to the masculine past-tense form of the verb. These forms occur in Russian literature of the 19th century, but are now considered obsolete:

Infinitive	*Masc. Past*	*Verbal Adverb*	
заперéть	зáпер	зáперши	*having locked*
помóчь	помóг	помóгши	*having helped*
испéчь	испёк	испёкши	*having baked*

Verbs which lose the suffix **-ну-** in the past tense, as well as those with a stem in **-р**, now normally form their perfective verbal adverb from the infinitive stem by adding **-в**:

заперéть	заперéв	*having locked*
вы́тереть	вы́терев	*having wiped (dry)*
привы́кнуть	привы́кнув	*having got used to*

Some perfective verbs with a basic stem in **з** or **с**, as well as those in **-д** or **-т** (especially prefixed motion verbs in **-йти**), form perfective verbal adverbs with the same suffix that imperfective verbs use, i.e., with **-я**:

привезти́	привез-	привезя́	*having brought by vehicle*
принести́	принес-	принеся́	*having brought, carried*
привести́	привед-	приведя́	*having brought, led on foot*
прийти́	при-ид-	придя́	*having arrived on foot*
сойти́	со-ид	сойдя́	*having stepped off*

Perfective verbal adverbs normally denote an action that is completed prior to the action denoted by the verb in the main clause.

Позáвтракав, **мáльчик пошёл в шкóлу.**
After having breakfast, the boy set out for school.

Perfective verbal adverb phrases may replace subordinate clauses introduced by conjunctions of time (**когдá** *when*), cause (**потому́ что** *because*), or condition (**éсли** *if*).

Прочитáв **газéту, óн пошёл погуля́ть с собáкой.**
Когдá óн прочитáл газéту, óн пошёл погуля́ть с собáкой.
When (After) he read the newspaper, he went for a walk with the dog.

Почу́вствовав **себя́ плóхо, онá рáно ушлá с рабóты.**
Not feeling well, she left work early.
Онá рáно ушлá с рабóты, потому́ что почу́вствовала себя́ плóхо.
She left work early because she didn't feel well.

Закóнчив **рабóту, óн смóжет позвони́ть тебé.**
Éсли óн закóнчит рабóту, . . .
If he finishes his work, he will be able to call you.

77. Replace the perfective verbal adverb phrase with a subordinate clause introduced by **когдá** *when* (*after*). The verb in the subordinate clause must have the same tense as that of the verb in the main clause. Follow the model.

Model: **Убрáв со столá, онá помы́ла посу́ду.**
         Когдá онá убралá со столá, . . .

1. *Умы́вшись,* óн сéл пообéдать.
2. *Закóнчив* рабóту, онá началá отдыхáть.
3. *Войдя́* в кóмнату, учи́тель срáзу нáчал урóк.
4. *Заперéв* двéрь, онá леглá спáть.
5. *Испёкши* пирóг, бáбушка позвалá детéй попрóбовать егó.

CHAPTER 8

Conjunctions

A conjunction is a part of speech consisting of one or more words which link or connect other words, phrases, or clauses in a sentence. There are two basic types of conjunctions: *coordinating* conjunctions and *subordinating* conjunctions.

COORDINATING CONJUNCTIONS

Coordinating conjunctions link elements of equal value in a sentence. The most common coordinating conjunctions in Russian are: **и** *and*; **и́ли** *or*; **но** *but*; **а** *and, but* (*rather*), *whereas*; **одна́ко** *but, however*; **и . . . и . . .** *both . . . and . . .*; **ни . . . ни . . .** *neither . . . nor. . .*; **и́ли . . . и́ли . . .** *either . . . or. . .*; **как . . . так и** *not only . . . but also*; and **не то́лько . . . но и** *not only . . . but also*. Coordinating conjunctions fall into the following subgroups: copulative, disjunctive, and adversative.

The elements connected by a coordinating conjunction must be equal and parallel. That is, the connected words, phrases, or clauses must perform an identical function in the sentence, e.g., as subjects or objects of the same verb, or modifiers of the same word.

In the following examples, the conjunction **и** joins two subjects, two predicates, and two clauses, respectively.

> **Та́ня** *и* **Ма́ша хорошо́ понима́ют по-англи́йски.**
> *Tanya and Maria understand English well.*

> **Они́ говоря́т** *и* **чита́ют по-англи́йски.**
> *They speak and read English.*

> **Та́ня ру́сская,** *и* **Ма́ша ру́сская.**
> *Tanya is Russian and Masha is Russian.*

In the following example, the conjunction **и́ли** joins two prepositional phrases:

> **Куда́ мы́ пое́дем ле́том, на пля́ж** *и́ли* **в го́ры?**
> *Where shall we go in the summer, to the beach or to the mountains?*

In the following example, the conjunction **но** joins two independent clauses.

> **Тама́ра родила́сь в Росси́и,** *но* **она́ не говори́т по-ру́сски.**
> *Tamara was born in Russia, but she doesn't speak Russian.*

Copulative (Connective) Coordinating Conjunctions

The copulative coordinating conjunctions connect two or more elements that have something in common.

и — *and*

Ле́том мы́ пое́дем на пля́ж *и* **в го́ры.**
In the summer we'll go to the beach and to the mountains.

и . . . и . . . — *both . . . and* (More emphatic than **и** *and*, the double **и . . . и** has one **и** before each parallel element.)

Ле́том мы́ пое́дем *и* **на пля́ж** *и* **в го́ры.**
In the summer we'll go both to the beach and to the mountains.

как . . . так и — *both . . . as well as* (a more literary, learned style used mainly in writing)

На конфере́нции обсужда́ли *как* **но́вые откры́тия в фи́зике,** *так и*
передовы́е взгля́ды совреме́нных филосо́фов.
At the conference they discussed new discoveries in physics, as well as the advanced views of modern philosophers.

не то́лько, . . . но и — *not only . . ., but also* (more emphatic and bookish in style)

Учёные на́шего институ́та интересу́ются *не то́лько* **эконо́микой Росси́и,**
но и **ро́лью Росси́и в европе́йском о́бществе.**
The scholars of our institute are interested not only in Russia's economy but also in Russia's role in European society.

The coordinating conjunction **а** can also be used in this copulative meaning if it is followed by the adverb **та́кже**. It conveys a more formal connotation than the usual conjunction **и**.

Алексе́ева преподаёт ру́сский язы́к, *а та́кже* **францу́зский язы́к.**
Alekseeva teaches Russian as well as French.

When **и** joins two complete sentences the adverb **то́же** *also, too, likewise* is often added to the second clause.

Ма́ма пошла́ в магази́н *и* **па́па** *то́же* **пошёл туда́.**
Mom went to the store, and Dad went there, too.

1. Rewrite the following sentences replacing **и** with **и . . . и . . .**.

Model: Ки́ра и Ла́ра чита́ют по-ру́сски.
  И Ки́ра *и* Ла́ра чита́ют по-неме́цки.

1. Жа́нна и Ма́ра занима́ются ру́сским языко́м.
2. Моя́ сестра́ говори́т по-ру́сски и по-испа́нски.
3. Ве́чером студе́нты смо́трят телеви́зор и слу́шают му́зыку.
4. Мы́ пригласи́ли к себе́ А́нну и Ива́на.

ни . . . ни — *neither . . . nor* (The negating particle **не** must be placed in front of the predicate (conjugated verb) of the clause.)

Мы́ не ви́дели *ни* **Ве́ру** *ни* **Ива́на.**
We saw neither Vera nor Ivan.

Соба́ки не́ было *ни* **в до́ме** *ни* **в гараже́.**
The dog was neither in the house nor in the garage.

However, if the negated parallel elements are themselves the predicates of the sentence, each of them is preceded by **ни**, and **не** is omitted.

Больно́й *ни* **ви́дит,** *ни* **слы́шит.**
The patient neither sees nor hears.

2. Negate the sentences, replacing **и . . . и** with **ни . . . ни**. Be sure to use **не** when necessary to negate the predicate. Follow the model.

   Model: Мэ́ри понима́ет *и* по-ру́сски *и* по-кита́йски.
         Мэ́ри *не* понима́ет *ни* по-ру́сски *ни* по-кита́йски.

   1. Мари́на лю́бит и фру́кты и о́вощи.
   2. Ле́том мы́ е́здили и в го́ры и на пля́ж.
   3. Э́та де́вушка и говори́т и чита́ет по-англи́йски.
   4. Слова́ э́той пе́сни и краси́вые и интере́сные.
   5. Ве́чером я́ писа́ла и пи́сьма и упражне́ния.

да — *and* (In informal conversation and in many folk sayings and idiomatic expressions, the unstressed conjunction **да** is often used to mean **и** *and*.)

Бли́зок ло́коть, *да* **не уку́сишь**. (Proverb)
So near and yet so far. (The elbow is near, but you can't bite it.)

Жи́ли-бы́ли стари́к *да* **стару́ха.**
Once upon a time there lived an old man and an old woman.

Disjunctive Coordinating Conjunctions

The disjunctive coordinating conjunctions present alternatives. The most common disjunctive conjunctions are **и́ли** *or* and **и́ли . . . и́ли** *either . . . or.*

и́ли — *or*
    Кто́ прие́дет сего́дня ве́чером, Никола́й *и́ли* **Ната́ша?**
    Who will arrive this evening, Nicholas or Natasha?

и́ли . . . и́ли — *either . . . or*
    И́ли **Никола́й** *и́ли* **Ната́ша прие́дет сего́дня ве́чером.**
    Either Nicholas or Natasha will arrive this evening.

Note. The double conjunction **ли́бо . . . ли́бо** is sometimes used in place of **и́ли . . . и́ли**, especially in conversation. **Ли́бо** can also be used singly to replace **и́ли**.

не то . . . не то — *either . . . or* (Used in conversational style to connote uncertainty and difficulty in specifying the exact nature of the action or thing described.)
    Де́ти услы́шали стра́нный зву́к — *не то* **кри́к** *не то* **пла́ч.**
    The children heard a strange sound—either a yell or a sob. (Not quite one and not quite the other.)

то ... то — *now ... now* (Used to connect changing actions or states.)

То óн смóтрит в окнó, *то* **óн хóдит по кóмнате.**
Now he looks out the window, now he paces the room.

3. Change the following sentences, replacing **и** with **и́ли** and **и ... и** with **и́ли ... и́ли**.

Model: (*a*) Вéчером я́ бýду читáть *и* отдыхáть.
Вéчером я́ бýду читáть *и́ли* отдыхáть.
(*b*) Дéти *и* бéгают *и* пры́гают.
Дéти *и́ли* бéгают *и́ли* пры́гают.

1. На ýжин у нáс бýдет сýп и салáт.
2. Мóй брáт хóчет купи́ть чёрные джи́нсы и си́ние брю́ки.
3. Купи́ мне, пожáлуйста, журнáл и газéту.
4. Возьми́те и молокó и лимонáд.
5. Нáш сы́н хóчет стáть и космонáвтом и президéнтом.

Adversative Coordinating Conjunctions

Adversative coordinating conjunctions join elements that seem contradictory or antithetical to one another.

но — *but* (The thought that follows **но** interrupts, adjusts, or contradicts what is asserted in the first clause.)

Герои́ня былá молодóй, *но* **си́льной и хрáброй.**
The heroine was young but (she was) strong and brave.

Э́тот áвтор хорошó пи́шет, *но* **никтó не покупáет егó кни́ги.**
This author writes well, but no one buys his books.

однáко — *but, however* (Synonymous with *но*, but must always be followed by a complete clause. It is used in more formal speaking and in writing, and emphasizes the antithesis between the two ideas more strongly than **но**.)

Герои́ня былá молодóй, *однáко* **онá былá си́льной и хрáброй.**
The heroine was young; she was, however, strong and brave.

Врáч дóлго объясня́л процедýру, *однáко* **для испýганного больнóго, егó словá не имéли никакóго значéния.**
The doctor spent a long time explaining the procedure; however, for the frightened patient his words had no meaning.

4. Join each pair of sentences into one sentence, using **и** if the elements have something in common and **но** if the second element appears to contradict the first.

Model: (*a*) Вчерá шёл си́льный дóждь. Вчерá бы́л си́льный вéтер.
Вчерá шёл си́льный дóждь *и* бы́л си́льный вéтер.
(*b*) Вчерá шёл си́льный дóждь. Вчерá бы́ло óчень теплó.
Вчерá шёл си́льный дóждь, *но* бы́ло óчень теплó.

1. Бáбушка хорошó понимáет по-англи́йски. Онá не читáет по-англи́йски.
2. Мой сёстры лю́бят танцевáть. Я́ не люблю́ танцевáть.
3. Вéчером мы́ переводи́ли статью́. Мы́ не кóнчили переводи́ть её.

　　4.　Вади́м пое́дет на Ура́л. Его́ брат то́же пое́дет туда́.
　　5.　Э́то дли́нный рома́н. Он о́чень интере́сный.
　　6.　В э́том рестора́не хлеб о́чень вку́сный. Суп то́же о́чень вку́сный.

The Adversative Conjunction A: Contrastive and Contradictory

The adversative conjunction **a** has both a *contrastive* meaning and a *contradictive* meaning. In its contrastive function it is used to join two or more *complete statements* that are juxtaposed. In this usage it is usually translated *and*, with the connotation *while, whereas*.

Ма́ша рабо́тает в институ́те, *а* **её подру́га рабо́тает в библиоте́ке.**
Masha works at the institute, and her girlfriend works at the library.

Ма́ма слу́шает ра́дио, *а* **па́па смо́трит фотогра́фии.**
Mom is listening to the radio, and Dad is looking at photos.

If both statements share the same predicate, that predicate is often omitted from the second clause and replaced with a dash.

Ты говори́шь бы́стро, *а* **я — ме́дленно.**
You speak quickly, and I (speak) slowly.

In its contradictive meaning, **a** joins words, phrases, or clauses, one of which is asserted to be correct as opposed to the other, which is declared incorrect. The incorrect element is preceded by *не*. In this function **a** is translated *and* when it precedes the *negated* element, and *but* (*rather*) when it precedes the *positive* element.

Ма́ша рабо́тает в институ́те, *а* **не в библиоте́ке.**
Masha works at the institute, (and) not at the library.

Подру́га Ма́ши рабо́тает не в институ́те, *а* **в библиоте́ке.**
Masha's girlfriend works, not at the institute, but (rather) at the library.

В библиоте́ке рабо́тает не Ма́ша, *а* **её подру́га.**
Not Masha, but (rather) her girlfriend, works at the library.

Подру́га, *а* **не Ма́ша, рабо́тает в библиоте́ке.**
The girlfriend, (and) not Masha, works at the library.

The conjunction **a** is also used in the meaning *and* to introduce follow-up questions.

— Э́то мой но́вый друг.	*This is my new friend*
— А как его́ зову́т?	*And what's his name?*

5. Translate the sentences and tell whether the **a** is contrastive or contradictive. See the above section for explanation and examples of each.

　　1.　Моя́ ста́ршая сестра́ живёт в Бо́стоне, а я живу́ в Вашингто́не.
　　2.　Моя́ ста́ршая сестра́ живёт не в Вашингто́не, а в Бо́стоне.
　　3.　Моя́ ста́ршая сестра́ живёт в Бо́стоне, а не в Вашингто́не.
　　4.　Тури́сты живу́т в гости́нице, а студе́нты — в общежи́тии.
　　5.　Москва́ нахо́дится на реке́, а Оде́сса нахо́дится на мо́ре.
　　6.　Оде́сса нахо́дится не на реке́, а на мо́ре.
　　7.　Санкт-Петербу́рг нахо́дится не на ю́ге, а на се́вере.

8. Моя́ сестра́ мно́го говори́т, а мо́й бра́т ма́ло.

9. Мы́ реши́ли пое́хать в го́ры, а не на мо́ре.

10. Ю́рий позвони́л мне́, не потому́ что о́н хоте́л со мно́й поговори́ть, а потому́ что ему́ нужна́ моя́ по́мощь.

Choosing И, А, or Но

Two independent clauses can be linked together by a coordinating conjunction into one compound sentence. The differences between **и**, **а**, and **но** can be subtle and therefore require special mention. The correct conjunction depends on the type of relationship between the connected elements.

(1) When to use **и**

The conjunction **и** joins independent clauses *only* (*a*) when the same statement is being made about two different subjects; (*b*) when each clause has the same subject and the word **та́кже** "*in addition*," can be inserted before the information in the second clause; or (*c*) whenever the second clause follows logically from the first.

(*a*) **Ма́рк лю́бит рисова́ть** *и* **Ла́ра (***то́же***)лю́бит рисова́ть.**
Mark likes to draw and Lara (also) likes to draw.

In such a sentence the word **то́же** is often inserted after the second subject. If such a compound sentence is split into two separate sentences, the conjunction **и** takes on the meaning *also*.

Ма́рк лю́бит рисова́ть. *И* Ла́ра лю́бит рисова́ть.
Mark likes to draw. Lara also likes to draw.

(*b*) **Мари́я о́чень хорошо́ танцу́ет,** *и* **она́ та́кже игра́ет на фле́йте.**
Maria dances very well, and, in addition, she plays the flute.

The subject of both clauses is Maria, and the word **та́кже** "*in addition*" pertains to the new information in the second clause.

(*c*) **Ма́рк лю́бит рисова́ть** *и* **он хо́чет ста́ть худо́жником.**
Mark likes to draw, and he wants to become an artist.

Пошёл до́ждь *и* **(поэ́тому) мы́ отмени́ли пикни́к.**
It began to rain, and (therefore) we canceled the picnic.

In both these sentences, the second statement follows logically from the first. In such cases, the adverb **поэ́тому** *therefore* is often inserted after the **и**.

(2) When to use **а**

If the statements in each clause have a parallel structure and are different but not conflicting, the statements are in *contrast* to each other, and the conjunction **а** is normally used. It can be translated *and*, *whereas*, or *while*, depending on the style. Usually there is a common element in both clauses, along with at least two contrasting elements.

Ма́рк лю́бит рисова́ть, *а* **Ла́ра бо́льше лю́бит чита́ть.**
Mark likes to draw, and (whereas, while) Lara prefers to read.

Сего́дня и за́втра я́ бу́ду рабо́тать, *а* **послеза́втра я́ бу́ду отдыха́ть.**
Today and tomorrow I'll work, and the day after tomorrow I'll rest.

То́м сиде́л на дива́не, *а* **я́ стоя́ла у окна́.**
Tom was sitting on the sofa, and I was standing by the window.

In the first example the common element is the verb **лю́бит**. The subjects are not the same and they like different things. In the second example, the common element is **я**. The adverbs of time and the activities are contrasted. In the third example, all three elements are contrasted.

(3)   When to use **но**

If the information in the second independent clause appears to contradict, or is at odds with, what is asserted in the first clause, the conjunction **но** is required. If, in the English translation, "*however*" can be used in place of "*but*," **но** is usually the correct choice.

> **Ма́рк лю́бит рисова́ть,** *но* **о́н не лю́бит пока́зывать свои́ рису́нки.**
> *Mark likes to draw, but (however) he doesn't like to show his drawings.*

In some instances either **а** or **но** can be used, with **но** expressing the stronger opposition.

> **Ма́рк лю́бит рисова́ть,** *а* **Ла́ра не лю́бит.**
> *Mark likes to draw, and Lara doesn't.*

> **Ма́рк лю́бит рисова́ть,** *но* **Ла́ра не лю́бит.**
> *Mark likes to draw, but Lara doesn't.*

6.   Complete the sentences with the appropriate conjunction: **и**, **а**, or **но**.

1.   Пе́рвого сентября́ начина́ется учёба в шко́ле _____ всё шко́льники ра́но выхо́дят из до́ма.
2.   Учёба в шко́ле начина́ется в сентябре́, _____ конча́ется в ию́не.
3.   Учёба в шко́ле начина́ется пе́рвого сентября́, _____ Бори́с не пойдёт на заня́тия. О́н бо́лен.
4.   Я́ хочу́ сего́дня ве́чером пойти́ в кино́, _____ моя́ сестра́ хо́чет пойти́ на конце́рт.
5.   Вади́м хо́чет пойти́ на футбо́льный ма́тч, _____ его́ ма́ма ему́ не разреша́ет.
6.   Вчера́ мы́ е́здили за́ город _____ на́ши друзья́ е́здили с на́ми.
7.   Я́ хорошо́ понима́ю бра́та _____ о́н хорошо́ понима́ет меня́.
8.   Ле́на хорошо́ у́чится _____ она́ о́чень хорошо́ сдаёт экза́мены.
9.   О́льга мно́го занима́ется, _____ она́ пло́хо сдаёт экза́мены.
10. Оле́г хорошо́ говори́т по-англи́йски, _____ его́ жена́ хорошо́ говори́т по-францу́зски.

SUBORDINATING CONJUNCTIONS

Subordinating conjunctions connect an independent, or main, clause with a dependent, or subordinate, clause which completes or modifies it. The subordinate clause is called "dependent" because it cannot stand on its own. The subordinating conjunction specifies the type of relationship between the main clause and the statement made in the dependent clause. The principal relationship types are: temporal (*when, before, after, until*), causal (*because, since*), purposive (*in order to*), resultative (*so that*), concessive (*although, whereas*), and conditional (*if*).

As in English, most subordinate clauses may either precede or follow the main clause, depending on the preference or intention of the speaker. Following are the most frequently encountered subordinating conjunctions, categorized according to the type of relationship they indicate between the main and the dependent clause.

Temporal Conjunctions

когда́ — *when, whenever, as, while, after*

The meaning of this conjunction depends on the aspect and tense sequence of the verbs in each clause. For example, **когда́** has the sense of *after*, when the predicate of the **когда́** clause is in the perfective aspect.

> *Когда́* **па́па прие́хал, все́ се́ли за сто́л.**
> *When (After) Dad had arrived, everyone sat down at the table.*

If the action is to take place in the future, the future tense must be used in the Russian **когда́** clause (whereas English uses the present tense).

> *Когда́* **па́па прие́дет, все́ ся́дут за сто́л.**
> *When (After) Dad arrives, everyone will sit down at the table.*

The conjunction **когда́** normally has the sense of *while* or *as* when the predicate of the **когда́** clause is in the imperfective aspect.

> *Когда́* **па́па шёл домо́й, о́н зашёл в магази́н.**
> *When (While/As) Dad was walking home, he stopped off at the store.*

> *Когда́* **Пе́тя учи́лся в институ́те, о́н жи́л в общежи́тии.**
> *When (While) Pete was a student at the institute, he lived in the dormitory.*

пока́ — *while* (Refers to an ongoing action or process; therefore, the predicate of the **пока́** clause is imperfective.)

> *Пока́* **ма́ма гото́вила обе́д, де́ти смотре́ли телеви́зор.**
> *While Mom was making lunch, the children watched television.*

> *Пока́* **ребёнок спи́т, ма́ма отдыха́ет.**
> *While the baby sleeps, Mom rests.*

Пока́ . . . не — *until* (The predicate of the *until* clause may be perfective future or past.)

> **Мы́ никуда́ не пойдём,** *пока́* **вы́** *не* **прекрати́те разгова́ривать.**
> *We won't go anywhere until you stop talking.*

> **Мы́ подожда́ли,** *пока́* **до́ждь** *не* **прекрати́лся.**
> *We waited until the rain stopped.*

Как — *when* (**Как** can replace **когда́** in situations which express unexpectedly sudden action or change. The idea conveyed is usually *hardly, barely, no sooner than*.)

> **Я́ едва́ вошла́ в ли́фт,** *как* **две́ри закры́лись.**
> *I had barely entered the elevator, when the doors closed.*

> **Не успе́ли мы́ се́сть в такси́,** *как* **води́тель пое́хал.**
> *We had hardly taken our seats in the taxi, when the driver took off.*

Many composite subordinating conjunctions are formed by joining **как** with other words to render a more specific time-related meaning.

Как то́лько — *as soon as* (As with **когда́**, a future action in the dependent clause must be expressed in the future tense.)

> **Я́ бу́ду де́лать дома́шнюю рабо́ту,** *как то́лько* **зако́нчится фи́льм.**
> *I will do my homework as soon as the film is over.*

> **Она́ обы́чно де́лает дома́шнюю рабо́ту,** *как то́лько* **прихо́дит домо́й.**
> *She usually does her homework as soon as she comes home.*

В то вре́мя как — *while* (The predicates of both clauses are usually imperfective.)

> **Де́ти игра́ли во дворе́ под присмо́тром учи́тельницы,** *в то вре́мя как* **и́х**
> **роди́тели бы́ли на шко́льном собра́нии.**
> *The children were playing in the yard under a teacher's supervision, while their*
> *parents were at the school meeting.*

Many composite subordinating conjunctions are formed by combining a preposition with the demonstrative **то** in the required case, followed by the conjunction **как**.

До того́ как — *before* (May be followed by a complete clause, or—if the subject of both clauses is the same—an infinitive may replace the finite (conjugated) predicate.)

> *До того́ как* **на́ш сы́н поступи́л в МГУ, мы́ никогда́ не е́здили в Москву́.**
> *Before our son entered Moscow University, we had never gone to Moscow.*

> *До того́ как* **поступи́ть в МГУ, о́н до́лжен рабо́тать го́д.**
> *Before entering Moscow University, he must work for a year.*

Пре́жде чем — *before* (Used in place of **до того́ как** whenever the *before* clause contains a precaution or an essential prerequisite to the action of the main clause. Usually the subjects of both clauses are the same, and **пре́жде чем** is followed by an infinitive.)

> *Пре́жде чем* **обвиня́ть друго́го, на́до че́стно оцени́ть свои́ со́бственные посту́пки.**
> *Before accusing another, one should honestly evaluate one's own actions.*

Пе́ред тем как — *(right) before* (May be followed by either a finite verb, or—if the subject of both clauses is the same—by an infinitive.)

> *Пе́ред тем как* **изве́стный актёр вы́шел на сце́ну, за́л зати́х.**
> *Right before the famous actor came out on stage, the hall became quiet.*

> **Включи́те све́т,** *пе́ред тем как* **войти́ в за́л.**
> *Turn on the light before entering the auditorium.*

По́сле того́ как — *after* (followed only by a finite verb)

> **Я́ реши́ла изуча́ть ру́сский язы́к,** *по́сле того́ как* **я́ побыва́ла в Москве́.**
> *I decided to study Russian after I visited Moscow.*

> *По́сле того́ как* **ты́ вернёшься из командиро́вки, позвони́ мне́.**
> *After you return from your business trip, phone me.*

С тех пор как — *since*

> **Прошло́ два́ го́да** *с тех пор как* **мы́ ви́делись в после́дний ра́з.**
> *Two years have passed since the last time we saw each other.*

До тех пор пока́ . . . не — *until* (This is a more formal version of **пока́ . . . не.**)

Зри́тели стоя́ли и аплоди́ровали *до тех пор пока́* **орке́стр** *не* **се́л и на́чал игра́ть.**
The audience stood and applauded until the orchestra sat down and began playing.

7. Combine each pair of simple sentences into a complex sentence, using the conjunction **когда́**. Determine whether **когда́** has the sense *while* or *after*.

Model: Све́та писа́ла пи́сьма. Она́ слу́шала му́зыку.
      Когда́ Све́та писа́ла пи́сьма, она́ слу́шала му́зыку.
      <u>While</u> Sveta was writing letters, she listened to music.

1. Друзья́ возвраща́лись домо́й. Они́ разгова́ривали обо всём.
2. Друзья́ верну́лись домо́й. Они́ легли́ и усну́ли.
3. Мы́ проща́лись. Мы́ кре́пко обнима́лись.
4. Мы́ прости́лись. Я́ пошёл домо́й.
5. Ма́ша смотре́ла ста́рые фотогра́фии. Она́ вспомина́ла про́шлое.
6. Ма́ша посмотре́ла переда́чу. Она́ вы́ключила телеви́зор.

8. Rewrite each pair of sentences as a single complex sentence beginning with a subordinate clause introduced by **по́сле того́ как**. Follow the model.

Model: Са́ша реши́л зада́чи. Пото́м о́н пошёл погуля́ть.
      По́сле того́ как Са́ша реши́л зада́чи, о́н пошёл погуля́ть.

1. Де́ти поза́втракали. Пото́м они́ пошли́ в шко́лу.
2. Ма́ма пригото́вилиа обе́д. Пото́м она́ позвала́ на́с се́сть за сто́л.
3. Андре́й сда́л экза́мен. Пото́м о́н пошёл с подру́гой в кафе́.
4. Ко́нчилась телепереда́ча. Пото́м ребя́та на́чали слу́шать но́вый ди́ск.
5. Оте́ц ко́нчил писа́ть докла́д. Пото́м о́н ста́л отдыха́ть.

9. Answer the questions, stating that one should perform the action *before* performing the second action in parentheses. Use the conjunction **до того́ как**, or **пе́ред тем как**, as appropriate. Follow the model.

Model: — Когда́ на́до чи́стить зу́бы?   (ложи́ться спа́ть)
      — На́до чи́стить зу́бы *пе́ред тем как* ложи́ться спа́ть.

1. — Когда́ на́до зако́нчить изуча́ть ру́сский язы́к?   (пое́дешь в Росси́ю)
2. — Когда́ на́до мы́ть ру́ки?   (обе́дать)
3. — Когда́ на́до побри́ться?   (уйти́ на рабо́ту)
4. — Когда́ на́до ко́нчить э́ту рабо́ту?   (уе́хать в о́тпуск)
5. — Когда́ на́до чи́стить фру́кты?   (и́х е́сть)
6. — Когда́ на́до вы́ключить све́т?   (уйти́ из ко́мнаты)

10. Combine each pair of simple sentences into a complex sentence, using the conjunction **до тех пор, пока́ не . . . .** Follow the model.

Model: Де́ти игра́ли во дворе́. Ма́ма позвала́ и́х обе́дать.
      Де́ти игра́ли во дворе́ *до тех пор, пока́* ма́ма *не* позвала́ и́х обе́дать.

1. Мы́ зде́сь бу́дем стоя́ть. Магази́н откро́ется.
2. Ребёнок пла́кал. Ма́ма покорми́ла его́.
3. Ви́ктор реша́л зада́чи. О́н уста́л.
4. Ребя́та загора́ли на пля́же. Ста́ло хо́лодно.
5. О́н пи́л пи́во. Он напи́лся.

11. Rewrite the sentence, stating how much time has passed *since* the given event occurred. Use the conjunction **с тех пор как**, as in the model.

Model: Я бы́л в Москве́ пя́ть ле́т наза́д.

Прошло́ пя́ть ле́т *с тех пор как* я́ бы́л в Москве́.

1. Па́влик купи́л маши́ну полтора́ ме́сяца наза́д.
2. Они́ перее́хали в но́вый до́м три́ го́да наза́д.
3. Ребёнок роди́лся ше́сть ме́сяцев наза́д.
4. Мы́ получи́ли письмо́ от Ли́и полтора́ го́да наза́д.

Causal Conjunctions

Causal subordinating conjunctions answer questions such as **Почему́?** *Why?* **По како́й причи́не?** *For what reason?*

Потому́ что — *because* (The subordinate clause containing **потому́ что** must always follow the main clause.)

Мы́ спеши́ли, *потому́ что* **опа́здывали на конце́рт.**
We were in a hurry because we were late for the concert.

A comma is inserted between **потому́** and **что** when special emphasis is placed on the cause. An emphatic or delimiting word such as **то́лько** *only*, **и́менно** *precisely*, may precede the conjunction:

Его́ взя́ли на рабо́ту то́лько *потому,* **что о́н дру́г нача́льника.**
They hired him only because he is a friend of the boss.

Президе́нт реши́л не е́хать на конфере́нцию, и́менно *потому,* **что о́н не мо́жет согласи́ться с пози́цией Европе́йского сообщества.**
The president decided not to go to the conference, precisely because he is unable to agree with the position of the European Community.

Та́к как — *since, because* (May precede or follow the main clause.)

Та́к как президе́нт не мо́жет согласи́ться с пози́цией ЕС, о́н реши́л не е́хать на конфере́нцию.
Since the president is unable to agree with the position of the EC, he has decided not to go to the conference.

Благодаря́ тому́ что — *because, thanks to the fact that* (Usually suggests a positive circumstance, and a sense of the speaker's satisfaction or appreciation. Often used in scientific and journalistic writing.)

Мы́ смогли́ зако́нчить э́ту рабо́ту, *благодаря́ тому́ что* **вы́ на́м помогли́.**
We were able to finish the work thanks to the fact that you helped us.

Из-за того́, что — *because, on account of* (Usually suggests a negative circumstance, and a sense of the speaker's disapproval or dissatisfaction.)

> *Из-за того́ что* **шёл до́ждь, я́рмарка не состоя́лась.**
> *Because it was raining, the fair did not take place.*

Поско́льку — *as long as, in so far as, since*

> *Поско́льку* **он зна́ет ру́сский, пу́сть он де́лает э́тот перево́д.**
> *As long as he knows Russian, let him do this translation.*

Other causal conjunctions, found primarily in official, bookish style, include:

Ввиду́ того́, что — *in view of* (*the fact that*)
Всле́дствие того́, что — *in consequence of* (*the fact that*)
В си́лу того́, что — *because of, on the strength of* (*the fact that*)

12. Combine each pair of simple sentences into a complex sentence, using the conjunction **потому́ что** or **так как**. Follow the model.

> *Model:* Студе́нты уста́ли. Они́ занима́лись 3 часа́ без переры́ва.
> Студе́нты уста́ли, *потому́ что* они́ занима́лись 3 часа́ без переры́ва.

1. Пётр бы́стро реши́л э́ту тру́дную зада́чу. Он хорошо́ зна́ет матема́тику.
2. Ле́на сего́дня о́чень уста́ла. Она́ не вы́спалась.
3. Ди́ма спеши́л. Он опа́здывал на ле́кцию.
4. Серёжа пошёл в библиоте́ку. Он до́лжен верну́ть кни́гу.
5. Лари́са не была́ на заня́тиях. Она́ была́ больна́.

13. Combine each pair of simple sentences into a complex sentence using the conjunction **благодаря́ тому́, что** or **из-за того́, что** depending on whether the events described are positive or negative. Follow the model.

> *Model:* Он отли́чно перево́дит. У него́ большо́й о́пыт и тала́нт.
> Он отли́чно перево́дит благодаря́ тому́, что у него́ большой о́пыт . . .

1. Экску́рсия была́ отменена́. Вы́пал большо́й сне́г.
2. Он выполня́ет свою́ рабо́ту в сро́к. Он о́чень организо́ванный челове́к.
3. Проду́кты испо́ртились. Они́ не храни́лись в холоди́льнике.
4. Хоро́шие результа́ты бы́ли дости́гнуты. Бы́л приме́нён но́вый ме́тод.
5. Она́ хорошо́ зако́нчила университе́т. Она́ усе́рдно рабо́тала.

Purposive Conjunctions

Subordinating conjunctions of purpose answer the question **Заче́м?** *Why? For what purpose?* They introduce clauses stating the purpose or goal of an action and the intention or desire of the subject of the main clause.

Что́бы — *in order to, so that,* or untranslated (With most verbs of desire, intention, request, or instruction, **что́бы** is used with the past-tense form of the verb, when the main clause and the subordinate clause contain different subjects. See pages 263–264.)

> **Мы́ покра́сили до́м,** *что́бы* **он бо́льше нра́вился потенциа́льным покупа́телям.**
> *We painted our house so that it would be more appealing to potential buyers.*

Профессора́ на́шей ка́федры хотя́т, *что́бы* **всё студе́нты пое́хали ле́том на пра́ктику.**
The professors in our department want all the students to do field training this summer.

Сестра́ сказа́ла, *что́бы* **всё друзья́ встре́тились у вхо́да в кинотеа́тр.**
My sister told all her friends to meet by the entrance to the movie theater.

If, however, the subject of the purpose clause is the same subject as in the main clause, **что́бы** is followed by an infinitive.

О́н серьёзно гото́вится к экза́менам, *что́бы* **поступи́ть в шко́лу би́знеса.**
He is seriously preparing for his exams in order to enter the business school.

Что́бы can be combined with the prepositions **для** *for* and **с** *with* and the demonstrative **то** in the required case to form more emphatic composite conjunctions:

Для того́, что́бы — *for the purpose of, so that*
С тем, что́бы — *with the purpose of, so that*
За тем, что́бы — *for the purpose of, so that*

Юри́ст гро́мко и уве́ренно защища́л своего́ клие́нта, *для того́, что́бы*
　　всё в суде́ утверди́лись в его́ невино́вности.
The lawyer defended his client loudly and confidently, so that everyone in the
　　courtroom would be convinced of his innocence.

Subordinating Conjunctions Что and Как

Что — *that*

The conjunction **что** (unstressed and always preceded by a comma) normally introduces a subordinate that is dependent on a main clause containing a verb meaning *say, think, know, hope, feel*, etc. Unlike English, which permits the omission of the word *that*, Russian does not normally permit the conjunction **что** to be dropped from the sentence. When reporting speech indirectly, observe the rule of reported speech and express the reported clause in the *same tense* that the speaker used in the original, direct speech.

Ла́ра сказа́ла, *что* **она́ на́с встре́тит по́сле конце́рта.**
Lara said (that) she would meet us after the concert.

Я́ зна́ю, *что* **она́ ска́жет,** *что* **фи́льм е́й понра́вился.**
I know (that) she'll say (that) she liked the film.

Мне́ ка́жется, *что* **ма́ма волну́ется почему́-то.**
It seems to me that Mom is upset for some reason.

In addition, **что** introduces subordinate clauses after short-form adjectives and adverbs that express states of mind, emotion, or perception.

Я́ о́чень ра́да, *что* **вы́ ра́но прие́хали.**
I'm very glad that you came early.

Ви́дно бы́ло, *что* **студе́нтам ста́ло ску́чно.**
It was evident that the students had gotten bored.

In all the above cases, **что** is an unstressed connective word which is not part of either clause. When the word **что** functions as a subject or object in the dependent clause, it is not a conjunction, but rather a stressed pronoun, and is translated *what*.

> **Я зна́ю,** *что́* **она́ ска́жет.** (**что́** is direct object of the verb **ска́жет.**)
> *I know what she'll say.*
> **Мне интере́сно,** *что́* **её волну́ет.** (**Что́** is subject of the verb **волну́ет.**)
> *I wonder what is upsetting her.*

14. Translate into Russian using the appropriate word: **что́бы, что** or **что́.**

  1. Dad said that Misha had called home.
  2. Dad told Misha to call home.
  3. I understand that you told the truth.
  4. We wanted you to tell the truth.
  5. We know what you said.
  6. Masha turned on the television in order to watch the film.
  7. Masha turned on the television so that we could watch the film.

Как — untranslated

To express the idea that someone *perceives* an action occurring (e.g., *I saw him leaving, We heard them talking*) the main clause contains the verb of perception, and the subordinate clause containing the action verb is normally introduced by the conjunction **как** (preceded by a comma, and not translated).

> **Та́ня заме́тила,** *как* **он подходи́л ко мне́.**
> *Tanya noticed him approaching me.*

> **Мы слы́шали,** *как* **она́ ушла́.**
> *We heard her leave.*

> **Все ви́дели,** *как* **он ходи́л по ко́мнате.**
> *Everyone saw him pacing the room.*

Such sentences can be rendered with the conjunction **что** *that*, but then the sentence does not convey the perception of the action, but instead reports a *fact*.

> **Все ви́дели,** *что* **он ходи́л по ко́мнате.**
> *Everyone saw that he was pacing the room.*

15. Translate into Russian using the appropriate conjunction: **как** or **что.**

  1. I saw him arrive.
  2. I saw that he had arrived.
  3. We heard her singing.
  4. We noticed that he had left.

Resultative Conjunctions

Subordinating conjunctions of result invariably follow the main clause, and express the logical result or consequence of the situation in the main clause.

та́к что — *so, so that*

> **Я́ не о́чень хорошо́ зна́ю его́,** *та́к что* **мне́ неудо́бно звони́ть ему́.**
> *I don't know him very well, so I feel uncomfortable calling him.*

Such a relationship can be expressed equally well by using the coordinating conjunction **и** and the adverb **поэ́тому** *therefore*.

> **Я́ не о́чень хорошо́ зна́ю его́** *и* *поэ́тому* **мне́ неудо́бно звони́ть ему́.**

16. Combine the two simple sentences into a complex sentence using the conjunction **та́к что**. Follow the model.

> *Model:* Я́ вчера́ бы́л бо́лен. Мне́ пришло́сь пропусти́ть заня́тия.
> Я́ вчера́ бы́л бо́лен, так что мне́ пришло́сь пропусти́ть заня́тия.

1. О́н опозда́л на авто́бус. О́н реши́л взя́ть такси́.
2. Мо́й дру́г до́лго жи́л в Ки́еве. О́н хорошо́ зна́ет э́тот го́род.
3. Э́то о́чень просто́й те́кст. Я́ его́ бы́стро перевёл.
4. Я́ уже́ прочита́л газе́ту. Я́ да́л её сосе́ду.
5. Я́ зна́л, что она́ лю́бит рок-му́зыку. Я́ пригласи́л её на рок-концерт.

Conditional Conjunctions

Е́сли — *if* (See discussion of real and unreal conditions in Chapter 7, page 260.)

The conjunction **е́сли** expresses a condition that

(*a*) may occur regularly:

> *Е́сли* **пого́да хоро́шая, мы́ гуля́ем в па́рке.**
> *If the weather is nice, we walk in the park.*

(*b*) is likely to occur in the future (when the event has yet to occur, the **е́сли** clause must be in the future tense)

> *Е́сли* **вы́ дади́те мне́ сво́й а́дрес, то́ я́ ва́м напишу́.**
> *If you give me your address, then I'll write to you.*

(*c*) or has perhaps already occurred.

> *Е́сли* **по́езд пришёл во́время, то́ па́па сейча́с до́лжен прийти́.**
> *If the train arrived on time, then Dad should be coming home any minute now.*

Е́сли ... не — *unless*

> **Я́ э́то не пойму́,** *е́сли* **ты́ мне́** *не* **объясни́шь.**
> *I won't understand that unless you explain it to me.*

Ра́з — *since, now that* (Used in both conversational and literary styles; expresses a real condition.)

> *Ра́з* **о́н пришёл, пу́сть о́н са́м расска́жет на́м об э́том.**
> *Since/Now that he's come, let him tell us about this himself.*

Concessive Conjunctions

Хотя́ (хоть) — *although* (The **хотя́** clause may contain the particle **и**, placed for emphasis before the key word or phrase of the clause. The main clause frequently is introduced with a contradictive conjunction such as **но**.)

Хотя́ о́н и челове́к небольши́х сре́дств, но о́н о́чень мно́го де́лает для свои́х дете́й.
Although he is a person of moderate means, he still does quite a lot for his children.

Хоть и тру́дно ему́ бы́ло, о́н всё-таки при́нял э́то реше́ние.
Although it was difficult for him, he nevertheless made this decision.

Несмотря́ на то, что — *despite the fact that* (more formal than **хотя́** and **хоть**)

Несмотря́ на то, что я живу́ в Москве́ уже́ два́ го́да, я ча́сто теря́ю доро́гу.
Despite the fact that I've been living in Moscow for two years, I often get lost.

17. Combine each pair of simple sentences into a complex sentence with either a conditional clause introduced by **е́сли**, or a concessive clause introduced by **хотя́**.

    Model: О́н мно́го занима́лся. О́н пло́хо сда́л экза́мен.
        Хотя́ о́н мно́го занима́лся, о́н пло́хо сда́л экза́мен.

    1. Мы́ угова́ривали его́. О́н не согласи́лся.
    2. Сне́г пойдёт. Мы́ бу́дем ката́ться на лы́жах.
    3. Ему́ предложи́ли большу́ю зарпла́ту. О́н не согласи́лся на э́ту рабо́ту.
    4. Все́ уста́нут. Мы́ остано́вим рабо́ту.
    5. Все́ уста́ли. Мы́ продолжа́ли рабо́тать.

Comparative Conjunctions

Как — *as, the (same) way that* (Expresses a similarity or comparison.)

Они́ лю́бят друг дру́га *как* **родны́е сёстры (лю́бят друг дру́га).**
They love each other like true sisters (love each other).

Often the words **так же** precede **как**, making the comparison more emphatic.

Тебе́ на́до относи́ться к свои́м заня́тиям *так же* **серьёзно,** *как* **ты́ отно́сишься к му́зыке.**
You should relate to your studies as seriously as you relate to music.

The conjunction **как** occurs regularly in similes such as the following:

бы́стрый *как* **мо́лния**	*fast as lightning*
голо́дный *как* **во́лк**	*hungry as a wolf*
пья́н *как* **сапо́жник**	*drunk as a shoemaker*
свобо́ден *как* **пти́ца**	*free as a bird*

как бу́дто/бу́дто бы/как бу́дто бы, сло́вно — *as though, as if* (Indicate that the similarity suggested is not the case in actual fact.)

Молодо́й води́тель смотре́л на полице́йского, *как бу́дто* **о́н бы́л ни в чём не винова́т.**
The young driver looked at the policeman, as though he were not guilty of anything.

Я́ по́мню то́т де́нь, когда́ роди́ла́сь моя́ до́чь так хорошо́, *как бу́дто э́то*
  бы́ло то́лько вчера́.
I remember the day my daughter was born as well, as if it were only yesterday.

18. Complete the sentences with the appropriate conjunction: **как** or **как бу́дто**.

    1. О́н ведёт себя́ так, _____ обы́чно.
    2. О́н ведёт себя́, _____ ничего́ не случи́лось.
    3. Пого́да была́, _____ э́то ча́сто быва́ет в а́вгусте, жа́ркая и вла́жная.
    4. Пого́да в ма́е была́ жа́ркая и вла́жная, _____ ле́то уже́ наступи́ло.

чем — *than* (Introduces the second term of a comparison.)

    Та́ня бо́лее серьёзная студе́нтка, *чем* **Ма́ша.**
    Tanya is a more serious student than Masha.

    О́н бо́лее спосо́бный челове́к, *чем* **я́ ду́мал.**
    He is a more capable person than I thought.

For discussion and exercises on the uses of **чем**, see Chapter 5 (page 163).

Answers to Exercises

Chapter 1

1.
1. Алаба́ма
2. Аризо́на
3. Вермо́нт
4. Индиа́на
5. Колора́до
6. Иллино́йс
7. Миннесо́та
8. Монта́на
9. Небра́ска
10. Нева́да
11. О́регон
12. Флори́да

2.
1. Аме́рика
2. Кана́да
3. Пакиста́н
4. Торо́нто
5. Бо́стон
6. Ло́ндон
7. Берли́н
8. Ерева́н
9. Мадри́д
10. Пана́ма

3.
1. student
2. professor
3. campus
4. college
5. hamburger
6. ketchup
7. hotdog
8. compact disk
9. computer
10. printer

4.
1. приве́т
2. спаси́бо
3. па́мять
4. письмо́
5. телеви́зор
6. сёрфинг
7. рюкза́к
8. го́сть
9. рэ́ппер
10. де́сять

5.
1. прямо́й
2. по́яс
3. еда́
4. съёмка
5. платье
6. Татья́на
7. я́блоко
8. ма́й
9. ю́мор
10. заём

6.
1. астроно́м
2. парадо́кс
3. тарака́н
4. голова́
5. мото́р
6. над до́мом
7. молоко́
8. газе́та
9. тала́нт
10. о кла́ссе

7.
1. о́рган
2. ко́локол
3. панара́ма
4. мо́ре
5. ю́мор
6. ме́сто
7. но́вое
8. дя́дя
9. потоло́к
10. кварти́ра

8.
1. телефо́н
2. мясно́й
3. ве́чер
4. рестора́н
5. эко́лог
6. па́мятник
7. ветерина́р
8. река́
9. эта́ж
10. сейча́с

9.
1. бы́стро
2. цеме́нт

3. жи́вопись
4. цыплёнок
5. ци́рк
6. жена́
7. жёны
8. шика́рный
9. шесто́й
10. шербе́т

10.
1. щи́
2. ещё
3. счита́ешь
4. щека́
5. мужчи́на
6. расска́зчик
7. подпи́счик
8. исчеза́ть
9. и́щут
10. щёлк

11.
1. гла́з
2. сбо́р
3. отде́л
4. кру́жка
5. круи́з
6. дро́бь
7. творо́г
8. вчера́
9. абсу́рд
10. к до́му

12.
1. ска-жи́-те
2. по-ни-ма́й-те
3. ла-бор-а-то́р-и-я
4. дир-е́-ктор
5. на-ча́ль-ник
6. сло-ва́рь
7. ко́м-на-та
8. ру́-чка
9. кар-ан-да́ш
10. ун-и-вер-си-те́т

13.
1. xerox
2. comics
3. sandwich
4. marketing
5. manager
6. know-how
7. disk player
8. fax
9. computer
10. happy end

14.
1. Agatha Christie
2. Jack London
3. Ernest Hemingway
4. Charles Dickens
5. Walt Disney
6. Richard Nixon
7. John Quincy Adams
8. Winston Churchill

Chapter 2

1.
1. N/hard
2. F/hard
3. M/soft
4. M/hard
5. F/soft
6. N/soft
7. M/soft
8. M/hard
9. N/soft
10. F/soft

2.
1. о́н
2. она́
3. оно́
4. о́н
5. о́н
6. она́
7. о́н
8. оно́
9. она́
10. оно́

3.
1. мо́й дом
2. моё место
3. моя́ ви́за
4. мо́й слова́рь
5. мо́й сту́л
6. моя́ ко́мната
7. моя́ крова́ть
8. моя́ фотогра́фия

4.
1. о́н
2. она́
3. о́н
4. о́н
5. она́
6. она́
7. о́н
8. она́
9. о́н
10. о́н

5.
1. но́вый
2. написа́ла
3. изве́стный
4. о́пытный
5. большо́й
6. занята́

6.
1. певи́ца
2. счастли́вец
3. америка́нка
4. кана́дка
5. испа́нец
6. писа́тельница
7. учи́тель
8. худо́жница
9. перево́дчик
10. танцо́вщица
11. англича́нка
12. грузи́н
13. по́ртни́ха
14. продаве́ц

7.
1. оно́
2. о́н
3. оно́
4. она́
5. она́
6. о́н
7. она́
8. о́н
9. о́н
10. о́н
11. о́н
12. оно́

8.
1. Э́то газе́ты.
2. Э́то уче́бники.
3. Э́то кни́ги.
4. Э́то кре́сла.
5. Э́то ру́чки.
6. Э́то тетра́ди.
7. Э́то пла́тья.
8. Э́то телефо́ны.
9. Э́то портфе́ли.
10. Э́то музе́и.
11. Э́то ла́мпы.
12. Э́то студе́нты.
13. Э́то студе́нтки.
14. Э́то институ́ты.
15. Э́то пля́жи.
16. Э́то пло́щади.

9.
1. Где́ значки́?
2. Где́ ножи́?
3. Где́ платки́?
4. Где́ словари́?
5. Где́ сёстры?
6. Где́ отцы́?
7. Где́ звёзды?
8. Где́ ключи́?
9. Где́ о́кна?
10. Где́ жёны?

10.
1. Мои́ сыновья́ учителя́.
2. Мои́ до́чери учи́тельницы.
3. Мои́ бра́тья врачи́.
4. Мои́ сёстры студе́нтки.
5. Мои́ друзья́ америка́нцы.

11.
1. Во́т на́ши де́ти.
2. Во́т на́ши паспорта́.
3. Во́т на́ши сту́лья.
4. Во́т на́ши имена́.
5. Во́т на́ши дере́вья.

12.
1. ру́сская молодёжь.
2. мо́дная оде́жда
3. кра́сные черни́ла
4. све́жая мали́на
5. желе́зные пери́ла
6. чи́стая посу́да
7. прия́тные духи́
8. сухи́е дрова́
9. но́вые де́ньги
10. весёлая детвора́

13.
1. Nominative
2. Nominative
3. Accusative
4. Nominative
5. Nominative
6. Accusative
7. Nominative
8. Accusative
9. Accusative
10. Accusative
11. Nominative
12. Nominative
13. Accusative
14. Nominative

14.
1. журна́лы
2. компью́теры
3. пи́сьма
4. студе́нтов
5. тетра́ди
6. словари́
7. пла́тья
8. свекро́вей

15.
1. литерату́ру
2. исто́рию
3. бра́та
4. соба́ку
5. преподава́теля
6. зада́ние
7. ра́дио
8. матема́тику
9. ма́ть
10. отца́

16.
1. Nom./Acc./Gen.
2. Nom./Gen.
3. Nom./Gen.
4. Nom./Acc./Gen.
5. Gen./Nom.
6. Acc./Gen.
7. Nom./Gen.
8. Nom./Gen.
9. Acc./Gen.
10. Nom./Gen.
11. Acc./Gen.
12. Nom./Gen.
13. Nom./Gen.
14. Acc./Gen.
15. Gen.
16. Nom./Gen.
17. Nom./Gen.
18. Acc./Gen.
19. Nom./Gen.
20. Nom./Gen.

17.
1. Э́то портфе́ль профе́ссора.
2. Э́то су́мка ма́мы.
3. Э́то кабине́т па́пы.

4. Это пода́рок го́стя.
5. Это пла́тье сестры́.
6. Это игру́шки дете́й.
7. Это маши́на отца́.
8. Это уче́бники студе́нтов.
9. Это кварти́ра бра́тьев.
10. Это жёны друзе́й.
11. Это брат студе́нтки.
12. Это рома́н писа́теля.
13. Это да́ча дя́ди.
14. Это плато́к ба́бушки.
15. Это крова́ть ребёнка.

18.
1. пло́щадь Пу́шкина
2. у́лица Королёва
3. бульва́р Го́голя
4. теа́тр Мейерхо́льда
5. библиоте́ка Ге́рцена

19.
1. выступле́ние арти́стки
2. пе́ние певца́
3. игра́ дете́й
4. про́сьба ученико́в
5. диа́гноз враче́й

20.
1. поку́пка маши́ны
2. приготовле́ние обе́да
3. прове́рка зада́ния
4. посеще́ние музе́я
5. изуче́ние литерату́ры

21.
1. темнота́ но́чи
2. ум студе́нтки
3. красота́ мо́ря
4. доброта́ ма́тери
5. бога́тство люде́й
6. све́тлость о́браза
7. ще́дрость друзе́й
8. изве́стность писа́телей
9. ую́т гости́ниц
10. серьёзность оши́бок

22.
1. Здесь не бу́дет гости́ницы.
2. Сего́дня нет семина́ра.
3. Вчера́ в клу́бе не́ было конце́рта.
4. У меня́ сейча́с нет вре́мени.
5. У нас вчера́ не́ было ле́кции.
6. Сего́дня в кла́ссе нет Ви́ктора.
7. Вчера́ Серге́я не́ было до́ма.
8. За́втра не бу́дет роди́телей.
9. Сего́дня не бу́дет дождя́.
10. В ка́ссе теа́тра не́ было биле́тов.

23.
1. теа́тров
2. музе́ев
3. библиоте́ки
4. де́вушек
5. спа́льни
6. пи́сем

7. лаборато́рий
8. карандаше́й
9. ру́чек
10. челове́к

24.
1. са́хару/са́хара
2. мёду/мёда и я́блок
3. пирожко́в
4. су́пу/су́па
5. коньяку́/коньяка́
6. де́нег
7. ри́су/ри́са и овоще́й
8. фру́ктов
9. грибо́в
10. сы́ру/сы́ра и хле́ба

25.
1. Же́нщины не име́ли пра́ва го́лоса.
2. Фильм не произвёл впечатле́ния.
3. Она́ не ви́дела авто́буса.
4. Он не пил спи́рта.
5. Студе́нт не по́нял отве́та.

26.
1. Dative
2. Accusative
3. Dative
4. Accusative
5. Dative
6. Accusative
7. Dative
8. Accusative
9. Dative
10. Dative

27.
1. сёстрам
2. друзья́м
3. чита́телям
4. гостя́м
5. слу́шателям
6. бра́тьям
7. матеря́м
8. дочеря́м
9. вну́кам
10. профессора́м

28.
1. Мы пи́шем сестре́.
2. Учени́к отвеча́ет учи́телю.
3. Ма́ма ве́рит до́чери.
4. Ба́бушка чита́ет вну́чке.
5. Андре́й звони́т врачу́.
6. Племя́нник благода́рен дя́де.
7. Го́род нра́вится го́стю.
8. Игру́шки нра́вятся де́тям.

29.
1. Де́тям на́до . . .
2. Сестре́ мо́жно . . .
3. Серёже нельзя́ . . .
4. Пожилы́м лю́дям мо́жно . . .
5. Врачу́ на́до . . .

30.
1. Ма́льчику не чита́ется.
2. До́чке не е́лось.
3. Певи́це не поётся.
4. Сы́ну сего́дня не игра́лось.
5. Тёте вчера́ не спало́сь.

31.
1. ме́лом
2. ру́чками
3. карандашо́м
4. ключо́м
5. платко́м
6. руко́й

7. па́льцем   9. уша́ми
8. глаза́ми   10. рука́ми

32.
1. мо́лнией
2. хо́ром
3. гру́ппой
4. хло́пьями
5. ты́сячами
6. самолётом
7. то́ном
8. у́лицей
9. трамва́ем
10. бе́регом

33.
1. зимо́й
2. вечера́ми
3. но́чью
4. весно́й
5. у́тром
6. о́сенью
7. днём

34.
1. Статья́ пи́шется журнали́стом.
2. Эконо́мика изуча́ется студе́нтами.
3. Посу́да мо́ется ма́терью.
4. Докуме́нты гото́вятся секретарём.
5. Пода́рки посыла́ются тётей.

35.
1. Ло́дку опроки́нуло волно́й.
2. Его́ ра́нило грана́той.
3. Кры́шу сорва́ло ве́тром.
4. Ко́мнату зали́ло све́том.
5. Соба́ку задави́ло маши́ной.

36.
1. учи́телем
2. студе́нткой
3. ветерина́ром
4. врачо́м
5. программи́стом
6. перево́дчицей
7. поэ́том
8. балери́ной
9. преседа́телем
10. секрета́ршей
11. столи́цей
12. дурако́м
13. ма́терью
14. ге́нием
15. геро́ем

37.
1. специали́стом
2. ме́неджером
3. Со́ней
4. преподава́телем
5. судьёй

38.
1. бале́том
2. футбо́лом
3. гимна́стикой
4. красото́й
5. до́черью
6. и́скренностью
7. кружко́м
8. кварти́рой
9. госуда́рством
10. сове́тами

39.
1. студе́нтами
2. анги́ной
3. едо́й
4. леса́ми и озёрами
5. красото́й
6. шитьём

Chapter 3

1.
1. за
2. че́рез
3. в
4. че́рез
5. про
6. че́рез
7. че́рез
8. про
9. сквозь
10. в

2.
1. по
2. по
3. с
4. по
5. о
6. с

3.
1. су́мку
2. дива́не
3. ры́нок
4. музе́е
5. скаме́йку
6. столе́
7. шка́ф
8. да́чу
9. по́лке
10. вера́нде

4.
1. на
2. в
3. на
4. на
5. в
6. на
7. в
8. в
9. на
10. в
11. в
12. на
13. в
14. на
15. в

5.
1. угол
2. угло́м
3. по́лку
4. ла́вку
5. кни́гой
6. кре́слом
7. ту́чу
8. но́сом
9. водо́й
10. вера́нду

6.
1. за
2. за
3. под
4. за
5. за
6. за
7. за
8. под
9. за
10. за
11. по́д
12. за

7.
1. по́сле
2. про́тив
3. ми́мо
4. о́коло
5. без
6. из-за
7. для
8. кро́ме
9. из-под
10. из-под
11. для
12. по́сле
13. о́коло
14. из-за
15. про́тив

8.
1. до
2. из
3. с
4. от
5. у
6. из
7. от
8. из
9. от
10. из
11. у … от
12. из … с
13. до
14. с … до
15. от
16. у
17. от
18. у

9.
1. путём
2. ра́ди
3. све́рх
4. вме́сто
5. ввиду́
6. вне́
7. вро́де

10.
1. во́зле
2. вокру́г
3. вдо́ль
4. вблизи́
5. вну́трь
6. впереди́
7. внутри́
8. ме́жду
9. пове́рх
10. сза́ди
11. среди́
12. посреди́
13. напро́тив

11.
1. на ... о
2. в ... на
3. при
4. по
5. при
6. в
7. на ... на
8. в
9. о
10. на
11. в
12. при
13. в
14. при
15. в
16. в
17. при
18. на
19. на ... в
20. в

12.
1. к
2. по
3. по
4. к
5. благодаря́
6. вопреки́
7. к
8. согла́сно
9. навстре́чу
10. по
11. к
12. по
13. по

13.
1. за
2. пе́ред
3. с
4. ме́жду
5. над
6. за
7. с
8. пе́ред
9. под
10. над
11. с
12. за
13. ме́жду
14. с
15. над
16. под
17. за
18. с

Chapter 4

1.
1. ты́/она́
2. вы́/я́
3. вы́/мы́
4. они́
5. они́
6. оно́
7. о́н

2.
1. его́
2. него́
3. него́
4. её
5. неё
6. и́х
7. ни́х
8. его́
9. её
10. неё
11. него́
12. на́с
13. меня́
14. тебя́
15. ва́с

3.
1. меня́
2. тебя́
3. его́
4. него́
5. неё
6. на́с
7. ва́с
8. ни́х

4.
1. о нём
2. обо мне́
3. о не́й
4. о ва́с
5. о ни́х
6. о тебе́

5.
1. Мы́ мно́го слы́шали о нём.
2. Де́ти говори́ли о ни́х.
3. О́н ча́сто ду́мает о не́й.
4. Она́ не забы́ла о нём.
5. Они́ спра́шивали о ни́х.

6.
1. ему́
2. и́м
3. е́й
4. тебе́
5. мне́

7.
1. ему́
2. е́й
3. нему́
4. ни́м
5. не́й
6. нему́

8.
1. тобо́й
2. мно́й
3. ни́м
4. на́ми
5. ни́ми
6. ни́м
7. не́й
8. и́м
9. ни́ми
10. е́й

9.
1. себе́
2. собо́й
3. себе́ ... себя́
4. себя́
5. себя́
6. собо́й
7. собо́й
8. себе́
9. себе́
10. собо́й
11. себя́
12. себя́
13. собо́й
14. себе́
15. себя́

10.
1. дру́г с дру́гом
2. дру́г дру́га
3. дру́г дру́гу/дру́г для дру́га
4. дру́г без дру́га
5. дру́г к дру́гу
6. дру́г на дру́га
7. дру́г за дру́га
8. дру́г на дру́га
9. дру́г от дру́га
10. дру́г к дру́гу

11.
1. ко́м
2. ке́м
3. кого́
4. кого́
5. кого́
6. кому́
7. кого́
8. ке́м
9. кого́
10. кого́

12.
1. чём
2. что
3. чего
4. что
5. чего
6. что
7. что
8. чего
9. чём
10. чём

13.
1. моего
2. нашими
3. твоей
4. вашу
5. чья
6. чьё
7. моей
8. чьей
9. чьём
10. твоего
11. нашем
12. твоей

14.
1. своём . . . своей . . . её
2. своему . . . его
3. своего . . . своём
4. свои . . . их
5. своей
6. его . . . свою
7. свой . . . его . . . своего
8. своей
9. своём
10. своя
11. свою . . . её
12. свой
13. её . . . своих
14. своей

15.
1. этой . . . той
2. эти . . . те
3. этом . . . том
4. это . . . то
5. эта . . . та
6. этим . . . тем
7. этот . . . тот
8. этими . . . теми
9. этому . . . тому
10. это . . . то

16.
1. тот
2. те
3. те
4. тот
5. тот
6. та

17.
1. был
2. было
3. было
4. была
5. были
6. был

18.
1. такая
2. такой
3. такую
4. такого
5. такая
6. такой

19.
1. сам
2. само
3. сами
4. саму
5. самого
6. самой
7. самих
8. самому
9. самой
10. самом
11. самим
12. самой
13. самом
14. самого

20.
1. самого
2. самой
3. самом
4. самого
5. самому

21.
1. Всё
2. всё
3. всех
4. всё
5. всём
6. всех . . . всё
7. всём
8. всеми
9. всех
10. всё

22.
1. Как зовут девушку, которая приехала недавно из Новосибирска?
2. Он живёт в доме, который находится в центре города.
3. Вот идут мальчики, которые учатся в школе вместе с нашим сыном.

23.
1. Я читал статью, которую рекомендовал профессор.
2. Как называется университет, который ты окончил?
3. Я знаю одного бизнесмена, которого зовут Владимир Сорокин.
4. Наши соседи нашли деньги, которые ты потерял.
5. Вчера к нам приехали друзья, которых мы давно не видели.

24.
1. Я позвонил другу, от которого я давно не получал письма.
2. Нас поместили в светлую комнату, окна которой смотрят на пляж.
3. Он работает в институте, около которого строят гостиницу.
4. Как фамилия студентки, родители которой живут в Ростове?
5. Он подарил ей духи, запах которых ей очень понравился.

25.
1. Ты читал книгу, о которой я тебе говорил?
2. Мы были на спектакле, в котором участвовала наша дочь.
3. Сегодня ко мне приедет друг, о котором я тебе рассказывал.
4. Через ворота Кремля проехал лимузин, в котором ехал президент.
5. Там строят общежития, в которых будут жить студенты.

26.
1. Они вышли из леса и увидели озеро, к которому они направлялись.
2. Как зовут девушку, которой я должен передать письмо?
3. Вот берег, по которому мы бегаем каждое утро.
4. Вчера я сдавала экзамен, к которому я долго готовилась.
5. Завтра к нам приедут друзья, к которым мы часто ездим.

27. 1. Я́ хочу́ познако́мить тебя́ с де́вушкой, с
которой я рабо́таю в институ́те.
2. Вдали́ мы́ уви́дели го́ры, ме́жду
которыми вила́сь доро́га.
3. Студе́нт подошёл к столу́, за кото́рым
сиде́л экзамена́тор.
4. Мы́ подошли́ к теа́тру, пе́ред кото́рым
тяну́лась дли́нная о́чередь.
5. Она́ вчера́ узна́ла результа́ты
экспериме́нта, кото́рыми она́ о́чень
дово́льна.

28. 1. како́й   5. кака́я
2. како́м   6. како́м
3. каки́х   7. каки́м
4. како́й   8. каки́е

29. 1. то́   6. те́м
2. то́м   7. то́м
3. те́м   8. те́м
4. че́м   9. чему́
5. че́м   10. тому́

30. 1. кого́   4. того́
2. кто́   5. тому́
3. то́т

31. 1. кто́-нубудь...кто́-то
2. каки́м-нубудь
3. кому́-то
4. кто́-нубудь...како́й-то
5. каки́е-нибудь...каку́ю-то
6. кому́-нибудь
7. кого́-то
8. кого́-нибудь
9. что́-нибудь
10. что́-то...како́й-то
11. че́й-нибудь
12. чыо́-то

32. 1. Мне́ никто́ не нра́вится.
2. Его́ ничто́ не интересу́ет.
3. Я́ ничего́ не де́лаю.
4. Я́ ни к кому́ не иду́.
5. Я́ ни о ко́м не мечта́ю.
6. Она́ ниче́м не занима́ется.
7. О́н ни с ке́м не встре́тился.
8. Я́ ни у кого́ не была́.
9. О́н ничего́ не бои́тся.
10. Я́ ни к чему́ не гото́влюсь.
11. Они́ не согласи́лись ни на каки́е усту́пки.
12. Она́ не слу́шала ничьи́ сове́ты.
13. Меня́ никаки́е вопро́сы не интересу́ют.
14. Я́ не води́л ничью́ маши́ну.
15. Я́ ни на кого́ не наде́юсь.

33. 1. не́кого   6. не́ с кем
2. не́ на что   7. не́ к кому
3. не́чего   8. не́кому
4. не́чем   9. не́ о чем
5. не́кому   10. не́ за что

Chapter 5

1. 1. лени́вая   9. ску́чный
2. ста́рой   10. молчали́вый
3. глу́пый   11. серьёзные
4. бе́лую   12. чёрными
5. гру́стный   13. ста́рый
6. бы́строе   14. некраси́вая
7. гру́бый   15. гря́зной
8. здо́бный   16. неопря́тный

2. 1. ра́ннего...по́зднего
2. ли́шнего
3. сосе́дней
4. после́днему
5. Вече́рнюю
6. дома́шними
7. у́треннем
8. сего́дняшней
9. ве́рхнюю
10. зде́шних

3. 1. жа́ркие   6. высо́кими
2. вели́ким   7. плохи́е
3. широ́ким   8. сла́дкую
4. таки́х дороги́х 9. бли́зкими
5. я́ркое   10. до́лгой

4. 1. чужи́е   7. мла́дшем
2. све́жим   8. ры́жей
3. горя́чее   9. настоя́щей
4. хоро́шей   10. рабо́чим
5. о́бщих   11. бу́дущему
6. больши́м   12. бы́вшего

5. 1. Ча́й кре́пок.
2. Сове́т поле́зен.
3. Пробле́ма серьёзна.
4. Де́нь прекра́сен.
5. Пиджа́к коро́ток.
6. Стари́к бе́ден.
7. Слова́рь ну́жен.
8. За́работок ни́зок.
9. Зачёт лёгок.
10. Апельси́н сла́док.
11. Ребёнок умён.
12. За́л по́лон.
13. По́рции равны́.
14. Места́ свобо́дны.
15. Су́мка легка́.

6.
1. здоро́вая … здоро́ва
2. заня́той … за́нят
3. больна́я
4. больна́
5. споко́йное … споко́йно

7.
1. мала́
2. ма́ленькая
3. ста́рые
4. ста́рый … стар
5. широки́
6. широ́кие
7. у́зкая … узка́
8. дли́нные … длинны́
9. молода́ … молода́
10. большо́е … велико́

8.
1. жива́я
2. жив
3. непра́вое
4. неправа́
5. смешно́й
6. смешно́
7. ужа́сны
8. ужа́сный

9.
1. тру́дная … трудна́
2. бога́т
3. дово́льный … дово́льна
4. досто́ин
5. досто́йная
6. пре́дан
7. пре́данная
8. по́лный
9. по́лон
10. свобо́дна
11. свобо́дной
12. близки́
13. бли́зкие
14. винова́т
15. винова́тыми
16. спосо́бный … спосо́бен
17. скло́нен
18. скло́нным
19. гото́вых … гото́вы
20. знако́мой … знако́мы
21. похо́жи
22. похо́жие
23. сильна́
24. си́льные
25. равноду́шна
26. равноду́шные
27. норма́льно
28. норма́льные
29. непоня́тно
30. непоня́тный

10.
1. каковы́
2. каки́е
3. тако́го
4. так
5. како́й
6. таково́

7. како́в
8. тако́й
9. как

11.
1. бу́лочную
2. пивно́й
3. про́шлом
4. ру́сской
5. больны́х
6. нали́чными
7. учёного
8. моро́женым
9. шампа́нского
10. живо́тных
11. вое́нных
12. взро́слыми

12.
1. ста́рого … нового
2. сла́дкое
3. дорого́е
4. ста́рое
5. зарабо́танное
6. смешно́го
7. о́стренького
8. о́строго
9. горя́чего
10. необходи́мое

13.
1. ма́миной
2. па́пином
3. соба́чкину
4. Та́ниного

14.
1. ме́нее тру́дную
2. бо́лее интере́сного
3. бо́лее дорого́й
4. вы́сшую
5. бо́лее но́вых
6. бо́лее серьёзных
7. ста́ршим
8. бо́лее ста́рые
9. лу́чший
10. бо́лее высо́кую
11. ме́ньшей
12. бо́лее молоды́е

15.
1. вы́ше
2. бо́льше
3. доро́же
4. ча́ще
5. симпати́чнее
6. лу́чше
7. вы́ше
8. ле́гче
9. быстре́е
10. ху́же

16.
1. Росси́я бо́льше Кита́я.
2. В Новосиби́рске холодне́е, чем в Торо́нто.
3. Ноя́брь коро́че октября́.
4. Здесь тепле́е в ма́е, чем в декабре́.
5. Жира́ф вы́ше кенгуру́.
6. Ки́ев да́льше Пари́жа от США.
7. Нью-Йо́рк ме́ньше Теха́са.
8. Москва́ старе́е Са́нкт-Петербу́рга.
9. «Мересе́дес» доро́же «Москвича́»
10. Байка́л глу́бже Мичига́на.
11. Мёд сла́ще со́ка.
12. Конья́к кре́пче шампа́нского.

13. Печа́тать на компью́тере удо́бнее, чём ...
14. Éсть фру́кты полéзнее, чём пи́ть ...
15. Во́лга длинéе Днепра́.
16. Чита́ть по-ру́сски лéгче, чём говори́ть.
17. На дискотéке веселéе, чём на лéкции.
18. На авто́бусе éздить быстрéе, чём на ...

17.
1. са́мое глубо́кое
2. са́мая ди́нная
3. са́мых популя́рных
4. са́мом большо́м
5. са́мым бли́зким

18.
1. крупнéйший
2. вкуснéйшие
3. здоровéйшими
4. высоча́йшая
5. строжа́йший

19.
1. мо́дно
2. аккура́тно
3. верхо́м
4. по-бра́тски
5. по-друго́му
6. по-ра́зному
7. понима́юще
8. одобря́юще
9. по-кита́йски
10. вслу́х
11. по-человéчески
12. угрожа́юще
13. по-прéжнему
14. осторо́жно
15. интерéсно
16. умоля́юще
17. босико́м
18. по-дура́цки
19. раздража́юще
20. бодря́ще-

20.
1. у́тром
2. давно́
3. тогда́
4. послеза́втра
5. позавчера́
6. снача́ла ... пото́м
7. тепéрь
8. сейча́с
9. лéтом
10. наконéц
11. днём
12. ско́ро
13. весно́й
14. по́здно
15. сра́зу
16. во́-время
17. ра́но ... ра́но

21.
1. навсегда́
2. до́лго
3. до́лго
4. давно́
5. надо́лго

22.
1. всегда́
2. рéдко
3. обы́чно
4. иногда́

23.
1. ужé не
2. всё ещё
3. ужé
4. ещё не
5. ужé

24.
1. до́ма
2. налéво ... напра́во
3. отку́да
4. вни́з
5. вездé
6. нару́жу
7. снару́жи
8. отовсю́ду
9. навéрх
10. изнутри́
11. вни́з
12. наза́д ... вперёд
13. свéрху
14. вну́трь
15. сюда́
16. та́м, гдé
17. сза́ди
18. впереди́
19. домо́й
20. слéва ... спра́ва

25.
1. та́к
2. о́чень
3. мно́го
4. почти́
5. ма́ло
6. немно́го
7. совершéнно
8. чу́ть чу́ть
9. совсéм
10. доста́точно
11. сли́шком
12. слегка́

26.
1. куда́-нибудь
2. гдé-то
3. ка́к-нибудь
4. почему́-нибудь
5. куда́-нибудь
6. куда́-нибудь
7. когда́-то
8. почему́-то
9. ка́к-то
10. когда́-нибудь

27.
1. Ва́м нéкуда пойти́ сего́дня вéчером.
2. Я́ никуда́ не пойду́ по́сле семина́ра.
3. Ва́м нéгде рабо́тать.
4. Вы́ нигдé не бу́дете рабо́тать.
5. Ему́ нéзачем чита́ть э́ту кни́гу.
6. О́н ника́к не спра́вится с э́тим.

Chapter 6

1.
1. оди́н
2. одну́
3. одни́
4. одну́
5. одно́й
6. одно́й
7. одна́
8. одни́
9. одно́м
10. одного́

2.
1. дву́м сыновья́м
2. трёх города́х
3. три́дцать четы́ре студéнта ... три́дцать два́ мéста
4. дву́х мужчи́н ... трёх жéнщин
5. два́дцать два́ студéнта
6. двé библиотéки
7. четырёх киломéтрах
8. трёх дéвушек
9. тремя́ до́чками
10. трём друзья́м

3.
1. 2 но́вых рестора́на
2. 3 ру́сских учёных
3. 3 больши́е гости́ницы
4. 2 свобо́дных ме́ста
5. 4 иностра́нных студе́нта
6. студе́нческие столо́вые

4.
1. двух живы́х крокоди́лов
2. двум но́вым студе́нткам
3. трёх ча́йных ло́жек
4. двумя́ ру́сскими ма́льчиками
5. четырёх университе́тских общежи́тиях

5.
1. шестью́ ру́сскими тури́стами
2. семь тру́дных зада́ч
3. десяти́ но́вым ученика́м
4. пять ча́стных университе́тов
5. двадцатью́ ста́рыми ко́шками
6. тридцати́ пяти́ хоро́шим друзья́м
7. ста́ небольши́х острова́х
8. трёхсот пяти́десяти о́пытных профессоро́в
9. двухсо́т пятна́дцади дождли́вых дне́й
10. пятисо́т сорока́ постоя́нных жи́телей

6.
1. десятью́ ты́сячами рубле́й
2. пятна́дцати ты́сяч посети́телей
3. два́дцать четы́ре ты́сячи студе́нтов
4. десяти́ ты́сячах ко́мнат
5. ста́ пяти́десяти ты́сяч до́лларов
6. двадцати́ миллио́нов сове́тских гра́ждан
7. пять биллио́нов до́лларов

7.
1. шестьдеся́т рубле́й два́дцать копе́ек
2. двена́дцать рубле́й два́дцать две́ копе́йки
3. три́дцать рубле́й со́рок одна́ копе́йка
4. оди́ннадцать рубле́й со́рок три́ копе́йки
5. се́мьдесят два́ рубля́
6. три́ ты́сячи рубле́й

8.
1. семьсо́т со́рок два́-ноль но́ль-шестьдеся́т ше́сть
2. две́сти три́дцать де́вять-двена́дцать-де́сять
3. четы́реста со́рок четы́ре-во́семьдесят се́мь-ноль де́вять
4. девятьсо́т девяно́сто три́-ноль три́-три́дцать
5. пятьсо́т два́дцать оди́н-пятьдеся́т пять-се́мьдесят се́мь

9.
1. пятёрку
2. деся́тку
3. деся́ток
4. шестёрку
5. семёрка
6. дво́йку

10.
1. о́бе
2. обо́их … обе́их
3. тро́е
4. дво́е
5. четверы́х
6. двои́х
7. тро́е
8. че́тверо
9. се́меро
10. семеры́х

11.
1. пе́рвом
2. второ́м
3. тре́тьей
4. пя́того
5. седьмо́м
6. девя́тую

12.
1. три́дцать втора́я глава́
2. семна́дцатый то́м
3. пятьдеся́т шесто́й ря́д
4. тре́тий кана́л
5. шестьдеся́т седьмо́й автобус
6. сто́ два́дцать пя́тое ме́сто

13.
1. полтора́ пирожка́
2. полторы́ мину́ты
3. полу́тора ты́сяч
4. полу́тора миллио́нах
5. полтора́ часа́

14.
1. три́ восьмы́х
2. ноль це́лых, семь деся́тых/ноль и се́мь деся́тых
3. две́ це́лых и три́ пя́тых
4. четы́ре це́лых и одна́ восьма́я
5. одна́ четвёртая/(одна́) че́тверть
6. две́ тре́тьих/две́ тре́ти
7. четы́ре це́лых, пять со́тых/четы́ре и пя́ть со́тых

15.
1. ноль два́дцать пять ли́тра/че́тверть ли́тра
2. ноль три́дцать три́ ли́тра/тре́ть ли́тра
3. ноль пя́ть/пол-ли́тра
4. ноль се́мьдесят пять ли́тра/три́ че́тверти ли́тра
5. оди́н ли́тр
6. полкило́

16.
1. в пя́тницу
2. на бу́дущей/сле́дующей неде́ле
3. в про́шлую сре́ду
4. в э́тот/то́т ве́чер
5. весно́й
6. в ию́не
7. в э́том году́
8. в ма́рте э́того го́да
9. в декабре́ бу́дущего го́да
10. на э́той неде́ле
11. в про́шлом ме́сяце
12. днём/во второ́й полови́не дня́
13. в бу́дущую суббо́ту
14. ле́том

15. в про́шлом ве́ке/столе́тии
16. про́шлой зимо́й

17. 1. седьмо́е ию́ня ты́сяча девятьсо́т девяно́сто восьмо́го го́да
2. шесто́го февраля́ ты́сяча девятьсо́т девяно́стого го́да
3. в ты́сяча девятьсо́т шестьдеся́т шесто́м году́
4. в восемьсо́т шестидеся́том году́ н. э.
5. с пя́того до двена́дцатого
6. два́дцать пе́рвое апре́ля
7. пя́того ию́ля девяно́сто девя́того го́да
8. с пятна́дцатого сентября́

18. 1. Ей два́дцать оди́н го́д.
2. Ему́ со́рок два́ го́да.
3. Ско́лько ребёнку ме́сяцев?
4. Ско́лько ле́т ма́тери?
5. Ребёнку го́д и три́ ме́сяца.
6. Ему́ идёт шестна́дцатый го́д.
7. В како́м во́зрасте о́н у́мер?
8. Он у́мер в (во́зрасте) се́мьдесят оди́н.

19. 1. Сейча́с се́мь часо́в утра́.
2. Сейча́с тре́тий ча́с.
3. ше́сть часо́в ве́чера
4. пятна́дцать мину́т/че́тверть девя́того
5. в полови́не деся́того/полдеся́того ве́чера
6. в по́лночь
7. в три́ часа́ но́чи
8. без че́тверти ча́с
9. Сейча́с ча́с дня́.
10. без трёх четы́ре
11. без одно́й мину́ты де́сять
12. по́лдень

20. 1. ше́сть (часо́в) со́рок (мину́т)
2. во́семь (часо́в) три́дцать пя́ть (мину́т)
3. де́сять (часо́в) два́дцать (мину́т)
4. трина́дцать часо́в
5. пятна́дцать (часо́в) пятна́дцать (мину́т)
6. восемна́дцать (часо́в) пя́ть (мину́т)
7. два́дцать (часо́в) де́сять (мину́т)
8. два́дцать три́ (часа́) со́рок (мину́т)
9. но́ль часо́в (но́ль но́ль мину́т)
10. но́ль (часо́в) пятьдеся́т (мину́т)

Chapter 7

1. 1. слу́шает
2. собира́ю
3. реша́ет
4. за́втракаем
5. де́лаешь
6. мечта́ет
7. покупа́ет
8. игра́ет
9. обе́дают
10. вспомина́ем
11. гуля́ет
12. выступа́ет
13. отдыха́ем
14. рабо́тает
15. опа́здывает
16. занима́ется
17. чита́ю
18. обсужда́ют
19. получа́ем
20. объясня́ет
21. понима́ете
22. начина́ет
23. конча́ет
24. расска́зывает
25. спра́шивает

2. 1. бледне́ет
2. боле́ет
3. красне́ет
4. неме́ет
5. гре́ет
6. желте́ют
7. лысе́ет
8. сме́ешь
9. успе́ем
10. худе́ет
11. слабе́ет
12. робе́ешь
13. седе́ют
14. владе́ют
15. голубе́ет
16. здорове́ет
17. беле́ет
18. пусте́ют
19. пьяне́ет
20. жале́ю
21. полне́ет
22. веселе́ет
23. име́ете
24. реде́ют
25. богате́ют
. . . бедне́ет

3. 1. организу́ют
2. тре́буете
3. импорти́рует
4. парку́ем
5. сове́тую
6. уча́ствует
7. ра́дуют
8. рису́ет
9. экспорти́рует
10. интересу́етесь
11. жа́луется
12. практику́ется
13. ремонти́руем
14. приватизи́рует
15. фотографи́руют
16. де́йствует
17. комбини́рует
18. реклами́рует
19. чу́вствую
20. путеше́ствуют
21. горю́ет
22. танцу́ют
23. сле́дует
24. копи́рует
25. рекоменду́ю

4. 1. тя́нет
2. па́хнет
3. отдохнём
4. га́снут
5. со́хнет
6. проснётся
7. пры́гнет
8. верну́сь
9. вы́кинет
10. вздохнём
11. ло́пнет
12. привы́кнете
13. ки́снет
14. мёрзну
15. кре́пнет

5.
1. поги́бли
2. поблёкли
3. дости́г
4. привы́кли
5. засну́л . . . замо́лкли
6. замёрзло
7. вздохну́ла
8. га́с
9. исче́з
10. па́хло
11. кре́пла
12. верну́лся
13. ру́хнула
14. рискну́л

6.
1. пи́шет
2. пря́чу
3. и́щет
4. ре́жут
5. ска́жете
6. ше́пчет
7. пла́чет
8. сви́щет
9. коле́блется
10. щеко́чет
11. дре́млет
12. вы́пишу
13. отка́жет
14. сы́плет

7.
1. ла́ет
2. та́ет
3. смею́сь
4. наде́емся
5. се́ет

8.
1. беру́
2. ржу́т
3. врёт
4. ждём
5. рвёт
6. лжёшь
7. зовёт
8. жрёт
9. деру́т

9.
1. передаёт
2. продаю́т
3. отстаёт
4. подаю́т
5. признаёт
6. преподаёт
7. сознаю́
8. отдаёт
9. узнаю́
10. устаёт
11. встаю́/раздаётся
12. остаётся

10.
1. ко́лет
2. бо́ремся
3. ме́лет
4. по́лют
5. по́рет

11.
1. хва́лит
2. ку́ришь
3. хожу́
4. но́сят
5. вожу́
6. говоря́т
7. у́чит
8. люблю́/ко́рмят
9. же́нится
10. ва́рит
11. плачу́
12. ло́вит/чи́щу

12.
1. зави́шу
2. те́рпит
3. лечу́/лети́шь
4. гори́т
5. храпи́т
6. свищу́
7. виси́т
8. шумя́т
9. ви́жу
10. боли́т

13.
1. стучи́т
2. слы́шу
3. молчи́т
4. держу́
5. дрожи́шь
6. кричи́шь
7. стоя́т
8. звучи́т
9. бои́тся
10. лежи́т

14.
1. хо́чет . . . хотя́т
2. хоти́те . . . хочу́
3. хоте́ла
4. бежи́шь . . . бегу́
5. бегу́т
6. бежи́м . . . хоти́м

15.
1. живём . . . живёт
2. плыву́ . . . плывёт
3. слывёт

16.
1. наде́нешь
2. ста́нет
3. вста́ну
4. разде́нется
5. оде́немся

17.
1. мо́ет
2. откро́ю
3. ро́ет
4. закро́ете
5. но́ют

18.
1. шью
2. льёт
3. вьёт
4. пьём
5. бьёт

19.
1. поёт
2. ду́ет
3. бре́ет
4. гниёт

20.
1. поймёт
2. возьму́
3. при́мет
4. отни́мет
5. займёт
6. наймём
7. начнёт
8. жмёт
9. жну́т
10. подни́мет
11. мнёт
12. сниму́

21.
1. тру́т
2. вы́тру
3. сотрёт
4. запрёт
5. отопрёт
6. умрёт

22.
1. ся́дет
2. скребёт
3. приобретёт
4. несли́
5. кладёшь
6. мёл
7. цвету́т
8. плёл
9. грёб
10. ползли́
11. ле́зла
12. трясу́т
13. спасло́
14. везла́
15. ведёт
16. упадёт

23.
1. ля́жет
2. бережёт
3. мо́жет
4. печёт
5. помо́жем
6. отвлечёт
7. стрижёт
8. обожгёт
9. течёт
10. привлечёт

24.
1. бу́дете де́лать
2. бу́дем смотре́ть
3. бу́дешь писа́ть
4. бу́ду рабо́тать
5. бу́дет изуча́ть
6. бу́дут реша́ть

25.
1. вы́пил
2. пригото́вила
3. реши́ли
4. нарисова́л
5. вы́учил
6. купи́ли
7. заплати́ла
8. отдохну́л
9. спроси́л
10. отве́тил

26.
1. собира́ет
2. запи́сывает
3. вызыва́ем
4. кладёт
5. берёт
6. говори́т
7. закрыва́ет
8. умыва́ет
9. и́щет
10. ло́вим

27.
1. привыка́ли ... привы́кли
2. угова́ривал ... уговори́л
3. сдава́ла ... сдала́
4. лови́л ... пойма́л
5. гото́вил
6. иска́л ... нашёл
7. буди́ла ... разбуди́ла

28.
1. посиде́ли
2. сиде́ла
3. гуля́ли
4. порабо́тал
5. рабо́тал
6. ду́мал
7. поду́мал

29.
1. запла́кала
2. пла́кала
3. пошёл
4. шёл
5. пошёл
6. запры́гали
7. пры́гали
8. рассерди́лась
9. услы́шали
10. слы́шали

30.
1. вста́л ... встава́л
2. написа́ла ... писа́ла
3. получи́ли ... получа́ли
4. ко́нчила ... конча́ла
5. испекла́ ... пекла́

31.
1. бу́ду объясня́ть ... объясню́
2. прочита́ю ... бу́ду чита́ть
3. бу́дет писа́ть ... напи́шет
4. позвони́т ... бу́дет звони́ть
5. сде́лаем ... бу́дем де́лать

32.
1. (*a*) поднима́лись
   (*b*) подняли́сь
2. (*a*) принёс
   (*b*) приноси́л
3. (*a*) включа́л ... включа́л
   (*b*) включи́л
4. (*a*) отдава́л
   (*b*) отда́л
5. (*a*) наде́л
   (*b*) надева́л

33.
1. отдыха́ли ... отдохну́ли
2. собира́л ... собра́л
3. переводи́л ... перевела́
4. писа́л ... написа́л
5. реши́л ... реши́л

34.
1. simultaneous
2. interrupted
3. sequential
4. interrupted
5. simultaneous
6. sequential
7. simultaneous
8. sequential

35.
1. (*a*) прочита́л ... прочита́л
   (*b*) чита́л ... чита́л
2. (*a*) купи́ла ... купи́ла
   (*b*) покупа́ла ... покупа́ла
3. (*a*) пока́зывала ... показа́ла
   (*b*) показа́ла

36.
1. говори́л
2. поздра́вил
3. открыва́л
4. включа́л
5. де́лал

37.
1. объясня́ть
2. обе́дать
3. поза́втракать
4. позвони́ть
5. изуча́ть
6. посети́ть
7. встреча́ться
8. отвеча́ть
9. игра́ть
10. реша́ть
11. встава́ть
12. пи́ть

38.
1. расска́зывать
2. звони́ть
3. встреча́ться
4. смотре́ть
5. ста́вить
6. говори́ть

39.
1. объясня́ть
2. узнава́ть
3. бра́ть
4. вызыва́ть
5. зака́зывать
6. спра́шивать

40.
1. прочита́ть
2. чита́ть
3. е́сть
4. разбуди́ть
5. буди́ть
6. бра́ть
7. оставля́ть
8. опа́здывать
9. отдохну́ть
10. поня́ть
11. позвони́ть
12. смотре́ть
13. лови́ть
14. продава́ть
15. вы́учить

41.
1. подожди́
2. включи́те
3. налейте
4. наре́жьте
5. спо́йте
6. наде́ньте
7. откро́йте
8. заплати́те
9. вы́пей
10. танцу́йте
11. отве́тьте
12. пригото́вьте

42.
1. напиши́те ... пиши́те
2. скажи́те ... говори́те
3. расскажи́те ... расска́зывайте
4. прочита́й ... чита́йте

43.
1. не включа́йте
2. не пока́зывайте
3. не переводи́те
4. не расска́зывайте
5. не дава́йте
6. не узнава́йте
7. не закрыва́йте
8. не е́шьте

44.
1. не звони́те
2. не помога́йте
3. не говори́те
4. не покупа́йте
5. не гото́вьте

45.
1. опозда́й
2. забу́дь
3. разбуди́
4. урони́
5. проле́й
6. возьми́те

46.
1. Дава́й вы́пьем
2. Дава́й отдохнём
3. Дава́й возьмём
4. Дава́й зака́жем
5. Дава́й подождём
6. Дава́й потанцу́ем
7. Дава́й рабо́тать
8. Дава́й погуля́ем
9. Дава́й сиде́ть и говори́ть
10. Дава́й игра́ть
11. Дава́й пое́дем
12. Дава́й съеди́м

47.
1. Дава́й не бу́дем убира́ть.
2. Дава́й не бу́дем пе́чь.
3. Дава́й не бу́дем вытира́ть.
4. Дава́й не бу́дем обе́дать.

48.
1. Пусть Ле́на помо́ет.
2. Пусть Па́ша запла́тит.
3. Пусть Та́ня ся́дет с ма́мой.
4. Пусть Ва́ня откро́ет.
5. Пусть Са́ша споёт.

49.
1. Е́сли за́втра бу́дет до́ждь, мы́ бу́дем сиде́ть до́ма.
2. Е́сли ты́ не оде́нешься быстре́е, опозда́ем на конце́рт.
3. Е́сли ты́ им позвони́шь, они́ бу́дут о́чень ра́ды.
4. Е́сли вы́ придёте к на́м, я́ пригото́влю вку́сный обе́д.
5. Е́сли у меня́ бу́дет вре́мя, я́ тебе́ помогу́.
6. Е́сли у на́с бу́дут де́ньги, мы́ ку́пим но́вую маши́ну.

50.
1. Е́сли бы она́ пришла́, я́ бы поговори́л с не́й.
2. Е́сли бы на́ши друзья́ позвони́ли, мы́ бы пригласи́ли и́х в го́сти.
3. Е́сли бы о́н захоте́л смотре́ть фи́льм, мы́ пошли́ бы в кино́.
4. Е́сли бы мы́ пригласи́ли его́, о́н пришёл бы на вечери́нку.
5. Е́сли бы ты́ проси́л меня́, я́ бы купи́л буты́лку вина́.

51.
1. Е́сли бы фи́льм ко́нчился в де́вять часо́в, мы́ бы встре́тились с ва́ми.
2. Е́сли бы о́н попроси́л, я́ бы ... помо́г ему́.
3. Е́сли бы мы́ успе́ли купи́ть биле́ты, мы́ бы пошли́ смотре́ть конце́рт.
4. Е́сли бы вы́ сказа́ли на́м доро́гу, мы́ бы пое́хали туда́.
5. Е́сли бы о́н сде́лал всё упражне́ния, о́н смо́г бы пойти́ в кино́.
6. Е́сли бы у меня́ бы́ло вре́мя, я́ бы ва́м позвони́л.

52.
1. Я́ бы хоте́л чита́ть но́вый ...
2. Я́ бы рекомендова́л ва́м сходи́ть ...
3. Я́ бы сове́товал ва́м поговори́ть ...
4. Что́ вы́ бы хоте́ли посмотре́ть ...
5. Како́й слова́рь ты́ бы сове́товал мне́ купи́ть?

53.
1. Я́ бы вы́пил ...
2. Я́ бы поспа́л ...
3. Я́ бы послу́шал ...
4. Я́ бы пое́л ...
5. Я́ бы пое́хал ...

54.
1. Помо́г бы ты́ ей ...
2. Посмотре́л бы ты́ ...
3. Убра́л бы ты́ ...
4. Послу́шал бы ты́ ...
5. Поговори́л бы ты́ ...

55.
1. Я́ посове́товал дру́гу, что́бы о́н бро́сил кури́ть.
2. Ми́ша попроси́л меня́, что́бы я́ купи́л ему́ газе́ту.
3. Мы́ уговори́ли дру́га, что́бы о́н пое́хал отдыха́ть ...
4. Я́ попроси́л бра́та, что́бы о́н помо́г мне́.
5. Учи́тель посове́товал ученика́м, что́бы они́ слу́шали внима́тельнее.

56.
1. перевести́
2. перевёл
3. посмотре́ли
4. показа́ть
5. поздоро́ваться
6. могла́

57.
1. Хорошо́ (бы́ло) бы отдыха́ть в Евро́пе.
2. Ва́жно, что́бы вы́ ко́нчили докла́д.
3. На́до, что́бы о́н отве́тил на письмо́.
4. То́лько бы о́н нашёл рабо́ту!
5. Бы́ло бы у меня́ бо́льше вре́мени.

58.
1. мо́ется
2. мо́ет
3. мо́ется
4. оде́лась
5. одева́ет
6. оде́ла
7. одева́ться
8. причёсывает
9. причёсывалась
10. причёсывает

59.
1. ви́делись
2. ви́дел
3. уви́димся
4. встреча́лись
5. встре́тил
6. поцелова́лся
7. поцелова́ла
8. обня́ли́сь
9. познако́мил
10. познако́мились

60.
1. обра́довало
2. обра́довались
3. беспоко́ит
4. беспоко́ится
5. интересу́ют
6. интересу́ется
7. волну́юсь
8. волну́ет
9. се́рдится
10. се́рдит
11. удиви́ли
12. удиви́лись

61.
1. Тру́дные зада́чи реша́ются студе́нтами в э́той гру́ппе.
2. Опро́с прово́дится социо́логами в э́том институ́те.
3. Матрёшки покупа́ются тури́стами.
4. Контро́льные рабо́ты проверя́ются преподава́телями.
5. Вся́кие ве́щи продаю́тся у́личными торго́вцами.

62.
1. Мето́дика преподава́ния изуча́ется на э́той ка́федре.
2. Но́вая карти́нная галере́я открыва́ется в го́роде.
3. Сво́дка пого́ды передаётся по Второ́й програ́мме в 21.00.
4. Рабо́та э́того а́втора публику́ется впервы́е в э́том журна́ле.
5. В Росси́и кни́ги Аксёного чита́ются с больши́м интере́сом.

63.
1. идём … хо́дим
2. шли́
3. идёт … хо́дит
4. е́ду … е́зжу
5. бежи́шь … бегу́
6. бе́гаешь … бе́гаю
7. ходи́ли
8. бе́гать … ходи́ть
9. пла́вает … пла́вает
10. е́здили
11. плывёт … плывёт
12. лета́л
13. лечу́ … лети́шь
14. е́здил
15. е́хал
16. иду́т
17. иду́т
18. идёт

64.
1. несу́т
2. везу́т
3. несу́т
4. ведёт
5. несёт
6. везу́т
7. несёт
8. везёт
9. несу́т
10. везёт

65.
1. во́зит
2. везли́
3. во́дит
4. вёл
5. но́сит
6. несёт
7. во́дит
8. вёл
9. но́сит
10. ношу́

66.
1. е́хала … пое́хала
2. е́хала … пое́хала
3. пое́хала
4. шли … пошли́
5. шли … пошли́
6. плы́л … поплы́л
7. плы́л … поплы́л
8. понёс
9. нёс

67.
1. попла́вали … поплы́ли
2. полета́ли … полете́ли
3. походи́ли … пошли́
4. побе́гали … побежа́ли

68.
1. уходи́ли
2. ушёл
3. уезжа́л
4. уе́хала
5. подходи́л
6. подошёл

69.
1. Де́вушка, кото́рая живёт в кварти́ре 7, …
2. Кни́ги, кото́рые лежа́т на столе́, …
3. Молодо́й челове́к, кото́рый занима́ется …
4. Профе́ссор, кото́рый чита́ет ле́кцию, …
5. Студе́нты, кото́рые реша́ют э́ту зада́чу, …

70.
1. А́втор, кото́рый написа́л э́ту кни́гу, …
2. Ма́льчик, кото́рый помо́г тебе́, …
3. Челове́к, кото́рый перевёл э́ту кни́гу, …
4. Я́ сего́дня познако́мился с челове́ком, кото́рый вы́рос …
5. Учени́к, кото́рый ушёл ра́но с уро́ка, …

71.
1. Зада́ча, кото́рую реша́ет студе́нт, …
2. Учи́тель, кото́рого лю́бят все́, …

3. Собы́тия, кото́рые опи́сывают в э́той кни́ге, . . .

4. Това́ры, кото́рые произво́дят на э́том заво́де, . . .

5. Ве́чер, кото́рый организу́ют студе́нты, . . .

72. 1. Я́ чита́л интере́сную кни́гу, кото́рую написа́л э́тот журнали́ст.

2. В э́той кни́ге мно́го краси́вых фотогра́фий, кото́рые сде́лал а́втор.

3. Я́ ви́дел фотогра́фию портре́та, кото́рый написа́л э́тот худо́жник.

4. Э́тот музе́й нахо́дится в зда́нии, кото́рое постро́или в девятна́дцатом ве́ке.

5. Я́ рассказа́л ему́ о письме́, кото́рое мы́ получи́ли вчера́.

6. В аудито́рии мы́ нашли́ су́мку, кото́рую кто́-то забы́л.

73. 1. Э́ту исто́рию давно́ забы́ли.

2. Телегра́мму получи́ли в суббо́ту.

3. Вы́ставку откры́ли на про́шлой неде́ле.

4. Рабо́ту сде́лали хорошо́.

5. До́м постро́или в про́шлом ве́ке.

74. 1. Когда́ она́ занима́ется аэро́бикой, . . .

2. Когда́ друзья́ возвраща́лись домо́й из кинотеа́тра, . . .

3. Когда́ студе́нты выходи́ли из аудито́рии, . . .

4. Когда́ о́н рабо́тает на компью́тере, . . .

5. Когда́ мы́ жи́ли в Москве́, . . .

75. 1. Та́к как они́ хоте́ли что́-нибудь е́сть, . . .

2. . . . та́к как наде́ялись найти́ поте́рянную су́мку.

3. Та́к как я́ не понима́ю по-ру́сски, . . .

4. Та́к как я́ не име́л де́нег, . . .

5. Та́к как о́н встава́л ра́но, . . .

76. 1. Е́сли ты́ бу́дешь та́к волнова́ться, . . .

2. Е́сли вы́ бу́дете изуча́ть иностра́нные языки́, . . .

3. Е́сли вы́ бу́дете путеше́ствовать по ра́зным стра́нам, . . .

4. Е́сли вы́ бу́дете занима́ться му́зыкой, . . .

77. 1. Когда́ о́н умы́лся, . . .

2. Когда́ она́ зако́нчила рабо́ту, . . .

3. Когда́ учи́тель вошёл в ко́мнату, . . .

4. Когда́ она́ заперла́ две́рь, . . .

5. Когда́ ба́бушка испекла́ пиро́г, . . .

Chapter 8

1. 1. И Жа́нна и Ма́ра занима́ются ру́сским языко́м.

2. Моя́ сестра́ говори́т и по-ру́сски и по-испа́нски.

3. Ве́чером студе́нты и смо́трят телеви́зор и слу́шают му́зыку.

4. Мы́ пригласи́ли к себе́ и А́нну и Ива́на.

2. 1. Мари́на не лю́бит ни фру́ктов ни овоще́й.

2. Ле́том мы́ не е́здили ни в го́ры ни на пля́ж.

3. Э́та де́вушка ни говори́т ни чита́ет по-англи́йски.

4. Слова́ э́той пе́сни ни краси́вые ни интере́сные.

5. Ве́чером я́ не писа́ла ни пи́сем ни упражне́ний.

3. 1. На у́жин у на́с бу́дет су́п и́ли сала́т.

2. Мо́й бра́т хо́чет купи́ть чёрные джи́нсы и́ли . . .

3. Купи́ мне пожа́луйста, журна́л и́ли газе́ту.

4. Возьми́те и́ли молоко́ и́ли лимона́д.

5. На́ш сы́н хо́чет ста́ть и́ли космона́втом и́ли . . .

4. 1. Ба́бушка хорошо́ понима́ет по-англи́йски, но . . .

2. Мои́ сёстры лю́бят танцева́ть, но . . .

3. Ве́чером мы́ переводи́ли статью́, но . . .

4. Вади́м пое́дет на Ура́л и . . .

5. Э́то дли́нный рома́н, но . . .

6. В э́том рестора́не хле́б о́чень вку́сный и су́п то́же . . .

5. 1. contrastive
2. contradictive
3. contradictive
4. contrastive
5. contrastive
6. contradictive
7. contradictive
8. contrastive
9. contradictive
10. contradictive

6.

1. и		6. и	
2. а (or и)		7. и	
3. но		8. и	
4. а		9. но	
5. но		10. а	

7. 1. Когда́ (*While*) друзья́ возвраща́лись домо́й, они́ разгова́ривали обо всём.
2. Когда́ (*After*) друзья́ верну́лись домо́й, они́ легли́ и усну́ли.
3. Когда́ (*While*) мы проща́лись, мы кре́пко обнима́лись.
4. Когда́ (*After*) мы прости́лись, я пошёл домо́й.
5. Когда́ (*While*) Ма́ша смотре́ла ста́рые фотогра́фии, она́ вспомина́ла про́шлое.
6. Когда́ (*After*) Ма́ша посмотре́ла переда́чу, она́ вы́ключила телеви́зор.

8. 1. По́сле того́ как де́ти поза́втракали, они́ пошли́ в шко́лу.
2. По́сле того́ как ма́ма пригото́вила обе́д, она́ позвала́ нас сесть за стол.
3. По́сле того́ как Андре́й сдал экза́мен, он пошёл с подру́гой в кафе́.
4. По́сле того́ как ко́нчилась телепереда́ча, ребя́та на́чали слу́шать но́вый диск.
5. По́сле того́ как оте́ц ко́нчил писа́ть докла́д, он стал отдыха́ть.

9. 1. На́до зако́нчить курс ру́сского языка́ до того́ как пое́дешь в Росси́ю.
2. На́до мыть ру́ки пе́ред тем как обе́дать.
3. На́до бри́ться пе́ред тем как уйти́ на рабо́ту.
4. На́до ко́нчить э́ту рабо́ту до того́ как уе́хать в о́тпуск.
5. На́до чи́стить фру́кты пе́ред тем как их есть.
6. На́до вы́ключить свет пе́ред тем как уйти́ из ко́мнаты.

10. 1. Мы здесь бу́дем стоя́ть до тех пор, пока́ магази́н не откро́ется.
2. Ребёнок пла́кал до тех пор, пока́ ма́ма не покорми́ла его́.
3. Ви́ктор реша́л зада́чи до тех пор, пока́ он не уста́л.
4. Ребя́та загора́ли на пля́же до тех пор, пока́ ста́ло хо́лодно.
5. Он пил пи́во до тех пор, пока́ он не напи́лся.

11. 1. Прошло́ полтора́ ме́сяца с тех пор как Па́влик купи́л маши́ну.
2. Прошло́ три го́да с тех пор как они́ перее́хали в но́вый дом.
3. Прошло́ шесть ме́сяцев с тех пор как роди́лся ребёнок.
4. Прошло́ полтора́ го́да с тех пор как мы получи́ли письмо́ от Ли́и.

12. 1. Пётр бы́стро реши́л э́ту тру́дную зада́чу, потому́ что он хорошо́ зна́ет матема́тику.
2. Ле́на сего́дня о́чень уста́ла, потому́ что она́ не вы́спалась.
3. Ди́ма спеши́л, потому́ что он опа́здывал на ле́кцию.
4. Серёжа пошёл в библиоте́ку, так как он до́лжен верну́ть кни́гу.
5. Лари́са не была́ на заня́тиях, потому́ что она́ была́ больна́.

13. 1. Экску́рсия была́ отменена́ из-за того́, что вы́пал большо́й снег.
2. Он выполня́ет свою́ рабо́ту в срок благодаря́ тому́, что он о́чень организо́ванный челове́к.
3. Проду́кты испо́ртились из-за того́, что они́ не храни́лись в холоди́льнике.
4. Хоро́шие результа́ты бы́ли дости́гнуты благодаря́ тому́, что был применён но́вый ме́тод.
5. Она́ хорошо́ зако́нчила университе́т благодаря́ тому́, что она́ усе́рдно рабо́тала.

14. 1. Па́па сказа́л, что Ми́ша звони́л домо́й.
2. Па́па сказа́л, чтобы Ми́ша звони́л домо́й.
3. Я понима́ю, что ты сказа́л пра́вду.
4. Мы хоте́ли, чтобы ты сказа́л пра́вду.
5. Мы зна́ем, что ты сказа́л.
6. Ма́ша включи́ла телеви́зор, чтобы смотре́ть фи́льм.
7. Ма́ша включи́ла телеви́зор, чтобы мы смотре́ли фи́льм.

15. 1. Я ви́дел, как он пришёл.
2. Я ви́дел, что он пришёл.
3. Мы слы́шали, как она́ пе́ла.
4. Мы заме́тили, что он ушёл.

16. 1. Он опозда́л на авто́бус, так что он реши́л взять такси́.
2. Мой друг до́лго жил в Ки́еве, так что он хорошо́ зна́ет э́тот го́род.
3. Э́то о́чень просто́й текст, так что я его́ бы́стро перевёл.
4. Я уже́ прочита́л газе́ту, так что я дал её сосе́ду.
5. Я знал, что она́ лю́бит рок-му́зыку, так что я пригласи́л её на рок-конце́рт.

17. 1. Хотя́ мы угова́ривали его́, он не согласи́лся.
2. Е́сли снег пойдёт, мы бу́дем ката́ться на лы́жах.

3. Хотя́ ему́ предложи́ли большу́ю
   зарпла́ту, о́н не согласи́лся на э́ту
   рабо́ту.
4. Éсли всé уста́нут, мы́ остано́вим рабо́ту.
5. Хотя́ всé уста́ли, мы́ продолжа́ли
   рабо́тать.

18. 1. О́н ведёт себя́ та́к, <u>как</u> обы́чно.
   2. О́н ведёт себя́, <u>как бу́дто</u> ничего́ не
      случи́лось.
   3. Пого́да была́, <u>как э́то</u> ча́сто быва́ет в
      а́вгусте, жа́ркая и вла́жная.
   4. Пого́да в ма́е была́ жа́ркая и вла́жная,
      <u>как бу́дто</u> ле́то уже́ наступи́ло.

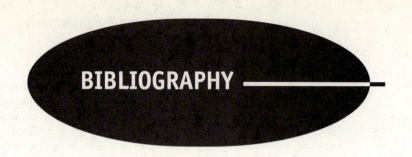

BIBLIOGRAPHY

DICTIONARIES

Apresyan, Yu, D. (and E. M. Mednikova for Vol. 1) (eds.) 1993–94. *Новый большой англо-русский словарь*, 3 vols., Moscow; Русский язык.

Avanesov, R. I. (ed.) 1988. *Орфоэпический словарь русского языка*, 4th edn., Moscow: Русский язык.

Chernyshev, V. I. et al. (eds.) 1950–65. *Словарь современного русского литературного языка*, 17 vols., Moscow: Академия наук СССР.

Ozhegov, S. I. 1968. *Словарь русского языка*, 7th edn., Moscow: Советская энциклопедия.

Wheeler, M. 1984. *The Oxford Russian–English Dictionary*, 2nd edn., Oxford: Clarendon Press.

Wilson, E. A. M. 1982. *The Modern Russian Dictionary for English Speakers*, Oxford and Moscow: Pergamon Press and Russky yazyk.

GRAMMARS AND GRAMMAR TEXTS

Baranova, N. et al. 1985. *Russian Stage Two*. Moscow: Russky yazyk.

Bogojavlensky, M. 1981. *Russian Review Grammar*, Columbus, OH: Slavica.

Borras, F. M. and R. F. Christian 1971. *Russian Syntax: Aspects of Modern Russian Syntax and Vocabulary*, 2nd edn., Oxford: Clarendon Press.

Davis, P. A. and D. V. Oprendek 1997, *Making Progress in Russian*, 2nd edn., revised by A. B. Bronstein and A. I. Fleszar, New York: John Wiley & Sons.

Martin, C. and I. Sokolova 1993. *Russian Stage Two* (American Edition), Dubuque, IA: ACTR and Kendall/Hunt.

Nakhimovsky, A. D. 1985. "An Overview of Russian Conjugation" (a grammar supplement contained in S. Paperno et al., *Intermediate Russian: The Twelve Chairs*, Columbus, OH: Slavica).

Nakhimovsky, A. D. and R. L. Leed 1987. *Advanced Russian*, 2nd edn., revised, Columbus, OH: Slavica.

Offord, D. 1996. *Using Russian: A Guide to Contemporary Usage*, Cambridge: Cambridge University Press.

Pulkina, I. M. and E. M. Zakhava-Nekrasova 1977. *Учебник русского языка*, 6th edn., Moscow: Русский язык.

Shvedova, N. Yu. et al. (eds.) 1980. *Русская грамматика*, 2 vols., Moscow: Наука.

Townsend, C. E. 1981. *Continuing with Russian*, Columbus, OH: Slavica.

Unbegaun, B. O. 1967. *Russian Grammar*, Oxford: Clarendon Press.

Wade, T. A. 1992. *A Comprehensive Russian Grammar*, Oxford: Blackwell.

OTHER WORKS ON RUSSIAN LANGUAGE AND LINGUISTICS

Babby, L. H. 1993. "A Theta-Theoretic Analysis of -en- Suffixation in Russian," *Journal of Slavic Linguistics* **1**, pp. 3–43.

Babby, L. H. 1994. "A Theta-Theoretic Analysis of Adversity Impersonal Sentences in Russian." In *Formal Approaches to Slavic Linguistics 2*, The MIT Meeting, Ann Arbor: Michigan Slavic Publications, pp. 25–67.

Bondarenko, B. S. 1961. *Предлоги в русском языке*, Moscow: Учпедгиз.

Brecht, R. D. and J. S. Levine 1985. "Conditions on Voice Marking in Russian," *Issues in Russian Morphosyntax* (UCLA Slavic Studies, Vol. 10, ed. by M. S. Flier and R. D. Brecht), Columbus, OH: Slavica, pp. 117–35.

Channon, R. 1975. "The Single-Stem Verb System Revisited," *Slavic and East European Journal* **19**, pp. 112–22.

Comrie, B. 1976. *Aspect*. Cambridge: Cambridge University Press.

Gerhart, G. 1995. *The Russian's World*. 2nd edn. revised, Fort Worth: Harcourt Brace.

Gerritsen, N. 1990. *Russian Reflexive Verbs: In Search of Unity in Diversity* (Studies in Slavic and General Linguistics, Vol. 15, ed. by A. A. Barentsen et al.), Amsterdam: Rodopi.

Hamilton, W. S. 1980. *Introduction to Russian Phonology and Word Structure*, Columbus, OH: Slavica.

Matveeva, V. M. and R. E. Nazarian 1972. *Пособие по развитию навыков устной речи*, Leningrad: Издательство Ленинградского университета.

Muravyova, L. S. 1975. *Verbs of Motion in Russian*, Moscow: Русский язык.

Nichols, J. 1981. *Predicate Nominals: A Partial Surface Syntax of Russian* (University of California Publications in Linguistics, Vol. 97), Berkeley and Los Angeles: University of California Press.

Rassudova, O. P. 1984. *Aspectual Usage in Modern Russian*, Moscow: Русский язык.

Timberlake, A. 1986. "Hierarchies in the Genitive of Negation," in *Case in Slavic*, ed. by R. D. Brecht and J. S. Levine, Columbus, OH: Slavica, pp. 338–60.

Timofeeva, G. G. 1995. *Новые английские заимствования в русском языке*, St. Petersburg: «Юна».

INDEX

Abbreviations B.C., A.D., 204 (note)
Abstract nouns:
  as object of negated transitive verb, 47
  occur only in singular, 32, 46
  predicate instrumental of, 61, 122
Accusative case:
  as direct object of transitive verb, 39
  expressing distance, cost, or weight, 39
  expressing duration and repetition of time, 39
  of animate nouns in masculine singular, 38
  of animate nouns in plural, 38–39
  of the numbers два/две, три, четыре modifying
    animate direct object, 182 (note)
  prepositions governing, 68–70
  tables of nouns in the three declensions, 38–39
  verbs followed by prepositions governing, 72, 73,
    75
Acronyms, pronunciation of, 1
Active participles (see Participles)
Active voice, 269
Address, forms of:
  first name and patronymic, 65
  ты vs. вы, 101–102
  use of nominative case as vocative, 37
Adjectival nouns:
  after два/две, три, четыре, 182 (note)
  categories of, 156
  derived from participles, 155, 157 (note)
  neuter singular with abstract meaning, 156
Adjectives:
  attributive use of, 140
  choosing predicative short or long form, 148
  comparative degree of, 159
  comparison of, 159
  family names declined as, 159
  governing the dative case, 55
  governing the genitive case, 48
  governing the instrumental case, 60
  какой vs. как, 154
  какой vs. каков, 154
  long and short forms of, 140
    long form:
      attributive and predicative use of, 141
      stem + ending structure of, 141
      with stem in a hard consonant, 141
      with stem in a soft -н, 143
      with stem in -г, -к, -х, 144
      with stem in -ж, -ч, -ш, -щ, 145
    short form:

Adjectives (Cont.):
    formation of, 146
    predicative use of, 146
    with inserted vowel, 146
  positive degree of, 159
  possessive in the suffix -ин, 158
  possessive of the type птичий, 157
  predicate, 141
  qualitative vs. relational, 140
  superlative degree of, 159
  такой vs. так, 154
  такой vs. таков, 154
  третий, 194
  целый in fractions, 196
  used as nouns, 155
  when preceding a number, 182 (note)
  with mixed declension, 158, 159
Adverbs:
  definition of, 168
  of manner, 169
  of measure or degree, 173
  of place, 172
  of time, 170
  очень vs. много, 173
  reinforcing durative meaning of imperfective,
    245
  reinforcing habitual meaning of imperfective,
    245
  также following the conjunction а, 290
  тоже following the conjunction и, 290
  used with comparatives, 164
  used with perfective to indicate completion,
    suddenness, or immediate start of action,
    243
  with meaning of superlative, 166
  with negative prefix ни-, 175
  with negative prefix не-, 175
  with -то and -нибудь, 174
Affirmative imperatives (see Imperatives)
Age, expressing with the dative case, 57, 204
Agent, 269, 270
Agreement:
  in the singular with collective nouns, 33
  of adjective/pronoun with "naturally masculine"
    2nd declension noun, 142
  of modifying adjective with subject noun, 21
  of modifying pronoun with subject noun, 21
  of predicate adjective with subject noun, 21, 36,
    147

Agreement (*Cont.*):
  of predicate adjective with subject pronoun **э́то, всё**, 151
  of predicate verb in past tense with subject noun, 22, 36, 211
  of predicate with **кто́**, 112
  of predicate with **что́**, 113
  of verb with **вы́**, 210
  with "characterizing" **э́то** as subject, 122
  with "identifying" **э́то** as subject, 121
  with indeclinable loanwords, 28
  with nouns denoting professions, 24
  with nouns of common gender, 23
Alphabet:
  Cyrillic (Russian), 1
  names of letters, 1
Alternations (*see* Consonants)
Animacy, animate and inanimate distinction, 35
Animate accusative:
  basic rule, 38, 115, 142
  in compound numbers ending in **два́/две́, три́, четы́ре**, 181
  motivation for, 35
  with **два́/две́, три́, четы́ре**, 181
  with numbers **пя́ть** and higher, 185
Annulled action verbs, 245–246, 279–280
Antecedent, 102, 103, 120, 127, 132
Apposition, 37
Approximation:
  expressed by **с** + accusative, 70
  expressed by **о́коло** + genitive, 79
  with numbers, 208
Articles, absence of, 19
Aspect (*See also* Imperfective/Perfective aspect):
  and first-person imperative, 259
  and second-person imperative, 256
  and third-person imperative, 260
  definition of, 210
  distinction between imperfective and perfective, 210
  formation of imperfective and perfective, 240–242
  in infinitive, 250–254
  in past or future tenses, 243–246
  in questions, 246–247
  negation and imperfective, 252
  uses of imperfective, 245–246
  uses of perfective, 243–245
Aspectual pairs:
  differentiated by prefixation, 240
  differentiated by suffixation, 241
  differentiated by suppletion, 242
  imperfective denotes process of "trying"/ perfective denotes "achievement of intended result," 243–244
  покупа́ть/купи́ть, 241 (note)

Basic stem of verb (*See also* Verbs):
  definition of, 213
Block style of Cyrillic letters, 13
Borrowed nouns (*See also* Loanwords):
  gender of, 26–27

Capitalization:
  compared with English, 11
  of **Вы́** in letter writing, 102
Cardinal numbers:
  as numerator of a fraction, 195
  declension and use of *1*, 178
  declension and use of *2*, *3*, and *4*, 180
  declension of *5–20* and *30*, 183
  declension of *50*, *60*, *70*, and *80*, 184
  declension of *40*, *90*, and *100*, 184
  declension of *200*, *300*, and *400*, 184
  declension of *500*, *600*, *700*, *800*, and *900*, 185
  declension and use of **ты́сяча**, 186
  declension and use of **миллио́н** and **миллиа́рд**, 187
  in compounds with ordinals, 193 (note)
  in telephone numbers, 188
  numerical nouns derived from, 189
  punctuation for writing "thousands" and "millions" in figures, 187
  table of nominative case forms, 177
  to express time on the hour, 205
  use of *5–999*, 185
  with nouns denoting male and female persons, 190
Case (*See also* Accusative; Dative; Genitive; Instrumental; Nominative; Prepositional):
  as a category of the Russian noun, 19, 34, 35
  definition and explanation of, 35
Clauses:
  conditional, 211, 260–261
  consequence, 211, 260–261
  dependent, 114, 295
  independent, 114, 289, 294, 295
  purpose, 264
  relative, 127, 280–283
  subordinate, 127, 263, 295
Collective nouns, 32
Collective numbers:
  declension and case government of **о́ба/о́бе**, 190
  declension and case government of **дво́е, тро́е, . . .**, 191
  uses of, 192
Comma:
  in decimal fractions, 187
  inserted between **потому́** and **что**, 299
  preceding **как**, 302
  preceding **кото́рый**, 127
  preceding **чем**, 164
  preceding **что**, 301

Commands (*See also* Imperatives):
  affirmative, 256
  negative, 257
Common gender, nouns of, 23
Common nouns, 19
Comparatives of adjectives:
  compound:
    formation of, 160
    use of, 161
  simple:
    formation of, 161
    use of, 163
Comparatives of adverbs:
  formation of, 162
  use of, 163
Conditional:
  real (likely) conditionals, 210, 260
  unreal (hypothetical/contrary-to-fact)
    conditionals, 210, 260
Conjugation (*See also* Verbs):
  definition of, 209
  endings of 1st and 2nd, 211–212
Conjunctions:
  coordinating:
    adversative, 292
    copulative, 290
    disjunctive, 291
    the choice of и, а, or но, 294
  definition of, 289
  subordinating:
    causal, 299
    comparative, 164, 304
    concessive, 304
    conditional, 303
    purposive, 300
    resultative, 302
    temporal, 296
    что and как, 301
Consonant alternations:
  in conjugation, 213
  in past passive participles, 283
  in simple comparatives, 162–163
Consonants:
  double softening of, 8
  hard and soft (palatalized), 4
  paired and unpaired, 7–9
  voiced and voiceless, 9
Contrary-to-fact:
  in subjunctive, 262
  in unreal conditionals, 210–211, 260–261
Conversational clock time, 205–207
Coordinating conjunctions (*see* Conjunctions)
Cursive style of Cyrillic letters, 14
Cyril, St., 1
Cyrillic alphabet, 1

Dash, 37, 293
Dates, expressing time in, 202–204
Dative case:
  after adjectives, 55
  after prepositions, 94–97
  after verbs, 54
  as "addressee," "recipient," "beneficiary," 55
  as "experiencer," 55
  as indirect object of verb, 54
  as logical subject, 55, 175
  expressing age, 57
  in impersonal constructions, 55–57
  table of noun endings, 53
Days of the week, 199
Decimal fractions, 197–199
Declension of nouns:
  of first names and patronymics, 65
  summary table of case endings in plural, 66
  summary table of case endings in singular, 65
  table illustrating three declension classes, 34
Demonstrative pronouns:
  э́тот vs. то́т, 119
  и то́т и друго́й, 120
  не то́т, 120
  тако́й, 122–123
  тако́й же, 123
  то́т же (са́мый), 120
Dependent clauses (*see* Clauses)
Derived imperfectives, 242
Determinative pronouns:
  ве́сь, 125–126
  са́м, 123–124
  са́мый, 125
Diminutive forms of male first names, 22
Diphthong, 5
Direct object:
  definition of, 39, 209
  in accusative case of transitive verbs, 39
  in genitive case of negated transitive verbs, 47
Distributive meaning, 70, 97

First names:
  declension of foreign, 65
  declension of Russian, 65
First-person imperative (*see* Imperatives)
Fleeting vowels:
  in genitive plurals, 41 (note)
  in nominative plurals, 30
Forms of address, formal/informal, 101–102
Fractions:
  decimal, 197
  declension of, 195
Future tense:
  formed from imperfective verbs, 239
  formed from perfective verbs, 212, 239

Future tense (*Cont.*):
  in **éсли-** clauses, 260, 303
  in **как тóлько-** clauses, 297
  in **когдá-** clauses, 296

Gender of nouns:
  common, 23
  denoting professions, 24
  differentiation by suffix, 25
  feminine:
    with stem ending in **-ь**, 23
  grammatical, 20
  masculine:
    of natural gender in **-а, -я**, 22
    with stem ending in **-ь**, 22
  natural, 20
  neuter:
    in **-мя**, 21
  of indeclinable loanwords, 26–27
  of indeclinable place names, 27
  of months, 22
  why important, 21
Genitive case:
  after adjectives, 48
  after adverbial expressions of quantity, 46
  after collective numbers, 191
  after comparatives, 48
  after fractions, 195
  after **мéжду** in idiomatic expressions, 85
  after negated forms of **бы́ть**, 47–48
  after numbers: **нóль/нýль**, 178; $1\frac{1}{2}$, 197; *2–4*, 45,
      180; **óба/óбе**, 46, 191; *5–999*, 185; **ты́сяча**,
      187; **миллиóн**, 187; **миллиáрд**, 187
  after **пол-** in compound nouns, 196
  after **половúна, трéть, чéтверть**, 196
  after prepositions, 77–86
  after verbs, 48
  as object of negated transitive verb, 47
  as object of transitive verb to express
      "partitive," 46
  denoting agent of an action, 45
  denoting container or specific quantity of an
      object, 45
  denoting entity to which a property is attributed,
      45
  denoting object of an action, 45
  denoting person after whom something is
      named, 45
  denoting possessor, 45
  denoting whole in relation to part, 45
  in expressing dates in months and years,
      202–204
  partitive genitive of nouns in **-у/-ю**, 46–47
  table of regular noun endings, 44
Genitive plurals of nouns:
  ending **-ов**, 41

Genitive plurals of nouns (*Cont.*):
  ending **-ев**, 42
  ending **-ей**, 42
  ending -$\varnothing$, 43
  of nouns in **-ие, -ия, -ея**, 43 (note)
  of **дя́дя, тётя, ю́ноша**, 43 (note)
  of **мóре, пóле**, 43 (note)
  of **óблако**, 43 (note)
  of **человéк**, 43, 44, 46 (note)
  with genitive plural = nominative singular, 44
  with inserted vowel, 43–44
Gerund (*see* Verbal Adverbs)
Glide, 3, 4, 5, 20

Hard sign:
  function of, 4
  in prefixed verbs of motion, 279
Hyphenated words, 10
Hypothetical:
  in subjunctive, 211
  in unreal conditional, 210

Imperatives, three types, 254
  first-person:
    давáй(те) + imperfective infinitive, 259
    давáй(те) + perfective 1st person plural, 259
    the meaning *Let's not do . . .*, 259
    the meaning *Let's do . . . instead*, 259
  second-person:
    formation of, 254
    irregular forms, 256
    uses of affirmative imperative, 256
    uses of negated imperative, 257
  third-person:
    пýсть + 3rd person singular or plural, 260
    use of aspect, 260
Imperfective aspect:
  definition of, 210, 243
  denoting action in progress or process, 245
  denoting annulled actions in the past, 245–246
  denoting denial of intent to perform action, 246
  denoting repeated (habitual) actions, 245
  denoting simultaneous ongoing actions, 245
  denoting statement of fact, 246
  denoting "trying" in the past, 244
  durative meaning of, 245
  general correlation with negation, 252
  in questions, 246
  infinitive:
    after expressions denoting lack of necessity, or
        inadvisability, 253
    after verbs denoting beginning, continuing, or
        finishing action, 251
    after verbs denoting habitual processes, 251
    denoting continuous process, 250
    denoting repeated action, 250

Imperfective aspect (*Cont.*):
    negated by **не**, 252
    with **нельзя́** denoting prohibition or
        inadvisability, 253
    second-person imperative:
        conveying polite invitations, 257
        expressing urgency, 256
        giving general advice, 256
        prompting someone to begin an action, 256
        requests for repeated actions, 256
        requests that an action *not* be performed, 257
        requests to modify action in progress, 256
Impersonal expressions, 55–57
Impersonal sentences, 175
Indeclinable nouns, 26
Indeclinable pronouns:
    "characterizing" **э́то**, 122
    "identifying" **э́то**, 121
Indefinite personal construction, 270
Indefinite pronouns in **-то, -нибудь**, 134–135
Indicative:
    definition of, 210
    in real conditionals, 211, 260
Indirect object, 35, 54
Infinitive (*See also* Imperfective aspect; Perfective
      aspect):
    as form of verb, 211
Inserted vowels:
    after consonantal prefix before verb stem **-йти**,
      279
    in forms of the verb **жéчь**, 237
    in forms of the verb **прочéсть**, 236
    in genitive plural of certain nouns, 43–44
Instrumental case:
    after adjectives, 60
    after prepositions, 97–100
    after verbs, 61
    as predicate instrumental, 37, 61
    as second object of transitive verb, 62
    denoting agent of action in passives, 59
    denoting force responsible for action in
      impersonals, 59
    denoting manner in which action is performed,
      59
    denoting means of travel, 60
    denoting route taken, 60
    denoting similarity, 60
    denoting time when something occurs, 60
    in plural subjects of type **Мы́ с ва́ми**, 108
    irregular noun plural in **-ьми́**, 59 (note)
    table of regular noun endings, 59
Interrogative pronouns:
    како́в, 154
    како́й, 154
    кто́, 112
    что́, 112

Intransitive verbs:
    definition of, 209
    marked by the particle **-ся/-сь**, 209, 212, 266
Italic style of Cyrillic letters, 13

Key forms of the verb, 213

Linking verbs, 36–37, 61, 62, 140, 147
Loanwords, 11
Location, expressed by nouns requiring
    на + prepositional, 89–92
Locative:
    nouns in stressed **-ý, -ю́**, 53
    prepositions governing, 52
    the noun **году́** in expressing years, 203
Logical subject (*see* Dative case)

Metric system, 198
Middle voice, 270
Modal words:
    followed by imperfective or perfective infinitive,
      250, 253
    followed by **что́бы** + past tense, 264
Monetary units, 188
Monophthong, 5
Months:
    gender of, 201
    stress in nouns denoting, 201
Mood (*See also* Conditional; Imperative;
      Indicative; Subjunctive):
    definition of, 210

Necessity, expressions of, 56
Negative adverbs:
    in **нé-**, 175
    in **ни-**, 175
Negative pronouns:
    in **нé-**, 137–138
    in **ни-**, 136–137
Nominative case:
    as form of direct address, 37
    as grammatical subject, 36
    as noun title in apposition, 37
    as predicate nominative, 36
    table of singular and plural noun endings, 36
Nominative plurals of nouns:
    and Spelling Rule 1, 28
    fleeting vowels in, 30
    in stressed **-á, -я́**, 30
    irregular in **-ья**, 30
    occurring only in the plural, 33
    of **до́чь** and **ма́ть**, 31
    of **ребёнок** and **челове́к**, 31
    stress shifts in, 29
    table of regular endings, 28
    with singular ending in **-мя**, 31

Non-past, 212, 239
Number (singular and plural):
   in indeclinable nouns, 28
   plural-only nouns, 33
   singular-only nouns, 32
Numbers (*See also* Cardinal; Collective; Ordinal):
   order of in dates, 204

Official (24-hour) clock time, 207–208
Ordinal numbers:
   as denominator of a fraction, 195
   as source of names for certain days, 199 (note)
   declension of **трéтий**, 194
   in Russian where English uses cardinals, 194
   to express dates in months, 202
   to express dates in years, 203
   to express decades, 204
   to express 60-minute period between hours, 206
   to indicate an approaching birthday, 205

Palatalized (*see* Consonants)
Participles:
   definition of, 280
   past active:
      formation of, 281
      use of, 282
   past passive:
      formation of, 283
      formation of short form, 284
      use of, 283
      uses of short form, 284
   present active:
      formation of, 280–281
      use of, 281
   present passive:
      formation of, 282
      use of, 282
Particles:
   бы, 211, 261, 262
   же, 120
   -ся/-сь, 109 (note), 111 (note), 266, 281, 285, 287
   -то/-нибудь, 134–135, 174
Partitive genitive:
   meaning and use of, 46–47
   nouns taking ending **-у/-ю**, 47
Passive participles (*see* Participles)
Passive voice, 269
Past tense:
   agreement with subject, 211
   aspect in, 211, 243–246
   corresponding to forms of English past, 210–211
   formation of, 211, 238
Patient, 269, 270
Patronymics:
   declension of, 65
   formation of, 65

Perfective aspect:
   definition of, 210, 242
   infinitive:
      denoting result to be achieved, 250
      denoting specific one-time action, 251
      verbs requiring perfective infinitive, 251
      with **нельзя** denoting impossibility, 253
   past and/or future tense:
      denoting achievement of intended result, 243
      denoting action that interrupts ongoing action, 245
      denoting actions of limited duration, 244
      denoting beginning of an action, 244
      denoting completion with attendant result, 243
      denoting instantaneous action, 244
      denoting sequential actions, 244
      denoting time in which action was/will be completed (with **за** + accusative), 244
   questions:
      about an intended/expected action, 247
   second-person imperative:
      denoting one-time concrete action, 256
      denoting warnings, 257
Period, 187, 204, 206
Permission/prohibition, expressions of, 56
Personal endings of verbs, 209
Personal names:
   family names (surnames), 159
   first names and patronymics, 65
Personal pronouns:
   я, 101
   ты vs. **вы**, 101
   он, онó, онá, онú, 102
Plural-only nouns (*see* Number)
Possessive adjectives:
   the type **птúчий**, 157
   with the suffix **-ин**, 158
Possessive pronouns:
   егó, её, úх, 116
   чей, мóй, твóй, нáш, вáш, 114–116
   свóй, 117
Predicate instrumental:
   after certain forms of **бы́ть**, 37 (note)
   after near-synonyms of **бы́ть**, 62
   definition of, 61
   of abstract or deverbal nouns, 61, 122
   of nouns denoting occupation, function, status, 37, 61
Predicate nominative, 36
Prefixes:
   вы- stressed in perfective verbs, 222 (note)
   denoting starting point of action, 244–245
   giving directional meaning to verbs of motion, 278
   perfectivizing basic imperfectives, 240–241

Prefixes (*Cont.*):
    perfectivizing and changing meaning of basic
        imperfectives, 213, 241
    по- and **про-** denoting "limited duration," 244
Prepositional case:
    of nouns in **-ие, -ия, -ий**, 52
    table of endings, 52
    the "locative" in stressed **-ý, -ю́**, 52–53
    to express location, 52
    to express other meanings, 87
Prepositions:
    definition of, 67
    governing accusative, 68–70
    governing dative, 94
    governing either accusative or instrumental, 74
    governing either accusative or prepositional,
        70–71
    governing genitive, 77–86
    governing instrumental, 97–100
    governing nominative, 67–68
    governing prepositional or locative, 87–93
    Russian rendering of English *for*, 67
Present tense:
    aspect in, 238
    corresponding to forms of English present, 211
    formed from imperfective verbs, 212
    used to refer to a future action, 273
Pretonic, 5
Productive/nonproductive verb classes, 215
Pronouns (*See also* Demonstrative; Determinative;
    Indeclinable; Interrogative; Negative;
    Personal; Possessive; Reciprocal; Reflexive;
    Relative):
    definition of, 101
    его́, её, их as possessives, 104, 116
    óн, онó, онá as object of preposition, 103
    свóй in impersonal sentences, 118
Pronunciation:
    of possessive pronoun **егó**, 103
    of genitive case adjective ending **-ого, -его**, 142
    of stressed vowels, 2, 5
    of unstressed vowels, 5–7
Proper nouns, 19
Proverbs:
    with **свóй** in nominative, 118
    with **тóт, ктó**, 132
Purpose clauses (*see* Clauses)

Reciprocal meaning, 111
Reciprocal pronoun **дрýг дрýга**, 110–111
Reflexive meaning of verbs, 109 (note)
Reflexive pronouns:
    reflexive personal **себя́**, 109–110
    reflexive possessive **свóй**, 117–118
Relative clauses (*see* Clauses)

Relative pronouns:
    какóй, 131
    котóрый, 127, 280, 282, 283
    ктó (тóт, ктó), 132
    такóй (же) ... какóй, 131
    чтó (тó, чтó), 132
Reversed actions (*See also* Annulled actions;
    Round-trip):
    expressed by verbs involving movement,
        245–246
    expressed by verbs of motion, 271, 273,
        279–280
Round-trip, meaning of, 271, 273, 279–280
Rule of "likes" and "unlikes," 214

Seasons (*see* Time expressions)
Soft sign, 4
Space, in representing numbers, 187
Spelling rules, statement of, 10–11
    Spelling Rule 1:
        and adjective with stem in **-г, -к, -х**, 144
        and adjective with stem in **-ж, -ч, -ш, -щ**, 145
        and genitive singular of feminine nouns, 41
        and nouns in nominative plural, 28
    Spelling Rule 2:
        and 1st singular, 3rd plural of verbs with stem
          in **-ж, -ч, -ш, -щ**, 212
        and genitive singular of masculine nouns in **-ч**,
          -щ, 41
    Spelling Rule 3:
        and genitive plural of nouns ending in **-ец**, 42
        and instrumental singular of nouns with stem
          in **-ж, -ч, -ш, -щ**, 58
Stem + ending structure:
    of adjectives, 141
    of nouns, 19
    of verbs, 213
Stress, 5 (*See also* Vowels)
Stress patterns in the non-past, 213
Subjunctive:
    definition of, 211, 262
    бы + past tense verb form:
        expressing a wish, 262
        expressing polite advice, 262
    чтóбы + past tense verb form:
        after verbs expressing wishes, desires,
          commands, 263
        after words expressing desire or necessity, 264
        expressing purpose, 264
Subordinating conjunctions (*see* Conjunctions)
Suffixes:
    as determiner of conjugation class, 214
    derived imperfectivizing, 242
    in noun structure, 19
    that build 1st conjugation verbs, 215

Suffixes (*Cont.*):
   that build 2nd conjugation verbs, 226
   -ёк, -ец, -ок with fleeting vowel, 30
   -ин in possessive adjectives, 158
   -ина denoting single item, 32
   -ка denoting single item, 32
   -ович and **-овна** in patronymics, 64
Superlatives of adjectives:
   form and use of compound, 166
   form and use of simple, 167
Superlatives of adverbs, 166
Surnames (*see* Personal names)
Syllabification, 10

Telephone numbers, 188
Telling time (*See also* Conversational clock time;
        Official (24-hour) clock time):
   at a given hour, 71
   at half past the hour, 88
   at number of minutes until the hour, 77
Tense:
   definition of, 210
   expressed by imperfective verb, 243
   expressed by perfective verb, 242
   formation of imperfective future, 239
   formation of past, 238
   in conditional statements, 260–261
   in reported speech, 301
   in the subjunctive, 262
   in verbal adverb constructions, 286
Time expressions:
   dates, 202
   days, 199
   months, 201
   seasons, 201
   weeks, 200
   years and centuries, 202
Transcription, phonetic, 2
Transitive/intransitive verbs:
   definition of, 209, 266
   intransitive verbs marked by **-ся**, 209, 212, 266
   transitive verbs and active voice, 269
Transliteration, 11
Truncate, 214

Verbal adjectives (*see* Participles)
Verbal adverbs (gerunds):
   definition of, 285
   imperfective:
      formation of, 285
      replacing subordinate clauses, 286
   perfective:
      formation of, 287
      replacing subordinate clauses, 288
Verbal government, 271

Verbs:
   definition of, 209
   first conjugation with nonsuffixed stem:
      in **-в-**, 231
      in **-н-**, 231
      in **-ой-**, 232
      in **-ий-**, 232
      in **-й-**, 233
      in **-м-** or **-н-**, 233
      in **-р-**, 235
      in **-з-** and **-с-**, 235
      in **-д-** and **-т-**, 235
      in **-б-**, 236
      in **-г-** and **-к-**, 236
      irregular with nonsuffixed stem, 237
   first conjugation with suffixed stem:
      in **-ай-**, 215
      in **-ей-**, 216
      in **-ова/уй-**, 217
      in **-ну-**, 219
      in **-а- (-я-)**, 221
      in **-а-вай-**, 224
      in **-о-**, 225
   followed by preposition + case:
      with **в** + accusative, 72
      with **в** + prepositional, 88–89
      with **за** + accusative, 75
      with **за** + instrumental, 98–99
      with **к** + dative, 95
      with **на** + accusative, 73
      with **на** + prepositional, 92–93
      with **над** + instrumental, 97–98
      with **от** + genitive, 80
      with **с** + instrumental, 100
      with **у** + genitive, 82–83
   followed only by imperfective infinitive, 251
   followed only by perfective infinitive, 251
   governing dative case, 54
   governing genitive case, 48
   governing instrumental case, 61
   irregular verbs of mixed conjugation, 229
   second conjugation with suffixed stem:
      in **-и-**, 226
      in **-е-**, 227
      in **-жа-**, 228
   table of verbs with nonsuffixed stems, 237
   table of verbs with suffixed stems, 230
Verbs in the particle **-ся**:
   and intransitivity, 209, 266
   denoting emotion, 267
   denoting reciprocal meaning, 109 (note), 267
   denoting reflexive meaning, 111 (note), 266
   governing an oblique object, 166, 267
   in impersonal constructions, 56–57
   lacking transitive counterparts, 268
   used in middle and passive voice, 269–270

Verbs of motion:
    characterization of unidirectional (determinate)
        and multidirectional (indeterminate), 271
    prefixed:
        meaning of multidirectional imperfective in
           по-, 277
        meanings of directional prefixes **при-, у-, в-,
           вы-, под-, от-, пере-, про-, за-**, 278
        pairs of prefixed imperfective/perfective verbs,
           278
        stem changes in prefixed multidirectionals, 279
        the meaning of annulled (round-trip) action,
           279
        uses of unidirectional perfective in **по-**, 276
        verbs that may denote annulled action, 280
    prefixless:
        correlating transitive and intransitive in same
           context, 275
        intransitive pairs of, 272

Verbs of motion (*Cont.*):
    transitive pairs of, 274
    uses of multidirectional, 273
    uses of unidirectional, 272
Vocative, 37
Voice (*See also* Active voice; Middle voice;
        Passive voice):
  and the particle **-ся**, 269
  definition of, 269
Voicing rules, 9
Vowels:
  hard and soft series, 4
  reduced, 5
  stressed and unstressed, 5

Word order, 33, 103

Zero ending, 20